Vauxhall/Opel Vectra
Service and Repair Manual

A K Legg LAE MIMI and Mark Coombs

Models covered

(3396 - 408 - 8AF3)

Vectra Saloon, Hatchback and Estate models, including special/limited editions

Petrol engines: 1.6 litre (1598cc), 1.8 litre (1796 & 1799cc) & 2.0 litre (1998cc) 4-cylinder
Turbo-Diesel engines: 1.7 litre (1686cc) & 2.0 litre (1994cc)

Does not cover 2.5 litre (2498cc) V6 petrol engine, "Super Touring" or GSi models

© Haynes Publishing 2002

ABCDE
FG

Printed in the USA

A book in the **Haynes Service and Repair Manual Series**

ISBN 1 85960 946 5

British Library Cataloguing in Publication Data
A catalogue record for this book is available from the British Library.

Haynes Publishing
Sparkford, Yeovil, Somerset BA22 7JJ, England

Haynes North America, Inc
861 Lawrence Drive, Newbury Park, California 91320, USA

Editions Haynes
4, Rue de l'Abreuvoir
92415 COURBEVOIE CEDEX, France

Haynes Publishing Nordiska AB
Box 1504, 751 45 UPPSALA, Sverige

Contents

LIVING WITH YOUR VAUXHALL VECTRA

MAINTENANCE

Routine Maintenance and Servicing

Contents

The Vauxhall Vectra was introduced in the UK in October 1995 as a replacement for the time-honoured Cavalier. It was originally available in Saloon and Hatchback versions with 1.6, 1.8, 2.0 and 2.5 litre petrol engines and 1.7 litre normally aspirated diesel engines. The 1.6 litre engines are in either 8-valve or 16-valve form, and the 1.8 and 2.0 litre engines are 16-valve. The 2.5 litre engine is a V6 and is not covered in this Manual. Models may be fitted with a five-speed manual transmission or four-speed automatic transmission mounted on the left-hand side of the engine.

All models have front-wheel-drive with fully-independent front and rear suspension.

Power steering (PAS) and Anti-Lock Braking (ABS) are fitted as standard to all models.

The Estate range was launched in October 1996, and at the same time the direct injection 2.0 litre diesel engine was introduced.

From February 1997, side air bags can be fitted as an option, and from April 1997 air conditioning was available as an option. Cruise control is fitted as standard on CDX models and is available as an option on certain other models.

For the home mechanic, the Vauxhall Vectra is a straightforward vehicle to maintain and repair since design features have been incorporated to reduce the actual cost of ownership to a minimum, and most of the items requiring frequent attention are easily accessible.

Vauxhall Vectra GLS Saloon

Your Vauxhall Vectra manual

The aim of this manual is to help you get the best value from your vehicle. It can do so in several ways. It can help you decide what work must be done (even should you choose to get it done by a garage), provide information on routine maintenance and servicing, and give a logical course of action and diagnosis when random faults occur. However, it is hoped that you will use the manual by tackling the work yourself. On simpler jobs, it may even be quicker than booking the car into a garage and going there twice, to leave and collect it. Perhaps most important, a lot of money can be saved by avoiding the costs a garage must charge to cover its labour and overheads.

The manual has drawings and descriptions to show the function of the various components, so that their layout can be understood. Then the tasks are described and photographed in a clear step-by-step sequence.

References to the 'left' or 'right' are in the sense of a person in the driver's seat, facing forward.

The Vauxhall Vectra Team

Haynes manuals are produced by dedicated and enthusiastic people working in close co-operation. The team responsible for the creation of this book included:

Authors	**A.K. Legg**
	Mark Coombs
Sub-editor	**Sophie Yar**
Editor & Page Make-up	**Steve Churchill**
Workshop manager	**Paul Buckland**
Photo Scans	**John Martin**
	Steve Tanswell
Cover illustration & Line Art	**Roger Healing**

We hope the book will help you to get the maximum enjoyment from your car. By carrying out routine maintenance as described you will ensure your car's reliability and preserve its resale value.

Acknowledgements

Thanks are due to Duckhams Oils, who provided lubrication data. Certain illustrations are the copyright of Vauxhall Motors Limited, and are used with their permission. Thanks are also due to Draper Tools Limited, who provided some of the workshop tools, and to all those people at Sparkford who helped in the production of this manual.

We take great pride in the accuracy of information given in this manual, but vehicle manufacturers make alterations and design changes during the production run of a particular vehicle of which they do not inform us. No liability can be accepted by the authors or publishers for loss, damage or injury caused by any errors in, or omissions from, the information given.

Project vehicles

The main vehicle used in the preparation of this manual, and which appears in many of the photographic sequences, was a 1997 Vauxhall Vectra DI fitted with a 2.0 litre turbocharged direct-injection diesel engine. Other vehicles used included 1.6 and 1.8 litre petrol models.

Working on your car can be dangerous. This page shows just some of the potential risks and hazards, with the aim of creating a safety-conscious attitude.

General hazards

Scalding

• Don't remove the radiator or expansion tank cap while the engine is hot.
• Engine oil, automatic transmission fluid or power steering fluid may also be dangerously hot if the engine has recently been running.

Burning

• Beware of burns from the exhaust system and from any part of the engine. Brake discs and drums can also be extremely hot immediately after use.

Crushing

• When working under or near a raised vehicle, always supplement the jack with axle stands, or use drive-on ramps. *Never venture under a car which is only supported by a jack.*
• Take care if loosening or tightening high-torque nuts when the vehicle is on stands. Initial loosening and final tightening should be done with the wheels on the ground.

Fire

• Fuel is highly flammable; fuel vapour is explosive.
• Don't let fuel spill onto a hot engine.
• Do not smoke or allow naked lights (including pilot lights) anywhere near a vehicle being worked on. Also beware of creating sparks (electrically or by use of tools).
• Fuel vapour is heavier than air, so don't work on the fuel system with the vehicle over an inspection pit.
• Another cause of fire is an electrical overload or short-circuit. Take care when repairing or modifying the vehicle wiring.
• Keep a fire extinguisher handy, of a type suitable for use on fuel and electrical fires.

Electric shock

• Ignition HT voltage can be dangerous, especially to people with heart problems or a pacemaker. Don't work on or near the ignition system with the engine running or the ignition switched on.

• Mains voltage is also dangerous. Make sure that any mains-operated equipment is correctly earthed. Mains power points should be protected by a residual current device (RCD) circuit breaker.

Fume or gas intoxication

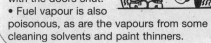

• Exhaust fumes are poisonous; they often contain carbon monoxide, which is rapidly fatal if inhaled. Never run the engine in a confined space such as a garage with the doors shut.
• Fuel vapour is also poisonous, as are the vapours from some cleaning solvents and paint thinners.

Poisonous or irritant substances

• Avoid skin contact with battery acid and with any fuel, fluid or lubricant, especially antifreeze, brake hydraulic fluid and Diesel fuel. Don't syphon them by mouth. If such a substance is swallowed or gets into the eyes, seek medical advice.
• Prolonged contact with used engine oil can cause skin cancer. Wear gloves or use a barrier cream if necessary. Change out of oil-soaked clothes and do not keep oily rags in your pocket.
• Air conditioning refrigerant forms a poisonous gas if exposed to a naked flame (including a cigarette). It can also cause skin burns on contact.

Asbestos

• Asbestos dust can cause cancer if inhaled or swallowed. Asbestos may be found in gaskets and in brake and clutch linings. When dealing with such components it is safest to assume that they contain asbestos.

Special hazards

Hydrofluoric acid

• This extremely corrosive acid is formed when certain types of synthetic rubber, found in some O-rings, oil seals, fuel hoses etc, are exposed to temperatures above 400°C. The rubber changes into a charred or sticky substance containing the acid. *Once formed, the acid remains dangerous for years. If it gets onto the skin, it may be necessary to amputate the limb concerned.*
• When dealing with a vehicle which has suffered a fire, or with components salvaged from such a vehicle, wear protective gloves and discard them after use.

The battery

• Batteries contain sulphuric acid, which attacks clothing, eyes and skin. Take care when topping-up or carrying the battery.
• The hydrogen gas given off by the battery is highly explosive. Never cause a spark or allow a naked light nearby. Be careful when connecting and disconnecting battery chargers or jump leads.

Air bags

• Air bags can cause injury if they go off accidentally. Take care when removing the steering wheel and/or facia. Special storage instructions may apply.

Diesel injection equipment

• Diesel injection pumps supply fuel at very high pressure. Take care when working on the fuel injectors and fuel pipes.

⚠ *Warning: Never expose the hands, face or any other part of the body to injector spray; the fuel can penetrate the skin with potentially fatal results.*

Remember...

DO

• Do use eye protection when using power tools, and when working under the vehicle.

• Do wear gloves or use barrier cream to protect your hands when necessary.

• Do get someone to check periodically that all is well when working alone on the vehicle.

• Do keep loose clothing and long hair well out of the way of moving mechanical parts.

• Do remove rings, wristwatch etc, before working on the vehicle – especially the electrical system.

• Do ensure that any lifting or jacking equipment has a safe working load rating adequate for the job.

DON'T

• Don't attempt to lift a heavy component which may be beyond your capability – get assistance.

• Don't rush to finish a job, or take unverified short cuts.

• Don't use ill-fitting tools which may slip and cause injury.

• Don't leave tools or parts lying around where someone can trip over them. Mop up oil and fuel spills at once.

• Don't allow children or pets to play in or near a vehicle being worked on.

The following pages are intended to help in dealing with common roadside emergencies and breakdowns. You will find more detailed fault finding information at the back of the manual, and repair information in the main chapters.

If your car won't start and the starter motor doesn't turn

☐ If it's a model with automatic transmission, make sure the selector is in 'P' or 'N'.
☐ Open the bonnet and make sure that the battery terminals are clean and tight.
☐ Switch on the headlights and try to start the engine. If the headlights go very dim when you're trying to start, the battery is probably flat. Get out of trouble by jump starting (see next page) using a friend's car.

If your car won't start even though the starter motor turns as normal

☐ Is there fuel in the tank?
☐ Is there moisture on electrical components under the bonnet? Switch off the ignition, then wipe off any obvious dampness with a dry cloth. Spray a water-repellent aerosol product (WD-40 or equivalent) on ignition and fuel system electrical connectors like those shown in the photos. Pay special attention to the ignition coil wiring connector and HT leads. (Note that Diesel engines don't normally suffer from damp.)

A Check the condition and security of the battery connections.

B Check the wiring to the airflow meter.

C Check the security of the HT leads on the spark plugs on petrol engines.

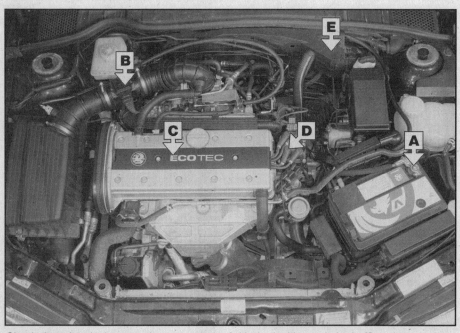

Check that electrical connections are secure (with the ignition switched off) and spray them with a water dispersant spray like WD-40 if you suspect a problem due to damp

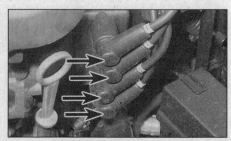

D Check that the HT leads are firmly connected to the coil on petrol engines.

E Check the wiring to the map sensor (where fitted).

Jump starting

When jump-starting a car using a booster battery, observe the following precautions:

✔ Before connecting the booster battery, make sure that the ignition is switched off.

✔ Ensure that all electrical equipment (lights, heater, wipers, etc) is switched off.

✔ Take note of any special precautions printed on the battery case.

✔ Make sure that the booster battery is the same voltage as the discharged one in the vehicle.

✔ If the battery is being jump-started from the battery in another vehicle, the two vehicles MUST NOT TOUCH each other.

✔ Make sure that the transmission is in neutral (or PARK, in the case of automatic transmission).

1 Connect one end of the red jump lead to the positive (+) terminal of the flat battery

2 Connect the other end of the red lead to the positive (+) terminal of the booster battery.

3 Connect one end of the black jump lead to the negative (-) terminal of the booster battery

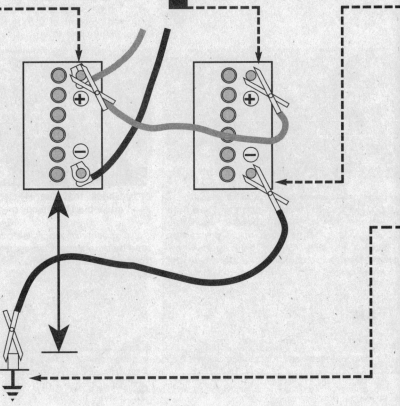

4 Connect the other end of the black jump lead to a bolt or bracket on the engine block, well away from the battery, on the vehicle to be started.

5 Make sure that the jump leads will not come into contact with the fan, drivebelts or other moving parts of the engine.

6 Start the engine using the booster battery and run it at idle speed. Switch on the lights, rear window demister and heater blower motor, then disconnect the jump leads in the reverse order of connection. Turn off the lights etc.

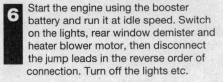

Wheel changing

Some of the details shown here will vary according to model. For instance, the location of the spare wheel and jack is not the same on all cars. However, the basic principles apply to all vehicles.

Warning: Do not change a wheel in a situation where you risk being hit by another vehicle. On busy roads, try to stop in a lay-by or a gateway. Be wary of passing traffic while changing the wheel - it is easy to become distracted by the job in hand.

Preparation

☐ When a puncture occurs, stop as soon as it is safe to do so.

☐ Park on firm level ground, if possible, and well out of the way of other traffic.

☐ Use hazard warning lights if necessary.

☐ If you have one, use a warning triangle to alert other drivers of your presence.

☐ Apply the handbrake and engage first or reverse gear (or Park on models with automatic transmission).

☐ Chock the wheel diagonally opposite the one being removed – a couple of large stones will do for this.

☐ If the ground is soft, use a flat piece of wood to spread the load under the jack.

Changing the wheel

1 On Saloon and Hatchback models the jack and wheel brace are stowed at the right-hand side of the luggage compartment, behind a cover. On Estate models they are beneath a cover in a compartment on the left-hand side of the luggage compartment.

2 The spare wheel is stored beneath a cover in the luggage compartment. Raise the cover, remove the securing screw and lift out the spare wheel. Place it beneath the sill as a precaution against the jack failing.

3 On models with steel wheels, use the special tool to pull the wheel trim from the wheel. On models with alloy wheels, use the screwdriver provided inserted at the wheel bolt holes, to prise off the trim. Where an anti-theft device is fitted, use the tool provided to remove the trim. Loosen each wheel bolt by half a turn.

4 Locate the jack head below the reinforced jacking point nearest the wheel to be changed, and on firm ground. The jacking point is indicated by the cut-outs in the sill. Turn the handle until the base of the jack touches the ground then make sure that the base is located directly below the sill. Raise the vehicle until the wheel is clear of the ground. If the tyre is flat make sure that the vehicle is raised sufficiently to allow the spare wheel to be fitted.

5 Remove the bolts and lift the wheel from the vehicle. Place it beneath the sill in place of the spare as a precaution against the jack failing. Fit the spare wheel and tighten the bolts moderately with the wheel brace.

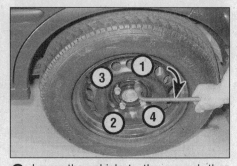

6 Lower the vehicle to the ground, then finally tighten the wheel bolts in a diagonal sequence. Refit the wheel trim. Note that the wheel bolts should be tightened to the specified torque at the earliest opportunity.

Finally...

☐ Remove the wheel chocks.

☐ Stow the jack and tools in the correct locations in the car.

☐ Check the tyre pressure on the wheel just fitted. If it is low, or if you don't have a pressure gauge with you, drive slowly to the nearest garage and inflate the tyre to the right pressure.

☐ Have the damaged tyre or wheel repaired as soon as possible.

Identifying leaks

Puddles on the garage floor or drive, or obvious wetness under the bonnet or underneath the car, suggest a leak that needs investigating. It can sometimes be difficult to decide where the leak is coming from, especially if the engine bay is very dirty already. Leaking oil or fluid can also be blown rearwards by the passage of air under the car, giving a false impression of where the problem lies.

 Warning: Most automotive oils and fluids are poisonous. Wash them off skin, and change out of contaminated clothing, without delay.

 HAYNES HiNT *The smell of a fluid leaking from the car may provide a clue to what's leaking. Some fluids are distinctively coloured. It may help to clean the car carefully and to park it over some clean paper overnight as an aid to locating the source of the leak.*

Remember that some leaks may only occur while the engine is running.

Sump oil

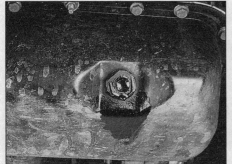

Engine oil may leak from the drain plug...

Oil from filter

...or from the base of the oil filter.

Gearbox oil

Gearbox oil can leak from the seals at the inboard ends of the driveshafts.

Antifreeze

Leaking antifreeze often leaves a crystalline deposit like this.

Brake fluid

A leak occurring at a wheel is almost certainly brake fluid.

Power steering fluid

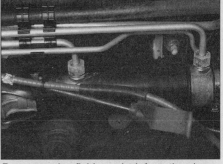

Power steering fluid may leak from the pipe connectors on the steering rack.

Towing

When all else fails, you may find yourself having to get a tow home – or of course you may be helping somebody else. Long-distance recovery should only be done by a garage or breakdown service. For shorter distances, DIY towing using another car is easy enough, but observe the following points:

☐ Use a proper tow-rope – they are not expensive. The vehicle being towed must display an 'ON TOW' sign in its rear window.

☐ Always turn the ignition key to the 'on' position when the vehicle is being towed, so that the steering lock is released, and that the direction indicator and brake lights will work.

☐ Before being towed, release the handbrake and select neutral on the transmission.

☐ Note that greater-than-usual pedal pressure will be required to operate the brakes, since the vacuum servo unit is only operational with the engine running.

☐ On models with power steering, greater-than-usual steering effort will also be required.

☐ The driver of the car being towed must keep the tow-rope taut at all times to avoid snatching.

☐ Make sure that both drivers know the route before setting off.

☐ Only drive at moderate speeds and keep the distance towed to a minimum. Drive smoothly and allow plenty of time for slowing down at junctions.

☐ On models with automatic transmission, special precautions apply. If in doubt, do not tow, or transmission damage may result.

☐ A towing eye is provided with the warning triangle and first aid kit in the luggage compartment.

☐ To fit the towing eye, prise the cover from the front bumper, then screw in the towing eye anti-clockwise as far as it will go using the handle of the wheel brace to turn the eye. **Note that the towing eye has a left-hand thread.** A rear towing eye is provided beneath the rear of the vehicle.

Introduction

There are some very simple checks which need only take a few minutes to carry out, but which could save you a lot of inconvenience and expense.

These "Weekly checks" require no great skill or special tools, and the small amount of time they take to perform could prove to be very well spent, for example;

☐ Keeping an eye on tyre condition and pressures, will not only help to stop them wearing out prematurely, but could also save your life.

☐ Many breakdowns are caused by electrical problems. Battery-related faults are particularly common, and a quick check on a regular basis will often prevent the majority of these.

☐ If your car develops a brake fluid leak, the first time you might know about it is when your brakes don't work properly. Checking the level regularly will give advance warning of this kind of problem.

☐ If the oil or coolant levels run low, the cost of repairing any engine damage will be far greater than fixing the leak, for example.

Underbonnet check points

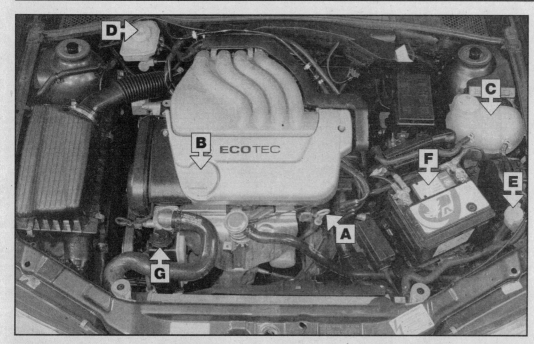

◀ **1.6 litre DOHC petrol**

A *Engine oil level dipstick*

B *Engine oil filler cap*

C *Coolant reservoir (expansion tank)*

D *Hydraulic fluid reservoir*

E *Washer fluid reservoir*

F *Battery*

G *Power steering fluid reservoir*

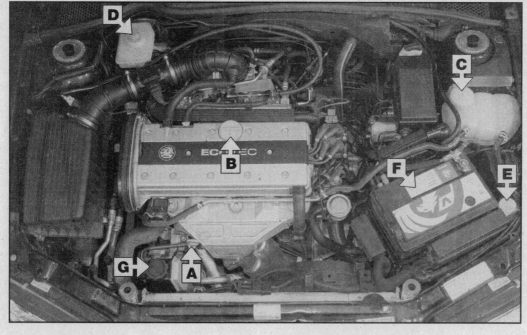

◀ **2.0 litre DOHC petrol**

A *Engine oil level dipstick*

B *Engine oil filler cap*

C *Coolant reservoir (expansion tank)*

D *Hydraulic fluid reservoir*

E *Washer fluid reservoir*

F *Battery*

G *Power steering fluid reservoir*

◀ **2.0 litre diesel**

A *Engine oil level dipstick*

B *Engine oil filler cap*

C *Coolant reservoir (expansion tank)*

D *Hydraulic fluid reservoir*

E *Washer fluid reservoir*

F *Battery*

G *Power steering fluid reservoir*

Engine oil level

Before you start

✔ Make sure that your car is on level ground.
✔ Check the oil level before the car is driven, or at least 5 minutes after the engine has been switched off.

HAYNES HiNT *If the oil is checked immediately after driving the vehicle, some of the oil will remain in the upper engine components, resulting in an inaccurate reading on the dipstick!*

The correct oil

Modern engines place great demands on their oil. It is very important that the correct oil for your car is used (See "Lubricants and fluids").

Car Care

● If you have to add oil frequently, you should check whether you have any oil leaks. Place some clean paper under the car overnight, and check for stains in the morning. If there are no leaks, the engine may be burning oil .

● Always maintain the level between the upper and lower dipstick marks (see photo 3). If the level is too low severe engine damage may occur. Oil seal failure may result if the engine is overfilled by adding too much oil.

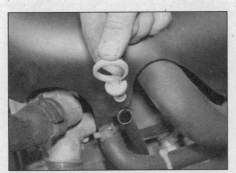
1 The dipstick is located on the front of the engine (see *"Underbonnet Check Points"* on pages 0•10 and 0•11 for exact location). Withdraw the dipstick.

2 Using a clean rag or paper towel remove all oil from the dipstick. Insert the clean dipstick into the tube as far as it will go, then withdraw it again.

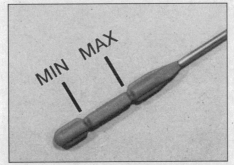
3 Note the oil level on the end of the dipstick, which should be between the upper ("MAX") mark and lower ("MIN") mark. Approximately 1.0 litre of oil will raise the level from the lower mark to the upper mark.

4 Oil is added through the filler cap. Rotate the cap through a quarter-turn anti-clockwise and withdraw it. Top-up the level. A funnel may help to reduce spillage. Add the oil slowly, checking the level on the dipstick often. Do not overfill.

Coolant level

 Warning: DO NOT attempt to remove the expansion tank pressure cap when the engine is hot, as there is a very great risk of scalding. Do not leave open containers of coolant about, as it is poisonous.

Car Care

● With a sealed-type cooling system, adding coolant should not be necessary on a regular basis. If frequent topping-up is required, it is likely there is a leak. Check the radiator, all hoses and joint faces for signs of staining or wetness, and rectify as necessary.

● It is important that antifreeze is used in the cooling system all year round, not just during the winter months. Don't top-up with water alone, as the antifreeze will become too diluted.

1 The coolant level varies with the temperature of the engine. When the engine is cold, the coolant level should be slightly above the KALT/COLD mark on the side of the tank. When the engine is hot, the level will rise.

2 If topping up is necessary, **wait until the engine is cold**. Slowly unscrew the expansion tank cap, to release any pressure present in the cooling system, and remove it.

3 Add a mixture of water and antifreeze to the expansion tank until the coolant is up to the MAX level mark. Refit the cap and tighten it securely.

Brake and clutch fluid level

 Warning:
● *Brake fluid can harm your eyes and damage painted surfaces, so use extreme caution when handling and pouring it.*
● *Do not use fluid that has been standing open for some time, as it absorbs moisture from the air, which can cause a dangerous loss of braking effectiveness.*

 HAYNES HINT ● *Make sure that your car is on level ground.*
● *The fluid level in the reservoir will drop slightly as the brake pads wear down, but the fluid level must never be allowed to drop below the "MIN" mark.*

Safety First!

● If the reservoir requires repeated topping-up this is an indication of a fluid leak somewhere in the system, which should be investigated immediately.

● If a leak is suspected, the car should not be driven until the braking system has been checked. Never take any risks where brakes are concerned.

1 The "MAX" and "MIN" marks are indicated on the front of the reservoir. The fluid level must be kept between the marks at all times.

2 If topping-up is necessary, first wipe clean the area around the filler cap to prevent dirt entering the hydraulic system.

3 Carefully add fluid, taking care not to spill it onto the surrounding components. Use only the specified fluid; mixing different types can cause damage to the system. After topping-up to the correct level, securely refit the cap and wipe off any spilt fluid.

Screen washer fluid level

Screenwash additives not only keep the windscreen clean during foul weather, they also prevent the washer system freezing in cold weather - which is when you are likely to need it most. Don't top up using plain water as the screenwash will become too diluted, and will freeze during cold weather. *On no account use coolant antifreeze in the washer system - this could discolour or damage paintwork.*

1 The reservoir for the windscreen and rear window (where applicable) washer systems is located on the front left-hand side of the engine compartment. If topping-up is necessary, open the cap.

2 When topping-up the reservoir(s) a screenwash additive should be added in the quantities recommended on the bottle.

Power steering fluid level

Before you start:
✔ Park the vehicle on level ground.
✔ With the engine idling, turn the steering wheel slowly from lock to lock 2 or 3 times and set the front wheels at the straight-ahead position, then stop the engine.

 HAYNES HINT *For the check to be accurate, the steering must not be turned once the engine has been stopped.*

Safety First!
● The need for frequent topping-up indicates a leak, which should be investigated immediately.

1 The power steering fluid reservoir is located at the front of the engine compartment. The fluid level should be checked with the engine stopped.

2 Unscrew the filler cap from the top of the reservoir, and wipe all fluid from the cap dipstick with a clean rag. Refit the filler cap, then remove it again. Note the fluid level on the dipstick.

3 When the engine is cold, the fluid level should be between the upper and lower marks on the dipstick where MIN and MAX marks are provided. Where only one mark is provided, the level should be between the bottom of the dipstick and the mark. Top up the fluid level using the specified type of fluid (do not overfill the reservoir), then refit and tighten the filler cap.

Tyre condition and pressure

It is very important that tyres are in good condition, and at the correct pressure - having a tyre failure at any speed is highly dangerous. Tyre wear is influenced by driving style - harsh braking and acceleration, or fast cornering, will all produce more rapid tyre wear. As a general rule, the front tyres wear out faster than the rears. Interchanging the tyres from front to rear ("rotating" the tyres) may result in more even wear. However, if this is completely effective, you may have the expense of replacing all four tyres at once! Remove any nails or stones embedded in the tread before they penetrate the tyre to cause deflation. If removal of a nail does reveal that the tyre has been punctured, refit the nail so that its point of penetration is marked. Then immediately change the wheel, and have the tyre repaired by a tyre dealer.

Regularly check the tyres for damage in the form of cuts or bulges, especially in the sidewalls. Periodically remove the wheels, and clean any dirt or mud from the inside and outside surfaces. Examine the wheel rims for signs of rusting, corrosion or other damage. Light alloy wheels are easily damaged by "kerbing" whilst parking; steel wheels may also become dented or buckled. A new wheel is very often the only way to overcome severe damage.

New tyres should be balanced when they are fitted, but it may become necessary to re-balance them as they wear, or if the balance weights fitted to the wheel rim should fall off. Unbalanced tyres will wear more quickly, as will the steering and suspension components. Wheel imbalance is normally signified by vibration, particularly at a certain speed (typically around 50 mph). If this vibration is felt only through the steering, then it is likely that just the front wheels need balancing. If, however, the vibration is felt through the whole car, the rear wheels could be out of balance. Wheel balancing should be carried out by a tyre dealer or garage.

1 Tread Depth - visual check
The original tyres have tread wear safety bands (B), which will appear when the tread depth reaches approximately 1.6 mm. The band positions are indicated by a triangular mark on the tyre sidewall (A).

2 Tread Depth - manual check
Alternatively, tread wear can be monitored with a simple, inexpensive device known as a tread depth indicator gauge.

3 Tyre Pressure Check
Check the tyre pressures regularly with the tyres cold. Do not adjust the tyre pressures immediately after the vehicle has been used, or an inaccurate setting will result. Tyre pressures are shown on page 0•18.

Tyre tread wear patterns

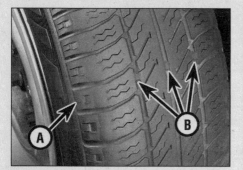

Shoulder Wear

Underinflation (wear on both sides)
Under-inflation will cause overheating of the tyre, because the tyre will flex too much, and the tread will not sit correctly on the road surface. This will cause a loss of grip and excessive wear, not to mention the danger of sudden tyre failure due to heat build-up.
Check and adjust pressures
Incorrect wheel camber (wear on one side)
Repair or renew suspension parts
Hard cornering
Reduce speed!

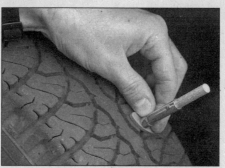

Centre Wear

Overinflation
Over-inflation will cause rapid wear of the centre part of the tyre tread, coupled with reduced grip, harsher ride, and the danger of shock damage occurring in the tyre casing.
Check and adjust pressures

If you sometimes have to inflate your car's tyres to the higher pressures specified for maximum load or sustained high speed, don't forget to reduce the pressures to normal afterwards.

Uneven Wear

Front tyres may wear unevenly as a result of wheel misalignment. Most tyre dealers and garages can check and adjust the wheel alignment (or "tracking") for a modest charge.
Incorrect camber or castor
Repair or renew suspension parts
Malfunctioning suspension
Repair or renew suspension parts
Unbalanced wheel
Balance tyres
Incorrect toe setting
Adjust front wheel alignment
Note: *The feathered edge of the tread which typifies toe wear is best checked by feel.*

Wiper blades

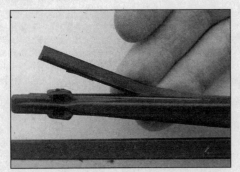

1 Check the condition of the wiper blades; if they are cracked or show any signs of deterioration, or if the glass swept area is smeared, renew them. Wiper blades should be renewed annually.

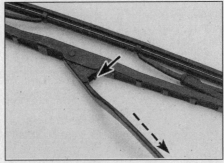

2 To remove a wiper blade, pull the arm fully away from the glass until it locks. Swivel the blade through 90º, then squeeze the locking clip, and detach the blade from the arm. When fitting the new blade, make sure that the blade locks securely into the arm, and that the blade is orientated correctly.

Battery

Caution: Before carrying out any work on the vehicle battery, read the precautions given in "Safety first" at the start of this manual.

✔ Make sure that the battery tray is in good condition, and that the clamp is tight. Corrosion on the tray, retaining clamp and the battery itself can be removed with a solution of water and baking soda. Thoroughly rinse all cleaned areas with water. Any metal parts damaged by corrosion should be covered with a zinc-based primer, then painted.

✔ Periodically (approximately every three months), check the charge condition of the battery as described in Chapter 5A.

✔ If the battery is flat, and you need to jump start your vehicle, see *Roadside Repairs*.

1 The battery is located on the left-hand side of the engine compartment. Unclip the fabric cover from the top of the battery for access to the terminals. The exterior of the battery should be inspected periodically for damage such as a cracked case or cover.

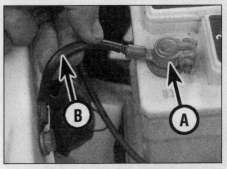

2 Check the tightness of battery clamps (A) to ensure good electrical connections. You should not be able to move them. Also check each cable (B) for cracks and frayed conductors.

HAYNES HiNT

Battery corrosion can be kept to a minimum by applying a layer of petroleum jelly to the clamps and terminals after they are reconnected.

3 If corrosion (white, fluffy deposits) is evident, remove the cables from the battery terminals, clean them with a small wire brush, then refit them. Automotive stores sell a tool for cleaning the battery post . . .

4 . . . as well as the battery cable clamps

Electrical systems

✔ Check all external lights and the horn. Refer to the appropriate Sections of Chapter 12 for details if any of the circuits are found to be inoperative.

✔ Visually check all accessible wiring connectors, harnesses and retaining clips for security, and for signs of chafing or damage.

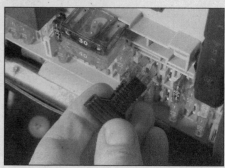

1 If a single indicator light, stop-light or headlight has failed, it is likely that a bulb has blown and will need to be replaced. Refer to Chapter 12 for details. If both stop-lights have failed, it is possible that the switch has failed (see Chapter 9).

2 If more than one indicator light or headlight has failed, it is likely that either a fuse has blown or that there is a fault in the circuit (see Chapter 12). The main fuses are located beneath a cover on the driver's side of the facia. Pull up and remove the cover, then pull out the bottom of the fusebox. Additional fuses and relays are located in the left-hand side of the engine compartment.

3 To replace a blown fuse, remove it, where applicable, using the plastic tool provided. Fit a new fuse of the same rating, available from car accessory shops. It is important that you find the reason that the fuse blew (see *"Electrical fault finding"* in Chapter 12).

Advanced driving

Many people see the words 'advanced driving' and believe that it won't interest them or that it is a style of driving beyond their own abilities. Nothing could be further from the truth. Advanced driving is straightforward safe, sensible driving - the sort of driving we should all do every time we get behind the wheel.

An average of 10 people are killed every day on UK roads and 870 more are injured, some seriously. Lives are ruined daily, usually because somebody did something stupid. Something like 95% of all accidents are due to human error, mostly driver failure. Sometimes we make genuine mistakes - everyone does. Sometimes we have lapses of concentration. Sometimes we deliberately take risks.

For many people, the process of 'learning to drive' doesn't go much further than learning how to pass the driving test because of a common belief that good drivers are made by 'experience'.

Learning to drive by 'experience' teaches three driving skills:

☐ Quick reactions. (Whoops, that was close!)
☐ Good handling skills. (Horn, swerve, brake, horn).
☐ Reliance on vehicle technology. (Great stuff this ABS, stop in no distance even in the wet...)

Drivers whose skills are 'experience based' generally have a lot of near misses and the odd accident. The results can be seen every day in our courts and our hospital casualty departments.

Advanced drivers have learnt to control the risks by controlling the position and speed of their vehicle. They avoid accidents and near misses, even if the drivers around them make mistakes.

The key skills of advanced driving are **concentration,** effective all-round **observation, anticipation** and **planning.** When **good vehicle handling** is added to

these skills, all driving situations can be approached and negotiated in a safe, methodical way, leaving nothing to chance.

Concentration means applying your mind to safe driving, completely excluding anything that's not relevant. Driving is usually the most dangerous activity that most of us undertake in our daily routines. It deserves our full attention.

Observation means not just looking, but seeing and seeking out the information found in the driving environment.

Anticipation means asking yourself what is happening, what you can reasonably expect to happen and what could happen unexpectedly. (One of the commonest words used in compiling accident reports is 'suddenly'.)

Planning is the link between seeing something and taking the appropriate action. For many drivers, planning is the missing link.

If you want to become a safer and more skilful driver and you want to enjoy your driving more, contact the Institute of Advanced Motorists on 0208 994 4403 or write to IAM House, Chiswick High Road, London W4 4HS for an information pack.

Lubricants and fluids

Engine:

Petrol . . . . Multigrade engine oil, viscosity range SAE 10W/40 to 20W/50, to API SG/CD or SH/CD
(Duckhams QXR Premium Petrol Engine Oil or Duckhams Hypergrade Petrol Engine Oil)

Diesel . . . . Multigrade engine oil, viscosity SAE 5W/40 to 15W/40 to CCMC-G5/PD2
(Duckhams QXR Premium Diesel Engine Oil)

Cooling system . . . . Ethylene-glycol based antifreeze
(Duckhams Antifreeze and Summer Coolant)

Manual gearbox . . . . Gear oil, Vauxhall part number 90 001 777
(Duckhams Hypoid Gear Oil 80W GL-4, or Duckhams Hypoid Gear Oil 75W-90 GL-4)

Automatic transmission . . . . Dexron II type ATF
(Duckhams ATF Autotrans III)

Power steering reservoir . . . . Dexron II type ATF
(Duckhams ATF Autotrans III)

Hydraulic fluid reservoir . . . . Hydraulic fluid to SAE J1703, DOT 3 or DOT 4
(Duckhams Universal Brake and Clutch Fluid)

Choosing your engine oil

Engines need oil, not only to lubricate moving parts and minimise wear, but also to maximise power output and to improve fuel economy. By introducing a simplified and improved range of engine oils, Duckhams has taken away the confusion and made it easier for you to choose the right oil for your engine.

HOW ENGINE OIL WORKS

• Beating friction

Without oil, the moving surfaces inside your engine will rub together, heat up and melt, quickly causing the engine to seize. Engine oil creates a film which separates these moving parts, preventing wear and heat build-up.

• Cooling hot-spots

Temperatures inside the engine can exceed 1000° C. The engine oil circulates and acts as a coolant, transferring heat from the hot-spots to the sump.

• Cleaning the engine internally

Good quality engine oils clean the inside of your engine, collecting and dispersing combustion deposits and controlling them until they are trapped by the oil filter or flushed out at oil change.

OIL CARE - FOLLOW THE CODE

To handle and dispose of used engine oil safely, always:

OIL CARE
FOLLOW THE CODE
OIL BANK LINE
0800 66 33 66
www.oilbankline.org.uk

• Avoid skin contact with used engine oil. Repeated or prolonged contact can be harmful.
• Dispose of used oil and empty packs in a responsible manner in an authorised disposal site. Call 0800 663366 to find the one nearest to you. Never tip oil down drains or onto the ground.

Tyre pressures (cold)

Note: *Pressures apply to original-equipment tyres, and may vary if any other make or type of tyre is fitted; check with the tyre manufacturer or supplier for correct pressures if necessary. The pressures are given on the inside of the fuel filler flap.*

Tyre size	Front	Rear
1.6 litre petrol engine models		
175/70:		
Up to 3 persons	33 psi (2.3 bar)	33 psi (2.3 bar)
Full load	34 psi (2.4 bar)	43 psi (3.0 bar)
185/70:		
Up to 3 persons	29 psi (2.0 bar)	29 psi (2.0 bar)
Full load	30 psi (2.1 bar)	39 psi (2.7 bar)
195/65:		
Up to 3 persons	29 psi (2.0 bar)	29 psi (2.0 bar)
Full load	30 psi (2.1 bar)	39 psi (2.7 bar)
1.8 and 2.0 litre petrol engine models		
175/70:		
Up to 3 persons	36 psi (2.5 bar)	36 psi (2.5 bar)
Full load	37 psi (2.6 bar)	46 psi (3.2 bar)
185/70:		
Up to 3 persons	32 psi (2.2 bar)	32 psi (2.2 bar)
Full load	33 psi (2.3 bar)	42 psi (2.9 bar)
195/65:		
Up to 3 persons	32 psi (2.2 bar)	32 psi (2.2 bar)
Full load	33 psi (2.3 bar)	42 psi (2.9 bar)
1.7 litre diesel engine models		
175/70:		
Up to 3 persons	36 psi (2.5 bar)	36 psi (2.5 bar)
Full load	36 psi (2.5 bar)	45 psi (3.1 bar)
185/70:		
Up to 3 persons	30 psi (2.1 bar)	30 psi (2.1 bar)
Full load	32 psi (2.2 bar)	40 psi (2.8 bar)
195/65:		
Up to 3 persons	30 psi (2.1 bar)	30 psi (2.1 bar)
Full load	32 psi (2.2 bar)	40 psi (2.8 bar)
2.0 litre diesel engine models:		
185/70:		
Up to 3 persons	33 psi (2.3 bar)	33 psi (2.3 bar)
Full load	34 psi (2.4 bar)	43 psi (3.0 bar)
195/65:		
Up to 3 persons	33 psi (2.3 bar)	33 psi (2.3 bar)
Full load	34 psi (2.4 bar)	43 psi (3.0 bar)

Chapter 1 Part A:
Routine maintenance and servicing - petrol engine models

Contents

Degrees of difficulty

Easy, suitable for novice with little experience	**Fairly easy,** suitable for beginner with some experience	**Fairly difficult,** suitable for competent DIY mechanic	**Difficult,** suitable for experienced DIY mechanic	**Very difficult,** suitable for expert DIY or professional

Lubricants and fluids .... Refer to *"Weekly checks"* on page 0•17

Capacities

Engine oil
Including oil filter:
1.6 litre engine	3.5 litres
1.8 and 2.0 litre engines:	
With one-part sump	4.25 litres
With two-part sump	5.00 litres
Difference between MIN and MAX on dipstick	1.0 litre

Cooling system

	Models without air conditioning	Models with air conditioning
1.6 litre SOHC engine	6.1 litres	6.4 litres
1.6 litre DOHC and 1.8 litre (X18XE1) engines	6.7 litres	7.0 litres
1.8 litre engine	7.3 litres	7.3 litres
2.0 litre engine	7.2 litres	7.2 litres

Transmission
Manual transmission:
1.6 litre SOHC engine	1.6 litres
1.6 litre DOHC engine:	
Early models (F15 transmission)	1.8 litres
Later models (F17 transmission)	1.6 litres
1.8 and 2.0 litre engines	1.9 litres
Automatic transmission:	
At fluid change	3.0 to 3.5 litres
From dry	5.0 litres (approximately)

Washer fluid reservoir
Without headlight washers	2.6 litres
With headlight washers	5.5 litres
Fuel tank	60 litres

Cooling system
Antifreeze mixture:
44% antifreeze	Protection down to -30°C
52% antifreeze	Protection down to -40°C

Note: *Refer to antifreeze manufacturer for latest recommendations.*

Ignition system

Spark plugs:	Type	Electrode gap
All engines	Bosch FLR 8 LD+U	1.0 mm

Brakes
Friction material minimum thickness (including backing plate):
Front brake pads	7.5 mm
Rear brake pads	7.0 mm
Rear brake shoes	0.5 mm above the rivet heads

Torque wrench settings

	Nm	lbf ft
Engine oil filter (spin-on canister type)	15	11
Engine oil filter housing cap (element type)	15	11
Engine oil filter housing-to-block bolt (element type)	45	33
Sump drain plug:		
1.6 litre SOHC engine:		
With an alloy sump	45	33
With a pressed-steel sump	55	41
All other engines:		
With rubber seal ring	10	7
With metal seal ring	45	33
Level plug:		
F13 and F18 transmission unit:		
Stage 1	4	3
Stage 2	Angle-tighten a further 45 to 180°	
All other transmission units	30	22
Ignition DIS module screws	8	5

1 The maintenance intervals in this manual are provided with the assumption that you, not the dealer, will be carrying out the work. These are the minimum maintenance intervals recommended by us for vehicles driven daily. If you wish to keep your vehicle in peak condition at all times, you may wish to perform some of these procedures more often. We encourage frequent maintenance, because it enhances the efficiency, performance and resale value of your vehicle. **2** If the vehicle is driven in dusty areas, used to tow a trailer, or driven frequently at slow speeds (idling in traffic) or on short journeys, more frequent maintenance intervals are recommended.
3 When the vehicle is new, it should be serviced by a factory-authorised dealer service department, in order to preserve the factory warranty.

Every 5000 miles (7500 km) or 6 months, whichever comes first

☐ Renew the engine oil and filter (Section 3)

Note: *Vauxhall recommend that the engine oil and filter are changed every 10 000 miles or 12 months. However, oil and filter changes are good for the engine and we recommend that the oil and filter are renewed more frequently, especially if the vehicle is used on a lot of short journeys.*

Every 10 000 miles (15 000 km) or 12 months, whichever comes first

☐ Check the condition and tension of the auxiliary drivebelts (Section 4)*
☐ Exhaust emission test (Section 5)
☐ Check the operation of all electrical systems (Section 6)*
☐ Check and if necessary adjust the headlight beam alignment (Section 7)
☐ Check the body and underbody for corrosion protection (Section 8)
☐ Check the front brake pads and discs for wear (Section 9)*
☐ Check the rear brake pads and discs (where applicable) for wear (Section 10)*
☐ Check all components, pipes and hoses for fluid leaks (Section 11)
☐ Check the roadwheel bolts are tightened to the specified torque (Section 12)*
☐ Check the rear suspension level control system (where applicable) (Section 13)*
☐ Renew the pollen filter (Section 14)*
  Note: *If the vehicle is used in dusty conditions, the pollen filter should be renewed more frequently.*
☐ Carry out a road test (Section 15)*

* On vehicles covering a high mileage (more than 20 000 miles/ 30 000 km annually) carry out the items marked with an asterisk every 10 000 miles/15 000 km, regardless of time, and carry out the items not marked with an asterisk at the 12 month interval.

Every 20 000 miles (30 000 km) or 2 years, whichever comes first

☐ Renew the air cleaner element (Section 16)
☐ Renew the fuel filter (Section 17)
☐ Check and if necessary top up the manual transmission oil level (Section 18)
☐ Check and if necessary top up the automatic transmission fluid level (Section 19)
☐ Lubricate all door locks and hinges, door stops, bonnet lock and release, and tailgate lock and hinges (Section 20)
☐ Check the rear brake shoes and drums for wear (Section 21)
☐ Check the steering and suspension components for condition and security (Section 22)
☐ Check the condition of the driveshaft gaiters (Section 23)

Every 40 000 miles (60 000 km) or 4 years, whichever comes first

☐ Renew the spark plugs and check the ignition system (Section 24)
☐ Renew the timing belt (Section 25)

Note: *From 1997 Model Year onwards, Vauxhall increased the specified interval for timing belt renewal to 80 000 (120 000 km) or 8 years. However, if the vehicle is used mainly for short journeys or a lot of stop-start driving it is recommended that the earlier (pre 1997) recommendation is adhered to. The actual belt renewal interval is very much up to the individual owner but, bearing in mind that severe engine damage will result if the belt breaks in use, we recommend you err on the side of caution.*

Every 2 years, regardless of mileage

☐ Renew the hydraulic fluid (Section 26)
☐ Renew the remote control batteries (Section 27)
☐ Renew the coolant (Section 28)

Underbonnet view of a 1.6 litre DOHC engine model

1 Engine oil filler cap
2 Air cleaner
3 Front suspension strut upper mounting
4 Hydraulic fluid reservoir
5 Auxiliary fuse and relay box
6 Cooling system expansion tank
7 Battery
8 Washer fluid reservoir
9 Radiator
10 Engine oil level dipstick
11 Air injection valve
12 Radiator top hose
13 Thermostat housing
14 Power steering fluid reservoir

Front underbody view of a 1.6 litre DOHC engine model

1 Exhaust front downpipe
2 Oil filter
3 Electric cooling fan motor
4 Engine oil drain plug
5 Front suspension lower arm
6 Steering track rod
7 Driveshaft
8 Subframe
9 Manual transmission
10 Washer fluid reservoir

Underbonnet view of a 2.0 litre engine model

1 Engine oil filler cap
2 Front suspension strut upper mounting
3 Hydraulic fluid reservoir
4 Air cleaner
5 Auxiliary fuse and relay box
6 Cooling system expansion tank
7 Battery
8 Washer fluid reservoir
9 Auxiliary fuse/relay box
10 Radiator
11 Air injection valve
12 Power steering fluid reservoir
13 Radiator top hose
14 Engine oil level dipstick

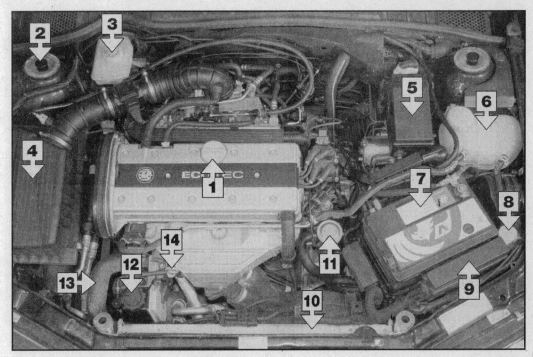

Front underbody view of a 2.0 litre engine model

1 Front suspension lower arm
2 Engine oil drain plug
3 Exhaust front downpipe
4 Manual transmission
5 Washer fluid reservoir
6 Steering track rod

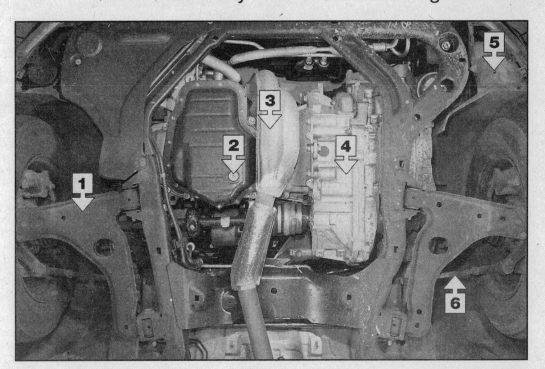

1A

Typical rear underbody

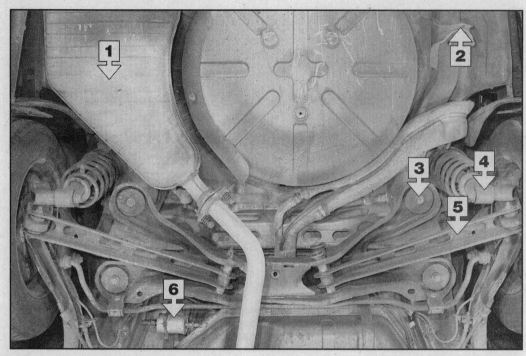

1 Exhaust rear silencer
2 Rear towing eye
3 Rear suspension crossmember
4 Rear suspension strut
5 Rear suspension lower arm
6 Fuel filter

1 General information

1 This Chapter is designed to help the home mechanic maintain his/her vehicle for safety, economy, long life and peak performance.
2 The Chapter contains a master maintenance schedule, followed by Sections dealing specifically with each task in the schedule. Visual checks, adjustments, component renewal and other helpful items are included. Refer to the accompanying illustrations of the engine compartment and the underside of the vehicle for the locations of the various components.
3 Servicing your vehicle in accordance with the mileage/time maintenance schedule and the following Sections will provide a planned maintenance programme, which should result in a long and reliable service life. This is a comprehensive plan, so maintaining some items but not others at the specified service intervals, will not produce the same results.
4 As you service your vehicle, you will discover that many of the procedures can - and should - be grouped together, because of the particular procedure being performed, or because of the proximity of two otherwise-unrelated components to one another. For example, if the vehicle is raised for any reason, the exhaust can be inspected at the same time as the suspension and steering components.

5 The first step in this maintenance programme is to prepare yourself before the actual work begins. Read through all the Sections relevant to the work to be carried out, then make a list and gather all the parts and tools required. If a problem is encountered, seek advice from a parts specialist, or a dealer service department.

2 Regular maintenance

1 If, from the time the vehicle is new, the routine maintenance schedule is followed closely, and frequent checks are made of fluid levels and high-wear items, as suggested throughout this manual, the engine will be kept in relatively good running condition, and the need for additional work will be minimised.
2 It is possible that there will be times when the engine is running poorly due to the lack of regular maintenance. This is even more likely if a used vehicle, which has not received regular and frequent maintenance checks, is purchased. In such cases, additional work may need to be carried out, outside of the regular maintenance intervals.
3 If engine wear is suspected, a compression test (refer to Chapter 2A or 2B, as applicable) will provide valuable information regarding the overall performance of the main internal components. Such a test can be used as a basis to decide on the extent of the work to be carried out. If, for example, a compression

test indicates serious internal engine wear, conventional maintenance as described in this Chapter will not greatly improve the performance of the engine, and may prove a waste of time and money, unless extensive overhaul work is carried out first.
4 The following series of operations are those most often required to improve the performance of a generally poor-running engine:

Primary operations

a) Clean, inspect and test the battery (refer to "Weekly checks").
b) Check all the engine-related fluids (refer to "Weekly checks").
c) Check the condition and tension of the auxiliary drivebelt (Section 4).
d) Renew the spark plugs (Section 25).
e) Check the condition of the air filter, and renew if necessary (Section 16).
f) Renew the fuel filter (Section 17).
g) Check the condition of all hoses, and check for fluid leaks (Section 11).
5 If the above operations do not prove fully effective, carry out the following secondary operations:

Secondary operations

All items listed under "Primary operations", plus the following:
a) Check the charging system (refer to Chapter 5A).
b) Check the ignition system (refer to Chapter 5B).
c) Check the fuel system (refer to Chapter 4A).

3.9a Using an oil filter removal tool to slacken the filter (viewed from underneath the vehicle)

3.9b Oil filter cap O-ring - 1.8 (X18XE1) litre engine

Every 5000 miles (7500 km) or 6 months

3 Engine oil and filter renewal

1 Frequent oil and filter changes are the most important preventative maintenance procedures which can be undertaken by the DIY owner. As engine oil ages, it becomes diluted and contaminated, which leads to premature engine wear.

2 Before starting this procedure, gather together all the necessary tools and materials. Also make sure that you have plenty of clean rags and newspapers handy, to mop up any spills. Ideally, the engine oil should be warm, as it will drain more easily, and more built-up sludge will be removed with it. Take care not to touch the exhaust or any other hot parts of the engine when working under the vehicle. To avoid any possibility of scalding, and to protect yourself from possible skin irritants and other harmful contaminants in used engine oils, it is advisable to wear gloves when carrying out this work.

3 Firmly apply the handbrake then jack up the front of the vehicle and support it on axle stands (see *"Jacking and Vehicle Support"*).

4 Remove the oil filler cap.

5 Using a spanner, or preferably a suitable socket and bar, slacken the drain plug about half a turn. Position the draining container under the drain plug, then remove the plug completely.

6 Allow some time for the oil to drain, noting that it may be necessary to reposition the container as the oil flow slows to a trickle.

7 After all the oil has drained, wipe the drain plug and the sealing washer with a clean rag. Examine the condition of the sealing washer, and renew it if it shows signs of scoring or other damage which may prevent an oil-tight seal. Clean the area around the drain plug opening, and refit the plug complete with the washer and tighten it to the specified torque.

8 Move the container into position under the oil filter. On 1.6 and 1.8 (X18XE1) litre models

the filter is located on the front of the cylinder block, on 1.8 (X18XE) and 2.0 litre engines it is located on the right-hand end of the rear of the engine, where it is screwed onto the oil pump housing

9 On 1.6, 1.8 (X18XE) and 2.0 litre engines, use an oil filter removal tool to slacken the filter initially, then unscrew it by hand the rest of the way (see illustration). On 1.8 (X18XE1) litre models, undo and remove the oil filter housing cap along with the filter element. Discard the O-ring (see illustration). Empty the oil from the old filter into the container.

10 Use a clean rag to remove all oil, dirt and sludge from the filter sealing area on the engine. On 1.8 (X18XE1) litre models, if required the oil filter housing can be removed from the cylinder block by unscrewing the retaining bolt (see illustration). The housing can then be thoroughly cleaned and refitted to the block with a new sealing ring. Tighten the retaining bolt to the specified torque.

11 On 1.6, 1.8 (X18XE) and 2.0 litre engines, apply a light coating of clean engine oil to the sealing ring on the new filter, then screw the filter into position on the engine. Tighten the filter firmly by hand only - do not use any tools. If a genuine filter is being fitted and the special oil filter tool (a socket which fits over the end of the filter) is available, tighten the filter to the specified torque. On 1.8 (X18XE1) litre models, insert the new filter element into the housing

cap and, using a new O-ring, screw the cap into the housing, and tighten the cap to the specified torque (see illustration).

12 Remove the old oil and all tools from under the vehicle then lower the vehicle to the ground.

13 Fill the engine through the filler hole, using the correct grade and type of oil (refer to *"Weekly Checks"* for details of topping-up). Pour in half the specified quantity of oil first, then wait a few minutes for the oil to drain into the sump. Continue to add oil, a small quantity at a time, until the level is up to the lower mark on the dipstick. Adding approximately a further 1.0 litre will bring the level up to the upper mark on the dipstick.

14 Start the engine and run it for a few minutes, while checking for leaks around the oil filter seal and the sump drain plug. Note that there may be a delay of a few seconds before the low oil pressure warning light goes out when the engine is first started, as the oil circulates through the new oil filter and the engine oil galleries before the pressure builds up.

15 Stop the engine, and wait a few minutes for the oil to settle in the sump once more. With the new oil circulated and the filter now completely full, recheck the level on the dipstick, and add more oil as necessary.

16 Dispose of the used engine oil safely with reference to *"General repair procedures"*.

1A

3.10 Oil filter housing bolt - 1.8 (X18XE1) litre engine

3.11 Insert the oil filter into the cap - 1.8 (X18XE1) litre engine

Every 10 000 miles (15 000 km) or 12 months

4 Auxiliary drivebelt check and renewal

Checking

1 Due to their function and material makeup, drivebelts are prone to failure after a long period of time and should therefore be inspected regularly.

2 With the engine stopped, inspect the full length of the drivebelt for cracks and separation of the belt plies. It will be necessary to turn the engine (using a spanner or socket and bar on the crankshaft pulley bolt) in order to move the belt from the pulleys so that the belt can be inspected thoroughly. Twist the belt between the pulleys so that both sides can be viewed. Also check for fraying, and glazing which gives the belt a shiny appearance. Check the pulleys for nicks, cracks, distortion and corrosion.

3 Check the position of the drivebelt tensioner assembly arm, the arm should be in between the stops on the backplate and should be free to move (see illustration).

4 If the belt shows signs of wear or damage, or the tensioner arm is against the stop, the belt must be renewed.

Renewal

5 To remove the drivebelt, first remove the air cleaner housing as described in Chapter 4A.

6 On models with air conditioning, it will be necessary to remove the engine/transmission right-hand front mounting in order to allow the belt to be removed/refitted. **Note:** *If the belt is being removed as part of another repair procedure (ie timing belt renewal) and is not to be renewed, the mounting can be left in position. Simply release the tensioner then disengage the belt from the pulleys and position it clear of the engine.*

7 Prior to removal, make a note of the correct routing of the belt around the various pulleys. If the belt is to be re-used, also mark the direction of rotation on the belt to ensure the belt is refitted the same way around.

8 Using a suitable spanner or socket fitted to the tensioner pulley centre bolt, lever the tensioner away from the belt until there is sufficient slack to enable the belt to be slipped off the pulleys. Carefully release the tensioner pulley until it is against its stop then remove the belt from the vehicle.

9 Manoeuvre the belt into position, routing it correctly around the pulleys; if the original belt is being fitted use the marks made prior to removal to ensure it is fitted the correct way around.

10 Lever the tensioner roller back against is spring, and seat the belt on the pulleys. Ensure the belt is centrally located on all pulleys then slowly release the tensioner pulley until the belt is correctly tensioned. **Do not** allow the tensioner to spring back and stress the belt.

11 On models equipped with air conditioning, refit the engine mounting as described in Chapter 2A.

12 On all models, refit the air cleaner housing as described in Chapter 4A.

5 Exhaust emission check

1 Vauxhall specify that this check should be carried out annually on all vehicles. The check involves checking the engine management system operation by plugging an electronic tester into the system diagnostic socket to check the electronic control unit (ECU) memory for faults (see Chapter 4A).

2 In reality, if the vehicle is running correctly and the engine management warning light in the instrument panel is functioning normally, then this check need not be carried out.

6 Electrical systems check

1 Check the operation of all electrical equipment, ie, lights, direction indicators, horn, wash/wipe system, etc. Refer to the appropriate Sections of Chapter 12 for details if any of the circuits are found to be inoperative.

2 Visually check all accessible wiring connectors, harnesses and retaining clips for security, and for signs of chafing or damage. Rectify any faults found.

7 Headlight beam alignment check

Refer to Chapter 12 for details

8 Body corrosion check

This work should be carried out by a Vauxhall/Opel dealer in order to validate the vehicle warranty. The work includes a thorough inspection of the vehicle paintwork and underbody for damage and corrosion

9 Front brake pad and disc check

1 Firmly apply the handbrake, then jack up the front of the vehicle and support it securely on axle stands (see *"Jacking and Vehicle Support"*). Remove the front roadwheels.

2 For a quick check, the pad thickness can be carried out via the inspection hole on the front of the caliper (see Haynes Hint). Using a steel rule, measure the thickness of the pad lining including the backing plate. This must not be less than that indicated in the Specifications.

3 The view through the caliper inspection hole gives a rough indication of the state of the brake pads. For a comprehensive check, the brake pads should be removed and cleaned. The operation of the caliper can then also be checked, and the condition of the brake disc itself can be fully examined on both sides. Chapter 9 contains a detailed description of how the brake disc should be checked for wear and/or damage.

4 If any pad's friction material is worn to the specified thickness or less, *all four pads must be renewed as a set*. Refer to Chapter 9 for details.

5 On completion, refit the roadwheels and lower the vehicle to the ground.

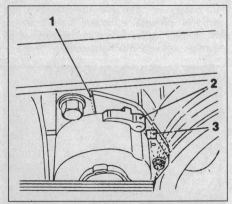

4.3 Check the auxiliary drivebelt tensioner arm indicator (2) is correctly positioned between the stops (1 and 3) on the backplate

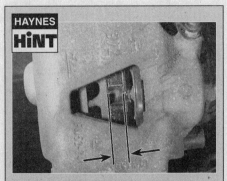

HAYNES HiNT

For a quick check, the thickness of friction material remaining on the inner brake pad can be measured through the aperture in the caliper body

10 Rear brake pad and disc check

1 Chock the front wheels, then jack up the rear of the vehicle and support it securely on axle stands (see *"Jacking and Vehicle Support"*). Remove the rear roadwheels.
2 For a quick check, the pad thickness can be carried out via the inspection hole on the rear of the caliper. Using a steel rule, measure the thickness of the pad lining including the backing plate. This must not be less than that indicated in the Specifications.
3 The view through the caliper inspection hole gives a rough indication of the state of the brake pads. For a comprehensive check, the brake pads should be removed and cleaned. The operation of the caliper can then also be checked, and the condition of the brake disc itself can be fully examined on both sides. Chapter 9 contains a detailed description of how the brake disc should be checked for wear and/or damage.
4 If any pad's friction material is worn to the specified thickness or less, *all four pads must be renewed as a set.* Refer to Chapter 9 for details.
5 On completion, refit the roadwheels and lower the vehicle to the ground.

11 Hose and fluid leak check

1 Visually inspect the engine joint faces, gaskets and seals for any signs of water or oil leaks. Pay particular attention to the areas around the cylinder head cover, cylinder head, oil filter and sump joint faces. Bear in mind that, over a period of time, some very slight seepage from these areas is to be expected - what you are really looking for is any indication of a serious leak. Should a leak be found, renew the offending gasket or oil seal by referring to the appropriate Chapters in this manual.
2 Also check the security and condition of all the engine-related pipes and hoses, and all braking system pipes and hoses and fuel lines. Ensure that all cable ties or securing clips are

in place, and in good condition. Clips which are broken or missing can lead to chafing of the hoses, pipes or wiring, which could cause more serious problems in the future.
3 Carefully check the radiator hoses and heater hoses along their entire length. Renew any hose which is cracked, swollen or deteriorated. Cracks will show up better if the hose is squeezed. Pay close attention to the hose clips that secure the hoses to the cooling system components. Hose clips can pinch and puncture hoses, resulting in cooling system leaks. If the crimped-type hose clips are used, it may be a good idea to replace them with standard worm-drive clips.
4 Inspect all the cooling system components (hoses, joint faces, etc) for leaks.

A leak in the cooling system will usually show up as white- or rust-coloured deposits on the area adjoining the leak.

5 Where any problems are found on system components, renew the component or gasket with reference to Chapter 3.
6 With the vehicle raised, inspect the fuel tank and filler neck for punctures, cracks and other damage. The connection between the filler neck and tank is especially critical. Sometimes a rubber filler neck or connecting hose will leak due to loose retaining clamps or deteriorated rubber.
7 Carefully check all rubber hoses and metal fuel lines leading away from the fuel tank. Check for loose connections, deteriorated hoses, crimped lines, and other damage. Pay particular attention to the vent pipes and hoses, which often loop up around the filler

neck and can become blocked or crimped. Follow the lines to the front of the vehicle, carefully inspecting them all the way. Renew damaged sections as necessary. Similarly, whilst the vehicle is raised, take the opportunity to inspect all underbody brake fluid pipes and hoses.
8 From within the engine compartment, check the security of all fuel, vacuum and brake hose attachments and pipe unions, and inspect all hoses for kinks, chafing and deterioration.
9 Check the condition of the power steering and, where applicable, the automatic transmission fluid pipes and hoses.

12 Wheel bolt tightness check

1 Remove the wheel trims and check the tightness of all the wheel bolts, using a torque wrench
2 Refit the wheel trims on completion.

13 Rear suspension level control system check

Where fitted on Estate models, check that the rear suspension level control system operates correctly. In the event of a fault, have the system checked by a Vauxhall/Opel dealer.

1A

14 Pollen filter renewal

1 Open the bonnet, and pull up the rubber weatherseal from the flange at the rear of the engine compartment **(see illustration)**.
2 Open the cover in the scuttle cover panel for access to the pollen filter **(see illustration)**.
3 Release the clips from each end, then lift out the filter **(see illustration)**.
4 Fit the new filter using a reversal of the removal procedure; make sure that the marking is visible on the right-hand end of the filter, as viewed through the cover.

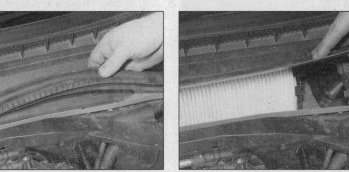

14.1 Pull up the rubber weatherseal . . .   **14.2 . . . then open the cover . . .**

14.3 . . . and lift out the pollen filter

15 Road test

Instruments and electrical equipment

1 Check the operation of all instruments and electrical equipment.
2 Make sure that all instruments read correctly, and switch on all electrical equipment in turn, to check that it functions properly.

Steering and suspension

3 Check for any abnormalities in the steering, suspension, handling or road 'feel'.
4 Drive the vehicle, and check that there are no unusual vibrations or noises.
5 Check that the steering feels positive, with no excessive 'sloppiness', or roughness, and check for any suspension noises when cornering and driving over bumps.

Drivetrain

6 Check the performance of the engine, clutch, transmission and driveshafts.

7 Listen for any unusual noises from the engine, clutch and transmission.
8 Make sure that the engine runs smoothly when idling, and that there is no hesitation when accelerating.
9 Check that, where applicable, the clutch action is smooth and progressive, that the drive is taken up smoothly, and that the pedal travel is not excessive. Also listen for any noises when the clutch pedal is depressed.
10 Check that all gears can be engaged smoothly without noise, and that the gear lever action is not abnormally vague or 'notchy'.
11 On automatic transmission models, make sure that all gearchanges occur smoothly, without snatching, and without an increase in engine speed between changes. Check that all of the gear positions can be selected with the vehicle at rest. If any problems are found, they should be referred to a Vauxhall/Opel dealer.
12 Listen for a metallic clicking sound from the front of the vehicle, as the vehicle is driven slowly in a circle with the steering on full-lock. Carry out this check in both directions. If a clicking noise is heard, this indicates wear in a driveshaft joint (see Chapter 8).

Check the operation and performance of the braking system

13 Make sure that the vehicle does not pull to one side when braking, and that the wheels do not lock prematurely when braking hard.
14 Check that there is no vibration through the steering when braking.
15 Check that the handbrake operates correctly, without excessive movement of the lever, and that it holds the vehicle stationary on a slope.
16 Test the operation of the brake servo unit as follows. Depress the footbrake four or five times to exhaust the vacuum, then start the engine. As the engine starts, there should be a noticeable 'give' in the brake pedal as vacuum builds up. Allow the engine to run for at least two minutes, and then switch it off. If the brake pedal is now depressed again, it should be possible to detect a hiss from the servo as the pedal is depressed. After about four or five applications, no further hissing should be heard, and the pedal should feel considerably harder.

Every 20 000 miles (30 000 km) or 2 years

16 Air cleaner element renewal

1 The air cleaner is located in the front right-hand corner of the engine compartment.
2 Release the securing clips, and lift the air cleaner cover sufficiently to enable removal of the filter element (see illustrations). Take care not to strain the wiring for the airflow meter/intake air temperature sensor wiring (as applicable) as the cover is lifted.

3 Lift out the filter element.
4 Wipe out the casing and the cover. Fit the new filter, noting that the rubber locating flange should be uppermost, and secure the cover with the clips.

17 Fuel filter renewal

1 The fuel filter is located under the rear of the vehicle where it is clipped onto the fuel tank retaining strap.

2 Depressurise the fuel system as described in Chapter 4A.
3 Chock the front wheels, then jack up the rear of the vehicle and support on axle stands (see "Jacking and Vehicle Support").
4 Release the retaining clip holding the filter to the underbody (see illustration). Before removing the filter, note the orientation of the fuel flow direction arrow.
5 Be prepared for fuel spillage, and take adequate fire precautions. Position a suitable container below the fuel filter, to catch spilt fuel.

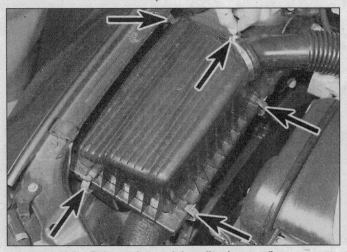

16.2a Release the retaining clips (arrowed) . . .

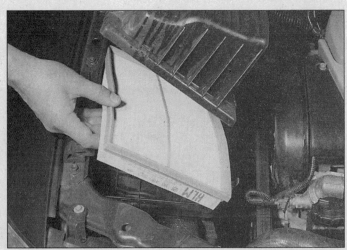

16.2b . . . then lift up the housing lid and remove the air cleaner filter element

17.4 Release the retaining clip . . .

17.6a . . . then disconnect the clip . . .

17.6b . . . and disconnect the fuel hoses from the fuel filter

6 Release the connectors and disconnect the fuel hoses from the fuel filter, noting their locations to ensure correct refitting. A Vauxhall/Opel special tool is available to disconnect the hose connectors, but provided care it taken, the connections can be released using a pair of pliers or a screwdriver **(see illustrations)**.
7 Withdraw the filter from under the vehicle **(see illustration)**.
8 Fitting the new filter is a reversal of removal, bearing in mind the following points.
  a) *Ensure that the filter is fitted with the flow direction arrow on the filter body pointing in the direction of fuel flow.*
  b) *Ensure that the hoses are reconnected to their correct locations, as noted before removal.*
  c) *On completion, run the engine and check for leaks. If leakage is evident, stop the engine immediately and rectify the problem without delay.*

18 Manual transmission oil level check

1 Position the vehicle over an inspection pit, on vehicle ramps, or jack it up, but make sure that it is level. The oil level must be checked before the car is driven, or at least 5 minutes after the engine has been switched off. If the oil is checked immediately after driving the car, some of the oil will remain distributed around the transmission components, resulting in an inaccurate level reading.
2 Wipe clean the area around the level plug. On 1.6 and 1.8 (X18XE1) litre models the level plug is located on the left-hand side of the transmission just behind the driveshaft inner joint, and on 1.8 (X18XE) and 2.0 litre models the level plug is located on the right-hand side of the transmission just behind the driveshaft inner joint. Unscrew the plug and clean it **(see illustration)**.
3 The oil level should reach the lower edge of the level plug hole.
4 If topping-up is necessary, unscrew the breather valve from the top of the transmission housing and add the specified type of oil through the valve hole until oil begins to trickle out from the level plug hole **(see illustrations)**.
5 Allow the excess oil to drain out from the level plug hole then refit the level plug, tightening it to the specified torque (see Chapter 7A).
6 Refit the breather valve to the top of the transmission unit, tightening it securely and wash off any spilt oil.

19 Automatic transmission fluid level check

1 Park the vehicle on level ground and firmly apply the handbrake. The fluid level is checked using the dipstick which is situated

17.7 Removing the fuel filter from under the vehicle

on the top of the transmission unit and is positioned between the battery and engine unit.
2 Start the engine and allow it to idle for a couple of minutes with the selector lever in the 'P' position.
3 With the engine idling, withdraw the dipstick from the tube, and wipe all the fluid from its end with a clean rag or paper towel. Insert the clean dipstick back into the tube as far as it will go, then withdraw it once more. Note the fluid level on the end of the dipstick and ensure it is between the upper (MAX) and lower (MIN) level markings **(see illustrations)**. If the transmission fluid is cold, use the markings on the side of the dipstick marked +20°C and if the transmission fluid is at operating temperature, use the markings on the +80°C side of the dipstick.

1A

18.2 Manual transmission oil level plug (arrowed) - 1.6 litre model shown

18.4a Unscrew the breather valve from the top of the transmission unit . . .

18.4b . . . and top up the oil level via the breather valve hole

19.3a The automatic transmission fluid dipstick is located between the engine and battery

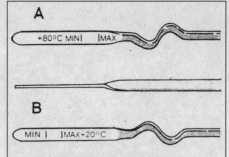

19.3b Automatic transmission fluid dipstick fluid level markings

A *Markings for use when fluid is at operating temperature*
B *Markings for use when fluid is cold*

4 If topping-up is necessary, add the required quantity of the specified fluid to the transmission via the dipstick tube. Use a funnel with a fine mesh gauze, to avoid spillage, and to ensure that no foreign matter enters the transmission. **Note:** *Never overfill the transmission so that the fluid level is above the relevant upper (MAX) mark.*

5 After topping-up, take the vehicle on a short run to distribute the fresh fluid, then recheck the level, topping-up if necessary.

6 Always maintain the level between the two dipstick marks. If the level is allowed to fall below the lower mark, fluid starvation may result, which could lead to severe transmission damage.

7 Frequent need for topping-up indicates that there is a leak, which should be found and corrected before it becomes serious.

20 Hinge and lock lubrication

1 Work around the vehicle and lubricate the hinges of the bonnet, doors and tailgate with a light machine oil.

2 Lightly lubricate the bonnet release mechanism and exposed section of inner cable with a smear of grease.

22.4 Check for wear in the hub bearings by grasping the wheel and trying to rock it

3 Check the security and operation of all hinges, latches and locks, adjusting them where required. Check the operation of the central locking system.

4 Check the condition and operation of the tailgate struts, renewing them both if either is leaking or no longer able to support the tailgate securely when raised.

21 Rear brake shoe and drum check

Refer to the detailed description given in Chapter 9.

22 Suspension and steering check

Front suspension and steering check

1 Raise the front of the vehicle, and securely support it on axle stands (see *"Jacking and Vehicle Support"*).

2 Visually inspect the balljoint dust covers and the steering rack-and-pinion gaiters for splits, chafing or deterioration. Any wear of these components will cause loss of lubricant, together with dirt and water entry, resulting in rapid deterioration of the balljoints or steering gear.

3 Check the power steering fluid hoses for chafing or deterioration, and the pipe and hose unions for fluid leaks. Also check for signs of fluid leakage under pressure from the steering gear rubber gaiters, which would indicate failed fluid seals within the steering gear.

4 Grasp the roadwheel at the 12 o'clock and 6 o'clock positions, and try to rock it **(see illustration)**. Very slight free play may be felt, but if the movement is appreciable, further investigation is necessary to determine the source. Continue rocking the wheel while an assistant depresses the footbrake. If the movement is now eliminated or significantly reduced, it is likely that the hub bearings are at fault. If the free play is still evident with the footbrake depressed, then there is wear in the suspension joints or mountings.

5 Now grasp the wheel at the 9 o'clock and 3 o'clock positions, and try to rock it as before. Any movement felt now may again be caused by wear in the hub bearings or the steering track-rod balljoints. If the outer balljoint is worn, the visual movement will be obvious. If the inner joint is suspect, it can be felt by placing a hand over the rack-and-pinion rubber gaiter and gripping the track-rod. If the wheel is now rocked, movement will be felt at the inner joint if wear has taken place.

6 Using a large screwdriver or flat bar, check for wear in the suspension mounting bushes by levering between the relevant suspension component and its attachment point. Some movement is to be expected, as the mountings are made of rubber, but excessive wear should be obvious. Also check the condition of any visible rubber bushes, looking for splits, cracks or contamination of the rubber.

7 With the car standing on its wheels, have an assistant turn the steering wheel back-and-forth, about an eighth of a turn each way. There should be very little, if any, lost movement between the steering wheel and roadwheels. If this is not the case, closely observe the joints and mountings previously described. In addition, check the steering column universal joints for wear, and also check the rack-and-pinion steering gear itself.

Rear suspension check

8 Chock the front wheels, then jack up the rear of the vehicle and support securely on axle stands (see *"Jacking and Vehicle Support"*).

9 Working as described previously for the front suspension, check the rear hub bearings, the suspension bushes and the strut or shock absorber mountings (as applicable) for wear.

Shock absorber check

10 Check for any signs of fluid leakage around the shock absorber body, or from the rubber gaiter around the piston rod. Should any fluid be noticed, the shock absorber is defective internally, and should be renewed. **Note:** *Shock absorbers should always be renewed in pairs on the same axle.*

11 The efficiency of the shock absorber may be checked by bouncing the vehicle at each corner. Generally speaking, the body will return to its normal position and stop after being depressed. If it rises and returns on a rebound, the shock absorber is probably suspect. Also examine the shock absorber upper and lower mountings for any signs of wear.

23 Driveshaft gaiter check

1 With the vehicle raised and securely supported on stands, turn the steering onto full lock then slowly rotate the roadwheel. Inspect the condition of the outer constant velocity (CV) joint rubber gaiters while squeezing the gaiters to open out the folds **(see illustration)**. Check for signs of cracking, splits or deterioration of the rubber which may allow the grease to escape and lead to water and grit entry into the joint. Also check the security and condition of the retaining clips. Repeat these checks on the inner CV joints. If any damage or deterioration is found, the gaiters should be renewed as described in Chapter 8.

2 At the same time, check the general condition of the CV joints themselves by first holding the driveshaft and attempting to rotate the wheel. Repeat this check by holding the inner joint and attempting to rotate the driveshaft. Any appreciable movement indicates wear in the joints, wear in the driveshaft splines or loose driveshaft retaining nut.

23.1 Check the condition of the driveshaft gaiters (1) and the retaining clips (2)

Every 40 000 miles (60 000 km) or 4 years

24 Spark plug renewal and ignition system check

Spark plug renewal

1 The correct functioning of the spark plugs is vital for the correct running and efficiency of the engine. It is essential that the plugs fitted are appropriate for the engine; suitable types are specified at the beginning of this Chapter, or in the vehicle's Owner's Handbook. If the correct type is used and the engine is in good condition, the spark plugs should not need attention between scheduled replacement intervals. Spark plug cleaning is rarely necessary, and should not be attempted unless specialised equipment is available, as damage can easily be caused to the firing ends.

2 On 1.6 litre DOHC and 1.8 (X18XE1) engines, remove the oil filler cap then undo the retaining screws and remove the cover from the top of the engine **(see illustration)**. Refit the oil filler cap.

3 On 1.8 (X18XE) and 2.0 litre engines, undo the retaining screws and lift off the spark plug cover from the top of the camshaft cover **(see illustration)**.

4 On 1.6 SOHC, 1.8 (X18XE) and 2.0 litre models, if the marks on the original-equipment spark plug (HT) leads cannot be seen, mark the leads to correspond to the cylinder the lead serves. Pull the leads from the plugs by gripping the end fitting, not the lead, otherwise the lead connection may be fractured. On DOHC engines use the tool clipped to one of the plug leads to pull the HT leads from the plugs **(see illustrations)**.

5 On 1.6 litre DOHC and 1.8 (X18XE1) engines, the ignition module is fitted directly above the spark plugs between the inlet and exhaust camshaft casings. Disconnect the ignition module wiring connector, undo the screws that secure the module to the cylinder head, and lift the module up and out of position. If the module proves reluctant to separate from the spark plugs, insert two long 8 mm bolts into the threaded holes in the top of the module, and pull up on the bolts to free the module from the plugs **(see illustration)**.

6 Unscrew the plugs from the cylinder head using a spark plug spanner, suitable box spanner or a deep socket and extension bar. Keep the socket aligned with the spark plug - if it is forcibly moved to one side, the ceramic insulator may be broken off.

7 Examination of the spark plugs will give a good indication of the condition of the engine. As each plug is removed, examine it as follows. If the insulator nose of the spark plug is clean and white, with no deposits, this is indicative of a weak mixture or too hot a plug (a hot plug transfers heat away from the electrode slowly, a cold plug transfers heat away quickly).

8 If the tip and insulator nose are covered with hard black-looking deposits, then this is

24.2 On 1.6 litre DOHC and 1.8 (X18XE1) engines, undo the retaining screws (arrowed) and remove the cover from the engine

24.3 On 1.8 and 2.0 litre engines undo the retaining screws (arrowed) and remove the spark plug cover

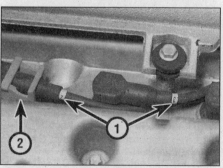

24.4a The HT leads should be numbered (1) for identification purposes. Note the HT lead removal tool (2) clipped to the cap

24.4b On DOHC engines use the removal tool to pull the HT leads off from the plugs

24.5 Lift the ignition module from the spark plugs - 1.8 (X18XE1) litre engine

1A

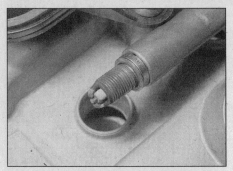

24.10 The multi-electrode plugs fitted as standard should not be adjusted

24.12a If single electrode plugs are being fitted, check the electrode gap using a feeler gauge . . .

24.12b . . . or a wire gauge . . .

24.13 . . . and if necessary adjust the gap by bending the electrode

indicative that the mixture is too rich. Should the plug be black and oily, then it is likely that the engine is fairly worn, as well as the mixture being too rich.

9 If the insulator nose is covered with light tan to greyish-brown deposits, then the mixture is correct and it is likely that the engine is in good condition.

10 All engines are fitted with multi-electrode plugs as standard by Vauxhall **(see illustration)**. On these plugs, the electrode gaps are all preset and no attempt should be

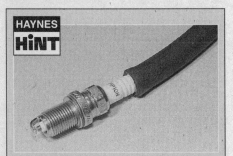

HAYNES HINT

It is very often difficult to insert spark plugs into their holes without cross-threading them. To avoid this possibility, fit a short length of rubber hose over the end of the spark plug. The flexible hose acts as a universal joint to help align the plug with the plug hole. Should the plug begin to cross-thread, the hose will slip on the spark plug, preventing thread damage to the aluminium cylinder head

made to bend the electrodes.

11 If non-standard single electrode plugs are to be installed, the spark plug electrode gap is of considerable importance. If the gap is too large or too small, the size of the spark and its efficiency will be seriously impaired and it will not perform correctly under all engine speed and load conditions. The gap should be set to the value specified by the manufacturer.

12 To set the gap, measure it with a feeler blade or spark plug gap gauge and then carefully bend the outer plug electrode until the correct gap is achieved. The centre electrode should never be bent, as this may crack the insulator and cause plug failure, if nothing worse. If using feeler blades, the gap is correct when the appropriate-size blade is a firm sliding fit **(see illustrations)**.

13 Special spark plug electrode gap adjusting tools are available from most motor accessory shops, or from some spark plug manufacturers **(see illustration)**.

14 Before fitting the spark plugs, check that the threaded connector sleeves are tight, and that the plug exterior surfaces and threads are clean **(see Haynes Hint)**.

15 Remove the rubber hose (if used), and tighten the plug to the specified torque using the spark plug socket and a torque wrench. Refit the remaining spark plugs in the same manner.

16 Where applicable, reconnect the HT leads in their original locations, or refit the ignition module to the top of the spark plugs. Tighten the ignition module retaining screws to the specified torque. Refit the engine/spark plug cover (where necessary).

Ignition system check

⚠ **Warning: Voltages produced by an electronic ignition system are considerably higher than those produced by conventional ignition systems. Extreme care must be taken when working on the system with the ignition switched on. Persons with surgically-implanted cardiac pacemaker devices should keep well clear of the ignition circuits, components and test equipment.**

Note: *The following applies to the 1.6 SOHC, 1.8 (X18XE) and 2.0 litre models.*

17 The spark plug (HT) leads should be checked whenever new spark plugs are fitted.

18 Ensure that the leads are numbered before removing them, to avoid confusion when refitting. Pull the leads from the plugs by gripping the end fitting, not the lead, otherwise the lead connection may be fractured.

19 Check inside the end fitting for signs of corrosion, which will look like a white crusty powder. Push the end fitting back onto the spark plug, ensuring that it is a tight fit on the plug. If not, remove the lead again and use pliers to carefully crimp the metal connector inside the end fitting until it fits securely on the end of the spark plug.

20 Using a clean rag, wipe the entire length of the lead to remove any built-up dirt and grease. Once the lead is clean, check for burns, cracks and other damage. Do not bend the lead excessively, nor pull the lead length-wise - the conductor inside might break.

21 Disconnect the other end of the lead from the DIS module and check for corrosion and a tight fit in the same manner as the spark plug end. Refit the lead securely on completion.

22 Check the remaining leads one at a time, in the same way.

23 If new spark plug (HT) leads are required, purchase a set for your car and engine.

24 Even with the ignition system in first-class condition, some engines may still occasionally experience poor starting attributable to damp ignition components. To disperse moisture, a water-dispersant aerosol can be very effective.

25 Timing belt renewal

Note: *From the 1997 Model Year onwards, Vauxhall increased the specified interval for timing belt renewal to 80 000 (120 000 km) or 8 years. However, if the vehicle is used mainly for short journeys or a lot of stop-start driving it is recommended that the earlier (pre 1997) recommendation is adhered to. The actual belt renewal interval is very much up to the individual owner but, bearing in mind that severe engine damage will result if the belt breaks in use, we recommend you err on the side of caution.*

1 Refer to the information given in Chapter 2A (SOHC engine) or 2B (DOHC engine).

Every 2 years, regardless of mileage

26 Hydraulic fluid renewal

⚠️ **Warning: Hydraulic fluid can harm your eyes and damage painted surfaces, so use extreme caution when handling and pouring it. Do not use fluid that has been standing open for some time, as it absorbs moisture from the air. Excess moisture can cause a dangerous loss of braking effectiveness.**

Note: *The brake and clutch hydraulic systems share a reservoir.*

1 The procedure is similar to that for the bleeding of the hydraulic systems as described in Chapters 6 and 9. Renew the fluid in the braking system first, then the clutch fluid.

2 Working as described in Chapter 9, open the first bleed screw in the sequence, and pump the brake pedal gently until nearly all the old fluid has been emptied from the master cylinder reservoir. Top-up to the MAX level with new fluid, and continue pumping until only the new fluid remains in the reservoir, and new fluid can be seen emerging from the bleed screw. Tighten the screw, and top the reservoir level up to the MAX level line.

 Old hydraulic fluid is invariably much darker in colour than the new, making it easy to distinguish the two.

3 Work through all the remaining bleed screws in the sequence until new fluid can be seen at all of them. Be careful to keep the master cylinder reservoir topped-up to above the MIN level at all times, or air may enter the system and greatly increase the length of the task.

4 Bleed the fluid from the clutch hydraulic system as described in Chapter 6.

5 When the operation is complete, check that all bleed screws are securely tightened, and that their dust caps are refitted. Wash off all traces of spilt fluid, and recheck the master cylinder reservoir fluid level.

6 Check the operation of the brakes and clutch before taking the car on the road.

27 Remote control battery renewal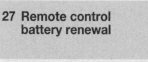

Note: *The following procedure must be performed within 3 minutes, otherwise the remote control unit will have to be re-programmed.*

1 Using a screwdriver inserted as shown prise the battery cover from the remote control unit **(see illustrations).**

2 Note how the battery is fitted, then carefully remove it from the contacts.

3 Fit the new battery and refit the cover making sure that it clips fully onto the base.

28 Coolant renewal

Cooling system draining

⚠️ **Warning: Wait until the engine is cold before starting this procedure. Do not allow antifreeze to come in contact with your skin, or with the painted surfaces of the vehicle. Rinse off spills immediately with plenty of water. Never leave antifreeze lying around in an open container, or in a puddle in the driveway or on the garage floor. Children and pets are attracted by its sweet smell, but antifreeze can be fatal if ingested.**

1 With the engine completely cold, remove the expansion tank filler cap. Turn the cap anti-clockwise, wait until any pressure remaining in the system is released, then unscrew it and lift it off.

2 Where applicable, remove the engine undershield, then position a suitable container beneath the left-hand side of the radiator.

3 Loosen the clip and disconnect the bottom hose from the radiator, and allow the coolant to drain into the container.

4 When the flow of coolant stops, refit the bottom hose and tighten the clip.

5 If the coolant has been drained for a reason other than renewal, then provided it is clean and less than two years old, it can be re-used, though this is not recommended.

Cooling system flushing

6 If coolant renewal has been neglected, or if the antifreeze mixture has become diluted, then in time, the cooling system may gradually lose efficiency, as the coolant passages become restricted due to rust, scale deposits, and other sediment. The cooling system efficiency can be restored by flushing the system clean.

7 The radiator should be flushed independently of the engine, to avoid unnecessary contamination.

Radiator flushing

8 Disconnect the top and bottom hoses and any other relevant hoses from the radiator, with reference to Chapter 3.

9 Insert a garden hose into the radiator top inlet. Direct a flow of clean water through the radiator, and continue flushing until clean water emerges from the radiator bottom outlet.

10 If after a reasonable period, the water still does not run clear, the radiator can be flushed with a good proprietary cleaning agent. It is important that the manufacturer's instructions are followed carefully. If the contamination is particularly bad, remove the radiator, insert the hose in the radiator bottom outlet, and reverse-flush the radiator.

Engine flushing

11 Remove the thermostat as described in Chapter 3 then, if the radiator top hose has been disconnected from the engine, temporarily reconnect the hose.

12 With the top and bottom hoses disconnected from the radiator, insert a garden hose into the radiator top hose. Direct a clean flow of water through the engine, and continue flushing until clean water emerges from the radiator bottom hose.

13 On completion of flushing, refit the thermostat and reconnect the hoses with reference to Chapter 3.

Cooling system filling

14 Before attempting to fill the cooling system, make sure that all hoses and clips are in good condition, and that the clips are tight. Note that an antifreeze mixture must be used all year round, to prevent corrosion of the engine components.

15 Remove the expansion tank filler cap.

16 On 1.6 litre SOHC engine models, remove the temperature gauge sender unit from the right-hand end of the inlet manifold with reference to Chapter 3. This is necessary to bleed air from the system. On other engines the system bleeds automatically during the warm-up period.

1A

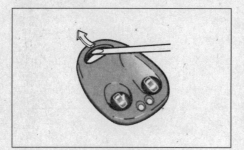

27.1a Insert a screwdriver as shown ...

27.1b ... to prise the cover from the remote control unit

17 Slowly fill the system until the coolant level reaches the KALT/COLD mark on the side of the expansion tank. On 1.6 litre SOHC engine models, refit the temperature gauge sender unit to the the inlet manifold as soon as bubble-free coolant emerges from the thermostat housing, then continue to fill the system until the coolant reaches the KALT/COLD mark on the expansion tank.

18 Refit and tighten the expansion tank filler cap.

19 Start the engine, and allow it to run until it reaches normal operating temperature (until the cooling fan cuts in and out).

20 Stop the engine, and allow it to cool, then re-check the coolant level with reference to *"Weekly checks"*. Top-up the level if necessary and refit the expansion tank filler cap. Where applicable, refit the engine undershield.

Antifreeze mixture

21 The antifreeze should always be renewed at the specified intervals. This is necessary not only to maintain the antifreeze properties, but also to prevent corrosion which would otherwise occur as the corrosion inhibitors become progressively less effective.

22 Always use an ethylene-glycol based antifreeze which is suitable for use in mixed-metal cooling systems. The quantity of antifreeze and levels of protection are given in the Specifications.

23 Before adding antifreeze, the cooling system should be completely drained, preferably flushed, and all hoses checked for condition and security.

24 After filling with antifreeze, a label should be attached to the expansion tank, stating the type and concentration of antifreeze used, and the date installed. Any subsequent topping-up should be made with the same type and concentration of antifreeze.

25 Do not use engine antifreeze in the windscreen/tailgate washer system, as it will cause damage to the vehicle paintwork. A screenwash additive should be added to the washer system in the quantities stated on the bottle.

Chapter 1 Part B:
Routine maintenance and servicing - diesel engine models

Contents

1B

Degrees of difficulty

  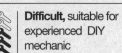

| Easy, suitable for novice with little experience | Fairly easy, suitable for beginner with some experience | Fairly difficult, suitable for competent DIY mechanic | Difficult, suitable for experienced DIY mechanic | Very difficult, suitable for expert DIY or professional |

Lubricants and fluids

Refer to *"Weekly checks"* on page 0•17

Capacities

Engine oil

Including oil filter:

1.7 litre engines	5.0 litres
2.0 litre engines	5.5 litres
Difference between MIN and MAX on dipstick	1.0 litre

Cooling system

	Models without air conditioning	Models with air conditioning
1.7 litre engines	6.8 litres	6.9 litres
2.0 litre engines:		
X 20 DTL	7.4 litres	7.4 litres
X 20 DTH	7.2 litres	7.2 litres

Transmission

Manual transmission	1.9 litres

Washer fluid reservoir

Without headlight washers	2.6 litres
With headlight washers	5.5 litres

Fuel tank

All models	60 litres

Cooling system

Antifreeze mixture:

44% antifreeze	Protection down to -30°C
52% antifreeze	Protection down to -40°C

Note: *Refer to antifreeze manufacturer for latest recommendations.*

Fuel system

Glow plugs:

1.7 litre engines	Bosch 0 250 312 003
2.0 litre engines:	
X 20 DTL:	
Chassis number up to V7999999	Bosch 0 250 202 027
Chassis numbers W1000001 and from XL000001	Bosch 0 250 202 042
X 20 DTH	Bosch 0 250 202 042

Idle speed:

1.7 litre models:	
Normal	780 to 880 rpm
Cold start	950 to 1000 rpm
2.0 litre models	750 to 850 rpm - controlled by ECU

Brakes

Friction material minimum thickness:

Front brake pads	7.5 mm
Rear brake pads	7.0 mm
Rear brake shoes	0.5 mm above the rivet heads

Torque wrench settings

	Nm	lbf ft
1.7 litre engine		
Compressor drivebelt tensioner centre bolt	45	33
Engine oil filter	15	11
Fuel filter mounting plate nuts	25	18
Manual transmission oil level plug:		
Stage 1	4	3
Stage 2	Angle-tighten a further 45 to 180°	
Roadwheel bolts	110	81
Sump drain plug	78	58
2.0 litre engine		
Engine oil filter housing cover	20 to 25	15 to 18
Fuel filter housing cover centre bolt	6	4
Manual transmission oil level plug:		
Stage 1	4	3
Stage 2	Angle-tighten a further 45 to 180°	
Roadwheel bolts	110	81
Sump drain plug	18	13

1 The maintenance intervals in this manual are provided with the assumption that you, not the dealer, will be carrying out the work. These are the minimum maintenance intervals recommended by us for vehicles driven daily. If you wish to keep your vehicle in peak condition at all times, you may wish to perform some of these procedures more often. We encourage frequent maintenance, because it enhances the efficiency, performance and resale value of your vehicle.
2 If the vehicle is driven in dusty areas, used to tow a trailer, or driven frequently at slow speeds (idling in traffic) or on short journeys, more frequent maintenance intervals are recommended.
3 When the vehicle is new, it should be serviced by a factory-authorised dealer service department, in order to preserve the factory warranty.

Every 5000 miles (7500 km) or 6 months, whichever comes first

☐ Renew the engine oil and filter (Section 3)

Note: *Vauxhall recommend that the engine oil and filter are changed every 10 000 miles or 12 months. However, oil and filter changes are good for the engine and we recommend that the oil and filter are renewed more frequently, especially if the vehicle is used on a lot of short journeys.*

Every 10 000 miles (15 000 km) or 12 months, whichever comes first

☐ Check the condition and tension of the auxiliary drivebelts (Section 4)*
☐ Drain water from the fuel filter (Section 5)
☐ Idle speed and exhaust emission check (Section 6)
☐ Check the operation of all electrical systems (Section 7)*
☐ Check and if necessary adjust the headlight beam alignment (Section 8)
☐ Check the body and underbody for corrosion protection (Section 9)
☐ Check the front brake pads and discs for wear (Section 10)*
☐ Check the rear brake pads and discs (where applicable) for wear (Section 11)*
☐ Check all components, pipes and hoses for fluid leaks (Section 12)
☐ Check the roadwheel bolts are tightened to the specified torque (Section 13)*
☐ Check the rear suspension level control system (where applicable) (Section 14)*
☐ Renew the pollen filter (Section 15)*
  Note: *If the vehicle is used in dusty conditions, the pollen filter should be renewed more frequently.*
☐ Carry out a road test (Section 16)*
* *On vehicles covering a high mileage (more than 20 000 miles/ 30 000 km annually) carry out the items marked with an asterisk every 10 000 miles/15 000 km (regardless of time), then carry out the items not marked with an asterisk at the 12 month interval.*

Every 20 000 miles (30 000 km) or 2 years, whichever comes first

☐ Renew the air cleaner element (Section 17)
☐ Renew the fuel filter (Section 18)
☐ Check and, if necessary, adjust the valve clearances - 1.7 litre engine (Section 19)
☐ Check and if necessary top up the manual transmission oil level (Section 20)
☐ Lubricate all door locks and hinges, door stops, bonnet lock and release, and tailgate lock and hinges (Section 21)
☐ Check the rear brake shoes and drums for wear (Section 22)
☐ Check the steering and suspension components for condition and security (Section 23)
☐ Check the condition of the driveshaft gaiters (Section 24)

Every 2 years, regardless of mileage

☐ Renew the hydraulic fluid (Section 25)
☐ Renew the remote control batteries (Section 26)
☐ Renew the coolant (Section 27)

Every 40 000 miles (60 000 km) or 4 years, whichever comes first

☐ Renew the timing belt - 1.7 litre engine (Section 28)

Note: *Although the normal interval for timing belt renewal is 80 000 miles/120 000 km or 8 years, it is strongly recommended that the interval is halved to 40 000 miles/60 000 km or 4 years on vehicles which are subjected to intensive use, ie. mainly short journeys or a lot of stop-start driving. The actual belt renewal interval is therefore up to the individual owner but, bearing in mind that severe engine damage will result should the belt break in use, we recommend you err on the side of caution.*

1B

Underbonnet view of a 2.0 litre engine model

1 Front suspension strut upper mounting
2 Hydraulic fluid reservoir
3 Turbocharger and heatshield
4 Fuel filter
5 Auxiliary fuse and relay box
6 Battery
7 Auxiliary relay box
8 Power steering fluid reservoir
9 Engine oil level dipstick
10 Air cleaner

Front underbody view of a 2.0 litre engine model

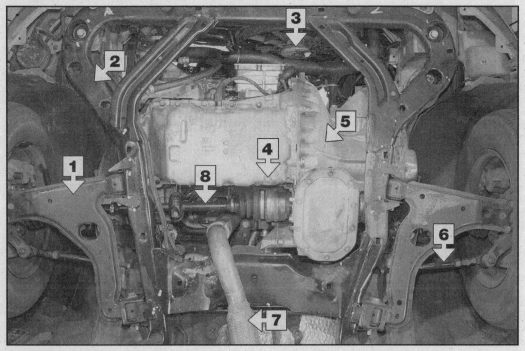

1 Front suspension lower arm
2 Front subframe
3 Electric cooling fan
4 Engine oil drain plug
5 Manual transmission
6 Steering track rod
7 Exhaust downpipe
8 Driveshaft

Rear underbody view of a 2.0 litre engine model

1 Anti-roll bar
2 Rear suspension crossmember mounting
3 Rear suspension strut lower mounting
4 Exhaust system rear silencer
5 Rear towing eye
6 Handbrake cable

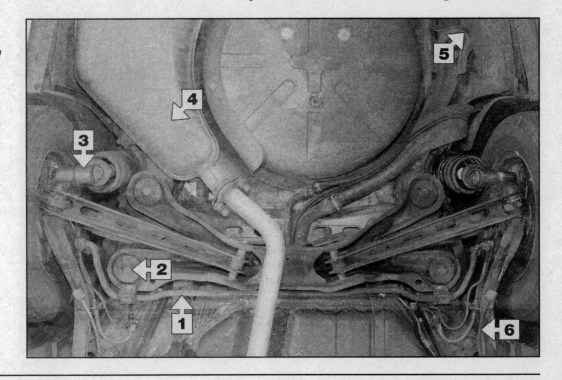

1 General information

1 This Chapter is designed to help the home mechanic maintain his/her vehicle for safety, economy, long life and peak performance.
2 The Chapter contains a master maintenance schedule, followed by Sections dealing specifically with each task in the schedule. Visual checks, adjustments, component renewal and other helpful items are included. Refer to the accompanying illustrations of the engine compartment and the underside of the vehicle for the locations of the various components.
3 Servicing your vehicle in accordance with the mileage/time maintenance schedule and the following Sections will provide a planned maintenance programme, which should result in a long and reliable service life. This is a comprehensive plan, so maintaining some items but not others at the specified service intervals, will not produce the same results.
4 As you service your vehicle, you will discover that many of the procedures can - and should - be grouped together, because of the particular procedure being performed, or because of the proximity of two otherwise-unrelated components to one another. For example, if the vehicle is raised for any reason, the exhaust can be inspected at the same time as the suspension and steering components.

5 The first step in this maintenance programme is to prepare yourself before the actual work begins. Read through all the Sections relevant to the work to be carried out, then make a list and gather all the parts and tools required. If a problem is encountered, seek advice from a parts specialist, or a dealer service department.

2 Regular maintenance

1 If, from the time the vehicle is new, the routine maintenance schedule is followed closely, and frequent checks are made of fluid levels and high-wear items, as suggested throughout this manual, the engine will be kept in relatively good running condition, and the need for additional work will be minimised.
2 It is possible that there will be times when the engine is running poorly due to the lack of regular maintenance. This is even more likely if a used vehicle, which has not received regular and frequent maintenance checks, is purchased. In such cases, additional work may need to be carried out, outside of the regular maintenance intervals.
3 If engine wear is suspected, a compression test or leakdown test (refer to Chapter 2C) will provide valuable information regarding the overall performance of the main internal components. Such a test can be used as a basis to decide on the extent of the work to

be carried out. If, for example, a compression or leakdown test indicates serious internal engine wear, conventional maintenance as described in this Chapter will not greatly improve the performance of the engine, and may prove a waste of time and money, unless extensive overhaul work is carried out first.
4 The following series of operations are those most often required to improve the performance of a generally poor-running engine:

Primary operations

a) Clean, inspect and test the battery (refer to "Weekly checks").
b) Check all the engine-related fluids (refer to "Weekly checks").
c) Check the condition and tension of the auxiliary drivebelt (Section 4).
d) Check the condition of the air filter, and renew if necessary (Section 17).
e) Renew the fuel filter (Section 18).
f) Check the condition of all hoses, and check for fluid leaks (Section 12).

5 If the above operations do not prove fully effective, carry out the following secondary operations:

Secondary operations

All items listed under "Primary operations", plus the following:

a) Check the charging system (refer to Chapter 5A).
b) Check the pre-heating system (refer to Chapter 5C).
c) Check the fuel system (refer to Chapter 4B).

1B

Every 5000 miles (7500 km) or 6 months

3 Engine oil and filter renewal

1 Frequent oil and filter changes are the most important preventative maintenance procedures which can be undertaken by the DIY owner. As engine oil ages, it becomes diluted and contaminated, which leads to premature engine wear.
2 Before starting this procedure, gather together all the necessary tools and materials. Also make sure that you have plenty of clean rags and newspapers handy, to mop up any spills. Ideally, the engine oil should be warm, as it will drain more easily, and more built-up sludge will be removed with it. Take care not to touch the exhaust or any other hot parts of the engine when working under the vehicle. To avoid any possibility of scalding, and to protect yourself from possible skin irritants and other harmful contaminants in used engine oils, it is advisable to wear gloves when carrying out this work.
3 Firmly apply the handbrake then jack up the front of the vehicle and support it on axle stands (see *"Jacking and Vehicle Support"*).
4 Remove the oil filler cap **(see illustration)**.
5 Using a spanner, or preferably a suitable socket and bar, slacken the drain plug about half a turn **(see illustration)**. Position the

3.4 Removing the oil filler cap - 2.0 litre engine

draining container under the drain plug, then remove the plug completely **(see Haynes Hint)**.

As the drain plug threads release, move it sharply away so the stream of oil issuing from the sump runs into the container, not up your sleeve

6 Allow some time for the oil to drain, noting that it may be necessary to reposition the container as the oil flow slows to a trickle.

1.7 litre engine

7 After all the oil has drained, wipe the drain plug and the sealing washer with a clean rag. Examine the condition of the sealing washer, and renew it if it shows signs of scoring or other damage which may prevent an oil-tight seal. Clean the area around the drain plug opening, and refit the plug complete with the washer and tighten it to the specified torque.
8 Move the container into position under the oil filter which is located on the rear of the cylinder block.
9 Use an oil filter removal tool to slacken the filter initially, then unscrew it by hand the rest of the way. Empty the oil from the old filter into the container.
10 Use a clean rag to remove all oil, dirt and sludge from the filter sealing area on the engine.

11 Apply a light coating of clean engine oil to the sealing ring on the new filter, then screw the filter into position on the engine. Tighten the filter firmly by hand only - **do not** use any tools. If a genuine filter is being fitted and the special oil filter tool (a socket which fits over the end of the filter) is available, tighten the filter to the specified torque.
12 Remove the old oil and all tools from under the vehicle then lower the vehicle to the ground.
13 Fill the engine through the filler hole, using the correct grade and type of oil (refer to *"Weekly Checks"* for details of topping-up). Pour in half the specified quantity of oil first, then wait a few minutes for the oil to drain into the sump. Continue to add oil, a small quantity at a time, until the level is up to the lower mark on the dipstick. Adding approximately a further 1.0 litre will bring the level up to the upper mark on the dipstick.
14 Start the engine and run it for a few minutes, while checking for leaks around the oil filter seal and the sump drain plug. Note that there may be a delay of a few seconds before the low oil pressure warning light goes out when the engine is first started, as the oil circulates through the new oil filter and the engine oil galleries before the pressure builds up.
15 Stop the engine, and wait a few minutes for the oil to settle in the sump once more. With the new oil circulated and the filter now completely full, recheck the level on the dipstick, and add more oil as necessary.
16 Dispose of the used engine oil safely with reference to *"General repair procedures"*.

2.0 litre engine

17 To gain access to the oil filter housing, undo the retaining screws and remove the plastic cover from the top of the engine **(see illustration)**.
18 Using a large socket, unscrew the cover and remove it from the top of the oil filter housing **(see illustration)**. Lift out the old filter element.

3.5 Sump drain plug - 1.7 litre engine

3.17 On 2.0 litre engines undo the retaining screws and remove the cover from the top of the engine

3.18 Unscrew the oil filter housing cover and lift out the old filter element

3.19 Fit the new filter element to the housing . . .

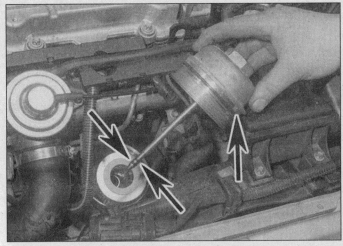

3.20 . . . then fit the new sealing rings to the cover recesses (arrowed) and refit the cover to the housing

19 Fit the new filter element to the housing (see illustration).

20 Renew the sealing rings then refit the oil filter cover and tighten it to the specified torque (see illustration). Refit the plastic cover to the engine and securely tighten its screws.

21 After all the oil has drained, wipe the drain plug and the sealing washer with a clean rag. Examine the condition of the sealing washer, and renew it if it shows signs of scoring or other damage which may prevent an oil-tight seal. Clean the area around the drain plug opening, and refit the plug complete with the washer and tighten it to the specified torque.

22 Fill the engine with oil as described in paragraphs 12 to 16.

Every 10 000 miles (15 000 km) or 12 months

1B

4 Auxiliary drivebelt check and renewal

Checking

Note: *On 1.7 litre models the alternator, power steering pump and (where fitted) air conditioning compressor are all driven by separate belts. On 2.0 litre engines a single belt is used to drive all auxiliary components.*

1 Drivebelts are prone to failure after a long period of time and should therefore be inspected regularly.

2 With the engine stopped, inspect the full length of the drivebelt(s) for cracks and separation of the belt plies. It will be necessary to turn the engine (using a spanner or socket and bar on the crankshaft pulley bolt) in order to move the belt from the pulleys so that the belt can be inspected thoroughly. Twist the belt between the pulleys so that both sides can be viewed. Also check for fraying, and glazing which gives the belt a shiny appearance. Check the pulleys for nicks, cracks, distortion and corrosion.

3 If the belt shows signs of wear or damage, it must be renewed..

Renewal

4 Remove the air cleaner housing as described in Chapter 4B then proceed as described under the relevant sub-heading.

Air conditioning compressor drivebelt - 1.7 litre engine

5 Slacken the tensioner pulley centre bolt then release the belt tension by rotating the adjuster bolt. Slip the belt off from the pulleys and remove it from the engine.

6 Manoeuvre the new belt into position and seat it on the pulleys. Tension the belt, using the adjuster bolt, so that under firm thumb pressure there is about 10 mm of movement at the mid-point on the longest run of the belt.

7 Once the belt is correctly tensioned, tighten the tensioner pulley centre bolt to the specified torque then refit the air cleaner housing (see Chapter 4B).

Power steering pump drivebelt - 1.7 litre engine

8 On models with air conditioning, remove the compressor drivebelt (see paragraph 5).

9 Slacken the pump mounting bolts to release the drivebelt tension and slip the belt off from the pulleys.

10 Manoeuvre the new belt into position and seat it on the pulleys. Tension the belt by positioning the pump so that under firm thumb pressure there is about 10 mm of movement at the mid-point on the longest run of the belt. Move the pump using an extension bar fitted to the square-section hole in the pump bracket and when its correctly positioned tighten its mounting bolts to the specified torque (see Chapter 10).

11 Refit the air conditioning compressor drivebelt (where fitted) then refit the air cleaner housing (see Chapter 4B).

Alternator drivebelt - 1.7 litre engine

12 Firmly apply the handbrake then jack up the front of the vehicle and support it on axle stands (see "Jacking and Vehicle Support"). To improve access, remove the right-hand front roadwheel then undo the fasteners and remove the undercover from beneath the wing.

13 Remove the power steering pump drivebelt as described in this Section.

14 Slacken the alternator mounting bolts to release the drivebelt tension and slip the belt off the pulleys.

15 Manoeuvre the new belt into position and seat it on the pulleys. Tension the belt by positioning the alternator so that under firm thumb pressure there is about 10 mm of movement at the mid-point on the longest run of the belt. Move the alternator using an extension bar fitted to the square-section hole in the bracket and when its correctly positioned tighten its mounting bolts to the specified torque (see Chapter 5A).

16 Fit the power steering pump and (where necessary) the air conditioning compressor drivebelt as described in this Section.

17 Refit the undercover and lower the vehicle to the ground and tighten the wheel bolts to the specified torque.

4.20 On 2.0 litre engines release the drivebelt tension and slip the belt off the pulleys

5.2 Draining water from the fuel filter (2.0 litre engine shown)

Auxiliary drivebelt - 2.0 litre engines

18 Firmly apply the handbrake then jack up the front of the vehicle and support it on axle stands (see *"Jacking and Vehicle Support"*). To improve access, remove the right-hand front roadwheel.

19 Prior to removal make a note of the correct routing of the belt around the various pulleys. If the belt is to be re-used, also mark the direction of rotation on the belt to ensure the belt is refitted the same way around.

20 Using a suitable spanner or socket fitted to the hexagonal section on the tensioner pulley backplate, lever the tensioner away from the belt until there is sufficient slack to enable the belt to be slipped off the pulleys (see illustration). Carefully release the tensioner pulley until it is against its stop then remove the belt from the vehicle.

21 Manoeuvre the belt into position, routing it correctly around the pulleys; if the original belt is being fitted, use the marks made prior to removal to ensure it is fitted the correct way around.

22 Lever the tensioner roller back against is spring, and seat the belt on the pulleys. Ensure the belt is centrally located on all pulleys then slowly release the tensioner pulley until the belt is correctly tensioned.

23 Lower the vehicle to the ground and tighten the wheel bolts to the specified torque

24 Refit the air cleaner housing as described in Chapter 4B.

5 Fuel filter water draining

Caution: Before starting any work on the fuel filter, wipe clean the filter assembly and the area around it; it is essential that no dirt or other foreign matter is allowed into the system. Obtain a suitable container into which the filter can be drained and place rags or similar material under the filter assembly to catch any spillages. Do not allow diesel fuel to contaminate components such as the alternator and starter motor, the coolant hoses and engine mountings, and any wiring.

1 In addition to taking the precautions noted above to catch any fuel spillages, connect a tube to the drain screw on the base of the fuel filter/filter housing. Place the other end of the tube in a clean jar or can.

2 Unscrew the drain screw and allow the filter to drain until clean fuel, free of dirt or water, emerges from the tube (approximately 100 cc is usually sufficient) (see illustration). Note that it maybe necessary to slacken the bleed screw (1.7 litre engine) or filter housing cover bolt (2.0 litre engine) to allow the fuel to drain.

3 Securely close the drain screw and remove the tube, containers and rag, mopping up any spilt fuel. Where necessary, securely tighten the bleed screw (1.7 litre engine) or tighten the housing cover screw (2.0 litre engine) to the specified torque.

4 On completion, dispose safely of the drained fuel. Check carefully all disturbed components to ensure that there are no leaks (of air or fuel) when the engine is restarted.

5 Start the engine and bleed the fuel system as described in Chapter 4B.

6 Idle speed and exhaust emission check

1.7 litre models

Idle speed check and adjustment

1 The usual type of tachometer (rev counter), which works from ignition system pulses, cannot be used on diesel engines. If it is not felt that adjusting the idle speed 'by ear' is satisfactory, it will be necessary to purchase or hire an appropriate tachometer, or else leave the task to a Vauxhall dealer or other suitably-equipped specialist.

2 Make sure that the accelerator cable is correctly adjusted (see Chapter 4B).

3 Warm the engine up to normal operating temperature and check that it idles at the specified speed.

4 If adjustment is necessary, slacken the locknut and rotate the idle speed adjustment screw (see illustration). Once the engine is idling at the specified speed, securely tighten the locknut.

5 Where applicable, disconnect the tachometer on completion.

Exhaust emission check

6 Specialised equipment is needed to check the exhaust gas emission levels so this check must be entrusted to a Vauxhall dealer or a

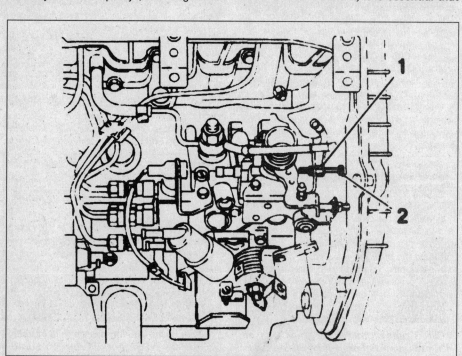

6.4 Engine idle speed adjustment screw (2) and locknut (1) - 1.7 litre engine

suitably-equipped garage. In reality, if the vehicle is running correctly and no problems have been noticed then this check need not be carried out (if the vehicle is over 3 years old, the exhaust emissions will be checked as part of the MoT test anyway).

2.0 litre models

7 Vauxhall specify that this check should be carried out annually on all vehicles. The check involves checking the engine management system operation by plugging an electronic tester into the system diagnostic socket to check the electronic control unit (ECU) memory for faults (see Chapter 4B).

8 In reality, if the vehicle is running correctly and the engine management warning light in the instrument panel is functioning normally, then this check need not be carried out.

7 Electrical systems check

1 Check the operation of all electrical equipment, ie, lights, direction indicators, horn, wash/wipe system, etc. Refer to the appropriate Sections of Chapter 12 for details if any of the circuits are found to be inoperative.

2 Visually check all accessible wiring connectors, harnesses and retaining clips for security, and for signs of chafing or damage. Rectify any faults found.

8 Headlight beam alignment check

Refer to Chapter 12 for details

9 Body corrosion check

This work should be carried out by a Vauxhall/Opel dealer in order to validate the vehicle warranty. The work includes a thorough inspection of the vehicle paintwork and underbody for damage and corrosion

10 Front brake pad and disc check

1 Firmly apply the handbrake, then jack up the front of the vehicle and support it securely on axle stands (see "Jacking and Vehicle Support"). Remove the front roadwheels.

2 For a quick check, the pad thickness can be carried out via the inspection hole on the front of the caliper (see Haynes Hint). Using a steel

rule, measure the thickness of the pad lining including the backing plate. This must not be less than that indicated in the Specifications.

3 The view through the caliper inspection hole gives a rough indication of the state of the brake pads. For a comprehensive check, the brake pads should be removed and cleaned. The operation of the caliper can then also be checked, and the condition of the brake disc itself can be fully examined on both sides. Chapter 9 contains a detailed description of how the brake disc should be checked for wear and/or damage.

4 If any pad's friction material is worn to the specified thickness or less, *all four pads must be renewed as a set*. Refer to Chapter 9 for details.

5 On completion, refit the roadwheels and lower the vehicle to the ground.

11 Rear brake pad and disc check

1 Firmly apply the handbrake, then jack up the rear of the vehicle and support it securely on axle stands (see "Jacking and Vehicle Support"). Remove the rear roadwheels.

2 For a quick check, the pad thickness can be carried out via the inspection hole on the rear of the caliper. Using a steel rule, measure the thickness of the pad lining including the backing plate. This must not be less than that indicated in the Specifications.

3 The view through the caliper inspection hole gives a rough indication of the state of the brake pads. For a comprehensive check, the brake pads should be removed and cleaned. The operation of the caliper can then also be checked, and the condition of the brake disc itself can be fully examined on both sides. Chapter 9 contains a detailed description of how the brake disc should be checked for wear and/or damage.

4 If any pad's friction material is worn to the specified thickness or less, *all four pads must be renewed as a set*. Refer to Chapter 9 for details.

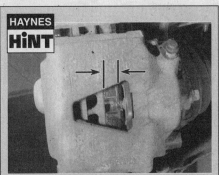

For a quick check, the thickness of friction material remaining on the inner brake pad can be measured through the aperture in the caliper body

5 On completion, refit the roadwheels and lower the vehicle to the ground.

12 Hose and fluid leak check

1 Visually inspect the engine joint faces, gaskets and seals for any signs of water or oil leaks. Pay particular attention to the areas around the cylinder head cover, cylinder head, oil filter and sump joint faces. Bear in mind that, over a period of time, some very slight seepage from these areas is to be expected - what you are really looking for is any indication of a serious leak. Should a leak be found, renew the offending gasket or oil seal by referring to the appropriate Chapters in this manual.

2 Also check the security and condition of all the engine-related pipes and hoses, and all braking system pipes and hoses and fuel lines. Ensure that all cable ties or securing clips are in place, and in good condition. Clips which are broken or missing can lead to chafing of the hoses, pipes or wiring, which could cause more serious problems in the future.

3 Carefully check the radiator hoses and heater hoses along their entire length. Renew any hose which is cracked, swollen or deteriorated. Cracks will show up better if the hose is squeezed. Pay close attention to the hose clips that secure the hoses to the cooling system components. Hose clips can pinch and puncture hoses, resulting in cooling system leaks. If the crimped-type hose clips are used, it may be a good idea to replace them with standard worm-drive clips.

4 Inspect all the cooling system components (hoses, joint faces, etc) for leaks.

5 Where any problems are found on system components, renew the component or gasket with reference to Chapter 3.

6 With the vehicle raised, inspect the fuel tank and filler neck for punctures, cracks and other damage. The connection between the filler neck and tank is especially critical.

A leak in the cooling system will usually show up as white- or rust-coloured deposits on the area adjoining the leak

1B

Sometimes a rubber filler neck or connecting hose will leak due to loose retaining clamps or deteriorated rubber.

7 Carefully check all rubber hoses and metal fuel lines leading away from the fuel tank. Check for loose connections, deteriorated hoses, crimped lines, and other damage. Pay particular attention to the vent pipes and hoses, which often loop up around the filler neck and can become blocked or crimped. Follow the lines to the front of the vehicle, carefully inspecting them all the way. Renew damaged sections as necessary. Similarly, whilst the vehicle is raised, take the opportunity to inspect all underbody brake fluid pipes and hoses.

8 From within the engine compartment, check the security of all fuel, vacuum and brake hose attachments and pipe unions, and inspect all hoses for kinks, chafing and deterioration.

9 Check the condition of the power steering fluid pipes and hoses.

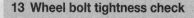

13 Wheel bolt tightness check

1 Remove the wheel trims and check the tightness of all the wheel bolts, using a torque wrench.

2 Refit the wheel trims on completion.

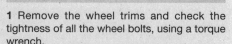

14 Rear suspension level control system check

Where fitted, on Estate models, check that the rear suspension level control system operates correctly. In the event of a fault, have the system checked by a Vauxhall/Opel dealer.

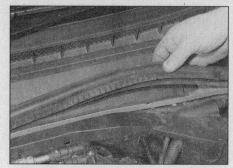

15.1 Pull up the rubber weatherseal . . .

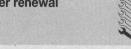

15 Pollen filter renewal

1 Open the bonnet, and pull up the rubber weatherseal from the flange at the rear of the engine compartment **(see illustration)**.

2 Open the cover in the scuttle cover panel for access to the pollen filter **(see illustration)**.

3 Release the clips from each end, then lift out the filter **(see illustration)**.

4 Fit the new filter using a reversal of the removal procedure; make sure that the marking is visible on the right-hand end of the filter, as viewed through the cover.

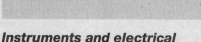

16 Road test

Instruments and electrical equipment

1 Check the operation of all instruments and electrical equipment.

2 Make sure that all instruments read correctly, and switch on all electrical equipment in turn, to check that it functions properly.

Steering and suspension

3 Check for any abnormalities in the steering, suspension, handling or road 'feel'.

4 Drive the vehicle, and check that there are no unusual vibrations or noises.

5 Check that the steering feels positive, with no excessive 'sloppiness', or roughness, and check for any suspension noises when cornering and driving over bumps.

Drivetrain

6 Check the performance of the engine, clutch, transmission and driveshafts.

7 Listen for any unusual noises from the engine, clutch and transmission.

8 Make sure that the engine runs smoothly when idling, and that there is no hesitation when accelerating.

9 Check that, where applicable, the clutch action is smooth and progressive, that the drive is taken up smoothly, and that the pedal travel is not excessive. Also listen for any noises when the clutch pedal is depressed.

10 Check that all gears can be engaged smoothly without noise, and that the gear lever action is not abnormally vague or 'notchy'.

11 Listen for a metallic clicking sound from the front of the vehicle, as the vehicle is driven slowly in a circle with the steering on full-lock. Carry out this check in both directions. If a clicking noise is heard, this indicates wear in a driveshaft joint (see Chapter 8).

Check the operation and performance of the braking system

12 Make sure that the vehicle does not pull to one side when braking, and that the wheels do not lock prematurely when braking hard.

15.2 . . . then open the cover . . .

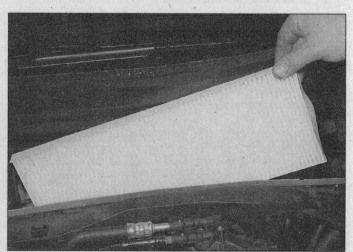

15.3 . . . and lift out the pollen filter

13 Check that there is no vibration through the steering when braking.
14 Check that the handbrake operates correctly, without excessive movement of the lever, and that it holds the vehicle stationary on a slope.

15 Test the operation of the brake servo unit as follows. Depress the footbrake four or five times to exhaust the vacuum, then start the engine. As the engine starts, there should be a noticeable 'give' in the brake pedal as vacuum builds up. Allow the engine to run for at least two minutes, and then switch it off. If the brake pedal is now depressed again, it should be possible to detect a hiss from the servo as the pedal is depressed. After about four or five applications, no further hissing should be heard, and the pedal should feel considerably harder.

Every 20 000 miles (30 000 km) or 2 years

17 Air cleaner element renewal

1 The air cleaner is located in the front right-hand corner of the engine compartment.

17.2 Release the clips then lift the air cleaner cover . . .

2 Release the securing clips, and lift the air cleaner cover sufficiently to enable removal of the filter element **(see illustration)**. On 2.0 litre engines take care not to strain the wiring for the airflow meter/intake air temperature sensor wiring (as applicable) as the cover is lifted.
3 Lift out the filter element **(see illustration)**.
4 Wipe out the casing and the cover **(see illustration)**. Fit the new filter, noting that the rubber locating flange should be uppermost, and secure the cover with the clips.

18 Fuel filter renewal

1.7 litre engine

1 Drain the fuel filter as described in Section 5.
2 Disconnect the wiring connectors from the

temperature switch and heating element which are fitted between the fuel filter and mounting plate.
3 Unscrew the union bolts and remove the fuel lines from the filter. Recover the sealing washers which are fitted on each side of the hose unions.
4 Unscrew the mounting nuts and remove the filter assembly from the bulkhead and separate the filter and its protective housing.
5 Retain the mounting plate and unscrew the filter. Remove the sealing rings from the filter head.
6 Ensure the mounting plate is clean then fit the new sealing rings to top of the new filter element.
7 Smear a little fuel on the new sealing rings and screw the new filter on the mounting plate, tightening securely by hand only.
8 Refit the filter assembly and protective housing to the bulkhead and tighten the mounting nuts to the specified torque.

17.3 . . . and remove the filter element

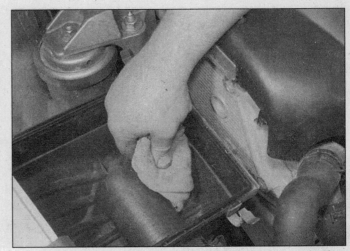

17.4 Wipe clean the air cleaner casing before fitting the new filter

18.12a On 2.0 litre engines, unscrew the centre bolt . . .

18.12b . . . and lift off the cover from the fuel filter housing

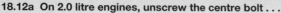

9 Reconnect the fuel lines, positioning a new sealing washer on each side of the unions, and refit the union bolts. Securely tighten both union bolts then reconnect the wiring to the temperature switch and heating element.
10 Start the engine and bleed the fuel system as described in Chapter 4B.

18.13a Remove the filter element . . .

2.0 litre engine

11 Drain the fuel filter housing as described in Section 5.
12 Unscrew the centre bolt and remove the cover from the filter housing (see illustrations).
13 Remove the filter element from the housing and discard it. Examine the housing cover and centre bolt sealing rings for signs of damage or deterioration and renew if necessary (see illustrations).
14 Fit the new filter in the body, then fill the filter housing with fresh fuel. Ideally the fuel level should be just below the rim of the body.
15 Refit the cover to the housing then refit the centre bolt, ensuring the sealing is in position, tightening it to the specified torque (see illustration). Do not overtighten the cover screw as the housing is easily damaged.
16 Start the engine and bleed the fuel system as described in Chapter 4B.

19 Valve clearance check and adjustment - 1.7 litre engine

Refer to Chapter 2C.

20 Manual transmission oil level check

1 Position the vehicle over an inspection pit, on vehicle ramps, or jack it up, but make sure that it is level. The oil level must be checked before the car is driven, or at least 5 minutes after the engine has been switched off. If the oil is checked immediately after driving the car, some of the oil will remain distributed around the transmission components, resulting in an inaccurate level reading.

18.13b . . . and check the cover sealing ring for signs of damage

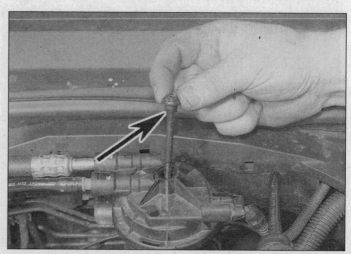

18.15 Refit the centre bolt, ensuring the sealing ring (arrowed) is in position, and tighten it to the specified torque

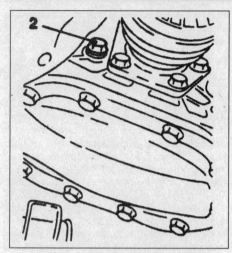

20.2 Transmission oil level plug (2) location

2 Wipe clean the area around the level plug which is located on the right-hand side of the transmission just behind the driveshaft inner joint. Unscrew the plug and clean it **(see illustration)**.
3 The oil level should reach the lower edge of the level plug hole.
4 If topping-up is necessary, unscrew the breather valve from the top of the transmission housing and add the specified type of oil through the valve hole until oil begins to trickle out from the level plug hole **(see illustrations)**.
5 Allow the excess oil to drain out from the level plug hole then refit the level plug, tightening it to the specified torque (see Chapter 7A).
6 Refit the breather valve to the top of the transmission unit, tightening it securely and wash off any spilt oil.

21 Hinge and lock lubrication

1 Work around the vehicle and lubricate the hinges of the bonnet, doors and tailgate with a light machine oil.
2 Lightly lubricate the bonnet release mechanism and exposed section of inner cable with a smear of grease.
3 Check carefully the security and operation of all hinges, latches and locks, adjusting them where required. Check the operation of the central locking system.
4 Check the condition and operation of the tailgate struts, renewing them both if either is leaking or no longer able to support the tailgate securely when raised.

22 Rear brake shoe and drum check

Refer to the detailed description given in Chapter 9.

23 Suspension and steering check

Front suspension and steering check

1 Raise the front of the vehicle, and securely support it on axle stands (see "*Jacking and Vehicle Support*").
2 Visually inspect the balljoint dust covers and the steering rack-and-pinion gaiters for splits, chafing or deterioration. Any wear of these components will cause loss of lubricant,

20.4a Unscrew the breather valve . . .

together with dirt and water entry, resulting in rapid deterioration of the balljoints or steering gear.
3 Check the power steering fluid hoses for chafing or deterioration, and the pipe and hose unions for fluid leaks. Also check for signs of fluid leakage under pressure from the steering gear rubber gaiters, which would indicate failed fluid seals within the steering gear.
4 Grasp the roadwheel at the 12 o'clock and 6 o'clock positions, and try to rock it **(see illustration)**. Very slight free play may be felt, but if the movement is appreciable, further investigation is necessary to determine the source. Continue rocking the wheel while an assistant depresses the footbrake. If the movement is now eliminated or significantly reduced, it is likely that the hub bearings are at fault. If the free play is still evident with the footbrake depressed, then there is wear in the suspension joints or mountings.
5 Now grasp the wheel at the 9 o'clock and 3 o'clock positions, and try to rock it as before. Any movement felt now may again be caused by wear in the hub bearings or the steering track-rod balljoints. If the outer balljoint is worn, the visual movement will be obvious. If

1B

20.4b . . . and top-up the transmission oil level via the breather valve hole

23.4 Check for wear in the hub bearings by grasping the wheel and trying to rock it

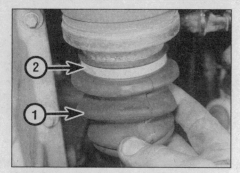

24.1 Check the condition of the driveshaft gaiters (1) and retaining clips (2)

the inner joint is suspect, it can be felt by placing a hand over the rack-and-pinion rubber gaiter and gripping the track-rod. If the wheel is now rocked, movement will be felt at the inner joint if wear has taken place.

6 Using a large screwdriver or flat bar, check for wear in the suspension mounting bushes by levering between the relevant suspension component and its attachment point. Some movement is to be expected, as the mountings are made of rubber, but excessive wear should be obvious. Also check the condition of any visible rubber bushes, looking for splits, cracks or contamination of the rubber.

7 With the car standing on its wheels, have an assistant turn the steering wheel back and forth, about an eighth of a turn each way.

There should be very little, if any, lost movement between the steering wheel and roadwheels. If this is not the case, closely observe the joints and mountings previously described. In addition, check the steering column universal joints for wear, and also check the rack-and-pinion steering gear itself.

Rear suspension check

8 Chock the front wheels, then jack up the rear of the vehicle and support securely on axle stands (see "Jacking and Vehicle Support").

9 Working as described previously for the front suspension, check the rear hub bearings, the suspension bushes and the strut or shock absorber mountings (as applicable) for wear.

Shock absorber check

10 Check for any signs of fluid leakage around the shock absorber body, or from the rubber gaiter around the piston rod. Should any fluid be noticed, the shock absorber is defective internally, and should be renewed. **Note:** Shock absorbers should always be renewed in pairs on the same axle.

11 The efficiency of the shock absorber may be checked by bouncing the vehicle at each corner. Generally speaking, the body will return to its normal position and stop after being depressed. If it rises and returns on a rebound, the shock absorber is probably

suspect. Also examine the shock absorber upper and lower mountings for any signs of wear.

24 Driveshaft gaiter check

1 With the vehicle raised and securely supported on stands, turn the steering onto full lock then slowly rotate the roadwheel. Inspect the condition of the outer constant velocity (CV) joint rubber gaiters while squeezing the gaiters to open out the folds **(see illustration)**. Check for signs of cracking, splits or deterioration of the rubber which may allow the grease to escape and lead to water and grit entry into the joint. Also check the security and condition of the retaining clips. Repeat these checks on the inner CV joints. If any damage or deterioration is found, the gaiters should be renewed as described in Chapter 8.

2 At the same time check the general condition of the CV joints themselves by first holding the driveshaft and attempting to rotate the wheel. Repeat this check by holding the inner joint and attempting to rotate the driveshaft. Any appreciable movement indicates wear in the joints, wear in the driveshaft splines or loose driveshaft retaining nut.

Every 2 years, regardless of mileage

25 Hydraulic fluid renewal

⚠️ **Warning: Hydraulic fluid can harm your eyes and damage painted surfaces, so use extreme caution when handling and pouring it. Do not use fluid that has been standing open for some time, as it absorbs moisture from the air. Excess moisture can cause a dangerous loss of braking effectiveness.**

Note: The brake and clutch hydraulic systems share a reservoir.

1 The procedure is similar to that for the bleeding of the hydraulic systems as described in Chapters 6 and 9. Renew the fluid in the braking system first, then the clutch fluid.

2 Working as described in Chapter 9, open the first bleed screw in the sequence, and pump the brake pedal gently until nearly all the old fluid has been emptied from the master cylinder reservoir. Top-up to the MAX level with new fluid, and continue pumping until only the new fluid remains in the reservoir, and new fluid can be seen emerging from the bleed screw. Tighten the screw, and top the reservoir level up to the MAX level line.

3 Work through all the remaining bleed screws

in the sequence until new fluid can be seen at all of them. Be careful to keep the master cylinder reservoir topped-up to above the MIN level at all times, or air may enter the system and greatly increase the length of the task.

HAYNES HiNT *Old hydraulic fluid is invariably much darker in colour than the new, making it easy to distinguish the two.*

4 Bleed the fluid from the clutch hydraulic system as described in Chapter 6.

5 When the operation is complete, check that all bleed screws are securely tightened, and that their dust caps are refitted. Wash off all

traces of spilt fluid, and recheck the master cylinder reservoir fluid level.

6 Check the operation of the brakes and clutch before taking the car on the road.

26 Remote control battery renewal

Note: The following procedure must be performed within 3 minutes, otherwise the remote control unit will have to be re-programmed.

1 Using a screwdriver inserted as shown prise the battery cover from the remote control unit **(see illustrations)**.

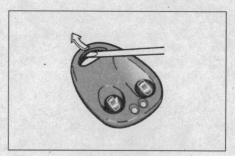

26.1a Insert a screwdriver as shown ...

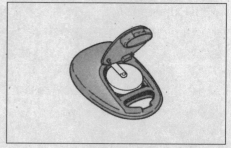

26.1b ... to prise the cover from the remote control unit

2 Note how the battery is fitted, then carefully remove it from the contacts.

3 Fit the new battery and refit the cover making sure that it clips fully onto the base.

27 Coolant renewal

Cooling system draining

 Warning: Wait until the engine is cold before starting this procedure. Do not allow antifreeze to come in contact with your skin, or with the painted surfaces of the vehicle. Rinse off spills immediately with plenty of water. Never leave antifreeze lying around in an open container, or in a puddle in the driveway or on the garage floor. Children and pets are attracted by its sweet smell, but antifreeze can be fatal if ingested.

1 With the engine completely cold, remove the expansion tank filler cap. Turn the cap anti-clockwise, wait until any pressure remaining in the system is released, then unscrew it and lift it off.

2 Where applicable, remove the engine undershield, then position a suitable container beneath the left-hand side of the radiator.

3 Loosen the clip and disconnect the bottom hose from the radiator, and allow the coolant to drain into the container.

4 When the flow of coolant stops, refit the bottom hose and tighten the clip.

5 If the coolant has been drained for a reason other than renewal, then provided it is clean and less than two years old, it can be re-used, though this is not recommended.

Cooling system flushing

6 If coolant renewal has been neglected, or if the antifreeze mixture has become diluted, then in time, the cooling system may gradually lose efficiency, as the coolant passages become restricted due to rust, scale deposits, and other sediment. The cooling system efficiency can be restored by flushing the system clean.

7 The radiator should be flushed independently of the engine, to avoid unnecessary contamination.

Radiator flushing

8 Disconnect the top and bottom hoses and any other relevant hoses from the radiator, with reference to Chapter 3.

9 Insert a garden hose into the radiator top inlet. Direct a flow of clean water through the radiator, and continue flushing until clean water emerges from the radiator bottom outlet.

10 If after a reasonable period, the water still does not run clear, the radiator can be flushed with a good proprietary cleaning agent. It is important that the manufacturer's instructions are followed carefully. If the contamination is particularly bad, remove the radiator, insert the hose in the radiator bottom outlet, and reverse-flush the radiator.

Engine flushing

11 Remove the thermostat as described in Chapter 3 then, if the radiator top hose has been disconnected from the engine, temporarily reconnect the hose.

12 With the top and bottom hoses disconnected from the radiator, insert a garden hose into the radiator top hose. Direct a clean flow of water through the engine, and continue flushing until clean water emerges from the radiator bottom hose.

13 On completion of flushing, refit the thermostat and reconnect the hoses with reference to Chapter 3.

Cooling system filling

14 Before attempting to fill the cooling system, make sure that all hoses and clips are in good condition, and that the clips are tight. Note that an antifreeze mixture must be used all year round, to prevent corrosion of the engine components.

15 Remove the expansion tank filler cap.

16 Slowly fill the system until the coolant level reaches the KALT/COLD mark on the side of the expansion tank.

17 Refit and tighten the expansion tank filler cap.

18 Start the engine, and allow it to run until it reaches normal operating temperature (until the cooling fan cuts in and out).

19 Stop the engine, and allow it to cool, then re-check the coolant level with reference to "*Weekly checks*". Top-up the level if necessary and refit the expansion tank filler cap. Where applicable, refit the engine undershield.

Antifreeze mixture

20 The antifreeze should always be renewed at the specified intervals. This is necessary not only to maintain the antifreeze properties, but also to prevent corrosion which would otherwise occur as the corrosion inhibitors become progressively less effective.

21 Always use an ethylene-glycol based antifreeze which is suitable for use in mixed-metal cooling systems. The quantity of antifreeze and levels of protection are given in the Specifications.

22 Before adding antifreeze, the cooling system should be completely drained, preferably flushed, and all hoses checked for condition and security.

23 After filling with antifreeze, a label should be attached to the expansion tank, stating the type and concentration of antifreeze used, and the date installed. Any subsequent topping-up should be made with the same type and concentration of antifreeze.

24 Do not use engine antifreeze in the windscreen/tailgate washer system, as it will cause damage to the vehicle paintwork. A screenwash additive should be added to the washer system in the quantities stated on the bottle.

Every 40 000 miles (60 000 km) or 4 years

28 Timing belt renewal - 1.7 litre engine

Note: *Although the normal interval for timing belt renewal is 80 000 miles/120 000 km or 8 years, it is strongly recommended that the interval is halved to 40 000 miles/60 000 km or 4 years on vehicles which are subjected to intensive use, ie. mainly short journeys or a lot of stop-start driving. The actual belt renewal interval is therefore up to the individual owner but, bearing in mind that severe engine damage will result should the belt break in use, we recommend you err on the side of caution.*

1 Refer to Chapter 2C.

Chapter 2 Part A:
SOHC petrol engine in-car repair procedures

Contents

Degrees of difficulty

| **Easy,** suitable for novice with little experience | **Fairly easy,** suitable for beginner with some experience | **Fairly difficult,** suitable for competent DIY mechanic | **Difficult,** suitable for experienced DIY mechanic | **Very difficult,** suitable for expert DIY or professional |

Specifications

General

Engine type	Four-cylinder, in-line, water-cooled. Single overhead camshaft, belt-driven, acting on hydraulic tappets
Manufacturer's engine code	X16SZR
Bore	79.0 mm
Stroke	81.5 mm
Capacity	1598 cc
Firing order	1-3-4-2 (No 1 cylinder at timing belt end)
Direction of crankshaft rotation	Clockwise (viewed from timing belt end of engine)
Compression ratio	9.6:1
Maximum power	55 kW at 5200 rpm
Maximum torque	128 Nm at 2800 rpm

Compression pressures

Standard	12 to 15 bar (172 to 217 psi)
Maximum difference between any two cylinders	1 bar (15 psi)

Camshaft

Endfloat	0.09 to 0.21 mm
Maximum permissible radial run-out	0.040 mm
Cam lift:	
Inlet valve	5.61 mm
Exhaust valve	6.12 mm

Lubrication system

Oil pump type	Gear type, driven directly from crankshaft
Minimum permissible oil pressure at idle speed, with engine at operating temperature (oil temperature of at least 80°C)	1.5 bar (22 psi)
Oil pump clearances:	
Gear teeth clearance	0.08 to 0.15 mm
Gear endfloat	0.10 to 0.20 mm

2A

Torque wrench settings	Nm	lbf ft
Camshaft cover bolts	8	6
Camshaft sprocket bolt	45	33
Camshaft thrustplate bolts	8	6
Camshaft housing end cover bolts	8	6
Connecting rod big-end bearing cap bolt: *		
Stage 1	25	18
Stage 2	Angle-tighten a further 30°	
Coolant pump bolts	8	6
Crankshaft pulley bolt: *		
Stage 1	55	41
Stage 2	Angle-tighten a further 45°	
Stage 3	Angle-tighten a further 15°	
Crankshaft sensor mounting bracket bolt	6	4
Cylinder head bolts: *		
Stage 1	25	18
Stage 2	Angle-tighten a further 60°	
Stage 3	Angle-tighten a further 60°	
Stage 4	Angle-tighten a further 60°	
Driveplate bolts	60	44
Engine/transmission mounting bolts:		
Front (left- and right-hand) mounting:		
Bracket-to-engine/transmission bolts	60	44
Mounting-to-bracket/subframe nuts	45	33
Rear mounting:		
Mounting-to-bracket bolts	45	33
Mounting-to-subframe bolts	20	15
Bracket-to-transmission bolts	60	44
Torque support rod bolts	60	44
Engine-to-transmission unit bolts:		
M8 bolts	20	15
M10 bolts	40	30
M12 bolts	60	44
Flywheel bolts: *		
Stage 1	35	26
Stage 2	Angle-tighten a further 30°	
Stage 3	Angle-tighten a further 15°	
Flywheel/driveplate lower cover plate bolts	8	6
Main bearing cap bolts: *		
Stage 1	50	37
Stage 2	Angle-tighten a further 45°	
Stage 3	Angle-tighten a further 15°	
Oil pump:		
Retaining bolts	8	6
Pump cover screws	6	4
Oil pressure relief valve bolt	30	22
Oil pump pick-up/strainer bolts	8	6
Sump drain plug	See Chapter 1A	
Sump bolts:		
Models without air conditioning (steel sump):		
Sump-to-cylinder block/oil pump bolts	10	7
Models with air conditioning (alloy sump):		
Sump-to-cylinder block/oil pump bolts	8	6
Sump flange-to-transmission bolts:		
M8 bolts	20	15
M10 bolts	40	30
Roadwheel bolts	110	81
Timing belt cover bolts:		
Upper and lower covers	4	3
Rear cover	12	9
Timing belt tensioner bolt	20	15

* **Note:** *The manufacturer states that all fasteners secured by the angle-tightening method must be renewed as a matter of course.*

1 General information

How to use this Chapter

1 This Part of Chapter 2 is devoted to in-car repair procedures for the engine. All procedures concerning engine removal and refitting, and engine block/cylinder head overhaul can be found in Chapter 2E.

2 Most of the operations included in this Part are based on the assumption that the engine is still installed in the car. Therefore, if this information is being used during a complete engine overhaul, with the engine already removed, many of the steps included here will not apply.

Engine description

3 The engine is a single overhead camshaft, four-cylinder, in-line unit, mounted transversely at the front of the car, with the clutch and transmission on its left-hand end.

4 The aluminium alloy cylinder block is of the dry-liner type. The crankshaft is supported within the cylinder block on five shell-type main bearings. Thrustwashers are fitted to number 3 main bearing, to control crankshaft endfloat.

5 The connecting rods are attached to the crankshaft by horizontally split shell-type big-end bearings, and to the pistons by interference-fit gudgeon pins. The aluminium alloy pistons are of the slipper type, and are fitted with three piston rings, comprising two compression rings and a scraper-type oil control ring.

6 The camshaft runs directly in the camshaft housing, which is mounted on top of the cylinder head, and driven by the crankshaft via a toothed rubber timing belt (which also drives the coolant pump). The camshaft operates each valve via a follower. Each follower pivots on a hydraulic self-adjusting valve lifter (tappet) which automatically adjust the valve clearances.

7 Lubrication is by pressure-feed from a gear-type oil pump, which is mounted on the right-hand end of the crankshaft. It draws oil through a strainer located in the sump, and then forces it through an externally-mounted full-flow cartridge-type filter. The oil flows into galleries in the main bearing cap bridge arrangement and cylinder block/crankcase, from where it is distributed to the crankshaft (main bearings) and camshaft(s). The big-end bearings are supplied with oil via internal drillings in the crankshaft, while the camshaft bearings also receive a pressurised supply. The camshaft lobes and valves are lubricated by splash, as are all other engine components.

8 A semi-closed crankcase ventilation system is employed; crankcase fumes are drawn from the cylinder head cover, and passed via a hose to the inlet manifold.

Repair operations possible with the engine in the car

9 The following operations can be carried out without having to remove the engine from the vehicle:

a) Removal and refitting of the cylinder head.
b) Removal and refitting of the timing belt and sprockets.
c) Renewal of the camshaft oil seal.
d) Removal and refitting of the camshaft housing and camshaft.
e) Removal and refitting of the sump.
f) Removal and refitting of the connecting rods and pistons*.
g) Removal and refitting of the oil pump.
h) Renewal of the crankshaft oil seals.
i) Renewal of the engine mountings.
j) Removal and refitting of the flywheel/driveplate.

* Although the operation marked with an asterisk can be carried out with the engine in the car after removal of the sump, it is better for the engine to be removed, in the interests of cleanliness and improved access. For this reason, the procedure is described in Chapter 2E.

2 Compression test - description and interpretation

1 When engine performance is down, or if misfiring occurs which cannot be attributed to the ignition or fuel systems, a compression test can provide diagnostic clues as to the engine's condition. If the test is performed regularly, it can give warning of trouble before any other symptoms become apparent.

2 The engine must be fully warmed-up to normal operating temperature, the battery must be fully charged, and the spark plugs must be removed (see Chapter 1). The aid of an assistant will also be required.

3 Disable the ignition system by disconnecting the wiring connector from the DIS module (see Chapter 5) and the fuel system by removing the fuel pump relay from the engine compartment relay box (see Chapter 4A, Section 8).

4 Fit a compression tester to the number 1 cylinder spark plug hole. The type of tester which screws into the plug thread is to be preferred (see illustration).

5 Have the assistant hold the throttle wide open and crank the engine on the starter motor; after one or two revolutions, the compression pressure should build up to a maximum figure, and then stabilise. Record the highest reading obtained.

6 Repeat the test on the remaining cylinders, recording the pressure in each.

7 All cylinders should produce very similar pressures; any difference greater than that specified indicates the existence of a fault. Note that the compression should build up

2.4 Compression tester fitted to No 1 spark plug hole

quickly in a healthy engine. Low compression on the first stroke, followed by gradually-increasing pressure on successive strokes, indicates worn piston rings. A low compression reading on the first stroke, which does not build up during successive strokes, indicates leaking valves or a blown head gasket (a cracked head could also be the cause). Deposits on the undersides of the valve heads can also cause low compression.

8 If the pressure in any cylinder is reduced to the specified minimum or less, carry out the following test to isolate the cause. Introduce a teaspoonful of clean oil into that cylinder through its spark plug hole, and repeat the test.

9 If the addition of oil temporarily improves the compression pressure, this indicates that bore or piston wear is responsible for the pressure loss. No improvement suggests that leaking or burnt valves, or a blown head gasket, may be to blame.

10 A low reading from two adjacent cylinders is almost certainly due to the head gasket having blown between them; the presence of coolant in the engine oil will confirm this.

11 If one cylinder is about 20 per cent lower than the others, and the engine has a slightly rough idle, a worn camshaft lobe could be the cause.

12 If the compression reading is unusually high, the combustion chambers are probably coated with carbon deposits. If this is the case, the cylinder head should be removed and decarbonised.

13 On completion of the test, refit the spark plugs (see Chapter 1), refit the fuel pump relay and reconnect the wiring connector to the DIS module.

3 Top dead centre (TDC) for No 1 piston - locating

1 In its travel up and down its cylinder bore, Top Dead Centre (TDC) is the highest point that each piston reaches as the crankshaft rotates. While each piston reaches TDC both at the top of the compression stroke and again at the top of the exhaust stroke, for the purpose of timing the engine, TDC refers to the piston position (usually number 1) at the top of its compression stroke.

2A

3.5a Align the camshaft sprocket timing mark with the cut-out on the timing belt cover . . .

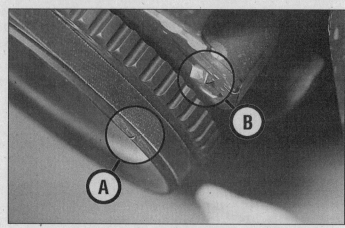

3.5b . . . and align the crankshaft pulley (A) notch with the timing belt pointer (B) to position No 1 piston at TDC on its compression stroke

2 Number 1 piston (and cylinder) is at the right-hand (timing belt) end of the engine, and its TDC position is located as follows. Note that the crankshaft rotates clockwise when viewed from the right-hand side of the car.

3 Disconnect the battery negative terminal. If necessary, remove all the spark plugs as described in Chapter 1 to enable the engine to be easily turned over.

4 To gain access to the camshaft sprocket timing mark, remove the timing belt upper cover as described in Section 6.

5 Using a socket and extension bar on the crankshaft pulley bolt, turn the crankshaft whilst keeping an eye on the camshaft sprocket. Rotate the crankshaft until the timing mark on the camshaft sprocket is correctly aligned with the cut-out on the top of the timing belt rear cover and the notch on the crankshaft pulley rim is correctly aligned with the pointer on the timing belt lower cover **(see illustrations)**.

6 With the crankshaft pulley and camshaft sprocket timing marks positioned as described, the engine is positioned with No 1 piston at TDC on its compression stroke.

4 Camshaft cover - removal and refitting

Removal

1 Release the retaining clips and disconnect the breather hoses from the camshaft cover **(see illustrations)**.

2 Slacken and remove the retaining bolts, noting the correct fitted location of any clips or brackets retained by the bolts (as applicable) then lift the camshaft cover from the camshaft housing **(see illustration)**. If the cover is stuck, do not lever between the cover and camshaft housing mating surfaces - if necessary, gently tap the cover sideways to free it. Recover the gasket; if it shows signs of damage or deterioration it must be renewed.

Refitting

3 Prior to refitting, examine the inside of the cover for a build-up of oil sludge or any other contamination, and if necessary clean the cover with paraffin, or a water-soluble solvent. Examine the condition of the crankcase ventilation filter inside the camshaft cover, and clean as described for the inside of the cover if clogging is evident (if desired, the filter can be removed from the cover, after removing the securing bolts). Dry the cover thoroughly before refitting.

4 Ensure the cover is clean and dry and seat the gasket in the cover recess then refit the cover to the camshaft housing, ensuring the gasket remains correctly seated **(see illustration)**.

5 Refit the retaining bolts, ensuring all relevant clips/brackets are correctly positioned, and tighten them to the specified torque working in a diagonal sequence **(see illustration)**.

6 Reconnect the breather hoses securely to the cover.

4.1a Slacken the retaining clips and disconnect the large . . .

4.1b . . . and small breather hose from the rear of the camshaft cover

4.2 Removing the camshaft cover from the engine

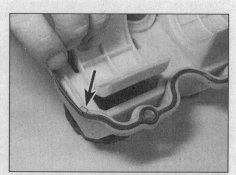

4.4 Ensure the gasket is correctly located in the camshaft cover recess

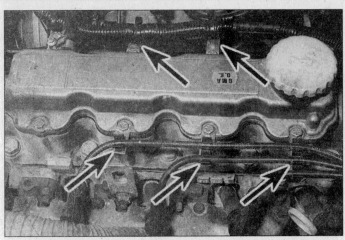

4.5 On refitting ensure the wiring and HT lead clips (arrowed) are fitted to the correct bolts

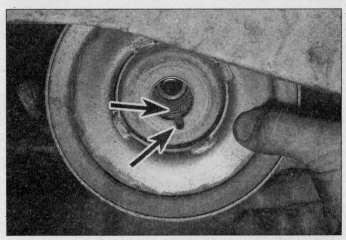
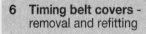

5.5 Refit the crankshaft pulley aligning the cut-out with the raised notch on the crankshaft sprocket (arrowed)

5 Crankshaft pulley - removal and refitting

Note: *A new pulley retaining bolt will be required on refitting.*

Removal

1 Apply the handbrake, then jack up the front of the car and support it on axle stands. Remove the right-hand roadwheel.
2 Remove the auxiliary drivebelt as described in Chapter 4. Prior to removal, mark the direction of rotation on the belt to ensure the belt is refitted the same way around.
3 Slacken the crankshaft pulley retaining bolt. To prevent crankshaft rotation on manual transmission models, have an assistant select top gear and apply the brakes firmly. On automatic transmission models prevent rotation by removing one of the torque converter retaining bolts and bolting the driveplate to the transmission housing using a metal bar, spacers and suitable bolts (see Chapter 7B). If the engine is removed from the vehicle it will be necessary to lock the flywheel/driveplate (see Section 15).
4 Unscrew the retaining bolt and washer and remove the crankshaft pulley from the end of

the crankshaft, taking care not to damage the crankshaft sensor.

Refitting

5 Refit the crankshaft pulley, aligning the pulley cut-out with the raised notch on the timing belt sprocket, then fit the washer and new retaining bolt **(see illustration)**.
6 Lock the crankshaft by the method used on removal, and tighten the pulley retaining bolt to the specified stage 1 torque setting then angle-tighten the bolt through the specified stage 2 angle, using a socket and extension bar, and finally through the specified stage 3 angle. It is recommended that an angle-measuring gauge is used during the final stages of the tightening, to ensure accuracy **(see illustration)**. If a gauge is not available, use white paint to make alignment marks between the bolt head and pulley prior to tightening; the marks can then be used to check that the bolt has been rotated through the correct angle.
7 Refit the auxiliary drivebelt as described in Chapter 1 using the mark made prior to removal to ensure the belt is fitted the correct way around.
8 Refit the roadwheel then lower the car to the ground and tighten the wheel bolts to the specified torque.

6 Timing belt covers - removal and refitting

Upper cover

Removal

1 Remove the air cleaner housing as described in Chapter 4.
2 Remove the auxiliary drivebelt as described in Chapter 1. Prior to removal, mark the direction of rotation on the belt to ensure the belt is fitted the same way around on refitting.
3 Undo the retaining screws then unclip the timing belt upper cover and remove it from the engine **(see illustration)**.

Refitting

4 Refitting is the reverse of removal, ensuring the auxiliary drivebelt is fitted the same way around as it was prior removal.

Lower cover

Removal

5 Remove the crankshaft pulley (see Section 5).
6 Remove the upper cover (see paragraphs 1 and 3) then undo the retaining screws and remove the lower cover from the engine **(see illustration)**.

2A

5.6 Fit the new retaining bolt and tighten it as described in text

6.3 Timing belt upper cover retaining bolts (arrowed)

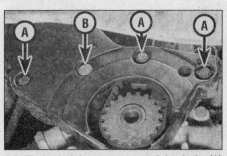

6.6 Timing belt lower cover retaining bolts (A)

There is no need to undo the timing belt tensioner bolt (B) to remove the cover

Refitting

7 Refitting is the reverse of removal, using a new crankshaft pulley retaining bolt.

Rear cover

Removal

8 Remove the camshaft and crankshaft timing belt sprockets and the timing belt tensioner as described in Section 8.

9 Slacken and remove the bolts securing the rear cover to the camshaft housing and oil pump housing, and remove the cover from the engine (see illustration).

Refitting

10 Refitting is the reverse of removal, tightening the cover retaining bolts to the specified torque.

7 Timing belt - removal and refitting

Note: *The timing belt must be removed and refitted with the engine cold.*

Removal

1 Remove the timing belt upper cover as described in Section 6.

2 Position No 1 cylinder at TDC on its compression stroke as described in Section 3.

3 Remove the crankshaft pulley as described in Section 5.

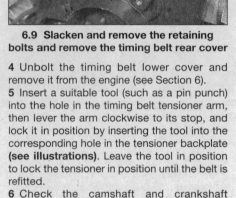

6.9 Slacken and remove the retaining bolts and remove the timing belt rear cover

4 Unbolt the timing belt lower cover and remove it from the engine (see Section 6).

5 Insert a suitable tool (such as a pin punch) into the hole in the timing belt tensioner arm, then lever the arm clockwise to its stop, and lock it in position by inserting the tool into the corresponding hole in the tensioner backplate (see illustrations). Leave the tool in position to lock the tensioner in position until the belt is refitted.

6 Check the camshaft and crankshaft sprocket timing marks are correctly aligned with the marks on the belt rear cover and oil pump housing.

7 Slacken the coolant pump retaining bolts then, using an open-ended spanner, carefully rotate the pump to relieve the tension in the timing belt. Adapters to fit the pump are available from most tool shops and allow the

pump to be easily turned using a ratchet or extension bar (see illustrations).

8 Slide the timing belt off from its sprockets and remove it from the engine (see illustration). If the belt is to be re-used, use white paint or similar to mark the direction of rotation on the belt. **Do not** rotate the crankshaft until the timing belt has been refitted.

9 Check the timing belt carefully for any signs of uneven wear, splitting or oil contamination, and renew it if there is the slightest doubt about its condition. If the engine is undergoing an overhaul and is approaching the manufacturers' specified interval for belt renewal (see Chapter 1) renew the belt as a matter of course, regardless of its apparent condition. If signs of oil contamination are found, trace the source of the oil leak and rectify it, then wash down the engine timing belt area and all related components to remove all traces of oil.

Refitting

10 On reassembly, thoroughly clean the timing belt sprockets then check that the camshaft sprocket timing mark is still correctly aligned with the cover cut-out and the crankshaft sprocket mark is still aligned with the mark on the oil pump housing (see illustration).

11 Fit the timing belt over the crankshaft and camshaft sprockets, ensuring that the belt front run is taut (ie, all slack is on the tensioner

7.5a Insert a tool (such as a punch) into the hole (arrowed) in the tensioner arm . . .

7.5b . . . then lever the arm clockwise and lock the tensioner in position by locating the tool in the backplate hole

7.7a Slacken the coolant pump bolts . . .

7.7b . . . and relieve the timing belt tension by rotating the pump with a suitable adapter

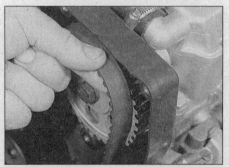

7.8 Slip the timing belt off from the sprockets and remove it from the engine

7.10 Ensure the timing mark on the crankshaft sprocket is correctly aligned with the mark on the oil pump housing

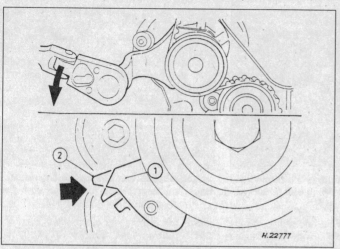

7.16 Rotate the coolant pump until the tensioner arm pointer (1) is correctly aligned with the cut-out (2) on the backplate

8.2 Using a home-made sprocket holding tool to retain the camshaft sprocket whilst the bolt is slackened

pulley side of the belt), then fit the belt over the coolant pump sprocket and tensioner pulley. Do not twist the belt sharply while refitting it. Ensure that the belt teeth are correctly seated centrally in the sprockets, and that the timing marks remain in alignment. If a used belt is being refitted, ensure that the arrow mark made on removal points in the normal direction of rotation, as before.

12 Carefully remove the punch from the timing belt tensioner to release the tensioner spring.

13 Check the sprocket timing marks are still correctly aligned. If adjustment is necessary, lock the tensioner in position again then disengage the belt from the sprockets and make any necessary adjustments.

14 If the marks are still correctly positioned, tension the timing belt by rotating the coolant pump whilst observing the movement of the tensioner arm. Position the pump so that the tensioner arm is fully over against its stop, without exerting any excess strain on the belt, then tighten the coolant pump retaining bolts.

15 Temporarily refit the crankshaft pulley bolt then rotate the crankshaft smoothly through two complete turns (720°) in the normal direction of rotation to settle the timing belt in position.

16 Check that both the camshaft and crankshaft sprocket timing marks are realigned then slacken the coolant pump bolts. Adjust the pump so that the tensioner arm pointer is aligned with the cut-out on the backplate then tighten the coolant pump bolts to the specified torque (see illustration). Rotate the crankshaft smoothly through another two complete turns in the normal direction of rotation, to bring the sprocket timing marks back into alignment. Check that the tensioner arm pointer is still aligned with the backplate cut-out.

17 If the tensioner arm is not correctly aligned with the backplate, repeat the procedure in paragraph 16.

18 Once the tensioner arm and backplate

remain correctly aligned, ensure the coolant pump bolts are tightened to the specified torque, then refit the timing belt covers and crankshaft pulley as described in Sections 5 and 6.

<h2>8 Timing belt tensioner and sprockets - removal and refitting</h2>

Camshaft sprocket

Removal

1 Remove the timing belt as described in Section 7.

2 The camshaft must be prevented from turning as the sprocket bolt is unscrewed, and this can be achieved in one of two ways as follows.

a) *Make up a sprocket-holding tool using two lengths of steel strip (one long, the other short), and three nuts and bolts; one nut and bolt forms the pivot of a forked tool, with the remaining two nuts and bolts at the tips of the 'forks' to engage with the sprocket spokes as shown (see illustration).*

8.5 Refit the camshaft sprocket making sure the locating pin (1) engages with the sprocket hole (2)

b) *Remove the camshaft cover as described in Section 4 and hold the camshaft with an open-ended spanner on the flats provided.*

3 Unscrew the retaining bolt and washer and remove the sprocket from the end of the camshaft.

Refitting

4 Prior to refitting check the oil seal for signs of damage or leakage, if necessary, renewing it as described in Section 9.

5 Refit the sprocket to the end of the camshaft, aligning its cut-out with the camshaft locating pin, then refit the retaining bolt and washer (see illustration).

6 Tighten the sprocket retaining bolt to the specified torque whilst preventing rotation using the method employed on removal (see illustration).

7 Refit the timing belt as described in Section 7 then (where necessary) refit the camshaft cover as described in Section 4.

Crankshaft sprocket

Removal

8 Remove the timing belt (see Section 7).

9 Slide the sprocket off from the end of the crankshaft, noting which way around it is fitted.

8.6 Using an open-ended spanner to retain the camshaft whilst the sprocket retaining bolt is tightened to the specified torque

2A

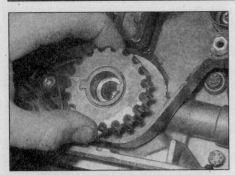

8.11 Refit the crankshaft sprocket making sure its timing marks are facing outwards

8.14 Slacken and remove the retaining bolt and remove the timing belt tensioner assembly

8.15 On refitting ensure the tensioner backplate lug (1) is correctly located in the oil pump housing hole (2)

Refitting

10 Ensure the Woodruff key is correctly fitted to the crankshaft.

11 Align the sprocket with the crankshaft groove then slide the sprocket into position, making sure its timing mark is facing outwards **(see illustration)**.

12 Refit the timing belt (see Section 7).

Tensioner assembly

Removal

13 Remove the timing belt (see Section 7).

14 Slacken and remove the retaining bolt and remove the tensioner assembly from the oil pump **(see illustration)**.

Refitting

15 Fit the tensioner to the oil pump housing, making sure that the lug on the backplate is correctly located in the oil pump housing hole **(see illustration)**. Ensure the tensioner is correctly seated then refit the retaining bolt and tighten it to the specified torque.

9 Camshaft oil seal - renewal

1 Remove the camshaft sprocket as described in Section 8.

2 Carefully punch or drill two small holes opposite each other in the oil seal. Screw a self-tapping screw into each, and pull on the screws with pliers to extract the seal **(see illustration)**.

3 Clean the seal housing, and polish off any burrs or raised edges which may have caused the seal to fail in the first place.

4 Lubricate the lips of the new seal with clean engine oil, and press it into position using a suitable tubular drift (such as a socket) which bears only on the hard outer edge of the seal **(see illustration)**. Take care not to damage the seal lips during fitting; note that the seal lips should face inwards.

5 Refit the camshaft sprocket as described in Section 8.

10 Camshaft - removal, inspection and refitting

Removal

Using Vauxhall service tool (tool no. MKM 891)

1 If access to the special service tool can be gained, the camshaft can be removed from the engine without disturbing the camshaft housing. The tool is fitted to the top of the camshaft housing, once the cover has been removed (see Section 4), and depresses the cam followers. This allows the camshaft to be withdrawn from the left-hand end of the housing once the timing belt sprocket has been removed (see Section 8) and the cover and thrustplate have been unbolted (see paragraphs 3 to 6).
Caution: Prior to fitting the special tool, rotate the crankshaft another 90° past the TDC position (see Section 3). This will position the pistons approximately mid-way in the bores and prevent the valves contacting them when the tool is fitted.

Without service tool

2 Assuming that such a tool is not available, the camshaft can only be removed once the camshaft housing has been removed from the engine. Since the camshaft housing is secured in position by the cylinder head bolts, it is not possible to remove the camshaft without removing the cylinder head (see Section 12).
Note: *In theory it is possible to remove the camshaft housing once the cylinder head bolts have been removed, and leave the head in position. However, this procedure carries a high risk of disturbing the head gasket, resulting in the head gasket 'blowing' once the camshaft and housing are refitted. If you wish to attempt this, remove the camshaft housing, as described in Section 12, noting that it will not be necessary to remove the manifolds, etc. Be warned though that, after refitting, you may find the head gasket will need renewing, meaning that the cylinder head will have to be removed after all and need another set of bolts. The decision is yours as to whether this is a chance worth taking.*

3 With the camshaft housing removed (where necessary), unbolt the DIS module and remove it from the end of the housing.

4 Undo the retaining bolts and remove the end cover from the left-hand end of the housing **(see illustration)**. Remove the sealing

9.2 Removing the camshaft oil seal

9.4 Fitting a new camshaft oil seal

10.4 Remove the cover from the left-hand end of the camshaft housing (sealing ring arrowed)

ring from the cover and discard it, a new one should be used on refitting.

5 Measure the camshaft endfloat by inserting feeler gauges between the thrustplate and the camshaft; if the endfloat is not within the limits given in the Specifications then the thrustplate will need to be renewed. Unscrew the two retaining bolts then slide out the camshaft thrustplate, noting which way round it is fitted **(see illustration)**.

6 Carefully withdraw the camshaft from the left-hand end of the housing, taking care not to damage the bearing journals **(see illustration)**.

Inspection

7 With the camshaft removed, examine the bearings in the camshaft housing for signs of obvious wear or pitting. If evident, a new camshaft housing will probably be required. Also check that the oil supply holes in the camshaft housing are free from obstructions.

8 The camshaft itself should show no marks or scoring on the journal or cam lobe surfaces. If evident, renew the camshaft. If the camshaft lobes show signs of wear also examine the followers (see Section 11).

9 Check the camshaft thrustplate for signs of wear or grooves, and renew if necessary.

Refitting

10 Carefully prise the old seal out of from the camshaft housing, using a suitable screwdriver. Ensure the housing is clean then press the in new seal, ensuring its sealing lip is facing inwards, until it is flush with the housing.

11 Liberally lubricate the camshaft and housing bearings and the oil seal lip with fresh engine oil.

12 Carefully insert the camshaft into the housing, taking care not to mark the bearing surfaces or damage the oil seal lip.

13 Slide the thrustplate into position, engaging it with the camshaft slot, and tighten its retaining bolts to the specified torque. Check the camshaft endfloat (see paragraph 5).

14 Fit a new sealing ring to the end cover recess then refit the cover to the camshaft housing and tighten its retaining bolts to the specified torque. Refit the DIS module to the housing cover.

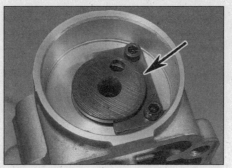

10.5 Undo the retaining bolts then remove the thrustplate (arrowed) . . .

15 If work is being carried out using the special service tool, remove the tool and refit the camshaft sprocket. Return the crankshaft to TDC and refit the timing belt (see Sections 7 and 8).

16 If the tool is not being used, refit the camshaft housing as described in Section 12.

---

11 Camshaft followers and hydraulic tappets - removal, inspection and refitting

Using Vauxhall service tool (tool no. KM-565)

Removal

1 If access to the special tool (KM-565) or a suitable equivalent can be gained, the cam followers and tappets can be removed as follows, without disturbing the camshaft.

2 Firmly apply the handbrake then jack up the front of the vehicle and support it on axle stands. Remove the right-hand front roadwheel.

3 Remove the camshaft cover as described in Section 4.

4 Using a socket and extension bar, rotate the crankshaft in the normal direction of rotation until the camshaft lobe of the first follower/tappet to be removed is pointing straight upwards.

5 Fit the service tool to the top of the camshaft housing, making sure the tool end is correctly engaged with the top of the valve. Screw the tool stud into one of the housing cover bolt holes until the valve is sufficiently

10.6 . . . and slide the camshaft out from the housing

depressed to allow the follower to be slid out from underneath the camshaft. The hydraulic tappet can then also be removed as can the thrust pad from the top of the valve. Inspect the components (see paragraphs 10 and 11) and renew if worn or damaged.

Refitting

6 Lubricate the tappet and follower with fresh engine oil then slide the tappet into its bore in the cylinder head. Manoeuvre the follower into position, ensuring it is correctly engaged with the tappet and valve stem, then carefully remove the service tool.

7 Repeat the operation on the remaining followers and tappets.

Without special tool

Removal

8 Without the use of the special tool, it will be necessary to remove the camshaft housing to allow the followers and tappets to be removed (see Section 10, paragraph 2).

9 With the housing removed, obtain eight small, clean plastic containers, and number them 1 to 8; alternatively, divide a larger container into eight compartments. Lift out each follower, thrust pad and hydraulic tappet in turn, and place them in their respective container. Do not interchange the cam followers, or the rate of wear will be much-increased **(see illustrations)**.

Inspection

10 Examine the cam follower bearing surfaces which contact the camshaft lobes for wear ridges and scoring. Renew any follower on which these conditions are apparent. If a

2A

11.9a Remove each follower . . .

11.9b . . . thrust pad . . .

11.9c . . . and hydraulic tappet from the cylinder head

12.12 Removing the camshaft housing

follower bearing surface is badly scored, also examine the corresponding lobe on the camshaft for wear, as it is likely that both will be worn. Also check the thrust pad for signs of wear or damage. Renew worn components as necessary.

11 If the hydraulic tappets are thought to be faulty they should be renewed; testing of the tappets is not possible.

Refitting

12 Lubricate the hydraulic tappets and their cylinder head bores with clean engine oil. Refit the tappets to the cylinder head, making sure they are fitted in their original locations.

13 Fit the thrust pads to the top of its respective valves.

14 Lubricate the followers with clean engine oil. Fit each follower, making sure it is correctly located with both the tappet and thrust pad, then refit the camshaft housing (see Section 12).

---

12 Camshaft housing and cylinder head - removal and refitting

Removal

Note: *The engine must be cold when removing the cylinder head. New cylinder head bolts must be used on refitting.*

1 Depressurise the fuel system as described in Chapter 4 then disconnect the battery negative lead.

2 Drain the cooling system and remove the spark plugs as described in Chapter 1.

3 Remove the timing belt as described in Section 7.

4 Remove the inlet and exhaust manifolds as described in Chapter 4. If no work is to be carried out on the cylinder head, the head can be removed complete with manifolds once the following operations have been carried out (see Chapter 4).

   a) *Disconnect the various wiring connectors from the throttle body and manifold and free the wiring harness from the inlet manifold.*

   b) *Disconnect the fuel hoses from the throttle body and the various vacuum and coolant hoses from the inlet manifold.*

12.13 Removing the cylinder head

   c) *Unbolt the inlet manifold support bracket and the alternator upper bracket.*

   d) *Disconnect the accelerator cable.*

   e) *Unbolt the exhaust front pipe from manifold and disconnect the oxygen sensor wiring connector.*

5 Remove the camshaft cover as described in Section 4.

6 Remove the camshaft sprocket as described in Section 8.

7 Undo the retaining bolts securing the timing belt rear cover to the camshaft housing.

8 Disconnect the wiring connectors from the DIS module, purge valve and the coolant temperature sender unit and on the left-hand end of the cylinder head. Free the wiring from its retaining clips, noting its correct routing, and position it clear of the cylinder head.

9 Slacken the retaining clip and disconnect the coolant hose from the thermostat housing

10 Make a final check to ensure that all relevant hoses, pipes and wires, etc, have been disconnected.

11 Working in the **reverse** of the tightening sequence **(see illustration 12.29a)**, progressively slacken the cylinder head bolts by a third of a turn at a time until all bolts can be unscrewed by hand. Remove each bolt in turn, along with its washer.

12 Lift the camshaft housing from the cylinder head **(see illustration)**. If necessary, tap the housing gently with a soft-faced mallet to free it from the cylinder head, but **do not** lever at the mating faces. Note the fitted positions of the two locating dowels, and remove them for safe keeping if they are loose.

12.22a Fit the new gasket to the cylinder block, engaging it with the locating dowels (arrowed) . . .

13 Lift the cylinder head from the cylinder block, taking care not to dislodge the cam followers or thrust pads **(see illustration)**. If necessary, tap the cylinder head gently with a soft-faced mallet to free it from the block, but **do not** lever at the mating faces. Note the fitted positions of the two locating dowels, and remove them for safe keeping if they are loose.

14 Recover the cylinder head gasket, and discard it.

Preparation for refitting

15 The mating faces of the cylinder head and block must be perfectly clean before refitting the head. Use a scraper to remove all traces of gasket and carbon, and also clean the tops of the pistons. Take particular care with the aluminium surfaces, as the soft metal is damaged easily. Also, make sure that debris is not allowed to enter the oil and water channels - this is particularly important for the oil circuit, as carbon could block the oil supply to the camshaft or crankshaft bearings. Using adhesive tape and paper, seal the water, oil and bolt holes in the cylinder block. To prevent carbon entering the gap between the pistons and bores, smear a little grease in the gap. After cleaning the piston, rotate the crankshaft so that the piston moves down the bore, then wipe out the grease and carbon with a cloth rag. Clean the other piston crowns in the same way.

16 Check the block and head for nicks, deep scratches and other damage. If slight, they may be removed carefully with a file. More serious damage may be repaired by machining, but this is a specialist job.

17 If warpage of the cylinder head is suspected, use a straight-edge to check it for distortion. Refer to Chapter 2E if necessary.

18 Ensure that the cylinder head bolt holes in the crankcase are clean and free of oil. Syringe or soak up any oil left in the bolt holes. This is most important in order that the correct bolt tightening torque can be applied and to prevent the possibility of the block being cracked by hydraulic pressure when the bolts are tightened.

19 Renew the cylinder head bolts regardless of their apparent condition.

Refitting

20 Position number 1 piston at TDC, and wipe clean the mating faces of the head and block.

21 Ensure that the two locating dowels are in position at each end of the cylinder block/crankcase surface.

22 Fit the new cylinder head gasket to the block, making sure it is fitted with the correct way up with its OBEN/TOP mark uppermost **(see illustrations)**.

23 Carefully refit the cylinder head, locating it on the dowels.

24 Ensure the mating surfaces of the cylinder head and camshaft housing are clean and dry.

12.22b . . . making sure its OBEN/TOP marking is uppermost

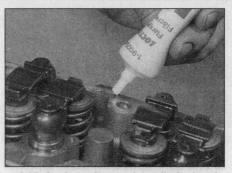

12.25 Apply sealant to the cylinder head upper mating surface then refit the camshaft housing

12.28 Fit the washers to the new cylinder head bolts and screw the bolts into position

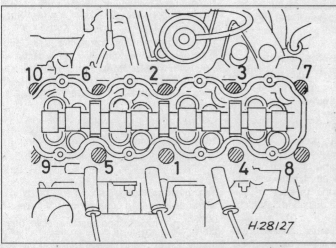

12.29a Cylinder head bolt tightening sequence

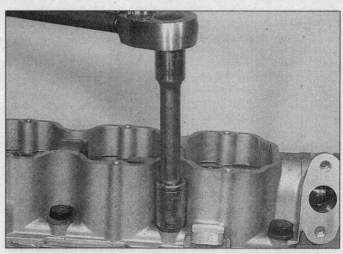

12.29b Working in the specified sequence, tighten the cylinder head bolts to the specified stage 1 torque setting . . .

2A

Check the camshaft is still correctly positioned by temporarily fitting the camshaft sprocket and checking that the sprocket timing mark is still uppermost.

25 Apply a bead of suitable sealant to the cylinder head mating surface **(see illustration)**.

26 Ensure the two locating dowels are in position then lubricate the camshaft followers with clean engine oil.

27 Carefully lower the camshaft housing assembly into position, locating it on the dowels.

28 Fit the washers to the new cylinder head bolts then carefully insert them into position (**do not drop**), tightening them finger-tight only at this stage **(see illustration)**.

29 Working progressively and in the sequence shown, first tighten all the cylinder head bolts to the stage 1 torque setting **(see illustrations)**.

30 Once all bolts have been tightened to the stage 1 torque, again working in the sequence shown, tighten each bolt through its specified stage 2 angle, using a socket and extension bar. It is recommended that an angle-measuring gauge is used during this stage of the tightening, to ensure accuracy **(see illustration)**.

31 Working in the specified sequence, go

around again and tighten all bolts through the specified stage 3 angle.

32 Finally go around in the specified sequence again and tighten all bolts through the specified stage 4 angle.

33 Refit the bolts securing the timing belt rear cover to the camshaft housing and tighten them to the specified torque.

34 Refit the camshaft sprocket as described in Section 8 then fit the timing belt as described in Section 7.

35 Reconnect the wiring connectors to the cylinder head components, ensuring all wiring is correctly routed, and secure it in position with the necessary clips.

36 Reconnect the coolant hose to the thermostat housing and securely tighten its retaining clip.

37 Refit/reconnect the manifolds as described in Chapter 4 (as applicable).

38 Refit the roadwheel then lower the vehicle to the floor and tighten the wheel bolts to the specified torque.

39 Ensure all pipes and hoses are securely reconnected then refill the cooling system and refit the spark plugs as described in Chapter 1.

40 Reconnect the battery then start the engine and check for signs of leaks.

13 Sump -
removal and refitting

Removal

1 Disconnect the battery negative terminal.

2 Firmly apply the handbrake then jack up the front of the car and support it on axle stands.

3 Drain the engine oil as described in Chapter 1, then fit a new sealing washer and refit the drain plug, tightening it to the specified torque.

12.30 . . . and then through the various specified angles (see text)

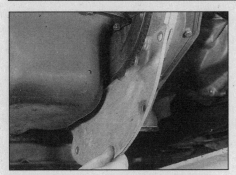

13.6 Removing the flywheel/driveplate lower cover plate - models without air conditioning

13.7 Removing the pressed-steel sump - models without air conditioning

13.10 On models with air conditioning remove the rubber plugs from the sump flange to access the remaining bolts

4 Remove the exhaust system front pipe as described in Chapter 4.

5 Where necessary, disconnect the wiring connector from the oil level sender unit on the sump.

Models not equipped with air conditioning (pressed-steel sump)

6 Slacken and remove the flywheel/driveplate lower cover retaining bolts and remove the cover from the base of the transmission unit **(see illustration)**.

7 Progressively slacken and remove the bolts securing the sump to the base of the cylinder block/oil pump. Break the sump joint by striking the sump with the palm of the hand, then lower the sump away from the engine and withdraw it **(see illustration)**. Remove the gasket and discard it.

8 While the sump is removed, take the opportunity to check the oil pump pick-up/strainer for signs of clogging or splitting. If necessary, unbolt the pick-up/strainer and remove it from the base of the oil pump housing along with its sealing ring. The strainer can then be cleaned easily in solvent or renewed.

Models with air conditioning (alloy sump)

9 Slacken and remove the bolts securing the sump flange to the transmission housing.

10 Remove the sump and (where necessary) the oil pump pick-up/strainer as described in paragraphs 7 and 8. Note that the bolts securing the transmission end of the sump to the cylinder block are accessed through the

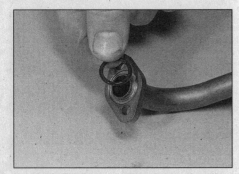

13.12 Fit a new sealing ring to the oil pump pick-up/strainer

cut-outs in the sump flange, once the rubber plugs have been removed **(see illustration)**.

Refitting

Models with pressed-steel sump

11 Remove all traces of dirt and oil from the mating surfaces of the sump and cylinder block and (where removed) the pick-up/strainer and oil pump housing. Also remove all traces of locking compound from the pick-up bolts (where removed).

12 Where necessary, position a new sealing ring on top of the oil pump pick-up/strainer and fit the strainer **(see illustration)**. Apply locking compound to the threads of the retaining bolts then fit the bolts and tighten to the specified torque.

13 Apply a smear of suitable sealant to the areas of the cylinder block mating surface around the areas of the of the oil housing and rear main bearing cap joints **(see illustration)**.

14 Fit a new gasket to the sump then offer up the sump to the cylinder block and refit the retaining bolts. Working out from the centre in a diagonal sequence, progressively tighten the sump retaining bolts to their specified torque setting.

15 Refit the cover plate to the transmission housing, tightening its retaining bolts to the specified torque.

16 Refit the exhaust front pipe (see Chapter 4) and reconnect the oil level sender wiring connector (where fitted).

17 Lower the vehicle to the ground then fill the engine with fresh oil, with reference to Chapter 1.

Models with alloy sump

18 Where necessary, refit the oil pump pick-up/strainer as described in paragraphs 11 and 12.

19 Ensure the sump and cylinder block mating surfaces are clean and dry and remove all traces of locking compound from the sump bolts.

20 Apply a smear of suitable sealant to the areas of the cylinder block mating surface around the areas of the oil housing and rear main bearing cap joints.

21 Fit a new gasket to the sump and apply a few drops of locking compound to the threads of the sump to cylinder block/oil pump bolts.

22 Offer up the sump, ensuring the gasket remains correctly positioned, and loosely refit all the retaining bolts. Working out from the

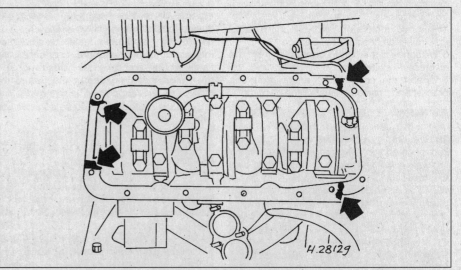

13.13 Apply sealant to the oil pump and rear main bearing cap joints (arrowed) before the sump is refitted

14.8 Undo the retaining screws and remove the oil pump cover

14.10 Removal of pump outer gear - outer face identification punch mark arrowed

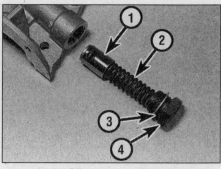

14.11 Oil pressure relief valve components

1 Plunger
2 Spring
3 Sealing washer
4 Valve bolt

centre in a diagonal sequence, progressively tighten the bolts securing the sump to the cylinder block/oil pump to their specified torque setting.

23 Tighten the bolts securing the sump flange to the transmission housing to their specified torque settings. Refit the rubber plugs to the sump flange cut-outs.

24 Refit the exhaust front pipe (see Chapter 4) and reconnect the oil level sender wiring connector (where fitted).

25 Lower the vehicle to the ground then fill the engine with fresh oil, with reference to Chapter 1.

14 Oil pump - removal, overhaul and refitting

Removal

Note: *The pressure relief valve can be removed with pump in position on the engine unit.*

1 Remove the timing belt (see Section 7).

2 Remove the camshaft and crankshaft timing belt sprockets and the tensioner as described in Section 8.

3 Unbolt the timing belt rear cover from the camshaft housing and oil pump and remove it from the engine.

4 Remove the sump and oil pump pick-up/strainer as described in Section 13.

5 Disconnect the wiring connector from the oil pressure switch.

6 Unbolt the crankshaft sensor mounting bracket and position it clear of the oil pump.

7 Slacken and remove the retaining bolts then slide the oil pump housing assembly off of the end of the crankshaft, taking great care not to lose the locating dowels. Remove the housing gasket and discard it.

Overhaul

8 Undo the retaining screws and lift off the pump cover from the rear of the housing **(see illustration)**.

9 Note any marks identifying the outer faces of the pump gears. If none can be seen, make your own using a suitable marker pen to ensure that the gears are refitted the correct way around.

10 Lift out the inner and outer gears from the pump housing **(see illustration)**.

11 Unscrew the oil pressure relief valve bolt from the front of the housing and withdraw the spring and plunger from the housing, noting which way around the plunger is fitted **(see illustration)**. Remove the sealing washer from the valve bolt.

12 Clean the components, and carefully examine the gears, pump body and relief valve plunger for any signs of scoring or wear. Renew any component which shows signs of wear or damage; if the gears or pump housing are marked then the complete pump assembly should be renewed.

13 If the components appear serviceable, measure the clearance between the inner gear and outer gear using feeler blades. Also measure the gear endfloat, and check the flatness of the end cover **(see illustrations)**. If the clearances exceed the specified tolerances, the pump must be renewed.

14 If the pump is satisfactory, reassemble the components in the reverse order of removal, noting the following.

a) *Ensure both gears are fitted the correct way around. Note that the outer gear is marked with a punch mark identifying its' "outer" face (i.e. that nearest the pump cover.*

b) *Fit a new sealing washer to the pressure relief valve bolt and tighten the bolt to the specified torque.*

c) *Remove all traces of locking compound from the cover screws. Apply a drop of fresh locking compound to each screw and tighten the screws to the specified torque.*

d) *On completion prime the oil pump by filling it with clean engine oil whilst rotating the inner gear.*

Refitting

15 Prior to refitting, carefully lever out the crankshaft oil seal using a flat-bladed screwdriver. Fit the new oil seal, ensuring its sealing lip is facing inwards, and press it squarely into the housing using a tubular drift which bears only on the hard outer edge of the seal **(see illustration)**. Press the seal into position so that it is flush with the housing and lubricate the oil seal lip with clean engine oil.

16 Ensure the mating surfaces of the oil pump and cylinder block are clean and dry and the locating dowels are in position.

17 Fit a new gasket to the cylinder block.

2A

14.13a Using a feeler blade to check gear clearance

14.13b Using a straight-edge and feeler blade to measure gear endfloat

14.15 Fitting a new crankshaft oil seal to the oil pump housing

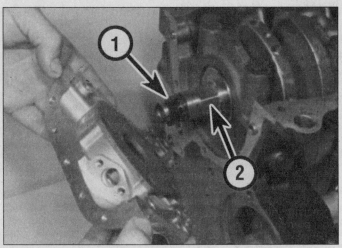

14.18 On refitting take care not to damage the oil seal on the crankshaft lip (1) and engage the inner gear with the crankshaft flats (2)

15.2 Lock the flywheel/driveplate ring gear with a tool similar to that shown

18 Carefully manoeuvre the oil pump into position and engage the inner gear with the crankshaft end (see illustration). Locate the pump on the dowels, taking great care not damage the oil seal lip.

19 Refit the pump housing retaining bolts in their original locations and tighten them to the specified torque.

20 Refit the crankshaft sensor bracket to the pump housing and tighten its mounting bolt to the specified torque. Reconnect the oil pressure sensor wiring connector.

21 Refit the oil pump pick-up/strainer and sump as described in Section 13.

22 Refit the rear timing belt cover to the engine, tightening its retaining bolts to the specified torque.

23 Refit the timing belt sprockets and tensioner then refit the belt as described in Sections 7 and 8.

24 On completion refill the engine with clean oil as described in Chapter 1.

15 Flywheel/driveplate - removal, inspection and refitting

Removal

Manual transmission models

Note: New flywheel retaining bolts will be required on refitting.

1 Remove the transmission as described in Chapter 7 then remove the clutch assembly as described in Chapter 6.

2 Prevent the flywheel from turning by locking the ring gear teeth with a similar arrangement to that shown (see illustration). Alternatively, bolt a strap between the flywheel and the cylinder block/crankcase. Make alignment marks between the flywheel and crankshaft using paint or a suitable marker pen.

3 Slacken and remove the retaining bolts and remove the flywheel. Do not drop it, as it is very heavy.

Automatic transmission models

4 Remove the transmission as described in Chapter 7 then remove the driveplate as described in paragraphs 2 and 3, noting that there is a retaining plate fitted between the retaining bolts and driveplate.

Inspection

5 On manual transmission models, examine the flywheel for scoring of the clutch face. If the clutch face is scored, the flywheel may be surface-ground, but renewal is preferable. Check for wear or chipping of the ring gear teeth. Renewal of the ring gear is also possible is not a task for the home mechanic; renewal requires the new ring gear to be heated (up to 180° to 230°C) to allow it to be fitted.

6 On automatic transmission models closely examine the driveplate and ring gear teeth for signs of wear or damage and check the driveplate surface for any signs of cracks.

7 If there is any doubt about the condition of the flywheel/driveplate, seek the advice of a Vauxhall dealer or engine reconditioning specialist. They will be able to advise if it is possible to recondition it or whether renewal is necessary.

Refitting

Manual transmission models

8 Clean the mating surfaces of the flywheel and crankshaft.

9 Offer up the flywheel and fit the new retaining bolts. If the original is being refitted align the marks made prior to removal.

10 Lock the flywheel by the method used on removal, and tighten the retaining bolts to the specified stage 1 torque setting then angle-tighten the bolts through the specified stage 2 angle, using a socket and extension bar, and finally through the specified stage 3 angle. It is recommended that an angle-measuring gauge is used during the final stages of the tightening, to ensure accuracy (see illustrations). If a gauge is not available, use white paint to make alignment marks between the bolt head and flywheel prior to tightening; the marks can then be used to check that the bolt has been rotated through the correct angle.

11 Refit the clutch as described in Chapter 6 then remove the locking tool, and refit the transmission as described in Chapter 7.

15.10a On manual transmission models, tighten the flywheel bolts to the specified stage 1 torque setting . . .

15.10b . . . then tighten them through the specified stage 2 and 3 angles

Automatic transmission models

12 Clean the mating surfaces of the driveplate and crankshaft and remove all traces of locking compound from the driveplate retaining bolt threads.

13 Apply a drop of locking compound to each of the retaining bolt threads then offer up the driveplate, if the original is being refitted align the marks made prior to removal. Refit the retaining plate and screw in the retaining bolts.

14 Lock the driveplate using the method employed on dismantling then, working in a diagonal sequence, evenly and progressively tighten the retaining bolts to the specified torque.

15 Remove the locking tool and refit the transmission as described in Chapter 7.

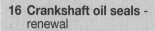

16 Crankshaft oil seals - renewal

Right-hand (timing belt end) oil seal

1 Remove the crankshaft sprocket as described in Section 8.

2 Carefully punch or drill two small holes opposite each other in the oil seal. Screw a self-tapping screw into each and pull on the screws with pliers to extract the seal **(see illustration)**.

Caution: Great care must be taken to avoid damage to the oil pump

3 Clean the seal housing and polish off any burrs or raised edges which may have caused the seal to fail in the first place.

4 Lubricate the lips of the new seal with clean engine oil and ease it into position on the end of the shaft. Press the seal squarely into position until it is flush with the housing. If necessary, a suitable tubular drift, such as a socket, which bears only on the hard outer edge of the seal can be used to tap the seal into position **(see illustration)**. Take great care not to damage the seal lips during fitting and ensure that the seal lips face inwards.

5 Wash off any traces of oil, then refit the crankshaft sprocket as described in Section 8.

16.4 Fitting a new crankshaft front oil seal

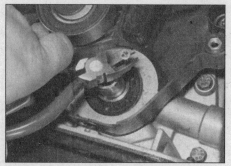

16.2 Removing the crankshaft front oil seal

Left-hand (flywheel/driveplate end) oil seal

6 Remove the flywheel/driveplate as described in Section 15.

7 Renew the seal as described in paragraphs 2 to 4.

8 Refit the flywheel/driveplate as described in Section 15.

17 Engine/transmission mountings - inspection and renewal

Inspection

1 If improved access is required, raise the front of the car and support it securely on axle stands. Where necessary, undo the retaining bolts and remove the undercover from beneath the engine/transmission unit.

2 Check the mounting rubber to see if it is cracked, hardened or separated from the metal at any point; renew the mounting if any such damage or deterioration is evident.

3 Check that all the mounting's fasteners are securely tightened; use a torque wrench to check if possible.

4 Using a large screwdriver or a pry bar, check for wear in the mounting by carefully levering against it to check for free play; where this is not possible, enlist the aid of an assistant to move the engine/transmission unit back and forth, or from side-to-side, while you watch the mounting. While some free play is to be expected even from new components, excessive wear should be obvious. If excessive free play is found, check first that the fasteners are correctly secured, then renew any worn components as described below.

Renewal

Torque support rod

5 Undo the mounting bolts and remove the torque support rod from the right-hand end of the engine. If necessary, unbolt the mounting bracket and remove it from the engine unit.

6 On refitting tightening the mounting bolts to the specified torque.

Front mounting

7 Undo the mounting bolts and remove the torque support rod from the right-hand end of the engine unit.

8 Firmly apply the handbrake then jack up the front of the vehicle and support it on axle stands.

9 Support the weight of the engine/transmission using a trolley jack with a block of wood placed on its head.

10 Slacken and remove the nut and washer securing the mounting to the front subframe and the upper nut securing the mounting to its bracket.

11 Raise the engine/transmission unit slightly and manoeuvre the mounting out of position, noting which way up it is fitted. If necessary, undo the bolts securing the mounting bracket to the cylinder block/transmission (as applicable) then manoeuvre the mounting and bracket out of position. **Note:** *Take great care not to place any excess stress on the exhaust system when raising the engine. If necessary, disconnect the front pipe from the manifold (see Chapter 4).*

12 Check all components for signs of wear or damage, and renew as necessary.

13 On reassembly, refit the mounting bracket (where removed) and tighten its bolts to the specified torque.

14 Locate the mounting in the subframe, ensuring it is fitted the correct way up, and lower the engine/transmission back down into position. Refit the mounting nuts and tighten them to the specified torque.

15 Lower the vehicle to the ground then refit the torque support rod and tighten its mounting bolts to the specified torque.

Rear mounting

16 Undo the mounting bolts and remove the torque support rod from the right-hand end of the engine unit.

17 Firmly apply the handbrake then jack up the front of the vehicle and support it on axle stands.

18 On manual transmission models, referring to Chapter 7A, slacken the gearchange mechanism selector rod clamp bolt and disengage the selector rod from the transmission linkage.

19 On automatic transmission models, referring to Chapter 7B, detach the selector cable from the transmission.

20 Support the weight of the engine/transmission using a trolley jack with a block of wood placed on its head. Position the jack underneath the transmission and raise the transmission slightly to remove all load from the rear mounting.

21 Slacken and remove the bolts securing the rear mounting to the subframe and transmission then manoeuvre the assembly out from underneath the vehicle. If necessary, undo the retaining bolts and separate the mounting and mounting bracket.

22 On refitting, reassemble the mounting and mounting bracket (where necessary) then refit

2A

the mounting bolts and tighten them to the specified torque.

23 Manoeuvre the assembly into position and refit the bolts securing it to the subframe. Clean the threads of the bracket-to-transmission bolts and apply a few drops of locking compound to each one. Refit the bolts and tighten both the bracket and mounting bolts to their specified torque settings. Remove the jack from underneath the engine/transmission.

24 On manual transmission models, reconnect the selector rod and adjust the gearchange mechanism as described in Chapter 7A.

25 On automatic transmission models, reconnect and adjust the selector cable as described in Chapter 7B.

26 Lower the vehicle to the ground then refit the torque support rod and tighten its mounting bolts to the specified torque.

Chapter 2 Part B:
DOHC petrol engine in-car repair procedures

Contents

Degrees of difficulty

Easy, suitable for novice with little experience	Fairly easy, suitable for beginner with some experience	Fairly difficult, suitable for competent DIY mechanic	Difficult, suitable for experienced DIY mechanic	Very difficult, suitable for expert DIY or professional 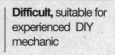

Specifications

General

Engine type . . . . Four-cylinder, in-line, water-cooled. Double overhead camshaft, belt-driven

Manufacturer's engine code:
1.6 litre	X16XEL
1.8 litre	X18XE
1.8 litre	X18XE1
2.0 litre	X20XEV

Bore:
1.6 litre	79.0 mm
1.8 litre:	
X18XE	81.6 mm
X18XE1	80.5 mm
2.0 litre	86.0 mm

Stroke:
1.6 litre	81.5 mm
1.8 litre:	
X18XE	86.0 mm
X18XE1	88.2 mm
2.0 litre	86.0 mm

Capacity:
1.6 litre	1598 cc
1.8 litre:	
X18XE	1799 cc
X18XE1	1796 cc
2.0 litre	1998 cc

Compression ratio:
1.6 litre	10.5:1
1.8 litre:	
X18XE	10.8:1
X18XE1	10.5:1
2.0 litre	10.8:1

2B

General (continued)

Maximum power (kW):
1.6 litre	74 at 6200 rpm
1.8 litre:	
X18XE	85 at 5400 rpm
X18XE1	85 at 5400 rpm
2.0 litre	100 at 5600 rpm

Maximum torque (Nm):
1.6 litre	150 at 3200 rpm
1.8 litre:	
X18XE	170 at 3600 rpm
X18XE1	170 at 3400 rpm
2.0 litre	188 at 3200 rpm
Firing order	1-3-4-2 (No 1 cylinder at timing belt end)
Direction of crankshaft rotation	Clockwise (viewed from timing belt end of engine)

Compression pressures

Standard	12 to 15 bar (174 to 218 psi)
Maximum difference between any two cylinders	1 bar (14.5 psi)

Camshaft

Endfloat	0.04 to 0.15 mm
Maximum permissible radial run-out	0.040 mm

Balancer shaft unit (X20XEV model)

Permissible backlash	0.02 to 0.06 mm
Shim code number:	**Shim thickness**
55	0.535 to 0.565 mm
58	0.565 to 0.595 mm
61	0.595 to 0.625 mm
64	0.625 to 0.655 mm
67	0.655 to 0.685 mm
70	0.685 to 0.715 mm
73	0.715 to 0.745 mm
76	0.745 to 0.775 mm
79	0.775 to 0.805 mm
82	0.805 to 0.835 mm
85	0.835 to 0.865 mm

Lubrication system

Oil pump type - depending on engine code	Rotor-type or crescent/gear-type driven directly from crankshaft
Minimum permissible oil pressure at idle speed, with engine at operating temperature (oil temperature of at least 80°C):	
1.6 litre engines	1.5 bar (22 psi)
1.8 and 2.0 litre engines	2.0 bar (29 psi)
Oil pump clearances crescent/gear-type:	
Inner-to-outer gear teeth clearance	0.10 to 0.20 mm
Gear endfloat:	
1.6 litre engines	0.08 to 0.15 mm
1.8 and 2.0 litre engines	0.03 to 0.10 mm
Oil pump clearances Rotor-type:	
Inner-to-outer rotor clearance	0.150 mm (max.)
Outer rotor-to-pump housing clearance	0.350 mm (max.)
Rotor endfloat	0.080 mm (max.)

Torque wrench settings

	Nm	lbf ft
X16XEL and X18XE1 models		
Baffle plate bolts	8	6
Camshaft bearing cap bolts	8	6
Camshaft cover bolts	8	6
Camshaft sprocket bolt*:		
Stage 1	50	37
Stage 2	Angle-tighten a further 60°	
Stage 3	Angle-tighten a further 15°	
Connecting rod big-end bearing cap bolt*:		
Stage 1	25	18
Stage 2	Angle-tighten a further 30°	

Torque wrench settings (continued)

	Nm	lbf ft

X16XEL and X18XE1 models (continued)

	Nm	lbf ft
Crankshaft pulley bolt*:		
Stage 1	95	70
Stage 2	Angle-tighten a further 30°	
Stage 3	Angle-tighten a further 15°	
Crankshaft sensor mounting bracket bolt	8	6
Cylinder head bolts*:		
Stage 1	25	18
Stage 2	Angle-tighten a further 90°	
Stage 3	Angle-tighten a further 90°	
Stage 4	Angle-tighten a further 90°	
Stage 5	Angle-tighten a further 45°	
Driveplate bolts	60	44
Engine/transmission mounting bolts:		
Front (left- and right-hand) mounting:		
Bracket-to-engine/transmission bolts	60	44
Mounting-to-bracket/subframe nuts	45	33
Rear mounting:		
Mounting-to-bracket bolts	45	33
Mounting-to-subframe bolts	20	15
Bracket-to-transmission bolts	60	44
Torque support rod bolts	60	44
Engine-to-transmission unit bolts:		
M8 bolts	20	15
M10 bolts	40	30
M12 bolts	60	44
Flywheel bolts*:		
Stage 1	35	26
Stage 2	Angle-tighten a further 30°	
Stage 3	Angle-tighten a further 15°	
Main bearing cap bolts*:		
Stage 1	50	37
Stage 2	Angle-tighten a further 45°	
Stage 3	Angle-tighten a further 15°	
Oil level sensor Torx screws	8	6
Oil pump:		
Retaining bolts	6	4
Pump cover screws	6	4
Oil pressure relief valve bolt	30	22
Oil pump pick-up/strainer and baffle bolts	8	6
Roadwheel bolts	110	81
Sump bolts:		
Sump to cylinder block/oil pump bolts	10	7
Sump flange-to-transmission bolts:		
M8 bolts	20	15
M10 bolts	40	30
Drain plug	45	33
Timing belt cover bolts:		
Upper and lower covers	4	3
Rear cover	6	4
Timing belt idler pulley bolt	25	18
Timing belt tensioner bolt	20	15

*Use new fasteners

X18XE and X20XEV models

	Nm	lbf ft
Baffle plate to Balancer shaft unit bolts	8	6
Baffle plate to crankshaft housing bolts	20	15
Balancer unit-to-cylinder block bolts*:		
Stage 1	20	15
Stage 2	Angle-tighten a further 45°	
Camshaft bearing cap bolts	8	6
Camshaft cover bolts	8	6
Camshaft sprocket bolt*:		
Stage 1	50	37
Stage 2	Angle-tighten a further 60°	
Stage 3	Angle-tighten a further 15°	

2B

Torque wrench settings (continued)

	Nm	lbf ft
X18XE and X20XEV models (continued)		
Connecting rod big-end bearing cap bolt*:		
Stage 1	35	26
Stage 2	Angle-tighten a further 45°	
Stage 3	Angle-tighten a further 15°	
Crankshaft pulley bolts	20	15
Crankshaft sprocket bolt*:		
Stage 1	130	96
Stage 2	Angle-tighten a further 40 to 50°	
Cylinder head bolts*:		
Stage 1	25	18
Stage 2	Angle-tighten a further 90°	
Stage 3	Angle-tighten a further 90°	
Stage 4	Angle-tighten a further 90°	
Stage 5	Angle-tighten a further 15°	
Driveplate bolts*	65	48
Engine/transmission mounting bolts:		
Front (left- and right-hand) mounting:		
Bracket-to-engine/transmission bolts	60	44
Mounting-to-bracket/subframe nuts	45	33
Rear mounting:		
Mounting-to-bracket bolts	45	33
Mounting-to-subframe bolts	20	15
Bracket-to-transmission bolts	60	44
Torque support rod and bracket bolts	60	44
Engine-to-transmission unit bolts:		
M8 bolts	20	15
M10 bolts	40	30
M12 bolts	60	44
Flywheel bolts*:		
Stage 1	65	48
Stage 2	Angle-tighten a further 30°	
Stage 3	Angle-tighten a further 15°	
Main bearing cap bolts*:		
Stage 1	50	37
Stage 2	Angle-tighten a further 45°	
Stage 3	Angle-tighten a further 15°	
Main bearing ladder casting bolts	20	15
Oil pump:		
Retaining bolts	6	4
Pump cover screws	6	4
Oil pressure relief valve bolt	30	22
Oil pump pick-up/strainer bolts:		
Pick-up-to-oil pump housing bolts	8	6
Pick-up-to-main bearing cap casting bolt	20	15
Roadwheel bolts	110	81
Sump bolts:		
Lower sump pan bolts*:		
Stage 1	8	6
Stage 2	Angle-tighten a further 30°	
Upper sump casting bolts:		
Upper sump-to-cylinder block/oil pump bolts	20	15
Sump flange-to-transmission bolts:		
M8 bolts	20	15
M10 bolts	40	30
Drain plug	10	7
Timing belt cover bolts	6	4
Timing belt idler pulley:		
Pulley bolt	25	18
Mounting bracket bolts	25	18
Timing belt tensioner bolt	20	15

*Use new fasteners

1 General information

How to use this Chapter

1 This Part of Chapter 2 is devoted to in-car repair procedures for the engine. All procedures concerning engine removal and refitting, and engine block/cylinder head overhaul can be found in Chapter 2E.

2 Most of the operations included in this Part are based on the assumption that the engine is still installed in the car. Therefore, if this information is being used during a complete engine overhaul, with the engine already removed, many of the steps included here will not apply.

Engine description

3 The engine is a double overhead camshaft, four-cylinder, in-line unit, mounted transversely at the front of the car, with the clutch and transmission on its left-hand end.

4 The aluminium alloy cylinder block is of the dry-liner type. The crankshaft is supported within the cylinder block on five shell-type main bearings. Thrustwashers are fitted to number 3 main bearing, to control crankshaft endfloat.

5 The connecting rods are attached to the crankshaft by horizontally-split shell-type big-end bearings, and to the pistons by interference-fit gudgeon pins. The aluminium alloy pistons are of the slipper type, and are fitted with three piston rings, comprising two compression rings and a scraper-type oil control ring.

6 The camshafts run directly in the cylinder head, and driven by the crankshaft via a toothed rubber timing belt (which also drives the coolant pump). The camshafts operate each valve via a follower. Each follower incorporates a hydraulic self-adjusting valve which automatically adjust the valve clearances.

7 Lubrication is by pressure-feed from either a crescent/gear-type or Rotor-type oil pump, which is mounted on the right-hand end of the crankshaft. It draws oil through a strainer located in the sump, and then forces it through an externally mounted full-flow cartridge-type filter. The oil flows into galleries in the main bearing cap bridge arrangement and cylinder block/crankcase, from where it is distributed to the crankshaft (main bearings) and camshafts. The big-end bearings are supplied with oil via internal drillings in the crankshaft, while the camshaft bearings also receive a pressurised supply. The camshaft lobes and valves are lubricated by splash, as are all other engine components.

8 A semi-closed crankcase ventilation system is employed; crankcase fumes are drawn from cylinder head cover, and passed via a hose to the inlet manifold.

Repair operations possible with the engine in the car

9 The following operations can be carried out without having to remove the engine from the vehicle.

a) Removal and refitting of the cylinder head.
b) Removal and refitting of the timing belt and sprockets.
c) Renewal of the camshaft oil seals.
d) Removal and refitting of the camshafts and followers.
e) Removal and refitting of the sump.
f) Removal and refitting of the connecting rods and pistons*.
g) Removal and refitting of the oil pump.
h) Renewal of the crankshaft oil seals.
i) Renewal of the engine mountings.
j) Removal and refitting of the flywheel/driveplate.

* Although the operation marked with an asterisk can be carried out with the engine in the car after removal of the sump, it is better for the engine to be removed, in the interests of cleanliness and improved access. For this reason, the procedure is described in Chapter 2E.

2 Compression test - description and interpretation

Refer to Chapter 2A, Section 2.

3 Top dead centre (TDC) for No 1 piston - locating

1 In its travel up and down its cylinder bore, Top Dead Centre (TDC) is the highest point that each piston reaches as the crankshaft rotates. While each piston reaches TDC both at the top of the compression stroke and again at the top of the exhaust stroke, for the purpose of timing the engine, TDC refers to the piston position (usually number 1) at the top of its compression stroke.

2 Number 1 piston (and cylinder) is at the right-hand (timing belt) end of the engine, and its TDC position is located as follows. Note that the crankshaft rotates clockwise when viewed from the right-hand side of the car.

3 Disconnect the battery negative terminal. If necessary, remove all the spark plugs as described in Chapter 1 to enable the engine to be easily turned over.

X16XEL and X18XE1 models

4 To gain access to the camshaft sprocket timing marks, remove the timing belt upper cover as described in Section 6.

5 Using a socket and extension bar on the crankshaft pulley bolt, rotate the crankshaft until the timing marks on the camshaft sprockets are facing towards each and are both correctly aligned with the cylinder head upper surface. With the camshaft sprocket marks correctly positioned, align the notch on the crankshaft pulley rim with the mark on the timing belt lower cover (see illustration). The engine is now positioned with No 1 piston at TDC.

2B

3.5 Align the camshaft sprocket timing marks so they are facing towards each other, an imaginary line can be drawn through the camshaft bolts and timing marks (as shown)

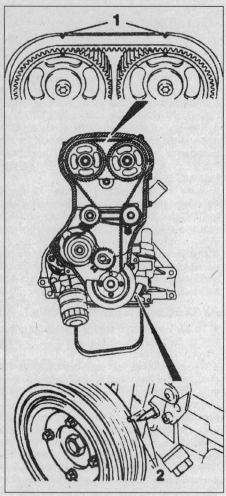

3.7 On 1.8 and 2.0 litre engines align the camshaft sprocket timing marks with the marks (1) on the cylinder head cover, and the crankshaft pulley notch with the pointer (2) to position No 1 cylinder at TDC on its compression stroke

X18XE and X20XEV models

6 To gain access to the camshaft sprocket timing marks, remove the timing belt outer cover as described in Section 6.

7 Using a socket and extension bar on the crankshaft sprocket bolt, rotate the crankshaft

4.1 Undo the two screws and disengage the locating lugs to remove the engine cover

until the timing marks on the camshaft sprockets are both at the top and are correctly aligned with the marks on the camshaft cover. With the camshaft sprocket marks correctly positioned, align the notch on the crankshaft pulley rim with the pointer on the cover (see illustration). The engine is now positioned with No 1 piston at TDC.

4 Camshaft cover - removal and refitting

X16XEL models

Removal

1 Remove the oil filler cap. Undo the retaining screws, disengage the engine cover from the locating lugs at the front of the camshaft cover, and remove the cover from the engine compartment (see illustration).

2 Disconnect the wiring plug, remove the retaining screws, and remove the ignition module. If necessary, refer to Chapter 5B.

3 Release the retaining clips and disconnect the breather hoses from the left-hand end of the camshaft cover (see illustration).

4 Evenly and progressively slacken and remove the camshaft cover retaining bolts.

5 Lift the camshaft cover away from the cylinder head and recover the cover's seals and the sealing rings which are fitted to each of the retaining bolt holes (see illustration). Examine the seals and sealing rings for signs of wear or damage and renew if necessary.

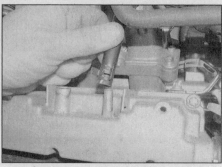

4.3 Disconnect the breather hoses

Refitting

6 Ensure the cover and cylinder head surfaces are clean and dry then fit the camshaft seals securely to the cover grooves. Fit the sealing rings to the recesses around each retaining bolt hole, holding them in position with a smear of grease (see illustrations).

7 Apply a smear of suitable sealant to areas of the cylinder head surface around the right-hand end inlet and exhaust camshaft bearing caps and also to the semi-circular cut-outs on the left-hand end of the head.

8 Carefully manoeuvre the camshaft cover into position, taking great care to ensure all the sealing rings remain correctly seated. Refit the cover retaining bolts and tighten the retaining bolts to the specified torque, working in a spiral pattern from the centre outwards.

9 Reconnect the breather hoses, securing them in position with the retaining clips.

10 Refit the ignition module with reference to Chapter 5B.

11 Refit the engine cover.

X18XE1 models

Removal

12 Remove the engine cover as described in paragraph 1.

13 Slacken the retaining clips and disconnect the breather hoses from the left-hand rear of the cover (see illustration).

14 Disconnect the wiring plug, undo the retaining screws, and remove the ignition module. Refer to Chapter 5B if necessary.

4.5 Lift the camshaft cover away from the engine

4.6a Ensure the seals are correctly seated in the cover recesses . . .

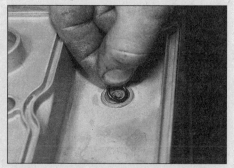

4.6b . . . and fit the sealing rings to the recess around each retaining bolt hole

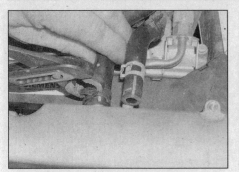

4.13 Disconnect the breather hoses

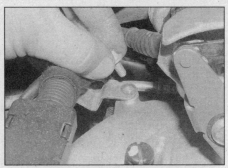

4.16 Remove the bolt supporting the coolant pipe across the camshaft cover

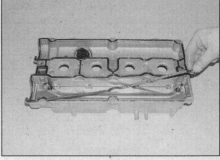

4.19 Carefully fit the camshaft cover seal

15 Disconnect the wiring plug from the coolant temperature sensor.

16 Disconnect the coolant pipe from the thermostat housing. Unbolt the retaining bracket from the camshaft cover and inlet manifold, release the retaining clip and move the pipe to one side (see illustration). Be prepared for coolant spillage.

17 Evenly and progressively slacken and remove the camshaft cover retaining bolts.

18 Lift the camshaft cover away from the cylinder head and recover the rubber seal. Examine the seal for signs of wear or damage and renew if necessary.

Refitting

19 Ensure the cover and cylinder head surfaces are clean and dry then fit the camshaft seal securely to the cover groove (see illustration).

20 Carefully manoeuvre the camshaft cover into position, taking great care to ensure the sealing ring remains correctly seated. Refit the cover retaining bolts and tighten the retaining bolts to the specified torque, working in a spiral pattern from the centre outwards.

21 Reconnect the coolant pipe to the thermostat housing, making sure it is secured by the retaining bracket on the camshaft cover and inlet manifold (see illustration). Top-up the cooling system as described in Chapter 1.

22 Refit the wiring plug to the coolant temperature sensor.

23 Reconnect the breather hoses, securing them in position with the retaining clips.

24 Refit the ignition module with reference to Chapter 5B.

25 Refit the engine cover.

X18XE and X20XEV models

Removal

26 With reference to Chapter 4A, remove the air filter housing.

27 Remove the timing belt upper cover as described in Section 6.

28 Disconnect the engine breather hoses from the right-hand rear and left-hand front of the cover (see illustration).

29 Undo the retaining screws and remove the spark plug cover. Disconnect the plug caps from the plugs then unclip the HT leads and position them clear of the cover.

30 Disconnect the wiring plug from the camshaft position sensor. Unclip the wiring harness from the cover.

31 Evenly and progressively slacken and remove the camshaft cover retaining bolts.

32 Lift the camshaft cover away from the cylinder head and recover the cover's seal and the sealing rings which are fitted to each of the retaining bolts holes. Examine the seal and sealing rings for signs of wear or damage and renew if necessary.

Refitting

33 Ensure the cover and cylinder head surfaces are clean and dry then fit the camshaft seals securely to the cover grooves. Fit the sealing rings to the recesses around each retaining bolt hole, holding them in position with a smear of grease.

34 Apply a smear of suitable sealant to areas of the cylinder head surface around the right-hand end inlet and exhaust camshaft bearing caps and also to the semi-circular cut-outs on the left-hand end of the head.

35 Carefully manoeuvre the camshaft cover into position, taking great care to ensure all the sealing rings remain correctly seated. Refit the cover retaining bolts and tighten the retaining bolts to the specified torque, working in a spiral pattern from the centre outwards.

36 Reconnect the breather hoses, securing them in position with the retaining clips.

37 Refit the plug caps to the spark plugs, and reposition the HT leads.

38 Position the spark plug cover in the centre of the camshaft cover, and tighten the retaining screws securely.

39 Refit the timing belt upper cover as described in Section 6.

40 Refit the air filter housing (see Chapter 4A).

5 Crankshaft pulley - removal and refitting

X16XEL and X18XE1 models

Note: A new pulley retaining bolt will be required on refitting.

Removal

1 Apply the handbrake, then jack up the front of the car and support it on axle stands. Remove the right-hand roadwheel.

2 Remove the auxiliary drivebelt as described in Chapter 1. Prior to removal, mark the direction of rotation on the belt to ensure the belt is refitted the same way around.

3 Slacken the crankshaft pulley retaining bolt. To prevent crankshaft rotation on manual transmission models, have an assistant select top gear and apply the brakes firmly. On automatic transmission models prevent rotation by removing one of the torque converter retaining bolts and bolting the driveplate to the transmission housing using a metal bar, spacers and suitable bolts (see Chapter 7B). If the engine is removed from the vehicle it will be necessary to lock the flywheel/driveplate (see Section 15).

4 Unscrew the retaining bolt and washer and remove the crankshaft pulley from the end of the crankshaft, taking care not to damage the crankshaft sensor.

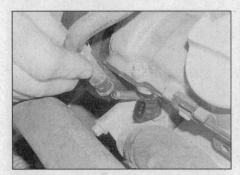

4.21 Reconnect the pipe to the thermostat housing

4.28 Disconnect the breather hoses from the camshaft cover (arrowed)

2B

5.5 Align the pulley cut-out with the raised notch

6.2 Undo the three screws and remove the timing belt upper cover

6.3 Ensure that the camshaft position sensor wiring is correctly routed

Refitting

5 Refit the crankshaft pulley, aligning the pulley cut-out with the raised notch on the timing belt sprocket, then fit the washer and new retaining bolt **(see illustration)**.

6 Lock the crankshaft by the method used on removal, and tighten the pulley retaining bolt to the specified stage 1 torque setting then angle-tighten the bolt through the specified stage 2 angle, using a socket and extension bar, and finally through the specified stage 3 angle. It is recommended that an angle-measuring gauge is used during the final stages of the tightening, to ensure accuracy. If a gauge is not available, use white paint to make alignment marks between the bolt head and pulley prior to tightening; the marks can then be used to check that the bolt has been rotated through the correct angle.

7 Refit the auxiliary drivebelt as described in Chapter 1 using the mark made prior to removal to ensure the belt is fitted the correct way around.

8 Refit the roadwheel then lower the car to the ground and tighten the wheel bolts to the specified torque.

X18XE and X20XEV models

Removal

9 Carry out the operations described in paragraphs 1 and 2.

10 Using a socket and extension bar on the crankshaft sprocket bolt, turn the crankshaft until the notch on the pulley rim is correctly aligned with the pointer on the cover.

11 Slacken and remove the small retaining

bolts securing the pulley to the crankshaft sprocket and remove the pulley from the engine. If necessary, prevent crankshaft rotation by holding the sprocket retaining bolt with a suitable socket.

Refitting

12 Check that the crankshaft sprocket mark is still aligned with the mark on the housing then manoeuvre the crankshaft pulley into position. Align the notch on the pulley rim with the pointer then seat the pulley on the sprocket and tighten its retaining bolts to the specified torque.

13 Carry out the operations described in paragraphs 7 and 8.

6 Timing belt covers - removal and refitting

X16XEL and X18XE1 models

Upper cover

1 Remove the air cleaner housing as described in Chapter 4.

2 Release the camshaft position sensor wiring from the retaining clip on the upper cover. Undo the three retaining screws then unclip the upper cover from the rear cover and remove it from the engine compartment **(see illustration)**.

3 Refitting is the reverse of removal, tighten the retaining bolts to the specified torque. Ensure that the camshaft position sensor wiring is correctly routed **(see illustration)**.

Lower cover

4 Remove the upper cover as described in paragraphs 1 and 2.

5 Hold the tensioner against the spring pressure, and disengage the auxiliary drivebelt from the pulleys (refer to Chapter 1 if necessary). Prior to removal, mark the direction of rotation on the belt to ensure the belt is refitted the same way around.

6 Apply the handbrake, then jack up the front of the car and support it on axle stands. Remove the right-hand roadwheel.

7 Remove the right-hand front lower wheelarch panel, as described in Chapter 11.

8 Undo the retaining bolt and remove the auxiliary drivebelt tensioner **(see illustration)**.

9 Remove the crankshaft pulley as described in Section 5.

10 Undo the retaining bolt then unclip the cover from the rear cover and manoeuvre it out of position **(see illustrations)**.

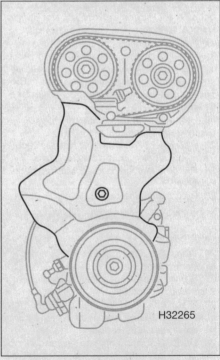

H32265

6.8 Remove the auxiliary drivebelt tensioner

6.10a Timing belt lower cover upper retaining bolt (arrowed) . . .

6.10b . . . and lower retaining bolt (arrowed)

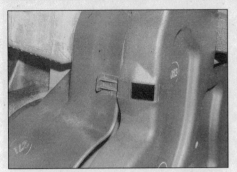

6.11 Clip the cover back into position

6.15 Engine mounting-to-cylinder block bracket retaining bolts

6.16 Lift the rear cover away from the engine

11 Refitting is the reverse of removal, clip the cover into position and tighten the cover bolts to the specified torque **(see illustration)**.

Rear cover

12 Remove the timing belt as described in Section 7.

13 Remove the camshaft cover as described in Section 4.

14 Remove the camshaft sprockets, crankshaft sprocket, timing belt tensioner, front idler pulley and the rear idler pulley as described in Section 8.

15 Slacken and remove the three retaining bolts, and withdraw the engine mounting bracket bolted to the cylinder block **(see illustration)**.

16 Undo the four retaining bolts and remove the rear cover upwards and away from the engine **(see illustration)**.

17 Refitting is the reverse of removal. Refit and tighten the cover bolts to the specified torque.

X18XE and X20XEV models

Upper cover

18 Remove the air cleaner housing as described in Chapter 4A.

19 Slacken and remove the upper cover retaining bolts **(see illustration)**.

20 Lift away the upper cover.

21 Refitting is a reversal of removal **(see illustration)**. Tighten the cover retaining bolts to the specified torque.

Lower cover

22 Remove the upper cover as described in paragraphs 18 to 20.

23 Hold the tensioner against the spring pressure, and disengage the auxiliary drivebelt from the pulleys (refer to Chapter 1 if necessary). Prior to removal, mark the direction of rotation on the belt to ensure the belt is refitted the same way around.

24 Models with air conditioning: Apply the handbrake, then jack up the front of the car and support it on axle stands. Remove the right-hand roadwheel. Remove the right-hand front lower wheelarch panel, as described in Chapter 11.

25 Undo the retaining bolt(s), and remove the auxiliary drivebelt tensioner from the alternator support bracket.

26 Remove the crankshaft pulley, as described in Section 5.

27 Slacken and remove the two retaining bolts, release the retaining clips and remove the cover from the engine unit along with its seal **(see illustration)**.

28 Refitting is the reverse of removal, ensure the cover seal is correctly fitted. Tighten all bolts to the specified torque.

Rear cover

29 Remove the timing belt as described in Section 7.

30 With reference to Section 4, remove the camshaft cover.

31 Remove the camshaft sprockets, crankshaft sprocket, the timing belt tensioner and the idler pulleys as described in Section 8.

32 Unbolt the camshaft sensor from the cylinder head.

33 Unscrew the retaining bolts and remove the engine mounting bracket from the cylinder block.

34 Undo the four retaining bolts and remove the rear cover from the engine unit.

35 Refitting is the reverse of removal, tightening all bolts to the specified torque.

7 Timing belt - removal and refitting

Note: *The timing belt must be removed and refitted with the engine cold.*

Removal

1 Position No 1 cylinder at TDC on its compression stroke as described in Section 3.

2 Remove the crankshaft pulley as described in Section 5.

3 On X16XEL and X18XE1 models, unbolt the timing belt lower cover and remove it from the engine (see Section 6).

4 On X16XEL and X18XE1 models, check the camshaft sprocket timing marks are correctly aligned with the cylinder head surface and the crankshaft sprocket timing mark is aligned

2B

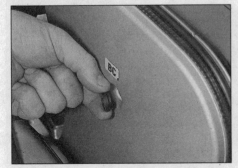

6.19 Undo the timing belt cover retaining bolt(s) and recover the rubber spacers

6.21 On refitting ensure the seal is correctly fitted to the outer cover

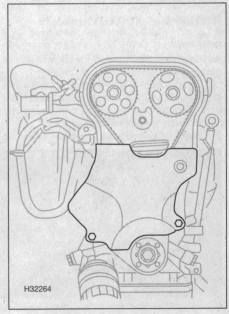

H32264

6.27 Lower cover retaining bolts

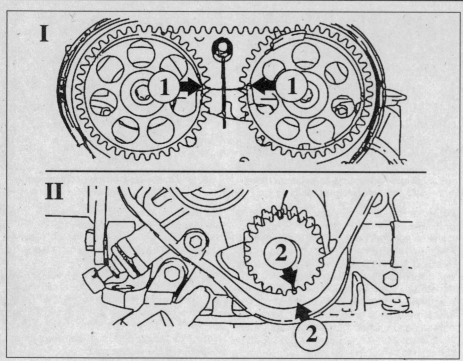

7.4b Unbolt the camshaft sensor and position it clear of the timing belt

7.4a Camshaft and crankshaft sprocket timing marks - X16XEL, Z16XE, X18XE1 and Z18XE engines

I *Camshaft sprocket timing marks aligned with the cylinder head upper surface*

II *Crankshaft sprocket timing mark aligned with mark on oil pump housing*

with the mark on the cover. Undo the two bolts securing the camshaft sensor to the cylinder head and position it clear of the engine **(see illustrations)**.

5 On X18XE and X20XEV models, check the camshaft sprocket timing marks are correctly aligned with the camshaft cover marks and the crankshaft sprocket timing mark is aligned with the pointer on the cover **(see illustration)**.

6 On all models, slacken the timing belt tensioner bolt. Using an Allen key, rotate the tensioner arm clockwise to its stop, to relieve

the tension in the timing belt, hold it in position and securely tighten the retaining bolt **(see illustration)**.

7 Slide the timing belt from its sprockets and remove it from the engine **(see illustration)**. If the belt is to be re-used, use white paint or similar to mark the direction of rotation on the belt. **Do not** rotate the crankshaft or camshafts until the timing belt has been refitted.

8 Check the timing belt carefully for any signs of uneven wear, splitting or oil contamination, and renew it if there is the slightest doubt about its

condition. If the engine is undergoing an overhaul and is approaching the manufacturer's specified interval for belt renewal (see Chapter 1) renew the belt as a matter of course, regardless of its apparent condition. If signs of oil contamination are found, trace the source of the oil leak and rectify it, then wash down the engine timing belt area and all related components to remove all traces of oil.

Refitting

9 On reassembly, thoroughly clean the timing belt sprockets and tensioner/idler pulleys.
10 Check that the camshaft sprocket timing marks are still correctly aligned with the cylinder head surface (X16XEL and X18XE1 models) or the camshaft cover marks (X18XE and X20XEV models) and the crankshaft sprocket mark is still aligned with the mark on the cover **(see illustration)**.
11 Fit the timing belt over the crankshaft and camshaft sprockets and around the idler pulleys, ensuring that the belt front run is taut (ie, all slack is on the tensioner side of the belt), then fit the belt over the coolant pump sprocket and tensioner pulley. Do not twist the belt sharply while refitting it. Ensure that the belt teeth are correctly seated centrally in the sprockets, and that the timing marks remain in alignment. If a used belt is being refitted, ensure that the arrow mark made on

7.5 On X18XE and X20XEV engines ensure the camshaft sprocket marks are correctly aligned with the marks on the camshaft cover (arrowed)

7.6 Slacken the timing belt tensioner bolt (1) and rotate the tensioner clockwise using an Allen key in the arm cut-out (2)

7.7 Removing the timing belt

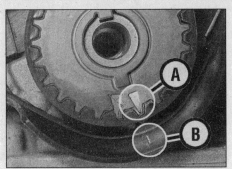

7.10 Crankshaft sprocket (A) and belt cover (B) timing marks - X16XEL, Z16XE, X18XE1 and Z18XE engines

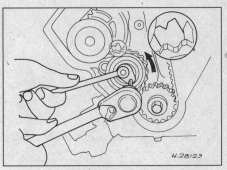

7.12 Tension the belt by rotating the tensioner arm fully anti-clockwise until the pointer is positioned as shown

removal points in the normal direction of rotation, as before.

12 Slacken the timing belt tensioner bolt to release the tensioner spring. Rotate the tensioner arm anti-clockwise until the tensioner pointer is fully over against its stop, without exerting any excess strain on the belt. Hold the tensioner in position and securely tighten its retaining bolt **(see illustration)**.

13 Check the sprocket timing marks are still correctly aligned. If adjustment is necessary, release the tensioner again then disengage the belt from the sprockets and make any necessary adjustments.

14 Using a socket on the crankshaft pulley/sprocket bolt (as applicable), rotate the crankshaft smoothly through two complete turns (720°) in the normal direction of rotation to settle the timing belt in position.

15 Check that both the camshaft and crankshaft sprocket timing marks are correctly realigned then slacken the tensioner bolt again.

16 If a new timing belt is being fitted, adjust the tensioner so that the pointer is aligned with the cut-out on the backplate **(see illustration)**. Hold the tensioner in the correct

position and tighten its retaining bolt to the specified torque. Rotate the crankshaft smoothly through another two complete turns in the normal direction of rotation, to bring the sprocket timing marks back into alignment. Check that the tensioner pointer is still aligned with the backplate cut-out.

17 If the original belt is being refitted, adjust the tensioner so that the pointer is positioned 4 mm to the left of the cut-out on the backplate **(see illustration)**. Hold the tensioner in the correct position and tighten its retaining bolt to the specified torque.

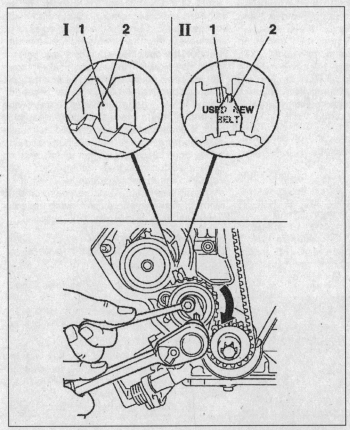

7.16 Timing belt tensioner pointer positions

I X16XEL, Z16XE, X18XE and X20XEV engines: Pointer (1) and backplate (2) for **new** belts

II X18XE1 and Z18XE engines: Pointer (1) and backplate (2) for **new** belts

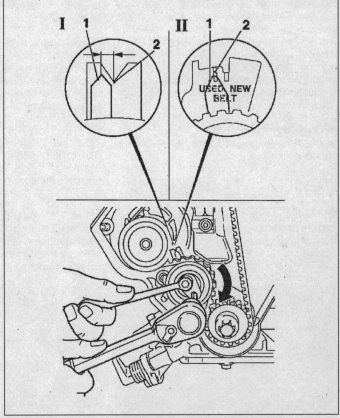

7.17 Timing belt tensioner pointer positions

I X16XEL, Z16XE, X18XE and X20XEV engines: Pointer (1) and backplate (2) for **used** belts

II X18XE1 and Z18XE engines: Pointer (1) and backplate (2) for **used** belts

2B

8.2 Using an open-ended spanner to retain the camshaft whilst the sprocket retaining bolt is slackened

8.7 On X16XEL, Z16XE, X18XE1 and Z18XE engines ensure the camshaft sprocket cut-out (arrowed) is correctly engaged with the locating pin

8.8 On X18XE and X20XEV engines ensure the locating pin is engaged in the correct sprocket hole on refitting (see text)

Rotate the crankshaft smoothly through another two complete turns in the normal direction of rotation, to bring the sprocket timing marks back into alignment. Check that the tensioner pointer is still correctly positioned in relation to the backplate cut-out.
18 If the tensioner pointer is not correctly positioned in relation to the backplate, repeat the procedure in paragraph 16 (new belt) or 17 (original belt) (as applicable).
19 Once the tensioner pointer and backplate remain correctly aligned, refit the timing belt covers and crankshaft pulley as described in Sections 5 and 6. On X16XEL and X18XE1 models, it will be necessary to refit the camshaft sensor to the cylinder head prior to refitting the upper cover.

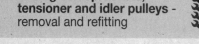

8 Timing belt sprockets, tensioner and idler pulleys - removal and refitting

Camshaft sprockets

Note: *New sprocket retaining bolt(s) will be required on refitting.*

Removal

1 Remove the timing belt as described in Section 7.
2 The camshaft must be prevented from turning as the sprocket bolt is unscrewed, and this can be achieved in one of two ways as follows.
 a) Make up a sprocket-holding tool using two

lengths of steel strip (one long, the other short), and three nuts and bolts; one nut and bolt forms the pivot of a forked tool, with the remaining two nuts and bolts at the tips of the 'forks' to engage with the sprocket spokes *(see illustration 8.2 in Chapter 2A).*
 b) Remove the camshaft cover as described in Section 4 and hold the camshaft with an open-ended spanner on the flats provided (see illustration).
3 Unscrew the retaining bolt and washer and remove the sprocket from the end of the camshaft. If the sprocket locating pin is a loose fit in the camshaft end, remove it and store it with the sprocket for safe-keeping.
4 If necessary, remove the remaining sprocket using the same method. On X16XEL and X18XE1 models the inlet and exhaust sprockets are different; the exhaust camshaft sprocket can be easily identified by the lugs which activate the camshaft position sensor.

Refitting

5 Prior to refitting check the oil seal(s) for signs of damage or leakage. If necessary, renew as described in Section 9.
6 Ensure the locating pin is in position in the camshaft end.
7 On X16XEL and X18XE1 models, refit the sprocket to the camshaft end, aligning its cut-out with the locating pin, and fit the washer and new retaining bolt **(see illustration)**. If both sprockets have been removed, ensure each sprocket is fitted to the correct shaft; the exhaust camshaft sprocket can be identified

by the lugs on the sprocket outer face which trigger the camshaft position sensor.
8 On X18XE and X20XEV litre models both inlet and exhaust camshaft sprockets are the same but each one is equipped with two locating pin cut-outs. If the sprocket is being fitted to the inlet camshaft engage the locating pin in the IN cut-out, and if the sprocket is being fitted to the exhaust camshaft engage the locating pin in the EX cut-out **(see illustration)**. Ensure the camshaft locating pin is engaged in the correct sprocket cut-out then fit the washer and new retaining bolt.
9 On all models, retain the sprocket by the method used on removal, and tighten the pulley retaining bolt to the specified stage 1 torque setting then angle-tighten the bolt through the specified stage 2 angle, using a socket and extension bar, and finally through the specified stage 3 angle **(see illustration)**. It is recommended that an angle-measuring gauge is used during the final stages of the tightening, to ensure accuracy. If a gauge is not available, use white paint to make alignment marks between the bolt head and pulley prior to tightening; the marks can then be used to check that the bolt has been rotated through the correct angle.
10 Refit the timing belt as described in Section 7 then (where necessary) refit the camshaft cover as described in Section 4.

Crankshaft sprocket - X16XEL and X18XE1 models

Removal

11 Remove the timing belt as described in Section 7.
12 Slide the sprocket off from the end of the crankshaft, noting which way around it is fitted.

Refitting

13 Align the sprocket locating key with the crankshaft groove then slide the sprocket into position, making sure its timing mark is facing outwards **(see illustration)**.
14 Refit the timing belt as described in Section 7.

Crankshaft sprocket - X18XE and X20XEV models

Note: *A new crankshaft sprocket retaining bolt will be required on refitting.*

8.9 Using a spanner to prevent camshaft rotation

8.13 Refit the crankshaft sprocket with the timing mark facing outwards

8.23a Engage the tensioner backplate lug with the locating hole in the oil pump housing . . .

8.23b . . . and rotate the tensioner arm clockwise until the roller is as far away from the belt run as possible

8.26 Idler pulley retaining bolt

Removal

15 Remove the timing belt as described in Section 7.

16 Slacken the crankshaft sprocket retaining bolt. To prevent crankshaft rotation on manual transmission models, have an assistant select top gear and apply the brakes firmly. On automatic transmission models prevent rotation by removing one of the torque converter retaining bolts and bolting the driveplate to the transmission housing using a metal bar, spacers and suitable bolts (see Chapter 7B). If the engine is removed from the vehicle it will be necessary to lock the flywheel/driveplate (see Section 15).

17 Unscrew the retaining bolt and washer and remove the crankshaft sprocket from the end of the crankshaft.

Refitting

18 Align the sprocket location key with the crankshaft groove and slide the sprocket into position, ensuring its timing mark is facing outwards. Fit the washer and new retaining bolt.

19 Lock the crankshaft by the method used on removal, and tighten the sprocket retaining bolt to the specified stage 1 torque setting then angle-tighten the bolt through the specified stage 2 angle, using a socket and extension bar. It is recommended that an angle-measuring gauge is used during the final stages of the tightening, to ensure accuracy. If a gauge is not available, use white paint to make alignment marks between the bolt head and sprocket prior to tightening; the

marks can then be used to check that the bolt has been rotated through the correct angle.

20 Refit the timing belt as described in Section 7.

Tensioner assembly

Removal

21 Remove the timing belt as described in Section 7.

22 Slacken and remove the retaining bolt and remove the tensioner assembly from the engine.

Refitting

23 Fit the tensioner to the engine, making sure that the lug on the backplate is correctly located in the oil pump housing hole (see illustrations). Ensure the tensioner is correctly seated then refit the retaining bolt. Using an Allen key, rotate the tensioner arm clockwise to its stop then securely tighten the retaining bolt.

24 Refit the timing belt as described in Section 7.

Idler pulleys

Removal

25 Remove the timing belt as described in Section 7.

26 Slacken and remove the retaining bolt(s) and remove the idler pulley(s) from the engine (see illustration). On X18XE and X20XEV models, if necessary, unbolt the pulley mounting bracket and remove it from the cylinder block.

Refitting

27 On X18XE and X20XEV models refit the pulley mounting bracket (where removed) to the cylinder block and tighten its retaining bolts to the specified torque.

28 On all models, refit the idler pulley(s) and tighten the retaining bolt(s) to the specified torque.

29 Refit the timing belt as described in Section 7.

9 Camshaft oil seals - renewal

1 Remove the relevant camshaft sprocket as described in Section 8.

2 Carefully punch or drill two small holes opposite each other in the oil seal. Screw a self-tapping screw into each, and pull on the screws with pliers to extract the seal (see illustration).

3 Clean the seal housing, and polish off any burrs or raised edges which may have caused the seal to fail in the first place.

4 Lubricate the lips of the new seal with clean engine oil, and press it into position using a suitable tubular drift (such as a socket) which bears only on the hard outer edge of the seal (see illustration). Take care not to damage the seal lips during fitting; note that the seal lips should face inwards.

5 Refit the camshaft sprocket as described in Section 8.

10 Camshaft and followers - removal, inspection and refitting

Removal

1 Prior to releasing the timing belt tension and removing the belt, rotate the crankshaft **backwards** by approximately 60° (4 teeth of movement); this will position the camshafts so that the valve spring pressure is evenly exerted along the complete length of the shaft, reducing the risk of the bearing caps being damaged on removal/refitting (see

9.2 Camshaft oil seal removal method

9.4 Using the old camshaft bolt and a suitable socket to fit the new camshaft oil seal

2B

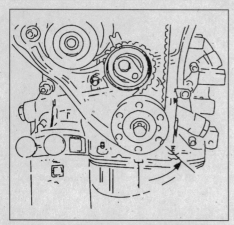

10.1 Prior to removing the timing belt, rotate the crankshaft 60° backwards to ensure the camshafts are correctly positioned (X18XE and X20XEV engine shown)

illustration). Remove the timing belt as described in Section 7.

2 Remove the camshaft sprockets as described in Section 8.

3 Starting on the inlet camshaft, working in a spiral pattern from the outside inwards, slacken the camshaft bearing cap retaining bolts by one turn at a time, to relieve the pressure of the valve springs on the bearing caps gradually and evenly (the reverse of illustration 10.15). Once the valve spring pressure has been relieved, the bolts can be fully unscrewed and removed along with the caps; the bearing caps and the cylinder head locations are numbered (inlet camshaft 1 to 5, exhaust camshaft 6 to 10) to ensure the caps are correctly positioned on refitting **(see illustrations)**. Take care not to loose the locating dowels (where fitted).

Caution: If the bearing cap bolts are carelessly slackened, the bearing caps might break. If any bearing cap breaks then the complete cylinder head assembly must be renewed; the bearing caps are matched to the head and are not available separately.

4 Lift the camshaft out of the cylinder head and slide off the oil seal.

5 Repeat the operations described in paragraphs 3 and 4 and remove the exhaust camshaft.

6 Obtain sixteen small, clean plastic containers, and label them for identification. Alternatively, divide a larger container into compartments. Lift the followers out from the top of the cylinder head and store each one in its respective fitted position **(see illustration)**. **Note:** *Store all the followers the correct way up to prevent the oil draining from the hydraulic valve adjustment mechanisms.*

Inspection

7 Examine the camshaft bearing surfaces and cam lobes for signs of wear ridges and scoring. Renew the camshaft if any of these conditions are apparent. Examine the condition of the bearing surfaces both on the camshaft journals and in the cylinder head. If the head bearing surfaces are worn excessively, the cylinder head will need to be renewed.

8 Support the camshaft end journals on V-blocks, and measure the run-out at the centre journal using a dial gauge. If the run-out exceeds the specified limit, the camshaft should be renewed.

9 Examine the follower bearing surfaces which contact the camshaft lobes for wear ridges and scoring. Check the followers and their bores in the cylinder head for signs of wear or damage. If any follower is thought to be faulty or is visibly worn it should be renewed.

Refitting

10 Where removed, lubricate the followers with clean engine oil and carefully insert each one into its original location in the cylinder head.

11 Lubricate the camshaft followers with molybdenum disulphide paste (or clean engine oil) then lay the camshafts in position. Ensure the crankshaft is still positioned approximately 60° BTDC and position each camshaft so that the lobes of No 1 cylinder are pointing upwards. Temporarily refit the sprockets to the camshafts and position each one so that its sprocket timing mark is approximately 4 teeth before its TDC alignment position.

12 Ensure the mating surfaces of the bearing caps and cylinder head are clean and dry and lubricate the camshaft journals and lobes with clean engine oil.

13 Apply a smear of sealant to the mating surfaces of both the inlet (No 1) and exhaust (No 6) camshaft right-hand bearing caps **(see illustration)**.

14 Ensure the locating dowels (where fitted) are in position then refit the camshaft bearing caps and the retaining bolts in their original

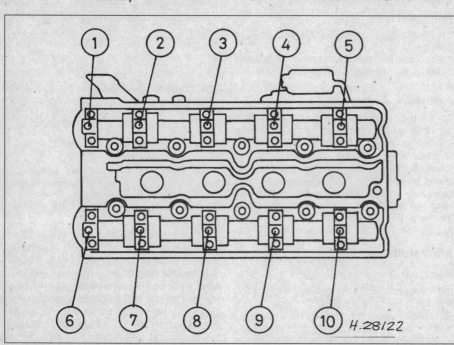

10.3a Camshaft bearing cap numbering sequence

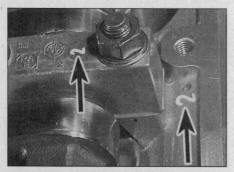

10.3b The identification numbers should be marked on both the bearing caps and the cylinder head (arrowed)

10.6 Using a rubber sucker to remove a camshaft follower

locations on the cylinder head **(see illustration)**. The caps are numbered (inlet camshaft 1 to 5, exhaust camshaft 6 to 10) from right to left, and the corresponding numbers are marked on the cylinder head upper surface. All bearing cap numbers should be the right way up when viewed from the front of the engine.

15 Working on the inlet camshaft, tighten the bearing cap bolts by hand only then, working in a spiral pattern from the centre outwards, tighten the bolts by one turn at a time to gradually impose the pressure of the valve springs on the bearing caps **(see illustration)**. Repeat this sequence until all bearing caps are in contact with the cylinder head then go around and tighten the camshaft bearing cap bolts to the specified torque.

Caution: If the bearing cap bolts are carelessly tightened, the bearing caps might break. If any bearing cap breaks then the complete cylinder head assembly must be renewed; the bearing caps are matched to the head and are not available separately.

16 Tighten the exhaust camshaft bearing cap bolts as described in paragraph 15.

17 Fit new camshaft oil seals as described in Section 9.

18 Refit the camshaft sprockets as described in Section 8.

19 Align all the sprocket timing marks to bring the camshafts and crankshaft back to TDC then refit the timing belt as described in Section 7.

20 Refit the camshaft cover and timing belt cover(s) as described in Sections 4 and 6.

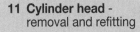

11 Cylinder head - removal and refitting

Removal

Note: *The engine must be cold when removing the cylinder head. New cylinder head bolts must be used on refitting.*

1 Depressurise the fuel system as described in Chapter 4 then disconnect the battery negative lead.

2 Drain the cooling system and remove the spark plugs as described in Chapter 1.

3 Prior to releasing the timing belt tension and removing the belt, rotate the crankshaft **backwards** by approximately 60° (4 teeth of movement); this will position the camshafts so that the valve spring pressure is evenly exerted along the complete length of the shafts, preventing the shafts turning and reducing the risk of the valves contacting the pistons **(see illustration)**. Remove the timing belt as described in Section 7. Proceed as described under the relevant sub-heading.

X16XEL and X18XE1 models

4 Remove the complete inlet manifold as described in Chapter 4. Remove the exhaust

10.13 Apply a smear of sealant to the right-hand bearing caps as shown

10.14 Refit the bearing caps using the identification markings to ensure each one is correctly fitted

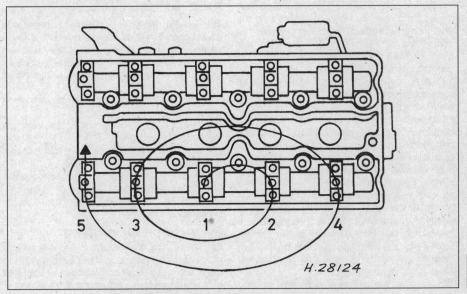

H.28124

10.15 Camshaft bearing cap tightening sequence (exhaust camshaft shown - inlet the same)

manifold as described in Chapter 4. If no work is to be carried out on the cylinder head, the head can be removed complete with the manifold once the following operations have been carried out (see Chapter 4).

a) *Unbolt the exhaust front pipe from manifold.*

b) *Disconnect the oxygen sensor wiring connector.*

c) *Disconnect the air hose and vacuum hose from the air injection valve.*

5 Remove the camshaft cover as described in Section 4.

6 Remove the camshaft sprockets and the timing belt idler pulleys as described in Section 8.

7 Undo the retaining bolts securing the timing belt rear cover to the cylinder head.

8 Referring to Chapter 10, unbolt the power steering pump and position it clear of the cylinder head.

9 Disconnect the wiring connectors from the DIS module and the coolant temperature sender units on the cylinder head. Free the wiring from its retaining clips, noting its correct routing, and position it clear of the cylinder head.

10 Release the retaining clips then disconnect and remove the upper coolant hose linking the cylinder head to the radiator. Release the retaining clip and disconnect the cylinder head coolant hose from the expansion tank.

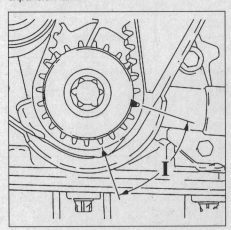

11.3 Prior to removing the timing belt, rotate the crankshaft 60° backwards to ensure the camshafts are correctly positioned

2B

11.29a Ensure the head gasket is fitted with its OBEN/TOP marking uppermost ...

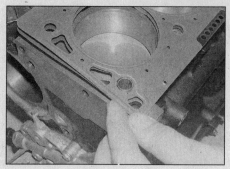

11.29b ... over the locating dowels

11.31 Fit the new head bolts tightening them by hand only

11 Referring to Chapter 3, unclip the coolant hoses from the heater matrix unions on the engine compartment bulkhead to drain the coolant from the cylinder block. Once the flow of coolant has stopped, reconnect both hoses and mop up any spilt coolant.

12 Make a final check to ensure that all relevant hoses, pipes and wires, etc, have been disconnected.

13 Working in the **reverse** of the tightening sequence **(see illustration 11.32a)**, progressively slacken the cylinder head bolts by a third of a turn at a time until all bolts can be unscrewed by hand. Remove each bolt in turn, along with its washer.

14 Lift the cylinder head from the cylinder block. If necessary, tap the cylinder head gently with a soft-faced mallet to free it from the block, but **do not** lever at the mating faces. Note the fitted positions of the two locating dowels, and remove them for safe-keeping if they are loose.

15 Recover the cylinder head gasket, and discard it.

X18XE and X20XEV models

16 Remove the inlet and exhaust manifolds as described in Chapter 4. If no work is to be carried out on the cylinder head, the head can be removed complete with manifolds once all the hoses/wiring etc have been disconnected (see Chapter 4).

17 Remove the camshaft cover as described in Section 4.

18 Remove the camshaft sprockets as described in Section 8.

19 Unbolt the torque support rod bracket from the end of the cylinder head.

20 Undo the retaining bolts securing the timing belt rear cover to the cylinder head.

21 Remove the cylinder head as described in paragraphs 10 to 15.

Preparation for refitting

22 The mating faces of the cylinder head and block must be perfectly clean before refitting the head. Use a scraper to remove all traces of gasket and carbon, and also clean the tops of the pistons. Take particular care with the

aluminium surfaces, as the soft metal is damaged easily. Also, make sure that debris is not allowed to enter the oil and water channels - this is particularly important for the oil circuit, as carbon could block the oil supply to the camshaft or crankshaft bearings. Using adhesive tape and paper, seal the water, oil and bolt holes in the cylinder block. To prevent carbon entering the gap between the pistons and bores, smear a little grease in the gap. After cleaning the piston, rotate the crankshaft so that the piston moves down the bore, then wipe out the grease and carbon with a cloth rag. Clean the other piston crowns in the same way.

23 Check the block and head for nicks, deep scratches and other damage. If slight, they may be removed carefully with a file. More serious damage may be repaired by machining, but this is a specialist job.

24 If warpage of the cylinder head is suspected, use a straight-edge to check it for distortion. Refer to Chapter 2E if necessary.

25 Ensure that the cylinder head bolt holes in the crankcase are clean and free of oil. Syringe or soak up any oil left in the bolt holes. This is most important in order that the correct bolt tightening torque can be applied and to prevent the possibility of the block being cracked by hydraulic pressure when the bolts are tightened.

26 Renew the cylinder head bolts regardless of their apparent condition.

Refitting

27 Ensure the crankshaft is still positioned approximately 60° BTDC and wipe clean the mating faces of the head and block.

28 Ensure that the two locating dowels are in position at each end of the cylinder block/crankcase surface.

29 Fit the new cylinder head gasket to the block, making sure it is fitted with the correct way up with its OBEN/TOP mark uppermost **(see illustrations)**.

30 Carefully refit the cylinder head, locating it on the dowels.

31 Fit the washers to the new cylinder head bolts then carefully insert them into position (**do not drop**), tightening them finger-tight only at this stage **(see illustration)**.

32 Working progressively and in the sequence shown, first tighten all the cylinder head bolts to the stage 1 torque setting **(see illustrations)**.

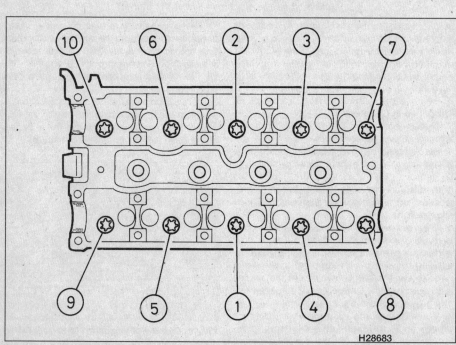

11.32a Cylinder head bolt tightening sequence (all models)

H28683

33 Once all bolts have been tightened to the stage 1 torque, again working in the sequence shown, tighten each bolt through its specified stage 2 angle, using a socket and extension bar. It is recommended that an angle-measuring gauge is used during this stage of the tightening, to ensure accuracy **(see illustration)**.

34 Working in the specified sequence, go around again and tighten all bolts through the specified stage 3 angle.

35 Working again in the specified sequence, go around and tighten all bolts through the specified stage 4 angle.

36 Finally go around in the specified sequence again and tighten all bolts through the specified stage 5 angle.

X16XEL and X18XE1 models

37 Reconnect the coolant hoses, securing them in position with the retaining clips.

38 Reconnect the wiring connectors to the cylinder head, ensuring the harness is correctly routed and retained by all the necessary clips.

39 Refit the power steering pump (see Chapter 10).

40 Refit the timing belt rear cover retaining bolts and tighten them to the specified torque.

41 Refit the camshaft sprockets and idler pulleys as described in Section 8.

42 Align all the sprocket timing marks to bring the camshafts and crankshaft back to TDC then refit the timing belt as described in Section 7.

43 Refit the camshaft cover and timing belt cover(s) as described in Sections 4 and 6.

44 Refit/reconnect the inlet and exhaust manifolds (see Chapter 4).

45 Refit the roadwheel then lower the vehicle to the floor and tighten the wheel bolts to the specified torque.

46 Ensure all pipes and hoses are securely reconnected then refill the cooling system and refit the spark plugs as described in Chapter 1.

47 Reconnect the battery then start the engine and check for signs of leaks.

X18XE and X20XEV models

48 Reconnect the coolant hoses, securing them in position with the retaining clips.

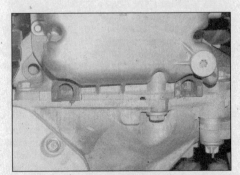

12.7 Remove the rubber plugs from the sump flange to access the remaining sump bolts

11.32b Tighten the cylinder head bolts to the specified stage 1 torque setting . . .

49 Refit the timing belt rear cover retaining bolts and tighten them to the specified torque.

50 Refit the torque support rod bracket to the side of the cylinder head and securely tighten its retaining bolts.

51 Refit the camshaft sprockets as described in Section 8.

52 Carry out the procedures described in paragraphs 42 to 47.

12 Sump -
removal and refitting

X16XEL and X18XE1 models

Removal

1 Disconnect the battery negative terminal.
Note: Before disconnecting the battery, refer to 'Disconnecting the battery' In the reference section at the rear of this manual.

2 Firmly apply the handbrake then jack up the front of the car and support it on axle stands. Where necessary, undo the retaining screws and remove the undercover from beneath the engine/transmission unit.

3 Drain the engine oil as described in Chapter 1, then fit a new sealing washer and refit the drain plug, tightening it to the specified torque.

4 Remove the exhaust system front pipe as described in Chapter 4.

5 Disconnect the wiring connector from the oil level sensor (where fitted).

6 Slacken and remove the bolts securing the sump flange to the transmission housing.

7 Remove the rubber plugs from the transmission end of the sump flange to gain access to the sump end retaining bolts **(see illustration)**.

8 Progressively slacken and remove the bolts securing the sump to the base of the cylinder block/oil pump. Break the sump joint by striking the sump with the palm of the hand, then lower the sump away from the engine and withdraw it. Where applicable, remove the gasket and discard it.

9 While the sump is removed, take the opportunity to check the oil pump pick-up/strainer for signs of clogging or splitting. If necessary, unbolt the pick-up/strainer and

11.33 . . . and then through the various specified angles as described in the text

remove it from the engine along with its sealing ring. The strainer can then be cleaned easily in solvent or renewed.

Refitting

10 Remove all traces of sealer and oil from the mating surfaces of the sump and cylinder block and (where removed) the pick-up/strainer. Also remove all traces of locking compound from the pick-up bolts (where removed).

11 Where necessary, position a new gasket/seal on top of the oil pump pick-up/strainer and fit the strainer **(see illustration)**. Apply locking compound to the threads of the retaining bolts then fit the bolts and tighten to the specified torque.

12 Ensure the sump and cylinder block mating surfaces are clean and dry and remove all traces of locking compound from the sump bolts.

13 Apply a smear of suitable sealant (available form Vauxhall dealers) to the areas of the cylinder block mating surface around the areas of the of the oil pump housing and rear main bearing cap joints **(see illustration)**.

14 On models with gasket: fit a new gasket to the sump and apply a few drops of locking compound to the threads of the sump to cylinder block/oil pump bolts.

15 On models with no gasket: apply a bead of suitable sealant (available from Vauxhall dealers) approximately 2.5 mm thick to the sealing surface of the oil pan. Around the No 5 main bearing cap area, increase the thickness of the bead to 3.5 mm **(see illustration)**.

12.11 Fit new seal/gasket to the oil pump pick-up pipe

2B

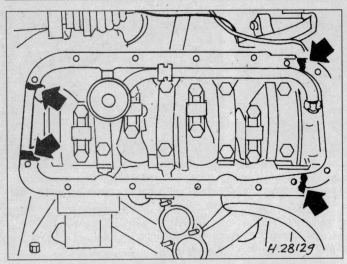

12.13 Apply sealant to the oil pump and rear main bearing cap joints (arrowed) before the sump is refitted

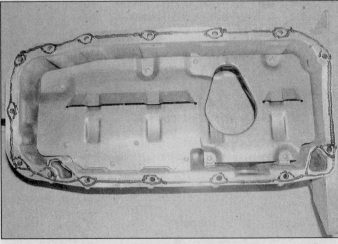

12.15 Apply a 2.5mm thick bead of sealant to the sump sealing surface - increase the thickness to 3.5mm around the No.5 main bearing cap area

16 Offer up the sump, ensuring the gasket sealer remains correctly positioned, and loosely refit all the retaining bolts. Working out from the centre in a diagonal sequence, progressively tighten the bolts securing the sump to the cylinder block/oil pump to their specified torque setting.

17 Tighten the bolts securing the sump flange to the transmission housing to their specified torque settings. Refit the rubber plugs to the sump flange cut-outs.

18 Refit the exhaust front pipe (see Chapter 4) and reconnect the oil level sender wiring connector (where fitted).

19 Lower the vehicle to the ground then fill the engine with fresh oil, with reference to Chapter 1.

X18XE and X20XEV models

Note: *New lower sump retaining bolts will be required on refitting.*

Removal

20 Carry out the operations described in paragraphs 1 to 3.

21 If an oil level sensor is fitted, disconnect the wiring connector from the sensor then slide off the retaining clip and push the sensor connector into the sump.

22 Slacken and remove the bolts securing the lower sump pan to the main casting then free the sump pan from the main casting and remove it along with its gasket (where applicable). On models with an oil level sensor, take care not to damage the sensor wiring as the pan is removed.

23 To remove the main casting from the engine, remove the oil filter (see Chapter 1). If the oil filter is damaged on removal (which is likely), a new one should be used on refitting and the engine should be filled with fresh oil.

24 Remove the exhaust system front pipe as described in Chapter 4.

25 Slacken and remove the bolts securing the sump flange to the transmission housing.

26 Progressively slacken and remove the bolts securing the main casting to the base of the cylinder block/oil pump. Break the joint by striking the casting with the palm of the hand, then lower it away from the engine and withdraw it. Where applicable, remove the gasket and discard it.

Note: *On some models it may be necessary to disconnect the right-hand driveshaft from the transmission in order to remove the main casting.*

27 If necessary, remove oil pump pick-up/strainer as described in paragraph 9.

Refitting

28 Remove all traces of sealer and oil from the mating surfaces of the sump main casting and pan, the cylinder block and (where removed) the pick-up/strainer. Also remove all traces of locking compound from the threads of the sump pan holes.

29 Where necessary, position a new gasket/seal on top of the oil pump pick-up/strainer. Fit the strainer to the engine and tighten its retaining bolts to their specified torque settings.

30 Ensure the main casting and cylinder block mating surfaces are clean and dry and remove all traces of locking compound from the retaining bolts.

31 Apply a smear of suitable sealant to the areas of the cylinder block mating surface around the areas of the of the oil housing and rear main bearing cap joints.

32 Fit a new gasket to the sump and apply a few drops of locking compound to the threads of the sump to cylinder block/oil pump bolts.

33 Offer up the main casting, ensuring the gasket remains correctly positioned, and loosely refit all the retaining bolts. Working out from the centre in a diagonal sequence, progressively tighten the bolts securing it to the cylinder block/oil pump to their specified torque setting.

34 Tighten the bolts securing the main

casting flange to the transmission housing to their specified torque settings.

35 Refit the exhaust front pipe (see Chapter 4) and, where necessary, refit the driveshaft (see Chapter 8).

36 Ensure the sump pan and main casting surfaces are clean and dry, place a new gasket on the top of the pan and offer it up to the main casting. On models with an oil level sensor, fit a new sealing ring to the wiring connector and seat the wiring connector in the main casting, securing it in position with the retaining clip, prior to seating the sump pan on the main casting.

37 Fit the new sump pan retaining bolts then go around in a diagonal sequence and tighten them to the specified stage 1 torque setting. Once all bolts have been tightened go around again and angle-tighten them through the specified stage 2 angle.

38 Fit a new oil filter and reconnect the oil level sender wiring connector (where necessary).

39 Lower the vehicle to the ground then fill the engine with fresh oil, with reference to Chapter 1.

13 Oil level sensor –
   removal and refitting

X16XEL and X18XE1 models

Removal

1 Firmly apply the handbrake then jack up the front of the car and support it on axle stands. Where necessary, undo the retaining screws and remove the undercover from beneath the engine/transmission unit.

2 Drain the engine oil as described in Chapter 1, then fit a new sealing washer and refit the drain plug, tightening it to the specified torque.

13.4 Manoeuvre the oil level sensor from the sump and renew the seal

3 Disconnect the oil level sensor wiring plug.
4 Slacken and remove the four screws, and manoeuvre the sensor out from the sump **(see illustration)**.

Refitting

5 If the original sensor is to be re-used, renew the sealing ring.
6 Refit the sensor to the sump, apply a little locking compound to the retaining screws, and tighten the screws to the specified torque setting.
7 Lower the vehicle to the ground then fill the engine with fresh oil, with reference to Chapter 1.

X18XE and X20XEV models

Removal

8 Firmly apply the handbrake then jack up the front of the car and support it on axle stands. Where necessary, undo the retaining screws and remove the undercover from beneath the engine/transmission unit.
9 Drain the engine oil as described in Chapter 1, then fit a new sealing washer and refit the drain plug, tightening it to the specified torque.
10 Disconnect the wiring connector from the oil level sensor then slide off the retaining clip and push the sensor connector into the sump.
11 Slacken and remove the bolts securing the lower sump pan to the main casting then free the sump pan from the main casting and remove it along with its gasket (see Section 12). Take care not to damage the oil level sensor wiring as the pan is removed.
12 Undo the two Torx screws and remove the sensor from the sump.

Refitting

13 Fit the sensor to the sump and tighten the Torx screws to the specified torque setting.
14 Ensure the sump pan and main casting surfaces are clean and dry, place a new gasket on the top of the pan and offer it up to the main casting. Fit a new sealing ring to the oil level sensor wiring connector and seat the wiring connector in the main casting, securing it in position with the retaining clip, prior to seating the sump pan on the main casting.
15 Fit the new sump pan retaining bolts then go around in a diagonal sequence and tighten them to the specified Stage 1 torque setting.

Once all bolts have been tightened go around again and angle-tighten them through the specified Stage 2 angle.
16 Lower the vehicle to the ground then fill the engine with fresh oil, with reference to Chapter 1.

14 Oil pump - removal, overhaul and refitting

Note: Depending on engine code the oil pump type could either be rotor-type or crescent/gear-type. At the time of writing the X18XE1 engine was shown to have the rotor type pump fitted, and all the other engines have the crescent/gear-type pump fitted.

Removal

Note: *The pressure relief valve can be removed with pump in position on the engine unit, although on some models it will be necessary to unbolt the mounting bracket assembly from the block to allow the valve to be removed.*
1 Remove the timing belt as described in Section 7.
2 Remove the rear timing belt cover as described in Section 6.
3 Remove the sump and oil pump pick-up/strainer as described in Section 12.
4 Disconnect the wiring connector from the oil pressure switch.
5 On models, with the crankshaft sensor on

14.7 Undo the retaining screws and remove the oil pump cover

14.9 Removal of the pump outer gear - outer face identification punch mark arrowed (crescent/gear-type pump shown)

the front pulley/vibration damper, unbolt the crankshaft sensor mounting bracket and position it clear of the oil pump.
6 Slacken and remove the retaining bolts then slide the oil pump housing assembly off of the end of the crankshaft, taking great care not to lose the locating dowels. Remove the housing gasket and discard it.

Overhaul

7 Undo the retaining screws and lift off the pump cover from the rear of the housing **(see illustration)**.
8 Using a suitable marker pen, mark the surface of both the pump inner and outer gears/rotors; the marks can then be used to ensure the gears/rotors are refitted the correct way around **(see illustration)**.
9 Lift out the inner and outer gears/rotors from the pump housing **(see illustration)**.
10 Unscrew the oil pressure relief valve bolt from the front of the housing and withdraw the spring and plunger from the housing, noting which way around the plunger is fitted. Remove the sealing washer from the valve bolt **(see illustration)**.
11 Clean the components, and carefully examine the gears/rotors, pump body and relief valve plunger for any signs of scoring or wear. Renew any component which shows signs of wear or damage; if the gears/rotors or pump housing are marked then the complete pump assembly should be renewed.
12 If the components appear serviceable, measure the clearance between the inner and

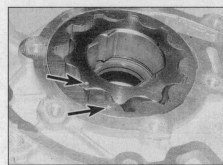

14.8 Oil pump rotors identifying marks (rotor-type pump shown)

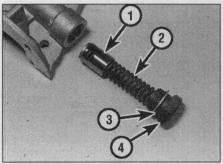

14.10 Oil pressure relief valve components

1 Plunger   *3 Sealing washer*
2 Spring   *4 Valve bolt*

14.12a Using a feeler blade to check gear clearance (crescent/gear-type pump shown)

14.12b Using a straight-edge and feeler blade to measure gear endfloat (crescent/gear-type pump shown)

outer gears/rotors using feeler blades. Also measure the gear/rotor endfloat, and check the flatness of the end cover **(see illustrations)**. If the clearances exceed the specified tolerances (in the specifications at the front of this Chapter), the pump must be renewed.

13 If the pump is satisfactory, reassemble the components in the reverse order of removal, noting the following.
  a) *Ensure both gears/rotors are fitted the correct way around.*
  b) *Fit a new sealing ring to the pressure relief valve bolt and tighten the bolt to the specified torque.*
  c) *Apply a small amount of locking compound to the threads, and tighten the pump cover screws to the specified torque (see illustration).*
  d) *On completion prime the oil pump by filling it with clean engine oil whilst rotating the inner gear.*

Refitting

14 Prior to refitting, carefully lever out the crankshaft oil seal using a flat-bladed screwdriver. Fit the new oil seal, ensuring its sealing lip is facing inwards, and press it squarely into the housing using a tubular drift which bears only on the hard outer edge of

the seal **(see illustration)**. Press the seal into position so that it is flush with the housing and lubricate the oil seal lip with clean engine oil.
15 Ensure the mating surfaces of the oil pump and cylinder block are clean and dry and the locating dowels are in position.
16 Fit a new gasket to the cylinder block.
17 Carefully manoeuvre the oil pump into position and engage the inner gear with the crankshaft end **(see illustration)**. Locate the pump on the dowels, taking great care not damage the oil seal lip.
18 Refit the pump housing retaining bolts in their original locations and tighten them to the specified torque.
19 On models with the crankshaft sensor on the front pulley/vibration damper, refit the crankshaft sensor bracket to the pump housing and tighten its mounting bolt to the specified torque.
20 Reconnect the oil pressure sensor wiring connector.
21 Refit the oil pump pick-up/strainer and sump as described in Section 12.
22 Refit the rear timing belt cover to the engine, tightening its retaining bolts to the specified torque.
23 Refit the timing belt sprockets, idler pulleys and tensioner then refit the belt as described in Sections 7 and 8.

24 On completion, fit a new oil filter and fill the engine with clean oil as described in Chapter 1.

15 Flywheel/driveplate - removal, inspection and refitting

Refer to Chapter 2A, Section 15.

16 Crankshaft oil seals - renewal

Right-hand (timing belt end) oil seal

1 Remove the crankshaft sprocket as described in Section 8.
2 Carefully punch or drill two small holes opposite each other in the oil seal. Screw a self-tapping screw into each and pull on the screws with pliers to extract the seal **(see illustration)**.

14.17 On refitting take care not to damage the oil seal on the crankshaft lip (1) and engage the inner gear with the crankshaft flats (2)

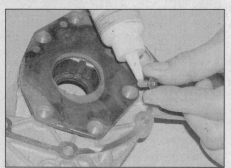

14.13 Apply thread locking compound to the oil pump cover screws

14.14 Fitting a new crankshaft oil seal to the oil pump housing

16.2 Removing the crankshaft front oil seal

16.4 Fitting a new crankshaft front oil seal

16.7 Left-hand crankshaft oil seal - transmission and flywheel removed

Caution: Great care must be taken to avoid damage to the oil pump

3 Clean the seal housing and polish off any burrs or raised edges which may have caused the seal to fail in the first place.

4 Lubricate the lips of the new seal with clean engine oil and ease it into position on the end of the shaft. Press the seal squarely into position until it is flush with the housing. If necessary, a suitable tubular drift, such as a socket, which bears only on the hard outer edge of the seal can be used to tap the seal into position **(see illustration)**. Take great care not to damage the seal lips during fitting and ensure that the seal lips face inwards.

5 Wash off any traces of oil, then refit the crankshaft sprocket as described in Section 8.

Left-hand (flywheel/driveplate end) oil seal

6 Remove the flywheel/driveplate as described in Section 15.

7 Renew the seal as described in paragraphs 2 to 4 **(see illustration)**.

8 Refit the flywheel/driveplate as described in Section 15.

17 Engine/transmission mountings - inspection and renewal

Refer to Chapter 2A, Section 17.

18 Balancer unit (X20XEV engine) - removal and refitting

Removal

1 Some models fitted with the 2.0 litre (X20XEV) DOHC engine are equipped with a balancer unit fitted between the cylinder block and the main sump casting. The unit consists of two counter-rotating balance shafts driven by the crankshaft **(see illustration)**.

2 Remove the sump main casting as described in Section 12.

3 Slacken the retaining bolts, and remove the balancer unit and shim.

Refitting

4 If operations have been carried out that might affect the backlash between the balancer shafts and the crankshaft (crankshaft, bearing cap or balancer unit replacement), then the backlash must be measured and, if necessary, adjusted. If none of theses mentioned operations have been carried out, the original shim can be reused.

5 In order to carry out the measurement and adjustment procedure, Vauxhall tool No. KM 949 must be used. If this tool is not available, take the cylinder block and balancer unit to a Vauxhall dealer or specialist to have the backlash measured and adjusted. If the tool is available, proceed as follows.

6 With reference to Section 3 if necessary, set the crankshaft at TDC on No 1 cylinder at the end of the compression stroke.

7 Position the two balance shafts so that when viewed from the right-hand of the engine, the two flat machined surfaces are exactly horizontal **(see illustration)**.

8 Fit the existing shim and balancer unit to the cylinder block. Insert the retaining bolts and tighten them to the specified torque.

9 Screw Vauxhall tool No. KM 949 with the long knurled bolt into the end of the inlet side balancer shaft. Position the measuring arm so that it points to the 9 o'clock position, when viewed from the end of the engine. Hand tighten the bolt.

2B

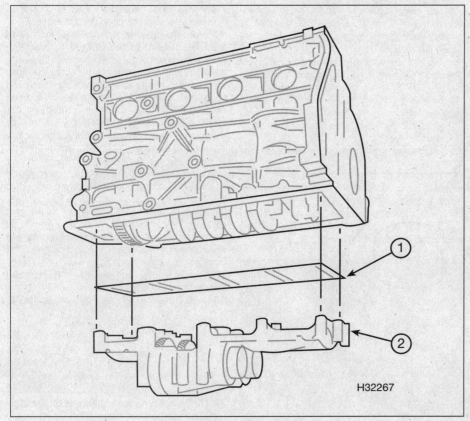

18.1 Balancer unit (2) and shim (1) - 2.0 litre engine

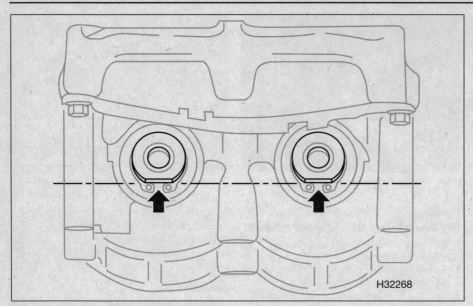

18.7 Position the balancer shafts so that the two flat machined surfaces are horizontal

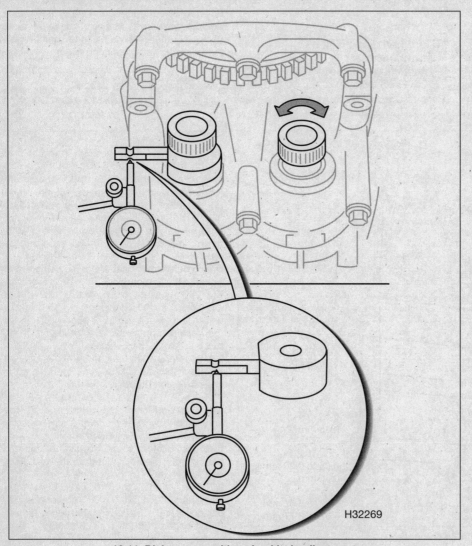

18.11 Dial gauge position - backlash adjustment

10 Screw the short knurled bolt of KM 949 into the exhaust side balancer shaft. Hand tighten the bolt.

11 Mount a dial gauge onto the balancer unit or cylinder block, so that the gauge probe acts vertically against the measuring arm between the notches of the flat machined surface **(see illustration)**.

12 Determine the 'beginning' and 'end' of the backlash by turning the exhaust side knurled bolt backwards and forwards. Position this balancer shaft at the 'beginning' of the backlash and zero the dial gauge.

13 Turn the exhaust side balancer shaft to the 'end' of the backlash, and read off the measurement from the dial gauge.

14 The backlash should be measured at four different balancer shaft positions. Using the crankshaft sprocket bolt, turn the crankshaft clockwise until the measuring arm on the inlet side balancer shaft points to the 6 o'clock position. Loosen the knurled bolt and reposition the arm back to the 9 o'clock position. Repeat the backlash measurement procedure in this position, and take two further readings repositioning the balancer shaft each time.

15 If any of the four reading are outside the value given in the Specifications, the backlash must be adjusted. Adjustment is achieved by inserting a shim of various thicknesses between the balancer unit and the cylinder block. Each shim is given a code number to represent its thickness (see Specifications). This code is also stamped onto the shim.

16 Having established the backlash, and the thickness of the existing shim (from the code number), it is then possible to determine the thickness (and code number) of the shim required to adjust the backlash to within the given tolerance. The next larger or smaller shim changes the backlash by approximately 0.02 mm. For example: The measured backlash with a shim code number '70' fitted was 0.08 mm. If this shim is replaced by one with the code number '67', the backlash is reduced to 0.06 mm. Only one shim may be fitted at a time.

17 After selecting the correct shim, and refitting the balancer unit and shim as described in paragraphs 6 to 8, repeat the measurement procedure to ensure the backlash is within tolerance.

18 Remove the dial gauge and the two knurled bolts of KM 949.

19 Refit the sump as described in Section 12.

Chapter 2 Part C:
1.7 litre diesel engine in-car repair procedures

Contents

Degrees of difficulty

Easy, suitable for novice with little experience		Fairly easy, suitable for beginner with some experience		Fairly difficult, suitable for competent DIY mechanic		Difficult, suitable for experienced DIY mechanic		Very difficult, suitable for expert DIY or professional	

Specifications

General

Engine type	Four-cylinder, in-line, water-cooled. Single overhead camshaft, belt-driven
Manufacturer's engine code	X17DT
Bore	79.0 mm
Stroke	86.0 mm
Capacity	1686 cc
Firing order	1-3-4-2 (No 1 cylinder at timing belt end)
Direction of crankshaft rotation	Clockwise (viewed from timing belt end of engine)
Compression ratio	22:1
Maximum power	60 kW at 4400 rpm
Maximum torque	168 Nm at 2400 rpm

Compression pressures

Standard	18.5 to 34.5 bar (268 to 500 psi)
Maximum difference between any two cylinders	1.5 bar (23 psi)

Valve clearances

Engine cold:	
Inlet	0.15 mm
Exhaust	0.25 mm

Camshaft

Endfloat	0.05 to 0.20 mm
Maximum permissible radial run-out	0.05 mm
Cam lift:	
Inlet valve	8.47 to 8.67 mm
Exhaust valve	8.57 to 8.77 mm
Bearing running clearance:	
Standard	0.040 to 0.082 mm
Service limit	0.110 mm

Lubrication system

Oil pump type	Gear-type, driven by timing belt	
Minimum permissible oil pressure at idle speed, with engine at operating temperature (oil temperature of at least 80°C)	2.0 bar (29 psi)	
Oil pump clearances:	**Standard**	**Service limit**
Outer rotor-to-body clearance	0.24 to 0.36 mm	0.40 mm
Inner-to-outer rotor clearance	0.13 to 0.15 mm	0.20 mm
Rotor endfloat	0.035 to 0.100 mm	0.150 mm

Torque wrench settings

	Nm	lbf ft
Baffle plate-to-cylinder block bolts	19	14
Camshaft bearing cap nuts	19	14
Camshaft cover bolts	8	6
Camshaft sprocket bolt	10	7
Coolant pump:		
Pump retaining bolts	20	15
Pulley retaining bolts	10	7
Connecting rod big-end bearing cap nuts: *		
Stage 1	25	18
Stage 2	Angle-tighten a further 100°	
Stage 3	Angle-tighten a further 15°	
Crankshaft pulley bolts	20	15
Crankshaft rear oil seal housing bolts	10	7
Crankshaft sprocket bolt	196	144
Cylinder head bolts: *		
Stage 1	40	30
Stage 2	Angle-tighten a further 60 to 75°	
Stage 3	Angle-tighten a further 60 to 75°	
Engine/transmission mounting bolts:		
Right-hand mounting:		
Mounting-to-bracket/subframe nuts	45	33
Bracket-to-engine bolts	60	44
Upper bracket nuts	45	33
Left-hand mounting:		
Mounting-to-bracket/subframe nuts	45	33
Bracket-to-transmission bolts	60	44
Rear mounting:		
Mounting-to-bracket bolts	45	33
Mounting-to-subframe bolts	20	15
Bracket-to-transmission bolts	60	44
Engine-to-transmission unit bolts:		
M8 bolts	20	15
M10 bolts	40	30
M12 bolts	60	44
Flywheel bolts: *		
Stage 1	30	22
Stage 2	Angle-tighten a further 45 to 60°	
Flywheel lower cover plate bolts	8	6
Injection pump sprocket nut	69	51
Main bearing cap bolts	88	65
Oil cooler centre bolt	49	36
Oil filter	See Chapter 1B	
Oil pressure (regulator) valve bolt	40	30
Oil pressure relief (safety) valve bolt	40	30
Oil pump cover retaining bolts	10	7
Oil pump pick-up/strainer bolts	19	14
Oil pump sprocket nut	44	32
Sump bolts:		
Main casting-to-block/oil pump cover nuts/bolts	10	7
Sump pan-to-main casting bolts	10	7
Drain plug	See Chapter 1B	
Roadwheel bolts	110	81
Timing belt cover bolts	8	6
Timing belt idler pulley bolt	76	57
Timing belt tensioner pulley bolts	19	14

* **Note:** *The manufacturer states that all fasteners secured by the angle-tightening method must be renewed as a matter of course.*

1 General information

1 This Part of Chapter 2 describes those repair procedures that can reasonably be carried out on the 1.7 litre diesel engine while it remains in the car. If the engine has been removed from the car and is being dismantled as described in Part E, any preliminary dismantling procedures can be ignored.

2 Note that, while it may be possible physically to overhaul items such as the piston/connecting rod assemblies while the engine is in the car, such tasks are not normally carried out as separate operations. Usually, several additional procedures (not to mention the cleaning of components and of oilways) have to be carried out. For this reason, all such tasks are classed as major overhaul procedures, and are described in Part E of this Chapter.

3 Part E describes the removal of the engine/transmission unit from the vehicle, and the full overhaul procedures that can then be carried out.

Engine description

4 The 1.7 litre (1686 cc) diesel engine is of the eight-valve, in-line four-cylinder, single overhead camshaft (SOHC) type, mounted transversely at the front of the car with the transmission attached to its left-hand end.

5 The crankshaft runs in five main bearings. Thrustwashers are fitted to No 2 main bearing (upper half) to control crankshaft endfloat.

6 The connecting rods rotate on horizontally-split bearing shells at their big-ends. The pistons are attached to the connecting rods by gudgeon pins, which are a sliding fit in the connecting rod small-end eyes being retained by circlips. The aluminium-alloy pistons are fitted with three piston rings - two compression rings and an oil control ring.

7 The cylinder block is made of cast iron and the cylinder bores are an integral part of the block. On this type of engine the cylinder bores are sometimes referred to as having dry liners.

8 The inlet and exhaust valves are each closed by coil springs, and operate in guides pressed into the cylinder head.

9 The camshaft is driven by the crankshaft by a timing belt and rotates directly in the head. The camshaft operates the valves via followers which are situated directly below the camshaft. Valve clearances are adjusted using shims which are fitted between the camshaft and follower.

10 Lubrication is by means of an oil pump, which is driven off the timing belt. It draws oil through a strainer located in the sump, and then forces it through an externally-mounted filter into galleries in the cylinder block/crankcase. From there, the oil is distributed to the crankshaft (main bearings) and camshaft. The big-end bearings are supplied with oil via internal drillings in the crankshaft, while the camshaft bearings also receive a pressurised supply. The camshaft lobes and valves are lubricated by splash, as are all other engine components. An oil cooler is fitted to keep the oil temperature stable under arduous operating conditions.

Repair operations possible with the engine in the car

11 The following work can be carried out with the engine in the car:

a) Compression pressure - testing.
b) Camshaft cover - removal and refitting.
c) Timing belt cover - removal and refitting.
d) Timing belt - removal and refitting.
e) Timing belt tensioner and sprockets - removal and refitting.
f) Valve clearances - checking and adjustment.
g) Camshaft and followers - removal, inspection and refitting.
h) Cylinder head - removal and refitting.
i) Connecting rods and pistons - removal and refitting*.
j) Sump - removal and refitting.
k) Oil pump - removal, overhaul and refitting.
l) Oil cooler - removal and refitting.
m) Crankshaft oil seals - renewal.
n) Engine/transmission mountings - inspection and renewal.
o) Flywheel - removal, inspection and refitting.

* Although the operation marked with an asterisk can be carried out with the engine in the car after removal of the sump, it is better for the engine to be removed, in the interests of cleanliness and improved access. For this reason, the procedure is described in Chapter 2E.

2 Compression test - description and interpretation

Refer to Chapter 2D, Section 2.

3 Top dead centre (TDC) for No 1 piston - locating

Note: *If the engine is to be locked in position with No 1 piston at TDC on its compression stroke then a M6 and M8 bolt will be required.*

1 In its travel up and down its cylinder bore, Top Dead Centre (TDC) is the highest point that each piston reaches as the crankshaft rotates. While each piston reaches TDC both at the top of the compression stroke and again at the top of the exhaust stroke, for the purpose of timing the engine, TDC refers to the piston position (usually number 1) at the top of its compression stroke.

2 Number 1 piston (and cylinder) is at the right-hand (timing belt) end of the engine, and its TDC position is located as follows. Note that the crankshaft rotates clockwise when viewed from the right-hand side of the car.

3.5 Align the crankshaft pulley notch with the pointer on the base of the oil pump cover

3 Disconnect the battery negative terminal. To improve access to the crankshaft pulley, apply the handbrake, then jack up the front of the vehicle and support it on axle stands and remove the right-hand front wheel.

4 Remove the timing belt upper cover as described in Section 6.

5 Using a socket and extension bar on the crankshaft sprocket bolt, rotate the crankshaft until the notch on the crankshaft pulley rim is aligned with the pointer on the base of the oil pump cover **(see illustration)**. Once the mark is correctly aligned, No 1 and 4 pistons are at TDC.

6 To determine which piston is at TDC on its compression stroke, check the position of the timing holes in the camshaft and injection pump sprockets. When No 1 piston is at TDC on its compression stroke, both sprocket holes will be aligned with the threaded holes in the cylinder head/block. If the timing holes are 180° out of alignment then No 4 cylinder is at TDC on its compression stroke; rotate the crankshaft through a further complete turn (360°) to bring No 1 cylinder to TDC on its compression stroke.

7 With No 1 piston at TDC on its compression stroke, if necessary, the camshaft and fuel injection pump sprockets can be locked in position. Secure the camshaft sprocket in position by screwing an M6 bolt through the sprocket hole and into the hole in the cylinder head, then lock the injection pump sprocket in position by screwing an M8 bolt through the arrowed sprocket hole - note that there are

3.7a Lock the camshaft sprocket in position by screwing an M6 bolt (arrowed) into position . . .

2C

3.7b . . . and lock the injection pump sprocket using an M8 bolt (arrowed) screwed into the block through the sprocket's arrowed hole

two holes in this sprocket; the correct hole for timing purposes being indicated by a stamped-in arrow mark – into the hole in the cylinder block **(see illustrations)**.

4 Camshaft cover - removal and refitting

Removal

1 Release the retaining clip and disconnect the breather hose from the rear of the camshaft cover.
2 Slacken and remove the camshaft cover retaining bolts, along with their spacers, and lift the camshaft cover and seal away from the cylinder head. Remove the semi-circular rubber seal from the cut-out on the left-hand end of the cylinder head upper surface **(see illustration)**.
3 Examine the cover seal and semi-circular seal for signs of damage or deterioration and renew if necessary.

Refitting

4 Ensure the cover and cylinder head surfaces are clean and dry then fit the seal to the cover groove **(see illustration)**.
5 Apply a smear of sealant to the semi-circular cut-out on the left-hand end of the cylinder head then fit the seal to the cut-out.
6 Carefully lower the cover into position, ensuring the seal remains correctly seated.

4.4 Ensure the seal is correctly located in the camshaft cover groove

4.2 Remove the semi-circular rubber seal from left-hand end of the cylinder head

Refit the spacers and retaining bolts and tighten them to the specified torque.
7 Reconnect the breather hose to the rear of the cover and secure in position with the retaining clip.

5 Crankshaft pulley - removal and refitting

Removal

1 Apply the handbrake, then jack up the front of the car and support it on axle stands. Remove the right-hand roadwheel.
2 Remove the auxiliary drivebelts as described in Chapter 1. Prior to removal, mark the direction of rotation on the belts to ensure each belt is refitted the same way around.
3 Slacken and remove the small retaining bolts securing the pulley to the crankshaft sprocket and remove the pulley from the engine. If necessary, prevent crankshaft rotation by holding the sprocket retaining bolt with a suitable socket.

Refitting

4 Refit the pulley to the crankshaft sprocket, aligning the pulley hole with the sprocket locating pin. Refit the pulley retaining bolts, tightening the to the specified torque **(see illustration)**.

5.4 Refit the crankshaft pulley, locating it on the sprocket pin (arrowed), and refit the retaining bolts

5 Refit the auxiliary drivebelt as described in Chapter 1 using the mark made prior to removal to ensure the belt is fitted the correct way around.
6 Refit the roadwheel then lower the car to the ground and tighten the wheel bolts to the specified torque.

6 Timing belt covers - removal and refitting

Removal

Upper cover

1 Apply the handbrake, then jack up the front of the car and support it on axle stands. Remove the right-hand roadwheel.
2 Remove the air cleaner housing as described in Chapter 4.
3 Remove the auxiliary drivebelts as described in Chapter 1. Prior to removal, mark the direction of rotation on each belt to ensure it is refitted the same way around.
4 On models equipped with air conditioning, unbolt the compressor drivebelt tensioner and remove it from the engine.
5 Referring to Section 19, support the engine/transmission unit then undo the retaining nuts and lift off the bracket from the right-hand mounting assembly. Unbolt the mounting bracket and remove it from the side of the cylinder block.
6 Slacken and remove the retaining bolts and remove the timing belt upper cover from the engine, along with its rubber sealing strips. Inspect the sealing strips for signs of damage or deterioration and renew if necessary **(see illustration)**.

Lower cover

7 Remove the upper cover as described in paragraphs 1 to 6.
8 Remove the crankshaft pulley as described in Section 5.
9 Undo the retaining bolts and remove the lower cover from the engine unit, along with its rubber sealing strips. Inspect the sealing strips for signs of damage or deterioration and renew if necessary.

Inner cover

10 Remove the timing belt as described in Section 7.
11 Remove the camshaft sprocket, the fuel injection pump sprocket, the timing belt idler pulley and the tensioner assembly as described in Section 8
12 Unbolt the inner cover from the cylinder head/block and remove it from the engine unit.

Refitting

13 Refitting is the reverse of removal, ensuring the cover sealing strips are correctly fitted and all retaining bolts are tightened to the specified torque **(see illustration)**.

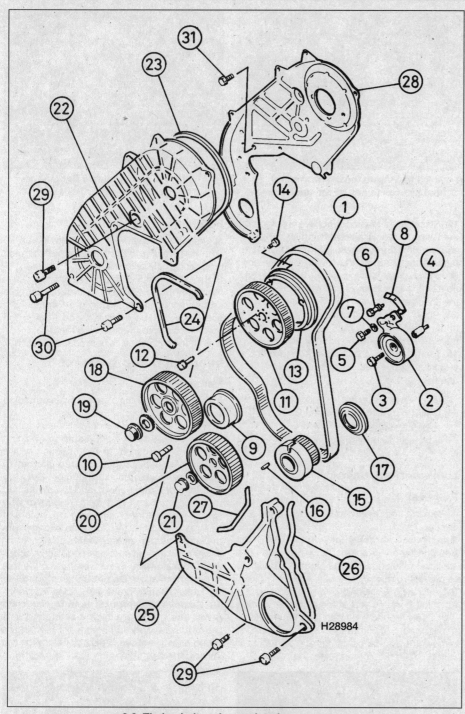

H28984

6.6 Timing belt and associated components

1 Timing belt	12 Camshaft sprocket bolt	21 Sprocket nut
2 Tensioner assembly	13 Camshaft sprocket	22 Upper cover
3 Tensioner bolt	flange	23 Sealing strip
4 Tensioner bolt	14 Flange screw	24 Sealing strip
5 Tensioner bolt	15 Crankshaft sprocket	25 Lower cover
6 Spring bolt	16 Locating pin	26 Sealing strip
7 Washer	17 Flanged spacer	27 Sealing strip
8 Tensioner spring	18 Injection pump	28 Rear cover
9 Idler pulley	sprocket	29 Cover bolts
10 Idler pulley bolt	19 Sprocket nut	30 Cover bolts
11 Camshaft sprocket	20 Oil pump sprocket	31 Cover bolts

7 Timing belt - removal and refitting

Note: *The timing belt must be removed and refitted with the engine cold.*

Removal

1 Position No 1 cylinder at TDC on its compression stroke as described in Section 3. Lock the camshaft and injection pump sprockets in position by screwing the bolts into the threaded holes in the cylinder head/block.

2 Remove the crankshaft pulley as described in Section 5.

3 Unbolt the timing belt lower cover and remove it along with its rubber sealing strips.

4 Slacken the timing belt tensioner retaining bolts, then carefully unhook the tensioner spring from its locating pins.

5 Slide the timing belt off from its sprockets and remove it from the engine. If the belt is to be re-used, use white paint or similar to mark the direction of rotation on the belt. **Do not** rotate the crankshaft until the timing belt has been refitted.

6 Check the timing belt carefully for any signs of uneven wear, splitting or oil contamination, and renew it if there is the slightest doubt about its condition. If the engine is undergoing an overhaul and is approaching the manufacturers' specified interval for belt renewal (see Chapter 1) renew the belt as a matter of course, regardless of its apparent condition. If signs of oil contamination are found, trace the source of the oil leak and rectify it, then wash down the engine timing belt area and all related components to remove all traces of oil.

Refitting

7 On reassembly, thoroughly clean the timing belt sprockets and ensure the camshaft and injection pump sprockets are locked correctly in position. Temporarily refit the crankshaft pulley to the sprocket and check that the pulley

2C

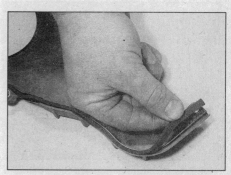

6.13 On refitting ensure the sealing strips are correctly seated in the cover grooves

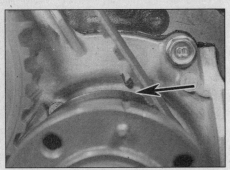

7.7 Check that the crankshaft sprocket cut-out is aligned with the mark on the oil pump cover (arrowed)

7.11a Rotate the crankshaft 60° backwards to adjust the timing belt tension . . .

7.11b . . . then securely tighten the tensioner pulley bolts

cut-out is still aligned with the pointer on the oil pump cover; the mark on the crankshaft sprocket should also be aligned with the mark on the oil pump cover (**see illustration**).

8 Remove the pulley and fit the timing belt over the crankshaft, oil pump, injection pump and camshaft sprockets, ensuring that the belt rear run is taut (ie, all slack is on the tensioner pulley side of the belt). Do not twist the belt sharply while refitting it. Ensure that the belt teeth are correctly seated centrally in the sprockets, and that the timing marks remain in alignment. If a used belt is being refitted, ensure that the arrow mark made on removal points in the normal direction of rotation, as before.

9 Tension the belt by refitting the tensioner pulley spring, ensuring it is correctly located on its pins.

10 Check that the crankshaft sprocket timing mark is still correctly positioned then unscrew the locking bolts from the injection pump and camshaft sprockets.

11 Slacken the tensioner pulley retaining bolt then rotate the crankshaft pulley approximately 60° **backwards** (anti-clockwise) to automatically adjust the timing belt tension. Hold the crankshaft pulley stationary and securely tighten the tensioner pulley retaining bolt (**see illustrations**).

12 Rotate the crankshaft smoothly through two complete turns (720°) in the normal direction of rotation to settle the timing belt in position. Realign the crankshaft sprocket timing mark and check that the camshaft and injection pump sprocket locking bolts can be refitted.

13 Slacken the tensioner pulley retaining bolt then rotate the crankshaft pulley approximately 60° **backwards** (anti-clockwise) to automatically adjust the timing belt tension. Hold the crankshaft pulley stationary and tighten the tensioner pulley retaining bolts to the specified torque.

14 Return the crankshaft to TDC and make a final check that the sprocket timing mark/holes are correctly positioned.

15 Refit the timing belt covers then refit the crankshaft pulley as described in Sections 5 and 6.

8 Timing belt tensioner and sprockets - removal and refitting

Camshaft sprocket

Removal

1 Remove the timing belt as described in Section 7.

2 Screw the sprocket locking bolt fully into position then slacken and remove the sprocket retaining bolts, using the locking bolt to prevent rotation.

3 Unscrew the locking bolt and remove the sprocket from the end of the camshaft, noting which way around it is fitted (**see illustration**). If the sprocket locating pin is a loose fit, remove it from the camshaft end and store it with the sprocket for safe-keeping.

Refitting

4 Ensure the locating pin is in position then refit the sprocket to the camshaft end aligning its locating hole with the pin.

5 Refit the sprocket retaining bolts then align the timing hole with the cylinder head hole and screw in the lock bolt. Use the locking bolt to retain the sprocket and tighten the sprocket bolts to the specified torque.

6 Refit the timing belt as described in Section 7.

Injection pump sprocket

Removal

7 Remove the timing belt as described in Section 7.

8 In order to prevent sprocket rotation as the retaining nut is slackened, a sprocket holding tool will be required. In the absence of the special Vauxhall tool, a suitable alternative can be made using two lengths of steel strip (one long, the other short), and three nuts and bolts; one nut and bolt forms the pivot of a forked tool, with the remaining two nuts and bolts at the tips of the 'forks' to engage with the sprocket spokes (**see illustration**).

9 Unscrew the pulley locking bolt and slacken the sprocket retaining nut whilst using the tool to prevent rotation. **Do not** be tempted to use the locking bolt to prevent sprocket rotation.

10 Remove the sprocket from the injection pump shaft, noting which way around it is fitted. If the Woodruff key is a loose fit in the pump shaft, remove it and store it with the sprocket for safe-keeping (**see illustration**).

8.3 Removing the camshaft sprocket (locating pin arrowed)

8.8 Using a sprocket holding tool to prevent rotation as the injection pump sprocket nut is slackened

8.10 Remove the sprocket and recover the Woodruff key from the injection pump shaft

8.17a Unscrew the retaining bolt and washer . . .

8.17b . . . and remove the crankshaft sprocket from the engine

8.18 Slide off the flanged spacer noting which way around it is fitted

Note: *The sprocket is a tapered-fit on the injection pump shaft and in some cases a suitable puller may be needed to free it from the shaft.*

Refitting

11 Ensure the Woodruff key is correctly fitted to the pump shaft then refit the sprocket, aligning the sprocket groove with the key.

12 Refit the retaining nut and tighten it to the specified torque whilst using the holding tool to prevent rotation.

13 Align the sprocket timing hole with the threaded hole in the cylinder block and screw in the locking bolt.

14 Refit the timing belt as described in Section 7.

Crankshaft sprocket

Removal

15 Remove the timing belt as described in Section 7.

16 Slacken the crankshaft sprocket retaining bolt. To prevent crankshaft rotation, have an assistant select top gear and apply the brakes firmly. If the engine is removed from the vehicle it will be necessary to lock the flywheel (see Section 17).

17 Unscrew the retaining bolt and washer and remove the crankshaft sprocket from the end of the crankshaft. If the sprocket is a tight fit, draw it off of the crankshaft using a suitable puller **(see illustrations)**. If the Woodruff key is a loose fit in the crankshaft,

remove it and store it with the sprocket for safe-keeping.

18 Slide the flanged spacer off of the crankshaft, noting which way around it is fitted **(see illustration)**.

Refitting

19 Refit the flanged spacer to the crankshaft with its convex surface facing away from the oil pump housing.

20 Ensure the Woodruff key is correctly fitted then slide on the crankshaft sprocket aligning its groove with the key.

21 Refit the retaining bolt and washer then lock the crankshaft by the method used on removal, and tighten the sprocket retaining bolt to the specified stage torque setting.

22 Refit the timing belt as described in Section 7.

Oil pump sprocket

Removal

23 Remove the timing belt as described in Section 7.

24 Prevent the oil pump sprocket from rotating using a socket and extension bar fitted to one of the oil pump cover bolts then slacken and remove the sprocket retaining nut **(see illustration)**.

25 Remove the sprocket from the oil pump shaft, noting which way around it is fitted.

Refitting

26 Refit the sprocket, aligning it with the flat on the pump shaft, and fit the retaining nut.

Tighten the sprocket retaining nut to the specified torque, using the socket and extension bar to prevent rotation.

27 Refit the timing belt as described in Section 7.

Tensioner assembly

Removal

28 Remove the timing belt as described in Section 7.

29 Unscrew the retaining bolts and remove the tensioner assembly from the engine **(see illustration)**.

Refitting

30 Fit the tensioner assembly to the engine tightening its retaining bolts by hand only.

31 Refit the timing belt as described in Section 7.

Idler pulley

Removal

32 Remove the timing belt as described in Section 7.

33 Slacken and remove the retaining bolt and remove the idler pulley from the engine **(see illustration)**.

Refitting

34 Refit the idler pulley and tighten the retaining bolt to the specified torque.

35 Refit the timing belt as described in Section 7.

2C

8.24 Lock the oil pump sprocket in position using a socket and extension bar then unscrew the sprocket retaining nut

8.29 Unscrew the retaining bolts and remove the tensioner assembly

8.33 Removing the idler pulley

9.2 Timing belt rear cover-to-cylinder head bolts (arrowed)

9 Camshaft oil seal - renewal

1 Remove the camshaft sprocket as described in Section 8.
2 Slacken and remove the bolts securing the timing belt rear cover to the cylinder head and block and ease the cover away from the head to gain access to the oil seal **(see illustration)**. To gain full access to the seal, remove the rear cover as described in Section 6.
3 Carefully punch or drill two small holes opposite each other in the oil seal. Screw a self-tapping screw into each, and pull on the screws with pliers to extract the seal.
4 Clean the seal housing, and polish off any burrs or raised edges which may have caused the seal to fail in the first place.
5 Lubricate the lips of the new seal with clean engine oil, and press it into position using a suitable tubular drift (such as a socket) which bears only on the hard outer edge of the seal. Take care not to damage the seal lips during fitting; note that the seal lips should face inwards.
6 Refit the timing belt rear cover bolts, tightening them to the specified torque setting.
7 Refit the camshaft sprocket as described in Section 8.

10 Valve clearances - checking and adjustment

Checking

1 The importance of having the valve clearances correctly adjusted cannot be overstressed, as they vitally affect the performance of the engine. Checking should not be regarded as a routine operation, however. It should only be necessary when the valve gear has become noisy, after engine overhaul, or when trying to trace the cause of power loss. The engine must be cold for the check to be accurate. The clearances are checked as follows.

2 Apply the handbrake, then jack up the front of the car and support it on axle stands. Remove the right-hand front roadwheel to gain access to the crankshaft pulley.
3 Remove the camshaft cover as described in Section 4.
4 Using a socket and extension on the crankshaft sprocket bolt, rotate the crankshaft in the normal direction of rotation (clockwise when viewed from the right-hand end of the engine) until the notch on the crankshaft pulley is correctly aligned with the pointer on the base of the oil pump cover. **Note:** *The engine will be easier to turn if the fuel injectors or glow plugs are removed.*
5 Check that the camshaft lobes of No 1 cylinder (nearest the timing belt end of the engine) are pointing away from the followers indicating No 1 cylinder is at TDC on its compression stroke. If the lobes are pointing downwards, rotate the crankshaft through one more complete turn (360°) and realign the notch and pointer.
6 On a piece of paper, draw the outline of the engine with the cylinders numbered from the timing belt end. Show the position of each valve, together with the specified valve clearance. Since the clearance is different for inlet and exhaust valves - make sure that you are aware which valve you are dealing with. The valve sequence from the timing belt end of the engine is:

   In - Ex - In - Ex - In - Ex - In - Ex

7 With No 1 cylinder at TDC on its compression stroke, using feeler blades, measure the clearance between the base of both No 1 cylinder cam lobes and their followers and record the clearances on the paper.
8 Rotate the crankshaft pulley through a half a turn (180°) to position No 3 cylinder at TDC on its compression stroke. Measure the clearance between the base of both No 3 cylinder cam lobes and their followers and record the clearances on the paper.
9 Rotate the crankshaft pulley through a half a turn (180°) and realign the pulley notch with the pointer so that No 4 cylinder is at TDC on its compression stroke. Measure the clearance between the base of both No 4 cylinder cam lobes and their followers and record the clearances on the paper.

10 Rotate the crankshaft pulley through a half a turn (180°) to position No 2 cylinder at TDC on its compression stroke. Measure the clearance between the base of both No 2 cylinder cam lobes and their followers and record the clearances on the paper.
11 If all the clearances are correct (or within 0.02 mm - the difference between shim sizes), refit the cylinder head cover (see Section 4), then refit the roadwheel and lower the vehicle to the ground and tighten the wheel bolts to the specified torque. If any clearance measured is not correct, adjustment must be carried out as described in the following paragraphs.

Adjustment

12 Rotate the crankshaft pulley until the lobe of the valve to be adjusted is pointing directly away from the follower.
13 Rotate the follower until the groove on its upper edge is facing towards the front of the engine.
14 In the absence of the special Vauxhall tool (KM-650), position a large flat-bladed screwdriver between the edge of the follower and the base of the camshaft. Use the screwdriver to carefully depress the follower until there is enough clearance to allow the shim to be slid out from between the follower and camshaft (a magnetic tool is particularly useful for this task) **(see illustration)**.
15 Clean the shim, and measure its thickness with a micrometer. The shims carry thickness markings, but wear may have reduced the original thickness, so be sure to check **(see illustration)**.
16 Add the measured clearance of the valve to the thickness of the original shim then subtract the specified valve clearance from this figure. This will give you the thickness of the shim required. For example:

Clearance measured of valve	0.35 mm
Plus thickness of the original shim	2.70 mm
Equals	3.05 mm
Minus clearance required	0.25 mm
Thickness of shim required	2.80 mm

17 Obtain the correct thickness of shim required lubricate it with clean engine oil. Carefully depress the follower and slide the shim into position, with the thickness number downwards, ensuring it is correctly located.

10.14 With the camshaft lobe pointing upwards, depress the follower and carefully remove the shim

10.15 The thickness of each shim should be stamped on one of its surfaces

11.5 Remove the camshaft bearing caps noting each caps identification marking (arrowed)

11.11a Refit each follower to the cylinder head . . .

11.11b . . . and refit the shim, ensuring it is correctly seated

HAYNES HiNT

It may be possible to correct the clearances by moving the shims around between the valves. Keep a note of all the shim thicknesses to assist valve clearance adjustment when they need to be done again.

18 Repeat the procedure given in paragraphs 12 to 17 on the remaining valves which require adjustment.

19 Rotate the crankshaft a few times to settle all shims in position the recheck the valve clearances before refitting the camshaft cover (see Section 4).

20 Refit the roadwheel then lower the vehicle to the ground and tighten the wheel bolts to the specified torque.

11 Camshaft and followers - removal, inspection and refitting

Removal

1 Remove the camshaft cover as described in Section 4.

2 Remove the camshaft sprocket as described in Section 8.

3 Slacken and remove the bolts securing the timing belt rear cover to the cylinder head.

4 Working in the **reverse** of the tightening sequence (see illustration 11.16), slacken the

11.12 Lubricate the bearings with clean engine oil then lay the camshaft in position

camshaft bearing cap retaining nuts by one turn at a time, to relieve the pressure of the valve springs on the bearing caps gradually and evenly. Once the valve spring pressure has been relieved, the nuts can be fully unscrewed and removed.

Caution: If the bearing cap nuts are carelessly slackened, the bearing caps might break. If any bearing cap breaks then the complete cylinder head assembly must be renewed; the bearing caps are matched to the head and are not available separately.

5 Remove the bearing caps, noting each caps correct fitted location. The bearing caps are numbered 1 to 5 and the arrow on each cap points towards the timing belt end of the engine **(see illustration)**.

6 Lift the camshaft out of the cylinder head and slide off the oil seal.

7 Obtain eight small, clean plastic containers, and label them for identification. Alternatively, divide a larger container into compartments. Lift the followers and shims out from the top of the cylinder head and store each one in its respective fitted position. Make sure the followers and shims are not mixed to ensure the valve clearances remain correctly adjusted on refitting.

Inspection

8 Examine the camshaft bearing surfaces and cam lobes for signs of wear ridges and scoring. Renew the camshaft if any of these conditions are apparent. Examine the condition of the bearing surfaces both on the camshaft journals and in the cylinder head. If the head bearing surfaces are worn excessively, the cylinder head will need to be renewed.

9 Support the camshaft end journals on V-blocks, and measure the run-out at the centre journal using a dial gauge. If the run-out exceeds the specified limit, the camshaft should be renewed.

10 Examine the followers and their bores in the cylinder head for signs of wear or damage. If any follower is visibly worn it should be renewed.

Refitting

11 Where removed, lubricate the followers with clean engine oil and carefully insert each one into its original location in the cylinder head. Ensure each shim is correctly located in the top of the its relevant follower **(see illustrations)**.

12 Lubricate the camshaft bearings with clean engine oil then lay the camshaft in position **(see illustration)**. Ensure the crankshaft pulley notch is still correctly aligned with the pointer on the oil pump cover and the injection pump sprocket is locked in position. Position the camshaft so that the lobes of No 1 cylinder are pointing upwards and the sprocket locating pin is uppermost.

13 Ensure the mating surfaces of the bearing caps and cylinder head are clean and dry and lubricate the camshaft journals and lobes with clean engine oil.

14 Apply a smear of sealant to the areas of the cylinder head No 1 bearing cap mating surface, on each side of the camshaft end **(see illustration)**.

15 Refit the camshaft bearing caps in their original locations on the cylinder head. The caps are numbered 1 to 5 (No 1 cap being at the timing belt end of the engine) and the arrow cast onto the top of each cap should point towards the timing belt end of the engine.

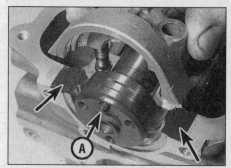

11.14 Apply sealant to the cylinder head mating surface of No 1 camshaft bearing cap (arrowed) then refit the caps ensuring the camshaft locating pin is correctly positioned (A)

2C

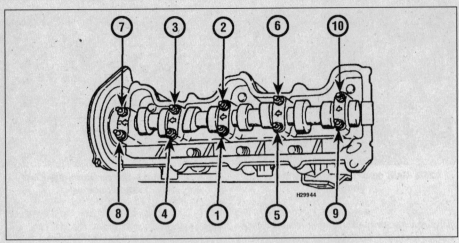

11.16 Camshaft bearing cap tightening sequence

16 Refit the bearing cap nuts, tightening them by hand only. Working in the specified sequence, tighten the nuts by one turn at a time to gradually impose the pressure of the valve springs on the bearing caps **(see illustration)**. Repeat this sequence until all bearing caps are in contact with the cylinder head then go around in the specified sequence and tighten them to the specified torque.

Caution: If the bearing cap bolts are carelessly tightened, the bearing caps might break. If any bearing cap breaks then the complete cylinder head assembly must be renewed; the bearing caps are matched to the head and are not available separately.

17 Fit a new camshaft oil seal as described in Section 9.

18 Refit the timing belt rear cover retaining bolts and tighten them to the specified torque.

19 Refit the camshaft sprocket and timing belt as described in Sections 7 and 8.

20 Check the valve clearances as described in Section 10 then refit the camshaft cover as described in Section 4.

12 Cylinder head - removal and refitting

Caution: Be careful not to allow dirt into the fuel injection pump or injector pipes during this procedure.

Note: *New cylinder head bolts will be required on refitting.*

Removal

1 Drain the cooling system as described in Chapter 1.

2 Remove the inlet and exhaust manifolds as described in Chapter 4.

3 Remove the camshaft sprocket (Section 8).

4 Slacken and remove the bolts securing the timing belt rear cover to the end of the cylinder head.

5 Release the retaining clips and disconnect the coolant hoses from thermostat housing and cylinder head.

6 Undo the retaining nut and disconnect the wiring connector from the glow plug.

7 Disconnect the wiring connectors from the coolant temperature sensors then free the wiring from its retaining clips and position it clear of the cylinder head.

8 Wipe clean the pipe unions then slacken the union nuts securing the injector pipes to the top of each injector and the four union nuts securing the pipes to the rear of the injection pump; as each pump union nut is slackened, retain the adapter with a suitable open-ended spanner to prevent it being unscrewed from the pump. With all the union nuts undone, remove the injector pipes from the engine unit and mop up any spilt fuel.

9 Working in the **reverse** of the sequence shown in illustration 12.27, progressively slacken the ten main cylinder head bolts by half a turn at a time, until all bolts can be unscrewed by hand.

10 Lift out the cylinder head bolts and recover the washers.

11 Lift the cylinder head away; seek assistance if possible, as it is a heavy assembly. Remove the gasket, noting the two locating dowels fitted to the top of the cylinder block. If they are a loose fit, remove the locating dowels and store them with the head for safe-keeping. Keep the head gasket for identification purposes (see paragraph 18).

12 If the cylinder head is to be dismantled for overhaul, then refer to Part E of this Chapter.

Preparation for refitting

13 The mating faces of the cylinder head and cylinder block/crankcase must be perfectly clean before refitting the head. Use a hard plastic or wood scraper to remove all traces of gasket and carbon; also clean the piston crowns. Take particular care, as the surfaces are damaged easily. Also, make sure that the carbon is not allowed to enter the oil and water passages - this is particularly important for the lubrication system, as carbon could block the oil supply to any of the engine's components. Using adhesive tape and paper, seal the

water, oil and bolt holes in the cylinder block/crankcase. To prevent carbon entering the gap between the pistons and bores, smear a little grease in the gap. After cleaning each piston, use a small brush to remove all traces of grease and carbon from the gap, then wipe away the remainder with a clean rag. Clean all the pistons in the same way.

14 Check the mating surfaces of the cylinder block/crankcase and the cylinder head for nicks, deep scratches and other damage. If slight, they may be removed carefully with a file, but if excessive, machining may be the only alternative to renewal.

15 Ensure that the cylinder head bolt holes in the crankcase are clean and free of oil. Syringe or soak up any oil left in the bolt holes. This is most important in order that the correct bolt tightening torque can be applied and to prevent the possibility of the block being cracked by hydraulic pressure when the bolts are tightened.

16 The cylinder head bolts must be discarded and renewed, regardless of their apparent condition.

17 If warpage of the cylinder head gasket surface is suspected, use a straight-edge to check it for distortion. Refer to Part E of this Chapter if necessary.

18 On this engine, the cylinder head-to-piston clearance is controlled by fitting different thickness head gaskets. The gasket thickness can be determined by looking at the left-hand front corner of gasket and checking on the number of holes **(see illustration)**.

Holes in gasket	Gasket thickness
No holes	1.40 mm
One hole	1.45 mm
Two hole	1.50 mm

The correct thickness of gasket required is selected by measuring the piston protrusions as follows.

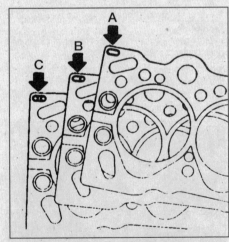

12.18 Cylinder head gasket thickness identification markings are found in the position shown

A No hole - 1.40 mm thickness
B One hole - 1.45 mm thickness
C Two holes - 1.50 mm thickness

12.19 Piston protrusion measuring points (arrowed)

12.23 Fit a new gasket to the cylinder block

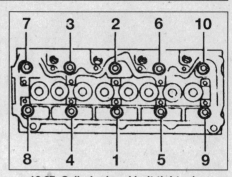

12.27 Cylinder head bolt tightening sequence

19 Ensure that the crankshaft is still correctly positioned in the TDC position. Mount a dial test indicator securely on the block so that its pointer can be easily pivoted between the piston crown and block mating surface. Zero the dial test indicator on the gasket surface of the cylinder block then carefully move the indicator over No 1 piston and measure its protrusion at the three points shown **(see illustration)**. Repeat this procedure on No 4 piston.
20 Rotate the crankshaft half a turn (180º) to bring No 2 and 3 pistons to TDC. Ensure the crankshaft is accurately positioned then measure the protrusions of No 2 and 3 pistons at the specified points. Once both pistons have been measured, rotate the crankshaft through a further one and a half turns (540º) to bring No 1 and 4 pistons back to TDC.
21 Find out the average piston protrusion by adding up the 12 different measurements taken (three for each piston) and dividing the total by 12. Using this average measurement, select the correct thickness of head gasket required using the following table.

Piston protrusion measurement	Gasket thickness required
0.58 to 0.64 mm	1.40 mm (no holes)
0.65 to 0.70 mm	1.45 mm (one hole)
0.71 to 0.78 mm	1.50 mm (two holes)

Note: *If any one of the piston protrusion measurements taken exceeds the average protrusion by more than 0.05 mm, select the gasket from the next available thickness up from the average. For example, if the average*

protrusion is 0.59 mm but one of the protrusion measurements taken was 0.67 mm (a difference of 0.08 mm) then use a 1.45 mm thick gasket instead of a 1.40 mm thick gasket.

Refitting

22 Wipe clean the mating surfaces of the cylinder head and cylinder block/crankcase.
23 Check that the two locating dowels are in position then fit a new gasket to the cylinder block **(see illustration)**.
24 Ensure the crankshaft pulley notch is still correctly aligned with the pointer on the oil pump cover with No 1 and 4 pistons at TDC and the camshaft is correctly positioned with the lobes of No 1 cylinder pointing upwards and the camshaft sprocket locating pin uppermost.
25 With the aid of an assistant, carefully refit the cylinder head assembly to the block, aligning it with the locating dowels.
26 Apply a smear of oil to the threads and the underside of the heads of the new cylinder head bolts and carefully enter each bolt into its relevant hole (do not drop them in). Screw all bolts in, by hand only, until finger-tight.
27 Working progressively and in the sequence shown, tighten the cylinder head bolts to their stage 1 torque setting, using a torque wrench and suitable socket **(see illustration)**.
28 Once all bolts have been tightened to the stage 1 torque, working again in the specified sequence, go around and tighten all bolts through the specified stage 2 angle. It is recommended that an angle-measuring gauge is used to ensure accuracy **(see illustration)**. If a gauge is not available, use white paint to make alignment marks prior to tightening; the marks can then be used to check that the bolt has been rotated through the correct angle.
29 Finally go around again in the specified sequence and angle tighten the bolts through the specified stage 3 angle.
30 Refit the injector pipes to the engine unit and tighten the union nuts to the specified torque setting (see Chapter 4).
31 Ensure the wiring is correctly routed and reconnect the connectors to the coolant temperature sensors. Reconnect the glow plug wiring and securely tighten its retaining nut.

32 Reconnect all coolant hoses to the cylinder head and thermostat housing, ensuring each one is securely held by its retaining clip.
33 Refit the bolts securing the timing belt cover to the cylinder head and tighten them to the specified torque.
34 Refit the camshaft sprocket and timing belt as described in Sections 7 and 8.
35 Refit the inlet and exhaust manifolds as described in Chapter 4.
36 On completion refill the cooling system as described in Chapter 1.

13 Sump - removal and refitting

Removal

1 Disconnect the battery negative terminal.
2 Firmly apply the handbrake then jack up the front of the car and support it on axle stands. Where necessary, undo the retaining screws and remove the undercover from beneath the engine/transmission unit.
3 Drain the engine oil as described in Chapter 1, then fit a new sealing washer and refit the drain plug, tightening it to the specified torque.
4 Slacken and remove the bolts securing the sump lower pan to the main casting then remove the sump pan from underneath the vehicle **(see illustration)**.
5 To remove the main casting from the engine, remove the exhaust system front pipe as described in Chapter 4.

13.4 If the lower pan is stuck to the main casting, carefully ease it away using a wide-bladed scraper

12.28 Use an angle-tightening gauge to ensure accuracy when tightening the cylinder head bolts

2C

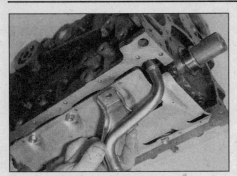

13.8 Removing the oil pump pick-up/strainer

13.10 On refitting fit a new sealing ring to the oil pump pick-up/strainer

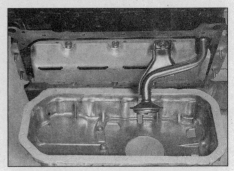

13.11 Apply a coat of sealant to the main casting upper surface prior to refitting

6 Undo the retaining bolts and remove the flywheel lower cover plate from the base of the transmission unit.

7 Progressively slacken and remove the nuts and bolts securing the main casting to the base of the cylinder block/oil pump cover. Break the joint by striking the casting with the palm of the hand, then lower it away from the engine and withdraw it from underneath the vehicle.

8 While the sump main casting is removed, take the opportunity to check the oil pump pick-up/strainer for signs of clogging or splitting. If necessary, unbolt the pick-up/strainer and remove it from the engine along with its sealing ring **(see illustration)**. The strainer can then be cleaned easily in solvent or renewed.

Refitting

9 Remove all traces of dirt and oil from the mating surfaces of the sump main casting and pan, the cylinder block and (where removed) the pick-up/strainer.

10 Where necessary, fit a new sealing ring to the oil pump pick-up/strainer and fit the strainer to the base of the cylinder block **(see illustration)**. Refit the strainer retaining bolt and tighten it to the specified torque.

11 Ensure the main casting and cylinder block mating surfaces are clean and dry and apply a coat of suitable sealant to the upper mating surface of the casting **(see illustration)**.

12 Offer up the main casting and loosely refit all the retaining nuts and bolts. Working out from the centre in a diagonal sequence,

progressively tighten the main casting retaining bolts to the specified torque setting.

13 Refit the flywheel lower cover plate and tighten its retaining bolts to the specified torque.

14 Refit the exhaust front pipe as described in Chapter 4.

15 Ensure the main casting and sump pan mating surfaces are clean and dry and apply a coat of suitable sealant to the upper mating surface of the pan. Refit the pan to the base of the main casting and tighten its retaining bolts to the specified torque.

16 Lower the vehicle to the ground then fill the engine with fresh oil, with reference to Chapter 1.

14 Oil pump - removal, inspection and refitting

Removal

Note: *Two valves control the flow and pressure of oil in the engine's lubricating system. Both are screwed into the rear of the cylinder block on its right-hand (timing belt) end and both will be difficult to reach as they are hidden behind the injection pump. The pressure relief (safety) valve is in fact behind the pump's mounting bracket, while the oil pressure (regulator) valve is located underneath the pump, just to the right of its mounting bracket. Both valves can therefore be serviced independently of the oil pump (see paragraph 7 below).*

1 Remove the timing belt as described in Section 7.

2 Remove the oil pump and crankshaft timing belt sprockets as described in Section 8.

3 Remove the sump main casting as described in Section 13.

4 Slacken and remove the retaining bolts then slide the oil pump cover off of the end of the crankshaft, taking great care not to lose the locating dowels. Remove the sealing ring which is fitted around the oil pump housing section of the cover and discard it.

5 Using a suitable marker pen, mark the surface of the pump outer rotor; the mark can then be used to ensure the rotor is refitted the correct way around.

6 Remove the oil pump inner and outer rotors from the cylinder block **(see illustrations)**.

7 Where necessary, unscrew the oil pressure (regulator) valve - take the necessary precautions to collect the oil which will escape **(see illustration)**. Collect the sealing washer. In the case of the pressure relief (safety) valve, remove first the injection pump's mounting bracket as described in Chapter 4B, then remove the valve in the same way.

Inspection

8 Clean the components, and carefully examine the rotors, pump housing and cover for any signs of scoring or wear. Renew any component which shows signs of wear or damage. If the pump housing in the cylinder block is marked then seek the advice of a Vauxhall dealer on the best course of action.

9 If the components appear serviceable, fit the rotors into the housing and measure the

14.6a Remove the oil pump inner rotor . . .

14.6b . . . and outer rotor from the cylinder block

14.7 Removing the oil pressure (regulator) valve

14.9a Using a feeler blade to measure inner rotor tip-to-outer rotor clearance

14.9b Checking outer rotor-to-pump housing clearance with a feeler blade

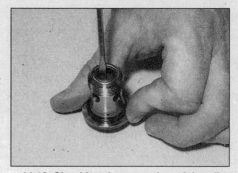

14.10 Checking the operation of the oil pressure (regulator) valve

clearance between the outer rotor and pump housing, and the inner rotor tip-to-outer rotor clearance using feeler blades **(see illustrations)**. Also measure the rotor endfloat, and check the flatness of the end cover. If the clearances exceed the specified tolerances, renew the worn components.

10 If either of the valves has been removed, clean carefully its component parts. Check that the valve piston moves freely and returns easily, with no signs of sticking, under spring pressure – especially in the case of the oil pressure valve **(see illustration)**. If this is not the case, renew the valve complete.

Refitting

11 If either valve has been removed, fit a new sealing washer and refit the valve to the cylinder block, tightening it to the specified torque wrench setting.

12 Lubricate the pump rotors with clean engine oil and refit them to the pump housing, using the mark made prior to removal to ensure the outer rotor is fitted the correct way around.

13 Prior to refitting, carefully lever out the crankshaft and oil pump oil seals using a flat-bladed screwdriver. Fit the new oil seals, ensuring that each seals sealing lip is facing inwards, and press them squarely into the housing using a tubular drift which bears only on the hard outer edge of the seal. Press each seal into position so that it is flush with the housing then lubricate the oil seal lips with clean engine oil.

14 Ensure the mating surfaces of the oil pump and cylinder block are clean and dry and the locating dowels are in position. Remove all traces of sealant from the threads of the pump cover bolts.

15 Apply a smear of sealant to the oil pump cover mating surface. Coat the new oil pump sealing ring with the same sealant and seat the sealing ring in the cover groove **(see illustration)**.

16 Carefully manoeuvre the oil pump cover into position, taking great care not to damage the oil seal lips on the crankshaft and inner rotor shaft. Locate the cover on the dowels making sure the pump sealing ring remains correctly positioned.

17 Apply a smear of sealant to the threads of each cover retaining bolt then refit all bolts and tighten them to the specified torque.

18 Refit the timing belt sprockets and belt as described in Sections 7 and 8 then refit the sump as described in Section 13.

19 On completion refill the engine with clean oil as described in Chapter 1.

15 Oil pump seal - renewal

1 Remove the oil pump sprocket as described in Section 8.

2 Carefully punch or drill two small holes opposite each other in the oil seal. Screw a self-tapping screw into each, and pull on the screws with pliers to extract the seal.

Caution: Great care must be taken to avoid damage to the oil pump

3 Clean the seal housing, and polish off any burrs or raised edges which may have caused the seal to fail in the first place.

4 Lubricate the lips of the new seal with clean engine oil, and press it into position using a suitable tubular drift (such as a socket) which bears only on the hard outer edge of the seal. Take care not to damage the seal lips during fitting; note that the seal lips should face inwards.

5 Refit the oil pump sprocket as described in Section 8.

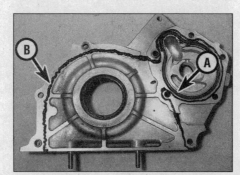

14.15 Coat the pump cover sealing ring (A) with sealant and apply a smear of sealant to the cover mating surface (B)

16 Oil cooler - removal and refitting

Removal

1 Firmly apply the handbrake, then jack up the front of the vehicle and support it on axle stands. Where necessary, undo the retaining screws and remove the undercover to gain access to the oil cooler which is situated on the rear of the cylinder block.

2 Drain the cooling system as described in Chapter 1. Alternatively, clamp the oil cooler coolant hoses directly above the cooler, and be prepared for some coolant loss as the hoses are disconnected.

3 Position a suitable container beneath the oil filter. Unscrew the filter using an oil filter removal tool if necessary, and drain the oil into the container. If the oil filter is damaged or distorted during removal, it must be renewed. Given the low cost of a new oil filter relative to the cost of repairing the damage which could result if a re-used filter springs a leak, it is probably a good idea to renew the filter in any case.

4 Release the clips and disconnect the coolant hoses from the oil cooler.

5 Note the correct fitted location of the oil cooler unions then unscrew the centre bolt and remove the cooler from the cylinder block. Discard the oil cooler sealing ring; a new one must be used on refitting.

Refitting

6 Fit a new sealing ring to the recess in the rear of the cooler, then offer the cooler to the cylinder block.

7 Ensure that the oil cooler unions are correctly positioned, then refit the centre bolt and tighten it to the specified torque.

8 Reconnect the coolant hoses to the cooler and secure them in position with the retaining clips.

9 Fit the oil filter, then lower the vehicle to the ground. Top-up the engine oil level as described in Chapter 1.

2C

17.2 Fabricate a locking tool similar to that shown to retain the flywheel

17.3 Remove the retaining bolts and lift off the retaining plate

17.10 Use an angle-tighten gauge to ensure accuracy when tightening the flywheel bolts

10 Refill or top-up the cooling system as described in Chapter 1 (as applicable). Start the engine, and check the oil cooler for signs of leakage.

17 Flywheel -
removal, inspection and refitting

Note: *New flywheel retaining bolts will be required on refitting.*

Removal

1 Remove the transmission as described in Chapter 7 then remove the clutch assembly as described in Chapter 6.
2 Prevent the flywheel from turning by locking the ring gear teeth with a similar arrangement to that shown **(see illustration)**. Alternatively, bolt a strap between the flywheel and the cylinder block/crankcase. Make alignment marks between the flywheel and crankshaft using paint or a suitable marker pen.
3 Slacken and remove the retaining bolts and retaining plate then remove the flywheel **(see illustration)**. Do not drop it, as it is very heavy.

Inspection

4 Examine the flywheel for wear or chipping of the ring gear teeth. Renewal of the ring gear is possible but is not a task for the home mechanic; renewal requires the new ring gear to be heated (up to 180° to 230°C) to allow it to be fitted.
5 Examine the flywheel for scoring of the clutch face. If the clutch face is scored, the flywheel may be surface-ground, but renewal is preferable.
6 If there is any doubt about the condition of the flywheel, seek the advice of a Vauxhall dealer or engine reconditioning specialist.

They will be able to advise if it is possible to recondition it or whether renewal is necessary.

Refitting

7 Clean the mating surfaces of the flywheel and crankshaft.
8 Apply a drop of locking compound to the threads of each of the new flywheel retaining bolts then refit the flywheel and retaining plate and install the new bolts. If the original is being refitted align the marks made prior to removal.
9 Lock the flywheel using the method employed on dismantling then, working in a diagonal sequence, evenly and progressively tighten the retaining bolts to the specified stage 1 torque setting.
10 Once all bolts have been tightened to the stage 1 torque, go around and tighten all bolts through the specified stage 2 angle. It is recommended that an angle-measuring gauge is used during the final stages of the tightening, to ensure accuracy **(see illustration)**. If a gauge is not available, use white paint to make alignment marks prior to tightening; the marks can then be used to check that the bolt has been rotated through the correct angle.
11 Refit the clutch as described in Chapter 6 then remove the locking tool and refit the transmission as described in Chapter 7.

18 Crankshaft oil seals -
renewal

Right-hand (timing belt end) oil seal

1 Remove the crankshaft sprocket as described in Section 8.

2 Carefully punch or drill two small holes opposite each other in the oil seal. Screw a self-tapping screw into each and pull on the screws with pliers to extract the seal.
3 Clean the seal housing and polish off any burrs or raised edges which may have caused the seal to fail in the first place.
4 Lubricate the lips of the new seal with clean engine oil and ease it into position on the end of the shaft. Press the seal squarely into position until it is flush with the housing. If necessary, a suitable tubular drift, such as a socket, which bears only on the hard outer edge of the seal can be used to tap the seal into position. Take great care not to damage the seal lips during fitting and ensure that the seal lips face inwards.
5 Wash off any traces of oil, then refit the crankshaft sprocket as described in Section 8.

Left-hand (flywheel end) oil seal

6 Remove the flywheel as described in Section 17.
7 Renew the seal as described in paragraphs 2 to 4.
8 Refit the flywheel as described in Section 17.

19 Engine/transmission mountings -
inspection and renewal

Refer to Chapter 2D, Section 17.

Chapter 2 Part D:
2.0 litre diesel engine in-car repair procedures

Contents

Degrees of difficulty

Easy, suitable for novice with little experience		**Fairly easy,** suitable for beginner with some experience		**Fairly difficult,** suitable for competent DIY mechanic		**Difficult,** suitable for experienced DIY mechanic		**Very difficult,** suitable for expert DIY or professional	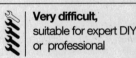

Specifications

General

Engine type	Four-cylinder, in-line, water-cooled. Single overhead camshaft, chain-driven, acting on hydraulic tappets
Manufacturer's engine code:	
Low-pressure turbo model	X20DTL
High-pressure turbo model	X20DTH
Bore	84 mm
Stroke	90 mm
Capacity	1994 cc
Injection sequence	1-3-4-2 (No 1 cylinder at timing chain end of engine)
Direction of crankshaft rotation	Clockwise (viewed from timing chain end of engine)
Compression ratio	18.5:1
Maximum power:	
Low-pressure turbo model	60 kW at 4300 rpm
High-pressure turbo model	74 kW at 4300 rpm
Maximum torque:	
Low-pressure turbo model	185 Nm at 1800 to 2500 rpm
High-pressure turbo model	205 Nm at 1600 to 2750 rpm

Compression pressures

Standard	25 to 28 bar (363 to 406 psi)
Maximum difference between any two cylinders	1 bar (15 psi)

Camshaft

Endfloat	0.04 to 0.14 mm
Maximum permissible radial run-out	0.06 mm
Cam lift (inlet and exhaust)	8.0 mm

Lubrication system

Oil pump type	Gear-type, driven directly from crankshaft
Minimum permissible oil pressure at idle speed, with engine at operating temperature (oil temperature of at least 80°C)	1.5 bar (22 psi)

2D

Torque wrench settings

	Nm	lbf ft
Auxiliary drivebelt tensioner assembly bolts:		
Pulley backplate pivot bolt	42	31
Strut mounting bolts	23	17
Camshaft bearing cap bolts	20	15
Camshaft cover bolts	8	6
Camshaft sprocket bolt: *		
Stage 1	90	66
Stage 2	Angle-tighten a further 60°	
Stage 3	Angle-tighten a further 30°	
Connecting rod big-end bearing cap bolt: *		
Stage 1	35	26
Stage 2	Angle-tighten a further 45°	
Stage 2	Angle-tighten a further 15°	
Crankshaft pulley bolt: *		
Stage 1	150	111
Stage 2	Angle-tighten a further 45°	
Stage 3	Angle-tighten a further 15°	
Cylinder head bolts: *		
Stage 1	25	18
Stage 2	Angle-tighten a further 65°	
Stage 3	Angle-tighten a further 65°	
Stage 4	Angle-tighten a further 65°	
Stage 5	Angle-tighten a further 65°	
Stage 6	Angle-tighten a further 15°	
Cylinder head-to-timing chain cover/block bolts	20	15
Engine/transmission mounting bolts:		
Right-hand mounting:		
Mounting-to-bracket/subframe nuts	45	33
Bracket-to-engine bolts	60	44
Upper bracket nuts	45	33
Left-hand mounting:		
Mounting-to-bracket/subframe nuts	45	33
Bracket-to-transmission bolts	60	44
Rear mounting:		
Mounting-to-bracket bolts	45	33
Mounting-to-subframe bolts	20	15
Bracket-to-transmission bolts	60	44
Engine-to-transmission unit bolts:		
M8 bolts	20	15
M10 bolts	40	30
M12 bolts	60	44
Flywheel bolts: *		
Stage 1	45	33
Stage 2	Angle-tighten a further 30°	
Stage 3	Angle-tighten a further 15°	
Injection pump sprocket bolts	20	15
Injection pump sprocket cover bolts	6	4
Main bearing cap bolts: *		
Stage 1	90	66
Stage 2	Angle-tighten a further 60°	
Stage 3	Angle-tighten a further 15°	
Main bearing ladder casting bolts	20	15
Oil pump:		
Oil pressure relief valve bolt	60	44
Pump cover screws	8	6
Pump pick-up/strainer bolts	8	6
Safety valve bolt	45	33
Cylinder block oil spray nozzle bolts	22	16
Sump bolts:		
Sump to cylinder block/timing chain cover bolts	20	15
Sump flange-to-transmission bolts:		
M8 bolts	20	15
M10 bolts	40	30
Drain plug	18	13
Roadwheel bolts	110	81
Timing chain cover bolts	20	15
Timing chain guide bolts	8	6
Timing chain tensioner blade pivot bolt	20	15
Timing chain tensioner cap	60	44

* **Note:** *The manufacturer states that all fasteners secured by the angle-tightening method must be renewed as a matter of course.*

1 General information

How to use this Chapter

1 This Part of Chapter 2 describes those repair procedures that can reasonably be carried out on the 2.0 litre diesel engine while it remains in the car. If the engine has been removed from the car and is being dismantled as described in Part E, any preliminary dismantling procedures can be ignored.

2 Note that, while it may be possible physically to overhaul items such as the piston/connecting rod assemblies while the engine is in the car, such tasks are not normally carried out as separate operations. Usually, several additional procedures (not to mention the cleaning of components and of oilways) have to be carried out. For this reason, all such tasks are classed as major overhaul procedures, and are described in Part E of this Chapter.

3 Part E describes the removal of the engine/transmission unit from the vehicle, and the full overhaul procedures that can then be carried out.

Engine description

4 The 2.0 litre (1994 cc) engine is a completely new engine designed by Vauxhall. It is of the sixteen-valve, in-line four-cylinder, single overhead camshaft (SOHC) type, mounted transversely at the front of the car with the transmission attached to its left-hand end.

5 The crankshaft runs in five main bearings. Thrustwashers are fitted to No 3 main bearing to control crankshaft endfloat.

6 The connecting rods rotate on horizontally-split bearing shells at their big-ends. The pistons are attached to the connecting rods by gudgeon pins, which are a sliding fit in the connecting rod small-end eyes being retained by circlips. The aluminium-alloy pistons are fitted with three piston rings - two compression rings and an oil control ring.

7 The cylinder block is made of cast iron and the cylinder bores are an integral part of the block. On this type of engine the cylinder bores are sometimes referred to as having dry liners.

8 The inlet and exhaust valves are each closed by coil springs, and operate in guides pressed into the cylinder head.

9 The camshaft is driven by the crankshaft via a dual timing chain arrangement; the lower timing chain links the crankshaft to the fuel injection pump and the upper chain links the injection pump to the camshaft. The camshaft rotates directly in the head and operates the sixteen valves via followers and hydraulic tappets. The followers are situated directly below the camshaft, each one operating two valves. Valve clearances are automatically adjusted by the hydraulic tappets.

10 Lubrication is by means of an oil pump, which is driven off the right-hand end of the crankshaft. It draws oil through a strainer located in the sump, and then forces it through an externally-mounted filter into galleries in the cylinder block/crankcase. From there, the oil is distributed to the crankshaft (main bearings) and camshaft. The big-end bearings are supplied with oil via internal drillings in the crankshaft, while the camshaft bearings also receive a pressurised supply. The camshaft lobes and valves are lubricated by splash, as are all other engine components. An oil cooler is fitted to keep the oil temperature stable under arduous operating conditions.

Repair operations possible with the engine in the car

11 The following work can be carried out with the engine in the car:

a) Compression pressure - testing.
b) Camshaft cover - removal and refitting.
c) Timing chain cover - removal and refitting.
d) Timing chains - removal and refitting.
e) Timing chain tensioners, guides and sprockets - removal and refitting.
f) Camshaft and followers - removal, inspection and refitting.
g) Cylinder head - removal and refitting.
h) Connecting rods and pistons - removal and refitting*.
i) Sump - removal and refitting.
j) Oil pump - removal, overhaul and refitting.
k) Oil cooler - removal and refitting.
l) Crankshaft oil seals - renewal.
m) Engine/transmission mountings - inspection and renewal.
n) Flywheel - removal, inspection and refitting.

* Although the operation marked with an asterisk can be carried out with the engine in the car after removal of the sump, it is better for the engine to be removed, in the interests of cleanliness and improved access. For this reason, the procedure is described in Chapter 2E.

2 Compression test - description and interpretation

Compression test

Note: A compression tester specifically designed for diesel engines must be used for this test.

1 When engine performance is down, or if misfiring occurs which cannot be attributed to the fuel system, a compression test can provide diagnostic clues as to the engine's condition. If the test is performed regularly, it can give warning of trouble before any other symptoms become apparent.

2 A compression tester specifically intended for diesel engines must be used, because of the higher pressures involved. The tester is connected to an adapter which screws into the glow plug or injector hole. On these models,

an adapter suitable for use in the glow plug holes will be required, due to the design of the injectors. It is unlikely to be worthwhile buying such a tester for occasional use, but it may be possible to borrow or hire one - if not, have the test performed by a garage.

3 Unless specific instructions to the contrary are supplied with the tester, observe the following points:

a) *The battery must be in a good state of charge, the air filter must be clean, and the engine should be at normal operating temperature.*
b) *All the glow plugs should be removed before starting the test (see Chapter 5).*
c) *Release the retaining clip and disconnect the wiring connector from the fuel injection pump control unit (see Chapter 4) to prevent the engine from running or fuel from being discharged.*

4 There is no need to hold the accelerator pedal down during the test, because the diesel engine air inlet is not throttled.

5 Crank the engine on the starter motor; after one or two revolutions, the compression pressure should build up to a maximum figure, and then stabilise. Record the highest reading obtained.

6 Repeat the test on the remaining cylinders, recording the pressure in each.

7 All cylinders should produce very similar pressures; any difference greater than that specified indicates the existence of a fault. Note that the compression should build up quickly in a healthy engine; low compression on the first stroke, followed by gradually-increasing pressure on successive strokes, indicates worn piston rings. A low compression reading on the first stroke, which does not build up during successive strokes, indicates leaking valves or a blown head gasket (a cracked head could also be the cause). Deposits on the undersides of the valve heads can also cause low compression.

Note: *The cause of poor compression is less easy to establish on a diesel engine than on a petrol one. The effect of introducing oil into the cylinders ('wet' testing) is not conclusive, because there is a risk that the oil will sit in the swirl chamber or in the recess on the piston crown instead of passing to the rings.*

8 On completion of the test, reconnect the injection pump wiring connector then refit the glow plugs as described in Chapter 5.

Leakdown test

9 A leakdown test measures the rate at which compressed air fed into the cylinder is lost. It is an alternative to a compression test, and in many ways it is better, since the escaping air provides easy identification of where pressure loss is occurring (piston rings, valves or head gasket).

10 The equipment needed for leakdown testing is unlikely to be available to the home mechanic. If poor compression is suspected, have the test performed by a suitably-equipped garage.

2D

3.6a When No 1 cylinder is at TDC on its compression stroke, its camshaft lobes (arrowed) will be pointing upwards . . .

3.6b . . . and the timing hole (arrowed) on the left-hand end of the camshaft will be at the top

3 Top dead centre (TDC) for No 1 piston - locating

1 In its travel up and down its cylinder bore, Top Dead Centre (TDC) is the highest point that each piston reaches as the crankshaft rotates. While each piston reaches TDC both at the top of the compression stroke and again at the top of the exhaust stroke, for the purpose of timing the engine, TDC refers to the piston position (usually number 1) at the top of its compression stroke.

2 Number 1 piston (and cylinder) is at the right-hand (timing chain) end of the engine, and its TDC position is located as follows. Note that the crankshaft rotates clockwise when viewed from the right-hand side of the car.

3 Disconnect the battery negative terminal. To improve access to the crankshaft pulley, apply the handbrake, then jack up the front of the vehicle and support it on axle stands.

4 To check the position of the camshaft either remove the camshaft cover (Section 5), so that the position of the cam lobes can be seen, or remove the braking system vacuum pump (Chapter 9) so the timing hole on the camshaft end can be seen.

5 Using a socket and extension bar on the crankshaft pulley bolt, rotate the crankshaft until the notch on the crankshaft pulley rim is aligned with the mark on the timing chain cover. Once the mark is correctly aligned, No 1 and 4 pistons are at TDC.

6 To determine which piston is at TDC on its compression stroke, check the position of the camshaft lobes/timing hole (as applicable). When No 1 piston is at TDC on its compression stroke, No 1 cylinder camshaft lobes will be pointing upwards and the timing hole on the left-hand of the camshaft will be at the top (12 o'clock position) with the camshaft slot parallel with the head surface (see illustrations). If No 1 cylinder camshaft lobes are pointing downwards and the camshaft end timing mark is at the bottom (6 o'clock position) then No 4 cylinder is at TDC on its compression stroke; rotate the crankshaft through a further complete turn (360°) to bring No 1 cylinder to TDC on its compression stroke.

7 With No 1 piston at TDC on its compression stroke, if necessary, the crankshaft can be locked in position by inserting a pin in through the crankshaft sensor bore on the front of the cylinder block. If access to the special Vauxhall tool (KM-929) cannot be gained, a home-made alternative will have to be manufactured (see Section 4). Remove the crankshaft sensor (see Chapter 4) and insert the pin, making sure it is correctly located in the crankshaft web slot (see illustrations).

4 Valve timing - checking and adjustment

Note: To check the valve (and fuel injection pump) timing, it will be necessary to use the following Vauxhall special tools (or suitable equivalents); the camshaft locking tool (KM-932), the injection pump flange locking pin (KM-927), the crankshaft locking pin (KM-929) and the camshaft sprocket wrench (KM-933). If access to these tools cannot be gained, this task must be entrusted to a Vauxhall dealer. If the necessary facilities are available to manufacture home-made tools, the dimensions of the locking pins are given in the accompanying illustrations (see illustrations). The camshaft locking tool (also pictured) ensures that the camshaft remains correctly positioned by keeping the camshaft slot parallel to the cylinder head surface.

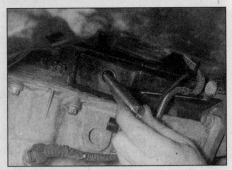

3.7a Remove the crankshaft sensor from the cylinder block and insert the locking pin . . .

3.7b . . . making sure it is correctly engaged with the crankshaft cut-out (arrowed - shown with sump removed)

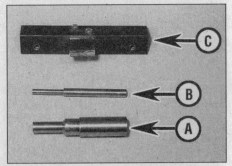

4.1a Home-made tools necessary to check/adjust the valve timing

A Crankshaft locking pin
B Injection pump flange locking pin
C Camshaft locking tool

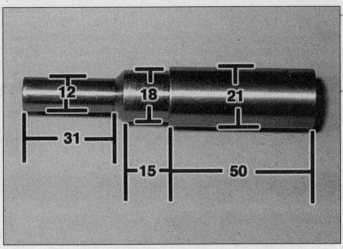

4.1b Crankshaft locking pin dimensions (in mm)

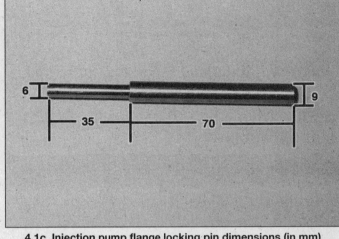

4.1c Injection pump flange locking pin dimensions (in mm)

1 Remove the auxiliary drivebelt as described in Chapter 1. Undo the auxiliary drivebelt tensioner pulley strut lower mounting bolt and the pulley backplate pivot bolt and remove the tensioner assembly from the engine. **Note:** *Store the assembly so the tensioner strut is the correct way up; if the strut is not stored properly it will have to be primed once it is refitted.*

2 Remove the braking system vacuum pump as described in Chapter 9.

3 To improve access to the injection pump sprocket cover and the pump, carry out the following.

a) *Remove the air cleaner housing and exhaust system front pipe (see Chapter 4).*

b) *Undo the nut from the top of the engine/transmission right-hand mounting then raise the right-hand end of the engine using a jack/engine support bar (see Section 17). Raise the engine as high as possible without placing any excess strain on the remaining mountings or any pipes/hoses or wiring.*

4 Remove the camshaft cover and position No 1 cylinder at TDC on it compression stroke as described in Section 3.

5 Remove the crankshaft sensor as described in Chapter 4, Section 10.

6 Undo the retaining screws and remove the injection pump sprocket cover from the timing chain cover.

7 Ensure the crankshaft pulley notch is correctly aligned with the timing chain cover mark then insert the crankshaft locking pin into the crankshaft sensor aperture and engage it with the slot in the crankshaft web **(see illustrations 3.7a and 3.7b).**

8 With the crankshaft locked in position, insert the injection pump flange locking pin into the hole in the flange and engage it with hole in the pump body, then slide the camshaft locking tool into position on the left-hand end of the camshaft **(see illustrations).**

9 If all the locking tools can be correctly fitted the valve timing is correctly set and no adjustment is necessary, proceed as described in paragraphs 21 to 26. If either of the tools can not be inserted, adjust the timing as follows noting that a new camshaft sprocket bolt and tensioner bolt sealing ring will be required.

10 Remove the camshaft/injection pump sprocket locking tool (as applicable) then unbolt the right-hand mounting bracket assembly from the cylinder head.

11 Unscrew the upper timing chain tensioner cap from the rear of the cylinder head and

remove the plunger, noting which way around it is fitted. Remove the sealing ring from the cap and discard it, a new one should be used on refitting.

12 Hold the camshaft, using an open-ended spanner on the flats provided, then slacken and remove the camshaft sprocket retaining bolt. Fit the new bolt, tightening it finger-tight only at this stage.

13 Slacken the bolts securing the injection pump sprocket to the pump flange.

14 With the crankshaft locked in position, ensure the timing mark on the injection pump upper timing chain sprocket is correctly aligned with the pump flange timing hole. Insert the flange locking pin making sure it is correctly seated then tighten the sprocket retaining bolts to the specified torque **(see illustration).**

15 Slide the camshaft locking tool into position making sure its pin engages centrally in the camshaft bore.

16 With all locking tools in position, fit the sprocket wrench to the camshaft sprocket; in the absence of the special wrench, pass two bolts through the sprocket holes and use a screwdriver to lever on the bolts. Have an assistant keep the timing chain taut on its

2D

4.8a Insert the locking pin in through the flange cut-out and engage it in the pump body hole

4.8b Engage the camshaft locking tool with the camshaft cut-out (arrowed)

4.14 Ensure the pump sprocket timing mark (arrowed) is correctly positioned then tighten the sprocket bolts to the specified torque

4.18 Adjust the upper timing chain tension as described in text then tighten the camshaft sprocket bolt to the Stage 1 torque setting

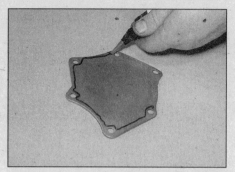

4.21 Apply a bead of sealant to the mating surface of the injection pump sprocket cover mating surface

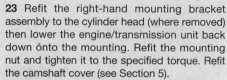

23 Refit the right-hand mounting bracket assembly to the cylinder head (where removed) then lower the engine/transmission unit back down onto the mounting. Refit the mounting nut and tighten it to the specified torque. Refit the camshaft cover (see Section 5).
24 Refit the exhaust front pipe and air cleaner housing as described in the Chapter 4.
25 Refit the vacuum pump to the cylinder head (see Chapter 9).
26 Fit the crankshaft sensor to the cylinder block (see Chapter 4) and reconnect the battery.

---

5 Camshaft cover - removal and refitting

guide (upper) side by applying **slight** pressure to the sprocket; this will ensure all slack in the chain is on the tensioner side of chain.
17 With the upper timing chain tensioned as described, check that the injection pump locking pin slides in and out of position with only a slight amount of drag. If excessive force is needed to move the pin, have your assistant decrease the pressure on the sprocket or if the pin moves easily increase the pressure.
18 Once the upper timing chain is correctly tensioned, retain the camshaft with an open-ended spanner and tighten the camshaft sprocket retaining bolt to the specified stage 1 torque setting **(see illustration)**. Check the injection pump pin action then tighten the bolt through the specified stage 2 angle and finally through the specified stage 3 angle. It is recommended that an angle-measuring gauge is used during the final stages of the tightening, to ensure accuracy. If a gauge is not available, use white paint to make alignment marks between the bolt head and pulley prior to tightening; the marks can then be used to check that the bolt has been rotated through the correct angle.
19 Remove all the locking tools and fit a new sealing ring to the upper timing chain tensioner cap. Insert the plunger into the cylinder head, ensuring its closed end is facing the timing chain, then install the cap

and tighten it to the specified torque. **Note:** *If a new tensioner is being fitted, release it by pushing the cap centre pin fully in until it is heard to 'click', the tensioner pin should then be able to be easily depressed and return smoothly.*
20 Rotate the crankshaft through two complete rotations (720°) in the correct direction of rotation (to bring number 1 piston back to TDC on its compression stroke) and check that all the locking tools can be inserted correctly.
21 Ensure the mating surfaces of the pump sprocket cover and timing chain cover are clean and dry. Where the cover was originally fitted with a gasket, fit the cover with a new gasket and tighten the retaining bolts to the specified torque. If no gasket was fitted, apply a bead of sealant (approximately 2 mm thick) to the cover mating surface then refit the cover and tighten its retaining bolts to the specified torque **(see illustration)**.
22 Refit the auxiliary drivebelt tensioner assembly to the engine unit, tightening the strut and backplate pivot bolts to their specified torque settings. If a new tensioner strut is being fitted, or the original was not stored properly, prime the strut by repeatedly compressing it using a socket on the backplate hexagonal section. Once the strut is functioning correctly, refit the auxiliary drivebelt as described in Chapter 1.

Removal

1 Undo the retaining screws and remove the plastic cover from the top of the camshaft cover **(see illustration)**.
2 Slacken the retaining clip and disconnect the breather hose from the rear of the cover.
3 On low-pressure turbo (X20DTL engine) models slacken the clamp securing the metal pipe to the turbocharger, and the clamp securing the intake duct to the manifold. Undo the two retaining bolts and remove the duct assembly from the engine along with the sealing ring which is fitted between the pipe and turbocharger **(see illustration)**.
4 On all models, carefully unclip the fuel hoses from the right-hand end of the cover and release the glow plug wiring guide from the rear of the cover. Undo the bolt securing the inlet manifold wiring harness tray to the cover.
5 Slacken and remove the camshaft cover retaining bolts along with their sealing washers then lift the camshaft cover and seal away from the cylinder head **(see illustration)**. Examine the cover seal and retaining bolt sealing washers for signs of damage or deterioration and renew if necessary.

Refitting

6 Ensure the cover and cylinder head

5.1 Undo the retaining screws and remove the plastic cover from the engine

5.3 On low-pressure turbo (X20DTL engine) models remove the metal pipe and intake duct linking the turbocharger to the manifold

5.5 Slacken and remove the camshaft cover retaining bolts noting the sealing washer (arrowed) which is fitted to each bolt

5.6 Fit the seal to the camshaft cover groove

5.8a Apply a smear of sealant to the semi-circular cut-out on the right-hand end of the cylinder head . . .

5.8b . . . and to the areas of the cylinder head surface on each side of the left-hand end camshaft cap (arrowed)

surfaces are clean and dry then fit the seal to the cover groove **(see illustration)**.

7 Fit the sealing washers to the retaining bolts, ensuring they are fitted the correct way up. Fit the retaining bolts to the cover making sure the cover seal is held firmly in position by the lower shoulder on each bolt.

8 Apply a smear of sealant to the circular cut-out on the right-hand end of the cylinder head mating surface and the areas of the cylinder head mating surface on either side of the left-hand end of the camshaft **(see illustrations)**.

9 Carefully lower the cover into position and screw in the retaining bolts. Once all bolts are hand-tight, go around and tighten them all to the specified torque setting.

10 Clip the fuel hoses and wiring back into position and reconnect the breather hose to the rear of the cover.

6.5a Slide the crankshaft pulley carefully into position engaging its slot (arrowed) with the Woodruff key . . .

6.5b . . . then fit the retaining bolt and washer

11 On low-pressure turbo models refit the intake duct and pipe, using a new sealing ring, and tighten its retaining clamps and bolts securely.

12 On all models, refit the plastic cover and securely tighten its retaining bolts.

6 Crankshaft pulley - removal and refitting

Note: *A new pulley retaining bolt will be required on refitting.*

Removal

1 Apply the handbrake, then jack up the front of the car and support it on axle stands. Remove the right-hand roadwheel.

2 Remove the auxiliary drivebelt as described in Chapter 1. Prior to removal, mark the direction of rotation on the belt to ensure the belt is refitted the same way around.

3 Slacken the crankshaft pulley retaining bolt. To prevent crankshaft rotation whilst the retaining bolt is slackened, have an assistant select top gear and apply the brakes firmly; if the engine is removed from the vehicle it will be necessary to lock the flywheel (see Section 16).

4 Unscrew the retaining bolt and washer and remove the crankshaft pulley from the end of the crankshaft. Whilst the pulley is removed check the oil seal for signs of wear or damage and, if necessary, renew as described in Section 15.

6.6 Lock the crankshaft then tighten the pulley retaining bolt as described in text

Refitting

5 Carefully locate the crankshaft pulley on the crankshaft end, aligning the pulley slot with the crankshaft key. Slide the pulley fully into position, taking great care not to damage the oil seal, then fit the washer and new retaining bolt **(see illustrations)**.

6 Lock the crankshaft by the method used on removal, and tighten the pulley retaining bolt to the specified stage 1 torque setting then angle-tighten the bolt through the specified stage 2 angle, using a socket and extension bar, and finally through the specified stage 3 angle. It is recommended that an angle-measuring gauge is used during the final stages of the tightening, to ensure accuracy **(see illustration)**. If a gauge is not available, use white paint to make alignment marks between the bolt head and pulley prior to tightening; the marks can then be used to check that the bolt has been rotated through the correct angle.

7 Refit the auxiliary drivebelt as described in Chapter 1 using the mark made prior to removal to ensure the belt is fitted the correct way around.

8 Refit the roadwheel then lower the car to the ground and tighten the wheel bolts to the specified torque.

7 Timing chain cover - removal and refitting

Removal

1 Remove the upper timing chain and sprockets as described in Section 9.

2 Remove the cylinder head as described in Section 11. **Note:** *In theory it is possible to remove the timing chain cover without disturbing the cylinder head. However, this procedure carries a high risk of damaging the head gasket, resulting in oil/coolant leakage once the cover is refitted. If you wish to attempt this, leave the cylinder head in position and just undo the retaining bolts securing the head to the top of the timing chain cover. Be warned though that, after refitting, you may find the head gasket will need renewing, meaning that the cylinder head will have to be*

7.9 Timing chain cover retaining bolt locations (arrowed)

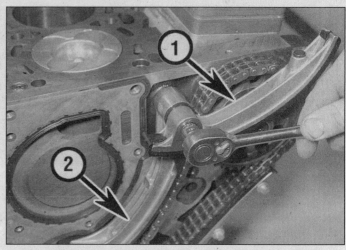

7.11 Unscrew the pivot bolt and remove the upper (1) and lower (2) timing chain tensioner blades

removed after all. The decision is yours as to whether this is a chance worth taking.

3 Remove the coolant pump as described in Chapter 3.

4 Remove the crankshaft pulley as described in Section 6. Prior to slackening the pulley bolt, temporarily remove the locking pin from the crankshaft to prevent damage. Refit the pin once the bolt is loose.

5 Remove the sump as described in Section 12.

6 Remove the alternator as described in Chapter 5.

7 Remove the power steering pump as described in Chapter 10.

7.12 Undo the retaining bolts (arrowed) and remove the lower timing chain guide

8 Unscrew the lower timing chain tensioner cap from the rear of the timing chain cover and remove the tensioner plunger, noting which way around it is fitted. Remove the sealing ring from the cap and discard it, a new one should be used on refitting.

9 Noting each bolts correct fitted location (the bolts are not all the same length), slacken and remove all the bolts securing the timing chain cover to the cylinder block (see illustration).

10 Carefully ease the timing cover squarely away from the cylinder block and manoeuvre it out of position, noting the correct fitted positions of its locating dowels. If the locating dowels are a loose fit, remove them and store with the cover for safe-keeping.

11 Undo the pivot bolt and remove the upper and lower timing chain tensioner blades from the cylinder block (see illustration).

12 Undo the retaining bolts and remove the lower timing chain guide from the cylinder block, noting which way around the guide is fitted (see illustration).

13 Temporarily free the lower timing chain sprocket from the injection pump and manoeuvre the timing chain cover gasket away from the cylinder block. Once the gasket has been removed, seat the sprocket back on the injection pump flange (see illustration).

Refitting

14 Prior to refitting the cover, it is recommended that the crankshaft oil seal should be renewed. Carefully lever the old seal out of the cover using a large flat-bladed screwdriver. Fit the new seal to the cover, making sure its sealing lip is facing inwards. Press/tap the seal into position until it is flush with the cover, using a suitable tubular drift, such as a socket, which bears only on the hard outer edge of the seal.

15 Ensure the mating surfaces of the cover and cylinder block are clean and dry and the locating dowels are in position.

16 Temporarily free the sprocket from the injection pump flange then manoeuvre the gasket into position and locate it on the dowels. Locate the sprocket back on the injection pump flange.

17 Refit the lower timing chain guide to the cylinder block and tighten its retaining bolts to the specified torque. Ensure the guide is fitted the correct way around with its stepped face on the inside (see illustration).

18 Manoeuvre the timing chain tensioner blades into position and refit the pivot bolt, tightening it to the specified torque setting (see illustration).

7.13 Free the sprocket from the injection pump and remove the timing chain cover gasket

7.17 Refit the lower timing chain guide and tighten its retaining bolts to the specified torque

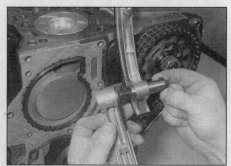

7.18 Refit the pivot bolt to the tensioner blades and tighten to the specified torque

8.3a Unscrew the tensioner cap from the rear of the cylinder head . . .

8.3b . . . and withdraw the plunger, noting which way around it is fitted

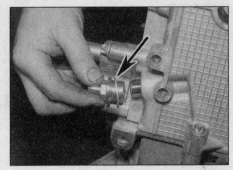

8.6a Insert the plunger, making sure its closed end facing the timing chain, then fit tensioner cap and sealing washer (arrowed)

19 Manoeuvre the timing cover into position. Align the oil pump drive gear with the crankshaft sprocket and slide the cover into position, locating it on the dowels.

20 Refit the timing chain cover retaining bolts, ensuring each one is fitted in its original location, and tighten them evenly and progressively to the specified torque.

21 Fit a new sealing ring to the lower timing chain tensioner cap. Insert the plunger, ensuring its closed end is facing the timing chain, then fit the cap to the timing chain cover and tighten to the specified torque. **Note:** *If a new tensioner is being fitted, release it by pushing the cap centre pin fully in until it is heard to 'click', the tensioner pin should then be able to be easily depressed and return smoothly.*

22 Refit the crankshaft pulley as described in Section 6.

23 Refit the cylinder head as described in Section 11.

24 Refit the upper timing chain and sprockets as described in Section 9.

25 Refit the sump as described in Section 12.

26 Refit the coolant pump, alternator and power steering pump (see Chapter 3, 5 and 10) and refit the auxiliary drivebelt (see Chapter 1).

27 On completion refill the engine with oil and coolant as described in Chapter 1. Start the engine and check for signs of oil leaks.

---

8 Timing chain tensioners - removal and refitting

Upper timing chain tensioner

Removal

1 Remove the air cleaner housing as described in Chapter 4.

2 Referring to Section 17, support the engine/transmission unit and unbolt the right-hand mounting assembly from the cylinder head.

3 Unscrew the tensioner cap from the rear of the cylinder head and remove the plunger, noting which way around it is fitted **(see illustrations)**. Remove the sealing ring from the cap and discard it, a new one should be used on refitting.

Caution: Do not rotate the engine whilst the tensioner is removed.

4 Inspect the tensioner plunger for signs of wear or damage and renew if necessary.

Refitting

5 Lubricate the tensioner plunger with clean engine oil and insert it into the cylinder head. Ensure the plunger is fitted the correct way around with its closed end facing the timing chain.

6 Fit a new sealing ring to the tensioner cap then fit the cap to the cylinder head, tightening it to the specified torque. **Note:** *If a new tensioner is being fitted, release it by pushing the cap centre pin fully in until it is heard to 'click', the tensioner pin should then be able to be easily depressed and return smoothly* **(see illustrations)**.

7 Refit the engine/transmission right-hand mounting assembly (see Section 17).

8 Refit the air cleaner housing as described in Chapter 4.

Lower timing chain tensioner

Removal

9 Firmly apply the handbrake then jack up the front of the vehicle and support it on axle stands.

10 Undo the retaining bolts/clips and remove the engine/transmission undercover (where fitted).

11 Unscrew the tensioner cap from the rear of the timing chain cover and remove the plunger, noting which way around it is fitted. Remove the sealing ring from the cap and discard it, a new one should be used on refitting **(see illustrations)**.

Caution: Do not rotate the engine whilst the tensioner is removed.

12 Inspect the tensioner plunger for signs of wear or damage and renew if necessary.

2D

8.6b If a new tensioner is being fitted, release it by depressing the cap centre pin until it is heard to click

8.11a Slacken and remove the lower timing chain tensioner cap and sealing washer from the rear of the timing chain cover . . .

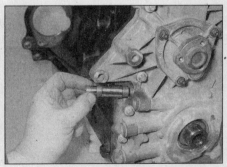

8.11b . . . then withdraw the tensioner plunger

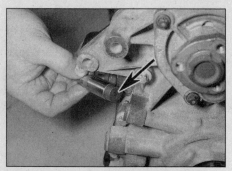

8.13 Ensure the plunger is fitted the correct way around with its closed end (arrowed) facing the timing chain

Refitting

13 Lubricate the tensioner plunger with clean engine oil and insert it into the timing chain cover. Ensure the plunger is fitted the correct way around with its closed end facing the timing chain **(see illustration)**.

14 Fit a new sealing ring to the tensioner cap then fit the cap to the cover, tightening it to the specified torque. **Note:** *If a new tensioner is being fitted, release it by pushing the cap centre pin fully in until it is heard to 'click', the tensioner pin should then be able to be easily depressed and return smoothly* **(see illustration)**.

15 Refit the undercover (where fitted) then lower the vehicle to the ground.

Upper and lower timing chain tensioner blades

16 Tensioner blade removal and refitting is part of the timing chain cover removal and

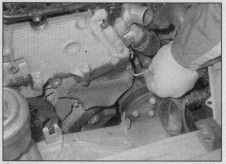

9.6a Undo the retaining screws . . .

9.8a To ease removal, heat the upper timing chain guide bolts with a hot air gun prior to removal

8.14 If a new tensioner is being fitted, release it by depressing the centre pin until it is heard to click

refitting procedure (see Section 7). The blades must be renewed if they show signs of wear or damage on their chain surfaces.

---

9 Timing chains and sprockets - removal, inspection and refitting 🔧

Note: *In order to set the valve timing accurately, several special Vauxhall service tools (or suitable alternatives) are required (see Section 4). If access to suitable tools cannot be gained then it is recommended that this task is entrusted to a Vauxhall dealer or suitably-equipped garage. If the task is to be carried out without the tools then accurate alignment marks must be made between the sprocket(s), chain(s) and the shaft(s) prior to removal to ensure the valve timing is correctly set on refitting.*

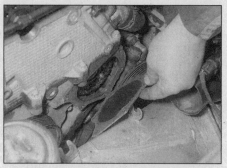

9.6b . . . and remove the injection pump sprocket cover from the engine

9.8b Unscrew both retaining bolts . . .

Note: *A new camshaft sprocket retaining bolt and new upper timing chain guide retaining bolts will be required on refitting.*

Removal

Upper timing chain and sprockets

Note: *A new camshaft sprocket bolt and new timing chain guide retaining bolts will be required on refitting.*

1 Disconnect the battery negative lead then remove the camshaft cover (see Section 5).

2 Position No 1 cylinder at TDC on its compression stroke as described in Section 3 and lock the crankshaft in position.

3 To improve access to the injection pump sprocket cover, carry out the following.
  a) *Remove the air cleaner housing and exhaust system front pipe (see Chapter 4).*
  b) *Remove the auxiliary drivebelt (Chapter 1).*
  c) *Undo the nut from the top of the engine/transmission right-hand mounting then raise the right-hand end of the engine using a jack/engine support bar (see Section 17). Raise the engine as high as possible without placing any excess strain on the remaining mountings or any pipes/hoses or wiring.*

4 Remove both the upper and lower timing chain tensioners as described in Section 8.

5 Undo the auxiliary drivebelt tensioner pulley strut lower mounting bolt and the pulley backplate pivot bolt and remove the tensioner assembly from the engine. **Note:** *Store the assembly so the tensioner strut is the correct way up; if the strut is not stored properly it will have to be primed once it is refitted.*

6 Undo the retaining bolts and remove the injection pump sprocket cover from the timing chain cover **(see illustrations)**.

7 If the special locking tools are available, lock the injection pump sprockets and camshaft in position (see Section 4). If the tools are not being used, make accurate alignment marks between the chain and sprockets, and the sprockets and the camshaft/pump flange.

8 Undo the retaining bolts then lift the upper chain guide out from the top of the cylinder head. **Note:** *The upper timing chain guide bolts should be heated with a hot air gun prior to removal; this loosens the locking compound on the bolt head and significantly eases removal of the bolts* **(see illustrations)**.

9.8c . . . and lift the upper guide out from the top of the cylinder head

9.9 Retain the camshaft with an open-ended spanner and unscrew the sprocket retaining bolt

9.10 Unbolt the sprocket from the injection pump then free it from the chain and remove it through the cover aperture

9.14 Free the sprocket from the injection pump flange and remove it complete with the lower timing chain

9.15a Slide the sprocket off from the end of the crankshaft . . .

9.15b . . . and remove the Woodruff key

9 Hold the camshaft using an open-ended spanner on the flats provided, then slacken and remove the camshaft sprocket retaining bolt **(see illustration)**. To ensure the camshaft sprocket and chain remain correctly mated, cable tie the chain to the sprocket. **Note:** *If the locking tools are being used, remove them prior to slackening the sprocket bolt and refit them once the bolt is loose.*

10 Remove the injection pump locking tool (where fitted) then slacken and remove the bolts securing the injection pump sprockets to the pump flange. Manoeuvre the injection pump upper chain sprocket out of position then free the camshaft sprocket from the camshaft end and lift the sprocket and upper timing chain out from the top of the cylinder head **(see illustration)**.

Lower timing chain and sprockets

11 Remove the upper timing chain and sprockets as described in paragraphs 1 to 10.
12 Remove the timing chain cover as described in Section 7.
13 Make alignment marks between the chain and sprockets and the injection pump sprocket and pump flange.
14 Free the pump sprocket from its flange and remove the sprocket and timing chain from the engine, noting which way around the sprocket is fitted **(see illustration)**.
15 Slide the crankshaft sprocket off from the crankshaft end and recover the Woodruff key from the crankshaft groove **(see illustrations)**.

Inspection

16 Examine the teeth on the sprockets for any sign of wear or damage such as chipped, hooked or missing teeth. If there is any sign of wear or damage on either sprocket, both sprockets and the relevant chain should be renewed as a set.
17 Inspect the links of each timing chain for signs of wear or damage on the rollers. The extent of wear can be judged by checking the amount by which the chain can be bent sideways; a new chain will have very little sideways movement. If there is an excessive amount of side play in a timing chain, it must be renewed.
18 Note that it is a sensible precaution to renew the timing chains, regardless of their apparent condition, if the engine has covered

a high mileage, or if it has been noted that the chain(s) have sounded noisy when the engine running. Although not strictly necessary, it is always worth renewing the chains and sprockets as a matched set, since it is false economy to run a new chain on worn sprockets and *vice-versa*. If there is any doubt about the condition of the timing chains and sprockets, seek the advice of a Vauxhall dealer service department, who will be able to advise you as to the best course of action, based on their previous knowledge of the engine.
19 Examine the chain guide(s) and tensioner blade(s) for signs of wear or damage to their chain contact faces, renewing any which are badly marked.

Refitting

Upper timing chain and sprockets

20 If any new components are being fitted,

9.24 Align the injection pump sprocket timing mark (arrowed) with the pump flange hole and refit the retaining bolts

transfer the alignment marks from the original components to aid refitting. Ensure the crankshaft is still locked in the TDC position.
21 Engage the camshaft sprocket with the chain and lower the assembly into position.
22 Manoeuvre the injection pump sprocket into position and engage it with the timing chain.
23 Ensure the marks made prior to removal are all correctly aligned then engage the sprockets with the camshaft and injection pump flange. Where necessary, remove the cable tie from camshaft sprocket.
24 Align the injection pump sprocket timing mark with the hole in the pump flange then refit the retaining bolts tightening them by hand only at this stage **(see illustration)**.
25 Fit the new sprocket retaining bolt to the camshaft end, tightening by hand only at this stage **(see illustration)**.

9.25 Fit the new camshaft sprocket retaining bolt and tighten it by hand only

2D

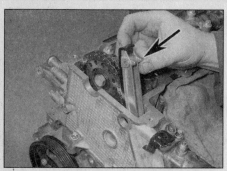

9.27 Refit the upper timing chain guide to the cylinder head making sure its locating lug (arrowed) is uppermost

26 Refit the lower timing chain tensioner as described in Section 8.

27 Slide the upper timing chain guide into position, ensuring its locating lug is uppermost, then fit the new retaining bolts and tighten them to the specified torque **(see illustration)**.

28 If the special tools are available, fit all the tools to ensure the pump, camshaft and crankshaft are correctly positioned. If the tools are not being used, ensure the marks made prior to removal are realigned.

29 If the special tools are available, adjust the valve timing as described in Section 4, paragraphs 14 to 18. Remove all the locking tools.

30 If the tools are not available, align the marks made prior to removal then tighten the injection pump sprocket bolts to the specified torque. Tighten the camshaft sprocket bolt to the specified stage 1 torque setting, whilst preventing the camshaft from rotating. Ensure the marks remain in alignment then tighten the bolt through the specified stage 2 angle and finally through the specified stage 3 angle. It is recommended that an angle-measuring gauge is used during the final stages of the tightening, to ensure accuracy. If a gauge is not available, use white paint to make alignment marks prior to tightening; the marks can then be used to check that the bolt has been rotated through the correct angle.

31 Refit the upper timing chain tensioner as described in Section 8.

32 Ensure the mating surfaces of the pump sprocket cover and timing chain cover are clean and dry. Where the cover was originally fitted with a gasket, fit the cover with a new gasket and tighten the retaining bolts to the specified torque. If no gasket was fitted, apply a bead of sealant (approximately 2 mm thick) to the cover groove then refit the cover and tighten its retaining bolts to the specified torque.

33 Refit the auxiliary drivebelt tensioner assembly to the engine unit, tightening the strut and backplate pivot bolts to their specified torque settings. If a new tensioner strut is being fitted, or the original was not stored properly, prime the strut by repeatedly compressing it using a socket on the backplate hexagonal section. Once the strut is functioning correctly, refit the auxiliary drivebelt as described in Chapter 1.

34 Refit the right-hand mounting assembly to the cylinder head then lower the engine/transmission unit back down onto the right-hand mounting. Refit the mounting nut and tighten it to the specified torque.

35 Refit the camshaft cover as described in Section 5.

36 Refit the exhaust front pipe, air cleaner housing and crankshaft sensor (see Chapter 4). Where the camshaft timing tool has have been used, refit the vacuum pump to the cylinder head (see Chapter 9).

Lower timing chain and sprockets

37 If any new components are being fitted transfer the alignment marks from the original components to aid refitting.

38 Refit the Woodruff key to the crankshaft then slide on the crankshaft sprocket, aligning the sprocket groove with the key.

39 Ensure the injection pump flange is still correctly positioned with the flange timing cut-out aligned with the hole in the pump body and the crankshaft is still locked at TDC.

40 Aligning the marks made prior to removal, engage the pump sprocket with the chain and manoeuvre the assembly into position. Engage the chain with the crankshaft sprocket and seat the pump sprocket on the flange, ensuring the sprocket is fitted the correct way around. Check that all the marks made prior to removal are correctly aligned and that the injection pump flange timing cut-out is correctly position in the oblong slot in the sprocket.

41 Refit the timing cover as described in Section 7 then refit the upper timing chain as described earlier in this Section.

10 Camshaft and followers - removal, inspection and refitting

Note: *A new camshaft sprocket retaining bolt and new upper timing chain guide retaining bolts will be required on refitting.*

Removal

1 Disconnect the battery negative lead then remove the camshaft cover as described in Section 5.

2 Remove the braking system vacuum pump as described in Chapter 9.

3 Position No 1 cylinder at TDC on its compression stroke as described in Section 3 and lock the crankshaft in position.

4 To improve access to the injection pump sprocket cover, carry out the following.

a) *Remove the air cleaner housing and exhaust system front pipe (see Chapter 4).*

b) *Remove the auxiliary drivebelt (see Chapter 1).*

c) *Undo the nut from the top of the engine/transmission right-hand mounting then raise the right-hand end of the engine using a jack/engine support bar (see Section 17). Raise the engine as high as possible without placing any excess strain on the remaining mountings or any pipes/hoses or wiring.*

5 Remove the upper timing chain tensioner as described in Section 8.

6 Undo the auxiliary drivebelt tensioner pulley strut lower mounting bolt and the pulley backplate pivot bolt and remove the tensioner assembly from the engine. **Note:** *Store the assembly so the tensioner strut is the correct way up; if the strut is not stored properly it will have to be primed once it is refitted.*

7 Undo the retaining bolts and remove the injection pump sprocket cover from the timing chain cover.

8 Make accurate alignment marks between the upper timing chain and sprockets, and the camshaft sprocket and camshaft.

9 Undo the retaining bolts then lift the upper chain guide out from the top of the cylinder head **(see illustration)**. **Note:** *The upper timing chain guide bolts should be heated with a hot air gun prior to removal; this loosens the locking compound on the bolt head and significantly eases removal of the bolts.*

10 Hold the camshaft, using an open-ended spanner on the flats provided, then slacken and remove the camshaft sprocket retaining bolt. Remove the crankshaft locking tool prior to slackening the sprocket bolt and refit it once the bolt is loose.

11 Disengage the camshaft sprocket from the upper timing chain and remove it from the engine. Pass a screwdriver or extension bar through the upper chain, to prevent it falling down into the cylinder head, and rest it on the head upper surface **(see illustrations)**.

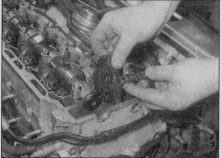

10.9 Remove the retaining bolts (arrowed) and lift out the upper timing chain guide

10.11a Free the camshaft sprocket from the timing chain . . .

10.11b ... then pass a screwdriver or extension bar through the chain to prevent it falling down into the engine

10.12 Each camshaft bearing cap should be stamped with an identification number (arrowed)

10.14 Removing a camshaft follower

12 Note the identification markings on the camshaft bearing caps. The caps are numbered 1 to 5 with all numbers being the right way up when viewed from the front of the engine; number 1 cap being at the timing chain end of the engine and number 5 at the flywheel end (see illustration). If the markings are not clearly visible, make identification marks to ensure each cap is fitted correctly on refitting.

13 Working in a spiral pattern from the outside inwards, slacken the camshaft bearing cap retaining bolts by one turn at a time, to relieve the pressure of the valve springs on the bearing caps gradually and evenly. Once the valve spring pressure has been relieved, the bolts can be fully unscrewed and removed, along with the caps. Take care not to loose the locating dowels which are fitted to left-hand end (No 5) bearing cap and lift the camshaft out from the head.

Caution: If the bearing cap bolts are carelessly slackened, the bearing caps might break. If any bearing cap breaks then the complete cylinder head assembly must be renewed; the bearing caps are matched to the head and are not available separately.

14 Obtain eight (twenty-four if the tappets are also to be removed) small, clean plastic containers, and label them for identification. Alternatively, divide a larger container into compartments. Lift the followers out from the top of the cylinder head and store each one in its respective fitted position (see illustration).

15 If the hydraulic tappets are also to be removed, remove the injector crosspipes as described in Chapter 4. Using a rubber sucker or magnet, withdraw each hydraulic tappet and place it in its container.

Inspection

16 Examine the camshaft bearing surfaces and cam lobes for signs of wear ridges and scoring. Renew the camshaft if any of these conditions are apparent. Examine the condition of the bearing surfaces both on the camshaft journals and in the cylinder head. If the head bearing surfaces are worn excessively, the cylinder head will need to be renewed.

17 Support the camshaft end journals on V-blocks, and measure the run-out at the centre journal using a dial gauge. If the run-out exceeds the specified limit, the camshaft should be renewed.

18 Examine the follower bearing surfaces which contact the camshaft lobes for wear ridges and scoring. Renew any followers on which these conditions are apparent.

19 Check the hydraulic tappets (where removed) and their bores in the cylinder head for signs of wear or damage. If any tappet is thought to be faulty it should be renewed.

Refitting

20 Where removed, lubricate the hydraulic tappets with clean engine oil and carefully insert each one into its original location in the cylinder head (see illustration). Refit the injector crosspipes as described in Chapter 4.

21 Refit the camshaft followers to the cylinder head. Ensure each follower is fitted in its original location and the punch marks on the follower upper surface are facing the injector crosspipe (see illustration).

22 Lubricate the camshaft followers with clean engine oil then lay the camshaft in position. Ensure the crankshaft is still locked in position and position the camshaft so that the lobes of No 1 cylinder are pointing upwards and the slot on the left-hand end of the camshaft is parallel with the cylinder head surface (timing hole at the top) (see illustrations).

2D

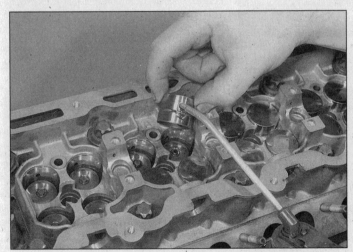

10.20 Lubricate the hydraulic tappets with clean engine oil and install them in the cylinder head

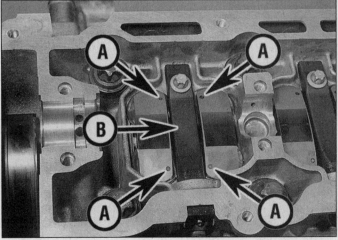

10.21 On refitting ensure that all followers are correctly positioned and that the punch marks (A) are facing towards the injector crosspipe (B)

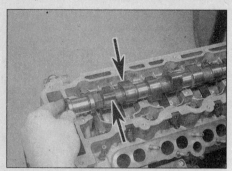

10.22a Refit the camshaft, positioning it so that No 1 cylinder lobes are pointing upwards (arrowed) . . .

10.22b . . . and the slot in its left-hand end is parallel to the cylinder head with the timing hole (arrowed) at the top

10.24 Apply sealant to the areas shown on the left-hand end of the cylinder head (arrowed)

23 Ensure the mating surfaces of the bearing caps and cylinder head are clean and dry and lubricate the camshaft journals and lobes with clean engine oil.

24 Apply a smear of sealant to the cylinder head mating surface of the left-hand (No 5) bearing cap and fit the cap locating dowels to the cylinder head (see illustration).

25 Refit the camshaft bearing caps and the retaining bolts in their original locations on the cylinder head (see illustration). The caps are numbered 1 to 5 from timing chain end of the cylinder head and all numbers should be the right way up when viewed from the front of the engine.

26 Tighten all bolts by hand only then, working in a spiral pattern from the centre outwards, tighten the bolts by one turn at a time to gradually impose the pressure of the valve springs on the bearing caps. Repeat this sequence until all bearing caps are in contact with the cylinder head then go around and tighten the camshaft bearing cap bolts to the specified torque (see illustration).

Caution: If the bearing cap bolts are carelessly tightened, the bearing caps might break. If any bearing cap breaks then the complete cylinder head assembly must be renewed; the bearing caps are matched to the head and are not available separately.

27 Using the marks made on removal, ensure that the upper timing chain is still correctly engaged with the injection pump sprocket then refit the camshaft sprocket to the chain. Seat the sprocket on the end of the camshaft and fit the new retaining bolt (see illustration).

28 Slide the upper timing chain guide into position, ensuring its locating lug is uppermost, then fit the retaining bolts and tighten them to the specified torque.

29 If the special tools are available, adjust the valve timing as described in Section 4, paragraphs 14 to 18. Remove all the locking tools.

30 If the tools are not available, align the marks made prior to removal on the camshaft and sprocket. Hold the camshaft with an open-ended spanner and tighten the sprocket bolt to the specified stage 1 torque setting. Ensure the marks have remained in alignment then tighten the bolt through the specified stage 2 angle and finally through the specified stage 3 angle. It is recommended that an angle-measuring gauge is used during the final stages of the tightening, to ensure accuracy (see illustrations). If a gauge is not available, use white paint to make alignment marks prior to tightening; the marks can then be used to check that the bolt has been rotated through the correct angle.

31 Refit the upper timing chain tensioner as described in Section 8.

32 Ensure the mating surfaces of the pump sprocket cover and timing chain cover are clean and dry. Where the cover was originally fitted with a gasket, fit the cover with a new gasket and tighten the retaining bolts to the specified torque. If no gasket was fitted, apply a bead of sealant (approximately 2 mm thick) to the cover groove then refit the cover and tighten its retaining bolts to the specified torque.

10.25 Refit the camshaft bearing caps using the identification markings to ensure each one is correctly positioned

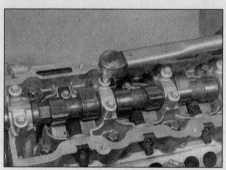

10.26 Working as described in text, tighten the bearing cap bolts to the specified torque

10.27 Refit the camshaft sprocket and install the new retaining bolt

10.30a If the timing tools are not available, align the marks made prior to removal then tighten the sprocket bolt to the stage 1 torque setting . . .

10.30b . . . and then through the specified stage 2 and 3 angles

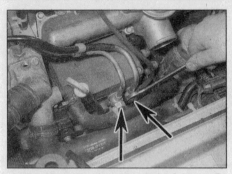

11.3a Unscrew the union bolts (arrowed) then disconnect the fuel feed and return hose unions from the injection pump . . .

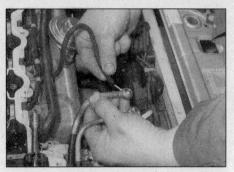

11.3b . . . and disconnect the return pipe

33 Refit the auxiliary drivebelt tensioner assembly to the engine unit, tightening the strut and backplate pivot bolts to their specified torque settings. If a new tensioner strut is being fitted, or the original was not stored properly, prime the strut by repeatedly compressing it using a socket on the backplate hexagonal section. Once the strut is functioning correctly, refit the auxiliary drivebelt as described in Chapter 1.

34 Refit the right-hand mounting assembly to the cylinder head then lower the engine/transmission unit back down onto the right-hand mounting. Refit the mounting nut and tighten it to the specified torque.

35 Refit the camshaft cover as described in Section 5.

36 Refit the exhaust front pipe, air cleaner housing and crankshaft sensor (see Chapter 4).

37 Refit the vacuum pump as described in Chapter 9.

11 Cylinder head - removal and refitting

Caution: Be careful not to allow dirt into the fuel injection pump or injector pipes during this procedure.

Note: *New cylinder head bolts, upper timing chain guide bolts and a camshaft sprocket retaining bolt will be required on refitting.*

Removal

1 Drain the cooling system as described in Chapter 1.

2 Carry out the operations described in paragraphs 1 to 11 of Section 10, noting that it will be necessary to raise the engine on a jack. Support the engine by inserting stout block of wood in between the right-hand end of the sump and the subframe. **Note:** *If the sump needs to be removed at the same time as the head, it will be necessary to fabricate a suitable alternative to the special Vauxhall service tool (KM-909-A). The tool is bolted to the suspension subframe and locates in the hole on the right-hand rear corner of the cylinder block, this supports the weight of the engine whilst the right-hand mounting assembly is removed yet still allows access to the sump.*

3 Wipe clean the area around the fuel hose unions on the injection pump then slacken and remove the union bolts and sealing washers. Disconnect the return pipe from the pump union then releasing the hoses from their retaining clips, and position them clear of the cylinder head **(see illustrations)**.

4 Remove the inlet and exhaust manifolds as described in Chapter 4. If no work is to be carried out on the cylinder head, the head can be removed complete with manifolds once the following operations have been carried out (see Chapter 4).

a) *On high-pressure turbo models, remove the intake ducts and metal pipe from the turbocharger.*

b) *Unbolt the wiring harness tray from the top of the inlet manifold, disconnect the wiring connectors and position it clear of the engine. Unclip the crankshaft sensor wiring from the manifold.*

c) *Remove the injector pipes linking the pump to the injectors.*

d) *Disconnect the vacuum hoses from the inlet manifold switchover valve and the EGR valve.*

e) *Disconnect/unbolt the wiring connectors from the glow plugs then remove the turbocharger heatshields.*

f) *Disconnect the turbocharger oil pipes from the cylinder block. Disconnect the wastegate diaphragm vacuum hose.*

g) *Remove the starter motor heatshield and unbolt the wiring harness guide and exhaust manifold support bracket from the rear of the block.*

5 Release the retaining clips and disconnect the coolant hoses from the front and rear of the right-hand end of the cylinder head **(see illustrations)**.

6 Slacken and remove the alternator upper mounting bolt, and pivot the alternator to the rear to position it clear of the cylinder head **(see illustration)**.

7 Slacken and remove the three bolts securing the right-hand end of the cylinder head to the top of the timing chain cover and the single bolt securing the head to the block **(see illustration)**.

8 Working in the **reverse** of the sequence shown in illustration 11.26, progressively

11.5a Disconnect the coolant hoses (arrowed) from the front of the cylinder head . . .

11.5b . . . and the hose from the rear of the cylinder head

11.6 Remove the upper mounting bolt and pivot the alternator away from the cylinder head

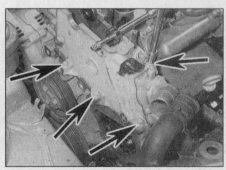

11.7 Unscrew the bolts (arrowed) securing the right-hand end of the cylinder head to the timing chain cover/block

2D

11.10a Lift off the cylinder head . . .

11.10b . . . and remove the gasket from
the block

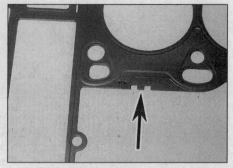

11.17 Cylinder head gasket thickness
identification cut-outs (arrowed)

slacken the ten main cylinder head bolts by half a turn at a time, until all bolts can be unscrewed by hand.

9 Lift out the cylinder head bolts and recover the washers.

10 Lift the cylinder head away; seek assistance if possible, as it is a heavy assembly (especially if complete with manifolds). Remove the gasket, noting the two locating dowels fitted to the top of the cylinder block. If they are a loose fit, remove the locating dowels and store them with the head for safe-keeping. Keep the head gasket for identification purposes (see paragraph 17) (see illustrations).

Caution: Do not lay the head on its lower mating surface; support the head on wooden blocks, ensuring each block only contacts the head mating surface not the glow plugs or injector nozzles. The glow plugs and injector nozzles protrude out the bottom of the head and they will be damaged if the head is placed directly onto a bench.

11 If the cylinder head is to be dismantled for overhaul, then refer to Part E of this Chapter.

Preparation for refitting

12 The mating faces of the cylinder head and cylinder block/crankcase must be perfectly clean before refitting the head. Use a hard plastic or wood scraper to remove all traces of gasket and carbon; also clean the piston crowns. Take particular care, as the surfaces are damaged easily. Also, make sure that the carbon is not allowed to enter the oil and water

passages - this is particularly important for the lubrication system, as carbon could block the oil supply to any of the engine's components. Using adhesive tape and paper, seal the water, oil and bolt holes in the cylinder block/crankcase. To prevent carbon entering the gap between the pistons and bores, smear a little grease in the gap. After cleaning each piston, use a small brush to remove all traces of grease and carbon from the gap, then wipe away the remainder with a clean rag. Clean all the pistons in the same way.

13 Check the mating surfaces of the cylinder block/crankcase and the cylinder head for nicks, deep scratches and other damage. If slight, they may be removed carefully with a file, but if excessive, machining may be the only alternative to renewal.

14 Ensure that the cylinder head bolt holes in the crankcase are clean and free of oil. Syringe or soak up any oil left in the bolt holes. This is most important in order that the correct bolt tightening torque can be applied and to prevent the possibility of the block being cracked by hydraulic pressure when the bolts are tightened.

15 The cylinder head bolts must be discarded and renewed, regardless of their apparent condition.

16 If warpage of the cylinder head gasket surface is suspected, use a straight-edge to check it for distortion. Refer to Part E of this Chapter if necessary.

17 On this engine, the cylinder head-to-piston clearance is controlled by fitting different thickness head gaskets. The gasket

thickness can be determined by looking at the tab situated directly in front of No 1 cylinder (see illustration).

Notches on tab	Gasket thickness
No notches	1.2 mm
One notch	1.3 mm
Two notches	1.4 mm

The correct thickness of gasket required is selected by measuring the piston protrusions as follows.

18 Ensure that the crankshaft is still locked in the TDC position. Mount a dial test indicator securely on the block so that its pointer can be easily pivoted between the piston crown and block mating surface. Zero the dial test indicator on the gasket surface of the cylinder block then carefully move the indicator over No 1 piston and measure its protrusion (see illustration). Repeat this procedure on No 4 piston.

19 Remove the crankshaft locking tool and rotate the crankshaft half a turn (180°) to bring No 2 and 3 pistons to TDC. Ensure the crankshaft is accurately positioned then measure the protrusions of No 2 and 3 pistons. Once both pistons have been measured, rotate the crankshaft through a further one and a half turns (540°) to bring No 1 and 4 pistons back to TDC and lock the crankshaft in position again.

Caution: When rotating the crankshaft, keep the upper timing chain taut to prevent the chain jamming around the injection pump sprocket.

20 Using the largest protrusion measurement of the four pistons, select the correct thickness of head gasket required using the following table.

Piston protrusion measurement	Gasket thickness required
0.40 to 0.50 mm	1.2 mm
0.51 to 0.60 mm	1.3 mm
0.61 to 0.70 mm	1.4 mm

Refitting

21 Wipe clean the mating surfaces of the cylinder head and cylinder block/crankcase.

22 Check that the two locating dowels are in position then fit a new gasket to the cylinder block (see illustration).

11.18 Measuring piston protrusion using
a dial gauge

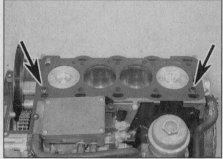

11.22 Ensure the locating dowels are in
position (arrowed) and fit the new gasket

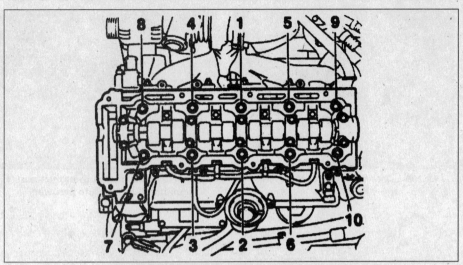

11.26 Cylinder head bolt tightening sequence

23 Ensure the crankshaft is locked in the TDC position and the camshaft is correctly positioned with the lobes of No 1 cylinder pointing upwards and the slot on the left-hand end of the camshaft parallel with the cylinder head surface (timing hole at the top).

24 With the aid of an assistant, carefully refit the cylinder head assembly to the block, aligning it with the locating dowels. As the head is fitted, pass the upper timing chain up through the cylinder head, holding it in position by passing a screwdriver through the upper chain and resting it on the head upper surface.

25 Apply a smear of oil to the threads and the underside of the heads of the new cylinder head bolts and carefully enter each bolt into its relevant hole (*do not drop them in*). Screw all bolts in, by hand only, until finger-tight.

26 Working progressively and in the sequence shown, tighten the cylinder head bolts to their stage 1 torque setting, using a torque wrench and suitable socket **(see illustration)**.

27 Once all bolts have been tightened to the stage 1 torque, working again in the specified sequence, go around and tighten all bolts through the specified stage 2 angle. It is

recommended that an angle-measuring gauge is used to ensure accuracy. If a gauge is not available, use white paint to make alignment marks prior to tightening; the marks can then be used to check that the bolt has been rotated through the correct angle.

28 Go around again in the specified sequence and angle tighten the bolts through the specified stage 3 angle.

29 Working again in the specified sequence, go around and tighten all bolts through the specified stage 4 angle.

30 Go around again in the specified sequence and angle tighten the bolts through the specified stage 5 angle.

31 Finally go around in the specified sequence and angle tighten the bolts through the specified stage 6 angle.

32 Refit the bolts securing the right-hand end of the cylinder head to the block/timing cover and tighten them to the specified torque setting.

33 Pivot the alternator back into position and tighten its upper mounting bolt to the specified torque (Chapter 5).

34 Reconnect the coolant hoses to the cylinder head and secure them in position with the retaining clips.

35 Refit/reconnect the inlet and exhaust manifolds and associated components as described in Chapter 4.

36 Refit the camshaft sprocket to the camshaft as described in paragraphs 27 to 37 of Section 10.

37 Position a new sealing washer on each side of the injection pump fuel hose unions then refit both union bolts and tighten them to the specified torque (Chapter 4).

38 On completion refill the cooling system as described in Chapter 1.

12 Sump - removal and refitting

Removal

1 Disconnect the battery negative terminal.

2 Firmly apply the handbrake then jack up the front of the car and support it on axle stands. Where necessary, undo the retaining screws and remove the undercover from beneath the engine/transmission unit.

3 Drain the engine oil as described in Chapter 1, then fit a new sealing washer and refit the drain plug, tightening it to the specified torque.

4 Disconnect the wiring connector(s) from the oil temperature sensor and (where fitted) the oil level sensor **(see illustration)**.

5 Slacken and remove the bolts securing the sump flange to the transmission housing **(see illustration)**.

6 Progressively slacken and remove the bolts securing the sump to the base of the cylinder block/oil pump. Break the sump joint by striking the sump with the palm of the hand, then lower the sump away from the engine and withdraw it. Remove the gasket and discard it.

7 While the sump is removed, take the opportunity to check the oil pump pick-up/strainer for signs of clogging or splitting. If necessary, unbolt the pick-up/strainer and remove it from the sump along with its sealing ring **(see illustration)**. The strainer can then be cleaned easily in solvent or renewed.

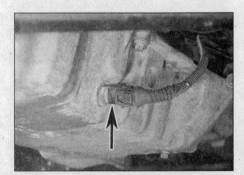

12.4 Disconnect the wiring connector from the oil temperature sensor (arrowed)

12.5 Slacken and remove the bolts securing the sump flange to the transmission housing (lower bolts arrowed)

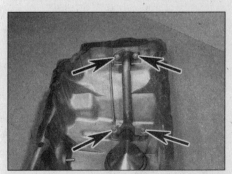

12.7 Oil pump pick-up/strainer retaining bolts (arrowed)

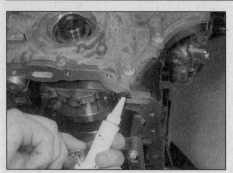

12.10a Apply a smear of sealant to the areas of the cylinder block/timing chain cover joints . . .

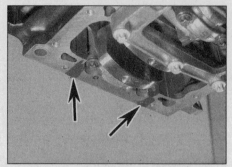

12.10b . . . and the rear main bearing cap/cylinder block joints

12.11 Fit a new gasket to the sump and manoeuvre it up into position

Refitting

8 Remove all traces of dirt and oil from the mating surfaces of the sump and cylinder block and (where removed) the pick-up/strainer.

9 Where necessary, position a new sealing ring on the oil pump pick-up/strainer flange and fit the strainer to the sump, tightening its retaining bolts to the specified torque.

10 Apply a smear of suitable sealant to the areas of the cylinder block mating surface around the oil pump housing and rear main bearing cap joints **(see illustrations)**.

11 Fit a new gasket to the sump then offer up the sump to the cylinder block and loosely refit all the retaining bolts **(see illustration)**.

12 Working out from the centre in a diagonal sequence, progressively tighten the bolts securing the sump to the cylinder block/oil pump to their specified torque setting.

13 Tighten the bolts securing the sump flange to the transmission housing to their specified torque settings.

14 Reconnect the oil temperature/level sensor wiring connector(s) (as applicable). Where necessary refit the undercover.

15 Lower the vehicle to the ground then fill the engine with fresh oil (see Chapter 1).

13 Oil pump - removal, inspection and refitting

Removal

1 The oil pump assembly is built into the timing chain cover. Removal and refitting is as described in Section 7. **Note:** *The oil pump safety valve can be removed with the timing*

chain cover in position on the engine and the pressure relief valve can be removed once the sump has been removed (see below).

Inspection

2 Undo the retaining screws and lift off the pump cover from the inside of the timing chain cover **(see illustration)**.

3 Using a suitable marker pen, mark the surface of both the pump inner and outer rotors; the marks can then be used to ensure the rotors are refitted the correct way around.

4 Lift out the inner and outer rotors from the cover **(see illustrations)**.

5 Unscrew the oil pressure relief valve bolt from the base of the timing chain cover and withdraw the spring, spring sleeve and plunger, noting which way around the plunger is fitted. Remove the sealing ring from the valve bolt **(see illustrations)**.

13.2 Remove the oil pump cover from the rear of the timing chain cover . . .

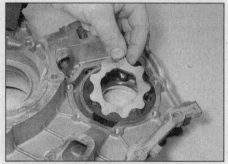

13.4a . . . then lift out the pump inner . . .

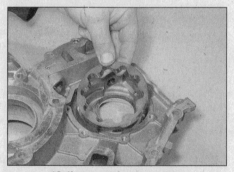

13.4b . . . and outer rotors

13.5a Unscrew the oil pressure relief valve bolt and sealing washer . . .

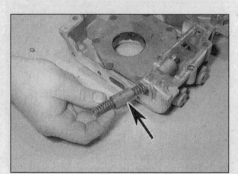

13.5b . . . and withdraw the spring, spring sleeve (arrowed) . . .

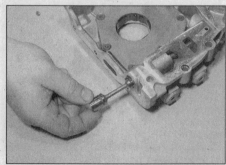

13.5c . . . and plunger from the timing chain cover

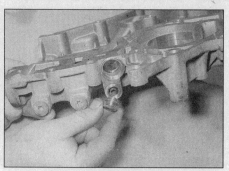

13.6a Unscrew the safety valve bolt and washer . . .

13.6b . . . then remove the spring and valve plunger from the timing chain cover

13.8 On refitting tighten the pump cover screws to the specified torque

6 Unscrew the safety valve bolt from the rear of the timing chain cover, the safety valve is the uppermost of the three bolts on the rear of the cover. Withdraw the spring and plunger from the cover, noting which way around the plunger is fitted **(see illustrations)**. Remove the sealing ring from the valve bolt.

7 Clean the components, and carefully examine the rotors, pump body and valve plungers for any signs of scoring or wear. Renew any component which shows signs of wear or damage; if the rotors or pump housing are marked then the complete pump assembly should be renewed.

8 If the pump is satisfactory, reassemble the components in the reverse order of removal, noting the following.

a) Ensure both rotors and the valve plungers are fitted the correct way around.

b) Fit new sealing rings to the pressure relief valve and safety valve bolts and tighten

both bolts to their specified torque settings.

c) Refit the pump cover tightening the cover screws to the specified torque **(see illustration)**.

d) On completion prime the oil pump by filling it with clean engine oil whilst rotating the inner rotor.

Refitting

9 Refit the timing chain cover as described in Section 7.

14 Oil cooler - removal and refitting

Removal

1 The oil cooler is mounted on the front, left-hand end of cylinder block. On early (pre-

1998) models, the cooler is housed inside the oil filter housing where as on later (1998-on) models it is bolted onto the front of the housing. To improve access, firmly apply the handbrake then jack up the front of the car and support it on axle stands. Where necessary, undo the retaining screws and remove the undercover from beneath the engine/transmission unit.

Early (pre-1998) models

2 To minimise coolant loss, clamp the coolant hoses on either side of the oil cooler then release the retaining clips and detach both hoses. Be prepared for some coolant loss and mop up any spilt coolant.

3 Wipe clean the area around the oil filter housing assembly then undo the retaining bolts and remove the complete housing assembly and gasket from the cylinder block. **Note:** On models with air conditioning, it may be necessary to remove the cooling fan to gain the clearance required to remove the housing (see Chapter 3).

4 Undo the retaining screws and remove the oil cooler cover and seal from the front of the filter housing **(see illustrations)**.

5 Slacken and remove the retaining bolts and washers from the rear of the oil filter housing and remove the oil cooler from the front of the housing, along with its sealing rings **(see illustrations)**.

Later (1998-on) models

6 To minimise coolant loss, clamp the coolant hoses on either side of the oil cooler then release the retaining clips and detach both

2D

14.4a On early models, undo the retaining screws and remove the oil cooler cover . . .

14.4b . . . and seal from the filter housing

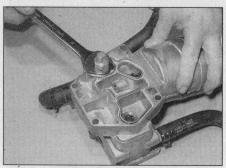

14.5a Slacken and remove the retaining bolts and washers . . .

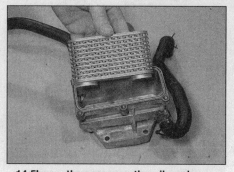

14.5b . . . then remove the oil cooler . . .

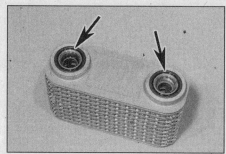

14.5c . . . noting the sealing rings (arrowed) which are fitted to the cooler recesses

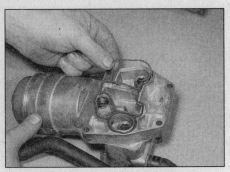

14.8 On early models, on refitting, fit a new seal to the rear of the oil filter housing

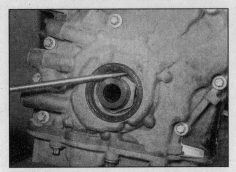

15.2 Lever the right-hand crankshaft oil seal out from the timing chain cover

15.4 Press/tap the new seal squarely into position until it is flush with the cover

hoses. Be prepared for some coolant loss and mop up any spilt coolant.

7 Wipe clean the area around the oil cooler then undo the retaining bolts and remove the cooler and gasket from the oil filter housing.

Refitting

8 Refitting is the reverse of removal, using a new gasket(s) and sealing rings (where fitted) **(see illustration)**.

15 Crankshaft oil seals - renewal

Right-hand (timing chain end) oil seal

1 Remove the crankshaft pulley as described in Section 6.

2 Using a large flat-bladed screwdriver, carefully lever the seal out from the timing chain cover **(see illustration)**.

3 Clean the seal housing and polish off any burrs or raised edges which may have caused the seal to fail in the first place.

4 Lubricate the lips of the new seal with clean

engine oil and press/tap it squarely into position until it is flush with the cover **(see illustration)**. If necessary, a suitable tubular drift, such as a socket, which bears only on the hard outer edge of the seal can be used to tap the seal into position.

5 Wash off any traces of oil, then refit the crankshaft pulley as described in Section 6.

Left-hand (flywheel/driveplate end) oil seal

6 Remove the flywheel as described in Section 16.

7 Carefully punch or drill two small holes opposite each other in the oil seal. Screw a self-tapping screw into each and pull on the screws with pliers to extract the seal **(see illustration)**.

8 Clean the seal housing and polish off any burrs or raised edges which may have caused the seal to fail in the first place.

9 Lubricate the lips of the new seal with clean engine oil and ease it into position on the end of the crankshaft. Press the seal squarely into position until it is flush with the bearing cap. If necessary, a suitable tubular drift, such as a socket, which bears only on the hard outer edge of the seal can be used to tap the seal

into position. Take great care not to damage the seal lips during fitting and ensure that the seal lips face inwards **(see illustration)**.

10 Refit the flywheel as described in Section 16.

16 Flywheel - removal, inspection and refitting

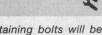

Note: New flywheel retaining bolts will be required on refitting.

Removal

1 Remove the transmission as described in Chapter 7 then remove the clutch assembly as described in Chapter 6.

2 Prevent the flywheel from turning by locking the ring gear teeth with a similar arrangement to that shown **(see illustration)**. Alternatively, bolt a strap between the flywheel and the cylinder block/crankcase. Make alignment marks between the flywheel and crankshaft using paint or a suitable marker pen.

3 Slacken and remove the retaining bolts and remove the flywheel **(see illustration)**. Do not drop it, as it is very heavy.

15.7 Removing the crankshaft left-hand oil seal

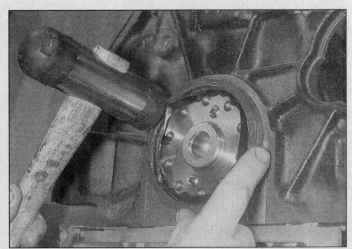

15.9 Carefully ease the new seal over the end of the crankshaft and tap/press it squarely into position

16.2 Lock the flywheel ring gear using a similar tool to that shown . . .

16.3 . . . then unscrew the retaining bolts and remove the flywheel

Inspection

4 Examine the flywheel for wear or chipping of the ring gear teeth. Renewal of the ring gear is possible but is not a task for the home mechanic; renewal requires the new ring gear to be heated (up to 180° to 230°C) to allow it to be fitted.

5 Examine the flywheel for scoring of the clutch face. If the clutch face is scored, the flywheel may be surface-ground, but renewal is preferable.

6 If there is any doubt about the condition of the flywheel, seek the advice of a Vauxhall dealer or engine reconditioning specialist. They will be able to advise if it is possible to recondition it or whether renewal is necessary.

Refitting

7 Clean the mating surfaces of the flywheel and crankshaft.

8 Offer up the flywheel and fit the new retaining bolts. If the original is being refitted align the marks made prior to removal.

9 Lock the flywheel using the method employed on dismantling then, working in a diagonal sequence, evenly and progressively tighten the retaining bolts to the specified stage 1 torque setting.

10 Once all bolts have been tightened to the stage 1 torque, go around and tighten all bolts through the specified stage 2 angle. It is recommended that an angle-measuring gauge is used during the final stages of the tightening, to ensure accuracy. If a gauge is not available, use white paint to make alignment marks prior to tightening; the marks can then be used to check that the bolt has been rotated through the correct angle.

11 Finally go around again and angle tighten the bolts through the specified stage 3 angle.

12 Refit the clutch as described in Chapter 6 then remove the locking tool and refit the transmission as described in Chapter 7.

17 Engine/transmission mountings - inspection and renewal

Inspection

1 If improved access is required, raise the front of the car and support it securely on axle stands. Where necessary, undo the retaining bolts and remove the undercover from beneath the engine/transmission unit.

2 Check the mounting rubber to see if it is cracked, hardened or separated from the metal at any point; renew the mounting if any such damage or deterioration is evident.

3 Check that all the mounting fasteners are securely tightened; use a torque wrench to check if possible.

4 Using a large screwdriver or a pry bar, check for wear in the mounting by carefully levering against it to check for free play; where this is not possible, enlist the aid of an assistant to move the engine/transmission unit back and forth, or from side-to-side, while you watch the mounting. While some free play is to be expected, even from new components, excessive wear should be obvious.

5 If excessive free play is found, check first that the fasteners are correctly secured, then renew any worn components as described below.

Renewal

Note: *Vauxhall recommend that both the right-hand and left-hand mountings should be renewed at the same time if either one is damaged.*

Right-hand mounting

6 Remove the air cleaner housing and intake duct assembly as described in Chapter 4.

7 Support the weight of the engine/transmission using a trolley jack with a block of wood placed on its head.

8 Slacken and remove the nuts securing the mounting bracket to the mounting and engine bracket and lift off the bracket. If necessary, the mounting bracket can then be unbolted from the side of the cylinder block.

9 Raise the engine/transmission unit slightly then unscrew the mounting lower retaining nut and remove the mounting from the body. **Note:** *Take great care not to place any excess stress on the exhaust system when raising the engine. If necessary, disconnect the front pipe from the manifold (see Chapter 4).*

10 Check all components for signs of wear or damage, and renew as necessary.

11 On reassembly, fit the mounting to the vehicle body and tighten its nut to the specified torque.

12 Refit the engine bracket (where removed) to the cylinder block and tighten its bolts to the specified torque. Then refit the mounting bracket to the top of the mounting/engine bracket and tighten its nuts to the specified torque.

Left-hand mounting

13 Slacken and remove the nut securing the right-hand mounting bracket to the mounting.

14 Firmly apply the handbrake then jack up the front of the vehicle and support it on axle stands. Where necessary, unbolt and remove the undercover.

15 Support the weight of the engine/transmission using a trolley jack with a block of wood placed on its head.

16 Slacken and remove the nut and washer securing the left-hand mounting to the front subframe and the upper nut securing the mounting to its bracket **(see illustration)**.

17 Raise the engine/transmission unit slightly then undo the bolts securing the mounting bracket to the transmission unit and manoeuvre the mounting and bracket out of position. Remove the nut and separate the mounting and bracket, noting which way up the mounting is fitted. **Note:** *Take great care*

2D

17.16 Left-hand mounting-to-subframe nut (arrowed)

not to place any excess stress on the exhaust system when raising the engine. If necessary, disconnect the front pipe from the manifold (see Chapter 4).

18 Check all components for signs of wear or damage, and renew as necessary.

19 On reassembly, refit the mounting to the bracket, ensuring it is fitted the right way up, and lightly tighten its nut.

20 Manoeuvre the mounting assembly into position and refit the bolts securing it to the transmission, tightening them to the specified torque.

21 Lower the engine/transmission unit and locate the mounting correctly in the subframe. Refit the lower mounting nut then tighten both the upper and lower nuts to the specified torque.

22 Lower the vehicle to the ground then refit the nut to the right-hand mounting and tighten it to the specified torque.

Rear mounting

23 Remove the right-hand driveshaft as described in Chapter 8.

24 Remove the exhaust system front pipe as described in Chapter 4.

25 Referring to Chapter 7, slacken the gearchange mechanism selector rod clamp bolt and disengage the selector rod from the transmission linkage.

26 Undo the retaining nut securing the mounting bracket to the top of the right-hand mounting.

27 Support the weight of the engine/transmission using a trolley jack with a block of wood placed on its head. Position the jack underneath the transmission and raise the transmission slightly to remove all load from the rear mounting.

28 Slacken and remove the bolts securing the rear mounting to the subframe and transmission then manoeuvre the assembly out from underneath the vehicle. If necessary, undo the retaining bolts and separate the mounting and mounting bracket.

29 On refitting, reassemble the mounting and mounting bracket (where necessary) then refit the mounting bolts and tighten them to the specified torque.

30 Manoeuvre the assembly into position and refit the bolts securing it to the subframe and transmission. Tighten the mounting bolts to their specified torque settings then remove the jack from underneath the engine/transmission.

31 Refit the nut to the right-hand mounting and tighten it to the specified torque.

32 Reconnect the selector rod and adjust the gearchange mechanism as described in Chapter 7.

33 Refit the right-hand driveshaft as described in Chapter 8.

34 Refit the exhaust front pipe as described in Chapter 4

Chapter 2 Part E:
Engine removal and overhaul procedures

Contents

Degrees of difficulty

Easy, suitable for novice with little experience	**Fairly easy,** suitable for beginner with some experience	**Fairly difficult,** suitable for competent DIY mechanic	**Difficult,** suitable for experienced DIY mechanic	**Very difficult,** suitable for expert DIY or professional

Specifications

Note: *Where specifications are given as N/A, no information was available at the time of writing. Refer to your Vauxhall dealer for the latest information available.*

1.6 litre SOHC petrol engine

Cylinder head

Maximum gasket face distortion	0.05 mm
Cylinder head height	95.90 to 96.10 mm
Valve seat width:	
Inlet	1.3 to 1.5 mm
Exhaust	1.6 to 1.8 mm

Valves and guides

	Inlet	Exhaust
Valve guide height in cylinder head	80.85 to 81.25 mm	
Valve stem diameter*:	**Inlet**	**Exhaust**
Standard (K)	6.998 to 7.012 mm	6.978 to 6.992 mm
1st oversize (0.075 mm - K1)	7.073 to 7.087 mm	7.053 to 7.067 mm
2nd oversize (0.150 mm - K2)	7.148 to 7.162 mm	7.128 to 7.142 mm
3rd oversize (0.250 mm - A)	7.248 to 7.262 mm	7.228 to 7.262 mm
Valve stem runout	Less than 0.03 mm	
Valve guide bore diameter*:		
Standard (K)	7.030 to 7.050 mm	
1st oversize (0.075 mm - K1)	7.105 to 7.125 mm	
2nd oversize (0.150 mm - K2)	7.180 to 7.200 mm	
3rd oversize (0.250 mm - A)	7.280 to 7.300 mm	
Stem-to-guide clearance:		
Inlet	0.018 to 0.052 mm	
Exhaust	0.038 to 0.072 mm	
Valve length:		
New	101.5 mm	
Service limit	101.1 mm	
Valve stem fitted height	13.75 to 14.35 mm	
Valve head diameter:		
Inlet	38 mm	
Exhaust	31 mm	

Identification marking in brackets

1.6 litre SOHC petrol engine (continued)

Cylinder block

Maximum gasket face distortion	0.05 mm
Cylinder bore diameter:	
Standard:	
Size group 6	78.955 to 78.965 mm
Size group 7	78.965 to 78.975 mm
Size group 8	78.975 to 78.985 mm
Oversize (0.5 mm)	79.465 to 79.475 mm
Maximum cylinder bore ovality	0.013 mm
Maximum cylinder bore taper	0.013 mm

Pistons and rings

Piston diameter:	
Standard:	
Size group 6	78.935 to 78.945 mm
Size group 7	78.945 to 78.955 mm
Size group 8	78.955 to 78.965 mm
Oversize (0.5 mm) - size group 7 + 0.5	79.445 to 79.455 mm
Piston-to-bore clearance	0.02 ± 0.01 mm
Piston ring end gaps (fitted in bore):	
Top and second compression rings	0.3 to 0.5 mm
Oil control ring	0.4 to 1.4 mm
Piston ring thickness:	
Top compression ring	1.2 mm
Second compression ring	1.5 mm
Oil control ring	3.0 mm
Piston ring-to-groove clearance	N/A

Gudgeon pins

Diameter	18 mm
Length	55 mm
Gudgeon pin-to-piston clearance	0.009 to 0.012 mm

Connecting rod

Big-end side clearance	0.07 to 0.24 mm

Crankshaft

Endfloat	0.1 to 0.2 mm
Main bearing journal diameter:	
Standard	54.980 to 54.997 mm
1st (0.25 mm) undersize	54.730 to 54.747 mm
2nd (0.50 mm) undersize	54.482 to 54.495 mm
Big-end bearing journal (crankpin) diameter:	
Standard	42.971 to 42.987 mm
1st (0.25 mm) undersize	42.721 to 42.737 mm
2nd (0.50 mm) undersize	42.471 to 42.487 mm
Journal out-of round	0.04 mm
Journal taper	N/A
Crankshaft runout	Less than 0.03 mm
Main bearing running clearance	0.017 to 0.047 mm
Big-end bearing (crankpin) running clearance	0.019 to 0.071 mm

Torque wrench settings	Refer to Chapter 2A Specifications

1.6 litre DOHC engine

Cylinder head

Maximum gasket face distortion	0.05 mm
Cylinder head height	135 mm
Valve seat width:	
Inlet	1.0 to 1.4 mm
Exhaust	1.4 to 1.8 mm

Gudgeon pins

Diameter	18 mm
Length	55 mm
Gudgeon pin-to-piston clearance	0.007 to 0.010 mm

1.6 litre DOHC engine (continued)

Crankshaft

Endfloat	0.1 to 0.2 mm
Main bearing journal diameter:	
Standard	54.980 to 54.997 mm
1st (0.25 mm) undersize	54.730 to 54.747 mm
2nd (0.50 mm) undersize	54.482 to 54.495 mm
Big-end bearing journal (crankpin) diameter:	
Standard	42.971 to 42.987 mm
1st (0.25 mm) undersize	42.721 to 42.737 mm
2nd (0.50 mm) undersize	42.471 to 42.487 mm
Journal out-of round	0.04 mm
Journal taper	N/A
Crankshaft runout	Less than 0.03 mm
Main bearing running clearance	0.017 to 0.047 mm
Big-end bearing (crankpin) running clearance	0.019 to 0.071 mm

Cylinder block

Maximum gasket face distortion	0.05 mm
Cylinder bore diameter:	
Standard:	
Size group 5	78.945 to 78.955 mm
Size group 6	78.955 to 78.965 mm
Size group 7	78.965 to 78.975 mm
Size group 8	78.975 to 78.985 mm
Size group 99	78.985 to 78.995 mm
Size group 00	78.995 to 79.005 mm
Size group 01	79.005 to 79.015 mm
Size group 02	79.015 to 79.025 mm
Size group 03	79.025 to 79.035 mm
Size group 04	79.035 to 79.045 mm
Size group 05	79.045 to 79.055 mm
Size group 06	79.055 to 79.065 mm
Size group 07	79.065 to 79.075 mm
Size group 08	79.075 to 79.085 mm
Size group 09	79.085 to 79.095 mm
Size group 1	79.095 to 79.105 mm
Oversize (0.5 mm)	79.465 to 79.475 mm
Maximum cylinder bore ovality and taper	0.013 mm

Pistons and rings

Piston diameter:	
Standard:	
Size group 5	78.915 to 78.955 mm
Size group 6	78.925 to 78.935 mm
Size group 7	78.935 to 78.945 mm
Size group 8	78.945 to 78.955 mm
Size group 99	78.955 to 78.965 mm
Size group 00	78.965 to 78.075 mm
Size group 01	78.075 to 78.085 mm
Size group 02	78.085 to 78.095 mm
Size group 03	78.095 to 79.005 mm
Size group 04	79.005 to 79.015 mm
Size group 05	79.015 to 79.025 mm
Size group 06	79.025 to 79.035 mm
Size group 07	79.035 to 79.045 mm
Size group 08	79.045 to 79.055 mm
Size group 09	79.055 to 79.065 mm
Size group 1	79.065 to 79.075 mm
Oversize (0.5 mm) - size group 7 + 0.5	79.435 to 79.445 mm
Piston-to-bore clearance	0.02 to 0.04 mm
Piston ring end gaps (fitted in bore):	
Top and second compression rings	0.3 to 0.5 mm
Oil control ring	0.4 to 1.4 mm
Piston ring thickness:	
Top compression ring	1.2 mm
Second compression ring	1.5 mm
Oil control ring	2.5 mm
Piston ring-to-groove clearance	N/A

2E

1.6 litre DOHC engine (continued)

Connecting rod
Big-end side clearance .... 0.11 to 0.24 mm

Valves and guides

	Inlet	Exhaust
Valve guide height in cylinder head .... 10.70 to 11.00 mm		
Valve stem diameter*:		
Standard (K)	5.955 to 5.970 mm	5.935 to 5.950 mm
1st oversize (0.075 mm - K1)	6.030 to 6.045 mm	6.010 to 6.025 mm
2nd oversize (0.150 mm - K2)	6.105 to 6.120 mm	6.085 to 6.100 mm
Valve stem runout .... Less than 0.03 mm		
Valve guide bore diameter*:		
Standard (K) .... 6.000 to 6.012 mm		
1st oversize (0.075 mm - K1) .... 6.075 to 6.090 mm		
2nd oversize (0.150 mm - K2) .... 6.150 to 6.165 mm		
Stem-to-guide clearance .... N/A		
Valve length:		
Inlet .... 103.1 mm		
Exhaust .... 102.2 mm		
Valve head diameter:		
Inlet .... 31.0 mm		
Exhaust .... 27.5 mm		

*Identification marking in brackets

Torque wrench settings .... Refer to Chapter 2B Specifications

1.8 (X18XE1) litre DOHC engine

Cylinder head
Maximum gasket face distortion .... 0.05 mm
Cylinder head height .... 135.00 to 136.00 mm
Cam lift:
  Inlet .... 8.50 mm
  Exhaust .... 8.00 mm
Camshaft radial runout .... 0.040 mm
Camshaft endfloat .... 0.040 to 0.144 mm
Valve seat angle in cylinder head .... 90° 30'
Valve seat width in cylinder head:
  Inlet .... 1.0 to 1.4 mm
  Exhaust .... 1.4 to 1.8 mm

Valves and guides

	Inlet	Exhaust
Valve stem runout .... Less than 0.03 mm		
Valve guide bore diameter*:		
Standard .... 5.000 to 5.012 mm		
1st oversize (0.075 mm) .... 5.075 to 5.087 mm		
2nd oversize (0.150 mm) .... 5.150 to 5.162 mm		
Length of valve guide:		
Inlet .... 38.70 to 39.30 mm		
Exhaust .... 38.70 to 39.30 mm		
Installation height of valve guide .... 10.70 to 11.00 mm		
Installation height of valves .... N/A		
Stem-to-guide clearance:		
Inlet .... 0.03 to 0.06 mm		
Exhaust .... 0.04 to 0.07 mm		
Valve length*:	**Inlet**	**Exhaust**
Standard	101.20 to 101.60	100.56 to 100.96
1st oversize (0.075 mm - K1)	N/A	N/A
2nd oversize (0.150 mm - K2)	N/A	N/A
Valve stem diameter*:	**Inlet**	**Exhaust**
Standard	4.955 to 4.970 mm	4.935 to 4.950 mm
1st oversize (0.075 mm - K1)	N/A	N/A
2nd oversize (0.150 mm - K2)	N/A	N/A
Valve head diameter:		
Inlet .... 31.2 mm		
Exhaust .... 27.5 mm		

Gudgeon pins
Diameter .... 17.997 to 18.000 mm
Length .... 55 mm

1.8 (X18XE1) litre DOHC engine (continued)

Gudgeon pins (continued)

Gudgeon pin clearance:

In con-rod (shrunk fit)	0.0 mm
In piston	0.09 to 0.015 mm

Crankshaft

Endfloat	0.100 to 0.202 mm
Main bearing journal diameter:	
Standard	54.980 to 54.997 mm
1st (0.25 mm) undersize	54.730 to 54.747 mm
2nd (0.50 mm) undersize	54.482 to 54.495 mm
Big-end bearing journal (crankpin) diameter:	
Standard	42.971 to 42.987 mm
1st (0.25 mm) undersize	42.721 to 42.737 mm
2nd (0.50 mm) undersize	42.471 to 42.487 mm
Big-end bearing journal shell thickness:	
Standard (264N)	1.485 to 1.497 mm
1st undersize (0.25 mm) (blue - 265A)	1.610 to 1.622 mm
2nd undersize (0.50 mm) (white - 266B)	1.735 to 1.747 mm
Main bearing shell thickness (Numbers 1, 2, 4 and 5):	
Standard (brown - 256N)	1.987 to 1.993 mm
Standard (green - 257N)	1.993 to 1.999 mm
1st undersize (0.25 mm) (brown/blue - 258A)	2.112 to 2.118 mm
1st undersize (0.25 mm) (green/blue - 259A)	2.118 to 2.124 mm
2nd undersize (0.50 mm) (brown/white - 260B)	2.237 to 2.243 mm
2nd undersize (0.50 mm) (green/white - 261B)	2.243 to 2.249 mm
Main bearing/thrust shell thickness (Number 3):	
Standard (brown - 859N)	1.987 to 1.993 mm
Standard (green - 860N)	1.993 to 1.999 mm
1st undersize (0.25 mm) (brown/blue - 861A)	2.112 to 2.118 mm
1st undersize (0.25 mm) (green/blue - 862A)	2.118 to 2.124 mm
2nd undersize (0.50 mm) (brown/white - 863B)	2.237 to 2.243 mm
2nd undersize (0.50 mm) (green/white - 864B)	2.243 to 2.249 mm
Main bearing/thrust shell width (Number 3):	
Standard (green/brown)	25.850 to 25.900 mm
1st undersize (0.25 mm) (brown/blue)	26.050 to 26.100 mm
2nd undersize (0.50 mm) (brown/white)	26.250 to 26.300 mm
Journal out-of round	0.04 mm
Journal taper	N/A
Crankshaft runout	Less than 0.03 mm
Main bearing running clearance	0.013 to 0.043 mm
Big-end bearing (crankpin) running clearance	0.019 to 0.071 mm

Cylinder block

Maximum gasket face distortion	0.05 mm
Cylinder bore diameter:	
Standard:	
Size group 5	80.445 to 80.455 mm
Size group 6	80.455 to 80.465 mm
Size group 7	80.465 to 80.475 mm
Size group 8	80.475 to 80.485 mm
Size group 99	80.485 to 80.495 mm
Size group 00	80.495 to 80.505 mm
Size group 01	80.505 to 80.515 mm
Size group 02	80.515 to 80.525 mm
Size group 03	80.525 to 80.535 mm
Size group 04	80.535 to 80.545 mm
Size group 05	80.545 to 80.555 mm
Size group 06	80.555 to 80.565 mm
Size group 07	80.565 to 80.575 mm
Size group 08	80.575 to 80.585 mm
Size group 09	80.585 to 80.595 mm
Size group 1	80.595 to 80.605 mm
Oversize (0.5 mm)	80.605 to 80.615 mm
Maximum cylinder bore ovality and taper	0.013 mm

2E

1.8 (X18XE1) litre DOHC engine (continued)

Pistons and rings

Piston diameter:
Standard:

Size group 5	80.415 to 78.955 mm
Size group 6	80.425 to 78.935 mm
Size group 7	80.435 to 78.945 mm
Size group 8	80.445 to 78.955 mm
Size group 99	80.455 to 80.465 mm
Size group 00	80.465 to 80.475 mm
Size group 01	80.475 to 80.485 mm
Size group 02	80.485 to 80.495 mm
Size group 03	80.495 to 80.505 mm
Size group 04	80.505 to 80.515 mm
Size group 05	80.515 to 80.525 mm
Size group 06	80.525 to 80.535 mm
Size group 07	80.535 to 80.545 mm
Size group 08	80.545 to 80.555 mm
Size group 09	80.555 to 80.565 mm
Size group 1	80.565 to 80.575 mm
Oversize (0.5 mm) - size group 7 + 0.5	80.965 to 80.975 mm
Piston-to-bore clearance	0.02 to 0.04 mm

Piston rings:
Top (rectangular) compression ring:

Height (thickness)	1.175 to 1.19 mm
Gap	0.20 to 0.40 mm
Vertical play	N/A

Middle (tapered) compression ring:

Height (thickness)	1.175 to 1.19 mm
Gap	0.40 to 0.60 mm
Vertical play	N/A

Bottom oil scraper ring:

Height (thickness)	1.88 to 1.96 mm
Gap	0.25 to 0.75 mm
Vertical play	N/A
Piston ring gap arrangement in cylinder	180°
Piston ring-to-groove clearance	N/A

Connecting rod

Big-end side clearance	0.11 to 0.24 mm

Identification marking in brackets

Torque wrench settings	Refer to Chapter 2B Specifications

1.8 (X18XE) and 2.0 litre DOHC petrol engines

Cylinder head

Maximum gasket face distortion	0.05 mm
Cylinder head height	134 mm

Valve seat width:

Inlet	1.0 to 1.5 mm
Exhaust	1.7 to 2.2 mm

Valves and guides

Valve guide height in cylinder head	13.70 to 14.00 mm

Valve stem diameter*:	**Inlet**	**Exhaust**
Standard (K)	5.955 to 5.970 mm	5.945 to 5.960 mm
1st oversize (0.075 mm - K1)	6.030 to 6.045 mm	6.020 to 6.035 mm
2nd oversize (0.150 mm - K2)	6.105 to 6.120 mm	6.095 to 6.110 mm
Valve stem runout	Less than 0.03 mm	

Valve guide bore diameter*:

Standard (K)	6.000 to 6.012 mm
1st oversize (0.075 mm - K1)	6.075 to 6.090 mm
2nd oversize (0.150 mm - K2)	6.150 to 6.165 mm

Stem-to-guide clearance:

Inlet	0.030 to 0.057 mm
Exhaust	0.040 to 0.067 mm

Valve length:

Inlet	102.0 mm
Exhaust	101.7 mm

Valve head diameter:

Inlet	31.9 to 32.1 mm
Exhaust	28.9 to 29.1 mm

Identification marking in brackets

1.8 (X18XE) and 2.0 litre DOHC petrol engines (continued)

Cylinder block

	1.8 litre engine	2.0 litre engine
Maximum gasket face distortion	0.05 mm	
Cylinder bore diameter:		
Standard:		
Size group 8	81.575 to 81.585 mm	85.975 to 85.985 mm
Size group 99	81.585 to 81.595 mm	85.985 to 85.995 mm
Size group 00	81.595 to 81.605 mm	85.995 to 86.005 mm
Size group 01	81.605 to 81.615 mm	86.005 to 86.015 mm
Size group 02	81.615 to 81.625 mm	86.015 to 86.025 mm
Oversize (0.5 mm)	82.065 to 82.075 mm	86.465 to 86.475 mm
Maximum cylinder bore ovality	0.013 mm	
Maximum cylinder bore taper	0.013 mm	

Pistons and rings

	1.8 litre engine	2.0 litre engine
Piston diameter:		
Standard:		
Size group 8	81.555 to 81.565 mm	85.955 to 85.965 mm
Size group 99	81.565 to 81.575 mm	85.965 to 85.975 mm
Size group 00	81.575 to 81.585 mm	85.975 to 85.985 mm
Size group 01	81.585 to 81.595 mm	85.985 to 85.995 mm
Size group 02	81.595 to 81.605 mm	85.995 to 86.005 mm
Oversize (0.5 mm) - size group 7 + 0.5	82.045 to 82.055 mm	86.445 to 86.455 mm
Piston-to-bore clearance	0.02 to 0.04 mm	
Piston ring end gaps (fitted in bore):		
Top and second compression rings	0.3 to 0.5 mm	
Oil control ring	0.4 to 1.4 mm	
Piston ring thickness:		
Top and second compression ring	1.5 mm	
Oil control ring	3.0 mm	
Piston ring-to-groove clearance	N/A	

Gudgeon pins

Diameter .... 21 mm
Length:
  1.8 litre engine .... 56.0 mm
  2.0 litre engine .... 61.5 mm
Gudgeon pin-to-piston clearance .... 0.011 to 0.014 mm

Connecting rod

Big-end side clearance .... 0.07 to 0.24 mm

Crankshaft

Endfloat .... 0.05 to 0.15 mm
Main bearing journal diameter:
  Standard:
    1st size group (white) .... 57.974 to 57.981 mm
    2nd size group (green) .... 57.981 to 57.988 mm
    3rd size group (brown) .... 57.988 to 57.995 mm
    1st (0.25 mm) undersize .... 57.732 to 57.745 mm
    2nd (0.50 mm) undersize .... 57.482 to 57.495 mm
Big-end bearing journal (crankpin) diameter:
  Standard .... 48.970 to 48.988 mm
  1st (0.25 mm) undersize .... 48.720 to 48.738 mm
  2nd (0.50 mm) undersize .... 48.470 to 48.488 mm
Journal out-of round .... 0.04 mm
Journal taper .... N/A
Crankshaft runout .... Less than 0.03 mm
Main bearing running clearance .... 0.015 to 0.040 mm
Big-end bearing (crankpin) running clearance .... 0.006 to 0.031 mm

Torque wrench settings .... Refer to Chapter 2B Specifications

1.7 litre diesel engine

Cylinder head

Maximum gasket face distortion .... 0.1 mm
Cylinder head height:
  Standard .... 131.45 to 131.55 mm
  Service limit .... 131.25 mm
Valve seat width:
  Standard .... 1.2 to 1.5 mm
  Service limit .... 2.0 mm
Swirl chamber protrusion .... 0.001 to 0.030 mm
Valve head depth below gasket face .... 0.5 to 1.0 mm

2E

1.7 litre diesel engine (continued)

Gudgeon pins

Diameter	27 mm
Length	60 mm
Gudgeon pin-to-piston clearance	0.002 to 0.012 mm
Gudgeon pin-to-connecting rod clearance	0.008 to 0.050 mm

Valves and guides

Valve stem diameter:

	Inlet	Exhaust
Inlet	6.959 to 6.977 mm	
Exhaust	6.960 to 6.978 mm	
Valve guide bore diameter	7.000 to 7.015 mm	

Stem-to-guide clearance:

	Inlet	Exhaust
Standard	0.023 to 0.056 mm	0.030 to 0.063 mm
Service limit	0.080 mm	0.095 mm
Valve length	104.05 mm	104.00 mm
Valve head diameter	34.6 mm	30.6 mm

Cylinder block

Cylinder bore diameter:

Size group A	79.000 to 79.009 mm
Size group B	79.010 to 79.019 mm
Size group C	79.020 to 79.029 mm
Maximum cylinder bore ovality	0.015 mm
Maximum cylinder bore taper	0.015 mm

Main bearing bore diameter (bearing shells removed):

Size group 1	55.992 to 56.000 mm
Size group 2	55.984 to 55.992 mm
Size group 3	55.976 to 55.984 mm

Pistons and rings

Piston diameter:

Size group A	78.975 to 78.984 mm
Size group B	78.965 to 78.994 mm
Size group C	78.995 to 79.004 mm
Piston-to-bore clearance	0.016 to 0.034 mm

Piston ring end gaps (fitted in bore):

Top compression ring	0.25 to 0.80 mm
Second compression ring	0.20 to 0.80 mm
Oil control ring	0.20 to 0.80 mm

Piston ring-to-groove clearance:

Top compression ring	0.12 to 0.18 mm
Second compression ring	0.05 to 0.15 mm
Oil control ring	0.02 to 0.15 mm

Piston ring thickness:

Top and second compression ring	2.0 mm
Oil control ring	3.0 mm

Connecting rod

Big-end side clearance	0.20 to 0.40 mm
Maximum permissible weight difference between connecting rods	4 grams

Crankshaft

Endfloat	0.06 to 0.30 mm

Main bearing journal diameter:

1st size group (single cutout)	51.928 to 51.938 mm
2nd size group (double cutout)	51.918 to 51.928 mm
Big-end bearing journal (crankpin) diameter	N/A
Journal out-of round	N/A
Journal taper	N/A
Crankshaft runout	Less than 0.06 mm
Main bearing running clearance	0.030 to 0.080 mm
Big-end bearing (crankpin) running clearance	0.025 to 0.100 mm

Torque wrench settings

Torque wrench settings	Refer to Chapter 2C Specifications

2.0 litre diesel engine

Cylinder head
Maximum gasket face distortion	N/A
Cylinder head height	140 mm
Valve seat width	1.4 to 1.8 mm

Valves and guides

Valve guide height in cylinder head .... 11.20 to 11.50 mm

Valve stem diameter*:	Inlet	Exhaust
Standard (K)	5.955 to 5.970 mm	5.945 to 5.960 mm
1st oversize (0.075 mm - K1)	6.030 to 6.045 mm	6.020 to 6.035 mm
2nd oversize (0.150 mm - K2)	6.105 to 6.120 mm	6.095 to 6.110 mm

Valve stem runout	Less than 0.03 mm

Valve guide bore diameter*:
Standard (K)	6.000 to 6.012 mm
1st oversize (0.075 mm - K1)	6.075 to 6.090 mm
2nd oversize (0.150 mm - K2)	6.150 to 6.165 mm
Stem-to-guide clearance	N/A

Valve length:
Inlet	97.1 to 97.2 mm
Exhaust	96.9 to 97.0 mm

Valve head diameter:
Inlet	28.9 to 29.1 mm
Exhaust	25.9 to 26.1 mm

Identification marking in brackets

Cylinder block

Maximum gasket face distortion	N/A

Cylinder bore diameter:
Standard:
Size group 8	83.975 to 83.985 mm
Size group 99	83.985 to 83.995 mm
Size group 00	83.995 to 84.005 mm
Size group 01	84.005 to 84.015 mm
Size group 02	84.015 to 84.025 mm
Oversize (0.5 mm)	N/A
Maximum cylinder bore ovality	N/A
Maximum cylinder bore taper	N/A

Pistons and rings

Piston diameter:
Standard:
Size group 8	N/A
Size group 99	N/A
Size group 00	N/A
Size group 01	N/A
Size group 02	N/A
Oversize (0.5 mm)	N/A
Piston-to-bore clearance	N/A

Piston ring end gaps (fitted in bore):
Top and second compression rings	0.3 to 0.5 mm
Oil control ring	0.4 to 1.4 mm

Piston ring-to-groove clearance:
Top and second compression rings	0.02 to 0.04 mm
Oil control ring	0.01 to 0.03 mm

Piston ring thickness:
Top compression ring:
X20DTL engine	2.00 mm
X20DTH engine	2.50 mm

Second compression ring:
X20DTL engine	1.75 mm
X20DTH engine	2.00 mm
Oil control ring	3.00 mm

Gudgeon pins
Diameter	29 mm
Length	68 mm

2E

2.0 litre diesel engine (continued)

Connecting rod
Big-end side clearance . . . .   0.07 to 0.28 mm

Crankshaft
Endfloat . . . .   0.05 to 0.15 mm

Main bearing journal diameter:
   Standard:
      1st size group (green) . . . .   67.966 to 67.974 mm
      2nd size group (brown) . . . .   67.974 to 67.982 mm
   1st (0.25 mm) undersize . . . .   67.716 to 67.732 mm
   2nd (0.50 mm) undersize . . . .   67.466 to 67.482 mm

Big-end bearing journal (crankpin) diameter:
   Standard . . . .   48.971 to 48.990 mm
   1st (0.25 mm) undersize . . . .   48.721 to 48.740 mm
   2nd (0.50 mm) undersize . . . .   48.471 to 48.490 mm

Journal out-of round 0.03
Journal taper . . . .   N/A
Crankshaft runout . . . .   Less than 0.03 mm
Main bearing running clearance . . . .   0.016 to 0.069 mm
Big-end bearing (crankpin) running clearance . . . .   0.010 to 0.061 mm

Torque wrench settings . . . .   Refer to Chapter 2D Specifications

1 General information

1 Included in this Part of Chapter 2 are details of removing the engine/transmission from the car and general overhaul procedures for the cylinder head, cylinder block and all other engine internal components.

2 The information given ranges from advice concerning preparation for an overhaul and the purchase of replacement parts, to detailed step-by-step procedures covering removal, inspection, renovation and refitting of engine internal components.

3 After Section 6, all instructions are based on the assumption that the engine has been removed from the car. For information concerning in-car engine repair, as well as the removal and refitting of those external components necessary for full overhaul, refer to the relevant in-car repair procedure section (Chapter 2A to 2D) of this Chapter and to Section 7. Ignore any preliminary dismantling operations described in the relevant in-car repair sections that are no longer relevant once the engine has been removed from the car.

4 Apart from torque wrench settings, which are given at the beginning of the relevant in-car repair procedure Chapter 2A to 2D, all specifications relating to engine overhaul are at the beginning of this Part of Chapter 2.

2 Engine overhaul - general information

1 It is not always easy to determine when, or if, an engine should be completely overhauled, as a number of factors must be considered.

2 High mileage is not necessarily an indication that an overhaul is needed, while low mileage does not preclude the need for an overhaul. Frequency of servicing is probably the most important consideration. An engine which has had regular and frequent oil and filter changes, as well as other required maintenance, should give many thousands of miles of reliable service. Conversely, a neglected engine may require an overhaul very early in its life.

3 Excessive oil consumption is an indication that piston rings, valve seals and/or valve guides are in need of attention. Make sure that oil leaks are not responsible before deciding that the rings and/or guides are worn. Perform a compression test, as described in the relevant Part A to D of this Chapter, to determine the likely cause of the problem.

4 Check the oil pressure with a gauge fitted in place of the oil pressure switch, and compare it with that specified. If it is extremely low, the main and big-end bearings, and/or the oil pump, are probably worn out.

5 Loss of power, rough running, knocking or metallic engine noises, excessive valve gear noise, and high fuel consumption may also point to the need for an overhaul, especially if they are all present at the same time. If a complete service does not remedy the situation, major mechanical work is the only solution.

6 An engine overhaul involves restoring all internal parts to the specification of a new engine. During an overhaul, the pistons and the piston rings are renewed. New main and big-end bearings are generally fitted; if necessary, the crankshaft may be renewed, to restore the journals. The valves are also serviced as well, since they are usually in less-than-perfect condition at this point. While the engine is being overhauled, other components, such as the starter and alternator, can be overhauled as well. The end result should be an as-new engine that will give many trouble-free miles. **Note:** *Critical cooling system components such as the hoses, thermostat and coolant pump should be renewed when an engine is overhauled. The radiator should be checked carefully, to ensure that it is not clogged or leaking. Also, it is a good idea to renew the oil pump whenever the engine is overhauled.*

7 Before beginning the engine overhaul, read through the entire procedure, to familiarise yourself with the scope and requirements of the job. Overhauling an engine is not difficult if you follow carefully all of the instructions, have the necessary tools and equipment, and pay close attention to all specifications. It can, however, be time-consuming. Plan on the car being off the road for a minimum of two weeks, especially if parts must be taken to an engineering works for repair or reconditioning. Check on the availability of parts and make sure that any necessary special tools and equipment are obtained in advance. Most work can be done with typical hand tools, although a number of precision measuring tools are required for inspecting parts to determine if they must be renewed. Often the engineering works will handle the inspection of parts and offer advice concerning reconditioning and renewal. **Note:** *Always wait until the engine has been completely dismantled, and until all components (especially the cylinder block and the crankshaft) have been inspected, before deciding what service and repair operations must be performed by an engineering works. The condition of these components will be the major factor to consider when determining whether to overhaul the original engine, or to buy a reconditioned unit. Do not, therefore, purchase parts or have overhaul work done on*

other components until they have been thoroughly inspected. As a general rule, time is the primary cost of an overhaul, so it does not pay to fit worn or sub-standard parts.

8 As a final note, to ensure maximum life and minimum trouble from a reconditioned engine, everything must be assembled with care, in a spotlessly-clean environment.

3 Engine removal - methods and precautions

1 If you have decided that the engine must be removed for overhaul or major repair work, several preliminary steps should be taken.

2 Locating a suitable place to work is extremely important. Adequate work space, along with storage space for the car, will be needed. If a workshop or garage is not available, at the very least, a flat, level, clean work surface is required.

3 Cleaning the engine compartment and engine/transmission before beginning the removal procedure will help keep tools clean and organised.

4 An engine hoist or A-frame will also be necessary. Make sure the equipment is rated in excess of the combined weight of the engine and transmission. Safety is of primary importance, considering the potential hazards involved in lifting the engine/transmission out of the car.

5 If this is the first time you have removed an engine, an assistant should ideally be available. Advice and aid from someone more experienced would also be helpful. There are many instances when one person cannot simultaneously perform all of the operations required when lifting the engine out of the vehicle.

6 Plan the operation ahead of time. Before starting work, arrange for the hire of or obtain all of the tools and equipment you will need. Some of the equipment necessary to perform engine/transmission removal and installation safely and with relative ease (in addition to an engine hoist) is as follows: a heavy duty trolley jack, complete sets of spanners and sockets as described in the back of this manual, wooden blocks, and plenty of rags and cleaning solvent for mopping up spilled oil, coolant and fuel. If the hoist must be hired, make sure that you arrange for it in advance, and perform all of the operations possible without it beforehand. This will save you money and time.

7 Plan for the car to be out of use for quite a while. An engineering works will be required to perform some of the work which the do-it-yourselfer cannot accomplish without special equipment. These places often have a busy schedule, so it would be a good idea to consult them before removing the engine, in order to accurately estimate the amount of time required to rebuild or repair components that may need work.

8 Always be extremely careful when removing and refitting the engine/transmission. Serious injury can result from careless actions. Plan ahead and take your time, and a job of this nature, although major, can be accomplished successfully.

4 Petrol engine and transmission unit - removal, separation and refitting

Removal

Note: *The engine can be removed from the car only as a complete unit with the transmission; the two are then separated for overhaul. The engine/transmission unit is lowered out of position, and withdrawn from under the vehicle. Bearing this in mind, ensure the vehicle is raised sufficiently so that there is enough clearance between the front of the vehicle and the floor to allow the engine/transmission unit to be slid out once it has been lowered out of position.*

1 Park the vehicle on firm, level ground then remove the bonnet as described in Chapter 11.

2 Depressurise the fuel system (see Chapter 4) then remove the battery and mounting plate as described in Chapter 5.

3 Chock the rear wheels, then firmly apply the handbrake. Jack up the front of the vehicle. Securely support it on axle stands, bearing in mind the note at the start of this Section. Where necessary, undo the retaining screws and remove the undercover from beneath the engine/ transmission unit.

4 If the engine is to be dismantled, working as described in Chapter 1, first drain the engine oil and remove the oil filter. Also drain the cooling system.

5 Referring to Chapter 4, carry out the following procedures.

a) *Remove the air cleaner housing and associated components.*

b) *Remove the exhaust front pipe.*

c) *Disconnect the fuel feed and return hoses from the fuel rail/throttle housing.*

d) *Disconnect the accelerator cable and position it clear of the engine.*

e) *Disconnect the brake servo hose and various vacuum hoses from the inlet manifold and exhaust manifolds, noting each hoses correct fitted location.*

f) *Disconnect the wiring connectors from the inlet manifold electrical components and free the wiring so it can be positioned clear of the engine unit.*

6 Referring to Chapter 3, carry out the following procedures.

a) *Release the retaining clips and disconnect the various coolant hoses from the cylinder head and the block.*

b) *On models with air conditioning, unbolt the compressor and position it clear of the engine.* **Do not** *open the refrigerant circuit.*

c) *Release the coolant/air-conditioning hoses/pipes (as applicable) from any relevant clips and ties and position them clear of the engine unit.*

7 Referring to Chapter 5, disconnect the wiring from the starter motor, alternator, oil pressure warning light switch and (where fitted) the oil level sensor. Unbolt any relevant earth leads from the cylinder block/transmission then unbolt/unclip the wiring from the engine unit and position it clear.

8 Referring to Chapter 10, unbolt the power steering pump and position it clear of the engine unit with its hoses still attached.

9 On models with a manual transmission unit, carry out the following procedures.

a) *Drain the transmission oil (see Chapter 7A) or be prepared for oil spillage as the engine/transmission unit is removed.*

b) *Disconnect the wiring connector from the reversing light switch.*

c) *Remove the gearchange linkage assembly from the top of the transmission unit (see Chapter 7).*

d) *Slide out the retaining clip and disconnect the clutch hose end fitting from the top of the transmission bellhousing (see Chapter 7A). Do not depress the clutch pedal whilst the hose is disconnected.*

10 On models with an automatic transmission unit, carry out the following procedures as described in Chapter 7B.

a) *Drain the transmission fluid.*

b) *Disconnect the selector cable and position it clear of the transmission.*

c) *Disconnect the transmission unit wiring connectors.*

d) *Disconnect the fluid cooler hoses from the transmission.*

11 Manoeuvre the engine hoist into position, and attach it to the lifting brackets bolted onto the engine/transmission. Raise the hoist until it is supporting the weight of the engine.

12 With the engine securely supported, remove the front suspension subframe assembly as described in Chapter 10.

13 Referring to Chapter 8, free the driveshaft inner constant velocity joints from the transmission unit and position them clear. Note that it is not necessary to remove the driveshafts, they can be left attached to the hub assemblies. **Note:** *Do not allow the shafts to hang down under their own weight as this could damage the constant velocity joints/gaiters.*

14 Make a final check that any components which would prevent the removal of the engine/transmission from the car have been removed or disconnected. Ensure that components such as the driveshafts are secured so that they cannot be damaged on removal.

15 Slacken and remove the mounting bolts then remove the torque support rod from the right-hand end of the cylinder head.

16 If available, a low trolley should be placed under the engine/transmission assembly, to facilitate its easy removal from under the

2E

vehicle. Lower the engine/transmission assembly, making sure that nothing is trapped, taking great care not to damage the radiator/cooling fan assembly. Enlist the help of an assistant during this procedure, as it may be necessary to tilt the assembly slightly to clear the body panels. Great care must be taken to ensure that no components are trapped and damaged during the removal procedure.

17 Detach the hoist and withdraw the engine/transmission unit from under the vehicle.

Separation

Manual transmission models

18 With the engine/transmission assembly removed, support the assembly on suitable blocks of wood, on a workbench (or failing that, on a clean area of the workshop floor).

19 On models with a pressed steel sump, undo the retaining bolts and remove the flywheel lower cover plate from the transmission.

20 Undo the retaining bolts and remove the starter motor from the transmission (see Chapter 5).

21 Ensure that both engine and transmission are adequately supported, then slacken and remove the remaining bolts securing the transmission housing to the engine. Note the correct fitted positions of each bolt (and the relevant brackets) as they are removed, to use as a reference on refitting.

22 Carefully withdraw the transmission from the engine, ensuring that the weight of the transmission is not allowed to hang on the input shaft while it is engaged with the clutch friction disc.

23 If they are loose, remove the locating dowels from the engine or transmission, and keep them in a safe place.

Automatic transmission models

24 With the engine/transmission assembly removed, support the assembly on suitable blocks of wood, on a workbench (or failing that, on a clean area of the workshop floor).

25 Undo the retaining bolts and remove the starter motor from the transmission (see Chapter 5).

26 Remove the rubber cover(s) from the cylinder block/sump flange to gain access to the torque converter retaining bolts. Slacken and remove the visible bolt(s) then, using a socket and extension bar to rotate the crankshaft pulley, undo the remaining bolts securing the torque converter to the driveplate as they become accessible. On 1.6 litre models there are three bolts in total and on 1.8 and 2.0 litre models there are six. Discard the bolts, new ones must be used on refitting.

27 To ensure that the torque converter does not fall out as the transmission is removed, slide the converter along the shaft and fully into the transmission housing.

28 Separate the engine and transmission as described in paragraphs 21 to 23.

Refitting

Manual transmission models

29 If the engine and transmission have been separated, perform the operations described below in paragraphs 30 to 33. If not, proceed as described from paragraph 34 onwards.

30 Ensure the locating dowels are correctly positioned then carefully offer the transmission to the engine, until the locating dowels are engaged. Ensure that the weight of the transmission is not allowed to hang on the input shaft as it is engaged with the clutch friction disc.

31 Refit the transmission housing-to-engine bolts, ensuring that all the necessary brackets are correctly positioned, and tighten them to the specified torque setting.

32 Refit the starter motor and tighten its mounting bolts to the specified torque (see Chapter 5).

33 On models with a pressed steel sump, refit the flywheel lower cover plate to the transmission, and tighten its retaining bolts to the specified torque.

34 Slide the engine/transmission unit into position and reconnect the hoist and lifting tackle to the engine lifting brackets.

35 With the aid of an assistant, carefully lift the assembly into position the engine compartment, manipulating the hoist and lifting tackle as necessary, taking great care not to trap any components.

36 Align the engine with the bracket on the right-hand side of the engine compartment then refit the torque support rod. Tighten the rod bolts by hand only at this stage.

37 Renew the driveshaft oil seals (see Chapter 7) then carefully engage the driveshaft inner constant velocity joints with the transmission (see Chapter 8).

38 Refit the front suspension subframe as described in Chapter 10.

39 With the subframe assembly correctly installed, tighten the torque rod mounting bolts to the specified torque.

40 The remainder of the refitting procedure is a direct reversal of the removal sequence, noting the following points:

a) Ensure that all wiring is correctly routed and retained by all the relevant retaining clips and that all connectors are correctly and securely reconnected.

b) Ensure that all disturbed hoses are correctly reconnected, and securely retained by their retaining clips.

c) Fit a new sealing ring to the clutch hose end fitting on the transmission unit and reconnect the end fitting, ensuring it is securely retained by the clip. On completion, bleed the hydraulic system as described in Chapter 6.

d) Refit the gearchange linkage to the transmission and adjust as described in Chapter 7A.

e) Adjust the accelerator cable as described in the Chapter 4.

f) Refill the transmission with correct quantity and type of oil, as described in Chapter A7. If the oil was not drained, top-up the level as described in Chapter 1.

g) Refill the engine with oil as described in Chapter 1 and also refill the cooling system.

Automatic transmission models

41 If the engine and transmission have been separated, perform the operations described below in paragraphs 42 to 46. If not, proceed as described from paragraph 47 onwards.

42 Remove all traces of old locking compound from the torque converter threads by running a tap of the correct thread diameter and pitch down the holes. In the absence of a suitable tap, use one of the old bolts with slots cut in its threads.

43 Ensure the engine/transmission locating dowels are correctly positioned and apply a smear of molybdenum disulphide grease to the torque converter locating pin and its centring bush in the crankshaft end.

44 Carefully offer the transmission to the engine, until the locating dowels are engaged. Refit the transmission housing-to-engine bolts, ensuring that all the necessary brackets are correctly positioned, and tighten them to the specified torque setting.

45 Fit the new torque converter-to-driveplate bolts and tighten them lightly only to start then go around and tighten them to the specified torque setting in a diagonal sequence. Refit the rubber covers to the sump flange.

46 Refit the starter motor and tighten its mounting bolts to the specified torque (see Chapter 5).

47 Slide the engine/transmission unit into position and reconnect the hoist and lifting tackle to the engine lifting brackets.

48 With the aid of an assistant, carefully lift the assembly into position the engine compartment, manipulating the hoist and lifting tackle as necessary, taking great care not to trap any components.

49 Align the engine with the bracket on the right-hand side of the engine compartment then refit the torque support rod. Tighten the rod bolts by hand only at this stage.

50 Renew the driveshaft oil seals (see Chapter 7B) then carefully engage the driveshaft inner constant velocity joints with the transmission (see Chapter 8).

51 Refit the front suspension subframe as described in Chapter 10.

52 With the subframe assembly correctly installed, tighten the torque rod mounting bolts to the specified torque.

53 The remainder of the refitting procedure is a direct reversal of the removal sequence, noting the following points:

a) Ensure that all wiring is correctly routed and retained by all the relevant retaining clips and that all connectors are correctly and securely reconnected.

b) Ensure that all disturbed hoses are correctly reconnected, and securely retained by their retaining clips.

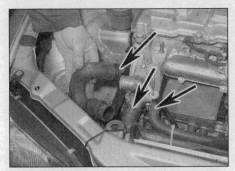

5.3 On 2.0 litre models, disconnect the coolant hoses (arrowed) from the right-hand end of the cylinder head

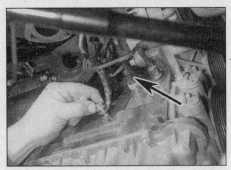

5.4a On 2.0 litre models, remove the bolt securing the earth lead to the rear of the cylinder block then disconnect the wiring from the oil pressure switch (arrowed) . . .

c) Fit new sealing rings to the transmission fluid cooler hose unions and ensure both unions are securely retained by their clips.

d) Adjust the accelerator cable as described in the Chapter 4.

e) Refill the transmission with the specified type and quantity of fluid and adjust the selector cable as described in Chapter 7B.

f) Refill the engine with correct quantity and type of oil, as described in Chapter 1.

g) Refill the cooling system as described in Chapter 1.

5 Diesel engine and transmission unit - removal, separation and refitting

Removal

Note: The engine can be removed from the car only as a complete unit with the transmission; the two are then separated for overhaul. The engine/transmission unit is lowered out of position, and withdrawn from under the vehicle. Bearing this in mind, ensure the vehicle is raised sufficiently so that there is enough clearance between the front of the vehicle and the floor to

allow the engine/transmission unit to be slid out once it has been lowered out of position.

1 Carry out the operations described in paragraphs 1 to 4 of Section 4, noting that it is not necessary to depressurise the fuel system.

2 Referring to Chapter 4, carry out the following procedures.

a) Remove the air cleaner housing and associated components.

b) Remove the exhaust front pipe.

c) Disconnect the fuel feed and return hoses from the injection pump.

d) Disconnect the brake servo hose and various vacuum hoses and from the inlet manifold and exhaust manifolds, noting each hoses correct fitted location.

e) Disconnect the wiring connectors from the inlet manifold electrical components and free the wiring so it can be positioned clear of the engine unit.

f) On 1.7 litre models, disconnect the accelerator cable and position it clear of the engine.

3 Referring to Chapter 3, carry out the following procedures.

a) Release the retaining clips and disconnect the various coolant hoses from the cylinder head and the block **(see illustration)**.

b) On models with air conditioning, unbolt the compressor and position it clear of the engine. **Do not** open the refrigerant circuit.

c) Release the coolant/air-conditioning hoses/pipes (as applicable) from any relevant clips and ties and position them clear of the engine unit.

4 Referring to Chapter 5, disconnect the wiring from the starter motor, alternator, oil pressure warning light switch and (where fitted) the oil level/oil temperature sensor. Unbolt any relevant earth leads from the cylinder block/transmission then unbolt/unclip the wiring from the engine unit and position it clear **(see illustrations)**.

5 Referring to Chapter 10, unbolt the power steering pump and position it clear of the engine unit with its hoses still attached.

6 Referring to Chapter 7A, carry out the following procedures.

a) Drain the transmission oil or be prepared for oil spillage as the engine/transmission unit is removed.

b) Disconnect the wiring connector from the reversing light switch.

c) Remove the gearchange linkage assembly from the top of the transmission unit.

d) Slide out the retaining clip and disconnect the clutch hose end fitting from the top of the transmission bellhousing. Do not depress the clutch pedal whilst the hose is disconnected.

7 Manoeuvre the engine hoist into position, and attach it to the lifting brackets bolted onto the engine/transmission **(see illustration)**. Raise the hoist until it is supporting the weight of the engine.

8 With the engine securely supported, remove the front suspension subframe assembly as described in Chapter 10.

9 Referring to Chapter 8, free the driveshaft inner constant velocity joints from the transmission unit and position them clear. Note that it is not necessary to remove the driveshafts, they can be left attached to the hub

2E

5.4b . . . alternator (A) and starter motor (B) then unbolt the wiring tray from the block

5.7 Attach the engine hoist to the lifting brackets on the cylinder head (2.0 litre model shown)

5.12a Ensure all components are disconnected then carefully lower the engine/transmission unit . . .

5.12b . . . and manoeuvre it out from underneath the vehicle

assemblies. **Note:** *Do not allow the shafts to hang down under their own weight as this could damage the constant velocity joints/gaiters.*

10 Make a final check that any components which would prevent the removal of the engine/transmission from the car have been removed or disconnected. Ensure that components such as the driveshafts are secured so that they cannot be damaged on removal.

11 Undo the retaining nuts and remove the bracket securing the right-hand engine mounting to the cylinder head.

12 If available, a low trolley should be placed under the engine/transmission assembly, to facilitate its easy removal from under the vehicle. Lower the engine/transmission assembly, making sure that nothing is trapped, taking great care not to damage the radiator/cooling fan assembly **(see illustrations)**. Enlist the help of an assistant during this procedure, as it may be necessary to tilt the assembly slightly to clear the body panels. Great care must be taken to ensure that no components are trapped and damaged during the removal procedure.

13 Detach the hoist and withdraw the engine/transmission unit from under the vehicle.

Separation

14 Refer to Section 4.

Refitting

15 If the engine and transmission have been separated, perform the operations described below in paragraphs 16 to 18. If not, proceed as described from paragraph 19 onwards.

16 Ensure the locating dowels are correctly positioned then carefully offer the transmission to the engine, until the locating dowels are engaged. Ensure that the weight of the transmission is not allowed to hang on the input shaft as it is engaged with the clutch friction disc.

17 Refit the transmission housing-to-engine bolts, ensuring that all the necessary brackets are correctly positioned, and tighten them to the specified torque setting.

18 Refit the starter motor and tighten its mounting bolts to the specified torque (see Chapter 5).

19 Slide the engine/transmission unit into position and reconnect the hoist and lifting tackle to the engine lifting brackets.

20 With the aid of an assistant, carefully lift the assembly into position the engine compartment, manipulating the hoist and lifting tackle as necessary, taking great care not to trap any components.

21 Align the engine with the right-hand mounting then refit the mounting bracket, tightening its nuts by hand only at this stage.

22 Renew the driveshaft oil seals (see Chapter 7A) then carefully engage the driveshaft inner constant velocity joints with the transmission (see Chapter 8).

23 Refit the front suspension subframe as described in Chapter 10.

24 With the subframe assembly correctly installed, tighten the right-hand mounting bracket nuts to the specified torque.

25 The remainder of the refitting procedure is a direct reversal of the removal sequence, noting the following points:

a) *Ensure that all wiring is correctly routed and retained by all the relevant retaining clips and that all connectors are correctly and securely reconnected.*

b) *Ensure that all disturbed hoses are correctly reconnected, and securely retained by their retaining clips.*

c) *Fit new sealing washers to the injection pump fuel hose unions and tighten the union bolts to the specified torque (see Chapter 4).*

d) *Fit a new sealing ring to the clutch fitting on the transmission unit and reconnect the end fitting, ensuring it is securely retained by the clip. On completion, check the bleed the hydraulic system as described in Chapter 6.*

e) *Refit the gearchange linkage to the transmission and adjust as described in Chapter 7A.*

f) *On 1.7 litre models, adjust the accelerator cable as described in the Chapter 4.*

g) *Refill the transmission with correct quantity and type of oil, as described in Chapter 7A. If the oil was not drained, top-up the level as described in Chapter 1.*

h) *Refill the engine with oil as described in Chapter 1 and also refill the cooling system.*

6 Engine overhaul - dismantling sequence

1 It is much easier to dismantle and work on the engine if it is mounted on a portable engine stand. These stands can often be hired from a tool hire shop. Before the engine is mounted on a stand, the flywheel/driveplate should be removed, so that the stand bolts can be tightened into the end of the cylinder block.

2 If a stand is not available, it is possible to dismantle the engine with it blocked up on a sturdy workbench, or on the floor. Be extra-careful not to tip or drop the engine when working without a stand.

3 If you are going to obtain a reconditioned engine, all the external components must be removed first, to be transferred to the replacement engine (just as they will if you are doing a complete engine overhaul yourself). These components include the following:

a) *Inlet and exhaust manifolds (Chapter 4).*

b) *Alternator/power steering pump/air conditioning compressor bracket(s) (as applicable).*

c) *Coolant pump (Chapter 3).*

d) *Fuel system components (Chapter 4).*

e) *Wiring harness and all electrical switches and sensors.*

f) *Oil filter (Chapter 1).*

g) *Flywheel/driveplate (relevant Part of this Chapter).*

Note: *When removing the external components from the engine, pay close attention to details*

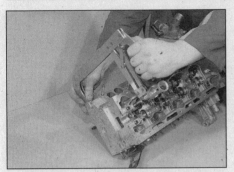

7.5a Using a valve spring compressor . . .

7.5b . . . compress the valve spring until the collets can be removed from the valve

7.5c Remove the compressor then lift off the spring retainer . . .

7.5d . . . and remove the valve spring

that may be helpful or important during refitting. Note the fitted position of gaskets, seals, spacers, pins, washers, bolts, and other small items.

4 If you are obtaining a 'short' engine (which consists of the engine cylinder block, crankshaft, pistons and connecting rods all assembled), then the cylinder head, sump, oil pump, and timing belt/chains (as applicable) will have to be removed also.

5 If you are planning a complete overhaul, the engine can be dismantled, and the internal components removed, in the order given below, referring to the relevant Part of this Chapter unless otherwise stated.

a) Inlet and exhaust manifolds (Chapter 4).
b) Timing belt, sprockets and tensioner - all models except 2.0 litre diesel engine
c) Cylinder head.
d) Flywheel/driveplate.
e) Sump.

f) Oil pump.
g) Timing chains and sprockets - 2.0 litre diesel engine.
h) Piston/connecting rod assemblies.
i) Crankshaft.

6 Before beginning the dismantling and overhaul procedures, make sure that you have all of the correct tools necessary. Refer to the "Tools and working facilities" Section of this manual for further information.

7 Cylinder head - dismantling

Note: *New and reconditioned cylinder heads are available from the manufacturer, and from engine overhaul specialists. Be aware that some specialist tools are required for the dismantling and inspection procedures, and new components may not be readily available. It may therefore be more practical and economical for the home mechanic to purchase a reconditioned head, rather than dismantle, inspect and recondition the original head.*

1 On 1.6 litre SOHC petrol engine, referring to Part A of this Chapter, remove the cylinder head from the engine then lift the camshaft followers, thrust pads and hydraulic tappets out from the cylinder head.

2 On all DOHC petrol engines remove the camshafts and followers as described in Part B of this Chapter then remove the cylinder head from the engine.

3 On 1.7 litre diesel engines, working as described in Part C of this Chapter, remove

the camshaft, followers and shims. Unscrew the glow plugs (Chapter 5) and injectors (Chapter 4) from the cylinder head then remove the cylinder head from the engine.

4 On 2.0 litre diesel engines, working as described in Part D of this Chapter, remove the camshaft, followers and hydraulic tappets from the cylinder head. Unscrew the glow plugs (Chapter 5) then remove the cylinder head from the engine.

5 On all models, using a valve spring compressor, compress each valve spring in turn until the split collets can be removed. Release the compressor, and lift off the spring retainer and spring. Using a pair of pliers, carefully extract the valve stem seal from the top of the guide then slide off the spring seat **(see illustrations)**.

6 If, when the valve spring compressor is screwed down, the spring retainer refuses to free and expose the split collets, gently tap the top of the tool, directly over the retainer, with a light hammer. This will free the retainer.

7 Withdraw the valve through the combustion chamber. It is essential that each valve is stored together with its collets, retainer, spring, and spring seat. The valves should also be kept in their correct sequence, unless they are so badly worn that they are to be renewed.

2E

7.5e Pull the seal off the top of the valve guide . . .

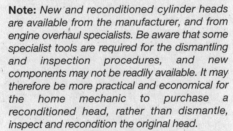

7.5f . . . then remove the spring seat

HAYNES HiNT

No.1 INLET

If the components are to be refitted, place each valve and its associated components in a labelled polythene bag or similar small container, and mark the bag/container with the relevant valve number to ensure that it is refitted in its original location

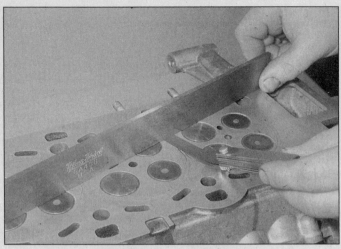

8.6 Using a straight edge and feeler gauge to check cylinder head surface distortion

8.11 Using a dial gauge to check swirl chamber protrusion - 1.7 litre diesel engines

8 Cylinder head and valves - cleaning and inspection

1 Thorough cleaning of the cylinder head and valve components, followed by a detailed inspection, will enable you to decide how much valve service work must be carried out during the engine overhaul. **Note:** *If the engine has been severely overheated, it is best to assume that the cylinder head is warped - check carefully for signs of this.*

Cleaning

2 Scrape away all traces of old gasket material from the cylinder head.
3 Scrape away the carbon from the combustion chambers and ports, then wash the cylinder head thoroughly with paraffin or a suitable solvent.
4 Scrape off any heavy carbon deposits that may have formed on the valves, then use a power-operated wire brush to remove deposits from the valve heads and stems.

Inspection

Note: *Be sure to perform all the following inspection procedures before concluding that the services of a machine shop or engine overhaul specialist are required. Make a list of all items that require attention.*

Cylinder head

5 Inspect the head very carefully for cracks, evidence of coolant leakage, and other damage. If cracks are found, a new cylinder head should be obtained.
6 Use a straight-edge and feeler gauge blade to check that the cylinder head surface is not distorted **(see illustration)**. If it is, it may be possible to resurface it, provided that the cylinder head is not reduced to less than the minimum specified height.
7 Examine the valve seats in each of the combustion chambers. If they are severely

pitted, cracked or burned, then they will need to be renewed (this is only possible on 1.7 litre diesel engines) or re-cut by an engine overhaul specialist. If they are only slightly pitted, this can be removed by grinding-in the valve heads and seats with fine valve-grinding compound, as described below.
8 If the valve guides are worn (indicated by a side-to-side motion of the valve, and accompanied by excessive blue smoke in the exhaust when running) new guides must be fitted. Measure the diameter of the existing valve stems (see below) and the bore of the guides, then calculate the clearance and compare the result with the specified value. If the clearance is not within the specified limits, renew the valves and/or guides as necessary.
9 The renewal of valve guides is best carried out by an engine overhaul specialist. If the work is to be carried out at home, however, use a stepped, double-diameter drift to drive out the worn guide towards the combustion chamber. On fitting the new guide, place it first in a deep-freeze for one hour, then drive it into its cylinder head bore from the camshaft side until it projects the specified amount above the cylinder head surface (where no measurement is given seek the advice of a Vauxhall dealer).

8.13 Using a micrometer to measure valve stem diameter

10 If the valve seats are to be re-cut this must be done only after the guides have been renewed.
11 On 1.7 litre diesel engines, inspect the swirl chambers for burning or damage such as cracking. Small cracks in the chambers are acceptable; renewal of the chambers will only be required if chamber tracts are badly burned and disfigured, or if they are no longer a tight fit in the cylinder head. If there is any doubt as to the swirl chamber condition, seek the advice of a Vauxhall dealer or a suitable repairer who specialises in diesel engines. Swirl chamber renewal should be entrusted to a specialist. Using a dial test indicator, check that the swirl chamber protrusion is within the limits given in the Specifications. Zero the dial test indicator on the gasket surface of the cylinder head, then measure the protrusion of the swirl chamber **(see illustration)**. If the protrusion is not within the specified limits, the advice of a Vauxhall dealer or suitable repairer who specialises in diesel engines should be sought.

Valves

12 Examine the head of each valve for pitting, burning, cracks and general wear, and check the valve stem for scoring and wear ridges. Rotate the valve, and check for any obvious indication that it is bent. Look for pitting and excessive wear on the tip of each valve stem. Renew any valve that shows any such signs of wear or damage.
13 If the valve appears satisfactory at this stage, measure the valve stem diameter at several points using a micrometer **(see illustration)**. Any significant difference in the readings obtained indicates wear of the valve stem. Should any of these conditions be apparent, the valve(s) must be renewed.
14 If the valves are in satisfactory condition, they should be ground (lapped) into their respective seats, to ensure a smooth gas-tight seal. If the seat is only lightly pitted, or if it has been re-cut, fine grinding compound

8.16 Grinding in a valve

only should be used to produce the required finish. Coarse valve-grinding compound should **not** be used unless a seat is badly burned or deeply pitted; if this is the case, the cylinder head and valves should be inspected by an expert to decide whether seat re-cutting, or even the renewal of the valve or seat insert, is required.

15 Valve grinding is carried out as follows. Place the cylinder head upside-down on a bench.

16 Smear a trace of the appropriate grade of valve-grinding compound on the seat face, and press a suction grinding tool onto the valve head. With a semi-rotary action, grind the valve head to its seat, lifting the valve occasionally to redistribute the grinding compound **(see illustration)**. A light spring

placed under the valve head will greatly ease this operation.

17 If coarse grinding compound is being used, work only until a dull, matt even surface is produced on both the valve seat and the valve, then wipe off the used compound and repeat the process with fine compound. When a smooth unbroken ring of light grey matt finish is produced on both the valve and seat, the grinding operation is complete. **Do not** grind in the valves any further than absolutely necessary, or the seat will be prematurely sunk into the cylinder head.

18 When all the valves have been ground-in, carefully wash off all traces of grinding compound using paraffin or a suitable solvent before reassembly of the cylinder head.

Valve components

19 Examine the valve springs for signs of damage and discoloration; if possible; also compare the existing spring free length with new components.

20 Stand each spring on a flat surface, and check it for squareness. If any of the springs are damaged, distorted or have lost their tension, obtain a complete new set of springs.

21 On 1.6 litre SOHC engines, the exhaust valve spring seats incorporate a bearing; the bearing rotates the valve which helps to keep the valve seat clean. If any spring seats bearing shows signs of wear or does not rotate smoothly then the seat should be renewed.

9 Cylinder head - reassembly

1 Lubricate the stems of the valves, and insert them into their original locations **(see illustration)**. If new valves are being fitted, insert them into the locations to which they have been ground.

2 Working on the first valve, refit the spring seat. Dip the new valve stem seal in fresh engine oil, then carefully locate it over the valve and onto the guide. Take care not to damage the seal as it is passed over the valve stem. Use a suitable socket or metal tube to press the seal firmly onto the guide. **Note:** *If genuine seals are being fitted, use the oil seal protector which is supplied with the seals; the protector fits over the valve stem and prevents the oil seal lip being damaged on the valve* **(see illustrations)**.

3 Locate the spring on the seat and fit the spring retainer **(see illustration)**.

4 Compress the valve spring, and locate the split collets in the recess in the valve stem **(see illustration)**. Release the compressor, then repeat the procedure on the remaining valves.

5 With all the valves installed, place the cylinder head flat on the bench and, using a hammer and interposed block of wood, tap the end of each valve stem to settle the components.

9.1 Lubricate the valve stem with engine oil and insert the valve into the correct guide

9.2a Fit the spring seat . . .

9.2b . . . then fit the seal protector (where supplied) to the valve . . .

9.2c . . . and install the new valve guide oil seal . . .

9.2d . . . pressing it onto the valve guide with a suitable socket

9.3 Refit the valve spring and fit the spring retainer

2E

9.4 Compress the valve and locate the collets in the recess on the valve stem

Use a little dab of grease to hold the collets in position on the valve stem while the spring compressor is released

10.3 On 1.7 litre diesel engines unbolt the baffle plate from the base of the cylinder block

6 On 1.6 litre SOHC engine, working as described in Part A, refit the hydraulic tappets, thrust pads and followers to the head then refit the cylinder head.

7 On all DOHC petrol engines, working as described in Part B, refit the cylinder head to the engine and install the followers and camshafts.

8 On 1.7 litre diesel engines, working as described in Part C, refit the cylinder head to the engine and install the followers, shims and camshaft. Refit the injectors and glow plugs as described in Chapters 4 and 5.

9 On 2.0 litre diesel engines, working as described in Part D, refit the cylinder head to the engine and install the hydraulic tappets, followers and camshaft.

10 Piston/connecting rod assembly - removal

Note: *New connecting rod big-end cap bolts (and nuts on 1.7 litre diesel engine) will be needed on refitting*

1 On 1.6 litre petrol engines, remove the cylinder head and sump then unbolt the pick-up/strainer from the base of the oil pump. Refer to Part A for information on SOHC engine and Part B for information on the DOHC engine.

2 On 1.8 and 2.0 litre DOHC engines, referring to Part B of this Chapter, remove the cylinder head and sump then unbolt the pick-up/strainer from the base of the oil pump. Undo the retaining screws and remove the baffle plate from the base of the cylinder block. To further improve access, evenly and progressively slacken the retaining bolts and remove the main bearing ladder casting from the base of the block.

3 On 1.7 litre diesel engines, referring to Part C of this Chapter, remove the cylinder head and sump then remove the pick-up/strainer from the base of the oil pump. Undo the retaining bolts and remove the baffle plate from the base of the cylinder block **(see illustration)**.

4 On 2.0 litre diesel engines, working as described in Part D of this Chapter, remove the cylinder head and sump and unbolt the pick-up/strainer from the base of the oil pump.

5 On all models, if there is a pronounced wear ridge at the top of any bore, it may be necessary to remove it with a scraper or ridge reamer, to avoid piston damage during removal. Such a ridge indicates excessive wear of the cylinder bore.

6 Prior to removal, using feeler blades, measuring the connecting rod big-end side clearance of each rod **(see illustration)**. If any rod exceeds the specified clearance, it must be renewed.

7 Using a hammer and centre-punch, paint or similar, mark each connecting rod and its bearing cap with its respective cylinder number on the flat machined surface provided; if the engine has been dismantled before, note carefully any identifying marks made previously **(see illustration)**. Note that No 1 cylinder is at the timing belt/chain (as applicable) end of the engine.

8 Turn the crankshaft to bring pistons 1 and 4 to BDC (bottom dead centre).

9 Unscrew the nuts (1.7 litre diesel engine) or bolts (all other engines) from No 1 piston big-end bearing cap. Take off the cap and recover the bottom half bearing shell. If the bearing shells are to be re-used, tape the cap and the shell together.

10.6 Checking connecting rod big-end side clearance

10.7 Prior to removal, make identification markings on the connecting rods and bearing caps (circled). Note that lug on the bearing cap faces towards the flywheel/driveplate end of the engine

Caution: *On some engines, the connecting rod/bearing cap mating surfaces are not machined flat; the big-end bearing caps are 'cracked' off from the rod during production and left untouched to ensure the cap and rod mate perfectly. Where this type of connecting rod is fitted, great care must be taken to ensure the mating surfaces of the cap and rod are not marked or damaged in anyway. Any damage to the mating surfaces will adversely affect the strength of the connecting rod and could lead to premature failure.*

10 Using a hammer handle, push the piston up through the bore, and remove it from the top of the cylinder block. Recover the bearing shell, and tape it to the connecting rod for safe-keeping.

11 Loosely refit the big-end cap to the connecting rod, and secure with the nuts/bolts - this will help to keep the components in their correct order.

12 Remove No 4 piston assembly in the same way.

13 Turn the crankshaft through 180° to bring pistons 2 and 3 to BDC (bottom dead centre), and remove them in the same way.

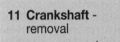

11 Crankshaft - removal

Note: *New main bearing cap bolts will be required on refitting.*

1.6 litre petrol engine

1 Remove the oil pump and flywheel/driveplate. Refer to Part A for information on SOHC engine and Part B for information on the DOHC engine.

2 Remove the piston and connecting rod assemblies as described in Section 10. If no work is to be done on the pistons and connecting rods, unbolt the caps and push the pistons far enough up the bores that the connecting rods are positioned clear of the crankshaft journals.

3 Check the crankshaft endfloat as described in Section 14, then proceed as follows.

4 The main bearing caps should be numbered 1 to 5 from the timing belt end of the engine and all identification numbers should be the right way up when read from the rear of the cylinder block **(see illustration)**. **Note:** *On some engines the flywheel/driveplate end (number 5) bearing cap may not be numbered but is easily identified anyway.* If the bearing caps are not marked, using a hammer and punch or a suitable marker pen, number the caps from 1 to 5 from the timing belt end of the engine and mark each cap to indicate its correct fitted direction to avoid confusion on refitting.

5 Working in a diagonal sequence, evenly and progressively slacken the ten main bearing cap retaining bolts by half a turn at a time until all bolts are loose. Remove all bolts.

11.4 Main bearing cap identification markings (arrowed)

6 Carefully remove each cap from the cylinder block, ensuring that the lower main bearing shell remains in position in the cap.

7 Carefully lift out the crankshaft, taking care not to displace the upper main bearing shells **(see illustration)**. Remove the rear oil seal and discard it.

8 Recover the upper bearing shells from the cylinder block, and tape them to their respective caps for safe-keeping.

1.8 and 2.0 litre petrol engines

9 Remove the flywheel/driveplate and the oil pump as described in Part B of the Chapter.

10 Undo the retaining screws and remove the baffle plate from the base of the cylinder block.

11 Evenly and progressively slacken the retaining bolts and remove the main bearing ladder casting from the base of the block.

12 Remove the crankshaft as described in paragraphs 2 to 8.

1.7 litre diesel engines

13 Working as described in Part C of this Chapter, remove the flywheel and unbolt the oil pump cover from the right-hand end of the cylinder block.

14 Unbolt the crankshaft rear oil seal housing and remove it from the cylinder block **(see illustration)**. If the housing locating dowels are a loose fit, remove them and store them with the housing for safe-keeping.

11.7 Removing the crankshaft

15 Remove the crankshaft as described in paragraphs 2 to 8 noting that the bearing cap identification markings are different. On this engine the caps should be numbered 1 to 5, number 1 cap being at the timing belt end, and the arrow on each cap should point towards the timing belt end of the engine.

16 With the crankshaft removed, remove the thrustwasher halves from the sides of number 2 main bearing.

2.0 litre diesel engine

17 Working as described in Part D of this Chapter, remove the crankshaft timing chain sprocket and the flywheel.

18 Evenly and progressively slacken and remove the retaining bolts then remove the main bearing ladder casting from the base of the bearing caps, noting which way around it is fitted.

19 Remove the crankshaft as described in paragraphs 2 to 8 noting that the bearing cap identification markings are different. On this engine, it will be necessary to make identification markings on each cap as only caps number 1 and 2 are marked by the manufacturer **(see illustration)**. Number the caps 1 to 5 from the timing chain end of the engine, marking each cap to indicate its correct fitted direction to avoid confusion on refitting.

2E

11.14 On 1.7 litre diesel engines unbolt the rear oil seal housing and remove it from the engine

11.19 On 2.0 litre diesel engines, only number 1 and 2 main bearing caps are marked by the manufacturer (arrowed)

12.2 On 2.0 litre diesel engines unscrew the retaining bolts and remove the piston oil spray nozzles from the cylinder block

12 Cylinder block - cleaning and inspection

Cleaning

1 Remove all external components and electrical switches/sensors from the block. For complete cleaning, the core plugs should ideally be removed. Drill a small hole in the plugs, then insert a self-tapping screw into the hole. Pull out the plugs by pulling on the screw with a pair of grips, or by using a slide hammer.

2 On diesel engines remove the piston oil spray nozzles from inside the cylinder block. On 1.7 litre engines the nozzles are a push-fit in the block and on 2.0 litre models they are retained by bolts (see illustration).

3 Scrape all traces of gasket from the cylinder block, and from the main bearing casting (where fitted), taking care not to damage the gasket/sealing surfaces.

4 Remove all oil gallery plugs (where fitted). The plugs are usually very tight - they may have to be drilled out, and the holes re-tapped. Use new plugs when the engine is reassembled.

5 If any of the castings are extremely dirty, all should be steam-cleaned.

6 After the castings are returned, clean all oil holes and oil galleries one more time. Flush all internal passages with warm water until the water runs clear. Dry thoroughly, and apply a

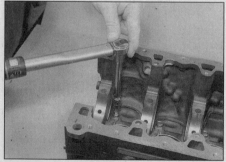

12.10 On 2.0 litre diesel engines refit the oil spray nozzles and tighten the retaining bolts to the specified torque

light film of oil to all mating surfaces, to prevent rusting. Also oil the cylinder bores. If you have access to compressed air, use it to speed up the drying process, and to blow out all the oil holes and galleries.

> ⚠️ Warning: Wear eye protection when using compressed air.

7 If the castings are not very dirty, you can do an adequate cleaning job with hot (as hot as you can stand), soapy water and a stiff brush. Take plenty of time, and do a thorough job. Regardless of the cleaning method used, be sure to clean all oil holes and galleries very thoroughly, and to dry all components well. Protect the cylinder bores as described above, to prevent rusting.

8 All threaded holes must be clean, to ensure accurate torque readings during reassembly. To clean the threads, run the correct-size tap into each of the holes to remove rust, corrosion, thread sealant or sludge, and to restore damaged threads. If possible, use compressed air to clear the holes of debris produced by this operation. A good alternative is to inject aerosol-applied water-dispersant lubricant into each hole, using the long spout usually supplied.

> ⚠️ Warning: Wear eye protection when cleaning out these holes in this way.

9 Apply suitable sealant to the new oil gallery plugs, and insert them into the holes in the block. Tighten them securely.

10 On diesel engines refit the piston oil spray nozzles to the cylinder block. On 1.7 litre engines press the nozzles securely into position ensuring that each one is positioned exactly at a right-angle to the crankshaft axis. On 2.0 litre models refit the nozzles to the block and tighten the retaining bolts to the specified torque (see illustration).

11 If the engine is not going to be reassembled right away, cover it with a large plastic bag to keep it clean; protect all mating surfaces and the cylinder bores as described above, to prevent rusting.

Inspection

12 Visually check the castings for cracks and corrosion. Look for stripped threads in the threaded holes. If there has been any history of internal water leakage, it may be worthwhile having an engine overhaul specialist check the cylinder block/crankcase with special equipment. If defects are found, have them repaired if possible, or renew the assembly.

13 Check the bore of each cylinder for scuffing and scoring.

14 Measure the diameter of each cylinder bore at the top (just below the wear ridge), centre and bottom of the bore, both parallel to the crankshaft axis and at right angles to it, so that a total of six measurements are taken. Note that there are various size groups of standard bore diameter to allow for manufacturing tolerances; the size group markings are stamped on the cylinder block.

15 Compare the results with the Specifications at the beginning of this Chapter; if any measurement exceeds the service limit specified, the cylinder block must be rebored if possible, or renewed and new piston assemblies fitted.

16 If the cylinder bores are badly scuffed or scored, or if they are excessively worn, out-of-round or tapered, or if the piston-to-bore clearance is excessive (see Section 13), the cylinder block must be rebored (if possible) or renewed and new pistons fitted. Oversize (0.5 mm) pistons are available for all engines except the 1.7 litre diesel engine.

17 If the bores are in reasonably good condition and not worn to the specified limits, then the piston rings should be renewed. If this is the case, the bores should be honed to allow the new rings to bed in correctly and provide the best possible seal. The conventional type of hone has spring-loaded stones, and is used with a power drill. You will also need some paraffin (or honing oil) and rags. The hone should be moved up and down the bore to produce a crosshatch pattern, and plenty of honing oil should be used. Ideally, the crosshatch lines should intersect at approximately a 60° angle. Do not take off more material than is necessary to produce the required finish. If new pistons are being fitted, the piston manufacturers may specify a finish with a different angle, so their instructions should be followed. Do not withdraw the hone from the bore while it is still being turned – stop it first. After honing a bore, wipe out all traces of the honing oil. If equipment of this type is not available, or if you are not sure whether you are competent to undertake the task yourself, an engine overhaul specialist will carry out the work at moderate cost.

13 Piston/connecting rod assembly - inspection

1 Before the inspection process can begin, the piston/connecting rod assemblies must be cleaned, and the original piston rings removed from the pistons.

2 Carefully expand the old rings over the top of the pistons. The use of two or three old feeler blades will be helpful in preventing the rings dropping into empty grooves (see illustration). Be careful not to scratch the piston with the ends of the ring. The rings are brittle, and will snap if they are spread too far. They're also very sharp - protect your hands and fingers. Note that the third (oil control) ring consists of a spacer and two side rails. Always remove the rings from the top of the piston. Keep each set of rings with its piston if the old rings are to be re-used.

3 Scrape away all traces of carbon from the top of the piston. A hand-held wire brush (or a piece of fine emery cloth) can be used, once the majority of the deposits have been scraped away. The piston identification markings should now be visible.

13.2 Using a feeler blade to remove a piston ring

4 Remove the carbon from the ring grooves in the piston, using an old ring. Break the ring in half to do this (be careful not to cut your fingers - piston rings are sharp). Be careful to remove only the carbon deposits - do not remove any metal, and do not nick or scratch the sides of the ring grooves.

5 Once the deposits have been removed, clean the piston/connecting rod assembly with paraffin or a suitable solvent, and dry thoroughly. Make sure that the oil return holes in the ring grooves are clear.

6 If the cylinder bores are not damaged or worn excessively, and if the cylinder block does not need to be rebored (see Section 12), check the pistons as follows.

7 Carefully inspect each piston for cracks around the skirt, around the gudgeon pin holes, and at the piston ring 'lands' (between the ring grooves).

8 Look for scoring and scuffing on the piston skirt, holes in the piston crown, and burned areas at the edge of the crown. If the skirt is scored or scuffed, the engine may have been suffering from overheating, and/or abnormal combustion which caused excessively high operating temperatures. The cooling and lubrication systems should be checked thoroughly. Scorch marks on the sides of the pistons show that blow-by has occurred. A hole in the piston crown, or burned areas at the edge of the piston crown, indicates that abnormal combustion (pre-ignition, knocking, or detonation) has been occurring. If any of the above problems exist, the causes must be investigated and corrected, or the damage will occur again. The causes may include

incorrect ignition/injection pump timing (as applicable), or a faulty injector.

9 Corrosion of the piston, in the form of pitting, indicates that coolant has been leaking into the combustion chamber and/or the crankcase. Again, the cause must be corrected, or the problem may persist in the rebuilt engine.

10 Measure the piston diameter at right angles to the gudgeon pin axis; compare the results with the Specifications at the beginning of this Chapter. Note that there are various size groups of standard piston diameter to allow for manufacturing tolerances; the size group markings are stamped on the piston crown.

11 To measure the piston-to-bore clearance, either measure the bore (see Section 12) and piston skirt as described and subtract the skirt diameter from the bore measurement, or insert each piston into its original bore, then select a feeler gauge blade and slip it into the bore along with the piston. The piston must be aligned exactly in its normal attitude, and the feeler gauge blade must be between the piston and bore, on one of the thrust faces, just up from the bottom of the bore. Divide the measured clearance by two, to provide the clearance when the piston is central in the bore. If the clearance is excessive, a new piston will be required. If the piston binds at the lower end of the bore and is loose towards the top, the bore is tapered. If tight spots are encountered as the piston/feeler gauge blade is rotated in the bore, the bore is out-of-round.

12 Repeat this procedure for the remaining pistons and cylinder bores. Any piston which is worn beyond the specified limits must be renewed.

13 Examine each connecting rod carefully for signs of damage, such as cracks around the big-end and small-end bearings. Check that the rod is not bent or distorted. Damage is highly unlikely, unless the engine has been seized or badly overheated. Detailed checking of the connecting rod assembly can only be carried out by a Vauxhall dealer or engine repair specialist with the necessary equipment.

Petrol engines

14 On all petrol engines, the gudgeon pins

are an interference fit in the connecting rod small-end bearing. Therefore, piston and/or connecting rod renewal should be entrusted to a Vauxhall dealer or engine repair specialist, who will have the necessary tooling to remove and install the gudgeon pins. If new pistons are to be fitted, ensure that the correct size group pistons are fitted to each bore. **Note:** *Vauxhall state that the piston/connecting rod assemblies should not be disassembled. If any components requires renewal, then the complete assembly must be renewed. Do not fit a new piston to an old connecting rod or vice versa.*

Diesel engines

15 On diesel engines, the gudgeon pins are of the floating type, secured in position by two circlips. On these engines, the pistons and connecting rods can be separated as follows.

16 Using a small flat-bladed screwdriver, prise out the circlips, and push out the gudgeon pin **(see illustration)**. Hand pressure should be sufficient to remove the pin. Identify the piston and rod to ensure correct reassembly. Discard the circlips - new ones *must* be used on refitting.

17 Examine the gudgeon pin and connecting rod small-end bearing for signs of wear or damage **(see illustration)**. Wear will require the renewal of both the pin and connecting rod. On 1.7 litre engines the small-end bush is available separately, however, bush renewal is a specialist job - press facilities are required, and the new bush must be reamed accurately.

18 The connecting rods themselves should not be in need of renewal, unless seizure or some other major mechanical failure has occurred. Check the alignment of the connecting rods visually, and if the rods are not straight, take them to an engine overhaul specialist for a more detailed check.

19 Examine all components, and obtain any new parts from your Vauxhall dealer. If new pistons are purchased, they will be supplied complete with gudgeon pins and circlips. Circlips can also be purchased individually.

20 On 1.7 litre engines, assemble the piston and connecting rod so that the timing mark (dot) on the piston crown is on the same side as the raised mark which is cast onto the side of the connecting rod **(see illustrations)**.

2E

13.16 On diesel engines prise out the circlips then remove the gudgeon pin and separate the piston and connecting rod

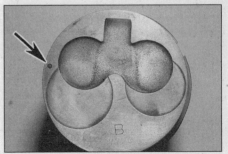

13.17 Measuring gudgeon pin diameter with a micrometer

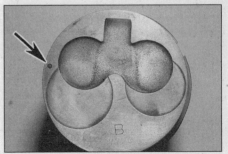

13.20a On 1.7 litre diesel engines assemble the piston and connecting rod so that the piston timing mark (arrowed) . . .

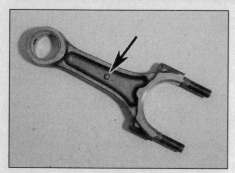

13.20b . . . is on the same side as the connecting rod raised mark (arrowed)

21 On 2.0 litre engines, assemble the piston and connecting rod so that the arrow on the piston crown is pointing away from the assembly mark which is cast onto one side of the connecting rod, on the top of the big-end bore **(see illustration)**.

22 Apply a smear of clean engine oil to the gudgeon pin. Slide it into the piston and through the connecting rod small-end. Check that the piston pivots freely on the rod, then secure the gudgeon pin in position with two new circlips, ensuring that each circlip is correctly located in its groove in the piston. On 2.0 litre engines make sure that both circlips are positioned so that their end gaps are at the top **(see illustrations)**.

13.22a Ensure the piston and connecting rod are correctly assembled then insert the gudgeon pin . . .

13.22b . . . and secure it in position with new circlips.

On 2.0 litre engines position the circlip end gap at the top

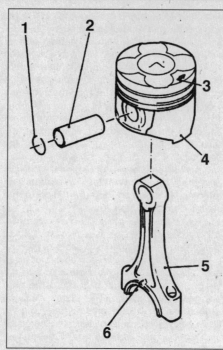

13.21 Piston/connecting rod assembly components

1 Circlip	4 Piston
2 Gudgeon pin	5 Connecting rod
3 Arrow on piston crown	6 Connecting rod assembly mark

14 Crankshaft - inspection

Checking crankshaft endfloat

1 If the crankshaft endfloat is to be checked, this must be done when the crankshaft is still installed in the cylinder block, but is free to move (see Section 11).

2 Check the endfloat using a dial gauge in contact with the end of the crankshaft. Push the crankshaft fully one way, and then zero the gauge. Push the crankshaft fully the other way, and check the endfloat **(see illustration)**. The result can be compared with

the specified amount, and will give an indication as to whether new thrustwasher halves (1.7 litre diesel engine) or main bearing shells (all other engines) are required.

3 If a dial gauge is not available, feeler gauges can be used. First push the crankshaft fully towards the flywheel/driveplate end of the engine, then use feeler gauges to measure the gap between the web of the crankpin and the side of thrustwasher **(see illustration)**. On 1.7 litre diesel engines separate thrustwashers are fitted to the sides of number 2 main bearing upper shell and on all other engines the thrustwashers are incorporated into number 3 main bearing shells.

Inspection

4 Clean the crankshaft using paraffin or a suitable solvent, and dry it, preferably with compressed air if available. Be sure to clean the oil holes with a pipe cleaner or similar probe, to ensure that they are not obstructed.

⚠ *Warning: Wear eye protection when using compressed air.*

5 Check the main and big-end bearing journals for uneven wear, scoring, pitting and cracking.

6 Big-end bearing wear is accompanied by distinct metallic knocking when the engine is running (particularly noticeable when the engine is pulling from low speed) and some loss of oil pressure.

7 Main bearing wear is accompanied by severe engine vibration and rumble - getting progressively worse as engine speed increases - and again by loss of oil pressure.

8 Check the bearing journal for roughness by running a finger lightly over the bearing surface. Any roughness (which will be accompanied by obvious bearing wear) indicates that the crankshaft requires regrinding (where possible) or renewal.

9 Check for burrs around the crankshaft oil holes (the holes are usually chamfered, so burrs should not be a problem unless regrinding has been carried out carelessly). Remove any burrs with a fine file or scraper, and thoroughly clean the oil holes as described previously.

14.2 Check the crankshaft endfloat using a dial gauge . . .

14.3 . . . or a feeler gauge

10 Using a micrometer, measure the diameter of the main and big-end bearing journals, and compare the results with the Specifications (see illustration). By measuring the diameter at a number of points around each journal's circumference, you will be able to determine whether or not the journal is out-of-round. Take the measurement at each end of the journal, near the webs, to determine if the journal is tapered. Compare the results obtained with those given in the Specifications.

11 Check the oil seal contact surfaces at each end of the crankshaft for wear and damage. If the seal has worn a deep groove in the surface of the crankshaft, consult an engine overhaul specialist; repair may be possible, but otherwise a new crankshaft will be required.

12 Set the crankshaft up in V-blocks, and position a dial gauge on the top of the crankshaft number 1 main bearing journal. Zero the dial gauge, then slowly rotate the crankshaft through two complete revolutions, noting the journal run-out. Repeat the procedure on the remaining four main bearing journals, so that a run-out measurement is available for all main bearing journals. If the difference between the run-out of any two journals exceeds the service limit given in the Specifications, the crankshaft must be renewed.

13 Undersize (0.25 mm and 0.50 mm) big-end and main bearing shells are produced by Vauxhall for all engines except the 1.7 litre diesel engine. If the crankshaft journals have not already been reground, it may be possible to have the crankshaft reconditioned, and to fit undersize shells. On 1.7 litre diesel engines, if the crankshaft has worn beyond the specified limits, it will have to be renewed.

15 Main and big-end bearings - inspection

1 Even though the main and big-end bearings should be renewed during the engine overhaul, the old bearings should be retained for close examination, as they may reveal valuable information about the condition of the engine (see illustration).

2 Bearing failure can occur due to lack of lubrication, the presence of dirt or other foreign particles, overloading the engine, or corrosion (see illustration). Regardless of the cause of bearing failure, the cause must be corrected (where applicable) before the engine is reassembled, to prevent it from happening again.

3 When examining the bearing shells, remove them from the cylinder block, the main bearing caps, the connecting rods and the connecting rod big-end bearing caps. Lay them out on a clean surface in the same general position as their location in the engine. This will enable you to match any bearing problems with the corresponding crankshaft journal.

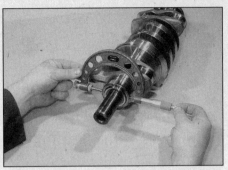

14.10 Using a micrometer to measure a crankshaft main bearing journal diameter

4 Dirt and other foreign matter gets into the engine in a variety of ways. It may be left in the engine during assembly, or it may pass through filters or the crankcase ventilation system. It may get into the oil, and from there into the bearings. Metal chips from machining operations and normal engine wear are often present. Abrasives are sometimes left in engine components after reconditioning, especially when parts are not thoroughly cleaned using the proper cleaning methods. Whatever the source, these foreign objects often end up embedded in the soft bearing material, and are easily recognised. Large particles will not embed in the bearing, and will score or gouge the bearing and journal. The best prevention for this cause of bearing failure is to clean all parts thoroughly, and keep everything spotlessly-clean during engine assembly. Frequent and regular engine oil and filter changes are also recommended.

5 Lack of lubrication (or lubrication breakdown) has a number of interrelated causes. Excessive heat (which thins the oil), overloading (which squeezes the oil from the bearing face) and oil leakage (from excessive bearing clearances, worn oil pump or high engine speeds) all contribute to lubrication breakdown. Blocked oil passages, which usually are the result of misaligned oil holes in a bearing shell, will also oil-starve a bearing, and destroy it. When lack of lubrication is the cause of bearing failure, the bearing material is wiped or extruded from the steel backing of the bearing. Temperatures may increase to the point where the steel backing turns blue from overheating.

6 Driving habits can have a definite effect on bearing life. Full-throttle, low-speed operation (labouring the engine) puts very high loads on bearings, tending to squeeze out the oil film. These loads cause the bearings to flex, which produces fine cracks in the bearing face (fatigue failure). Eventually, the bearing material will loosen in pieces, and tear away from the steel backing.

7 Short-distance driving leads to corrosion of bearings, because insufficient engine heat is produced to drive off the condensed water and corrosive gases. These products collect in the engine oil, forming acid and sludge. As the oil is carried to the engine bearings, the acid attacks and corrodes the bearing material.

8 Incorrect bearing installation during engine assembly will lead to bearing failure as well. Tight-fitting bearings leave insufficient bearing running clearance, and will result in oil starvation. Dirt or foreign particles trapped behind a bearing shell result in high spots on the bearing, which lead to failure.

9 As mentioned at the beginning of this Section, the bearing shells should be renewed as a matter of course during engine overhaul; to do otherwise is false economy.

15.1 Typical main bearing shell identification markings

16 Engine overhaul - reassembly sequence

1 Before reassembly begins, ensure that all new parts have been obtained, and that all necessary tools are available. Read through the entire procedure to familiarise yourself with the work involved, and to ensure that all items necessary for reassembly of the engine are at hand. In addition to all normal tools and materials, thread-locking compound will be needed. A good quality tube of liquid sealant

2E

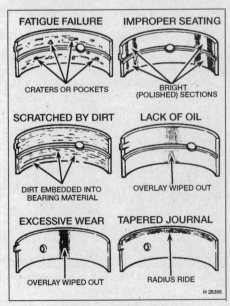

15.2 Typical bearing failures

17.4 Measuring a piston ring end gap using a feeler gauge

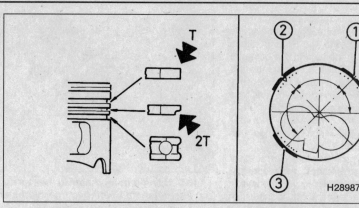

17.10 Piston ring identification and end gap locations - 1.7 litre diesel engine

1 Top compression ring
2 Second compression ring
3 Oil scraper ring
F Timing mark (dot) on piston crown

will also be required for the joint faces that are fitted without gaskets.

2 In order to save time and avoid problems, engine reassembly can be carried out in the following order:

a) *Crankshaft.*
b) *Piston/connecting rod assemblies.*
c) *Timing chains and sprockets - 2.0 litre diesel engine.*
d) *Oil pump.*
e) *Sump.*
f) *Flywheel/driveplate.*
g) *Cylinder head.*
h) *Timing belt tensioner and sprockets, and belts - all models except 2.0 litre diesel engine.*
i) *Inlet and exhaust manifolds (Chapter 4).*
j) *Engine external components.*

3 At this stage, all engine components should be absolutely clean and dry, with all faults repaired. The components should be laid out (or in individual containers) on a completely clean work surface.

17 Piston rings - refitting

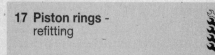

1 Before fitting new piston rings, the ring end gaps must be checked as follows.

2 Lay out the piston/connecting rod assem-blies and the new piston ring sets, so that the ring sets will be matched with the same piston and

cylinder during the end gap measurement and subsequent engine reassembly.

3 Insert the top ring into the first cylinder, and push it down the bore using the top of the piston. This will ensure that the ring remains square with the cylinder walls. Push the ring down into the bore until it is positioned 15 to 20 mm down from the top edge of the bore, then withdraw the piston.

4 Measure the end gap using feeler gauges, and compare the measurements with the figures given in the Specifications **(see illustration)**.

5 If the gap is too small (unlikely if genuine Vauxhall parts are used), it must be enlarged, or the ring ends may contact each other during engine operation, causing serious damage. Ideally, new piston rings providing the correct end gap should be fitted. As a last resort, the end gap can be increased by filing the ring ends very carefully with a fine file. Mount the file in a vice with soft jaws, slip the ring over the file with the ends contacting the file face, and slowly move the ring to remove material from the ends. Take care, as piston rings are sharp, and are easily broken.

6 With new piston rings, it is unlikely that the end gap will be too large. If the gaps are too large, check that you have the correct rings for your engine and for the particular cylinder bore size.

7 Repeat the checking procedure for each ring in the first cylinder, and then for the rings in the remaining cylinders. Remember to keep rings, pistons and cylinders matched up.

8 Once the ring end gaps have been checked and if necessary corrected, the rings can be fitted to the pistons.

9 Fit the piston rings using the same technique as for removal. Fit the bottom (oil control) spacer first then install both the side rails, noting that both the spacer and side rails can be installed either way up.

10 On 1.7 litre diesel engines, the second and top rings are different and can be identified by the marks on the ring top surface; the top ring has a square cross-section and is marked 'T' whilst the second ring has a stepped cross-section and is marked '2T'. Fit the second and top compression rings ensuring that each ring is fitted the correct way up with its identification mark uppermost **(see illustration)**. **Note:** *Always follow any instructions supplied with the new piston ring sets - different manufacturers may specify different procedures. Do not mix up the top and second compression rings.*

11 On all other engines, the second and top compression rings are different and can be identified by their cross-sections; the top ring is square whilst the second ring is tapered. Fit the second and top compression rings ensuring

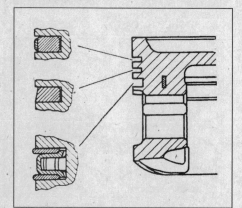

17.11 Sectional view of piston rings (1.6 litre engine shown - others similar)

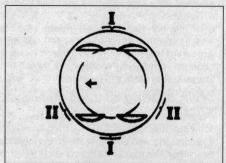

17.12a Piston ring end gap positions - petrol engine

I Top and second compression rings
II Oil control ring side rails

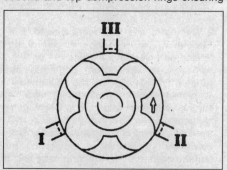

17.12b Piston ring end gap positions - 2.0 litre diesel engine

I Top compression ring
II Second compression ring
III Oil control ring

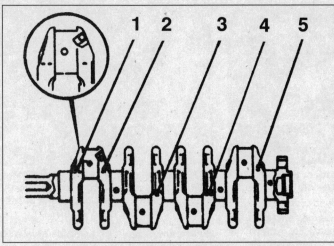

18.2 Crankshaft main bearing journal size group markings - 1.7 litre diesel engine

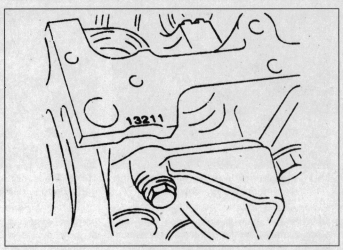

18.3 Cylinder block main bearing bore size group markings - 1.7 litre diesel engine

that each ring is fitted the correct way up with its identification ('TOP') mark uppermost **(see illustration)**. **Note:** *Always follow any instructions supplied with the new piston ring sets - different manufacturers may specify different procedures. Do not mix up the top and second compression rings. On some engines the top ring will not have an identification marking and can be fitted either way up.*

12 With the piston rings correctly installed, check that each ring is free to rotate easily in its groove. Check the ring-to-groove clearance of each ring using feeler gauges and check that the clearance is within the specified range then position the ring end gaps as shown **(see illustrations)**.

18 Crankshaft - refitting and main bearing running clearance check

Note: *It is recommended that new main bearing shells are fitted regardless of the condition of the original ones.*

Selection of bearing shells

1.7 litre diesel engine

1 The main bearing running clearance is controlled in production by selecting one of four grades of bearing shell. The grades are indicated by a colour-coding marked on the edge of each shell which governs the shell's thickness. In order, from the thinnest to the thickest, the shell grades are: Green, Brown, Black and Blue. Bearing shells are produced in standard size only, no undersize shells are available from Vauxhall.

2 If the bearing shells are to be renewed, first check and record the identification marking stamped on the crankshaft adjacent to each main bearing journal. The marking is in the form of a either single or double line on the crankshaft web. Number 1 (timing belt end of the engine) bearing code is situated to the

right of the journal; whereas all other codes are on the left-hand side of the relevant journal **(see illustration)**.

3 Secondly, check and record the main bearing bore size code identification markings which are stamped on the right-hand, rear end of the cylinder block lower mating surface **(see illustration)**. The markings are in the form of numbers (1 to 3). The first marking indicates the size group of number 1 (timing belt end) main bearing bore and the last number 5.

4 Match the relevant main bearing bore code with its crankshaft journal code, and select a new set of bearing shells using the following table. The crankshaft codes are listed down the left-hand side, and the main bearing bore codes along the top; the required bearing grade is indicated in the box where the two columns intersect.

	1	2	3
Single line	Black	Brown	Green
Double line	Blue	Black	Brown

All other engines

5 On all engines except the 1.7 litre diesel, although the original bearing shells fitted at the factory maybe of various grades, all replacement bearing shells sold are of the same grade. Vauxhall supply both standard size bearing shells and undersize shells for use when the crankshaft has been reground. The required size of shell required can be determined by measuring the crankshaft journals (see Section 14).

Main bearing running clearance check

6 Clean the backs of the bearing shells and the bearing locations in both the cylinder block and the main bearing caps.

7 Press the bearing shells into their locations, ensuring that the tab on each shell engages in the notch in the cylinder block or main bearing cap **(see illustration)**. If the original bearing shells are being used for the check, ensure they are refitted in their original locations. The

clearance can be checked in either of two ways.

8 One method (which will be difficult to achieve without a range of internal micrometers or internal/external expanding calipers) is to refit the main bearing caps to the cylinder block, with bearing shells in place. With the cap retaining bolts correctly tightened (use the original bolts for the check, not the new ones), measure the internal diameter of each assembled pair of bearing shells. If the diameter of each corresponding crankshaft journal is measured and then subtracted from the bearing internal diameter, the result will be the main bearing running clearance.

9 The second (and more accurate) method is to use a product known as Plastigauge. This consists of a fine thread of perfectly round plastic which is compressed between the bearing shell and the journal. When the shell is removed, the plastic is deformed and can be measured with a special card gauge supplied with the kit. The running clearance is determined from this gauge. Plastigauge is sometimes difficult to obtain but enquiries at one of the larger specialist quality motor factors should produce the name of a stockist in your area. The procedure for using Plastigauge is as follows.

2E

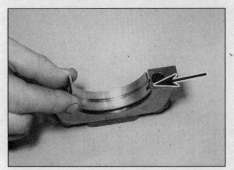

18.7 Fit the bearing shells making sure their tabs are correctly located in the slots in the bearing cap/block (arrowed)

18.11 Plastigauge in place on a crankshaft main bearing journal

18.13 Measure the width of the deformed Plastigauge using the scale on the card

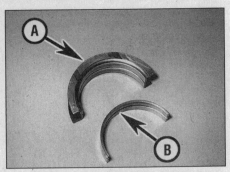

18.19 On all engines except the 1.7 litre diesel, the centre main bearing shells (A) incorporate the thrust flanges and all other shells are plain (B)

10 With the main bearing upper shells in place, carefully lay the crankshaft in position. Do not use any lubricant; the crankshaft journals and bearing shells must be perfectly clean and dry.

11 Cut several lengths of the appropriate size Plastigauge (they should be slightly shorter than the width of the main bearings) and place one length on each crankshaft journal axis **(see illustration)**.

12 With the main bearing lower shells in position, refit the main bearing caps, using the identification marks to ensure each one is correctly positioned. Refit the original retaining bolts and tighten them to the specified torque (1.7 litre diesel engine - see paragraph 41) or to the specified stage 1 torque and then through the stage 2 and 3 angles (all other engines - see paragraphs 24 to 26). Take care not to disturb the Plastigauge and **do not** rotate the crankshaft at any time during this operation. Evenly and progressively slacken and remove the main bearing cap bolts then lift off the caps again taking great care not to disturb the Plastigauge or rotate the crankshaft.

13 Compare the width of the crushed Plastigauge on each journal to the scale printed on the Plastigauge envelope to obtain the main bearing running clearance **(see illustration)**. Compare the clearance measured with that given in the Specifications at the start of this Chapter.

14 If the clearance is significantly different from that expected, the bearing shells may be the wrong size (or excessively worn if the original shells are being re-used). Before deciding that the crankshaft is worn, make sure that no dirt or oil was trapped between the bearing shells and the caps or block when the clearance was measured. If the Plastigauge was wider at one end than at the other, the crankshaft journal may be tapered.

15 Before condemning the components concerned, seek the advice of your Vauxhall dealer or suitable engine repair specialist. They will also be able to inform as to the best course of action or whether renewal will be necessary.

16 Where necessary, obtain the correct size of bearing shell and repeat the running clearance checking procedure as described above.

17 On completion, carefully scrape away all traces of the Plastigauge material from the crankshaft and bearing shells using a fingernail or other object which is unlikely to score the bearing surfaces.

Final crankshaft refitting

1.6 litre petrol engine models

18 Carefully lift the crankshaft out of the cylinder block.

19 Place the bearing shells in their locations as described above in paragraphs 6 and 7 **(see illustration)**. If new shells are being fitted, ensure that all traces of the protective

grease are cleaned off using paraffin. Wipe dry the shells and caps with a lint-free cloth.

20 Lubricate the upper shells with clean engine oil then lower the crankshaft into position **(see illustration)**.

21 Ensure the crankshaft is correctly seated then check the endfloat as described in Section 14.

22 Ensure the bearing shells are correctly located in the caps and refit the caps number 1 to 4 to the cylinder block **(see illustration)**. Ensure the caps are fitted in their correct locations, with number 1 cap at the timing belt end, and are fitted the correct way around so that all the numbers are the correct way up when read from the rear of the cylinder block.

23 Ensure the rear (number 5) bearing cap is clean and dry then fill the groove on each side of the cap with sealing compound (Vauxhall recommend the use of sealant, part no 90485251, available from your Vauxhall dealer) **(see illustration)**. Fit the bearing cap to the engine, ensuring it is fitted the correct way around.

24 Apply a smear of clean engine to oil to the threads and underneath the heads of the new main bearing cap bolts. Fit the bolts, tightening them all by hand **(see illustration)**.

25 Working in a diagonal sequence from the centre outwards, tighten the main bearing cap bolts to the specified Stage 1 torque setting **(see illustration)**.

18.20 Lubricate the upper bearing shells with clean engine oil then fit the crankshaft

18.22 Lubricate the crankshaft journals then refit bearing caps number 1 to 4, ensuring each one is fitted in its original location

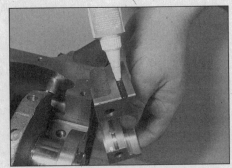

18.23 Fill the side grooves of the rear (number 5) bearing cap with sealant prior to refitting it to the engine

18.24 Lubricate the threads of the new main bearing cap bolts . . .

18.25 . . . then tighten the bolts to the specified stage 1 torque setting . . .

18.26 . . . and then through the specified stages 2 and 3 angles

26 Once all bolts are tightened to the specified Stage 1 torque, go around again and tighten all bolts through the specified Stage 2 angle then go around for once more and tighten all bolts through the specified Stage 3 angle. It is recommended that an angle-measuring gauge is used during the final stages of the tightening, to ensure accuracy **(see illustration)**. If a gauge is not available, use white paint to make alignment marks between the bolt head and cap prior to tightening; the marks can then be used to check that the bolt has been rotated through the correct angle.

27 Once all the bolts have been tightened, inject more sealant down the grooves in the rear main bearing cap until sealant is seen to be escaping through the joints. Once you are sure the cap grooves are full of sealant, wipe off all excess sealant using a clean cloth.

28 Check that the crankshaft is free to rotate smoothly; if excessive pressure is required to turn the crankshaft, investigate the cause before proceeding further.

29 Refit/reconnect the piston connecting rod assemblies to the crankshaft as described in Section 19.

30 Referring to Part A (SOHC engine) or Part B (DOHC engine), fit a new left-hand crankshaft oil seal, then refit the flywheel/driveplate, oil pump, cylinder head, timing belt sprocket(s) and fit a new timing belt.

1.8 and 2.0 litre petrol engines

31 Refit the crankshaft as described in paragraphs 18 to 29.

32 Ensure the bearing cap and main bearing ladder casting surfaces are clean and dry then refit the casting to the engine. Refit the retaining bolts and tighten them to the specified torque, working in a diagonal sequence from the centre outwards.

33 Refit the baffle plate to the base of the cylinder block assembly and tighten its retaining bolts to the specified torque.

34 Working as described in Part B of this Chapter, fit a new left-hand crankshaft oil seal then refit the flywheel/driveplate, oil pump, cylinder head, timing belt sprocket(s) and fit a new timing belt.

1.7 litre diesel engine

35 Carefully lift the crankshaft out of the cylinder block.

36 Place the bearing shells in their locations as described above in paragraphs 6 and 7. If new shells are being fitted, ensure that all traces of the protective grease are cleaned off using paraffin. Wipe dry the shells and caps with a lint-free cloth.

37 Using a little grease, stick the thrustwashers to each side of the number 2 main bearing upper location; ensure that the oilway grooves on each thrustwasher face outwards **(see illustration)**.

38 Lubricate the upper shells with clean engine oil then lower the crankshaft into position.

39 Ensure the crankshaft is correctly seated then check the endfloat as described in Section 14.

40 Ensure the bearing shells are correctly located in the caps and refit the caps to the cylinder block **(see illustration)**. Ensure the caps are fitted in their correct locations, with number 1 cap at the timing belt end, and are fitted the correct way around so that the arrows all point towards the timing belt end of the engine. Prior to refitting number 1 cap, apply a smear of sealant to its mating surface.

41 Apply a smear of clean engine to oil to the threads and underneath the heads of the new main bearing cap bolts. Fit the bolts tightening them all by hand then working in a diagonal sequence from the centre outwards, evenly and progressively tighten them to the specified torque setting **(see illustration)**.

42 Check that the crankshaft is free to rotate smoothly; if excessive pressure is required to turn the crankshaft, investigate the cause before proceeding further.

43 Ensure that the mating surfaces of rear oil seal housing and cylinder block are clean and dry. Note the correct fitted depth of the oil seal then tap/lever the seal out of the housing **(see illustration)**.

2E

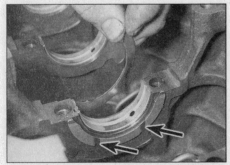

18.37 On 1.7 litre diesel engines, fit the thrustwasher to each side of number 2 main bearing ensuring the oilway grooves (arrowed) are facing outwards

18.40 Refit the main bearing caps . . .

18.41 . . . then fit the new retaining bolts and tighten them evenly and progressively to the specified torque

18.43 Remove the oil seal from the rear housing prior to refitting

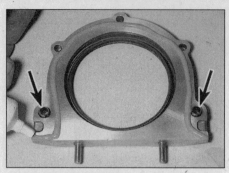

18.44 Apply a bead of sealant to the rear oil seal housing mating surface and refit the housing to the engine (locating dowels arrowed)

18.46a With the rear bearing cap in position, inject sealant down the groove . . .

18.46b . . . until it is seen to be forced out through the hole in the cap (arrowed)

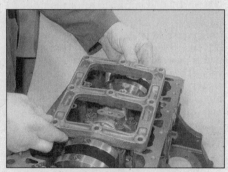

18.47a Refit the main bearing ladder casting . . .

18.47b . . . ensuring its arrow is pointing towards the timing chain end of the engine, and tighten its retaining bolts to the specified torque

44 Apply a smear of sealant to the oil seal housing mating surface, and make sure that the locating dowels are in position **(see illustration)**. Slide the housing over the end of the crankshaft, and into position on the cylinder block, then tighten the retaining bolts to the specified torque setting.

45 Refit/reconnect the piston connecting rod assemblies to the crankshaft as described in Section 19. Referring to Part C of this Chapter fit a new crankshaft rear oil seal, then refit the flywheel, oil pump cover, cylinder head, timing belt sprocket(s) and fit a new timing belt.

2.0 litre diesel engine

46 Refit the crankshaft as described in paragraphs 18 to 29, using the marks made on removal to ensure the bearing caps are correctly positioned (see Section 11) **(see illustrations)**.

47 Ensure the bearing cap and main bearing ladder casting surfaces are clean and dry. Refit the casting to the engine, ensuring that the arrow on the casting is pointing towards the timing chain end of the engine, then refit the retaining bolts and tighten them to the specified torque, working in a diagonal sequence from the centre outwards **(see illustrations)**.

48 Working as described Part D of this Chapter, fit a new left-hand oil crankshaft oil seal then refit the flywheel, timing chains and sprockets and cylinder head.

19 Piston/connecting rod assembly - refitting and big-end running clearance check

Note: *It is recommended that new piston rings and big-end bearing shells are fitted regardless of the condition of the original ones.*

Selection of bearing shells

1.7 litre diesel engine

1 The big-end bearing running clearance is controlled in production by selecting one of three grades of bearing shell. The grades are indicated by a colour-coding marked on the edge of each shell which governs the shell's thickness. In order, from the thinnest to the

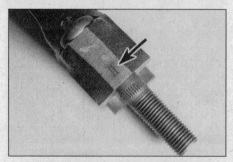

19.2 Connecting rod big-end bore size group marking (arrowed) - 1.7 litre diesel engine

thickest, the shell grades are: Brown, Black and Blue. Bearing shells are produced in standard size only, no undersize shells are available from Vauxhall.

2 If the bearing shells are to be renewed, first check and record the identification marking stamped on the side face of each connecting rod **(see illustration)**. The markings are used to select the correct grade of bearing shell required as follows.

Connecting rod mark	Bearing shell grade required
I	Blue
II	Black
III	Brown

All other engines

3 On all engines except the 1.7 litre diesel, although the original bearing shells fitted at the factory maybe of various grades, all replacement bearing shells sold are of the same grade. Vauxhall supply both standard size bearing shells and undersize shells for use when the crankshaft has been reground. The required size of shell required can be determined by measuring the crankshaft journals (see Section 14).

Big-end bearing running clearance check

4 Clean the backs of the bearing shells and the bearing locations in both the connecting rod and bearing cap.

19.5 Fit the bearing shells making sure their tabs are correctly located in the connecting rod/cap groove (arrowed)

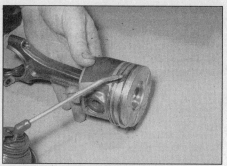

19.9 Lubricate the piston rings with clean engine oil

19.10 Ensure the piston ring end gaps are correctly spaced then fit the ring compressor

5 Press the bearing shells into their locations, ensuring that the tab on each shell engages in the notch in the connecting rod and cap **(see illustration)**. If the original bearing shells are being used for the check ensure they are refitted in their original locations. The clearance can be checked in either of two ways.

6 One method is to refit the big-end bearing cap to the connecting rod, with bearing shells in place. With the cap retaining bolts/nuts (use the original bolts for the check) correctly tightened, use an internal micrometer or vernier caliper to measure the internal diameter of each assembled pair of bearing shells. If the diameter of each corresponding crankshaft journal is measured and then

subtracted from the bearing internal diameter, the result will be the big-end bearing running clearance.

7 The second method is to use Plastigauge as described in Section 18, paragraphs 9 to 17. Place a strand of Plastigauge on each (cleaned) crankpin journal and refit the (clean) piston/connecting rod assemblies, shells and big-end bearing caps. Tighten the bolts/nuts (as applicable) correctly taking care not to disturb the Plastigauge. Dismantle the assemblies without rotating the crankshaft and use the scale printed on the Plastigauge envelope to obtain the big-end bearing running clearance. On completion of the measurement, carefully scrape off all traces of Plastigauge from the journal and shells using a fingernail or other object which will not score the components.

Final piston/connecting rod assembly refitting

8 Ensure the bearing shells are correctly refitted as described above in paragraphs 4 and 5. If new shells are being fitted, ensure that all traces of the protective grease are cleaned off using paraffin. Wipe dry the shells and connecting rods with a lint-free cloth.

9 Lubricate the bores, the pistons and piston rings then lay out each piston/connecting rod assembly in its respective position **(see illustration)**.

10 Starting with assembly number 1, make sure that the piston rings are still spaced as

described in Section 17, then clamp them in position with a piston ring compressor **(see illustration)**.

Petrol engines

11 Insert the piston/connecting rod assembly into the top of cylinder No 1, ensuring that the arrow marking on the piston crown is pointing towards the timing belt end of the engine. Using a block of wood or hammer handle against the piston crown, tap the assembly into the cylinder until the piston crown is flush with the top of the cylinder **(see illustrations)**.

12 Taking care not to mark the cylinder bore, liberally lubricate the crankpin and both bearing shells, then pull the piston/connecting rod assembly down the bore and onto the crankpin and refit the big-end bearing cap using the markings to ensure it is fitted the correct way around (the lug on the bearing cap base should be facing the flywheel/driveplate end of the engine) and screw in the new retaining bolts **(see illustration)**.

13 On 1.6 litre engines, tighten both bearing cap bolts to the specified Stage 1 torque setting and then tighten them through the specified Stage 2 angle. It is recommended that an angle-measuring gauge is used to ensure accuracy **(see illustrations)**. If a gauge is not available, use white paint to make alignment marks between the bolt head and cap prior to tightening; the marks can then be used to check that the bolt has been rotated through the correct angle.

2E

19.11a Insert the piston connecting rod into the correct bore ensuring the arrow on the piston crown (circled) is pointing towards the timing belt end of the engine

19.11b Tap the piston gently into the bore using handle of a hammer

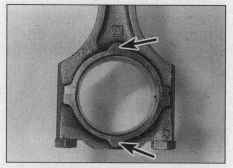

19.12 Refit the bearing cap to the connecting rod making sure its lug (arrowed) is facing the flywheel/driveplate end of the engine

19.13a Tighten the big-end bearing cap bolts to the specified stage 1 torque . . .

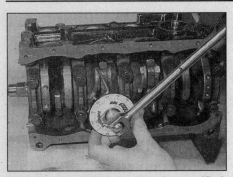

19.13b . . . and then through the specified angle(s)

14 On 1.8 and 2.0 litre engines, tighten both bearing cap bolts to the specified Stage 1 torque setting then tighten them through the specified Stage 2 angle, and finally through the specified Stage 3 angle. It is recommended that an angle-measuring gauge is used during the final stages of the tightening, to ensure accuracy. If a gauge is not available, use white paint to make alignment marks between the bolt head and cap prior to tightening; the marks can then be used to check that the bolt has been rotated through the correct angle.

15 Refit the remaining three piston and connecting rod assemblies in the same way.

16 Rotate the crankshaft, and check that it turns freely, with no signs of binding or tight spots.

17 On 1.8 and 2.0 litre engines, where removed, ensure the bearing cap and main bearing ladder casting surfaces are clean and dry. Refit the casting to the engine and tighten its retaining bolts to the specified torque, working in a diagonal sequence from the centre outwards. Refit the baffle plate to the base of the cylinder block and tighten its retaining bolts to the specified torque.

18 On all engines, refit the oil pump strainer, sump and the cylinder head as described in Part A or B (as applicable) of this Chapter.

1.7 litre diesel engines

19 Prior to refitting, carefully tap the original bolts out from the connecting rod and install the new bolts **(see illustration)**.

20 Insert the piston/connecting rod assembly into the top of cylinder No 1, ensuring that the timing mark (dot) on the piston crown is pointing towards the timing belt end of the engine. Using a block of wood or hammer handle against the piston crown, tap the assembly into the cylinder until the piston crown is flush with the top of the cylinder **(see illustrations)**.

21 Taking care not to mark the cylinder bore, liberally lubricate the crankpin and both bearing shells, then pull the piston/connecting rod assembly down the bore and onto the crankpin and refit the big-end bearing cap, using the markings to ensure it is fitted the correct way around and fit the new retaining nuts **(see illustration)**.

22 Tighten both bearing cap nuts to the specified Stage 1 torque setting then tighten them through the specified Stage 2 angle, and finally through the specified Stage 3 angle **(see illustration)**. It is recommended that an angle-measuring gauge is used during the final stages of the tightening, to ensure accuracy. If a gauge is not available, use white paint to make alignment marks between the nut and cap prior to tightening; the marks can then be used to check that the nut has been rotated through the correct angle.

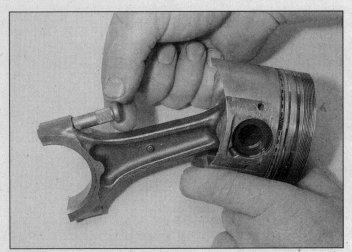

19.19 On 1.7 litre diesel engines renew the connecting rod bearing cap bolts before refitting the piston/connecting rod assemblies

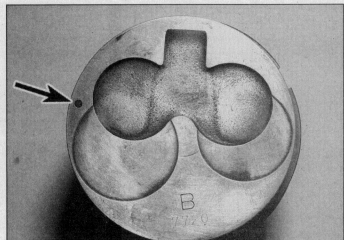

19.20a Insert the piston connecting rod into the correct bore ensuring the timing mark (arrowed) on the piston crown is pointing towards the timing belt end of the engine

19.20b Tap the piston gently into the bore using handle of a hammer

19.21 Refit the bearing cap to the connecting rod

19.22 Tighten the connecting rod nuts to the specified stage 1 torque and then through the specified stages 2 and 3 angles

19.27 On 2.0 litre diesel engines, tap the piston/connecting rod gently into the bore using handle of a hammer

19.28 Lubricate the bearing shell with clean engine oil and then refit the bearing cap to the connecting rod . . .

23 Refit the remaining three piston and connecting rod assemblies in the same way.

24 Rotate the crankshaft, and check that it turns freely, with no signs of binding or tight spots.

25 Refit the baffle plate to the base of the cylinder block and tighten its retaining bolts to the specified torque.

26 Refit the oil pump strainer, sump and the cylinder head as described in Part C of this Chapter.

2.0 litre diesel engine

27 Insert the piston/connecting rod assembly into the top of cylinder No 1, ensuring that the arrow marking on the piston crown is pointing towards the timing chain end of the engine. Using a block of wood or hammer handle against the piston crown, tap the assembly into the cylinder until the piston crown is flush with the top of the cylinder **(see illustration)**.

28 Taking care not to mark the cylinder bore, liberally lubricate the crankpin and both bearing shells, then pull the piston/connecting

rod assembly down the bore and onto the crankpin and refit the big-end bearing cap using the markings to ensure it is fitted the correct way around (the lug on the bearing cap base should be facing the flywheel end of the engine) and screw in the new retaining bolts **(see illustration)**.

29 Tighten both bearing cap bolts to the specified Stage 1 torque setting then tighten them through the specified Stage 2 angle, and finally through the specified Stage 3 angle. It is recommended that an angle-measuring gauge is used during the final stages of the tightening, to ensure accuracy **(see illustrations)**. If a gauge is not available, use white paint to make alignment marks between the bolt head and cap prior to tightening; the marks can then be used to check that the bolt has been rotated through the correct angle.

30 Refit the remaining three piston and connecting rod assemblies in the same way.

31 Rotate the crankshaft, and check that it turns freely, with no signs of binding or tight spots.

32 Refit the oil pump strainer, sump and the cylinder head as described in Part D of this Chapter.

20 Engine -
initial start up after overhaul

1 With the engine refitted in the vehicle, double-check the engine oil and coolant levels. Make a final check that everything has been reconnected, and that there are no tools or rags left in the engine compartment.

2 On petrol engine models, disable the ignition system by disconnecting the wiring connector from the ignition DIS module, and the fuel system by removing the fuel pump relay from the engine compartment relay box (see Chapter 4A, Section 8). Turn the engine on the starter until the oil pressure warning light goes out then stop and reconnect the wiring connector and refit the relay.

2E

19.29a . . . making sure its lug (arrowed) is facing the flywheel end of the engine. Tighten the bearing cap bolts to the specified stage 1 torque . . .

19.29b . . . and then through the specified stages 2 and 3 angles

3 On diesel engine models, switch on the ignition and immediately turn the engine on the starter (without allowing the glow plugs to heat up) until the oil pressure warning light goes out.

4 On all models, start the engine as normal noting that this may take a little longer than usual, due to the fuel system components having been disturbed.

5 While the engine is idling, check for fuel, water and oil leaks. Don't be alarmed if there are some odd smells and smoke from parts getting hot and burning off oil deposits.

6 Assuming all is well, keep the engine idling until hot water is felt circulating through the top hose, then switch off the engine.

7 Allow the engine to cool then recheck the oil and coolant levels as described in "*Weekly Checks*", and top-up as necessary.

8 If new pistons, rings or crankshaft bearings have been fitted, the engine must be treated as new, and run-in for the first 500 miles (800 km). *Do not* operate the engine at full-throttle, or allow it to labour at low engine speeds in any gear. It is recommended that the oil and filter be changed at the end of this period.

Chapter 3
Cooling, heating and air conditioning systems

Contents

Degrees of difficulty

Easy, suitable for novice with little experience	**Fairly easy,** suitable for beginner with some experience	**Fairly difficult,** suitable for competent DIY mechanic	**Difficult,** suitable for experienced DIY mechanic 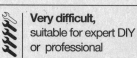	**Very difficult,** suitable for expert DIY or professional

Specifications

System type . . . . Pressurised, with remote expansion tank.

Thermostat
Opening temperatures:
  Petrol engines:
    Starts to open . . . . 92°C
    Fully open . . . . 107°C
  1.7 litre diesel engine:
    Starts to open:
      Main valve . . . . 86 to 90°C
      Auxiliary valve . . . . 83 to 87°C
    Fully open:
      Main valve . . . . 103°C
      Auxiliary valve . . . . 100°C
  2.0 litre diesel engine:
    Starts to open . . . . 92°C
    Fully open . . . . 107°C

Oil cooler thermostat (X17DT diesel engine)
Opening temperatures:
  Starts to open . . . . 107°C
  Fully open . . . . 120°C

Electric cooling fan operating temperature
Cooling fan on . . . . 100°C
Cooling fan off . . . . 95°C

Expansion tank cap
Opening pressure:
  Petrol engines . . . . 1.2 to 1.5 bars
  Diesel engines . . . . 1.4 to 1.5 bars
Boiling point . . . . 123°C

Torque wrench settings

	Nm	lbf ft
Air conditioning compressor mounting bolt:		
Except X20DTL diesel engine	35	26
X20DTL diesel engine	20 to 24	15 to 18
Air conditioning refrigerant line	27	20

3

Torque wrench settings (continued)

	Nm	lbf ft
Temperature gauge sender unit:		
X16SZR engine	10 to 14	7 to 10
X16XEL and X18XE1 engines	14	10
X18XE and X20XEV engines	10	7
X17DT engine	8	6
X20DTL and X20DTH engines	10	7
Coolant temperature sensor:		
X16SZR engine - fuel injection system	20	15
X16XEL and X18XE1 engines - fuel injection system	14	10
X18XE and X20XEV engines - fuel injection system	10	7
X17DT engine - fuel injection system	10	7
X20DTL and X20DTH engines - fuel injection system	18	13
Coolant pump:		
X16SZR, X16XEL and X18XE1 engines	8	6
X18XE and X20XEV engines	25	19
X17DT engine	20	15
X20DTL and X20DTH engines	20	15
Coolant pump pulley securing nuts:		
X17DT engine	10	7
X20DTL and X20DTH engines	20	15
Thermostat cover:		
X16SZR	10	7
X16XEL and X18XE1 engines	8	6
X18XE and X20XEV engines	15	11
X17DT engine	24	18
X20DTL and X20DTH engine:		
Standard thermostat	8	6
Oil cooler thermostat*	20	15
Thermostat housing:		
X16XEL and X18XE1 engines	20	15
X18XE and X20XEV engines	15	11
X17DT engine	24	18
X20DTL and X20DTH engine:		
To cylinder block	20	15
To cylinder head	8	6
Right-hand engine mounting nut	45	33

* **Note:** *This thermostat is only fitted to early models*

1 General information and precautions

General information

The cooling system is of pressurised type, comprising a pump driven by the timing belt on petrol engines or the auxiliary drivebelt on diesel engines, a crossflow radiator, electric cooling fan(s), and thermostat(s). The system functions as follows. Cold coolant from the radiator passes through the bottom hose to the coolant pump, where it is pumped around the cylinder block, head passages and heater matrix. After cooling the cylinder bores, combustion surfaces and valve seats, the coolant reaches the underside of the thermostat, which is initially closed. The coolant passes through the heater, and is returned to the coolant pump.

When the engine is cold, the coolant circulates only through the cylinder block, cylinder head and heater. When the coolant reaches a predetermined temperature, the thermostat opens and the coolant passes through to the radiator. As the coolant circulates through the radiator, it is cooled by

the inrush of air when the car is in forward motion. Airflow is supplemented by the action of the electric cooling fan when necessary. Once the coolant has passed through the radiator, and has cooled, the cycle is repeated.

The electric cooling fan, mounted on the rear of the radiator, is controlled by a thermostatic switch. At a predetermined coolant temperature, the switch actuates the fan.

On 1.7 litre diesel engine models an auxiliary electric coolant pump is fitted to the bottom right-hand side of the electric cooling fan assembly on the radiator. This pump directs coolant to the water-cooled turbocharger. An additional cooling fan is also fitted to the rear of the radiator.

On 2.0 litre diesel engine models an additional thermostat was originally fitted in the left-hand end of the cylinder block in the outlet to the oil cooler, however later models are not fitted with this thermostat.

An expansion tank is fitted to the left-hand side of the engine compartment to accommodate expansion of the coolant when hot. The expansion tank is connected to the top of the radiator.

Refer to Section 12 for information on the air conditioning system.

Precautions

Warning: Do not attempt to remove the expansion tank filler cap, or disturb any part of the cooling system, while the engine is hot; there is a high risk of scalding. If the cap must be removed before the engine and radiator have fully cooled (even though this is not recommended) the pressure in the cooling system must first be relieved. Cover the cap with a thick layer of cloth, to avoid scalding, and slowly unscrew the filler cap until a hissing sound can be heard. When the hissing has stopped, indicating that the pressure has reduced, slowly unscrew the filler cap until it can be removed; if more hissing sounds are heard, wait until they have stopped before unscrewing the cap completely. At all times, keep well away from the filler cap opening.

Warning: Do not allow antifreeze to come into contact with the skin, or with the painted surfaces of the vehicle. Rinse off spills immediately, with plenty of water. Never leave antifreeze lying around in an open container, or in a puddle on the driveway or garage floor. Children and pets are attracted by its sweet smell, but antifreeze can be fatal if ingested.

3.5 Disconnecting the expansion tank hose from the top of the radiator

3.8a Disconnect the electric cooling fan wiring . . .

 Warning: If the engine is hot, the electric cooling fan may start rotating even if the engine is not running; be careful to keep hands, hair and loose clothing well clear when working in the engine compartment.

 Warning: Refer to Section 12 for precautions to be observed when working on models equipped with air conditioning.

2 Cooling system hoses -
disconnection and renewal

Note: *Refer to the warnings given in Section 1 of this Chapter before proceeding. Do not attempt to disconnect any hose while the system is still hot.*

1 If the checks described in Chapter 1 reveal a faulty hose, it must be renewed as follows.

2 First drain the cooling system (see Chapter 1). If the coolant is not due for renewal, it may be re-used if it is collected in a clean container.

3 Before disconnecting a hose, first note its routing in the engine compartment, and whether it is secured by any clips or ties. Use a screwdriver to slacken the clips, then move the clips along the hose, clear of the relevant inlet/outlet union. Carefully work the hose free.

4 Note that the radiator inlet and outlet unions are fragile; do not use excessive force when attempting to remove the hoses. If a hose proves to be difficult to remove, try to release it by rotating the hose ends before attempting to free it.

 If all else fails, cut the coolant hose with a sharp knife, then slit it so that it can be peeled off in two pieces. Although this may prove expensive if the hose is otherwise undamaged, it is preferable to buying a new radiator.

5 When fitting a hose, first slide the clips onto the hose, then work the hose into position. If clamp-type clips were originally fitted, it is a

good idea to replace them with screw-type clips when refitting the hose. If the hose is stiff, use a little soapy water (washing-up liquid is ideal) as a lubricant, or soften the hose by soaking it in hot water.

6 Work the hose into position, checking that it is correctly routed and secured. Slide each clip along the hose until it passes over the flared end of the relevant inlet/outlet union, before tightening the clips securely.

7 Refill the cooling system with reference to Chapter 1.

8 Check thoroughly for leaks as soon as possible after disturbing any part of the cooling system.

3 Radiator -
removal, inspection and refitting

Removal

Models without air conditioning

1 Disconnect the battery negative (earth) lead (see Chapter 5A).

2 Apply the handbrake, then jack up the front of the vehicle and support it on axle stands (see *"Jacking and Vehicle Support"*).

3 Drain the cooling system as described in Chapter 1 by disconnecting the bottom hose from the radiator.

4 Except on 1.6 litre engine models, remove the electric fan assembly from the rear of the radiator as described in Section 5.

5 Disconnect the expansion tank hose and where necessary, remove the small thermostat hose from the top of the radiator **(see illustration)**.

6 Disconnect the top hose from the left-hand side of the radiator.

7 On models with automatic transmission, disconnect the fluid cooler hoses by extracting the spring clips. Be prepared for some loss of fluid by placing a suitable container beneath the hoses.

8 Disconnect the electric cooling fan wiring harness plug(s) and the wiring from the fan thermoswitch(es). Also release the wiring from the top of the radiator **(see illustrations)**.

9 Remove the radiator grille as described in Chapter 11.

10 Where necessary, detach the air guides from the left- and right-hand side of the radiator and unclip the power steering cooler hose from the bracket.

11 Detach the bracket from the air deflector panel where applicable.

12 On 2.0 litre diesel engine models unbolt the power steering fluid reservoir from the top of the radiator and support to one side. Also release the power steering cooler hose from the support **(see illustrations)**.

13 Unscrew the mounting bolts and remove the brackets from the top of the radiator. Examine the rubbers and if necessary obtain new ones **(see illustrations)**.

14 Lift the radiator (together with the electric fan assembly where applicable) upwards from the rubber mountings in the subframe.

3

3.8b . . . and release the wiring from the top of the radiator

3.8c Wiring on the fan thermoswitch (arrowed)

3.12a On 2.0 litre diesel engine models, unbolt the power steering fluid reservoir from the top of the radiator

3.12b Release the power steering cooler hose from the support

3.13a Unscrew the mounting bolts . . .

Withdraw the radiator from the engine compartment **(see illustrations)**.

15 If a new radiator is to be fitted, remove the fan assembly and, where applicable, the automatic transmission fluid cooler pipes, and transfer them to the new radiator.

Models with air conditioning

16 Disconnect the battery negative (earth) lead (see Chapter 5A).

17 Apply the handbrake, then jack up the front of the vehicle and support it on axle stands (see *"Jacking and Vehicle Support"*).

18 Drain the cooling system as described in Chapter 1 by disconnecting the bottom hose from the radiator.

19 Except on 1.6 litre engine models, remove the electric fan assembly from the rear of the radiator as described in Section 5.

20 Disconnect the expansion tank hose and release the small thermostat hose from the top of the radiator.

21 Disconnect the top hose from the left-hand side of the radiator.

22 On models with automatic transmission, disconnect the fluid cooler hoses. Be prepared for some loss of fluid by placing a suitable container beneath the hoses.

23 Disconnect the electric cooling fan(s) wiring harness plug and the wiring from the fan thermoswitch. Also disconnect the wiring from the air conditioning thermoswitch.

24 Remove the front bumper as described in Chapter 11.

25 Unbolt the air conditioning condenser and auxiliary electric fan assembly from the front of the radiator and position to one side. Do not disconnect the refrigerant lines.

26 Where necessary, unscrew the mounting bolt from the drier.

27 On diesel models with an intercooler, remove the air inlet pipe and the charge hose with pipe. Note that the intercooler is removed together with the radiator.

28 Unscrew the mounting bolts and remove the brackets from the top of the radiator, then withdraw the radiator (together with the electric fan assembly where applicable) upwards from the lower mounting rubbers.

29 If a new radiator is to be fitted, remove the fan assembly and, where applicable, the

3.13b . . . and remove the radiator upper mounting brackets

automatic transmission fluid cooler pipes, and transfer them to the new radiator.

Inspection

30 If the radiator has been removed due to suspected blockage, reverse-flush it as described in Chapter 1. Clean dirt and debris from the radiator fins, using an air line (in which case, wear eye protection) or a soft brush.
Caution: Be careful, as the fins are easily damaged, and are sharp!
31 If necessary, a radiator specialist can perform a "flow test" on the radiator, to establish whether an internal blockage exists.
32 A leaking radiator must be referred to a specialist for permanent repair. Do not attempt to weld or solder a leaking radiator, as damage may result.
33 In an emergency, minor leaks from the radiator can be cured by using a suitable

3.13c Check the upper mounting rubbers for wear and damage

radiator sealant (in accordance with its manufacturer's instructions) with the radiator fitted in the vehicle.

34 Inspect the radiator mounting rubbers, and renew them if necessary.

Refitting

35 Refitting is a reversal of removal, bearing in mind the following points.

a) Ensure that the lower mounting rubbers are correctly located in the front valance.
b) Ensure that all hoses are correctly reconnected, and their retaining clips securely tightened.
c) On completion, refill the cooling system as described in Chapter 1 and, on models with automatic transmission, check and if necessary top-up the automatic transmission fluid level as described in Chapter 1.

3.14a Lifting the radiator from the engine compartment (2.0 litre diesel engine model)

3.14b The radiator lower mounting rubbers (arrowed) are located in the front subframe

4 Thermostat - removal, testing and refitting

SOHC 1.6 litre engine

Note: *A new sealing ring will be required on refitting.*

Removal

1 Disconnect the battery negative (earth) lead (see Chapter 5A).
2 Drain the cooling system as described in Chapter 1.
3 Loosen the clip and disconnect the top hose from the thermostat cover on the right-hand side of the engine.
4 Remove the timing belt and idler, camshaft sprocket, and rear timing belt cover with reference to Chapter 2.
5 Unscrew the mounting bolts and remove the thermostat cover from the cylinder head.
6 Carefully prise the thermostat from the cylinder head and remove the sealing ring.

Testing

7 A rough test of the thermostat's operation may be made by suspending it with a piece of string in a container full of water. Heat the water to bring it to the boil - the thermostat must open by the time the water boils. If not, renew it **(see illustration)**.
8 The opening temperature is usually marked on the thermostat. If a thermometer is available, the precise opening temperature of the thermostat may be determined, and compared with the value marked on the thermostat.
9 A thermostat which fails to close as the water cools must also be renewed.

Refitting

10 Thoroughly clean the mating faces of the thermostat cover and the cylinder head.
11 Locate the thermostat in the cylinder head together with a new sealing ring. Make sure that the spring and capsule end is facing into the head and position the thermostat with the outer bar vertical.
12 Refit the thermostat cover and tighten the bolts to the specified torque.
13 Refit the rear timing belt cover, camshaft sprocket, and timing belt and idler with reference to Chapter 2.
14 Reconnect the top hose to the thermostat cover and tighten the clip.
15 Refill and bleed the cooling system with reference to Chapter 1.
16 Reconnect the battery negative (earth) lead.

DOHC 1.6, 1.8 and 2.0 litre petrol engines

Removal

17 Disconnect the battery negative (earth) lead (see Chapter 5A).
18 Drain the cooling system as described in Chapter 1.

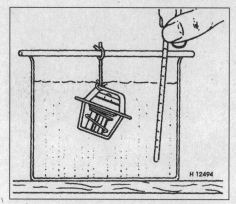
4.7 Testing the thermostat opening temperature

19 Loosen the clip and disconnect the top hose from the thermostat cover on the right-hand side of the engine. On 1.6 litre engines the cover is attached to a further housing bolted to the right-hand end of the engine. On 1.8 (X18XE) and 2.0 litre engines the cover is bolted directly to the cylinder head and it is necessary to disconnect the small hose in addition to the top hose. On 1.8 (X18XE1) engines, disconnect the wiring from the temperature sensor.
20 Unscrew the bolts and remove the thermostat cover which has an integral thermostat. On 1.6 litre engines, remove the sealing ring **(see illustrations)**. On 1.8 (X18XE) and 2.0 litre engines remove the gasket. On 1.8 (X18XE1) engines, the cover is sealed with sealant, and there is no gasket fitted.

Testing

21 Refer to paragraphs 7 to 9 inclusive.

Refitting

22 Thoroughly clean the mating faces of the thermostat cover and housing/head.
23 Fit the thermostat and cover together with a new sealing ring (1.6 litre engines), gasket (1.8 X18XE and 2.0 litre engines) or apply sealant to the surfaces of the cover and cylinder head (1.8 X18XE1 engines). Tighten the bolts to the specified torque.
24 Reconnect the top hose (and small hose on 1.8 and 2.0 litre engines) to the thermostat cover and tighten the clip(s).
25 Refill and bleed the cooling system with reference to Chapter 1.

26 Refit the wiring connector to the temperature sensor on 1.8 (X18XE1) engines, then reconnect battery negative (earth) lead.

1.7 litre diesel engine

Removal

27 Disconnect the battery negative (earth) lead (see Chapter 5A).
28 Drain the cooling system as described in Chapter 1.
29 Remove the battery and support bracket as described in Chapter 5A.
30 Loosen the clip and disconnect the top hose from the thermostat cover located on the left-hand side of the cylinder head.
31 Unscrew the bolts and remove the thermostat cover noting the location of the wiring support bracket on the top bolt. Recover the gasket.

Testing

32 Refer to paragraphs 7 to 9 inclusive.

Refitting

33 Thoroughly clean the mating faces of the thermostat cover and housing.
34 Locate the thermostat in the housing with the vent hole at the top.
35 Refit the cover together with a new gasket and tighten the bolts to the specified torque.
36 Refit the top hose and tighten the clip.
37 Refit the battery support bracket and battery with reference to Chapter 5A.
38 Refill and bleed the cooling system as described in Chapter 1.
39 Reconnect the battery negative (earth) lead.

2.0 litre diesel engine

Removal

40 Disconnect the battery negative (earth) lead (see Chapter 5A).
41 Drain the cooling system as described in Chapter 1.
42 Apply the handbrake, then jack up the front of the vehicle and support it on axle stands (see *Jacking and Vehicle Support*).
43 Remove the splash guard from under the engine.
44 To remove the standard thermostat located at the right-hand front of the cylinder

4.20a Removing the thermostat and cover on DOHC 1.6 litre petrol engines

4.20b Removing the sealing ring on DOHC 1.6 litre petrol engines

3

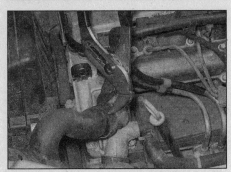

4.44a Release the clip . . .

4.44b . . . and disconnect the top hose from the thermostat housing cover

4.44c Unscrew the mounting bolts . . .

head, first disconnect the wiring from the temperature sensor, then disconnect the three hoses including the top hose. Unscrew the bolts and remove the housing which includes the integral thermostat. Recover the gasket **(see illustrations)**.

45 To remove the oil cooler thermostat located on the left-hand end of the cylinder block, first disconnect the hose then unscrew the bolts and remove the housing which includes the integral thermostat. Recover the gasket.

Testing

46 Refer to paragraphs 7 to 9 inclusive. If the thermostat is faulty, unscrew the temperature sensor and transfer it to the new housing.

Refitting

47 Thoroughly clean the mating faces of the thermostat cover and cylinder head/block.

48 Refit the housing together with a new gasket and tighten the mounting bolts to the specified torque.

49 Reconnect the hoses and wiring as applicable.

50 Refit the splash guard, and lower the vehicle to the ground.

51 Refill and bleed the cooling system as described in Chapter 1.

52 Reconnect the battery negative (earth) lead.

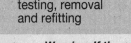

5 Electric cooling fan - testing, removal and refitting

⚠️ *Warning: If the engine is hot, the cooling fan may start up at any time. Take extra precautions when working in the vicinity of the fan.*

Testing

1 The cooling fan is supplied with current via the ignition switch, relay(s) and a fuse (see Chapter 12). The circuit is completed by the cooling fan thermostatic switch, which is mounted in the right-hand end of the radiator. **Note:** *On models with air conditioning, there are two switches fitted to the radiator; both switches operate the cooling fan and the air conditioning auxiliary cooling fan simultaneously.*

2 If a fan does not work, run the engine until normal operating temperature is reached, then allow it to idle. If the fan does not cut in within a few minutes (or before the temperature gauge indicates overheating), switch off the ignition and disconnect the wiring plug from the cooling fan switch. Bridge the two contacts in the wiring plug using a length of spare wire, and switch on the ignition. If the fan now operates, the switch is probably faulty, and should be renewed.

3 If the fan still fails to operate, check that full battery voltage is available at the feed wire to the switch; if not, then there is a fault in the feed wire.

4 If the switch and the wiring are in good condition, the fault must be in the motor itself. The motor can be checked by disconnecting the motor wiring connector and connecting a 12-volt supply directly to the motor terminals. If the motor fails this test, it is proved faulty, and must be renewed complete.

Removal

Petrol engine models without air conditioning

5 Disconnect the wiring plug from the fan motor and release the wiring from the support clip.

6 Unscrew the upper mounting bolts securing the fan assembly to the rear of the radiator.

7 Carefully lift the fan assembly from the bottom mounting brackets and withdraw it from the engine compartment.

8 With the assembly on the bench, unscrew

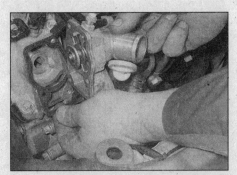

4.44d . . . then remove the thermostat and cover together with the gasket

the motor mounting nuts and extract the retaining circlip then remove the motor from the housing and the fan from the motor.

Petrol engine models with air conditioning

9 Disconnect the battery negative (earth) **and** positive leads (see Chapter 5A), then remove the relay and fusebox located in front of the battery.

10 Disconnect the wiring plug for the auxiliary cooling fan, and also disconnect the rotary wiring plug.

11 Unbolt the earth cable from the body.

12 Disconnect the wiring from both air conditioning pressure switches located on the engine compartment bulkhead.

13 Drain the cooling system as described in Chapter 1.

14 Loosen the clips and disconnect the top hose from the radiator and thermostat housing.

15 Unbolt the refrigerant line bracket from the right-hand side of the radiator.

16 Disconnect the wiring from the two air conditioning switches on the bottom right-hand side of the radiator.

17 Disconnect the wiring from the air conditioning compressor.

18 Release the refrigerant line from the bracket.

19 Detach the left-hand side of the fan assembly from the radiator then carefully lift the assembly upwards and remove from the engine compartment.

20 Disconnect the wiring plug then unscrew the motor mounting bolts and remove the motor and fan.

21 Extract the clip and remove the fan from the motor.

Diesel engine models

22 Remove the battery and support bracket as described in Chapter 5A.

23 Remove the front bumper as described in Chapter 11.

24 Remove the lower right-hand wheel arch liner (see Chapter 11), then disconnect the wiring plugs leading to the fan assembly.

25 On models with air conditioning, disconnect the wiring from the pressure switch at the rear of the engine.

26 On 1.7 litre diesel engine models, remove

5.30a Unscrew the mounting bolts from the radiator . . .

5.30b . . . and lift the assembly upwards from the engine compartment

the auxiliary coolant pump as described in Section 7. Also disconnect the hoses from the radiator.

27 Where necessary, disconnect the air inlet ducts from the intercooler on the left-hand side of the radiator.

28 Disconnect all wiring plugs from the fan assembly.

29 On models with air conditioning, disconnect the wiring from the auxiliary fan and compressor.

30 Unscrew the mounting bolts from the radiator, then carefully lift the assembly upwards from the lower right-hand bracket taking care not to damage the radiator fins **(see illustrations)**.

31 Extract the circlip and remove the fan.

32 Unscrew the mounting bolts and remove the motor from the assembly.

Refitting

33 Refitting is a reversal of removal. Refill and bleed the cooling system (see Chapter 1).

---

6 Auxiliary electric cooling fan (1.7 litre diesel engine) - testing, removal and refitting

Testing

1 Refer to Section 5.

Removal

2 Remove the front bumper (see Chapter 11).

3 Remove the right-hand headlight as described in Chapter 12.

4 Unbolt the fan shroud.

5 Disconnect the wiring for the auxiliary cooling fan.

6 Remove the turbocharger intercooler mounting bracket.

7 On models with air conditioning, remove the condenser and support to one side.

8 Unscrew the bolts securing the auxiliary cooling fan assembly to the radiator, then carefully lift the assembly upwards and withdraw from the engine compartment.

9 Unscrew the mounting bolts and remove the fan motor from the housing.

Refitting

10 Refitting is a reversal of removal.

---

7 Auxiliary electric coolant pump (1.7 litre diesel engine) - testing, removal and refitting

Testing

1 The auxiliary coolant pump is supplied with current via the ignition switch, a relay and a fuse (see Chapter 12).

2 If the pump does not work, disconnect the wiring plug and check that battery voltage is available at the feed wire; if not, then there is a fault in the feed wire.

3 The pump can be checked by disconnecting the wiring and connecting a 12-volt supply directly to the pump terminals. If the pump fails this test, it is proved faulty, and must be renewed.

Removal

4 Remove the electric cooling fan assembly as described in Section 5.

5 Disconnect the hoses and remove the pump from the fan assembly.

Refitting

6 Refitting is a reversal of removal, referring to Section 5 for the refitting of the electric cooling fan assembly.

---

8 Cooling system electrical switches and sensors - testing, removal and refitting

Coolant temperature sensor - fuel injection system

Note: *The temperature gauge sender unit can usually be distinguished by its single electrical wire from the fuel injection system's coolant temperature sensor (which has a multi-pin block connector). On X 17 DT engines, the preheating system's coolant temperature sensor can be identified by its integral wire from the temperature gauge sender unit. The location of the temperature sensor is as follows:*

X 16 SZR engine - the sensor is screwed into the inlet manifold underneath the throttle body

X16XEL and X18XE1 engines - the sensor is screwed into the thermostat housing on the right-hand end of the cylinder head

X 18 XE and X 20 XEV engines - the sensor is screwed into the housing on the left-hand end of the cylinder head

X 17 DT engine - the sensor is screwed into the thermostat housing on the left-hand end of the cylinder head

X 20 DTL and X 20 DTH engines - the sensor is screwed into the right-hand end of the cylinder head, behind the thermostat housing **(see illustration)**

Testing

1 Testing of the coolant temperature sensor circuit must be entrusted to a Vauxhall/Opel dealer, who will have the necessary specialist diagnostic equipment.

Removal

2 Drain the cooling system as described in Chapter 1.

3 On X 16 SZR-engined models, remove the cover from the throttle body, disconnecting the air intake duct and the vacuum and breather hoses from the cover as described in Section 12 of Chapter 4A. On models with X 18 XE or X 20 XEV engines, remove the DIS module (see Chapter 5B).

4 Disconnect the coolant temperature sensor wiring.

5 Unscrew the sensor and withdraw it.

Refitting

6 Refitting is a reversal of removal. Carefully remove all traces of sealant from the sensor's threads and from the threads and mating surfaces on the engine. Where the sensor is fitted with a sealing washer, this must be renewed as a matter of course: where no sealing washer is fitted, apply a smear of suitable sealant to the sensor's threads. Refit the sensor, tightening it to the specified torque wrench setting, then reconnect its wiring. Refit all components removed for access, then refill the cooling system with reference to Chapter 1.

Temperature gauge sender unit

Note: *The temperature gauge sender unit can usually be distinguished by its single electrical wire from the fuel injection system's coolant temperature sensor (which has a multi-pin block connector). On X 17 DT engines, the preheating system's coolant temperature sensor can be*

8.1 Coolant temperature sensor located on the right-hand front of the cylinder head (2.0 litre diesel engines)

3

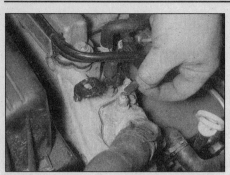

8.10 Disconnecting the single electrical wire of the temperature gauge sender unit

identified by its integral wire from the temperature gauge sender unit. The location of the temperature sender unit is as follows:

X 16 SZR engine - the sender unit is screwed into the right-hand end of the inlet manifold

X16XEL and X18XE1 engines - the sender unit is screwed into the thermostat housing on the right-hand end of the cylinder head

X 18 XE and X 20 XEV engines - the sender unit is screwed into the housing on the left-hand end of the cylinder head

X 17 DT engine - the sender unit is screwed into the thermostat housing on the left-hand end of the cylinder head

X 20 DTL and X 20 DTH engines - the sender unit is screwed into the right-hand end of the cylinder head, behind the thermostat housing

Testing

7 Testing of the sender is by the substitution of a unit known to be in good working order.

Removal

8 Drain the cooling system as described in Chapter 1.

9 On X 16 SZR-engined models, the sender can be reached with no need for the prior removal of other components; if, however the additional working space is required, proceed as described in paragraph 4 above. On models with X 18 XE or X 20 XEV engines, remove the DIS module (see Chapter 5B).

10 Disconnect the temperature gauge sender unit wiring **(see illustration)**.

11 Unscrew the sender and withdraw it.

9.9 On 1.6 litre DOHC engines align the flange edge with the mark on the cylinder block

Refitting

12 Refitting is a reversal of removal. Carefully remove all traces of sealant from the sender's threads and from the threads and mating surfaces on the engine. Where the sender is fitted with a sealing washer, this must be renewed as a matter of course: where no sealing washer is fitted, apply a smear of suitable sealant to the sender's threads. Refit the sender, tightening it to the specified torque wrench setting, then reconnect its wiring. Refit all components removed for access, then refill the cooling system with reference to Chapter 1.

Cooling fan/auxiliary fan temperature switch

Removal

13 Drain the cooling system as described in Chapter 1.

14 Disconnect the wiring from the switch located on the right-hand side of the radiator. The upper switch is for the cooling fan and the lower switch is for the auxiliary fan.

15 Unscrew and remove the switch from the radiator.

Refitting

16 Refitting is a reversal of removal, but refill the cooling system with reference to Chapter 1.

Coolant level warning switch

Removal

17 The switch is located in the expansion tank. With the engine cold, unscrew the expansion tank filler cap to dissipate any remaining pressure.

18 Draw off the coolant from the expansion tank until its level is below the switch.

19 Disconnect the wiring, then unscrew the switch from the tank.

Refitting

20 Refitting is a reversal of removal.

9 Coolant pump - removal and refitting

1.6 and 1.8 (X18XE1) litre petrol engines

Removal

1 Disconnect the battery negative (earth) lead (see Chapter 5A).

2 Drain the cooling system as described in Chapter 1.

3 Remove the timing belt and timing belt rear cover as described in Chapter 2.

4 Unscrew and remove the three coolant pump securing bolts.

5 Withdraw the coolant pump from the cylinder block, noting that it may be necessary to tap the pump lightly with a soft-faced mallet to free it from the cylinder block.

6 Recover the pump sealing ring, and discard it; a new one must be used on refitting.

7 Note that it is not possible to overhaul the pump. If it is faulty, the unit must be renewed complete.

Refitting

8 Ensure that the pump and cylinder block mating surfaces are clean and dry, and apply a smear of silicone grease to the pump mating surface in the cylinder block.

9 Fit a new sealing ring to the pump, and install the pump in the cylinder block. Make sure that the lugs on the pump and cylinder block are aligned with each other on SOHC engines. On DOHC engines align the edge of the coolant pump flange with the mark on the cylinder block **(see illustration)**.

10 Insert the securing bolts and tighten to the specified torque.

11 Refit the timing belt rear cover and timing belt as described in Chapter 2.

12 Refill the cooling system with reference to Chapter 1.

13 Reconnect the battery negative lead (see Chapter 5A).

1.8 (X18XE) and 2.0 litre petrol engines

Removal

14 Disconnect the battery negative (earth) lead (see Chapter 5A).

15 Drain the cooling system as described in Chapter 1.

16 Remove the timing belt, it's rear cover and the tensioner as described in Chapter 2B.

17 Unscrew and remove the three coolant pump securing bolts.

18 Withdraw the coolant pump from the cylinder block, noting that it may be necessary to tap the pump lightly with a soft-faced mallet to free it from the cylinder block.

19 Recover the pump sealing ring, and discard it; a new one must be used on refitting.

20 Note that it is not possible to overhaul the pump. If it is faulty, the unit must be renewed complete.

Refitting

21 Ensure that the pump and cylinder block mating surfaces are clean and dry, and apply a smear of silicone grease to the pump mating surface in the cylinder block.

22 Fit a new sealing ring to the pump, and install the pump in the cylinder block. Make sure that the lugs on the pump and cylinder block are aligned with each other.

23 Insert the securing bolts and tighten to the specified torque.

24 Refit the timing belt rear cover and timing belt as described in Chapter 2.

25 Reconnect the battery negative lead (see Chapter 5A).

26 Refill the cooling system with reference to Chapter 1.

1.7 litre diesel engine

Removal

27 Disconnect the battery negative (earth) lead (see Chapter 5A).

9.51 Unscrew the mounting bolts . . .

9.52 . . . withdraw the coolant pump from the cylinder block . . .

9.53 . . . and recover the sealing ring

28 Drain the cooling system (see Chapter 1).
29 Remove the auxiliary drivebelt (see Chapter 1).
30 Hold the coolant pump pulley stationary using an old auxiliary drivebelt or an oil filter strap wrench, then unscrew and remove the nuts and remove the pulley from the drive flange on the coolant pump.
31 Unscrew and remove the coolant pump securing bolts.
32 Withdraw the coolant pump from the cylinder block, noting that it may be necessary to tap the pump lightly with a soft-faced mallet to free it from the cylinder block. Remove the coolant duct-to-cylinder block guide.
33 Recover the gasket and discard it; a new one must be used on refitting.
34 Note that it is possible to obtain overhaul parts for the coolant pump, however a press is required to fit the bearing. If the pump is worn excessively, it will probably be more economical to obtain a replacement pump rather than overhaul the old one.

Refitting

35 Ensure that the pump and cylinder block mating surfaces are clean and dry.
36 Refit the coolant duct then install the coolant pump to the cylinder block together with a new gasket.
37 Insert the securing bolts and tighten progressively to the specified torque.
38 Refit the pulley and tighten the securing nuts to the specified torque while holding the pulley stationary using the method used on removal.
39 Refit and tension the auxiliary drivebelt as described in Chapter 1.
40 Reconnect the battery negative lead (see Chapter 5A).
41 Refill and bleed the cooling system with reference to Chapter 1.

2.0 litre diesel engine

Removal

42 Disconnect the battery negative (earth) lead (see Chapter 5A).
43 Drain the cooling system (see Chapter 1).
44 Remove the auxiliary drivebelt (see Chapter 1).
45 Remove the air cleaner assembly as described in Chapter 4.
46 Apply the handbrake, then jack up the

front of the vehicle and support it on axle stands (see *"Jacking and Vehicle Support"*).
47 Remove the splash guard from beneath the engine.
48 Unscrew the nut from the top of the right-hand engine mounting.
49 The engine must now be lifted slightly off the right-hand mounting to provide room to remove the coolant pump. To do this, either use a trolley jack and block of wood beneath the engine, or alternatively connect a hoist to the right-hand side of the engine. Whichever method is used, make sure the equipment is adequate for the job and can be used safely.
50 Hold the coolant pump pulley stationary using an old auxiliary drivebelt or an oil filter strap wrench, then unscrew and remove the bolts and remove the pulley from the drive flange on the coolant pump.
51 Unscrew and remove the three coolant pump securing bolts **(see illustration)**.
52 Withdraw the coolant pump from the cylinder block, noting that it may be necessary to tap the pump lightly with a soft-faced mallet to free it from the cylinder block **(see illustration)**.
53 Recover the pump sealing ring, and discard it; a new one must be used on refitting **(see illustration)**.
54 Note that it is not possible to overhaul the pump. If it is faulty, the unit must be renewed complete.

Refitting

55 Ensure that the pump and cylinder block mating surfaces are clean and dry, and apply a smear of silicone grease to the pump mating surface in the cylinder block.
56 Fit a new sealing ring to the pump, and install the pump in the cylinder block.
57 Insert the securing bolts and tighten to the specified torque.
58 Refit the pulley and tighten the securing bolts to the specified torque.
59 Lower the engine and refit the nut to the top of the right-hand mounting. Tighten the nut to the specified torque.
60 Refit the splash guard and lower the vehicle to the ground.
61 Refit the air cleaner assembly as described in Chapter 4.
62 Refit and tension the auxiliary drivebelt as described in Chapter 1.

63 Reconnect the battery negative lead (see Chapter 5A).
64 Refill and bleed the cooling system as described in Chapter 1.

10 Heating and ventilation system - general information

The heater/ventilation system consists of a four-speed blower motor (housed behind the facia), face-level vents in the centre and at each end of the facia, and air ducts to the front and rear footwells.

The heater controls are located in the centre of the facia, and the controls operate flap valves to deflect and mix the air flowing through the various parts of the heater/ventilation system. The flap valves are contained in the air distribution housing, which acts as a central distribution unit, passing air to the various ducts and vents.

Cold air enters the system through the grille at the rear of the engine compartment.

The air (boosted by the blower fan if required) then flows through the various ducts, according to the settings of the controls. Stale air is expelled through ducts at the rear of the vehicle. If warm air is required, the cold air is passed through the heater matrix, which is heated by the engine coolant.

A recirculation switch enables the outside air supply to be closed off, while the air inside the vehicle is recirculated. This can be useful to prevent unpleasant odours entering from outside the vehicle, but should only be used briefly, as the recirculated air inside the vehicle will soon deteriorate.

11 Heater/ventilation system components - removal and refitting

Air vents

Removal

1 To remove an air vent from the centre of the facia, insert a small screwdriver between the two vents and carefully lever out either one. On the driver's side it will be necessary to remove the

3

11.13a Removing the heater control panel

11.13b Removing the heater control knobs

side light switch assembly first. With the vents removed the housing can be removed by undoing the three retaining screws.

2 To remove the vent from the driver's side of the facia, first lever out the light control switch then remove the steering column shrouds. Undo the three screws and withdraw the vent assembly - the upper screw is located behind the vent grilles. Disconnect the wiring and remove the vent.

3 To remove the vent from the passenger's side of the facia, first remove the glovebox as described in Chapter 11. Undo the three screws and withdraw the vent assembly.

4 To remove the windscreen air duct panel located along the bottom of the windscreen, first on models fitted with electronic climate control remove the sun sensor as described in paragraphs 69 to 71 of this Section. Release the 10 clips and withdraw the air duct panel taking care not to damage the facia panel. Vauxhall/Opel technicians use a special tool (KM-595-1) to release the clips, and if the clips are difficult to remove it may be possible to obtain the tool from a Vauxhall/Opel dealer.

Refitting

5 Refitting is a reversal of removal.

Blower motor resistor

Note: *The resistor is not fitted to models with electronic climate control.*

Removal

6 Remove the heater blower motor as described below.

7 Pull the resistor upwards then sideways then disconnect the wiring.

Refitting

8 Refitting is a reversal of removal.

Heater blower motor

Removal

9 Remove the pollen filter housing. This involves removing the windscreen wiper motor and disconnecting the vacuum hoses from the housing. On 2.0 litre diesel engine models also remove the ambient temperature sensor for the auxiliary heating.

10 Unscrew the bolts securing the heater blower motor cover, then release the clips and remove the cover.

11 Disconnect the wiring plug then withdraw the heater motor and disconnect the remaining wiring.

Refitting

12 Refitting is a reversal of removal.

Heater control - models without Electronic Climate Control

Removal

13 Using a small screwdriver inserted at each bottom corner in turn, carefully prise the heater control panel from the facia, over the heater control knobs. Place a wad of cloth beneath the screwdriver to avoid damage to the facia - when the lower pair of retaining clips are disengaged, lift the panel and release the upper two clips (using a long, slim-bladed screwdriver, if required). Pull off the heater control knobs **(see illustrations)**.

14 Undo the upper retaining screws and withdraw the heater control assembly by moving it slightly upwards then removing from the facia **(see illustration)**.

15 Disconnect the wiring from the rear of the control assembly.

16 Note the position of the cables then release the clips and disconnect the cables. To remove

the cables completely disconnect them from the heater housing **(see illustration)**.

Refitting

17 Refitting is a reversal of removal. Before refitting the panel, make sure that the bulbs are correctly fitted. When refitting the knobs, make sure that the conductor engages with the lug on the spindle.

Heater housing

Note: *On models with air conditioning it is necessary to drain the refrigerant. This work* ***must*** *be carried out by qualified personnel.*

Removal

18 Remove the facia panel (see Chapter 11).

19 Remove the front doors (see Chapter 1).

20 Using a Torx key, unscrew the bolts securing the outer ends of the steering crossmember to the A-pillars on each side, then remove the crossmember from the guides and unscrew the tolerance bolts from the ends of the crossmember, noting that they are left-hand thread.

21 Remove the rear footwell air distribution housing.

22 On models with air conditioning, the refrigerant must now be evacuated by a refrigerant engineer.

⚠️ **Warning: Do not attempt to drain the refrigerant without the specialist equipment as this is potentially a dangerous job.**

23 On models with air conditioning, working in the engine compartment disconnect the lines from the evaporator and remove the condensation drain flange.

24 Working in the engine compartment, use two hose clamps to clamp the hoses leading to the heater matrix. The hoses are located on the bulkhead, just above the steering gear. Alternatively, drain the cooling system completely as described in Chapter 1.

25 Disconnect the hoses from the heater matrix stubs by pressing the bar and pulling back the locking ring. Note that the connections are of quick release design. Be prepared for some loss of coolant as the hoses are released, by placing cloth rags beneath them.

26 Unscrew the three bolts securing the heater housing to the bulkhead. The bolts are located in the engine compartment.

27 Remove the pollen filter housing. This involves removing the windscreen wiper motor and disconnecting the vacuum hoses from the housing. On 2.0 litre diesel engine models also remove the ambient temperature sensor for the auxiliary heating.

28 On models with electronic climate control, release the wiring harness plug for the power supply from the servo motors and fan.

29 Withdraw the heater housing from inside the vehicle.

Refitting

30 Refitting is a reversal of removal, but refill the cooling system as described in Chapter 1. On models with air conditioning, have the

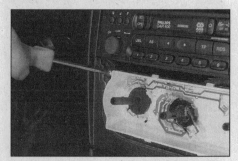

11.14 Unscrewing the heater control assembly mounting screws

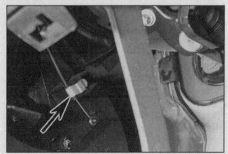

11.16 The heater control cables are clipped to the housing

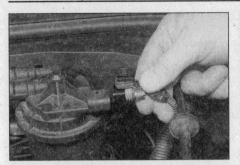

11.31a For improved access to the heater hoses in the engine compartment on 2.0 litre diesel models, disconnect the wiring . . .

11.31b . . . and remove the fuel filter

11.31c Using hose clamps to clamp the heater matrix hoses in the engine compartment

system charged by the refrigerant engineer. When refitting the steering crossmember, make sure that the upper guides are located first before tightening the bolts.

Heater matrix

Removal

31 Working in the engine compartment, use two hose clamps to clamp the hoses leading to the heater matrix. The hoses are located on the bulkhead, just above the steering gear. Alternatively, drain the cooling system completely as described in Chapter 1. For improved access remove the fuel filter on diesel engine models (see illustrations).

32 Disconnect the hoses from the heater matrix stubs by pressing the bar and pulling back the locking ring. Note that the connections are of quick release design. Tape over or plug the stubs to prevent dust or dirt entering the cooling system (see illustrations). Be prepared for some loss of coolant as the hoses are released, by placing cloth rags beneath them.

33 Remove the centre console as described in Chapter 11.

34 Remove the facia panel support bracket from beneath the centre of the facia (see illustration).

35 Remove the rear footwell air distribution housing from beneath the centre of the facia. First pull up the extensions from the lower outlets, then undo the retaining screw and withdraw the housing. Finally remove the support bracket (see illustrations).

36 Release the clips and remove the cover to expose the heater matrix (see illustrations). On models with air conditioning, the cover is retained with bolts.

37 Carefully withdraw the heater matrix from the housing (see illustration). On models with air conditioning it is necessary to move the matrix to the right before removing it.

11.32a Pull back the locking ring to disconnect the quick-release connections

11.32b Seal the ends of the matrix stubs before removing the matrix

11.34 Removing the facia panel support bracket (arrowed)

11.35a Pull up the extensions from the lower outlets . . .

11.35b . . . then undo the screw . . .

11.35c . . . and withdraw the rear footwell air distribution housing . . .

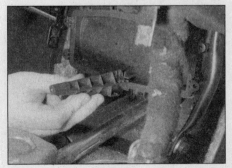

11.35d . . . followed by the support bracket

3

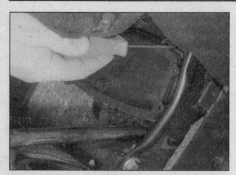

11.36a Use a screwdriver to release the clips . . .

11.36b . . . then remove the cover from the heater matrix

Refitting

38 Refitting is a reversal of removal. If the matrix cover clips are damaged on removal, drill four holes in the cover and use self-tapping screws to secure the cover. Press the matrix firmly into the housing before refitting the cover **(see illustration)**. On completion refill the cooling system as described in Chapter 1. Make sure that the quick release hose fittings are correctly engaged by checking that the green lock ring is released.

Heater switch

Removal

39 Remove the heater control assembly as described in paragraphs 13 to 16.
40 Carefully release the lugs and remove the switch from the assembly.

Refitting

41 Refitting is a reversal of removal.

Facia-mounted heating control switches

Removal

42 Using a small screwdriver, carefully prise the switch from the facia taking care not to damage the facia. Position a wad of cloth on the facia as a precaution.

Refitting

43 Refitting is a reversal of removal.

Vacuum tank

Removal

44 With the bonnet open, remove the water deflector from the right-hand (LHD models) or left-hand (RHD models) rear side of the engine compartment for access to the vacuum tank.
45 Note the location of the vacuum hoses then disconnect them **(see illustration)**.
46 Unscrew the two mounting nuts and withdraw the vacuum tank.

Refitting

47 Refitting is a reversal of removal.

Vacuum unit

Removal

48 Remove the glovebox (see Chapter 11).
49 On left-hand drive models remove the lower trim panel from the right-hand footwell.
50 Disconnect the wiring and vacuum hose from the vacuum unit.
51 Remove the air recirculation vacuum unit and lower it until the flap in the air distribution housing is open.
52 Press the linkage towards the front of the vehicle and withdraw the vacuum unit from inside the vehicle.

Refitting

53 Refitting is a reversal of removal.

Heater control - models with Electronic Climate Control

Removal

54 On vehicles with a "full" heater control panel (surrounding the radio as well as the heater controls), using a small screwdriver inserted at the top of the panel, carefully prise the heater control panel outwards from the facia until the four retaining clips are disengaged from the panel's upper edge, then lift the panel to withdraw it. Place a wad of cloth beneath the screwdriver to avoid damage to the facia.
55 On vehicles with a heater control panel surrounding only the heater controls, using a small screwdriver inserted at each bottom corner in turn, carefully prise the heater control panel from the facia. Place a wad of cloth beneath the screwdriver to avoid damage to the facia - when the lower pair of retaining clips are disengaged, lift the panel and release the upper two clips (using a long, slim-bladed screwdriver, if required).
56 On all vehicles, remove the radio, then remove the hazard warning and other pushbutton switches from above the radio aperture - refer to the relevant Sections of Chapter 12. Remove the radio mounting bracket and the switch mounting strip.
57 Using a small screwdriver to release their locking bars, unplug the two electrical connectors from the front (ie, engine compartment side) of the control assembly. On vehicles with a "full" heater control panel, unscrew the control assembly's two upper mounting bolts. On all vehicles, use a screwdriver to release the control assembly's two lower retaining lugs (by pressing them in), then push the assembly towards the front of the vehicle (until the two locating pins have been disengaged from the facia) and lift it to withdraw it.

Refitting

58 Refitting is the reverse of removal, noting the following points:
a) Manoeuvre the control assembly into position and pull it against the facia so that the two locating pins enter their respective apertures and the two lower retaining lugs engage correctly
b) Ensuring that the connections are clean and properly made, plug the two electrical connectors back into the front of the control assembly, then refit their locking bars to secure them
c) On vehicles with a "full" heater control panel, tighten securely the control assembly's two upper mounting bolts
d) On all vehicles, refit all other components removed for access. On vehicles with a "full" heater control panel, ensure that the

11.37 Carefully withdraw the heater matrix from the housing

11.38 Press the heater matrix firmly into the housing before refitting the cover

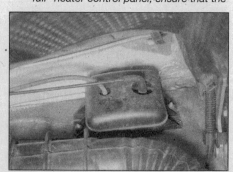

11.45 The heater vacuum tank is located in the rear corner of the engine compartment

panel is located from the top first, so that its four retaining clips are correctly seated before the panel's lower end is pressed into place

e) When reassembly is complete, synchronise the servomotors by switching on the ignition and depressing simultaneously the "Auto On" and "Auto Off" controls for approximately 5 seconds

Electronic Climate Control Air Temperature Sensor

Removal

59 Remove the climate control unit as described earlier.
60 Disconnect the wiring plug from the air outlet temperature sensor.
61 Twist the temperature sensor anti-clockwise and remove from the housing.

Refitting

62 Refitting is a reversal of removal.

Electronic Climate Control Fan Regulator

Removal

63 Remove the left-hand side footwell air duct.
64 Remove the heater chamber casing from the driver's side.
65 On petrol engine models, remove the accelerator pedal.
66 On diesel engine models, remove the accelerator.
67 Unscrew the retaining bolts and remove the regulator from the heater housing.

Refitting

68 Refitting is a reversal of removal.

Electronic Climate Control Sun Sensor

Removal

69 Carefully prise out the sensor from the top of the air duct panel taking care not to damage the panel. Use a wad of cloth when levering as a precaution.
70 Tape or clip the wiring to the facia to prevent it dropping inside.
71 Disconnect the wiring and remove the sensor.

Refitting

72 Refitting is a reversal of removal.

---

12 Air conditioning system - general information and precautions

General information

Air conditioning is standard on top of the range models, and optional on certain other models. It enables the temperature of incoming air to be lowered, and also dehumidifies the air, which makes for rapid demisting and increased comfort.

The cooling side of the system works in the same way as a domestic refrigerator. Refrigerant gas is drawn into a belt-driven compressor, and passes into a condenser mounted in front of the radiator, where it loses heat and becomes liquid. The liquid passes through an expansion valve to an evaporator, where it changes from liquid under high pressure to gas under low pressure. This change is accompanied by a drop in temperature, which cools the evaporator. The refrigerant returns to the compressor, and the cycle begins again.

Air blown through the evaporator passes to the heater assembly, where it is mixed with hot air blown through the heater matrix, to achieve the desired temperature in the passenger compartment.

The heating side of the system works in the same way as on models without air conditioning (see Section 10).

The operation of the system is controlled electronically. Any problems with the system should be referred to a Vauxhall/Opel dealer or an air conditioning specialist.

Precautions

It is necessary to observe special precautions whenever dealing with any part of the system, its associated components, and any items which necessitate disconnection of the system.

⚠️ **Warning: The refrigeration circuit contains a liquid refrigerant (Freon). This refriger-ant is potentially dangerous, and should only be handled by qualified persons. If it is splashed onto the skin, it can cause frostbite. It is not itself poisonous, but in the presence of a naked flame it forms a poisonous gas; inhalation of the vapour through a lighted cigarette could prove fatal. Uncontrolled discharging of the refrigerant is dangerous, and potentially damaging to the environment. It is therefore dangerous to disconnect any part of the system without specialised knowledge and equipment. If for any reason the system must be disconnected, entrust this task to an authorised dealer or an air conditioning specialist.**
Caution: Do not operate the air conditioning system if it is known to be short of refrigerant, as this may damage the compressor.

---

13 Air conditioning system components - removal and refitting

Compressor

⚠️ **Warning: Read the precautions given in Section 12, and have the system discharged by a Vauxhall/ Opel dealer or an air conditioning specialist. Do not carry out the following work unless the system has been discharged.**

Removal

4-cylinder petrol and X20DTL diesel engine models
1 Have the air conditioning system evacuated by a qualified engineer.
2 Where necessary, remove the air filter housing as described in Chapter 4.
3 Remove the auxiliary drivebelt as described in Chapter 1.
4 Apply the handbrake, then jack up the front of the vehicle and support it on axle stands (see "Jacking and Vehicle Support"). Remove the splash guard from under the engine compartment.
5 On petrol engine models, remove the front exhaust downpipe as described in Chapter 4.
6 Disconnect the refrigerant lines from the compressor, then tape over or plug the lines.
7 Disconnect the wiring plug from the compressor.
8 On models with the X20DTL diesel engine, disconnect the wiring plug at the sump.
9 Unscrew the mounting bolts and withdraw the compressor from the engine.

X17DTL diesel engine models
10 Have the air conditioning system evacuated by a qualified engineer.
11 Remove the air filter housing as described in Chapter 4.
12 Unscrew the bolts from the line support brackets on the right-hand side of the cylinder head and at the rear of the compressor.
13 Disconnect the wiring from the plug beneath the compressor.
14 Detach the refrigerant lines from the compressor and tape over or plug the lines.
15 Unbolt and remove the heat shield from the exhaust manifold.
16 Remove the auxiliary drivebelt as described in Chapter 1, then remove the tension roller.
17 Unscrew the mounting bolts and withdraw the compressor from the engine. Recover the spacer.

Refitting

18 Refitting is a reversal of removal but tighten the mounting bolts to the specified torque and tension the auxiliary drivebelt with reference to Chapter 1. On completion, have the refrigerant engineer charge the system and fit new O-rings to the line connections. If a new compressor is being fitted, make sure that the oil level is topped up before fitting it.

Evaporator

Removal

19 Have the air conditioning system evacuated by a qualified engineer.
20 Remove the heater blower motor as described in Section 11.
21 Remove the expansion valve.
22 Remove the glovebox (see Chapter 11).
23 On left-hand drive models, remove the trim panel from the right-hand footwell (see Chapter 11).
24 Remove the coolant line cover, and on

3

left-hand drive models the right-hand side footwell air duct.

25 Carefully cut around the edge of the housing and remove the evaporator. Note that the new evaporator is provided with a new cover which is screwed into position.

Refitting

26 Refitting is a reversal of removal, but before fitting the new evaporator apply sealing compound to the edge of the new cover. On completion, have the refrigerant engineer charge the system and fit new O-rings to the line connections.

Condenser

Removal

27 Have the air conditioning system evacuated by a qualified engineer.

28 Remove the radiator grille (see Chapter 11).

29 Unbolt the auxiliary electric cooling fan and disconnect the wiring.

30 Detach the refrigerant lines from the condenser and tape over or plug them.

31 Disconnect the radiator cooling fan wiring at the plug.

32 Carefully lift the condenser from the radiator and withdraw from the vehicle.

33 If necessary, detach the receiver-dryer from the condenser.

Refitting

34 Refitting is a reversal of removal. On completion, have the refrigerant engineer charge the system and fit new O-rings to the line connections.

Receiver-dryer

Removal

35 Have the air conditioning system evacuated by a qualified engineer.

36 Remove the front bumper as described in Chapter 11.

37 The receiver-dryer is located on the front left-hand side of the radiator.

38 Detach the refrigerant lines and tape over or plug them.

39 Unbolt the receiver-dryer from the condenser.

Refitting

40 Refitting is a reversal of removal. On completion, have the refrigerant engineer charge the system and fit new O-rings to the line connections.

Auxiliary fan triple switch

Removal

41 The auxiliary fan switch is located on the left-hand rear of the radiator. First, have the air conditioning system evacuated by a qualified engineer.

42 Apply the handbrake, then jack up the front of the vehicle and support it on axle stands (see "Jacking and Vehicle Support").

43 Disconnect the wiring from the switch, then unscrew the switch from the refrigerant line.

Refitting

44 Refitting is a reversal of removal. On completion, have the refrigerant engineer charge the system and fit new O-rings to the line connections.

Chapter 4 Part A:
Fuel and exhaust systems - petrol engine models

Contents

Degrees of difficulty

Easy, suitable for novice with little experience	**Fairly easy,** suitable for beginner with some experience	**Fairly difficult,** suitable for competent DIY mechanic	**Difficult,** suitable for experienced DIY mechanic	**Very difficult,** suitable for expert DIY or professional

Specifications

System type
1.6 litre SOHC (X16SZR) engine .... Multec (single-point injection)
1.6 litre DOHC (X16XEL) engine .... Multec S (multi-point injection)
1.8 litre (X18XE1) engine .... Simtec 70 (multi-point injection)
1.8 litre (X18XE) and 2.0 litre (X20XEV) engines .... Simtec 56.5 (multi-point injection)

Fuel system data
Fuel pump type .... Electric, immersed in tank
Fuel pump regulated constant pressure (approximate):
  Single-point injection system .... 0.8 bar
  Multi-point injection system* .... 3.0 to 3.5 bar
Specified idle speed .... Not adjustable - controlled by ECU
Idle mixture CO content .... Not adjustable - controlled by ECU
*Fuel pressure regulator vacuum hose disconnected and plugged (on X16XEL, X18XE and X20XEV models)

Recommended fuel
Minimum octane rating .... 95 RON* unleaded (UK premium unleaded).
Leaded fuel (4-star/LRP) must **NOT** be used

*91 RON unleaded fuel can be used but a slight power loss maybe noticeable.

Torque wrench settings

	Nm	lbf ft
Accelerator pedal nuts	20	15
Accelerator pedal position sensor nuts	20	15
Braking system vacuum hose union nut	15	11
Camshaft sensor*:		
All engines except X18XE and X20XEV	8	6
X18XE and X20XEV engines	6	4
Crankshaft sensor bolt:		
All engines except X18XE and X20XEV	8	6
X18XE and X20XEV engines	6	4
Exhaust front pipe-to-manifold bolts*:		
X16XEL and X18XE1 engines	25	18
X16SZR, X18XE and X20XEV engines	20	15
Exhaust manifold nuts*	22	16
Exhaust manifold shroud/heat shield bolts/nuts	8	6
Fuel hose union nuts	15	11
Fuel pressure regulator clamp	5	4
Fuel rail bolts	8	6
Fuel tank retaining strap bolts	20	15
Inlet manifold nuts and bolts:		
X16XEL and X18XE1 engines:		
Manifold to manifold flange	8	6
Manifold to cylinder head	20	15
Support bracket to manifold	20	15
Support bracket to cylinder block	35	26
X16SZR, X18XE and X20XEV engines	22	16
Knock sensor bolt	20	15
Spark plug heat shields - 1.6 litre SOHC engine	30	22
Throttle body - X16SZR (SOHC) engine:		
Retaining nuts	22	16
Upper body-to-lower body screws	6	4
Throttle housing - X16XEL and X18XE1 engines	8	6
Throttle housing - X18XE and X20XEV engines	9	7
Throttle potentiometer bolts - X16SZR (SOHC) engine	2	1

*Use new bolts/nuts

1 General information and precautions

The fuel system consists of a fuel tank (which is mounted under the rear of the car, with an electric fuel pump immersed in it), a fuel filter and the fuel feed and return lines. On single-point injection models the fuel is supplied by a throttle body assembly which incorporates the single fuel injector and the fuel pressure regulator. On multi-point injection models the fuel pump supplies fuel to the fuel rail, which acts as a reservoir for the four fuel injectors which inject fuel into the inlet tracts. In addition, there is an Electronic Control Unit (ECU) and various sensors, electrical components and related wiring.

Refer to Section 7 for further information on the operation of each fuel injection system, and to Section 18 for information on the exhaust system.

⚠️ *Warning: Many of the procedures in this Chapter require the removal of fuel lines and connections, which may result in some fuel spillage. Before carrying out any operation on the fuel system, refer to the precautions given in "Safety first!" at the beginning of this manual, and follow them implicitly. Petrol is a highly-dangerous and volatile liquid, and the precautions necessary when handling it cannot be overstressed.*
Note: *Residual pressure will remain in the fuel lines long after the vehicle was last used. Before disconnecting any fuel line, first depressurise the fuel system as described in Section 8.*

2 Air cleaner assembly and intake ducts - removal and refitting

Removal

1 To remove the air cleaner housing, slacken the retaining clip securing the inlet trunking to the throttle body. Release the clips securing the trunking to the air cleaner housing by levering up the edge of the clip, then unscrew the retaining screw/nut(s) and remove the housing from the engine compartment (see illustration).

2 Where applicable, disconnect the wiring connector from the intake air temperature sensor and unclip the tank vent (canister purge) valve from the bracket on the housing (see illustrations).

3 On single-point injection models, it will be necessary to disconnect the vacuum hose and the hot air intake hose from the housing as it is being removed.

4 The various air intake pipes/ducts can be disconnected and removed once the retaining clips have been slackened. In some cases it will be necessary to disconnect breather hoses, vacuum pipes and wiring connectors to allow the pipe/duct to be removed; the pipe/duct may also be bolted to a support bracket

2.1 Use a small screwdriver to release the trunking retaining clip

Refitting

5 Refitting is the reverse of removal, making sure all the air intake ducts/hoses are securely reconnected.

3 Intake air temperature control system (single-point injection)

General information

1 The system is controlled by a heat-sensitive vacuum switch, mounted in the throttle body cover. When the temperature of the air passing through the cover is cold (below approximately 35°C), the vacuum switch is open, allowing inlet manifold depression to act on the air temperature control valve diaphragm in the base of the air cleaner housing. This vacuum causes the diaphragm to rise, drawing a flap valve across the cold-air intake, allowing only warmed air from the exhaust manifold shroud to enter the air cleaner.

2 As the temperature of the exhaust-warmed air entering the throttle body rises, the wax capsule in the vacuum switch deforms and closes the switch, cutting off the vacuum supply to the air temperature control valve assembly. As the vacuum supply is cut, the flap is gradually lowered across the hot-air intake until, when the temperature of the air in the duct is fully warmed-up (approximately 40°C), the control valve closes, allowing only cold air from the front of the car to enter the air cleaner.

Testing

3 To check the system, allow the engine to cool down completely, then detach the intake duct from the front of the air cleaner housing; the control valve assembly flap valve in the housing duct should be securely seated across the hot-air intake. Start the engine: the flap should immediately rise to close off the cold-air intake, and should then lower steadily as the engine warms up, until it is eventually seated across the hot-air intake again.

4 To check the vacuum switch, disconnect the vacuum pipe from the control valve when the engine is running, and place a finger over the pipe end. When the engine is cold, full inlet manifold vacuum should be felt in the pipe, and when the engine is at normal operating temperature, there should be no vacuum in the pipe.

5 To check the air temperature control valve assembly, detach the intake duct from the air cleaner housing; the flap valve should be securely seated across the hot-air intake. Disconnect the vacuum pipe and, using a suitable length of hose, suck hard at the control valve stub; the flap should rise to shut off the cold-air intake.

6 If either component is faulty, it must be renewed. The vacuum switch is an integral part of the throttle body cover and the

2.2a Disconnect any wiring connectors from the air intake trunking

2.2b Removing the intake pipe assembly - 1.8 and 2.0 litre models

temperature control valve is an integral part of the air cleaner housing; neither component is available separately.

7 On completion of the check, ensure all disturbed items are securely reconnected.

4 Accelerator cable - removal, refitting and adjustment

Removal

1 Working in the engine compartment, release the inner cable retaining clip then slide the clip out of the end fitting and release the cable from the throttle cam (**see illustration**).

2 Free the accelerator outer cable from its mounting bracket, taking care not to lose the adjusting clip (**see illustration**). Work back along the length of the cable, free it from any

retaining clips or ties, noting its correct routing. On models with automatic transmission it will be necessary to disconnect the wiring from the kickdown switch which is built into the cable.

3 From inside the vehicle, unscrew the fasteners and remove the lower trim panel from underneath the driver's side of the facia to gain access to the accelerator pedal.

4 Reaching up behind the facia, unclip the accelerator inner cable from the top of the accelerator pedal (**see illustration**).

5 Return to the engine compartment then free the cable sealing grommet from the bulkhead and remove the cable and grommet from the vehicle.

6 Examine the cable for signs of wear or damage and renew if necessary. Check the rubber grommet for signs of damage or deterioration and renew it if necessary (**see illustration**).

4.1 Remove the retaining clip then free the inner cable end fitting from its ball joint . . .

4.2 . . . and detach the outer cable from its bracket

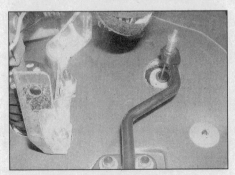

4.4 Pull the cable grommet up and out from the end of the pedal

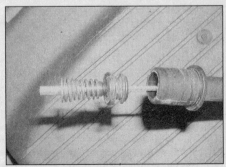

4.6 Accelerator cable grommet - pedal end

4A

Refitting

7 Feed the cable into position from the engine compartment and seat the outer cable grommet in the bulkhead.

8 From inside the vehicle, clip the inner cable into position in the pedal end and check to make sure the grommet is correctly located in the bulkhead. Check that the cable is securely retained, then refit the trim panel to the facia.

9 From within the engine compartment, ensure the outer cable is correctly seated in the bulkhead, then work along the cable, securing it in position with the retaining clips and ties, ensuring that the cable is correctly routed. On models with automatic transmission, reconnect the wiring connector to the kickdown switch.

10 Connect the inner cable to the throttle cam and secure it in position with the retaining clip. Clip the outer cable into its mounting bracket and adjust the cable as described below.

Adjustment

11 Working in the engine compartment, slide the adjustment clip from accelerator outer cable **(see illustration)**.

12 With the clip removed, ensure that the throttle cam is fully against its stop. Gently pull the cable out of its grommet until all free play is removed from the inner cable.

13 With the cable held in this position, refit the spring clip to the last exposed outer cable groove in front of the rubber grommet. When the clip is refitted and the outer cable is released, there should be only a small amount of free play in the inner cable.

14 Have an assistant depress the accelerator pedal, and check that the throttle cam opens fully and returns smoothly to its stop.

5 Accelerator pedal - removal and refitting

1 From inside the vehicle, unscrew the fasteners and remove the lower trim panel from underneath the driver's side of the facia to gain access to the accelerator pedal.

2 Reach up behind the facia, unclip the accelerator inner cable from the top of the accelerator pedal **(see illustration 4.4)**.

3 Unscrew the retaining nuts and remove the pedal assembly from the bulkhead **(see illustration)**.

4 Inspect the pedal assembly for signs of wear, paying particular attention to the pedal bushes, and renew as necessary. To dismantle the assembly, unhook the return spring then slide off the retaining clip and separate the pedal, mounting bracket, return spring and pivot bushes.

5 If the assembly has been dismantled, apply a smear of multi-purpose grease to the pedal pivot shaft and bushes. Fit the bushes and return spring to the mounting bracket and

4.11 Removing the accelerator cable adjustment clip

insert the pedal, making sure it passes through the return spring bore. Secure the pedal in position with the retaining clip and hook the return spring back behind the pedal.

6 Refit the pedal assembly and tighten its retaining nuts to the specified torque setting.

7 Clip the accelerator cable into position on the pedal then refit the trim panel to the facia.

8 On completion, adjust the accelerator cable as described in Section 4.

6 Unleaded petrol - general information and usage

Note: *The information given in this Chapter is correct at the time of writing. If updated information is thought to be required, check with a Vauxhall dealer. If travelling abroad, consult one of the motoring organisations (or a similar authority) for advice on the fuel available.*

1 The fuel recommended by Vauxhall is given in the Specifications Section of this Chapter, followed by the equivalent petrol currently on sale in the UK.

2 All petrol models are designed to run on fuel with a minimum octane rating of 95 RON. Lower octane fuel, down to minimum of rating 91 RON, can be safely used since the engine management system automatically adjusts the ignition timing to suit (using the information supplied by the knock sensor). However, a slight power loss is likely if fuel with a octane rating of less than 95 RON is used.

5.3 Undo the three pedal bracket retaining bolts

3 All models have a catalytic converter, and so must be run on unleaded fuel **only**. Under no circumstances should leaded fuel (UK 4-star/LRP) be used, as this may damage the converter.

4 Super unleaded petrol (98 octane) can also be used in all models if wished, though there is no advantage in doing so.

7 Fuel injection systems - general information

Multec single-point system

1 The Multec engine management (fuel injection/ignition) system **(see illustration)** incorporates a closed-loop catalytic converter, an evaporative emission control system and an exhaust gas recirculation (EGR) system, and complies with the latest emission control standards. The fuel injection side of the system operates as follows; refer to Chapter 5 for information on the ignition system.

2 The fuel pump, immersed in the fuel tank, pumps fuel from the fuel tank to the fuel injector, via a filter mounted underneath the rear of the vehicle. Fuel supply pressure is controlled by the pressure regulator in the throttle body assembly. The regulator operates by allowing excess fuel to return to the tank.

3 The electrical control system consists of the ECU, along with the following sensors.

a) *Throttle potentiometer - informs the ECU of the throttle position, and the rate of throttle opening or closing.*

b) *Coolant temperature sensor - informs the ECU of engine temperature.*

c) *Oxygen sensor - informs the ECU of the oxygen content of the exhaust gases (explained in greater detail in Part C of this Chapter).*

d) *Crankshaft sensor - informs the ECU of engine speed and crankshaft position.*

e) *Knock sensor - informs the ECU when pre-ignition ('pinking') is occurring.*

f) *Manifold absolute pressure (MAP) sensor - informs the ECU of the engine load by monitoring the pressure in the inlet manifold.*

g) *ABS control unit - informs the ECU of the vehicle speed.*

h) *Air conditioning system compressor switch (where fitted) - informs ECU when the air conditioning system is switched on.*

4 All the above information is analysed by the ECU and, based on this, the ECU determines the appropriate ignition and fuelling requirements for the engine. The ECU controls the fuel injector by varying its pulse width - the length of time the injector is held open - to provide a richer or weaker mixture, as appropriate. The mixture is constantly varied by the ECU, to provide the best setting

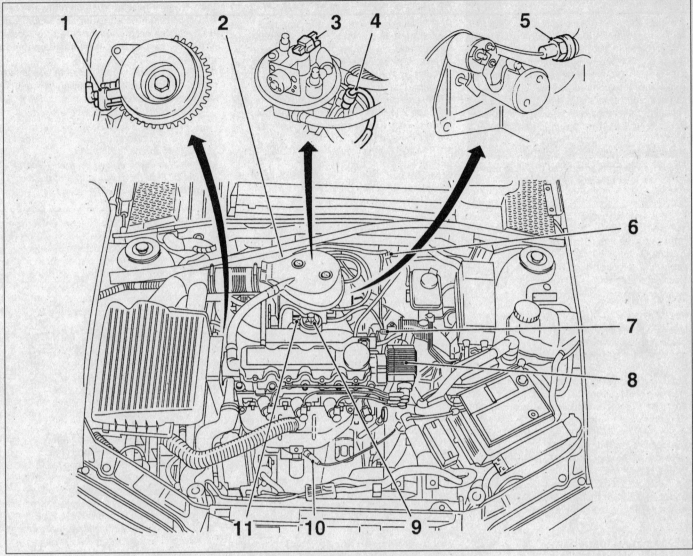

**7.1 Multec single-point injection system components -
X16SZR engine**

1 Crankshaft sensor
2 Throttle body
3 Fuel injector

4 Throttle potentiometer
5 Knock sensor
6 MAP sensor

7 Evaporative emission
   system purge valve
8 Ignition module

9 Exhaust gas
   recirculation (EGR)
   valve

10 Oxygen sensor
11 Idle speed control
   stepper motor

for cranking, starting (with either a hot or cold engine), warm-up, idle, cruising, and acceleration.

5 The ECU also has full control over the engine idle speed, via a stepper motor which is fitted to the throttle body. The motor pushrod controls the opening of an air passage which bypasses the throttle valve. When the throttle valve is closed (accelerator pedal released), the ECU uses the motor to vary the amount of air entering the engine and so controls the idle speed.

6 The ECU also controls the exhaust and evaporative emission control systems, which are described in detail in Part C of this Chapter.

7 If there is an abnormality in any of the readings obtained from any sensor, the ECU enters its back-up mode. In this event, the ECU ignores the abnormal sensor signal, and assumes a pre-programmed value which will allow the engine to continue running (albeit at reduced efficiency). If the ECU enters this back-up mode, the warning light on the instrument panel will come on, and the relevant fault code will be stored in the ECU memory.

8 If the warning light comes on, the vehicle should be taken to a Vauxhall dealer at the earliest opportunity. A complete test of the engine management system can then be carried out, using a special electronic diagnostic test unit which is simply plugged into the system's diagnostic connector. The connector is located behind the centre console; unclip the trim panel situated just in front of the handbrake lever to gain access **(see illustrations)**.

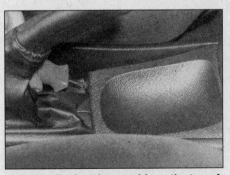

**7.8a Unclip the trim panel from the top of
the centre console . . .**

4A

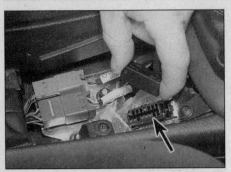

7.8b ... to gain access to the diagnostic connector (arrowed)

Multec S multi-point system

9 The Multec S engine management (fuel injection/ignition) system **(see illustration)** incorporates a closed-loop catalytic converter, an evaporative emission control system, an exhaust gas recirculation (EGR) system and a secondary air system, and complies with the latest emission control standards. The fuel injection side of the system operates as follows; refer to Chapter 5 for information on the ignition system.

10 The fuel pump, immersed in the fuel tank, pumps fuel from the fuel tank to the fuel rail, via a filter mounted underneath the rear of the vehicle. Fuel supply pressure is controlled by the pressure regulator which allows excess fuel to be returned to the tank. **Note:** *On some later models the pressure regulator is located in the fuel tank as part of the fuel tank sender unit/pump.*

11 The electrical control system consists of the ECU, along with the following sensors.

a) *Throttle potentiometer - informs the ECU of the throttle position, and the rate of throttle opening or closing.*

b) *Coolant temperature sensor - informs the ECU of engine temperature.*

c) *Intake air temperature sensor - informs the ECU of the temperature of the air entering the manifold.*

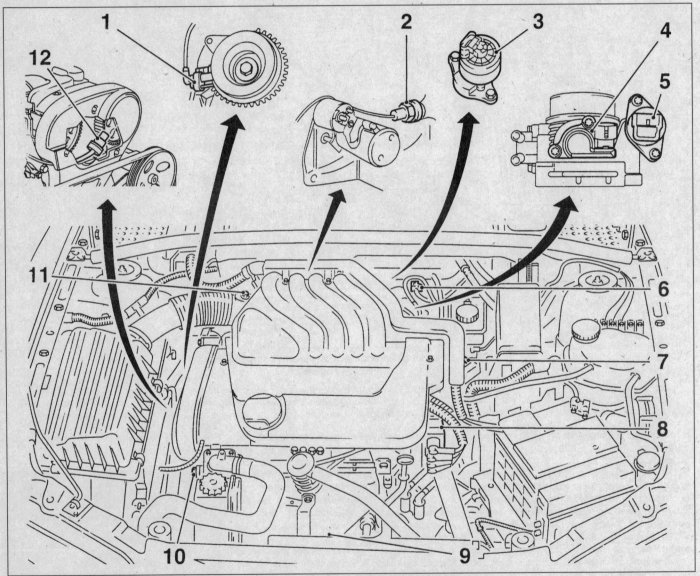

7.9 Multec S multi-point injection system components - X16XEL engine

1 Crankshaft sensor
2 Knock sensor
3 Exhaust gas recirculation (EGR) valve
4 Throttle potentiometer
5 Idle speed control stepper motor
6 MAP sensor
7 Evaporative emission system purge valve
8 Ignition module
9 Oxygen sensor
10 Coolant temperature sensor
11 Intake air temperature sensor
12 Camshaft position sensor

d) Oxygen sensor - informs the ECU of the oxygen content of the exhaust gases (explained in greater detail in Part C of this Chapter).

e) Crankshaft sensor - informs the ECU of engine speed and crankshaft position.

f) Camshaft sensor - informs the ECU of speed and position of the exhaust camshaft.

g) Knock sensor - informs the ECU when pre-ignition (pinking) is occurring.

h) Manifold absolute pressure (MAP) sensor - informs the ECU of the engine load by monitoring the pressure in the inlet manifold.

i) ABS control unit - informs the ECU of the vehicle speed.

j) Air conditioning system compressor switch (where fitted) - informs ECU when the air conditioning system is switched on.

12 All the above information is analysed by the ECU and, based on this, the ECU determines the appropriate ignition and fuelling requirements for the engine. The ECU controls the fuel injector by varying its pulse width - the length of time the injector is held open - to provide a richer or weaker mixture, as appropriate. The mixture is constantly varied by the ECU, to provide the best setting for cranking, starting (with either a hot or cold engine), warm-up, idle, cruising, and acceleration. The Multec S system is a 'sequential' fuel injection system. This means that each of the four injectors is triggered individually just before the inlet valve of the relevant cylinder is about to open.

13 The ECU also has full control over the engine idle speed, via a stepper motor which is fitted to the throttle housing. The motor controls the opening of an air passage which bypasses the throttle valve. When the throttle valve is closed (accelerator pedal released), the ECU uses the motor to vary the amount of air entering the engine and so controls the idle speed.

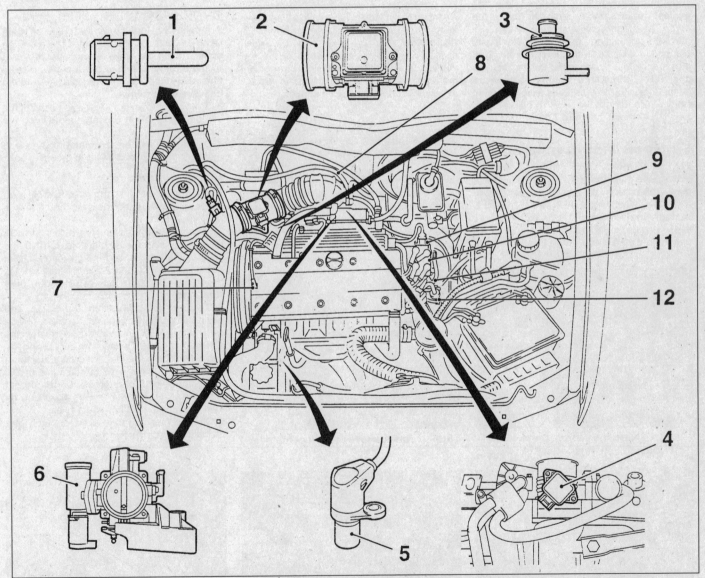

7.17 Simtec 56.5 and 70 multi-point fuel injection system components - X18XE, X18XE1 and X20XEV engines

1 Intake air temperature sensor
2 Hot film mass airflow meter
3 Fuel pressure regulator
4 Throttle potentiometer
5 Crankshaft sensor
6 Idle speed control stepper motor
7 Camshaft position sensor
8 Knock sensor (on rear of the cylinder block)
9 Evaporative emission system purge valve
10 Ignition module
11 Coolant temperature sensor
12 Exhaust gas recirculation (EGR) valve

4A

14 The ECU also controls the exhaust and evaporative emission control systems, which are described in detail in Part C of this Chapter.

15 If there is an abnormality in any of the readings obtained from any sensor, the ECU enters its back-up mode. In this event, the ECU ignores the abnormal sensor signal, and assumes a pre-programmed value which will allow the engine to continue running (albeit at reduced efficiency). If the ECU enters this back-up mode, the warning light on the instrument panel will come on, and the relevant fault code will be stored in the ECU memory.

16 If the warning light comes on, the vehicle should be taken to a Vauxhall dealer at the earliest opportunity. A complete test of the engine management system can then be carried out, using a special electronic diagnostic test unit which is simply plugged into the system's diagnostic connector. The connector is located behind the centre console; unclip the trim panel situated just in front of the handbrake lever to gain access **(see illustrations 7.8a and 7.8b).**

Simtec multi-point systems

17 The Simtec 56.5 and 70 engine management (fuel injection/ignition) systems **(see illustration on previous page)** are almost identical in operation to the Multec S system (see paragraphs 9 to 16). The only major change to the system is that a Hot Film Mass airflow sensor is fitted in place of the manifold pressure (MAP) sensor. The airflow meter informs the ECU of the amount of air entering the inlet manifold.

18 Another additional feature of the Simtec system is that it incorporates a variable tract inlet manifold to help increase torque output at low engine speeds. Each inlet manifold tract is fitted with a valve. The valve is controlled by the ECU via a solenoid valve and vacuum diaphragm unit.

19 At low engine speeds (below approximately 3600 rpm) the valves remain closed. The air entering the engine is then forced to take the long inlet path through the manifold which leads to an increase in the engine torque output.

20 At higher engine speeds, the ECU switches the solenoid valve which then allows vacuum to act on the diaphragm unit. The diaphragm unit is linked to the valve assemblies and opens up each of the four valves allowing the air passing through the manifold to take the shorter inlet path which is more suited to higher engine speeds.

---

8 Fuel injection system - depressurisation

⚠️ **Warning: Refer to the warning note in Section 1 before proceeding. The following procedure will merely relieve the pressure in the fuel system - remember that fuel will still be present in the system components, and take precautions accordingly before disconnecting any of them.**

1 The fuel system referred to in this Section is defined as the tank-mounted fuel pump, the fuel filter, the fuel injector(s) and the pressure regulator, and the metal pipes and flexible hoses of the fuel lines between these components. All these contain fuel which will be under pressure while the engine is running, and/or while the ignition is switched on. The pressure will remain for some time after the ignition has been switched off, and it must be relieved in a controlled fashion when any of these components are disturbed for servicing work.

SOHC engines

2 Ensure the ignition is switched off then remove the cover from the engine compartment relay box, which is situated next to the battery. Remove the fuel pump relay (the relay should be coloured purple) from the box **(see illustrations).**

3 Start the engine and allow it to idle until the engine starts to run roughly then switch the ignition off.

4 Disconnect the battery negative terminal then refit the relay and cover to the relay box.

DOHC engines

5 On these engines, the fuel system can either be depressurised as described above in paragraphs 2 to 4, or as follows.

6 Locate the valve assembly which is fitted to the fuel rail on the inlet manifold. On 1.6 litre engines the valve is on the right-hand end of the rail and on 1.8 and 2.0 litre engines it can be found on the top of the rail **(see illustrations).**

7 Unscrew the cap from the valve and position a container beneath the valve. Hold a wad of rag over the valve and relieve the pressure in the fuel system by depressing the valve core with a suitable screwdriver **(see illustration).** Be prepared for the squirt of fuel as the valve core is depressed and catch it with the rag. Hold the valve core down until no more fuel is expelled from the valve.

8 Once all pressure is relieved, securely refit the valve cap.

8.2a Unclip the lid from the engine compartment main relay box . . .

8.2b . . . and remove the fuel pump relay

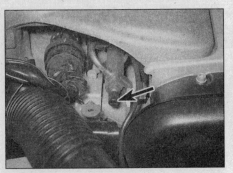

8.6a Fuel depressurisation valve - 1.6 litre engines

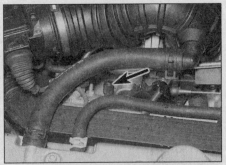

8.6b Fuel depressurisation valve - 1.8 and 2.0 litre engines

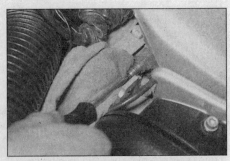

8.7 Unscrew the cap, and depress the valve core. Catch all the expelled fuel using a rag

9.3 Fuel pump access cover

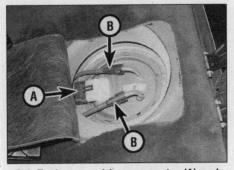

9.4 Fuel pump wiring connector (A) and fuel hoses (B)

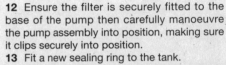

9.6 Undo the locking ring

9 Fuel pump - removal and refitting

> **Warning: Refer to the warning note in Section 1 before proceeding.**

Note: On X18XE1 models the pressure regulator is located in the fuel tank as part of the fuel tank sender unit/pump.

Removal

1 Depressurise the fuel system as described in Section 8 then disconnect the battery negative lead.

2 Fold the rear seat cushion forwards and lift up the flap in the carpet to reveal the fuel pump access cover.

3 Using a screwdriver, carefully prise the plastic access cover from the floor to expose the fuel pump **(see illustration)**.

4 Disconnect the wiring connector from the fuel pump, and tape the connector to the vehicle body, to prevent it disappearing behind the tank **(see illustration)**.

5 Mark the fuel hoses for identification purposes. The hoses are equipped with quick-release fittings to ease removal. To disconnect each hose, compress the clips located on each side of the fitting and ease the fitting off of its union. Disconnect both hoses from the top of the pump, noting the correct fitted position of the sealing rings and plug the hose ends to minimise fuel loss.

6 Unscrew the locking ring and remove it from the tank. This is best accomplished by using a screwdriver on the raised ribs of the locking ring. Carefully tap the screwdriver to turn the ring anti-clockwise until it can be unscrewed by hand **(see illustration)**.

7 Carefully lift the fuel pump cover away from tank until the wiring connector can be disconnected from its underside **(see illustration)**. Make alignment marks between the cover and hoses then release the retaining clips and remove the cover from the vehicle along with its sealing ring. Discard the sealing ring; a new one must be used on refitting.

8 Release the three retaining clips by pressing them inwards then lift the fuel pump

housing assembly out of the fuel tank, taking great care not to drop the fuel filter which is fitted to the pump base **(see illustrations)**. Also try not to spill fuel onto the interior of the vehicle.

9 Inspect the fuel filter for signs of damage or deterioration and renew if necessary **(see illustration)**.

10 If necessary the pump housing assembly can be dismantled and the pump removed, noting the wiring connectors correct locations.

Refitting

Note: A new fuel pump cover sealing ring will be required on refitting.

11 Where necessary, reassemble the pump and housing components ensuring the wiring connectors are correctly and securely reconnected.

9.7 Disconnect the wiring connector from the underside of the fuel pump cover

9.8b . . . and remove it from the vehicle

12 Ensure the filter is securely fitted to the base of the pump then carefully manoeuvre the pump assembly into position, making sure it clips securely into position.

13 Fit a new sealing ring to the tank.

14 Reconnect the fuel hoses to the pump cover, using the marks made on removal, and securely tighten their retaining clips. Reconnect the wiring connector then seat the pump cover on the tank.

15 Refit the locking ring to the fuel tank and tighten it securely.

16 Reconnect the fuel hoses to the pump cover, ensuring each fitting clicks securely into position, and reconnect the wiring connector.

17 Reconnect the battery then start the engine and check for fuel leaks. If all is well, refit the access cover and fold the seat back into position.

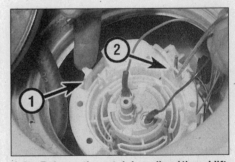

9.8a Release the retaining clips (1) and lift the housing assembly upwards (use a hook engaged with the eye - 2) . . .

9.9 Removing the fuel filter from the base of the pump assembly

4A

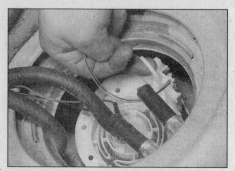

10.2 Unclip the fuel gauge sender unit . . .

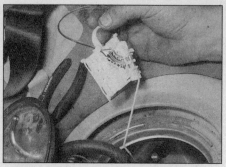

10.3 . . . and manoeuvre it out from the tank

10 Fuel gauge sender unit - removal and refitting

⚠️ **Warning: Refer to the warning note in Section 1 before proceeding.**

Note: *A new fuel pump cover sealing ring will be required on refitting.*

1 Carry out the operations described in paragraphs 1 to 7 of Section 9 to remove the fuel pump cover.

2 The fuel gauge sender unit is clipped to the side of the fuel pump mounting reservoir. Carefully release the retaining clip then slide the sender unit upwards to release it from its mounting **(see illustration)**.

3 Manoeuvre the sender unit through the fuel tank aperture, taking great care not damage the float arm **(see illustration)**.

4 Manoeuvre the sender unit carefully in through the tank aperture and slide it into position on the side of the fuel pump reservoir.

5 Ensure the sender unit is clipped securely in position then refit the fuel pump cover as described in paragraphs 12 to 16 of Section 9.

11 Fuel tank - removal and refitting

⚠️ **Warning: Refer to the warning note in Section 1 before proceeding.**

1 Depressurise the fuel system as described in Section 8 then disconnect the battery negative terminal.

2 Before removing the fuel tank, all fuel must be drained from the tank. Since a fuel tank

drain plug is not provided, it is therefore preferable to carry out the removal operation when the tank is nearly empty. The remaining fuel can then be siphoned or hand-pumped from the tank.

3 Remove the exhaust system and relevant heat shield(s) as described in Section 18.

4 Disconnect the wiring connector from the fuel pump as described in paragraphs 1 to 4 of Section 9.

5 Open up the fuel filler flap and remove the rubber cover from around the filler neck aperture. Slacken and remove the retaining bolt which secures the filler neck to the body **(see illustrations)**.

6 Remove the right-hand rear wheel then remove the retaining screws and clips and remove the plastic wheelarch liner.

7 Make alignment marks between the small hoses and the top of the filler neck assembly then release the retaining clips and disconnect both hoses.

8 Slacken the retaining clips and disconnect the main hoses from the base of the filler neck. Unscrew the filler neck lower retaining bolt and manoeuvre the assembly out from underneath the vehicle.

9 Trace the fuel feed and return hoses from the tank to their unions in front of the tank **(see illustration)**. Make alignment marks between the hoses then release the retaining clips and disconnect both hoses. If the hoses are equipped with quick-release fittings, disconnect each hose by depressing the clips on each side of the fitting and easing the fitting of the pipe.

10 Unclip the fuel filter from the fuel tank retaining strap **(see illustration)**.

11 Place a trolley jack with an interposed block of wood beneath the tank, then raise the jack until it is supporting the weight of the tank.

12 Slacken and remove the retaining bolts and remove the two retaining straps from underneath the fuel tank **(see illustration)**.

13 Slowly lower the fuel tank out of position, disconnecting any other relevant vent pipes as they become accessible (where necessary), and remove the tank from underneath the vehicle.

14 If the tank is contaminated with sediment or water, remove the fuel pump cover (Section 9),

11.5a Remove the rubber cover from the fuel tank filler neck . . .

11.5b . . . then undo the retaining screw (arrowed)

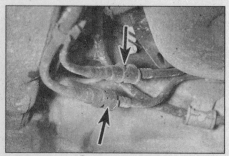

11.9 Disconnect the fuel feed and return hoses (arrowed) at the unions in front of the tank

11.10 Unclip the fuel filter from the fuel tank retaining strap

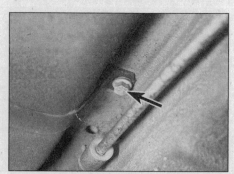

11.12 Fuel tank retaining strap bolt (arrowed)

12.2a Slacken and remove the retaining screws . . .

12.2b . . . and detach the intake duct and sealing ring from the throttle body

12.3 Disconnect the injector wiring connector and free it from the throttle body

and swill the tank out with clean fuel. The tank is injection-moulded from a synthetic material - if seriously damaged, it should be renewed. However, in certain cases, it may be possible to have small leaks or minor damage repaired. Seek the advice of a specialist before attempting to repair the fuel tank.

15 Refitting is the reverse of the removal procedure, noting the following points:

a) *When lifting the tank back into position, take care to ensure that none of the hoses become trapped between the tank and vehicle body. Refit the retaining straps and tighten the bolts to the specified torque.*

b) *Ensure all pipes and hoses are correctly routed and all hoses unions are securely joined.*

c) *On completion, refill the tank with a small amount of fuel, and check for signs of leakage prior to taking the vehicle out on the road.*

12 Throttle body/housing - removal and refitting

⚠ **Warning: Refer to the warning note in Section 1 before proceeding.**

SOHC engine

1 Depressurise the fuel system as described in Section 8 then disconnect the battery negative terminal.

2 Slacken the retaining clip and disconnect

the air intake duct from the throttle body cover. Disconnect the vacuum and breather hoses from the cover then undo the retaining screws and remove the cover and sealing ring from the top of the throttle body **(see illustrations)**.

3 Depress the retaining clips and disconnect the wiring connectors from the throttle potentiometer, the idle control stepper motor and the injector and release the wiring from the throttle body **(see illustration)**.

4 Disconnect the fuel hoses from the side of the throttle body.

5 Unclip the accelerator linkage link rod from the ball joint on the throttle housing **(see illustration)**.

6 Disconnect the breather/vacuum hoses from the throttle body (as applicable).

7 Slacken and remove the nuts securing the throttle body assembly to the inlet manifold, then remove the assembly along with its gasket **(see illustration)**. Discard the gasket, a new one should be used on refitting.

8 If necessary, undo the retaining screws and separate the upper and lower sections of the throttle body assembly **(see illustration)**. Remove the gasket and discard it, a new one should be used on refitting.

9 Where necessary, ensure the mating surfaces are clean and dry then fit a new gasket and rejoin the upper and lower sections of the throttle body. Apply locking compound to the retaining screw threads then fit the screws and tighten them evenly and progressively to the specified torque.

10 Ensure the throttle body and manifold mating surfaces are clean and dry and remove

all traces of locking compound from the studs and nuts.

11 Fit the new gasket to the manifold then refit the throttle body. Apply a few drops of locking compound to the threads of each retaining nut then refit the nuts and tighten them evenly and progressively to the specified torque setting.

12 Reconnect the vacuum/breather hoses (as applicable) and clip the accelerator linkage back onto its ball joint.

13 Reconnect the fuel hoses to the throttle body, tightening the union nuts to the specified torque, and reconnect the wiring connectors.

14 Ensure the sealing ring is in position then refit the cover to the throttle body. Securely tighten the cover retaining screws then reconnect the intake duct and vacuum hoses.

15 Reconnect the battery then start the engine and check for signs of fuel leaks before taking the vehicle on the road.

1.6 litre DOHC engine

16 Depressurise the fuel system as described in Section 8 then disconnect the battery.

17 Remove the engine oil filler cap then undo the retaining screws and lift off the engine cover. Refit the oil filler cap.

18 Slacken and remove the bolts securing the wiring harness plastic tray to the rear of the inlet manifold. Starting at the front and working back, disconnect the wiring connectors from the oxygen sensor, DIS module, purge valve and the various connectors on the left-hand side of the manifold. Undo the nuts securing the earth

4A

12.5 Unclip the accelerator link rod (arrowed) from the throttle housing balljoint

12.7 Removing the throttle body assembly

12.8 Undo the retaining screws and separate the upper and lower sections of the throttle body

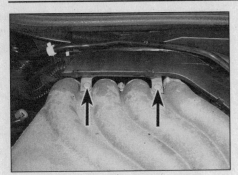

12.18a Undo the retaining bolts (arrowed) . . .

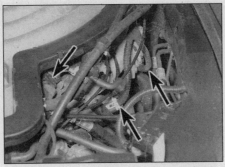

12.18b . . . then disconnect the various wiring connectors (arrowed) . . .

12.18c . . . and free the wiring harness tray from the manifold

leads to the cylinder head and manifold then unclip the plastic tray and position it clear of the manifold **(see illustrations)**.

19 Remove the DIS module as described in Chapter 5.

20 Unclip the evaporative emission system purge valve from the left-hand end of the manifold and disconnect the valve hose from the manifold **(see illustration)**.

21 Slacken the union nut and disconnect the braking system vacuum servo hose from the manifold. Also disconnect the breather/vacuum hoses which are situated next to the servo unit union **(see illustration)**.

22 Slacken the retaining clip and disconnect the intake duct from the throttle housing.

23 Slacken and remove the bolts securing the accelerator cable mounting bracket to the manifold. Remove the retaining clip then free the cable end fitting from the throttle cam and position it clear of the housing.

24 Slacken and remove the throttle housing retaining bolts and free the housing from the manifold. Recover the housing gasket and discard it, a new one should be used on refitting.

25 Slacken the union nuts and disconnect the fuel hoses from the fuel rail. Retain the fuel rail adapters with an open-ended spanner whilst the union nuts are slackened.

26 Rotate the throttle housing until access can be gained to the housing coolant hoses. Make alignment marks between the hoses and housing then release the retaining clips and disconnect both from the housing. Plug the hose ends to minimise coolant loss.

27 Disconnect the wiring connectors from the throttle valve potentiometer and the idle control stepper motor then manoeuvre the throttle housing assembly out from the engine compartment.

28 Refitting is the reverse of removal, bearing in mind the following points.

a) Ensure the wiring connectors and coolant hoses are correctly and securely reconnected before bolting the housing to the manifold.

b) Fit a new gasket and tighten the housing bolts to the specified torque.

c) Tighten the fuel hose union nuts to the specified torque setting.

d) Ensure all hoses are correctly and securely reconnected.

e) On completion adjust the accelerator cable as described in Section 4.

1.8 and 2.0 litre engines

29 Disconnect the battery negative terminal.

30 Where applicable, disconnect the wiring connectors from the intake air temperature sensor and the Hot film mass airflow meter **(see illustration)**.

31 Release the retaining clip and disconnect the breather hose from the cylinder head cover.

32 Slacken the retaining clips then disconnect the intake pipe from the air cleaner and throttle housing and remove the air intake pipe assembly from the engine compartment.

33 Remove the retaining clip and detach the accelerator cable from the throttle cam ball joint and unclip the cable from its mounting bracket. On models with cruise control it will also be necessary to detach the cruise control cable.

34 Undo the retaining bolts and free the cable mounting bracket from the throttle housing.

35 Clamp the coolant hoses which are connected to the rear of the throttle body then release the retaining clips and disconnect both hoses **(see illustration)**. Wipe away any spilt coolant.

36 Disconnect the wiring connectors from the throttle potentiometer and the idle control stepper motor.

37 Where applicable, disconnect the vacuum/breather hoses from the throttle body, noting their correct fitted locations, then undo the retaining nuts and remove the housing from the manifold. Remove the gasket and discard it, a new one should be used on refitting **(see illustration)**.

12.20 Unclip the purge valve from the left-hand end of the manifold

12.21 Disconnect the vacuum servo unit hose (1) and vacuum hose (2) from the manifold

12.30 Disconnect the Hot Film Mass airflow sensor

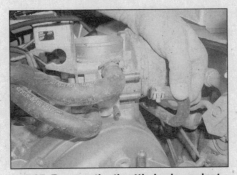

12.35 Remove the throttle body coolant hoses

38 Refitting is the reverse of removal, bearing in mind the following points.

  a) *Ensure the mating surfaces are clean and dry then fit a new gasket and tighten the housing nuts to the specified torque.*

  b) *Ensure all hoses are correctly and securely reconnected.*

  c) *On completion adjust the accelerator cable as described in Section 4.*

13 Fuel injection system - testing and adjustment

Testing

1 If a fault appears in the fuel injection system, first ensure that all the system wiring connectors are securely connected and free of corrosion. Ensure that the fault is not due to poor maintenance; ie, check that the air cleaner filter element is clean, the spark plugs are in good condition and correctly gapped, the cylinder compression pressures are correct, and that the engine breather hoses are clear and undamaged, referring to Chapters 1, 2 and 5 for further information (as applicable).

2 If these checks fail to reveal the cause of the problem, the vehicle should be taken to a suitably-equipped Vauxhall dealer for testing. A wiring block connector is incorporated in the engine management circuit, into which a special electronic diagnostic tester can be plugged (see Section 7). The tester will locate the fault quickly and simply, alleviating the need to test all the system components individually, which is a time-consuming operation that carries a risk of damaging the ECU.

Adjustment

3 Experienced home mechanics with a considerable amount of skill and equipment (including a tachometer and an accurately calibrated exhaust gas analyser) may be able to check the exhaust CO level and the idle speed. However, if these are found to be in need of adjustment, the car will have to be taken to a suitably-equipped Vauxhall dealer who has access to the necessary diagnostic equipment required to test and adjust the settings.

12.37 Renew the throttle body to manifold gasket

14 Single-point injection system components - removal and refitting

⚠️ *Warning: Refer to the warning note in Section 1 before proceeding.*

Fuel injector

Note: *Before condemning an injector, if a faulty injector is suspected, it is worth trying the effect of one of the proprietary injector-cleaning treatments.*

1 Depressurise the fuel system as described in Section 8 then disconnect the battery negative terminal.

2 Slacken the retaining clip and disconnect the air intake duct from the throttle body cover. Disconnect the vacuum and breather hoses from the cover then undo the retaining

14.3 Disconnect the wiring connector from the fuel injector . . .

screws and remove the cover and sealing ring from the top of the throttle body.

3 Release the retaining clips and disconnect the wiring connector from the injector **(see illustration)**.

4 Undo the retaining screw and remove the injector retaining plate **(see illustrations)**.

5 Ease the injector out from the throttle body along with its sealing rings **(see illustration)**. Discard the sealing rings, they must be renewed whenever the injector is disturbed.

6 Refitting is a reversal of the removal procedure using new injector sealing rings. When refitting the retaining clip, ensure it is correctly engaged with the injector and securely tighten its retaining screw.

Fuel pressure regulator

Note: *At the time of writing it appears that the regulator assembly is not available separately; if it is faulty the complete throttle body upper section must be renewed. Although the unit can be dismantled for cleaning, if required, it should not be disturbed unless absolutely necessary.*

7 Depressurise the fuel system as described in Section 8 then disconnect the battery negative terminal.

8 Slacken the retaining clip and disconnect the air intake duct from the throttle body cover. Disconnect the vacuum and breather hoses from the cover then undo the retaining screws and remove the cover and sealing ring from the top of the throttle body.

9 Using a marker pen, make alignment marks between the regulator cover and throttle body, then slacken and remove the cover retaining screws **(see illustration)**.

14.4a . . . then undo the retaining screw . . .

14.4b . . . and remove the injector retaining plate

14.5 Remove the injector from the throttle body, noting the sealing rings (arrowed)

14.9 Fuel pressure regulator retaining screws (arrowed)

4A

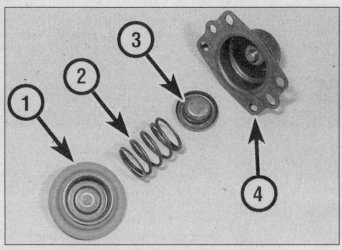

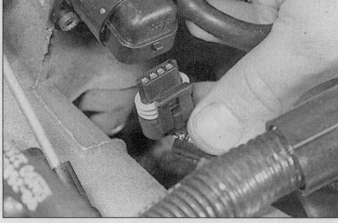

14.10 Fuel pressure regulator components

1 Diaphragm   2 Spring   3 Spring seat   4 Cover

14.14 Disconnecting the idle speed stepper motor

10 Lift off the cover, then remove the spring seat and spring then withdraw the diaphragm, noting its correct fitted orientation **(see illustration)**. Remove all traces of dirt, and examine the diaphragm for signs of splitting. If damage is found, it will probably be necessary to renew the throttle body assembly.

11 Refitting is a reverse of the removal procedure, ensuring that the diaphragm and cover are fitted the correct way round, and that the retaining screws are securely tightened.

Idle speed control stepper motor

12 Disconnect the battery negative terminal.

13 To improve access to the motor, slacken the retaining clip and disconnect the air intake duct from the throttle body cover. Disconnect the vacuum and breather hoses from the cover then undo the retaining screws and remove the cover and sealing ring from the top of the throttle body.

14 Release the retaining clip and disconnect the wiring connector from the motor which is fitted to the front of the throttle body assembly **(see illustration)**.

15 Undo the retaining screws and carefully manoeuvre the motor out of position, taking great care not to damage the motor plunger.

Remove the sealing ring from the motor and discard it; a new one should be used on refitting **(see illustration)**.

16 Refitting is the reverse of removal, using a new sealing ring. To ensure the motor plunger is not damaged on refitting, prior to installation, check that the plunger tip does not extend more than 28 mm from the motor mating flange **(see illustration)**. If necessary, **gently** push the plunger into the body until it is correctly positioned.

Throttle potentiometer

17 Disconnect the battery negative terminal then release the retaining clip and disconnect the wiring connector from the throttle potentiometer which is fitted to the left-hand side of the throttle body **(see illustration)**.

18 Slacken and remove the retaining screws and remove the potentiometer **(see illustration)**.

19 Prior to refitting, clean the threads of the retaining bolts and apply a drop of fresh locking compound to each one. Ensure the potentiometer is correctly engaged with the throttle valve spindle then tighten its retaining bolts to the specified torque and reconnect the wiring connector.

Coolant temperature sensor

20 The coolant temperature sensor is screwed into the rear of the inlet manifold. Refer to Chapter 3 for removal and refitting details.

Manifold absolute pressure (MAP) sensor

21 The MAP sensor is mounted onto the engine compartment bulkhead, just to the left of the throttle body **(see illustration)**. Ensure the ignition is switched off then disconnect the wiring connector and vacuum hose from the sensor. The MAP sensor can then be unclipped and removed from its mounting.

22 Refitting is the reverse of removal.

14.15 Remove the motor from the throttle body noting the sealing ring (arrowed)

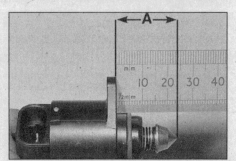

14.16 Ensure that the plunger does not extend more than the specified distance (A) from the mating flange (see text)

14.17 Disconnect the wiring connector . . .

14.18 . . . then undo the retaining screws and remove the potentiometer from the throttle housing

Crankshaft sensor

23 The sensor is mounted on the rear of the cylinder block and is accessible from underneath the vehicle. Firmly apply the handbrake then jack up the front of the vehicle and support it on axle stands.

24 Trace the wiring back from the sensor, releasing it from all the relevant clips and ties whilst noting its correct routing. Disconnect the wiring connector so the wiring is free to be removed with the sensor.

25 Unscrew the retaining bolt and remove the sensor from underneath the vehicle **(see illustration)**.

26 Refitting is the reverse of removal, tightening the retaining bolt to the specified torque. Ensure the wiring is correctly routed and retained by all the necessary clips and ties.

27 On completion, using feeler gauges, check that the clearance between the sensor tip and the crankshaft pulley teeth is 1.0 ± 0.7 mm. If the clearance is not within the specified range, renew the sensor mounting bracket.

Knock sensor

28 The knock sensor is mounted on the rear of the cylinder block and is accessible from underneath the vehicle. Firmly apply the handbrake then jack up the front of the vehicle and support it on axle stands.

29 Trace the wiring back from the sensor, noting its correct routing, and disconnect it at the connector.

30 Slacken and remove the retaining bolt and remove the sensor from the engine.

31 On refitting ensure the mating surfaces are clean and dry then fit the sensor and tighten its retaining bolt to the specified torque. Ensure the wiring is correctly routed and securely reconnected then lower the vehicle to the ground.

Electronic control unit (ECU)

32 The ECU is located behind the water deflector panel at the base of the windscreen.

33 Disconnect the battery negative terminal then remove both windscreen wiper arms as described in Chapter 12.

34 Peel off the rubber seal from the engine compartment bulkhead then unclip the water deflector panel from the base of the windscreen and remove it from the vehicle.

35 Undo the retaining nuts and remove the protective cover to gain access to the ECU.

36 Disconnect the wiring connectors then undo the retaining nuts and remove the ECU from the vehicle.

37 Refitting is the reverse of removal, ensuring the wiring connectors are securely reconnected and the ECU cover and water deflector are correctly seated.

Fuel pump relay

38 The fuel pump relay is located in the engine compartment main relay box.

39 Unclip the cover and remove it from the relay box, the fuel pump relay is coloured

14.21 MAP (manifold absolute pressure) sensor

purple. Ensure the ignition is switched off then pull out the relay.

40 Refitting is the reverse of removal.

Air conditioning system switch

41 The air conditioning system switch is screwed into one of the refrigerant pipes and cannot be removed without first discharging the refrigerant (see Chapter 3). Renewal of the switch should therefore be entrusted to a suitably-equipped garage.

---

15 Multi-point injection system components - removal and refitting

> ⚠ **Warning: Refer to the warning note in Section 1 before proceeding.**

Multec-S

Fuel rail and injectors

Note: *If a faulty injector is suspected, before condemning the injector, it is worth trying the effect of one of the proprietary injector-cleaning treatments.*

1 Depressurise the fuel system as described in Section 8 then disconnect the battery negative terminal.

2 Remove the upper section of the inlet manifold as described in Section 16.

3 Disconnect the wiring connectors from the four injectors then free the wiring harness from the fuel rail.

4 Unscrew the union nuts and disconnect the

15.9 On X16XEL engines the fuel pressure regulator (arrowed) is located on the left-hand end of the fuel rail

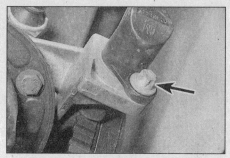

14.25 Crankshaft sensor retaining bolt (arrowed) - viewed from underneath the vehicle

fuel hoses from the fuel rail. Whilst the unions are being slackened, retain the fuel rail adapters with an open-ended spanner.

5 Slacken and remove the three retaining bolts then carefully ease the fuel rail and injector assembly out of position and remove it from the manifold. Remove the lower sealing rings from the injectors and discard them; they must be renewed whenever they are disturbed.

6 Slide off the relevant retaining clip and withdraw the injector from the fuel rail. Remove the upper sealing ring from the injector and discard it; all disturbed sealing rings must be renewed.

7 Refitting is a reversal of the removal procedure, noting the following points.

 a) Renew all disturbed sealing rings and apply a smear of engine oil to them to aid installation.
 b) Ease the injector(s) into the fuel rail, ensuring that the sealing ring(s) remain correctly seated, and secure in position with the retaining clips.
 c) On refitting the fuel rail, take care not to damage the injectors and ensure that all sealing rings remain in position. Once the fuel rail is correctly seated, tighten its retaining bolts to the specified torque.
 d) On completion start the engine and check for fuel leaks.

Fuel pressure regulator

8 Depressurise the fuel system as described in Section 8 then disconnect the battery negative terminal.

9 Access to the fuel regulator is poor and can be improved slightly by freeing the wiring harness plastic tray from the inlet manifold (see Section 16) **(see illustration)**.

10 Retain the regulator with an open-ended spanner and unscrew the fuel hose union nut. Disconnect the fuel hose and the vacuum hose from the regulator.

11 Slacken and remove the retaining bolt and free the wiring bracket from the fuel rail.

12 Ease the regulator out from the end of the fuel rail and remove it along with its sealing ring.

13 Refitting is the reverse of removal, using a new sealing ring. On completion start the engine and check for fuel leaks.

4A

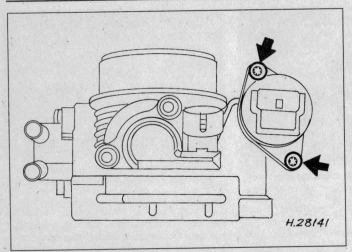

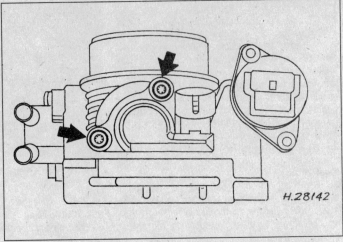

15.15 Idle speed control motor retaining screws (arrowed) - shown with the throttle housing removed

15.18 Throttle potentiometer retaining screws (arrowed) - shown with the throttle housing removed

Idle speed control stepper motor

14 Access to the idle control stepper motor is very poor, to improve it remove the throttle housing as described in Section 12.

15 Undo the retaining screws and remove the motor from the housing along with its sealing ring (see illustration).

16 Refitting is the reverse of removal, noting the following points.

a) Prior to installation, check that the plunger tip does not extend more than 33 mm from the motor mating flange (see illustration 14.16). If necessary, **gently** push the plunger into the body until it is correctly positioned. Failure to do this could lead to the motor being damaged.

b) Apply locking compound to the motor screws.

Throttle potentiometer

17 Remove the throttle housing as described in Section 12.

18 Undo the retaining screws and remove the potentiometer from the side of the housing (see illustration).

19 On refitting, fit the potentiometer, ensuring it is correctly engaged with the throttle valve spindle. Apply locking compound to the retaining screws and tighten them securely. Check the operation of the

throttle valve then refit the housing as described in Section 12.

Coolant temperature sensor

20 The coolant temperature sensor is screwed into the thermostat housing. Refer to Chapter 3 for removal and refitting details.

Intake air temperature sensor

21 The intake air temperature sensor is mounted in the intake duct which connects the air cleaner housing to the inlet manifold.

22 Ensure the ignition is switched off, then disconnect the wiring connector from the sensor.

23 Carefully ease the sensor out of position and remove its sealing grommet from the intake duct. If the sealing grommet shows signs of damage or deterioration it should be renewed.

24 Refitting is the reverse of removal, ensuring the sensor and grommet are correctly located in the duct.

Manifold absolute pressure (MAP) sensor

25 The MAP sensor is mounted onto the engine compartment bulkhead, just to the left of the inlet manifold (see illustration).

26 Ensure the ignition is switched off then disconnect the wiring connector and vacuum

hose from the sensor. The MAP sensor can then be unclipped and removed from its mounting.

27 Refitting is the reverse of removal.

Crankshaft sensor

28 The sensor is mounted on a bracket at the rear of the right-hand end of the cylinder block and is accessible from underneath the vehicle (see illustration). Firmly apply the handbrake then jack up the front of the vehicle and support it on axle stands.

29 Trace the wiring back from the sensor, releasing it from all the relevant clips and ties whilst noting its correct routing. Disconnect the wiring connector so the wiring is free to be removed with the sensor. Unscrew the retaining bolt and remove the sensor.

30 Refitting is the reverse of removal, tightening the retaining bolt to the specified torque. Ensure the wiring is correctly routed and retained by all the necessary clips and ties.

31 Using feeler gauges, check that the clearance between the sensor tip and the crankshaft pulley teeth is 1.0 ± 0.7 mm. If the clearance is not within the specified range, renew the sensor mounting bracket.

Camshaft sensor

32 Remove the timing belt upper cover as described in Chapter 2.

33 Trace the wiring back from the sensor, releasing it from all the relevant clips and ties whilst noting its correct routing. Disconnect the wiring connector so the wiring is free to be removed with the sensor.

34 Unscrew the retaining bolts and remove the sensor from the side of the cylinder head (see illustration).

35 Refitting is the reverse of removal, tightening the retaining bolts to the specified torque. Ensure the wiring is correctly routed and retained by all the necessary clips and ties.

15.25 MAP (manifold absolute pressure) sensor on the engine compartment bulkhead

15.28 Crankshaft position sensor (X16XEL engines)

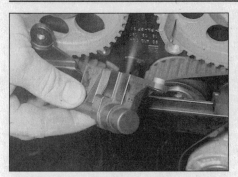

15.34 Removing the camshaft sensor

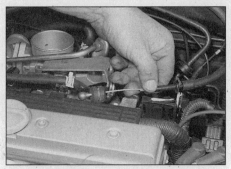

15.54 Detach the accelerator cable from the throttle housing and its mounting bracket

15.56 Release the retaining clips (arrowed) and disconnect the wiring cover assembly from the top of the injectors

Knock sensor

36 Firmly apply the handbrake then jack up the front of the vehicle and support it on axle stands. The knock sensor is mounted onto the rear of the cylinder block, just to the right of the starter motor, and is accessible from underneath the vehicle.

37 Trace the wiring back from the sensor, noting its correct routing, and disconnect it at the connector.

38 Slacken and remove the retaining bolt and remove the sensor from the engine.

39 On refitting ensure the mating surfaces are clean and dry then fit the sensor and tighten its retaining bolt to the specified torque. Ensure the wiring is correctly routed and securely reconnected then lower the vehicle to the ground.

Electronic control unit (ECU)

40 The ECU is located behind the water deflector panel at the base of the windscreen.

41 Disconnect the battery negative terminal then remove both windscreen wiper arms as described in Chapter 12.

42 Peel off the rubber seal from the engine compartment bulkhead then unclip the water deflector panel from the base of the windscreen and remove it from the vehicle.

43 Undo the retaining nuts and remove the protective cover to gain access to the ECU.

44 Release the retaining clip(s) then disconnect the wiring connector(s) from the ECU. Undo the retaining nuts and remove the ECU from the vehicle.

45 Refitting is the reverse of removal, ensuring the wiring connectors are securely reconnected and the ECU cover and water deflector are correctly seated.

Fuel pump relay

46 The fuel pump relay is located in the engine compartment main relay box.

47 Unclip the cover and remove it from the relay box, the fuel pump relay is coloured purple. Ensure the ignition is switched off then pull out the relay.

48 Refitting is the reverse of removal.

Air conditioning system switch

49 The air conditioning system switch is screwed into one of the refrigerant pipes and

cannot be removed without first discharging the refrigerant (see Chapter 3). Renewal of the switch should therefore be entrusted to a suitably-equipped garage.

Simtec 56.5 and 70

Fuel rail and injectors

Note: *Before condemning an injector, if a faulty injector is suspected, it is worth trying the effect of one of the proprietary injector-cleaning treatments.*

50 Depressurise the fuel system as described in Section 8 then disconnect the battery negative terminal.

51 Disconnect the wiring connectors from the intake air temperature sensor and the Hot Film Mass airflow meter.

52 Release the retaining clips and disconnect the breather hoses from the rear of the cylinder head cover.

53 Slacken the retaining clips then disconnect the intake duct from the air cleaner and throttle housing and remove the duct assembly from the engine compartment, freeing it from the wiring harness.

54 Remove the retaining clip and detach the accelerator cable from the throttle cam ball joint and unclip the cable from its mounting bracket **(see illustration)**. On models with cruise control it will also be necessary to detach the cruise control cable.

55 Disconnect the wiring connector from the idle control stepper motor then undo the retaining bolts and free the cable mounting bracket from the throttle housing.

56 Carefully release the retaining clips and lift the injector wiring cover assembly squarely away from the top of the injectors; the wiring connectors are an integral part of the cover **(see illustration)**.

57 Position the injector wiring cover assembly clear of the fuel rail.

58 Unscrew the union nuts and disconnect the fuel hoses from the fuel rail. Whilst the unions are being slackened, retain the fuel rail adapters with an open-ended spanner **(see illustration)**.

59 Slacken and remove the three retaining bolts then carefully ease the fuel rail and injector assembly out of position and remove it from the manifold. Remove the lower sealing rings from the injectors and discard them; they must be renewed whenever they are disturbed.

60 Slide off the relevant retaining clip and withdraw the injector from the fuel rail **(see illustration)**. Remove the upper sealing ring from the injector and discard it; all disturbed sealing rings must be renewed.

61 Refitting is a reversal of the removal procedure, noting the following points.

a) *Renew all disturbed sealing rings and apply a smear of engine oil to them to aid installation.*

b) *Ease the injector(s) into the fuel rail, ensuring that the sealing ring(s) remain correctly seated, and secure in position with the retaining clips.*

c) *On refitting the fuel rail, take care not to damage the injectors and ensure that all sealing rings remain in position. Once the*

4A

15.58 Fuel supply pipe

15.60 Lever out the spring clip and carefully pull apart the connector

15.62 Fuel pressure regulator - X18XE1 models

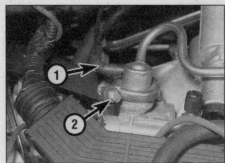

15.64 Fuel pressure regulator vacuum hose (1) and retaining clamp (2)

fuel rail is correctly seated, tighten its retaining bolts to the specified torque.

d) On completion start the engine and check for fuel leaks.

Fuel pressure regulator

Note: *On X18XE1 models: Fuel pressure regulation is a function of the fuel tank pump module. The regulator is located under the fuel pump access cover. However, the regulator does not appear to be available as a separate part – check with your Vauxhall dealer. To remove the regulator, follow the procedure for fuel pump renewal, as described in Section 9, and disconnect the regulator from the fuel pipes and wiring connector located on the underside of the fuel pump access cover (see illustration).*

62 On X18XE and X20XEV models, depressurise the fuel system as described in Section 8 then disconnect the battery negative terminal.

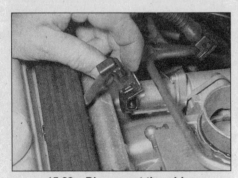

15.68a Disconnect the wiring connector . . .

15.74 Disconnect the intake air temperature wiring connector

63 To improve access to the regulator, release the retaining clips and disconnect the breather hose from the rear of the cylinder head cover.

64 Disconnect the vacuum hose from the regulator **(see illustration)**.

65 Slacken the retaining clamp then carefully ease the pressure regulator out from the top of the fuel rail. Remove the both sealing rings from the regulator and discard them; new ones must be used on refitting.

66 Refitting is the reverse of removal, using new sealing rings. Lubricate the sealing rings with a smear of engine oil to ease installation and tighten the retaining clamp screw to the specified torque. On completion check for signs of fuel leakage.

Idle speed control stepper motor

67 Disconnect the wiring connectors from the intake air temperature sensor and the

15.68b . . . then undo the retaining screws (one hidden) and remove the idle speed control motor from the throttle housing

15.78 Disconnect the (Hot Film Mass) airflow meter wiring connector

airflow meter. Release the retaining clip and disconnect the breather hose from the rear of the cylinder head cover then slacken the retaining clips and remove the intake duct assembly from the engine compartment.

68 Disconnect the wiring connector then undo the retaining screws and remove the motor assembly from the side of the throttle housing **(see illustrations)**. Remove the gasket and discard it; a new one should be used on refitting.

69 Refitting is the reverse of removal using a new gasket.

Throttle potentiometer

70 Ensure the ignition is switched off then disconnect the wiring connector from the throttle potentiometer which is fitted to the rear of the throttle housing.

71 Slacken and remove the retaining screws then remove the potentiometer from the housing.

72 Refitting is the reverse of removal, making sure the potentiometer is correctly engaged with the throttle valve spindle.

Coolant temperature sensor

73 The coolant temperature sensor is screwed into the housing on the left-hand end of the cylinder head. Refer to Chapter 3 for removal and refitting details.

Intake air temperature sensor

74 Ensure the ignition is switched off then disconnect the wiring connector from the sensor **(see illustration)**.

75 Slacken the retaining clips then detach the intake duct from the airflow meter and air cleaner housing and remove it from the vehicle.

76 Carefully ease the sensor out of position, taking great care not to damage the duct.

77 Refitting is the reverse of removal, noting that the sensor must be fitted so that its flat edge aligns with the flat on the intake duct.

Hot Film Mass airflow meter

78 Ensure the ignition is switched off then disconnect the wiring connector from the airflow meter **(see illustration)**.

79 Slacken the retaining clips then disconnect the intake ducts and remove the airflow meter from the vehicle. Inspect the meter for signs of damage and renew if necessary.

80 Refitting is the reverse of removal, ensuring the intake ducts are correctly engaged with the meter recesses.

Crankshaft sensor

81 On X18XE1 engines, the sensor is mounted on a bracket at the rear of the right-hand end of the cylinder block. Follow the procedures as described in paragraphs 28 to 31 for the X16XEL engine.

82 On X18XE and X20XEV engines, the sensor is mounted on the front of the cylinder block at the timing belt end. Remove the air cleaner housing with reference to Section 2, and unbolt the engine lifting shackle from the

15.89 Remove the camshaft sensor - note the location dowel

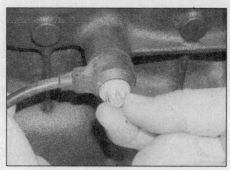

15.94 Knock sensor retaining bolt

top of the engine. At the rear of the cylinder head, disconnect the wiring connector so the wiring is free to be removed with the sensor.

83 Trace the wiring back from the sensor, releasing it from all the relevant clips and ties whilst noting its correct routing.

84 Unscrew the retaining bolt and remove the sensor from the front of the cylinder block, along with its sealing ring. Discard the sealing ring, a new one should be used on refitting.

85 Refitting is the reverse of removal using a new sealing ring and tightening the sensor bolt to the specified torque. Ensure the wiring cover assembly is clipped securely in position.

Camshaft sensor

86 Undo the retaining screws and remove the spark plug cover from the top of the cylinder head cover.

87 Ensure the ignition is switched off then disconnect the wiring connector from the camshaft sensor.

88 Remove the timing belt front cover as described in Chapter 2.

89 Unscrew the retaining bolt and remove the camshaft sensor from the top of the cylinder head (**see illustration**).

90 Refitting is the reverse of removal, tightening the sensor retaining bolt to the specified torque.

Knock sensor

91 The knock sensor is mounted on the rear of the cylinder block and is accessible from underneath the vehicle. Firmly apply the handbrake then jack up the front of the vehicle and support it on axle stands. Depending on model, it may be necessary to remove the starter motor as described in Chapter 5 to make access easier.

92 Trace the wiring back from the sensor, releasing it from all the relevant clips and ties whilst noting its correct routing.

93 Carefully release the retaining clips and lift the wiring cover assembly squarely away from rear of the cylinder head to gain access to the sensor wiring connector. Disconnect the connector so the wiring is free to be removed with the sensor.

94 Slacken and remove the retaining bolt and remove the sensor from the engine (**see illustration**).

95 On refitting, ensure the mating surfaces are clean and dry then fit the sensor and tighten its retaining bolt to the specified torque. Ensure the wiring is correctly routed and securely reconnected then clip the wiring cover assembly back into position.

Electronic control unit (ECU)

96 Refer to paragraphs 40 to 45.

Fuel pump relay

97 Refer to paragraphs 46 to 48.

Air conditioning system switch

98 The air conditioning system switch is screwed into one of the refrigerant pipes and cannot be removed without first discharging the refrigerant (see Chapter 3). Renewal of the switch should therefore be entrusted to a suitably-equipped garage.

Inlet manifold valve switching solenoid

99 The solenoid which operates the inlet manifold valve assemblies is mounting on the left-hand end of the manifold (**see illustration**).

100 Ensure the ignition is switched off then disconnect the wiring connector from the solenoid.

101 Disconnect both vacuum hoses then remove the solenoid from the manifold.

102 Refitting is the reverse of removal.

Inlet manifold valve vacuum diaphragm unit

103 The inlet manifold valve vacuum diaphragm unit is fitted to the left-hand end of the manifold (**see illustration 15.99**).

15.99 Inlet manifold valve switching solenoid and diaphragm

104 Disconnect the vacuum hose, unclip the diaphragm rod from the its ball joint and remove the unit from the manifold.

105 Refitting is the reverse of removal.

16 Inlet manifold - removal and refitting

SOHC engine

1 Depressurise the fuel system as described in Section 8 then disconnect the battery negative terminal.

2 Remove the auxiliary drivebelt then drain the cooling system as described in Chapter 1.

3 Remove the air cleaner housing and intake duct as described in Section 2.

4 Disconnect the vacuum and breather hoses from the throttle body cover then undo the retaining screws and remove the cover and sealing ring from the top of the throttle body.

5 Disconnect the wiring connectors from the throttle potentiometer, the idle control motor, the throttle body injector, the coolant temperature sender and the exhaust gas recirculation (EGR) valve. Note the correct routing of the wiring then free it from all the relevant clips and ties. Unclip the wiring duct from the rear of the cylinder head and position it clear of the inlet manifold.

6 Undo the retaining bolts and remove the support bracket and alternator mounting bracket from the right-hand side of the manifold.

7 Slacken the unions nuts and disconnect the fuel hoses from the side of the throttle body. Whilst slackening the nuts, retain the throttle body adapters with an open-ended spanner.

8 Unclip and slide out the retaining clip securing the accelerator cable end fitting in position and detach the cable from the ball joint. Free the outer cable from its mounting bracket and position it clear of the manifold.

9 Disconnect the breather/vacuum hoses from the throttle body (as applicable) noting each ones correct fitted location.

10 Slacken the retaining clip and disconnect the coolant hose from the rear of the manifold.

11 Unscrew the union nut and disconnect the braking system servo unit hose from the manifold.

12 Check that all the necessary vacuum/breather hoses have been disconnected then slacken and remove the manifold retaining nuts.

13 Remove the manifold from the engine and recover the manifold gasket, noting which way around it is fitted.

14 Refitting is the reverse of removal bearing in mind the following points.

a) *Prior to refitting, check the manifold studs and renew any that are worn or damaged.*

b) *Ensure the manifold and cylinder mating surfaces are clean and dry and fit the new gasket. Refit the manifold and tighten the retaining nuts evenly and progressively to the specified torque.*

4A

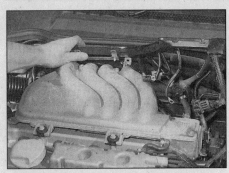

16.16 Free the wiring harness from the rear of the manifold (X16XEL shown)

16.17 Unclip the purge valve (arrowed) from the left-hand end of the manifold (X16XEL shown)

c) *Ensure that all relevant hoses are reconnected to their original positions, and are securely held (where necessary) by their retaining clips.*

d) *Tighten the fuel hose and vacuum servo hose union nuts to their specified torque settings.*

e) *Refit the auxiliary drivebelt and refill the cooling system as described in Chapter 1.*

f) *On completion, adjust the accelerator cable as described in Section 4.*

1.6 litre DOHC engine

Removal

Note: *If only the upper section of the manifold is to be removed carry out the operations described in paragraphs 15 to 20.*

15 Remove the oil filler cap then undo the retaining screws and lift off the cover from the top of the engine. Refit the oil filler cap. Drain the coolant system with reference to Chapter 1.

16 Slacken and remove the bolts securing the wiring harness plastic tray to the rear of the inlet manifold. Starting at the front and working back, disconnect the wiring connectors from the oxygen sensor, DIS module, purge valve and the various connectors on the left-hand side of the manifold. Undo the nuts securing the earth leads to the cylinder head and manifold then unclip the plastic tray and position it clear of the manifold **(see illustration)**.

17 Unclip the evaporative emission system purge valve from the left-hand end of the manifold and disconnect the valve hose from the manifold **(see illustration)**.

18 Slacken the union nut and disconnect the braking system vacuum servo hose from the manifold. Also disconnect the breather/vacuum hoses which are situated next to the servo unit union. Disconnect the vacuum hose from the fuel pressure regulator.

19 Release the retaining clips and disconnect the coolant pipes from the throttle housing.

20 Slacken and remove the retaining nuts and bolts from the front and rear of the manifold upper section **(see illustration)**. Lift the manifold section out of position, freeing it from the connecting hose, and recover the gasket from the lower section.

21 To remove the lower section of the manifold, first depressurise the fuel system as described in Section 8.

22 Slacken the unions nuts and disconnect the fuel hoses from the fuel rail. Whilst slackening the nuts, retain the fuel rail adapters with an open-ended spanner.

23 Slacken the lower retaining clip and remove the connecting piece from the throttle housing.

24 Disconnect the crankshaft sensor wiring connector and free it from the manifold, noting its correct routing.

25 Free the accelerator cable from the throttle housing and mounting bracket (see Section 4) and disconnect the wiring connectors from the throttle valve body.

26 Undo the retaining bolts and remove the throttle housing from the its mounting flange. Recover the housing gasket and discard.

27 Unbolt the throttle housing mounting flange and remove it from the side of the manifold. Note each bolt's fitted location as they are different lengths.

28 Remove the auxiliary drivebelt (see Chapter 1) then undo the retaining bolts and remove the alternator mounting bracket from the right-hand end of the manifold.

29 Release the retaining clip and disconnect the coolant hose from the base of the manifold.

30 Slacken and remove the retaining nuts then manoeuvre the lower section of the manifold away from the cylinder head and out of the engine compartment.

31 Unbolt the coolant housing from the right-

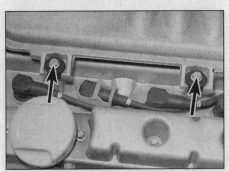

16.20 Manifold upper section-to-camshaft cover bolts (arrowed)

hand end of the cylinder head then remove the manifold gasket and discard it.

32 Refitting is the reverse of removal bearing in mind the following points.

a) *Prior to refitting, check the manifold studs and renew any that are worn or damaged.*

b) *Ensure the manifold and cylinder mating surfaces are clean and dry and fit the new gasket. Fit the manifold and coolant housing and tighten the retaining nuts and bolts evenly and progressively to the specified torque.*

c) *Fit the throttle housing using a new gasket and tighten its retaining bolts to the specified torque.*

d) *Ensure that all relevant hoses are reconnected to their original positions, and are securely held (where necessary) by their retaining clips.*

e) *Tighten the fuel hose and vacuum servo hose union nuts to their specified torque settings.*

f) *Refill the cooling system as described in Chapter 1.*

g) *On completion, adjust the accelerator cable as described in Section 4.*

1.8 and 2.0 litre engines

33 Remove the auxiliary drivebelt as described in Chapter 1.

34 Depressurise the fuel system as described in Section 8 then disconnect the battery negative terminal.

35 Carry out the operations described in paragraphs 30 to 37 of Section 12 noting that it is not necessary to unbolt the throttle housing from the manifold.

36 Slacken the unions nuts and disconnect the fuel hoses from the fuel rail. Whilst slackening the nuts, retain the fuel rail adapters with an open-ended spanner.

37 Disconnect the wiring connectors from the DIS module, the purge valve, the manifold valve switchover solenoid, the coolant temperature sensor, the EGR valve and the oxygen sensor.

38 Carefully release the retaining clips and lift the wiring cover assembly squarely away from rear of the cylinder head. Disconnect the crankshaft sensor and knock sensor wiring connectors from the base of the cover then position the cover and wiring clear of the manifold.

39 Unscrew the union nut and disconnect the braking system servo unit hose from the manifold. Disconnect all remaining vacuum/breather hoses from the manifold, noting each ones correct fitted location.

40 Undo the retaining bolts and remove the alternator mounting brackets from the right-hand side of the inlet manifold **(see illustration)**.

41 Undo the retaining bolts and remove the support bracket from the base of the manifold **(see illustration)**.

42 Slacken and remove the retaining nuts and bolts and manoeuvre the manifold assembly away from the engine. Remove the

gasket and discard it. **Note:** *The manifold assembly must be treated as a sealed unit; do not attempt to dismantle it as no components, other than the switchover diaphragm and solenoid, are available separately.*
43 Refitting is the reverse of removal noting the following.
a) *Prior to refitting, check the manifold studs and renew any that are worn or damaged.*
b) *Ensure the manifold and cylinder mating surfaces are clean and dry and fit the new gasket. Refit the manifold and tighten the retaining nuts and bolts evenly and progressively to the specified torque.*
c) *Ensure that all relevant hoses are reconnected to their original positions, and are securely held (where necessary) by their retaining clips.*
d) *Tighten the fuel hose and vacuum servo hose union nuts to their specified torque settings.*
e) *Refit the auxiliary drivebelt as described in Chapter 1.*
f) *On completion, adjust the accelerator cable as described in Section 4.*

17 Exhaust manifold - removal and refitting

Warning: *When disconnecting the front pipe from the manifold, support the front pipe to prevent any damage to the exhaust system, catalytic convertor or oxygen sensor wiring.* **Note:** *New manifold nuts will be required on refitting.*

SOHC engine

1 Trace the wiring back from the oxygen sensor and disconnect its wiring connector. Free the wiring from all the necessary clips and ties so the sensor is free to be removed with the manifold.
2 Slacken and remove the bolts and springs securing the front pipe flange joint to the manifold.
3 Disconnect the hot air hose from the exhaust manifold shroud then undo the retaining bolts and remove the shroud from the manifold.
4 Remove the engine oil dipstick and pull the plug caps off from the centre (No 2 and 3) spark plugs. Unscrew the centre spark plug heat shields and remove them from the manifold (a special socket, number KM-834, is available to ease removal of the heat shields).
5 Undo the retaining nuts securing the manifold to the head. Manoeuvre the manifold out of the engine compartment, complete with the gasket.
6 Examine all the exhaust manifold studs for signs of damage and corrosion; remove all traces of corrosion, and repair or renew any damaged studs.
7 Ensure that the manifold and cylinder head

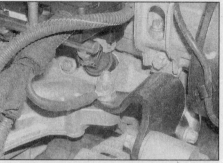
16.40 Alternator support bracket (X18XE1 shown) - note the earth connection

sealing faces are clean and flat, and fit the new gasket.
8 Refit the manifold then fit the new retaining nuts and tighten them to the specified torque.
9 Apply a smear of high-temperature grease to the threads of the spark plug heat shields then refit the shields and tighten them to the specified torque. Reconnect the plug caps and refit the dipstick.
10 Refit the shroud to the manifold, tightening its retaining bolts to the specified torque, and reconnect the hot air hose.
11 Reconnect the oxygen sensor wiring connector making sure the wiring is correctly routed and retained by all the necessary clips.
12 Refit the front pipe as described in Section 18.

1.6 litre DOHC engine

13 Where fitted, remove the secondary air injection system air valve and connecting pipe as described in Chapter 4C.
14 Remove the oil filler cap, undo the retaining screws, and remove the engine cover. Trace the wiring back from the oxygen sensor and disconnect its wiring connector. Free the wiring from all the necessary clips and ties so the sensor is free to be removed with the manifold.
15 Where fitted, remove the heat shield, then slacken and remove the bolts securing the front pipe to the manifold and recover the gasket.
16 Undo the retaining nuts securing the manifold to the head. Manoeuvre the manifold out of the engine compartment, complete with the gasket.

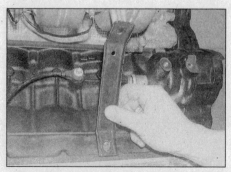
16.41 Unbolt the manifold support bracket

17 Refit the manifold as described in paragraphs 6 to 8.
18 Fit a new gasket between the manifold and front pipe then refit the front pipe bolts and tighten them to the specified torque.
19 Reconnect the oxygen sensor wiring connector making sure the wiring is correctly routed and retained by all the necessary clips.
20 Refit the secondary air injection system connecting pipe and air valve as described in Chapter 4C.

1.8 (X18XE1) litre engine

21 Undo the retaining screws, remove the oil filler cap, and remove the engine cover. Slacken and remove the bolts securing the front pipe to the manifold and recover the gasket.
22 Drain the coolant system as described in Chapter 1.
23 Release the retaining clip and disconnect the large coolant hose from the thermostat housing.
24 Undo the three bolts and remove the heat shield from the manifold.
25 Undo the engine oil dipstick guide bracket retaining bolt, and twist the dipstick guide tube to one side.
26 Slacken and remove the manifold retaining nuts, remove the manifold and recover the gasket.
27 Refit the manifold as described in paragraphs 6 to 8.
28 Realign the dipstick guide tube, and tighten the mounting bracket bolt securely.
29 Refit the heat shield to the manifold (noting that the lower bolt is the shorter of the three), and reconnect the coolant hose to the thermostat. Refill the cooling system as described in Chapter 1.
30 Reconnect the front exhaust pipe to the manifold, using a new gasket.
31 Refit the engine cover.

1.8 (X18XE) and 2.0 litre engines

32 Remove the two engine transport brackets from the cylinder head. Slacken and remove the bolts securing the front pipe to the manifold and recover the gasket.
33 Loosen the front coolant hose from the cylinder head, but do not disconnect the pipe.
34 Undo the retaining screws and remove the heat shield from the manifold.
35 Slacken and remove the retaining nuts, and manoeuvre the manifold out of the engine compartment. Recover the gasket.
36 Refit the manifold as described in paragraphs 6 to 8.
37 Reconnect the front exhaust pipe, using a new gasket. Tighten the bolts to the specified torque.
38 Align the heat shield with the manifold, and tighten the screws to the specified torque.
39 Fasten the front coolant pipe to the cylinder head.
40 Re-attach the transport shackles to the cylinder head. Tighten the bolts securely.

4A

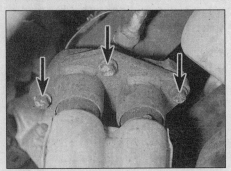

18.7 Exhaust front pipe-to-manifold bolts (arrowed) . . .

18.8 . . . and front pipe mounting nut - 1.6 litre DOHC engine

18.18 Slacken and remove the bolts (arrowed) securing the intermediate pipe to the front pipe

18 Exhaust system - general information, removal and refitting

General information

1 On most models, the exhaust system consists of three sections: the front pipe which incorporates the catalytic converter, the intermediate pipe and centre silencer, and the tailpipe and main silencer box. On models equipped with an automatic transmission unit, the exhaust system is split into four sections; the system is identical to that described above except that the catalytic converter is a separate item and not an integral part of the front pipe.

2 All exhaust sections are joined by flanged joints which are secured by bolts. Some of the joints are of the spring-loaded ball type, to allow for movement in the exhaust system. The system is suspended throughout its entire length by rubber mountings.

Removal

3 Each exhaust section can be removed individually, or alternatively, the complete system can be removed as a unit. Even if only one part of the system needs attention, it is often easier to remove the whole system and separate the sections on the bench.

4 To remove the system or part of the system, first jack up the front or rear of the car and support it securely on axle stands. Alternatively, position the car over an inspection pit or on car ramps.

Front pipe - 1.6 litre SOHC engine

5 Slacken and remove the bolts and springs securing the front pipe flange joint to the manifold.

6 Undo the bolts securing the front pipe to the intermediate pipe and remove the pipe from underneath the vehicle. Recover the gasket from the pipe-to-manifold joint.

Front pipe - 1.6 litre DOHC engine

7 Slacken and remove the bolts securing the front pipe flange joint to the manifold (see illustration).

8 On manual transmission models, unscrew the nut securing the front pipe to its mounting bracket and remove the washer, spacer and mounting rubber (see illustration). Slacken and remove the bolts securing the front pipe to the intermediate pipe and remove the front pipe from the vehicle. Recover the gasket from the front pipe-to-manifold joint.

9 On automatic transmission models, unscrew the nuts securing the front pipe to its mounting bracket and remove the retaining plate. Slacken and remove the bolts and springs securing the front pipe to the catalytic converter and remove the front pipe from the vehicle. Recover the gaskets from the front pipe joints.

Front pipe - 1.8 and 2.0 litre engines

10 Trace the wiring back from the oxygen sensor, noting its correct routing, and disconnect its wiring connector. Free the wiring from any clips so the sensor is free to be removed with the front pipe.

11 Slacken and remove the bolts securing the front pipe flange joint to the manifold.

12 Unscrew the nuts securing the front pipe to its mounting bracket and remove the retaining plate.

13 On manual transmission models, slacken and remove the bolts securing the front pipe to the intermediate pipe and remove the front pipe from the vehicle. Recover the gasket from the front pipe-to-manifold joint.

14 On automatic transmission models, slacken and remove the bolts and springs securing the front pipe to the catalytic converter and remove the front pipe from the vehicle. Recover the gaskets from the front pipe joints.

Catalytic converter - automatic transmission models

15 Slacken and remove the bolts and springs securing the converter to the front pipe and bolts securing it to the intermediate pipe. Remove the catalytic converter from underneath the vehicle and recover the gasket from its front pipe joint.

Intermediate pipe - SOHC engines

16 Slacken and remove the bolts securing the intermediate pipe to the front pipe and slacken the clamp securing the pipe to the tailpipe.

17 Free the intermediate pipe from its mounting rubbers and manoeuvre it out from underneath the vehicle.

Intermediate pipe - DOHC engines

18 Slacken and remove the bolts securing the intermediate pipe to the front pipe and the bolts and springs securing it to the tailpipe (see illustration).

19 Free the intermediate pipe from its mounting rubbers and manoeuvre it out from underneath the vehicle (see illustration). Recover the gasket from the rear tailpipe joint.

Tailpipe - SOHC engines

20 Slacken the clamp securing the tailpipe to the intermediate pipe.

21 Free the tailpipe from its mounting rubbers and remove it from the underneath the vehicle.

Tailpipe - DOHC engines

22 Slacken and remove the bolts and springs securing the tailpipe joint to the intermediate pipe (see illustration).

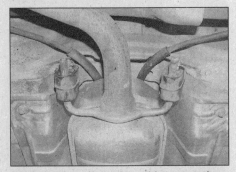

18.19 Intermediate pipe rubber mountings

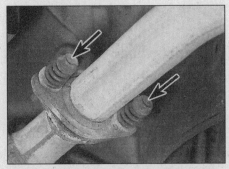

18.22 Intermediate pipe-to-tail pipe bolts and springs (arrowed)

23 Free the tailpipe from its mounting rubbers and remove it along with its gasket.

Complete system - SOHC engines

24 Undo the bolts and spring securing the front pipe flange joint to the manifold.

25 Free the system from all its mounting rubbers and lower it from under the vehicle. Recover the gasket from the front pipe joint.

Complete system - DOHC engines

26 Where applicable, trace the wiring back from the oxygen sensor, noting its correct routing, and disconnect its wiring connector. Free the wiring from any clips so the sensor is free to be removed with the front pipe.

27 Unscrew the nuts securing the front pipe to its mounting bracket and remove the retaining plate.

28 Slacken and remove the bolts securing the front pipe flange joint to the manifold and recover the gasket.

29 Free the exhaust system from all its mounting rubbers and lower it from underneath the vehicle.

Heat shield(s)

30 The heat shields are secured to the underside of the body by various nuts and bolts. Each shield can be removed once the relevant exhaust section has been removed. If a shield is being removed to gain access to a component located behind it, it may prove sufficient in some cases to remove the retaining nuts and/or bolts, and simply lower the shield, without disturbing the exhaust system.

Refitting

31 Each section is refitted by reversing the removal sequence, noting the following points:

   a) Ensure that all traces of corrosion have been removed from the flanges and renew all necessary gaskets.

   b) Inspect the rubber mountings for signs of damage or deterioration, and renew as necessary.

   c) Where no gasket is fitted to a joint, apply a smear of exhaust system jointing paste to ensure a gas-tight seal.

   d) Prior to tightening the exhaust system fasteners, ensure that all rubber mountings are correctly located, and that there is adequate clearance between the exhaust system and vehicle underbody.

4A

Notes

Chapter 4 Part B:
Fuel and exhaust systems - diesel engine models

Contents

Degrees of difficulty

Easy, suitable for novice with little experience	Fairly easy, suitable for beginner with some experience	Fairly difficult, suitable for competent DIY mechanic 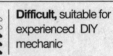	Difficult, suitable for experienced DIY mechanic	Very difficult, suitable for expert DIY or professional 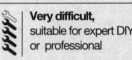

Specifications

General

System type:

1.7 litre models . . . .
  Indirect injection system incorporating a distributor fuel injection pump with integral transfer pump. Turbocharger and intercooler fitted to all models.

2.0 litre models . . . .
  Direct injection system incorporating an electronically-controlled fuel injection pump. Turbocharger fitted to all models and intercooler fitted to high-pressure turbo (X20DTH engine) models.

4B

Adjustment data

Idle speed . . . .   See Chapter 1B

Maximum speed:

1.7 litre models . . . .   5200 rpm

2.0 litre models . . . .   4900 to 5100 rpm - controlled by ECU

Injection pump

Direction of rotation . . . .   Clockwise, viewed from sprocket end

Pump timing (static):

1.7 litre models:

  Engine position . . . .   No 1 piston at TDC

  Pump timing measurement . . . .   0.55 ± 0.05 mm

2.0 litre models . . . .   Preset - controlled by ECU

Injectors

Opening pressure:

1.7 litre models . . . .   142 to 162 bar

2.0 litre models:

  Low-pressure turbo models (X20DTL) . . . .   180 to 365 bar

  High-pressure turbo models (X20DTH) . . . .   220 to 380 bar

Torque wrench settings

	Nm	lbf ft
1.7 litre models		
Exhaust front pipe-to-turbocharger nuts	65	48
Exhaust manifold:		
Retaining nuts and bolts	24	18
Support bracket bolts	51	38
Fuel injector return pipe nuts	29	21
Fuel injectors	50	37
Fuel pipe union nuts	25	18
Inlet manifold nuts and bolts	24	18
Injection pump:		
Front mounting nuts	23	17
Rear mounting bracket bolts:		
M8 bolts	25	18
M10 bolts	40	30
Timing access hole plug	20	15
Timing belt sprocket nut	See Chapter 2C	
Turbocharger:		
Coolant pipe bolts	8	6
Exhaust flange nuts	27	20
Turbocharger-to-manifold nuts	27	20
2.0 litre models		
Accelerator pedal nuts	20	15
Auxiliary drivebelt tensioner assembly bolts:		
Pulley backplate pivot bolt	42	31
Strut mounting bolts	23	17
Boost pressure sensor bolt	8	6
Camshaft sprocket bolt	See Chapter 2D	
Coolant temperature sensor	See Chapter 3	
Crankshaft sensor bolt	8	6
Exhaust front pipe:		
Pipe-to-intermediate pipe bolts	12	9
Pipe-to-turbocharger nuts	20	15
Exhaust manifold:		
Retaining nuts	22	16
Support bracket bolts	25	18
Fuel pipe union nuts	25	18
Injection pump:		
Front mounting bolts	25	18
Fuel pipe union bolts	15	11
Rear mounting bracket bolts	20	15
Sprocket cover bolts	See Chapter 2D	
Sprocket retaining bolts	See Chapter 2D	
Inlet manifold:		
Lower section-to-cylinder head nuts	22	16
Upper section-to-lower section bolts	8	6
Timing chain:		
Tensioner cap (upper and lower)	See Chapter 2D	
Upper chain guide bolts	See Chapter 2D	
Turbocharger:		
Exhaust flange bolts	30	22
Oil feed pipe:		
Pipe-to-cylinder block union nut	20	15
Pipe-to-turbo charger union bolt	20	15
Oil return pipe:		
Pipe-to-cylinder block union nut	25	18
Pipe-to-turbocharger bolts	8	6
Turbocharger-to-manifold bolts	30	22

1 General information and precautions

General information - 1.7 litre models

1 The fuel system consists of a rear-mounted fuel tank, a fuel filter with integral water separator, a fuel injection pump, injectors and associated components. Before passing through the filter, the fuel is heated by an electric heating element which is fitted to the filter housing.

2 Fuel is drawn from the fuel tank to the fuel injection pump by a vane-type transfer pump incorporated in the fuel injection pump. Before reaching the pump, the fuel passes through a fuel filter, where foreign matter and water are removed. Excess fuel lubricates the moving components of the pump, and is then returned to the tank.

3 The fuel injection pump is driven at half-crankshaft speed by the timing belt. The high pressure required to inject the fuel into the compressed air in the swirl chambers is achieved by a cam plate acting on a single piston. The fuel passes through a central rotor with a single outlet drilling which aligns with ports leading to the injector pipes.

4 Fuel metering is controlled by a centrifugal governor, which reacts to accelerator pedal position and engine speed. The governor is linked to a metering valve, which increases or decreases the amount of fuel delivered at each pumping stroke.

5 Basic injection timing is determined when the pump is fitted. When the engine is running, it is varied automatically to suit the prevailing engine speed by a mechanism which turns the cam plate or ring.

6 The four fuel injectors produce a spray of fuel into the swirl chambers located in the cylinder head. The injectors are calibrated to open and close at critical pressures to provide efficient and even combustion. Each injector needle is lubricated by fuel, which accumulates in the spring chamber and is channelled to the injection pump return hose by leak-off pipes.

7 Cold starting is assisted by preheater or 'glow' plugs fitted to each swirl chamber. A thermostatic capsule on the injection pump increase the idling speed when the engine is cold.

8 A stop solenoid cuts the fuel supply to the injection pump rotor when the ignition is switched off.

9 A turbocharger is fitted to increase engine efficiency by raising the pressure in the inlet manifold above atmospheric pressure. Instead of the air simply being sucked into the cylinders, it is forced in. Additional fuel is supplied by the injection pump in proportion to the increased air intake.

10 Energy for the operation of the turbocharger comes from the exhaust gas.

The gas flows through a specially-shaped housing (the turbine housing) and in so doing, spins the turbine wheel. The turbine wheel is attached to a shaft, at the end of which is another vaned wheel known as the compressor wheel. The compressor wheel spins in its own housing, and compresses the inlet air on the way to the inlet manifold.

11 Between the turbocharger and the inlet manifold, the compressed air passes through an intercooler. This is an air-to-air heat exchanger is mounted next to the radiator, and supplied with cooling air from the front of the vehicle. The purpose of the intercooler is to remove some of the heat gained in being compressed from the inlet air. Because cooler air is denser, removal of this heat further increases engine efficiency.

12 Boost pressure (the pressure in the inlet manifold) is limited by a wastegate, which diverts the exhaust gas away from the turbine wheel in response to a pressure-sensitive actuator. A pressure-operated switch operates a warning light on the instrument panel in the event of excessive boost pressure developing.

13 The turbo shaft is pressure-lubricated by an oil feed pipe from the engine main oil so that the shaft 'floats' on a cushion of oil. A drain pipe returns the oil to the sump. The turbo is also connected into the cooling system to prevent it overheating.

14 Provided that regular maintenance is carried out, the fuel injection equipment will give long and trouble-free service. The injection pump itself may well outlast the engine. The main potential cause of damage to the injection pump and injectors is dirt or water in the fuel.

15 Servicing of the injection pump and injectors is very limited for the home mechanic, and any dismantling or adjustment other than that described in this Chapter must be entrusted to a Vauxhall dealer or fuel injection specialist.

General information - 2.0 litre models

Note: *Two versions of the 2.0 litre engine are available; a low-pressure turbo (X20DTL) version and a high-pressure (X20DTH) version. Refer to "Vehicle identification" for information on engine number location to determine which engine is fitted to your vehicle.*

16 The fuel system consists of a rear-mounted fuel tank, a fuel filter with integral water separator, a fuel injection pump, injectors and associated components.

17 Fuel is drawn from the fuel tank by the fuel injection pump. Before reaching the pump, the fuel passes through a fuel filter, where foreign matter and water are removed. Excess fuel lubricates the moving components of the pump, and is then returned to the tank.

18 The fuel injection pump is driven at half-crankshaft speed by the lower timing chain. The high pressure required to inject the fuel into the compressed air in the cylinder is

achieved by a radial piston pump.

19 The injection pump is electronically-controlled to meet the latest emission standards. The system consists of the electronic control unit (ECU), the injection pump control unit and the following sensors.

a) *Accelerator pedal position sensor - informs the ECU of the accelerator pedal position.*

b) *Coolant temperature sensor - informs the ECU of engine temperature.*

c) *Intake air temperature sensor - informs the ECU of the temperature of the air passing through the intake duct.*

d) *Oil temperature sensor - informs ECU of the temperature of the engine oil.*

e) *Airflow meter - informs the ECU of the amount of air passing through the intake duct.*

f) *Crankshaft sensor - informs the ECU of engine speed and crankshaft position.*

g) *Boost pressure sensor - informs ECU of the pressure in the inlet manifold.*

h) *ABS control unit - informs the ECU of the vehicle speed.*

i) *Air conditioning system compressor switch (where fitted) - informs ECU when the air conditioning system is switched on.*

20 All the above information is analysed by the ECU and, based on this, the ECU determines the appropriate injection requirements for the engine. The ECU controls the injection pump timing, via the pump control unit, to provide the best setting for cranking, starting (with either a hot or cold engine), warm-up, idle, cruising, and acceleration.

21 The ECU also controls the exhaust gas recirculation (EGR) system (see Chapter 4C) and the preheating system (see Chapter 5C).

22 The four fuel injectors produce a spray of fuel directly into the cylinders. The injectors are calibrated to open and close at critical pressures to provide efficient and even combustion. Each injector needle is lubricated by fuel, which accumulates in the spring chamber and is channelled to the injection pump return hose by leak-off pipes.

23 The inlet manifold is fitted with a butterfly valve arrangement to improve efficiency at low engine speeds. Each cylinder has two intake tracts in the manifold, one of which is fitted a valve; the operation of the valve is controlled by the ECU via a solenoid valve and vacuum diaphragm unit. At low engine speeds (below approximately 1500 rpm) the valves remain closed, meaning that air entering each cylinder is passing through only one of the two manifold tracts. At higher engine speeds, the ECU opens up each of the four valves allowing the air passing through the manifold to pass through both inlet tracts.

24 Refer to paragraphs 9 to 13 for information on the turbocharger, noting that an intercooler is only fitted to high-pressure turbo (X20DTH engine) models. The boost

4B

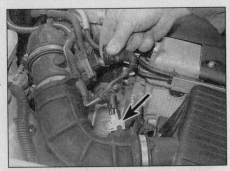

2.4 Disconnect the wiring connector from the airflow meter and (where fitted) the intake air temperature sensor (arrowed)

2.5 Removing the intake duct assembly - 2.0 litre models (shown with air cleaner housing lid)

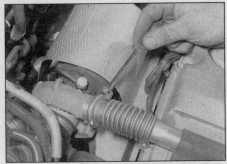

2.7a On low-pressure turbo models slacken the retaining clamp securing the metal pipe to the turbocharger . . .

pressure wastegate is controlled by the ECU via a solenoid valve.

25 If there is an abnormality in any of the readings obtained from any sensor, the ECU enters its back-up mode. In this event, the ECU ignores the abnormal sensor signal, and assumes a pre-programmed value which will allow the engine to continue running (albeit at reduced efficiency). If the ECU enters this back-up mode, the warning light on the instrument panel will come on, and the relevant fault code will be stored in the ECU memory.

26 If the warning light comes on, the vehicle should be taken to a Vauxhall dealer at the earliest opportunity. A complete test of the injection system can then be carried out, using a special electronic diagnostic test unit which is simply plugged into the system's diagnostic connector. The connector is located behind the centre console; unclip the trim panel situated just in front of the handbrake lever to gain access.

Precautions

Warning: It is necessary to take certain precautions when working on the fuel system components, particularly the fuel injectors. Before carrying out any operations on the fuel system, refer to the precautions given in "Safety first!" at the beginning of this manual, and to any additional warning notes at the start of the relevant Sections.
Caution: Do not operate the engine if any of air intake ducts are disconnected or the filter element is removed. Any debris

entering the engine will cause severe damage to the turbocharger
Caution: To prevent damage to the turbocharger, do not race the engine immediately after start-up, especially if it is cold. Allow it to idle smoothly to give the oil a few seconds to circulate around the turbocharger bearings. Always allow the engine to return to idle speed before switching it off - do not blip the throttle and switch off, as this will leave the turbo spinning without lubrication.
Caution: Observe the recommended intervals for oil and filter changing, and use a reputable oil of the specified quality. Neglect of oil changing, or use of inferior oil, can cause carbon formation on the turbo shaft, leading to subsequent failure.

2	Air cleaner assembly and intake ducts - removal and refitting

Removal - 1.7 litre models

1 Slacken the retaining clip and detach the intake duct from the air cleaner housing. If necessary, slacken the other retaining clip then detach the duct from the manifold and remove it from the engine compartment.
2 Undo the nuts securing the air cleaner mountings to the body then free the housing from its air intake and remove the assembly from the engine compartment.

3 The remaining ducts linking the turbocharger, intercooler and inlet manifold can be removed once their retaining clips and (where necessary) bolts have been slackened.

Removal - 2.0 litre models

4 Disconnect the battery negative terminal then disconnect the wiring connector(s) from the airflow meter and (where fitted) the intake air temperature sensor **(see illustration)**.
5 Disconnect the breather hose from the intake duct then slacken the retaining clips and remove the duct assembly, complete with airflow meter, from the engine compartment **(see illustration)**.
6 Unclip the air cleaner housing lid and remove the filter element, noting which way up it is fitted. Undo the retaining nuts and remove the housing from the engine compartment, freeing it from its intake.
7 On low-pressure turbo (X20DTL engine) models, to remove the ducts linking the turbocharger and inlet manifold, first undo the retaining screws and remove the plastic cover from the top of the engine. Slacken the retaining clip securing the duct connecting the metal pipe to the manifold. Undo the bolts securing the pipe to the cylinder head cover, then slacken the retaining clamp and detach the pipe from the turbocharger. Remove the pipe and duct assembly from the top of the engine and recover the sealing ring which is fitted between the pipe and turbocharger **(see illustrations)**.
8 On high-pressure turbo (X20DTH engine) models, the ducts linking the intercooler to

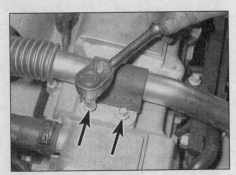

2.7b . . . then undo the two retaining bolts (arrowed) . . .

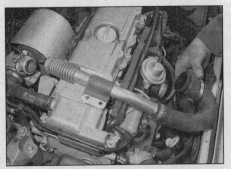

2.7c . . . and remove the metal pipe and intake duct . . .

2.7d . . . noting the sealing ring which is fitted to the turbocharger (arrowed)

the manifold and turbocharger pipe can be removed once their retaining clips have been slackened. To remove the metal pipe, detach the duct then slacken the clamp securing it to the turbocharger. Undo the retaining bolt and remove the pipe from the engine, noting the sealing ring which is fitted between the pipe and turbocharger.

Refitting

9 Refitting is the reverse of removal, ensuring that all intake ducts are properly reconnected and their retaining clips securely tightened. On 2.0 litre models, renew the sealing ring if the metal pipe has been disconnected from the turbocharger.

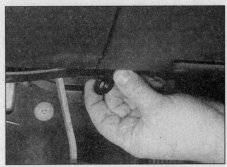

4.2a Unscrew the fasteners . . .

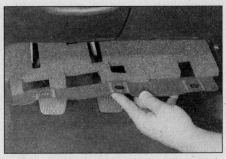

4.2b . . . and remove the lower trim panel from underneath the driver's side of the facia

3 Accelerator cable - removal, refitting and adjustment

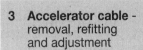

1.7 litre models

1 Refer to Section 4 of Chapter 4A substituting in 'injection pump accelerator lever' for all references to the 'throttle cam'. Access to the injection pump is very poor and can only be significantly improved by removing the inlet manifold (see Section 17).

2.0 litre models

2 On 2.0 litre models there is no accelerator cable. The injection pump is electronically controlled by the ECU via the control unit which is bolted to the top of the pump. The accelerator pedal is connected to a position sensor and the position sensor informs the ECU of the accelerator pedal position (see Section 1).

4 Accelerator pedal - removal and refitting

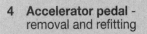

1.7 litre models

1 Refer to Section 5 of Chapter 4A.

2.0 litre models

2 From inside the vehicle, unscrew the fasteners and remove the lower trim panel from underneath the driver's side of the facia to gain access to the accelerator pedal (see illustrations).
3 Disconnect the wiring connector from the accelerator pedal position sensor.
4 Unscrew the retaining nuts and remove the pedal assembly from the bulkhead.
5 Inspect the pedal assembly for signs of wear, paying particular attention to the pedal bushes, and renew as necessary. To dismantle the assembly, remove the position sensor (see Section 10) then unhook the return spring then slide off the retaining clip and separate the pedal, mounting bracket, return spring and pivot bushes.
6 If the assembly has been dismantled, apply

a smear of multi-purpose grease to the pedal pivot shaft and bushes. Fit the bushes and return spring to the mounting bracket and insert the pedal, making sure it passes through the return spring bore. Secure the pedal in position with the retaining clip and hook the return spring back behind the pedal. Refit the position sensor (see Section 10).
7 Refit the pedal assembly and tighten its retaining nuts to the specified torque setting.
8 Reconnect the wiring connector then refit the trim panel to the facia.

5 Fuel system - priming and bleeding

1 It is not always necessary to manually prime and bleed the fuel system after any operation on the system components. Start the engine (this may take longer than usual, especially if the fuel system has been allowed to run dry - operate the starter in ten second bursts with 5 seconds rest in between each operation) and run it a fast idle speed for a minute or so to purge any trapped air from the fuel lines. After this time the engine should idle smoothly at a constant speed.
2 If the engine idles roughly, then there is still some air trapped in the fuel system. Increase the engine speed again for another minute or so then recheck the idle speed. Repeat this procedure as necessary until the engine is idling smoothly.

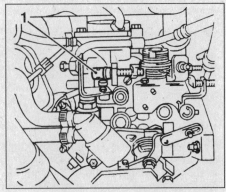

8.3 On 1.7 litre models the maximum speed adjusting screw (1) is sealed with a lead seal

3 If there is difficulty in bleeding the system, then it may be necessary to contact your Vauxhall dealer as they have equipment (Tool No. KM948) to bleed the system.

6 Fuel gauge sender unit - removal and refitting

1 Refer to Section 10 of Chapter 4A, noting that there is no fuel pump in the tank reservoir, just a fuel pick-up filter.

7 Fuel tank - removal and refitting

1 Refer to Section 11 of Chapter 4A, noting that there is no fuel filter clipped to the tank strap. Plug the fuel hose ends to prevent the fuel draining from the system; this will enable the engine to be started more easily once the fuel tank has been refitted (see Section 5).

8 Maximum speed - checking and adjustment

4B

Caution: The maximum speed adjustment screw is sealed by the manufacturers at the factory, using paint or a locking wire and a lead seal. There is no reason why it should require adjustment. Do not disturb the screw if the vehicle is still within the warranty period, otherwise the warranty will be invalidated. This adjustment requires the use of a tachometer - refer to Chapter 1 for alternative methods.

1.7 litre models

1 Run the engine to normal operating temperature.
2 Have an assistant fully depress the accelerator pedal, and check that the maximum engine speed is as given in the Specifications. Do not keep the engine at maximum speed for more than two or three seconds.
3 If adjustment is necessary, stop the engine, then loosen the locknut, turn the maximum speed adjustment screw as necessary, and retighten the locknut (see illustration).

9.4a On 1.7 litre engines measure the clearance between cold start advance lever screw and the accelerator lever . . .

9.4b . . . and, if necessary, adjust by slackening the locknut and rotating the adjustment screw

4 Repeat the procedure in paragraph 2 to check the adjustment.
5 Stop the engine and disconnect the tachometer.

2.0 litre models

6 The maximum speed is controlled by the ECU and cannot be adjusted by the home mechanic. The speed can be checked as described above (see paragraphs 1 and 2) but if adjustment is needed it will have be necessary to take the vehicle to a Vauxhall dealer. They will have access to the necessary diagnostic equipment required to test and adjust the settings.

9 Cold start advance (CSA) system - general information and adjustment

General information

1 On 1.7 litre models, a cold start advance (CSA) capsule is fitted to the injection pump to improve the running and lessen exhaust emissions when the engine is cold. The coolant circulates around the thermostatic capsule which contains an expandable element. When the engine is cold, the element advances the injection timing and raises the engine idle speed approximately 150 rpm. This prevents the engine stalling and also lessens exhaust smoke.
2 On 2.0 litre models, the engine idle speed and injection timing are constantly monitored and controlled by the ECU to provide optimum performance under all operating conditions (see Section 1). Therefore there is no auxiliary cold start advance system.

Adjustment

3 Check and, if necessary, adjust the idle speed as described in Chapter 1 then allow the engine to cool fully.
4 With the engine cool, measure the clearance

between the cold start advance lever adjustment screw and the injection pump accelerator lever. At a coolant temperature of 20°C (68°F) the clearance should be 0.8 to 1.1 mm. **Note:** *If the coolant temperature is hotter or colder than 20°C (68°F) then this should be taken into consideration when making the measurement; the cooler the temperature the larger the clearance and the warmer the temperature the smaller the clearance.* If necessary, slacken the locknut and adjust the clearance by rotating the cold start lever adjustment screw **(see illustrations)**. Once the clearance is correctly set, hold the screw and securely tighten the locknut.
5 Once the clearance is correctly set, start the engine and check that the engine idles at the recommended speed given in the Specifications. If adjustment is necessary, slacken the locknut and adjust the idle speed screw until the speed is within the specified range then securely tighten the locknut.
6 Warm the engine up to normal operating temperature and recheck the idle speed. As the engine warms, the gap between the cold start advance lever and the accelerator lever should steadily decrease until the two are in contact. If this is not the case, there is a fault in the cold start advance system and the vehicle should be taken to a Vauxhall dealer for testing.
7 Where applicable, disconnect the tachometer on completion.

10 Injection system electrical components - removal and refitting

1.7 litre models

1 The only electrical component in the injection system is the stop solenoid. The solenoid is located on the top of the fuel injection pump, at the rear, its purpose being to cut the fuel supply when the ignition is switched off. If an open-circuit occurs in the

solenoid or supply wiring, it will be impossible to start the engine, as the fuel will not reach the injectors. The same applies if the solenoid plunger jams in the 'stop' position. If the solenoid jams in the 'run' position, the engine will not stop when the ignition is switched off. *Caution: Be careful not to allow dirt into the injection pump during this procedure.*

Models fitted with a Vauxhall immobiliser

Note: *New solenoid control unit shear bolts will be required on refitting.*
2 Remove the inlet manifold as described in Section 17.
3 Remove the oil cooler as described in Chapter 2.
4 Disconnect the solenoid control unit wiring connector. Remove the rubber cover from the top of the solenoid then slacken and remove the retaining nut and washer and disconnect the feed wire.
5 Taking great care to not damage the solenoid control unit, carefully drill off the control unit retaining bolt heads. Slide the control unit off from the rear of the injection pump and unscrew the remains of retaining bolts.
6 Carefully clean around the solenoid, then unscrew and withdraw the solenoid, and recover the sealing washer/ring (as applicable). Recover the solenoid plunger and spring if they remain in the pump. If the solenoid is to be removed for any length of time cover the injection pump to prevent the entry of dirt.
7 Refitting is a reversal of removal, using a new sealing washer/ring and tightening the solenoid securely. Secure the control unit in position with new shear bolts tightening them evenly and progressively until their heads break off.

Models not fitted with a Vauxhall immobiliser

8 Remove the inlet manifold as described in Section 17.
9 Remove the rubber cover from the top of the solenoid then slacken and remove the nut

10.9 Stop solenoid electrical lead (arrowed) - 1.7 litre engine

10.10 Stop solenoid, sealing ring, spring and plunger - 1.7 litre engine

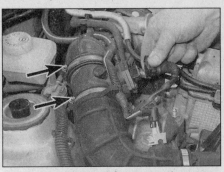

10.12 On 2.0 litre engines disconnect the wiring connector then slacken the retaining clips (arrowed) and remove the airflow meter

and washer and disconnect the feed wire **(see illustration)**.

10 Carefully clean around the solenoid, then unscrew and withdraw the solenoid, and recover the sealing washer/ring (as applicable). Recover the solenoid plunger and spring if they remain in the pump **(see illustration)**. If the solenoid is to be removed for any length of time, cover the injection pump to prevent the entry of dirt.

11 Refitting is a reversal of removal, using a new sealing washer/ring and tightening the solenoid securely.

2.0 litre models

Airflow meter

12 Ensure the ignition is switched off then disconnect the wiring connector from the airflow meter **(see illustration)**.

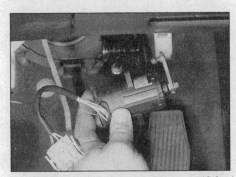

10.20 Removing the accelerator pedal position sensor

13 Slacken the retaining clips then free the airflow meter from the intake ducts and remove it from the engine compartment.

14 Refitting is the reverse of removal, ensuring the intake ducts are correctly seated and their retaining clips are securely tightened.

Intake air temperature sensor - low-pressure turbo (X20DTL engine)

Note: *On high-pressure turbo (X20DTH engine) models, the air temperature sensor is built into the airflow meter.*

15 Ensure the ignition is switched off, then disconnect the wiring connector and carefully ease the sensor out from the intake duct.

16 Refitting is the reverse of removal ensuring the sensor is correctly located in the duct.

Accelerator pedal position sensor

17 From inside the vehicle, unscrew the fasteners and remove the lower trim panel from underneath the driver's side of the facia to gain access to the accelerator pedal.

18 Disconnect the wiring connector from the sensor which is mounted onto the top of the accelerator pedal.

19 Remove the retaining clip from the link rod balljoint then unclip the rod from the sensor.

20 Undo the retaining screws and remove the sensor from the pedal bracket **(see illustration)**.

21 Refitting is the reverse of removal.

Crankshaft sensor

22 Undo the retaining screws and remove the

plastic cover from the top of the cylinder head.

23 To gain access to the sensor from below, firmly apply the handbrake then jack up the front of the vehicle and support it on axle stands. Where necessary, undo the retaining bolts and remove the undercover from beneath the engine/transmission unit.

24 Trace the wiring back from the crankshaft sensor to its wiring connector then free the connector from its bracket and disconnect it from the main harness **(see illustration)**.

25 Wipe clean the area around the crankshaft sensor then slacken and remove the retaining bolt. Remove the sensor from the front of the cylinder block and recover the sealing ring **(see illustration)**.

26 Refitting is the reverse of removal, using a new sealing ring. Tighten the sensor retaining bolt to the specified torque.

Coolant temperature sensor

27 The coolant temperature sensor is screwed into the front of the cylinder head, at the right-hand end. Refer to Chapter 3 for removal and refitting details.

Boost pressure sensor

28 Undo the retaining screws and remove the plastic cover from the top of the cylinder head.

29 Slacken and remove the screws securing the wiring harness tray to the top of the inlet manifold and disconnect the wiring connector from the boost pressure sensor **(see illustration)**.

4B

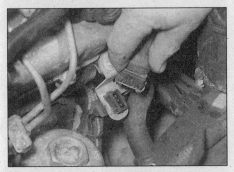

10.24 Disconnect the wiring connector . . .

10.25 . . . then undo the retaining screw and remove the crankshaft sensor from the front of the cylinder block (sealing ring arrowed)

10.29 Disconnect the wiring connector then undo the retaining bolt (arrowed) and remove the boost pressure sensor

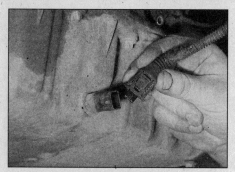

10.34 Disconnect the oil temperature sensor wiring connector

11.5 The fuel injection pump cold start advance capsule (arrowed) - 1.7 litre engine

30 Undo the retaining bolt and remove the sensor from the top of the inlet manifold, noting the sealing ring fitted to the sensor shaft.

31 Refitting is the reverse of removal, using a new sealing ring and tightening the retaining bolt to the specified torque.

Oil temperature sensor

32 Firmly apply the handbrake then jack up the front of the vehicle and support it on axle stands. Where necessary, undo the retaining bolts and remove the undercover from beneath the engine/transmission unit.

33 Drain the engine oil as described in Chapter 1. Once the oil has finished draining, fit a new sealing ring then refit the drain plug and tighten it to the specified torque.

34 Disconnect the wiring connector then unscrew the sensor from the front of the sump (see illustration).

35 On refitting is the reverse of removal, refilling the engine with oil as described in Chapter 1.

Electronic control unit (ECU)

36 Remove the windscreen wiper arms as described in Chapter 12 then disconnect the battery negative terminal.

37 Unscrew the plastic nuts from the wiper arm spindles.

38 Peel off the rubber sealing strip from the top of the engine compartment bulkhead.

39 Carefully unclip the plastic vent panel from the base of the windscreen and remove it from the vehicle to gain access to the ECU.

40 Undo the retaining nuts and free the ECU protective cover from the body.

41 Release the retaining clip and disconnect the wiring connector from the ECU.

42 Undo the retaining nuts and remove the ECU from the vehicle.

43 Refitting is the reverse of removal, ensuring the wiring connector is securely reconnected.

Injection pump control unit

44 The control unit is an integral part of the injection pump and should not be disturbed. **Never** attempt to separate the control unit and pump.

Inlet manifold switchover solenoid valve

45 Remove the battery (see Chapter 5) to gain access to the valve which is located in the front left-hand corner of the engine compartment. Note that there are two valves, the EGR system valve and the manifold switchover valve; the manifold switchover valve can be identified by its grey wiring connector.

46 Disconnect the wiring connector and vacuum hoses from the valve then undo the retaining screws and remove the valve from its mounting bracket.

47 Refitting is the reverse of removal.

Turbocharger wastegate solenoid valve

48 The solenoid valve is located in the right-hand rear corner of the engine compartment.

49 To gain access to the valve, remove the intake duct assembly linking the air cleaner housing to the turbocharger (see Section 2).

50 Disconnect the wiring connector and vacuum hoses from the valve then undo the retaining screws and remove the valve from its mounting bracket.

51 Refitting is the reverse of removal.

11 Fuel injection pump - removal and refitting

Caution: Be careful not to allow dirt into the injection pump or injector pipes during this procedure.

1.7 litre models

1 Disconnect the battery negative lead then remove the inlet manifold as described in Section 17.

2 Remove the injection pump timing belt sprocket as described in Chapter 2.

3 Remove the engine oil filter as described in Chapter 1. If the oil filter is damaged on removal (which is likely), drain the engine oil then fit a new filter on refitting and refill the engine with fresh oil.

4 Remove the retaining clip and free the accelerator cable from the injection pump.

5 Clamp the coolant hoses to minimise coolant loss then release the retaining clips and disconnect both hoses from the injection pump cold start advance capsule (see illustration). Mop up any spilt coolant.

6 Remove all traces of dirt and make identification marks between the fuel feed and return hoses and their pump unions. Release the retaining clips and disconnect both hoses from the pump. Plug the hose ends to minimise fuel loss and prevent the entry of dirt.

7 Wipe clean the pipe unions then slacken the union nuts securing the injector pipes to the top of each injector and the four union nuts securing the pipes to the rear of the injection pump; as each pump union nut is slackened, retain the adapter with a suitable open-ended spanner to prevent it being unscrewed from the pump. With all the union nuts undone, remove the injector pipes from the engine unit and mop up any spilt fuel.

8 Disconnect the wiring connector from the injection pump solenoid/solenoid control unit (as applicable).

9 Mark the fuel injection pump front flange in relation to the mounting bracket, using a scriber or felt tip pen. This will ensure the correct pump timing is retained when refitting.

10 Slacken and remove the retaining bolts securing the pump rear mounting bracket to the cylinder block bracket (see illustration).

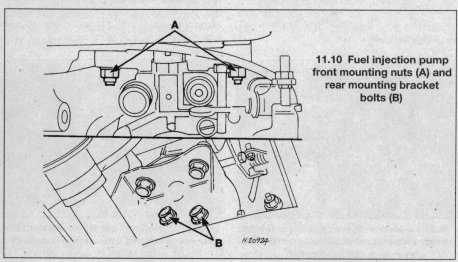

11.10 Fuel injection pump front mounting nuts (A) and rear mounting bracket bolts (B)

H20924

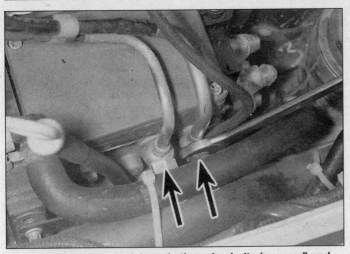

11.26 On 2.0 litre models undo the union bolts (arrowed) and disconnect the feed and return pipes from the pump

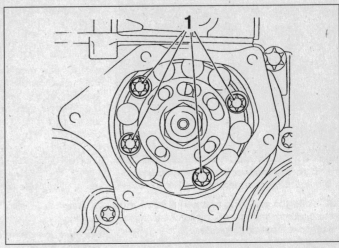

11.28 Slacken and remove the injection pump front mounting bolts (1) through the holes in the lower timing chain sprocket

11 Slacken and remove the pump front mounting nuts and remove the pump assembly from the engine.
Caution: Never attempt to dismantle the pump assembly. If there is a problem, take the pump to a Vauxhall dealer/diesel injection specialist for testing/repair.

12 Manoeuvre the pump into position and loosely refit its front mounting nuts and rear mounting bolts.

13 Align the marks made on the pump and mounting bracket before removal and lightly tighten the mounting nuts and bolts. If a new pump is being fitted, transfer the mark from the old pump to give an approximate setting.

14 Refit the injection pump sprocket and timing belt as described in Chapter 2.

15 Adjust the injection timing, as described in Section 13 then tighten the pump mounting nuts and bolts to the specified torque.

16 Ensure the unions are clean and dry then refit the injector pipes, tightening their union nuts to the specified torque.

17 Reconnect the wiring to the injection pump solenoid/solenoid control unit (as applicable).

18 Reconnect the feed and return hoses to the injection pump, securing them in position with the retaining clips.

19 Reconnect the coolant hoses to the cold start advance capsule and secure in position with the retaining clips.

20 Reconnect the accelerator cable to the pump and secure it position with the retaining clip.

21 Refit the inlet manifold as described in Section 17.

22 Fit the oil filter and top-up/refill the engine with oil (see Chapter 1 and *"Weekly checks"*).

23 Reconnect the battery negative lead then start the engine and bleed the fuel system as described in Section 5.

24 Warm the engine up to normal operating temperature then check and, if necessary, adjust the idle speed as described in Chapter 1.

2.0 litre models

Note: *Since it is necessary to remove the upper timing chain and sprockets to remove the injection pump, several special Vauxhall service tools (or suitable alternatives) will be required on refitting to enable the valve timing to be accurately adjusted (see Section 4 of Chapter 2D). If access to suitable tools cannot be gained then it is recommended that this task is entrusted to a Vauxhall dealer or suitably-equipped garage. If the task is to be carried out without the tools then accurate alignment marks must be made between the sprockets, camshaft and injection pump flange prior to removal. It is also likely that the special socket (MKM-604-30) will also be needed to unscrew the pump front mounting bolts.*

Note: *A new camshaft sprocket bolt and upper timing chain guide bolts will be required on refitting.*

25 Remove the inlet manifold as described in Section 17

26 Remove all traces of dirt from around the injection pump fuel feed and return pipe unions. Slacken and remove the union bolts and sealing washers then disconnect both pipes and position them clear of the pump **(see illustration)**.

27 Remove the upper timing chain and sprockets as described in Chapter 2.

28 Working through the holes in the lower timing chain sprocket, slacken and remove the pump front mounting bolts **(see illustration)**.

29 Slacken and remove the retaining bolts and remove the pump rear mounting bracket. Manoeuvre the pump out of position along with its sealing ring. Discard the sealing ring, a new one must be used on refitting **(see illustrations)**.

Caution: Never attempt to dismantle the pump assembly. If there is a problem, take the pump to a Vauxhall dealer/diesel injection specialist for testing/repair.

30 Prior to refitting, ensure the timing cut-out in the pump sprocket flange is correctly aligned with the locating hole in the pump body and check that the camshaft and crankshaft are still correctly positioned.

31 Ensure the mating surfaces are clean and dry and fit a new sealing ring to the pump flange.

32 Manoeuvre the pump into position, engaging the lower timing chain sprocket with the pump flange. Refit the pump front mounting bolts and tighten them to the specified torque setting.

4B

11.29a Slacken and remove the retaining bolts (arrowed - one hidden) and remove the rear mounting bracket . . .

11.29b . . . then remove the pump from the engine noting the sealing ring (arrowed)

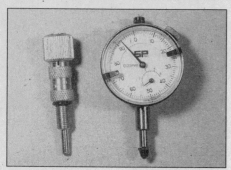

12.3 Dial gauge and adapter needed to check the injection timing on 1.7 litre models

33 Refit the mounting bracket to the rear of the injection pump and tighten its retaining bolts to the specified torque.
34 Refit the upper timing chain and sprockets as described in Chapter 2.
35 Position a new sealing washer on each side of the injection pump feed and return pipe unions then refit the union bolts, tightening them to the specified torque.
36 Refit the inlet manifold as described in Section 17.
37 Reconnect the battery negative lead then start the engine and bleed the fuel system as described in Section 5.

12 Injection timing - checking methods

1.7 litre models

1 Checking the injection timing is not a routine operation. It is only necessary after the injection pump has been disturbed.
2 Dynamic timing equipment does exist, but it is unlikely to be available to the home mechanic. The equipment works by converting pressure pulses in an injector pipe into electrical signals. If such equipment is available, use it in accordance with its maker's instructions.
3 Static timing as described in this Chapter gives good results if carried out carefully. A dial gauge will be needed, with probes and adapters appropriate to the type of injection

pump **(see illustration)**. Read through the procedures before starting work, to find out what is involved.

2.0 litre models

4 On these models the injection timing is determined by the ECU using the information supplied by the various sensors. Checking of the injection system can only be carried out using specialist diagnostic equipment (see Section 1).

13 Injection timing - checking and adjustment

Caution: Be careful not to allow dirt into the injection pump or injector pipes during this procedure.
Caution: Some of the injection pump settings and access plugs may be sealed by the manufacturers at the factory, using paint or locking wire and lead seals. Do not disturb the seals if the vehicle is still within the warranty period, otherwise the warranty will be invalidated. Also do not attempt the timing procedure unless accurate instrumentation is available.

1.7 litre models

1 If the injection timing is being checked with the pump in position on the engine unit, rather than as part of the pump refitting procedure, disconnect the battery negative lead. Firmly apply the handbrake then jack up the front of the vehicle and support it on axle stands, where necessary, undo the retaining screws and remove the undercover. Remove all traces of dirt from the unions of cylinder No 1 and 2 injector pipes then slacken the union nuts and remove the pipes from the engine; as each pump union nut is slackened, retain the adapter with a suitable open-ended spanner to prevent it being unscrewed from the pump. With all the union nuts undone, remove the injector pipe assembly from the engine unit and mop up and spilt fuel.
2 On all models, unscrew the access screw, situated in the centre of the four injector pipe unions, from the rear of the injection pump **(see illustration)**. As the screw is removed,

position a suitable container beneath the pump to catch any escaping fuel. Mop up any split fuel with a clean cloth.
3 Deactivate the cold start advance mechanism by passing a screwdriver through the two holes in the advance lever as shown and by turning the lever anti-clockwise **(see illustration)**.
4 Referring to Chapter 2, position No 1 cylinder at TDC on its compression stroke then from that position turn the crankshaft **backwards** (anti-clockwise) approximately a quarter of a turn.
5 Screw the adapter into the rear of the pump and mount the dial gauge in the adapter **(see illustration)**. If access to the special adapter and dial gauge cannot be gained (Vauxhall tool No. KM-798), they can be purchased from most good motor factors. Position the dial gauge so that its plunger is at the mid-point of its travel and securely tighten the adapter locknut.
6 Slowly rotate the crankshaft back and forth whilst observing the dial gauge, to determine when the injection pump piston is at the bottom of its travel (BDC). When the piston is correctly positioned, zero the dial gauge.
7 Rotate the crankshaft slowly in the correct direction until the crankshaft pulley mark is correctly realigned with the pointer (No 1 cylinder at TDC on its compression stroke).
8 The reading obtained on the dial gauge should be equal to the specified pump timing measurement given in the Specifications at the start of this Chapter. If adjustment is necessary, slacken the pump front mounting nuts and rear mounting bolts and slowly rotate the pump body until the point is found where the specified reading is obtained. When the pump is correctly positioned, tighten both its front and rear mounting nuts and bolts to the specified torque.
9 Rotate the crankshaft through one and three quarter rotations in the normal direction of rotation. Find the injection pump piston BDC as described in paragraph 6 and zero the dial gauge.
10 Rotate the crankshaft slowly in the correct direction of rotation until the crankshaft pulley mark is realigned with the pointer (bringing the engine back to TDC). Recheck the timing measurement.

13.2 On 1.7 litre models, remove the access screw from the rear of the pump

13.3 Deactivate the cold start advance mechanism by turning the advance lever anti-clockwise

13.5 Screw the adapter into the rear of the pump and fit the dial gauge

14.7a On 1.7 litre engines, fit the heat sleeve to the cylinder head . . .

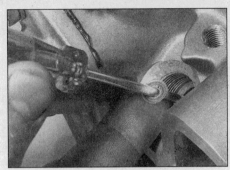

14.7b . . . followed by the fire seal washer . . .

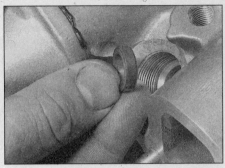

14.7c . . . and sealing ring, ensuring each component is fitted the correct way up

11 If adjustment is necessary, slacken the pump sprocket bolts and repeat the operations in paragraphs 8 to 10.

12 When the pump timing is correctly set unscrew the adapter and remove the dial gauge. Also, reset the cold start advance mechanism by turning the advance lever clockwise, then remove the screwdriver.

13 Refit the screw and sealing washer to the pump and tighten it to the specified torque.

14 If the procedure is being carried out as part of the pump refitting sequence, proceed as described in Section 11.

15 If the procedure is being carried out with the pump fitted to the engine, refit the fuel pipes to the pump and injectors and tighten the union nuts to the specified torque. Lower the vehicle to the ground then reconnect the battery. Start the engine and bleed the fuel system as described in Section 5. On completion check and, if necessary, adjust the idle speed as described in Chapter 1.

2.0 litre models

16 On these models the injection timing is determined by the ECU using the information supplied by the various sensors. Checking and adjustment of the injection system can only be carried out using specialist diagnostic equipment (see Section 1).

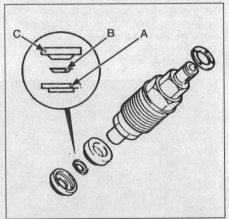

14.7d Correct fitted locations of injector components - 1.7 litre engine

A Heat sleeve   C Sealing ring
B Fire seal washer

14 Fuel injectors - removal and refitting

Warning: Exercise extreme caution when working on the fuel injectors. Never expose the hands or any part of the body to injector spray, as the high working pressure can cause the fuel to penetrate the skin, with possibly fatal results. You are strongly advised to have any work which involves testing the injectors under pressure carried out by a dealer or fuel injection specialist.

Caution: Be careful not to allow dirt into the injection pump, injectors or pipes during this procedure.

Caution: Take care not to drop the injectors, or allow the needles at their tips to become damaged. The injectors are precision-made to fine limits, and must not be handled roughly. In particular, never mount them in a bench vice.

1.7 litre models

1 To gain access to the injectors, remove the inlet manifold as described in Section 17.

2 Wipe clean the pipe unions then slacken the union nuts securing the injector pipes to the top of each injector and the four union nuts securing the pipes to the rear of the injection pump; as each pump union nut is slackened, retain the adapter with a suitable open-ended spanner to prevent it being unscrewed from the pump. With all the union nuts undone, remove the injector pipes from the engine unit and mop up any spilt fuel.

3 Unscrew the nut from the top of each injector then lift off the fuel return pipe assembly. Recover the sealing washer from the top of each injector and discard them; new ones must be used on refitting.

4 Clean around the base of the injector(s) to be removed then unscrew the injector(s) and remove them from the cylinder head.

Caution: Ensure you unscrew each injector holder from the cylinder head and remove the complete injector assembly rather than unscrewing the injector body from the holder. If the body is unscrewed from the

holder, the small internal components of the injector will be disturbed and it will be necessary to take them to a specialist to have them reassembled and tested prior to refitting.

5 Remove the sealing ring, fire seal washer and heat sleeve from the injector/cylinder head and discard; new ones must be used on refitting. **Do not** attempt to dismantle the injectors any further.

6 Testing of the injectors requires the use of special equipment. If any injector is thought to be faulty have it tested and, if necessary, reconditioned by a diesel engine specialist or Vauxhall dealer.

7 Commence refitting by inserting the heat sleeves, fire seal washers and sealing rings into the cylinder head, ensuring that each component is fitted the correct way up **(see illustrations)**.

8 Carefully fit the injector(s) and tighten to the specified torque. When each injector is correctly tightened, the mark (either a punch mark or a coloured dot) on the injector body should align with the projection on the cylinder head **(see illustration)**.

9 Fit a new sealing washer to the top of each injector then refit the return pipe assembly, tightening its retaining nuts to the specified torque.

10 Refit the injector pipes to the engine and tighten the union nuts to the specified torque.

11 Refit the inlet manifold as described in Section 17.

12 On completion start the engine and bleed the fuel system as described in Section 5.

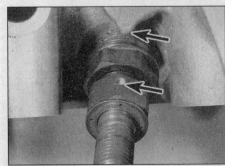

14.8 When the injector is tightened to the specified torque, its mark should align with the cylinder head projection (arrowed)

4B

14.16 On 2.0 litre engines, remove the injector crosspipe from the cylinder head (sealing ring arrowed) . . .

14.17 . . . then remove the sealing ring from the top of the injector nozzle

14.19a Fit a new sealing washer to the base of the nozzle . . .

2.0 litre models

Note: *If the injector nozzle is to be removed from the cylinder head, it is likely that the special Vauxhall puller (KM-928-B) and adapter (KM-931) will be needed. New injector crossover pipe bolts should be used on refitting.*

13 Remove the upper section of the inlet manifold as described in Section 17.

14 Remove the camshaft and followers as described in Chapter 2.

15 Disconnect the return pipe from the injector crossover pipe.

16 Unscrew the retaining bolt then carefully free the crossover pipe from the top of the injector nozzle and ease it from the cylinder head **(see illustration)**.

17 Remove the sealing rings from the crossover pipe and the top of the injector nozzle and discard, new ones must be used on refitting **(see illustration)**.

18 Fit the adapter and puller to the top of the injector nozzle and carefully pull the nozzle squarely out of the top of the cylinder head. Recover the sealing washer which is fitted to the base of the nozzle and discard it.

19 Fit a new sealing washer to the base of the injector nozzle then carefully ease the nozzle into position in the cylinder head, aligning its locating pin with the cylinder head cut-out **(see illustrations)**.

20 Ensure the injector nozzle is pushed fully into the cylinder head then fit a new sealing ring to its upper end.

21 Fit a new sealing ring to the crosspipe recess. Ease the crossover pipe into position in the cylinder head, seating it correctly on the top of the injector nozzle, fit the new retaining bolt. Tighten the retaining bolt as tight as possible by hand, using a socket and extension bar, then tighten it through a further complete rotation (360°) **(see illustrations)**.

22 Connect the return pipe to the crossover pipe then refit the inlet manifold section as described in Section 17.

23 Refit the camshaft and followers as described in Chapter 2

24 On completion start the engine and bleed the fuel system as described in Section 5.

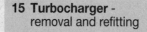

15 Turbocharger - removal and refitting

Removal

1 Remove the exhaust manifold and turbocharger assembly as described in Section 18 and proceed as described under the relevant sub-heading.

1.7 litre models

2 With the assembly on bench, undo the retaining nuts and remove the exhaust connection flange and gasket from the turbocharger.

3 Undo the retaining bolts and remove the coolant pipe assembly and gasket from the turbocharger.

4 Unscrew the union nut and remove the oil feed pipe along with the sealing washers which are fitted on each side of the pipe union.

5 Undo the retaining bolts and remove the oil return pipe union and gasket.

6 Slacken and remove the mounting nuts then remove the turbocharger and gasket from the manifold.

7 Do not attempt to dismantle the turbocharger any further. If the unit is thought to be faulty take it to a turbo specialist or Vauxhall dealer for testing and examination. They will be able to inform you if the unit can be overhauled or will need renewing.

2.0 litre models

8 With the assembly on bench, undo the retaining bolts and remove the exhaust connection flange and gasket from the turbocharger.

9 Unscrew the union bolt and remove the oil feed pipe. Recover the sealing washers fitted on each side of the pipe union.

10 Undo the retaining bolts and remove the oil return pipe and gasket.

11 Slacken and remove the mounting bolts then remove the turbocharger and gasket from the manifold.

12 Do not attempt to dismantle the turbocharger any further. If the unit is thought to be faulty take it to a turbo specialist or Vauxhall dealer for testing and examination. They will be able to inform you if the unit can be overhauled or will need renewing.

14.19b . . . then refit the nozzle to the cylinder head, aligning its locating pin with the head cut-out (arrowed)

14.21a Tighten the injector crosspipe bolt as tight as possible by hand . . .

14.21b . . . then tighten the bolt by one further complete turn

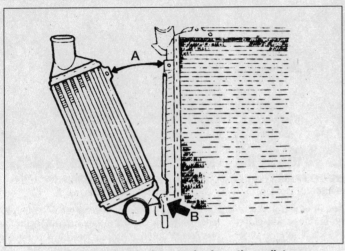

16.2 Removing the intercooler from the radiator
(1.7 litre model shown)

A Upper retaining screw location   B Lower locating point

17.17a On 2.0 litre engines, slacken and remove the retaining
bolts (arrowed) . . .

Refitting

13 Refitting is the reverse of removal, using new gaskets/sealing washers, and tightening the fasteners to their specified torque settings (where given). Refit the manifold and turbocharger assembly as described in Section 18.

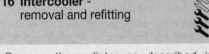

16 Intercooler -
removal and refitting

1 Remove the radiator as described in Chapter 3.
2 Undo the retaining bolts and remove the intercooler from the side of the radiator **(see illustration)**.
3 Refitting is the reverse of removal.

17 Inlet manifold -
removal and refitting

1.7 litre models

1 Disconnect the battery negative terminal.
2 Slacken the retaining clips securing the air cleaner housing intake duct in position and remove it from the engine compartment.
3 Slacken the retaining clips and bolt securing the turbocharger intake duct in position and remove the duct from the engine, disconnecting the breather hose from the cylinder head.
4 Slacken and remove the bolts securing the intercooler air intake pipe to the manifold and cylinder head then separate the pipe from the manifold. Recover the gasket then slacken the hose retaining clip and remove the pipe from the engine.
5 Release the retaining clip and disconnect the injection pump vacuum hose from the rear of the manifold.

6 Undo the retaining screws and detach the wiring harness brackets from the manifold.
7 Evenly and progressively slacken and remove the nuts and bolts securing the inlet manifold to the cylinder head, noting the correct fitted position of the odd bolt.
8 Manoeuvre the inlet manifold out of position and remove the gasket.
9 Ensure the manifold and cylinder mating surfaces are clean and dry and fit a new gasket over the manifold studs.
10 Refit the manifold and fit the retaining nuts and bolts. Working in a diagonal sequence, evenly and progressively tighten the manifold nuts and bolts to the specified torque setting.
11 Refit the wiring harness brackets to the manifold and (where necessary) reconnect the manifold heater wiring connector.
12 Reconnect the injection pump vacuum hose to the manifold and secure it in position with the retaining clip.
13 Ensure the mating surfaces are clean and dry then refit the intercooler air intake pipe using a new gasket. Securely tighten the pipe bolts then reconnect the intake hose, tightening its retaining clip securely.
14 Refit the intake ducts and reconnect the battery.

17.17b . . . then disconnect the various
wiring connectors and position the wiring
harness tray clear of the manifold

2.0 litre models

Note: *New lower manifold section retaining nuts will be required on refitting.*
15 Disconnect the battery negative terminal then undo the retaining screws and remove the plastic cover from the top of the cylinder head.
16 Referring to Section 2, on low-pressure turbo (X20DTL engine) models remove the metal pipe and duct linking the inlet manifold to the turbocharger, and on high-pressure turbo (X20DTH engine) models remove the duct linking the manifold to the intercooler.
17 Undo the retaining screws securing the wiring harness tray to the top of the inlet manifold. Disconnect the wiring connectors from the coolant sensors, the fuel injection pump (slide out the retaining clip to release the connector), the crankshaft sensor and the manifold boost pressure sensor then position the tray clear of the manifold **(see illustrations)**.
18 Disconnect the vacuum pipe from the exhaust gas recirculation (EGR) valve on the top of the manifold **(see illustration)**.
19 Wipe clean the pipe unions then slacken the union nuts securing the injector pipes to

17.18 Disconnect the EGR valve vacuum
pipe

4B

17.19a Slacken the union nuts securing the injector pipes to the injectors ...

17.19b ... and injection pump ...

17.19c ... and remove them from the engine

the injectors and the four union nuts securing the pipes to the rear of the injection pump; as each pump union nut is slackened, retain the adapter with a suitable open-ended spanner to prevent it being unscrewed from the pump. With all the union nuts undone, remove the injector pipes from the engine unit and mop up any spilt fuel **(see illustrations)**. Seal the pipe end fittings to minimise fuel loss and prevent the entry of dirt.

20 Evenly and progressively slacken and remove the retaining bolts then lift off the upper part of the manifold **(see illustration)**. Recover the gasket and discard it.

21 To remove the lower section of the manifold, disconnect the vacuum pipe from the manifold switchover valve diaphragm unit and unbolt the wiring connector bracket from the manifold. Evenly and progressively slacken and remove the retaining nuts then remove the manifold lower section and gasket

from the cylinder head **(see illustrations)**.

22 Ensure the all mating surfaces are clean and dry.

23 Fit a new gasket to the cylinder head then refit the lower manifold section **(see illustration)**. Fit the new retaining nuts and, working in a diagonal sequence, evenly and progressively tighten them to the specified torque setting. Reconnect the switchover valve hose and refit the wiring bracket.

24 Fit a new gasket to the top of the manifold lower section then refit the upper section of the manifold, tightening its retaining bolts to the specified torque.

25 Refit the injector pipes, tightening the union nuts to the specified torque.

26 Refit the wiring harness tray to the top of the manifold, tightening its retaining bolts securely, and reconnect the wiring connectors. Reconnect the vacuum pipe to the EGR valve.

27 Refit the intake duct/pipe (see Section 2) then refit the plastic cover to the cylinder head.

28 Reconnect the battery then start the engine and bleed the fuel system as described in Section 5.

18 Exhaust manifold - removal and refitting

1.7 litre models

1 The exhaust manifold should be removed with the turbocharger. Firmly apply the handbrake then jack up the front of the vehicle so access can be gained both from above and below. Where necessary, unbolt the undercover and remove it from beneath the engine/transmission unit.

2 Remove the radiator cooling fan as described in Chapter 3.

3 Slacken the retaining clips and bolt securing the turbocharger intake duct in position and remove the duct from the engine, disconnecting the breather hose from the cylinder head.

4 Slacken and remove the bolts securing the intercooler air intake pipe to the manifold and cylinder head then separate the pipe from the manifold. Recover the gasket then slacken the hose retaining clip and remove the pipe from the engine.

5 Slacken the retaining clips and remove the duct connecting the turbocharger to the intercooler.

17.20 Slacken and remove the retaining bolts and remove the upper section of the inlet manifold

17.21a Disconnect the vacuum pipe from the manifold switchover valve ...

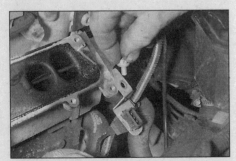

17.21b ... then remove the bolt securing the crankshaft sensor wiring to the manifold lower section

17.21c Unscrew the retaining nuts and remove the inlet manifold lower section from the engine

17.23 On refitting, use a new manifold gasket

18.11 Exhaust manifold retaining nut and bolt locations - 1.7 litre engine

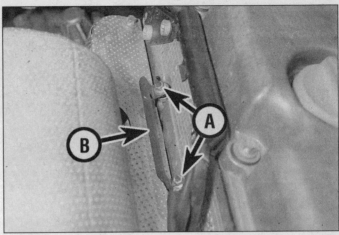

18.15 On 2.0 litre engines undo the retaining nuts (A) and remove the connector straps (B) from the glow plugs (left-hand arrangement shown)

6 Trace the coolant pipes/hoses back from the rear of the turbocharger to their unions on the thermostat and coolant pump housings. Being prepared for coolant loss, release the retaining clips and detach both hoses from the housings. Plug the housing unions to minimise coolant loss and mop up any spilt coolant. Free the coolant hoses from any relevant clips or ties so they are free to be removed with the manifold assembly.

7 Undo the retaining bolts and remove the heatshield from the turbocharger.

8 Slacken and remove the nuts then free exhaust front pipe from the turbocharger and recover the gasket.

9 Remove all traces of dirt from around the turbocharger oil feed pipe and return hose unions. Undo the union bolt securing the turbocharger oil feed pipe to the cylinder block and recover the sealing washers then release the retaining clip and disconnect the oil return hose. Mop up any spilt oil.

10 Undo the retaining bolts and remove the mounting bracket from the side of the turbocharger.

11 Working in a diagonal sequence, evenly and progressively slacken and remove the exhaust manifold retaining nuts and bolts. Manoeuvre the manifold assembly out of position and recover the gasket (see illustration). If

necessary, separate the turbo-charger from the manifold as described in Section 15.

12 Refitting is the reverse of removal, noting the following points.

a) Ensure all mating surfaces are clean and dry and renew all gaskets.

b) Tighten the manifold nuts and bolts and the support bracket bolts to their specified torque settings.

c) Securely reconnect the turbocharger oil and coolant pipes/hoses.

d) Refit the intake ducts ensuring then are securely reconnected.

e) On completion check and, if necessary, top-up the oil and coolant levels as described in "Weekly checks".

f) Before starting the engine for the first time, disconnect the wiring from the injection pump stop solenoid (see Section 10) then turn the engine over on the starter until the oil pressure warning light goes out; this will allow oil to be circulated around the turbocharger bearings before the engine is started. Reconnect the solenoid then start the engine as normal.

2.0 litre models

Note: New manifold retaining nuts and exhaust front pipe nuts will be required on refitting.

13 Disconnect the battery negative terminal then undo the retaining screws and remove the plastic cover from the top of the cylinder head.

14 Referring to Section 2, remove the air cleaner housing duct assembly and remove the metal pipe linking the turbocharger to the manifold/intercooler duct (as applicable).

15 Undo the retaining nuts and washers (where fitted) from the top of each glow plug then disconnect the wiring connectors and lift off the connector straps (see illustration). On later models simply disconnect the connector from the top of the each glow plug.

16 Undo the retaining screws and remove the heatshields from the top of the manifold assembly (see illustrations).

17 Undo the nuts securing the exhaust system front pipe to the manifold and free the pipe from the manifold (see illustration).

18 Working underneath the vehicle, undo the retaining bolts and remove the heatshield from the rear of the starter motor.

19 Undo the retaining bolts and remove the wiring harness guide from the rear of the cylinder block.

20 Remove all traces of dirt from around the turbocharger oil feed and return pipe unions. Slacken the union nuts securing the pipes to the cylinder block and allow the oil to drain into a suitable container. Mop up any spilt oil.

4B

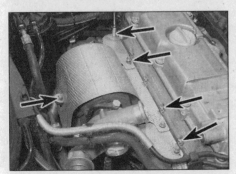

18.16a Undo the retaining screws (arrowed) . . .

18.16b . . . and remove the heatshields from the manifold assembly

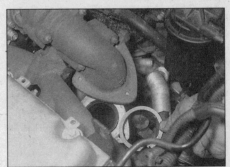

18.17 Separate the exhaust front pipe from the manifold and collect the gasket

18.21 Disconnect the vacuum hose from the turbocharger wastegate

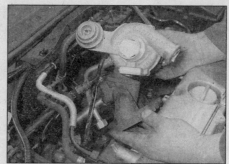

18.22a Remove the manifold assembly from the engine . . .

18.22b . . . and remove the gasket

21 Slacken and remove the retaining bolts and remove the manifold support bracket. Disconnect the vacuum hose from the turbocharger wastegate diaphragm **(see illustration)**.

22 Working in a diagonal sequence, evenly and progressively slacken and remove the exhaust manifold retaining nuts. Manoeuvre the manifold assembly out of position and recover the gasket **(see illustrations)**. If necessary, separate the turbocharger from the manifold as described in Section 15.

23 Refitting is the reverse of removal, noting the following points.
 a) *Ensure all mating surfaces are clean and dry and renew all gaskets.*
 b) *Fit the new manifold nuts and tighten them evenly and progressively to the specified torque, working in a diagonal sequence. Also tighten the support bracket bolts to the specified torque.*
 c) *Tighten the turbocharger oil pipe union nuts to the specified torque.*
 d) *Ensure the intake duct and metal pipe are securely reconnected (see Section 2).*
 e) *Fit the exhaust front pipe as described in Section 19.*
 f) *On completion check and, if necessary, top-up the oil and coolant levels as described in "Weekly checks".*
 g) *On start the engine for the first time, allow the engine to idle for a few minutes before increasing the engine speed; this will allow oil to be circulated around the turbocharger bearings.*

19 Exhaust system - general information, removal and refitting

General information

1 The exhaust system consists of three sections: the front pipe (which incorporates the catalytic converter), the intermediate pipe and the tailpipe. The front pipe is fitted with a flexible section to allow for movement in the exhaust system. On 2.0 litre models, the intermediate pipe to tailpipe joint is also spring-loaded to allow for movement in the system.

2 The system is suspended throughout its entire length by rubber mountings.

Removal

3 Each exhaust section can be removed individually, or the complete system can be removed as a unit. Even if only one part of the system needs attention, in some case it can be easier to remove the whole system and separate the sections on the bench.

4 To remove the system or part of the system, first jack up the front or rear of the car, and support it on axle stands. Alternatively, position the car over an inspection pit, or on car ramps. Where necessary, undo the retaining bolts and remove the undercover from beneath the engine/transmission unit.

Front pipe (incorporating the catalytic converter)

Note: *On 2.0 litre models new pipe-to-manifold nuts should be used on refitting.*

5 Undo the nuts securing the front pipe to the turbocharger. Slacken and remove the bolts securing the front pipe to the intermediate pipe.

6 Free the front pipe from the turbocharger, recovering the gasket, and intermediate pipe then remove it from underneath the vehicle.

Intermediate pipe - 1.7 litre models

Note: *If the intermediate pipe is corroded into the tailpipe, remove the intermediate pipe and tailpipe as an assembly and separate them on the bench.*

7 Slacken and remove the bolts securing the intermediate pipe to the front pipe and the clamp securing it to the tailpipe.

8 Remove the securing clips and release the intermediate pipe from its mounting rubbers. Disengage the intermediate pipe from the front pipe and tailpipe and remove it from underneath the vehicle.

Intermediate pipe - 2.0 litre models

9 Slacken and remove the bolts securing the intermediate pipe to the front pipe and the bolts and springs securing it to the tailpipe.

10 Remove the securing clips and release the intermediate pipe from its mounting rubbers. Disengage the intermediate pipe from the front pipe and tailpipe and remove it from underneath the vehicle. Recover gasket which is fitted to the tailpipe joint.

Tailpipe - 1.7 litre models

11 Slacken the clamp securing the tailpipe to the intermediate pipe and disengage the clamp from the joint.

12 Remove the securing clips then unhook the tailpipe from its mounting rubbers, and free it from the intermediate pipe.

Tailpipe - 2.0 litre models

13 Slacken and remove the bolts and springs securing the tailpipe to the intermediate pipe joint.

14 Remove the securing clips then unhook the tailpipe from its mounting rubbers, and free it from the intermediate pipe. Recover the gasket from the joint.

Complete system - all models

Note: *On 2.0 litre models new pipe-to-manifold nuts should be used on refitting.*

15 Slacken and remove the nuts securing the front pipe flange joint to the turbocharger.

16 Remove the securing clips then free the system from its mounting rubbers and remove it from underneath the vehicle. Recover the gasket from the front pipe joint.

Heat shield(s)

17 The heat shields are secured to the underside of the body by various nuts and bolts. Each shield can be removed once the relevant exhaust section has been removed. If a shield is being removed to gain access to a component located behind it, it may prove sufficient in some cases to remove the retaining nuts and/or bolts, and simply lower the shield, without disturbing the exhaust system.

Refitting

18 Each section is refitted by reversing the removal sequence, noting the following points:
 a) *On 2.0 litre models, renew the front pipe nuts whenever they are disturbed.*
 b) *Ensure that all traces of corrosion have been removed from the flanges, and renew all necessary gaskets. Where no gasket is fitted, apply a smear of exhaust system jointing paste to the joint to ensure a gas-tight seal.*
 c) *Inspect the rubber mountings for signs of damage or deterioration, and renew as necessary.*
 d) *Prior to tightening the exhaust system fasteners, ensure that all rubber mountings are correctly located, and that there is adequate clearance between the exhaust system and vehicle underbody.*

Chapter 4 Part C:
Emission control systems

Contents

Degrees of difficulty

Easy, suitable for novice with little experience	**Fairly easy,** suitable for beginner with some experience	**Fairly difficult,** suitable for competent DIY mechanic

Difficult, suitable for experienced DIY mechanic

Very difficult, suitable for expert DIY or professional

Specifications

Torque wrench settings	Nm	lbf ft
Exhaust gas recirculation (EGR) solenoid bolts	4	3
Exhaust gas recirculation (EGR) valve bolts	20	15
Exhaust manifold shroud bolts	8	6
Oxygen sensor for catalytic converter (in front exhaust pipe):		
X16SZR and X16XEL	30	22
X18XE1	40	30
X18XE and X20XEV	55	41
Secondary air injection system:		
Air valve connecting pipe bolts:		
M6 bolt	8	6
M8 bolt	20	15
Support bracket bolts - 1.6 litre engine	8	6

1 General information

1 All petrol engine models use unleaded petrol and also have various other features built into the fuel system to help minimise harmful emissions. All models are equipped with a crankcase emission-control system, a catalytic converter, an exhaust gas recirculation (EGR) system and an evaporative emission control system to keep fuel vapour/exhaust gas emissions down to a minimum. All models except those with a 1.6 litre SOHC engine are also fitted with the secondary air injection system to further improve the exhaust gas emissions during engine warm-up.

2 All diesel engine models are also designed to meet strict emission requirements. All models are fitted with a crankcase emission control system and a catalytic converter to keep exhaust emissions down to a minimum. All 2.0 litre models are also fitted with an exhaust gas recirculation (EGR) system to further decrease exhaust emissions.

3 The emission control systems function as follows.

Petrol models

Crankcase emission control

4 To reduce the emission of unburned hydrocarbons from the crankcase into the atmosphere, the engine is sealed and the blow-by gases and oil vapour are drawn from inside the crankcase, through a wire mesh oil separator, into the inlet tract to be burned by the engine during normal combustion.

5 Under conditions of high manifold depression (idling, deceleration) the gases will be sucked positively out of the crankcase. Under conditions of low manifold depression (acceleration, full-throttle running) the gases are forced out of the crankcase by the (relatively) higher crankcase pressure; if the engine is worn, the raised crankcase pressure (due to increased blow-by) will cause some of the flow to return under all manifold conditions.

Exhaust emission control

6 To minimise the amount of pollutants which escape into the atmosphere, all models are fitted with a catalytic converter in the exhaust system. The system is of the closed-loop type, in which a oxygen sensor in the exhaust system provides the fuel-injection/ignition system ECU with constant feedback, enabling the ECU to adjust the mixture to provide the best possible conditions for the converter to operate.

7 The oxygen sensor's tip is sensitive to oxygen and sends the ECU a varying voltage depending on the amount of oxygen in the exhaust gases; if the intake air/fuel mixture is too rich, the exhaust gases are low in oxygen so the sensor sends a low-voltage signal, the voltage rising as the mixture weakens and the amount of oxygen rises in the exhaust gases.

Peak conversion efficiency of all major pollutants occurs if the intake air/fuel mixture is maintained at the chemically-correct ratio for the complete combustion of petrol of 14.7 parts (by weight) of air to 1 part of fuel (the 'stoichiometric' ratio). The sensor output voltage alters in a large step at this point, the ECU using the signal change as a reference point and correcting the intake air/fuel mixture accordingly by altering the fuel injector pulse width.

Evaporative emission control

8 To minimise the escape into the atmosphere of unburned hydrocarbons, an evaporative emissions control system is also fitted to all models. The fuel tank filler cap is sealed and a charcoal canister is mounted behind the right-hand front wing. The canister collects the petrol vapours generated in the tank when the car is parked and stores them until they can be cleared from the canister (under the control of the fuel-injection/ignition system ECU) via the purge valve into the inlet tract to be burned by the engine during normal combustion.

9 To ensure that the engine runs correctly when it is cold and/or idling and to protect the catalytic converter from the effects of an over-rich mixture, the purge control valve is not opened by the ECU until the engine has warmed up, and the engine is under load; the valve solenoid is then modulated on and off to allow the stored vapour to pass into the inlet tract.

4C

Exhaust gas recirculation (EGR) system

10 This system is designed to recirculate small quantities of exhaust gas into the inlet tract, and therefore into the combustion process. This process reduces the level of unburnt hydrocarbons present in the exhaust gas before it reaches the catalytic converter. The system is controlled by the fuel-injection/ignition ECU, using the information from its various sensors, via the EGR valve.

11 On 1.6 litre models the EGR valve is an electrically-operated valve mounted on the inlet manifold.

12 On 1.8 and 2.0 litre models the EGR valve assembly is mounted on the cylinder head. The valve assembly contains the vacuum-operated valve and the electrical solenoid valve which is used to switch the valve on and off.

Secondary air injection system - DOHC engine models

13 The purpose of the secondary air injection system is to decrease exhaust gas emissions when the engine is cold. The system achieves this by raising the temperature of the exhaust gases which has the effect of quickly warming the catalytic converter up to its normal operating temperature. Once the catalytic converter is up to temperature the air injection system is switched off.

14 The system consists of the pump, the air valve and the solenoid valve and is controlled by the fuel-injection/ignition ECU. When the engine is cold, the solenoid valve switches the air valve to open and the pump injects a controlled amount of air into the cylinder head exhaust ports. The air then mixes with the exhaust gases, causing any unburned particles of the fuel in the mixture to be burnt in the exhaust port/manifold which effectively raises the temperature of the exhaust gases. Once the catalytic converter is up to temperature, the solenoid valve closes the air valve and the pump is switched off. A non-return valve prevents the exhaust gases passing through the air valve.

Diesel models

Crankcase emission control

15 Refer to paragraphs 4 and 5.

Exhaust emission control

16 To minimise the level of exhaust pollutants released into the atmosphere, a catalytic converter is fitted in the exhaust system of some models.

17 The catalytic converter consists of a canister containing a fine mesh impregnated with a catalyst material, over which the hot exhaust gases pass. The catalyst speeds up the oxidation of harmful carbon monoxide, unburned hydrocarbons and soot, effectively reducing the quantity of harmful products released into the atmosphere via the exhaust gases.

Exhaust gas recirculation (EGR) system - 2.0 litre models

18 This system is designed to recirculate small quantities of exhaust gas into the inlet tract, and therefore into the combustion process. This process reduces the level of unburnt hydrocarbons present in the exhaust gas before it reaches the catalytic converter. The system is controlled by the injection system ECU, using the information from its various sensors, via the EGR valve on the upper section of the inlet manifold. The EGR valve is vacuum operated and is switched on and off by an electrical solenoid valve.

2 Petrol engine emission control systems - testing and component renewal

Crankcase emission control

1 The components of this system require no attention other than to check that the hose(s) are clear and undamaged at regular intervals.

Evaporative emission control system

Testing

2 If the system is thought to be faulty, disconnect the hoses from the charcoal canister and purge control valve and check that they are clear by blowing through them. Full testing of the system can only be carried out using specialist electronic equipment which is connected to the engine management system diagnostic wiring connector (see Chapter 4A). If the purge control valve or charcoal canister are thought to be faulty, they must be renewed.

Charcoal canister - renewal

3 The charcoal canister is located behind the right-hand front wing. To gain access to the canister, firmly apply the handbrake then jack up the front of the vehicle and support it on axle stands.

4 Remove the retaining screws and fasteners and remove the wheelarch liner to gain access to the canister.

5 Slacken and remove the retaining clamp nut and free the canister from its mounting bracket. Mark the hoses for identification purposes then disconnect them and remove the canister from the vehicle.

6 Refitting is a reverse of the removal procedure, ensuring the hoses are correctly and securely reconnected.

Purge valve renewal - 1.6 litre models

7 The purge valve is mounted onto the left-hand side of the inlet manifold.

8 To renew the valve, ensure the ignition is switched off then depress the retaining clip and disconnect the wiring connector from the valve.

9 Disconnect the hoses from the valve, noting their correct fitted locations then unbolt the valve mounting bracket from the manifold and remove it from the engine. The valve and bracket can then be separated.

10 Refitting is a reversal of the removal procedure, ensuring the valve is fitted the correct way around and the hoses are securely connected.

Purge valve renewal - 1.8 and 2.0 litre models

11 On X18XE and X20XEV engines, the purge valve is mounted on the left-hand end of the cylinder head. On X18XE1 engines, the purge valve is mounted on the right-hand side of the engine compartment, behind the air cleaner housing. Unclip the valve from the air cleaner housing to remove.

12 To improve access to the valve retaining bolts, remove the DIS module as described in Chapter 5A **(see illustration)**.

13 Disconnect the wiring connector from the purge valve then disconnect the vacuum hoses, noting their correct fitted locations.

14 Undo the retaining bolts and remove the purge valve and mounting bracket from the cylinder head.

15 Refitting is a reversal of the removal procedure, ensuring the valve is fitted the correct way around and the hoses are securely connected.

Exhaust emission control

Testing

16 The performance of the catalytic converter can be checked only by measuring the exhaust gases using a good-quality, carefully-calibrated exhaust gas analyser, as described in Chapter 1.

17 If the CO level at the tailpipe is too high, the vehicle should be taken to a Vauxhall dealer so that the complete fuel-injection and ignition systems, including the oxygen sensor, can be thoroughly checked using the special diagnostic equipment. Once these have been checked and are known to be free from faults, the fault must be in the catalytic converter, which must be renewed.

Catalytic converter - renewal

18 Refer to Chapter 4A.

Oxygen sensor renewal - 1.6 litre models

Note: *The oxygen sensor is delicate and will not work if it is dropped or knocked, if its power supply is disrupted, or if any cleaning materials are used on it.*

19 Warm the engine up to normal operating temperature then stop the engine and disconnect the battery negative terminal.

20 Trace the wiring back from the oxygen sensor, which is screwed into the left-hand side of the exhaust manifold and disconnect its wiring connector, freeing the wiring from any relevant retaining clips or ties **(see illustration)**.

21 Unscrew the sensor and remove it from the manifold.

Caution: Take great care not burn yourself on the hot manifold/sensor.

2.12 Purge valve location (arrowed) 1.8 and 2.0 litre petrol engine

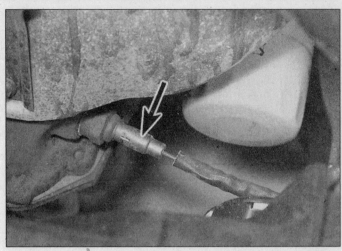

2.20 On 1.6 litre petrol engines the oxygen sensor (arrowed) is screwed into the exhaust manifold

22 Refitting is a reverse of the removal procedure. Prior to installing the sensor apply a smear of high temperature grease to the sensor threads (Vauxhall recommend the use of grease 19 48 602, part no. 90 295 397 - available from your Vauxhall dealer). Tighten the sensor to the specified torque and ensure that the wiring is correctly routed and in no danger of contacting either the exhaust manifold or engine.

Oxygen sensor renewal - 1.8 and 2.0 litre models

Note: *The oxygen sensor is delicate and will not work if it is dropped or knocked, if its power supply is disrupted, or if any cleaning materials are used on it.*

23 Firmly apply the handbrake then jack up the front of the vehicle and support it on axle stands. Disconnect the battery negative terminal.

24 Trace the wiring back from the oxygen sensor, which is screwed into the exhaust front pipe, to its connector which is clipped to the left-hand end of the cylinder head **(see illustration)**. Disconnect the wiring connector and free the wiring from any relevant retaining clips or ties, noting its correct routing.

25 Unscrew the sensor and remove it from the exhaust system front pipe. Recover the sealing washer and discard; it a new one should be used on refitting.

26 Refitting is a reverse of the removal procedure, using a new sealing washer. Prior to installing the sensor, apply a smear of high temperature grease to the sensor threads (Vauxhall recommend the use of special grease 19 48 602, part no. 90 295 397 - available from your Vauxhall dealer). Tighten the sensor to the specified torque and ensure that the wiring is correctly routed and in no danger of contacting either the exhaust system or engine.

Exhaust gas recirculation (EGR) system

Testing

27 Comprehensive testing of the system can only be carried out using specialist electronic equipment which is connected to the engine management system diagnostic wiring connector (see Chapter 4A). If the EGR valve is thought to be faulty, it must be renewed.

Exhaust gas recirculation (EGR) valve renewal - 1.6 litre models

28 Ensure the ignition is switched off, then disconnect the wiring connector from the valve. On SOHC engines the valve is fitted to the centre of the inlet manifold and on DOHC engines it is mounted on the left-hand end of the manifold **(see illustration)**.

4C

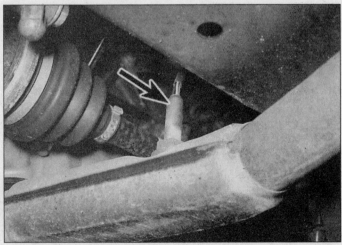

2.24 On 1.8 and 2.0 litre petrol engines the oxygen sensor (arrowed) is screwed into the front pipe

2.28 On 1.6 litre SOHC petrol engines, disconnect the wiring connector . . .

2.29 . . . then undo the retaining screws (arrowed) and remove the EGR valve from the inlet manifold

2.31 EGR valve location (arrowed) - 1.8 and 2.0 litre petrol engines

29 Undo the retaining screws and remove the valve and its gasket from the manifold **(see illustration)**.

30 Refitting is the reverse of removal, using a new gasket and tightening the valve bolts to the specified torque.

Exhaust gas recirculation (EGR) valve renewal - 1.8 and 2.0 litre models

31 Ensure the ignition is switched off then disconnect the wiring connector and vacuum hose from the EGR valve which is mounted on the left-hand end of the cylinder head **(see illustration)**.

32 Undo the retaining screws and remove the valve and its gasket from the end of the cylinder head.

33 Refitting is the reverse of removal using a new gasket and tightening the valve bolts to the specified torque.

Secondary air injection system - DOHC engine models

Testing

34 Comprehensive testing of the system can only be carried out using specialist electronic equipment which is connected to the engine management system diagnostic wiring connector (see Chapter 4A). If any component is thought to be faulty, it must be renewed.

Air injection valve - renewal

35 The air injection valve is located at the front of the cylinder head. On 1.6 litre engines the valve is situated above the exhaust manifold, and on 1.8 and 2.0 litre engines it is on the left-hand end of the head **(see illustration)**.

36 Disconnect the vacuum pipe from the valve then release the retaining clip and disconnect the air hose **(see illustration)**.

37 Slacken and remove the bolts securing the valve to the metal pipe and remove the valve and its gasket from the metal pipe.

38 Refitting is the reverse of removal, using a new gasket.

Air injection valve connecting pipe renewal - 1.6 litre engine

39 Remove the air injection valve as described in paragraphs 35 to 37.

40 Undo the retaining bolts securing the pipe support bracket and the exhaust manifold shroud in position and remove both items from the manifold.

41 Slacken and remove the pipe retaining bolts then remove the pipe and gasket from the front of the cylinder head.

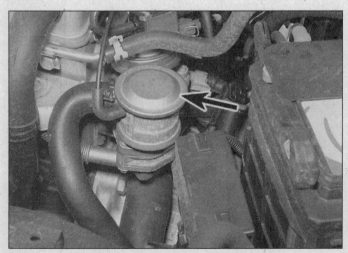

2.35 Air injection valve location (arrowed) - 1.8 and 2.0 litre petrol engines

2.36 Air injection valve vacuum pipe (A) and air hose (B) - 1.6 litre DOHC petrol engine

42 Refitting is the reverse of removal, noting the following.

a) *Ensure the mating surfaces are clean and dry and use a new gasket.*

b) *Apply a smear of high-temperature grease to the threads of the pipe retaining bolts prior to refitting.*

c) *Tighten all bolts to their specified torque settings (where given).*

Air injection valve connecting pipe renewal - 1.8 and 2.0 litre engine

43 Remove the air injection valve as described in paragraphs 35 to 37.

44 Undo the retaining bolts and remove the shroud from the exhaust manifold.

45 Undo the retaining bolts and remove the connecting pipe from the front of the cylinder head. Recover the gaskets which are fitted between the pipe and cylinder head, and the gasket which is fitted between the pipe and cylinder head bracket.

46 Refitting is the reverse of removal, noting the following.

a) *Ensure the mating surfaces are clean and dry and use new gaskets.*

b) *Apply a smear of high-temperature grease to the threads of the pipe retaining bolts prior to refitting.*

c) *Tighten all bolts to their specified torque settings (where given).*

Air injection pump renewal

47 To gain access to the pump, remove the battery and mounting plate (see Chapter 5A) (see illustration).

48 Disconnect the air hoses from the pump then undo the pump mounting bracket retaining nuts.

49 Remove the pump assembly from the engine compartment, disconnecting the wiring connector as it becomes accessible. If necessary the pump and mounting bracket can then be separated.

50 Refitting is the reverse of removal, tightening the retaining nuts securely.

Air injection pump filter renewal

51 To gain access to the filter, open up the bonnet then undo the retaining screws and remove the radiator grille (see Chapter 11). The filter is clamped to the centre of the vehicle front crossmember, behind the bumper.

52 Slacken the clamp bolt then disengage the filter from the clamp and disconnect it from the air hose.

53 Refitting is the reverse of removal.

Solenoid valve renewal

54 The solenoid valve is mounted on the left-hand side of the engine compartment. To locate the valve, trace the vacuum hose back from the air valve on the front of the engine. On 1.8 and 2.0 litre models it will be necessary to remove the battery to gain access to the valve.

55 Disconnect the wiring connector from the valve and detach the vacuum hoses, noting each ones correct fitted location.

56 Undo the retaining screws and remove the valve from the engine compartment.

57 Refitting is the reverse of removal, ensuring the vacuum hoses are correctly reconnected.

<table>
<tr><td>3</td><td>Diesel engine emission control systems - testing and component renewal</td><td></td></tr>
</table>

Crankcase emission control

1 The components of this system require no attention other than to check that the hose(s) are clear and undamaged at regular intervals.

Exhaust emission control

Testing

2 The performance of the catalytic converter can be checked only by measuring the exhaust gases using a good-quality, carefully-calibrated exhaust gas analyser as described in Chapter 1.

3 If the catalytic converter is thought to be faulty, before assuming the catalytic converter is faulty, it is worth checking the problem is not due to a faulty injector(s). Refer to your Vauxhall dealer for further information.

Catalytic converter - renewal

4 The catalytic converter is an integral part of the exhaust system front pipe. Refer to Chapter 4B for removal and refitting details.

Exhaust gas recirculation (EGR) system

Testing

5 Comprehensive testing of the system can only be carried out using specialist electronic equipment which is connected to the injection system diagnostic wiring connector (see Chapter 4B). If the EGR valve or solenoid valve are thought to be faulty, they must be renewed.

Exhaust gas recirculation (EGR) valve - renewal

6 If the EGR valve is to be renewed, it will be necessary to renew the complete upper section of the inlet manifold (see Chapter 4B). The valve assembly is not available separately and should not be removed from the manifold.

Exhaust gas recirculation (EGR) system solenoid valve - renewal

7 Remove the battery (see Chapter 5) to gain access to the valve which is located in the front left-hand corner of the engine compartment. Note that there are two valves, the EGR system valve and the inlet manifold switchover valve; the EGR system valve can be identified by its black wiring connector.

8 Disconnect the wiring connector and vacuum hoses from the valve then undo the retaining screws and remove the valve from its mounting bracket.

9 Refitting is the reverse of removal.

4C

2.47 The air injection pump is located beside the battery

4 Catalytic converter - general information and precautions

1 The catalytic converter is a reliable and simple device which needs no maintenance in itself, but there are some facts of which an owner should be aware if the converter is to function properly for its full service life.

Petrol models

a) DO NOT use leaded petrol in a car equipped with a catalytic converter - the lead will coat the precious metals, reducing their converting efficiency and will eventually destroy the converter.

b) Always keep the ignition and fuel systems well-maintained in accordance with the manufacturer's schedule.

c) If the engine develops a misfire, do not drive the car at all (or at least as little as possible) until the fault is cured.

d) DO NOT push- or tow-start the car - this will soak the catalytic converter in unburned fuel, causing it to overheat when the engine does start.

e) DO NOT switch off the ignition at high engine speeds.

f) DO NOT use fuel or engine oil additives - these may contain substances harmful to the catalytic converter.

g) DO NOT continue to use the car if the engine burns oil to the extent of leaving a visible trail of blue smoke.

h) Remember that the catalytic converter operates at very high temperatures. DO NOT, therefore, park the car in dry undergrowth, over long grass or piles of dead leaves after a long run.

i) Remember that the catalytic converter is FRAGILE - do not strike it with tools during servicing work.

j) In some cases a sulphurous smell (like that of rotten eggs) may be noticed from the exhaust. This is common to many catalytic converter-equipped cars and once the car has covered a few thousand miles the problem should disappear.

k) The catalytic converter, used on a well-maintained and well-driven car, should last for between 50 000 and 100 000 miles - if the converter is no longer effective it must be renewed.

Diesel models

2 Refer to the information given in parts f, g, h, i and k of the petrol models information given above.

Chapter 5 Part A:
Starting and charging systems

Contents

Degrees of difficulty

| Easy, suitable for novice with little experience | Fairly easy, suitable for beginner with some experience | Fairly difficult, suitable for competent DIY mechanic 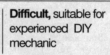 | Difficult, suitable for experienced DIY mechanic | Very difficult, suitable for expert DIY or professional |

Specifications

System type	12-volt, negative earth

Battery

Charge condition:	
Poor	12.5 volts
Normal	12.6 volts
Good	12.7 volts

Torque wrench settings	Nm	lbf ft
Alternator fixings:		
Diesel models:		
1.7 litre models:		
M8 bolts	24	18
M10 bolts	48	35
2.0 litre models	35	26
Petrol models:		
Alternator to bracket bolts	35	26
Alternator bracket to cylinder block bolts	35	26
Support bracket bolts	18	13
Engine torque support rod bolts	60	44
Oil pressure switch:		
Diesel models	30	22
Petrol models:		
X16SZR, X16XEL and X18XE1 engines	30	22
X18XE and X20XEV engines	40	30
Starter motor bolts:		
Diesel models:		
Starter to cylinder block	45	33
Starter bracket to cylinder block	25	18
Starter bracket to starter	7	5
Petrol models:		
X16SZR engine:		
Starter fastening nut	45	33
Starter fastening bolt	25	18
X16XEL and X18XE1 engines:		
Starter to transmission	40	30
Starter to cylinder block	25	18
X18XE and X20XEV engines	60	44
Starter heat shield (where fitted)	6	4

1 General information and precautions

General information

1 The engine electrical system consists mainly of the charging and starting systems. Because of their engine-related functions, these components are covered separately from the body electrical devices such as the lights, instruments, etc (which are covered in Chapter 12). On petrol-engine models refer to Part B for information on the ignition system, and on diesel models refer to Part C for information on the preheating system.

2 The electrical system is of the 12-volt negative earth type.

3 The battery is of the low maintenance or 'maintenance-free' (sealed for life) type and is charged by the alternator, which is belt-driven from the crankshaft pulley.

4 The starter motor is of the pre-engaged type incorporating an integral solenoid. On starting, the solenoid moves the drive pinion into engagement with the flywheel ring gear before the starter motor is energised. Once the engine has started, a one-way clutch prevents the motor armature being driven by the engine until the pinion disengages from the flywheel.

Precautions

5 Further details of the various systems are given in the relevant Sections of this Chapter. While some repair procedures are given, the usual course of action is to renew the component concerned. The owner whose interest extends beyond mere component renewal should obtain a copy of the *"Automobile Electrical & Electronic Systems Manual"*, available from the publishers of this manual.

6 It is necessary to take extra care when working on the electrical system to avoid damage to semi-conductor devices (diodes and transistors), and to avoid the risk of personal injury. In addition to the precautions given in *"Safety first!"* at the beginning of this manual, observe the following when working on the system:

7 *Always remove rings, watches, etc before working on the electrical system.* Even with the battery disconnected, capacitive discharge could occur if a component's live terminal is earthed through a metal object. This could cause a shock or nasty burn.

8 *Do not reverse the battery connections.* Components such as the alternator, electronic control units, or any other components having semi-conductor circuitry could be irreparably damaged.

9 If the engine is being started using jump leads and a slave battery, connect the batteries *positive-to-positive* and *negative-to-negative* (see *"Jump starting"*). This also applies when connecting a battery charger.

10 Never disconnect the battery terminals, the alternator, any electrical wiring or any test instruments when the engine is running.

11 Do not allow the engine to turn the alternator when the alternator is not connected.

12 Never 'test' for alternator output by 'flashing' the output lead to earth.

13 Never use an ohmmeter of the type incorporating a hand-cranked generator for circuit or continuity testing.

14 Always ensure that the battery negative lead is disconnected when working on the electrical system.

15 Before using electric-arc welding equipment on the car, disconnect the battery, alternator and components such as the fuel injection/ignition electronic control unit to protect them from the risk of damage.

16 The radio/cassette unit fitted as standard equipment by Vauxhall is equipped with a built-in security code to deter thieves. If the power source to the unit is cut, the anti-theft system will activate. Even if the power source is immediately reconnected, the radio/cassette unit will not function until the correct security code has been entered. Therefore, if you do not know the correct security code for the radio/cassette unit **do not** disconnect the battery negative terminal of the battery or remove the radio/cassette unit from the vehicle. Refer to *"Radio/cassette unit anti-theft system - precaution"* Section for further information.

2 Electrical fault finding - general information

Refer to Chapter 12.

3 Battery - testing and charging

Traditional-style and low maintenance battery - testing

1 If the vehicle covers a small annual mileage, it is worthwhile checking the specific gravity of the electrolyte every three months to determine the state of charge of the battery. Use a hydrometer to make the check and compare the results with the following table.

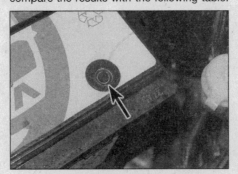

3.5 Battery charge condition indicator - 'Delco' type battery

Note that the specific gravity readings assume an electrolyte temperature of 15°C (60°F); for every 10°C (18°F) below 15°C (60°F) subtract 0.007. For every 10°C (18°F) above 15°C (60°F) add 0.007.

	Ambient temperature above 25°C (77°F)	Ambient temperature below 25°C (77°F)
Fully-charged	1.210 to 1.230	1.270 to 1.290
70% charged	1.170 to 1.190	1.230 to 1.250
Discharged	1.050 to 1.070	1.110 to 1.130

2 If the battery condition is suspect, first check the specific gravity of electrolyte in each cell. A variation of 0.040 or more between any cells indicates loss of electrolyte or deterioration of the internal plates.

3 If the specific gravity variation is 0.040 or more, the battery should be renewed. If the cell variation is satisfactory but the battery is discharged, it should be charged as described later in this Section.

Maintenance-free battery - testing

4 In cases where a 'sealed for life' maintenance-free battery is fitted, topping-up and testing of the electrolyte in each cell is not possible. The condition of the battery can therefore only be tested using a battery condition indicator or a voltmeter.

5 Certain models may be fitted with a 'Delco' type maintenance-free battery, with a built-in charge condition indicator. The indicator is located in the top of the battery casing, and indicates the condition of the battery from its colour **(see illustration)**. If the indicator shows green, then the battery is in a good state of charge. If the indicator turns darker, eventually to black, then the battery requires charging, as described later in this Section. If the indicator shows clear/yellow, then the electrolyte level in the battery is too low to allow further use, and the battery should be renewed. **Do not** attempt to charge, load or jump start a battery when the indicator shows clear/yellow.

All battery types

6 If testing the battery using a voltmeter, connect the voltmeter across the battery and compare the result with those given in the Specifications under 'charge condition'. The test is only accurate if the battery has not been subjected to any kind of charge for the previous six hours. If this is not the case, switch on the headlights for 30 seconds, then wait four to five minutes before testing the battery after switching off the headlights. All other electrical circuits must be switched off, so check that the doors and tailgate are fully shut when making the test.

7 If the voltage reading is less than 12.2 volts, then the battery is discharged, whilst a reading of 12.2 to 12.4 volts indicates a partially discharged condition.

8 If the battery is to be charged, remove it from the vehicle (Section 4) and charge it as described later in this Section.

Traditional-style and low maintenance battery - charging

Note: *The following is intended as a guide only. Always refer to the manufacturer's recommendations (often printed on a label attached to the battery) before charging a battery.*

9 Charge the battery at a rate of 3.5 to 4 amps and continue to charge the battery at this rate until no further rise in specific gravity is noted over a four hour period.

10 Alternatively, a trickle charger charging at the rate of 1.5 amps can safely be used overnight.

11 Specially rapid 'boost' charges which are claimed to restore the power of the battery in 1 to 2 hours are not recommended, as they can cause serious damage to the battery plates through overheating.

12 While charging the battery, note that the temperature of the electrolyte should never exceed 37.8°C (100°F).

Maintenance-free battery - charging

Note: *The following is intended as a guide only. Always refer to the manufacturer's recommendations (often printed on a label attached to the battery) before charging a battery.*

13 This battery type takes considerably longer to fully recharge than the standard type, the time taken being dependent on the extent of discharge, but it can take anything up to three days.

14 A constant voltage type charger is required, to be set, when connected, to 13.9 to 14.9 volts with a charger current below 25 amps. Using this method, the battery should be usable within three hours, giving a voltage reading of 12.5 volts, but this is for a partially discharged battery and, as mentioned, full charging can take considerably longer.

15 If the battery is to be charged from a fully discharged state (condition reading less than 12.2 volts), have it recharged by your Vauxhall

4.2 Always disconnect the battery negative terminal (1) first and the positive terminal (2) second

dealer or local automotive electrician, as the charge rate is higher and constant supervision during charging is necessary.

---

4 Battery - removal and refitting

Note: *If a Vauxhall radio/cassette unit is fitted, refer to "Radio/cassette unit anti-theft system - precaution".*

Note: *Whenever the battery is reconnected, it will be necessary to reprogram the electric windows (if fitted). Refer to Chapter 11, Section 22.*

Removal

1 The battery is located on the left-hand side of the engine compartment. On some models the battery will be housed in a protective casing.

2 Unclip the cover (where fitted) then slacken the clamp nut and disconnect the clamp from the battery negative (earth) terminal **(see illustration)**.

3 Lift the insulation cover and disconnect the positive terminal lead in the same way.

4 Unscrew the bolt and remove the battery retaining clamp and lift the battery out of the engine compartment **(see illustration)**.

5 If necessary, unclip the fusebox/wiring

4.4 Battery clamp retaining bolt (arrowed)

bracket assembly from the rear of the battery mounting plate and unclip the relay box(es) from the front of the battery mounting plate. Unbolt the mounting plate and remove it from the engine compartment, freeing all the relevant wiring from its retaining clips **(see illustrations)**.

Refitting

6 Refitting is a reversal of removal, but smear petroleum jelly on the terminals when reconnecting the leads, and always reconnect the positive lead first, and the negative lead last.

---

5 Charging system - testing

Note: *Refer to the warnings given in "Safety first!" and in Section 1 of this Chapter before starting work.*

1 If the ignition warning light fails to illuminate when the ignition is switched on, first check the alternator wiring connections for security. If satisfactory, check that the warning light bulb has not blown, and that the bulbholder is secure in its location in the instrument panel. If the light still fails to illuminate, check the continuity of the warning light feed wire from the alternator to the bulbholder. If all is

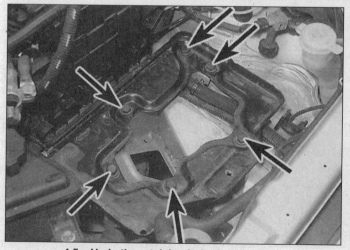

4.5a Undo the retaining bolts (arrowed) . . .

4.5b . . . then unclip the battery mounting plate from the relay boxes and remove it from the engine compartment

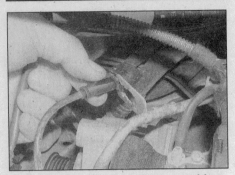

7.9 Remove the camshaft sensor wiring plug from the bracket

satisfactory, the alternator is at fault and should be renewed or taken to an auto-electrician for testing and repair.

2 If the ignition warning light illuminates when the engine is running, stop the engine and check that the drivebelt is correctly tensioned (see Chapter 1) and that the alternator connections are secure. If all is so far satisfactory, have the alternator checked by an auto-electrician for testing and repair.

3 If the alternator output is suspect even though the warning light functions correctly, the regulated voltage may be checked as follows.

4 Connect a voltmeter across the battery terminals and start the engine.

5 Increase the engine speed until the voltmeter reading remains steady; the reading should be approximately 12 to 13 volts, and no more than 14 volts.

6 Switch on as many electrical accessories

(eg, the headlights, heated rear window and heater blower) as possible, and check that the alternator maintains the regulated voltage at around 13 to 14 volts.

7 If the regulated voltage is not as stated, the fault may be due to worn brushes, weak brush springs, a faulty voltage regulator, a faulty diode, a severed phase winding or worn or damaged slip rings. The alternator should be renewed or taken to an auto-electrician for testing and repair.

6 Alternator drivebelt - removal, refitting and tensioning

1 Refer to the procedure given for the auxiliary drivebelt(s) in Chapter 1.

7 Alternator - removal and refitting

Removal

1 Firmly apply the handbrake then jack up the front of the vehicle and support it securely on axle stands. Where necessary, undo the retaining bolts and remove the undercover from beneath the engine/transmission unit. Disconnect the battery negative lead and proceed as described under the relevant sub-heading.

2 Remove the air cleaner housing and air ducts as described in Chapter 4.

3 Push the auxiliary drivebelt tensioner against the spring pressure, and disengage the belt from the pulleys (refer to Chapter 1 if necessary)

1.6 litre SOHC engine

4 Slacken and remove the mounting bolts and remove the support bracket from the alternator to the inlet manifold.

5 Undo the bolts and remove the support bracket securing the alternator to the cylinder head. Swing the alternator to the rear.

6 Unclip the wiring harness from the bracket, and remove the bracket.

7 Remove the rubber covers (where fitted) from the alternator terminals, then unscrew the retaining nuts and disconnect the wiring from the rear of the alternator.

8 Slacken and remove the lower alternator mounting bolt, and manoeuvre the alternator out of position.

1.6 DOHC and 1.8 (X18XE1) litre engines

9 On 1.8 litre models, disconnect the camshaft sensor wiring plug and unclip it from the mounting bracket **(see illustration)**.

10 Remove the upper alternator mounting bolt **(see illustration)**.

11 Slacken the lower alternator bolt, and swing the alternator to the rear.

12 Undo the bolt(s) and remove the alternator drivebelt tensioner.

13 On 1.8 litre models, disconnect the wiring plugs for the crankshaft sensor and oil pressure switch. Place the cables out of the way.

14 Remove the rubber covers (where fitted) from the alternator terminals, then unscrew the retaining nuts and disconnect the wiring from the rear of the alternator **(see illustration)**.

15 Slacken and remove the bolts securing the alternator mounting bracket to the cylinder block, then manoeuvre the alternator and bracket assembly upwards and out of position. On models fitted with air conditioning, manoeuvre the alternator and bracket assembly downwards and out of position **(see illustration)**.

16 Slacken and remove the bolts securing the alternator to its mounting bracket and separate the two components **(see illustration)**.

1.8 (X18XE) and 2.0 litre engines

17 Models without air conditioning: Remove the alternator drivebelt tensioner.

18 Undo the retaining bolts and remove the alternator support brackets from the alternator to the inlet manifold and cylinder had.

19 Remove the rubber covers (where fitted) from the alternator terminals, then unscrew the retaining nuts and disconnect the wiring from the rear of the alternator.

20 Remove the three bolts securing the alternator mounting bracket to the cylinder block, and manoeuvre the alternator and bracket assembly downwards and out of the engine compartment.

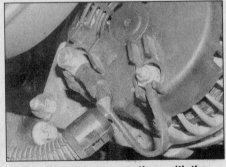

7.14 Alternator connections with the covers removed

7.10 Remove the alternator upper mounting bolt

7.15 Alternator mounting bracket bolts (X18XE1 engine shown)

7.16 Withdraw the alternator lower mounting bolt

21 Slacken and remove the bolts securing the alternator to its mounting bracket and separate the two components.

Diesel engines

22 With reference to Chapter 4 if necessary, remove the intake ducting complete with hot film mass airflow meter.

23 Unscrew the three bolts securing the rear wiring trough, and disconnect the wiring connections from the alternator

24 Remove the heat shields, and slacken the lower alternator retaining bolt **(see illustration)**.

25 Where applicable, disconnect the vacuum pipe and wiring plug, and remove the turbocharger wastegate solenoid valve as described in Chapter 4.

26 Unscrew the nut and remove the upper alternator retaining bolt **(see illustration 7.24)**.

27 Drain the cooling system as described in Chapter 1, or be prepared for coolant spillage. Disconnect the coolant flange from the right-hand end of the cylinder head.

28 Remove the lower retaining bolt, and remove the alternator upwards and out of the engine compartment.

Refitting

29 Refitting is the reverse of removal tightening all mounting bolts to their specified torque settings (where given). Ensure the drivebelt is correctly refitted and tensioned as described in Chapter 1.

Note: If the alternator is thought to be suspect, it can be removed from the vehicle and taken to an auto-electrician for testing. Most auto-electricians will be able to supply and fit brushes at a reasonable cost. However, check on the cost of repairs and availability of parts before proceeding as it may prove more economical to obtain a new or exchange alternator.

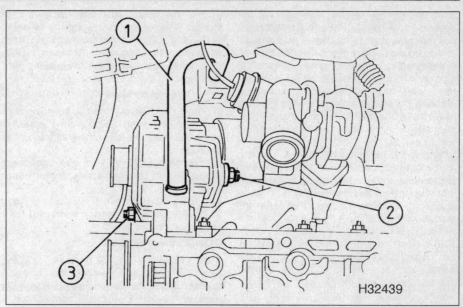

7.24 Lower alternator mounting bolt (3), upper mounting bolt (2), and coolant hose (1)

9 Starting system - testing

Note: *Refer to the precautions given in "Safety first!" and in Section 1 of this Chapter before starting work.*

1 If the starter motor fails to operate when the ignition key is turned to the appropriate position, the following possible causes may be to blame.

  a) The battery is faulty.

  b) The electrical connections between the switch, solenoid, battery and starter motor are somewhere failing to pass the necessary current from the battery through the starter to earth.

  c) The solenoid is faulty.

  d) The starter motor is mechanically or electrically defective.

8 Alternator brush renewal - typical

1 Remove the alternator (see Section 7).

2 Place the alternator on a clean work surface, with the pulley facing down.

3 Undo the retaining screws, and lift away the outer plastic cover **(see illustration)**.

4 Unscrew the two retaining screws and ease the wire from the connector **(see illustrations)**.

5 If the brushes are damaged or excessively worn, the brush pack must be renewed.

6 Clean and inspect the surfaces of the slip rings, at the end of the alternator shaft. If they are excessively worn, or damaged, the alternator must be renewed.

7 Reassemble the alternator by following the dismantling procedure in reverse, taking care to ease the brushes over the end of the slip rings **(see illustration)**. On completion, refer to previous Section to refit the alternator.

8.3 Undo the screws and lift away the cover

8.4a Unscrew the brush pack screws . . .

8.4b . . . and ease the connector apart

8.7 Compress the brushes and refit the brush pack

5A

2 To check the battery, switch on the headlights. If they dim after a few seconds, this indicates that the battery is discharged - recharge (see Section 3) or renew the battery. If the headlights glow brightly, operate the ignition switch and observe the lights. If they dim, then this indicates that current is reaching the starter motor, therefore the fault must lie in the starter motor. If the lights continue to glow brightly (and no clicking sound can be heard from the starter motor solenoid), this indicates that there is a fault in the circuit or solenoid - see following paragraphs. If the starter motor turns slowly when operated, but the battery is in good condition, then this indicates that either the starter motor is faulty, or there is considerable resistance somewhere in the circuit.

3 If a fault in the circuit is suspected, disconnect the battery leads (including the earth connection to the body), the starter/solenoid wiring and the engine/transmission earth strap. Thoroughly clean the connections, and reconnect the leads and wiring, then use a voltmeter or test lamp to check that full battery voltage is available at the battery positive lead connection to the solenoid, and that the earth is sound. Smear petroleum jelly around the battery terminals to prevent corrosion - corroded connections are amongst the most frequent causes of electrical system faults.

4 If the battery and all connections are in good condition, check the circuit by disconnecting the wire from the solenoid blade terminal. Connect a voltmeter or test lamp between the wire end and a good earth (such as the battery negative terminal), and check that the wire is live when the ignition switch is turned to the 'start' position. If it is, then the circuit is sound - if not the circuit wiring can be checked as described in Chapter 12.

5 The solenoid contacts can be checked by connecting a voltmeter or test lamp between the battery positive feed connection on the starter side of the solenoid, and earth. When the ignition switch is turned to the 'start' position, there should be a reading or lighted bulb, as applicable. If there is no reading or lighted bulb, the solenoid is faulty and should be renewed.

6 If the circuit and solenoid are proved sound, the fault must lie in the starter motor. In this event, it may be possible to have the starter motor overhauled by a specialist, but check on the cost of spares before proceeding, as it may prove more economical to obtain a new or exchange motor.

10 Starter motor - removal and refitting

Removal

1 Disconnect the battery negative lead then firmly apply the handbrake then jack up the front of the vehicle and support it on axle stands. Where necessary, undo the retaining bolts and remove the undercover from beneath the engine/transmission unit. Proceed as described under the relevant sub-heading.

SOHC petrol models

2 Slacken and remove the two retaining nuts and disconnect the wiring from the starter motor solenoid. Recover the washers under the nuts.

3 Unscrew the retaining nut and disconnect the earth lead from the starter motor upper bolt.

4 Slacken and remove the retaining bolts then manoeuvre the starter motor out from underneath the engine.

DOHC petrol engines

5 On X18XE and X20XEV engines, undo the retaining bolts and remove the support bracket from the underside of the inlet manifold. Where necessary, disconnect the oil level sensor wiring connector.

6 Where necessary, undo the nut/bolt(s) (as applicable) and remove the starter motor mounting bracket.

7 Slacken and remove the two retaining nuts and disconnect the wiring from the starter motor solenoid. Recover the washers under the nuts.

8 Slacken and remove the retaining bolts then manoeuvre the starter motor out from underneath the engine.

1.7 litre diesel models

9 Slacken and remove the two retaining nuts and disconnect the wiring from the starter motor solenoid. Recover the washers under the nuts.

10 Slacken and remove the retaining bolts then manoeuvre the starter motor out from underneath the engine.

2.0 litre diesel engine

11 To improve access, remove the exhaust system front pipe as described in Chapter 4.

12 Undo the retaining bolts and remove the heatshield from the rear of the starter motor.

13 Slacken and remove the retaining bolts and remove the exhaust manifold support bracket.

14 Slacken and remove the two retaining nuts and disconnect the wiring from the starter motor solenoid. Recover the washers under the nuts.

15 Undo the retaining nuts/bolt and remove the mounting bracket from the rear of the starter motor.

16 Slacken and remove the retaining bolts then manoeuvre the starter motor out from underneath the engine.

Refitting

17 Refitting is a reversal of removal tightening the retaining bolts to the specified torque. Ensure all wiring is correctly routed and its retaining nuts are securely tightened.

11 Starter motor - testing and overhaul

1 If the starter motor is thought to be suspect, it should be removed from the vehicle and taken to an auto-electrician for testing. Most auto-electricians will be able to supply and fit brushes at a reasonable cost. However, check on the cost of repairs before proceeding as it may prove more economical to obtain a new or exchange motor.

12 Ignition switch - removal and refitting

1 The ignition switch is integral with the steering column lock, and can be removed as described in Chapter 12.

13 Oil pressure warning light switch - removal and refitting

Removal

Petrol models

1 The switch is screwed into the rear of the oil pump housing which is located on the right-hand end of the engine, on the end of the crankshaft. To improve access to the switch, firmly apply the handbrake then jack up the front of the vehicle and support it on axle stands. Where necessary, undo the retaining bolts and remove the undercover from beneath the engine/transmission unit.

2 Disconnect the wiring connector then unscrew the switch and recover the sealing washer. Be prepared for oil spillage, and if the switch is to be left removed from the engine for any length of time, plug the switch aperture.

Diesel models

3 On 1.7 litre models, the oil pressure switch is screwed into the left-hand end of the cylinder block and can be reached from above.

4 On 2.0 litre models the switch is screwed into the rear of the cylinder block. To gain access to the switch, firmly apply the handbrake then jack up the front of the vehicle and support it on axle stands. Where necessary, undo the retaining bolts and remove the undercover from beneath the engine/transmission unit. The switch can then be reached from underneath the vehicle.

5 Disconnect the wiring connector then unscrew the switch and recover the sealing washer. Be prepared for oil spillage, and if the switch is to be left removed from the engine for any length of time, plug the switch aperture.

Refitting

6 Examine the sealing washer for signs of damage or deterioration and if necessary renew.

7 Refit the switch and washer, tightening it to the specified torque, and reconnect the wiring connector.

8 Lower the vehicle to the ground (where necessary) then check and, if necessary, top up the engine oil as described in *"Weekly checks"*.

14 Oil level sensor - removal and refitting

X16XEL and X18XE1 engines

Removal

1 The oil level sensor (where fitted) is located on the rear face of the engine sump.

2 To gain access to the sensor, firmly apply the handbrake then jack up the front of the vehicle and support it on axle stands. Where necessary, undo the retaining bolts and remove the undercover from beneath the engine/transmission unit.

3 Drain the engine oil into a clean container then refit the drain plug and tighten it to the specified torque setting (see Chapter 1).

4 Disconnect the wiring connector(s) from the sensor.

5 On models with a pressed steel sump, unscrew the retaining bolts then ease the sensor out from the sump and remove it along with its sealing ring. Discard the sealing ring, a new one should be used on refitting.

6 On models with a cast aluminium sump, unscrew the sensor and remove it from the

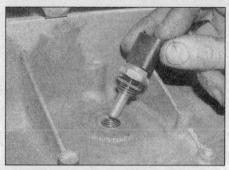

15.4 Unscrew the oil temperature sensor from the sump

sump. Discard the sealing washer, a new one should be used on refitting.

Refitting

7 Refitting is the reverse of removal ensuring the wiring is correctly routed and securely reconnected. On completion refill the engine with oil (see Chapter 1)

All other models

Removal

8 The oil level sensor (where fitted) is located inside the sump which must first be removed (see Chapter 2).

9 With the sump removed, slide off the retaining clip and free the sensor wiring connector from the sump.

10 Note the correct routing of the wiring then undo the retaining screws and remove the sensor assembly from the sump. Check the wiring connector seal for signs or damage and renew if necessary.

Refitting

11 Prior to refitting remove all traces of

locking compound from the sensor retaining screw and sump threads. Apply a drop of fresh locking compound to the screw threads and lubricate the wiring connector seal with a smear of engine oil.

12 Fit the sensor, making sure the wiring is correctly routed, and securely tighten its retaining screws. Ease the wiring connector through the sump, taking care not to damage its seal, and secure it in position with the retaining clip.

13 Ensure the sensor is correctly refitted then fit the sump as described in Chapter 2.

15 Oil temperature sensor (diesels) - removal and refitting

Removal

1 Where fitted, release the retaining clips/screws and remove the engine under tray.

2 Undo the sump plug and drain the engine oil as described in Chapter 1.

3 The sensor (where fitted) is located at the front of the sump. Disconnect the wiring plug from the sensor.

4 Unscrew the sensor from the sump **(see illustration)**.

Refitting

5 With a new sealing ring fitted, apply a few drops of locking compound to the threads of the sensor, securely refit the sensor to the sump. Take care not to over tighten.

6 Reconnect the sensor wiring plug.

7 Refit the engine under tray.

8 On completion refill the engine with oil (see Chapter 1).

Notes

Chapter 5 Part B:
Ignition system - petrol models

Contents

Degrees of difficulty

| Easy, suitable for novice with little experience | | Fairly easy, suitable for beginner with some experience | | Fairly difficult, suitable for competent DIY mechanic | | Difficult, suitable for experienced DIY mechanic | | Very difficult, suitable for expert DIY or professional | |

Specifications

System type	Distributorless ignition system controlled by engine management ECU
Firing order	1-3-4-2 (No 1 cylinder at timing belt end)

Torque wrench setting	Nm	lbf ft
DIS module screws	8	5

1 Ignition system - general information

1 The ignition system is integrated with the fuel injection system to form a combined engine management system under the control of one ECU (See Chapter 4 for further information). The ignition side of the system is of the distributorless type, and consists of the DIS (distributorless ignition system) module and the knock sensor.
2 On X16SZR, X18XE and X20XEV engines, the ignition module is actually a four output ignition coil. The module consists of two separate HT coils which supply two cylinders each (one coil supplies cylinders 1 and 4, and the other cylinders 2 and 3). Under the control of the ECU, the module operates on the 'wasted spark' principle, ie, each spark plug sparks twice for every cycle of the engine, once on the compression stroke and once on the exhaust stroke. On X16XEL and X18XE1 engines, the ignition module consists of four ignition coils, one per cylinder, in one casing mounted longitudinally directly above the spark plugs. This module eliminates the need for any HT leads as the coils locate directly onto the relevant spark plug. The ECU uses its inputs from the various sensors to calculate the required ignition advance setting and coil charging time.
3 The knock sensor is mounted onto the cylinder block and informs the ECU when the engine is 'pinking' under load. The sensor is sensitive to vibration and detects the knocking which occurs when the engine starts to 'pink' (pre-ignite). The knock sensor sends an electrical signal to the ECU which in turn retards the ignition advance setting until the 'pinking' ceases.

Warning: Voltages produced by an electronic ignition system are considerably higher than those produced by conventional ignition systems. Extreme care must be taken when working on the system with the ignition switched on. Persons with surgically-implanted cardiac pacemaker devices should keep well clear of the ignition circuits, components and test equipment.

3.2a Ignition module - X16SZR engine

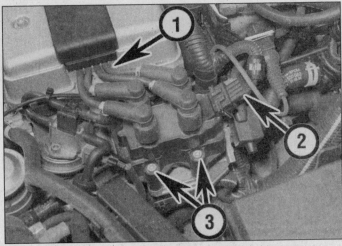

3.2b Ignition module - X18XE and X20XEV engines

1 HT leads   2 Wiring connector   3 Retaining screws

2 Ignition system - testing

1 If a fault appears in the engine management (fuel injection/ignition) system first ensure that the fault is not due to a poor electrical connection or poor maintenance; ie, check that the air cleaner filter element is clean, the spark plugs are in good condition and correctly gapped, that the engine breather hoses are clear and undamaged, referring to Chapter 1 for further information. Also check that the accelerator cable is correctly adjusted as described in Chapter 4. If the engine is running very roughly, check the compression pressures and (where necessary) the valve clearances as described in Chapter 2.

2 If these checks fail to reveal the cause of the problem the vehicle should be taken to a suitably equipped Vauxhall dealer for testing. A wiring block connector is incorporated in the engine management circuit into which a special electronic diagnostic tester can be plugged. The tester will locate the fault quickly and simply alleviating the need to test all the system components individually which is a time consuming operation that carries a high risk of damaging the ECU.

3 The only ignition system checks which can be carried out by the home mechanic are those described in Chapter 1, relating to the spark plugs. If necessary, the system wiring and wiring connectors can be checked as described in Chapter 12 ensuring that the ECU wiring connector(s) have first been disconnected.

3 DIS module - removal and refitting

Removal

X16SZR, X18XE and X20XEV engines

1 Disconnect the battery negative terminal.
2 Disconnect the wiring connector and HT leads from the ignition module (see illustrations). The module HT lead terminals are numbered (the leads should also be numbered) with their respective cylinder number to avoid confusion on refitting.
3 Slacken and remove the retaining screws and remove the ignition module from the end of the cylinder head.

X16XEL and X18XE1 engines

4 Undo the retaining bolts, unscrew the oil filler cap, and remove the engine cover.

5 The ignition module is mounted at the top of the engine, between the inlet and exhaust camshaft casings. Disconnect the wiring plug at the left-hand end of the module (see illustration).
6 Undo the retaining screws, and lift the module up and out of position. If the module proves reluctant to separate from the spark plugs, insert two long 8 mm bolts into the threaded holes in the top of the module, and pull up on the bolts to free the module from the plugs (see illustration).

Refitting

7 Refit the module to the cylinder head and tighten its retaining screws to the specified torque setting.
8 On X16SZR, X18XE and X20XEV models, reconnect each HT lead to its corresponding terminal on the ignition module using the numbers on the leads and modules.
9 Reconnect the wiring connector to the ignition module, making sure it is fitted securely
10 Refit the engine cover and reconnect the battery.

4 Ignition timing - checking and adjustment

1 There are no timing marks on the flywheel or crankshaft pulley. The timing is constantly being monitored and adjusted by the engine management ECU, and nominal values cannot be given. Therefore, it is not possible for the home mechanic to check the ignition timing.
2 The only way in which the ignition timing can be checked and (where possible) adjusted is by using special electronic test equipment, connected to the engine management system diagnostic connector (refer to Chapter 4 for further information). Refer to your Vauxhall dealer for further information.

3.5 Ignition module wiring plug - X16XEL and X18XE1 engines

3.6 Pull the ignition module up and away from the top of the spark plugs

Chapter 5 Part C:
Preheating system - diesel models

Contents

Degrees of difficulty

Easy, suitable for novice with little experience	**Fairly easy,** suitable for beginner with some experience	**Fairly difficult,** suitable for competent DIY mechanic	**Difficult,** suitable for experienced DIY mechanic	**Very difficult,** suitable for expert DIY or professional

Specifications

Torque wrench settings	Nm	lbf ft
Glow plugs:		
1.7 litre models	20	15
2.0 litre models	10	7

---

1 Preheating system - description and testing

Description

1 Each cylinder of the engine is fitted with a heater plug (commonly called a glow plug) screwed into it. The plugs are electrically-operated before and during start-up when the engine is cold. Electrical feed to the glow plugs is controlled via a relay and the preheating system control unit (1.7 litre models) or the injection system ECU (2.0 litre models).

2 A warning light in the instrument panel tells the driver that preheating is taking place. When the light goes out, the engine is ready to be started. The voltage supply to the glow plugs continues for several seconds after the light goes out. If no attempt is made to start, the timer then cuts off the supply, in order to avoid draining the battery and overheating the glow plugs.

3 The glow plugs also provide a 'post-heating' function, whereby the glow plugs remain switched on for a period after the engine has started. The length of time 'post-heating' takes place for is also determined by the control unit but it can be anything up to 6 minutes, depending on engine temperature.

4 On 1.7 litre models the fuel filter is also fitted with a heating element to prevent the fuel 'waxing' in extreme conditions and to improve combustion. The heating element is fitted between the filter and its housing and is controlled by the preheating system control unit via the temperature switch on the filter housing. The heating element is switched on if the temperature of the fuel passing through the filter is less than 5°C (41°F) and switches off when the fuel temperature reaches 16°C (61°F).

Testing

5 If the system malfunctions, testing is ultimately by substitution of known good units, but some preliminary checks may be made as follows.

6 Connect a voltmeter or 12-volt test lamp between the glow plug supply cable and earth (engine or vehicle metal). Make sure that the live connection is kept clear of the engine and bodywork.

7 Have an assistant switch on the ignition, and check that voltage is applied to the glow plugs. Note the time for which the warning light is lit, and the total time for which voltage is applied before the system cuts out. Switch off the ignition.

8 At an under-bonnet temperature of 20°C (68°F), typical times noted should be approximately 3 seconds for warning light operation. Warning light time will increase with lower temperatures and decrease with higher temperatures.

9 If there is no supply at all, the control unit, relay or associated wiring is at fault.

10 To locate a defective glow plug, slacken and remove the nuts and washers (where fitted) then disconnect the main supply lead(s) and the electrical supply rail from the plugs. On later models simply pull off the wiring connector from each plug

11 Use a continuity tester, or a 12-volt test lamp connected to the battery positive terminal, to check for continuity between each glow plug terminal and earth. The resistance of a glow plug in good condition is very low (less than 1 ohm), so if the test lamp does not light or the continuity tester shows a high resistance, the glow plug is certainly defective.

12 If an ammeter is available, the current draw of each glow plug can be checked. After an initial surge of 15 to 20 amps, each plug should draw 12 amps. Any plug which draws much more or less than this is probably defective.

13 As a final check, the glow plugs can be removed and inspected as described in the following Section.

2 Glow plugs - removal, inspection and refitting

Caution: If the preheating system has just been energised, or if the engine has been running, the glow plugs will be very hot.

Removal

1.7 litre models

1 Disconnect the battery negative lead. To improve access, disconnect the breather hose from the rear of the cylinder head cover.

2 Slacken the nut securing the electrical supply rail to each glow plug then slide the rail to the rear to disengage it from the glow plugs.

2.5a On 2.0 litre engines, unscrew the retaining nut from each glow plug . . .

3 Unscrew the glow plug(s) and remove from the cylinder head.

2.0 litre models

4 Disconnect the battery negative lead. If necessary, to improve access, remove the metal pipe linking the turbocharger to the manifold/intercooler duct (see Chapter 4).

5 On early models undo the retaining nuts and washers from the top of each glow plug then disconnect the wiring connectors and lift off the electrical connecting rails **(see illustrations)**. On later models simply disconnect the connector from the top of the each glow plug.

6 Unscrew the glow plug(s) and remove them from the cylinder head.

Inspection

7 Inspect each glow plug for physical damage. Burnt or eroded glow plug tips can be caused by a bad injector spray pattern. Have the injectors checked if this sort of damage is found.

8 If the glow plugs are in good physical condition, check them electrically using a 12 volt test lamp or continuity tester as described in the previous Section.

9 The glow plugs can be energised by applying 12 volts to them to verify that they heat up evenly and in the required time. Observe the following precautions.

 a) *Support the glow plug by clamping it carefully in a vice or self-locking pliers. Remember it will become red-hot.*

 b) *Make sure that the power supply or test lead incorporates a fuse or overload trip*

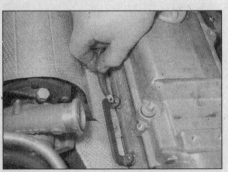

2.5b . . . then disconnect the wiring . . .

to protect against damage from a short-circuit.

 c) *After testing, allow the glow plug to cool for several minutes before attempting to handle it.*

10 A glow plug in good condition will start to glow red at the tip after drawing current for 5 seconds or so. Any plug which takes much longer to start glowing, or which starts glowing in the middle instead of at the tip, is defective.

Refitting

1.7 litre models

11 Carefully refit the plug(s) and tighten to the specified torque. Do not overtighten, as this can damage the glow plug element.

12 Ease the electrical supply rail into position, ensuring it is correctly engaged with each of the four glow plugs, and securely tighten the glow plug nuts.

13 Reconnect the breather hose then connect the battery and check the operation of the glow plugs.

2.0 litre models

14 Carefully refit the plug(s) and tighten to the specified torque. Do not overtighten, as this can damage the glow plug element.

15 On early models, refit the supply rail(s) to the glow plugs, reconnect the wiring connector(s) then refit the washers and retaining nuts and tighten securely. On later models reconnect the connectors securely to the plugs.

16 Refit the metal pipe (where removed) to the turbocharger/duct (see Chapter 4) then reconnect the battery and check the operation of the glow plugs.

---

3 Preheating system components - removal and refitting

1.7 litre models

Preheating system control unit

1 The unit is located on the left-hand side of the engine compartment where it is mounted onto the rear of the battery box.

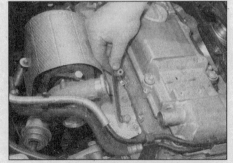

2.5c . . . and lift off the electrical connecting rails

2 Disconnect the battery negative lead.

3 Unscrew the retaining nut securing the unit to the battery box.

4 Disconnect the wiring connector from the base of the unit then unscrew the two retaining nuts and free the main feed and supply wires from the unit. Remove the unit from the engine compartment.

5 Refitting is a reversal of removal, ensuring that the wiring connectors are correctly connected.

Coolant temperature sensor

6 The coolant temperature switch is screwed into the thermostat housing. Refer to Chapter 3 for removal and refitting details.

Fuel filter heating element

7 Remove the fuel filter as described in Chapter 1. If the filter is damaged on removal (which is likely), a new one should be used on refitting.

8 Disconnect the battery negative terminal then disconnect the wiring connector from the heating element.

9 Unscrew the centre bolt and remove the heating element from the filter housing. Recover the sealing ring and discard, a new one should be used on refitting.

10 Fit a new sealing ring the heating element recess then refit the element to the filter housing and securely tighten the centre bolt.

11 Reconnect the battery then fit the fuel filter as described in Chapter 1.

Fuel filter heating element temperature switch

12 Disconnect the battery negative terminal then disconnect the wiring connector from the temperature switch which is screwed into the fuel filter housing.

13 Position a wad of rag beneath the filter housing to catch any spilt fuel then unscrew the switch and remove it from the housing. Plug the housing aperture to prevent the entry of dirt and minimise fuel loss. Remove the sealing ring from the switch and renew them.

14 Fit new sealing rings to the switch recesses then refit the switch to the filter housing and tighten securely. Reconnect the wiring connector to the switch then reconnect the battery.

Relays and fuses

15 The glow plug and fuel heating element relays and fuses are located in the box in the engine compartment. Refer to Chapter 12 for further details.

2.0 litre models

16 The operation of the preheating system is controlled by the injection system ECU and its sensors. Refer to Chapter 4 for further information.

Chapter 6
Clutch

Contents

Degrees of difficulty

Easy, suitable for novice with little experience	**Fairly easy,** suitable for beginner with some experience	**Fairly difficult,** suitable for competent DIY mechanic 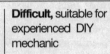	**Difficult,** suitable for experienced DIY mechanic	**Very difficult,** suitable for expert DIY or professional

Specifications

Type . . . . Single dry plate with diaphragm spring, hydraulically operated

Friction plate

Diameter:

Petrol models:

1.6 litre SOHC models	200 mm

1.6 litre DOHC models:

Early models	200 mm
Later models	205 mm
1.8 litre models	216 mm
2.0 litre models	228 mm

Diesel models:

1.7 litre models	200 mm
2.0 litre models	228 mm

Torque wrench settings	Nm	lbf ft
Hydraulic pipe union nut	14	10
Master cylinder retaining nuts	20	15
Pedal mounting bracket nuts	20	15
Pressure plate retaining bolts	15	11
Release cylinder mounting bolts	5	4

1 General information

1 The clutch consists of a friction plate, a pressure plate assembly, and the hydraulic release cylinder (which incorporates the release bearing); all of these components are contained in the large cast-aluminium alloy bellhousing, sandwiched between the engine and the transmission.

2 The friction plate is fitted between the engine flywheel and the clutch pressure plate, and is allowed to slide on the transmission input shaft splines.

3 The pressure plate assembly is bolted to the engine flywheel. When the engine is running, drive is transmitted from the crankshaft, via the flywheel, to the friction plate (these components being clamped securely together by the pressure plate assembly) and from the friction plate to the transmission input shaft.

4 To interrupt the drive, the spring pressure must be relaxed. This is achieved using a hydraulic release mechanism which consists of the master cylinder, the release cylinder and the pipe/hose linking the two components. Depressing the pedal pushes on the master cylinder pushrod which hydraulically forces the release cylinder piston against the pressure plate spring fingers. This causes the springs to deform and releases the clamping force on the friction plate.

5 The clutch is self-adjusting and requires no manual adjustment.

2 Clutch hydraulic system - bleeding

Warning: *Hydraulic fluid is poisonous; wash off immediately and thoroughly in the case of skin contact, and seek immediate medical advice if any fluid is swallowed or gets into the eyes. Certain types of hydraulic fluid are flammable, and may ignite when allowed into contact with hot components; when servicing any hydraulic system, it is safest to assume that the fluid is flammable, and to take precautions against the risk of fire as though it is petrol that is being handled. Hydraulic fluid is also an effective paint stripper, and will attack plastics; if any is spilt, it should be washed off immediately, using copious quantities of fresh water. Finally, it is hygroscopic (it absorbs moisture from the air) - old fluid may be contaminated and unfit for further use. When topping-up or renewing the fluid, always use the recommended type, and ensure that it comes from a freshly-opened sealed container.*

1 The correct operation of any hydraulic system is only possible after removing all air from the components and circuit; this is achieved by bleeding the system.

2 During the bleeding procedure, add only clean, unused hydraulic fluid of the recommended type; never re-use fluid that has already been bled from the system. Ensure that sufficient fluid is available before starting work.

3 If there is any possibility of incorrect fluid being already in the system, the hydraulic circuit must be flushed completely with uncontaminated, correct fluid.

4 If hydraulic fluid has been lost from the system, or air has entered because of a leak, ensure that the fault is cured before continuing further.

5 The bleed screw is screwed into the hose end fitting which is situated on the top of the transmission housing. On some models access to the bleed screw is limited and it may be necessary to jack up the front of the vehicle and support it on axle stands so that the screw can be reached from below.

6 Check that all pipes and hoses are secure, unions tight and the bleed screw is closed. Clean any dirt from around the bleed screw.

7 Unscrew the master cylinder fluid reservoir cap (the clutch shares the same fluid reservoir as the braking system), and top the master cylinder reservoir up to the upper (MAX) level line. Refit the cap loosely, and remember to maintain the fluid level at least above the lower (MIN) level line throughout the procedure, or there is a risk of further air entering the system.

8 There are a number of one-man, do-it-yourself bleeding kits currently available from motor accessory shops. It is recommended that one of these kits is used whenever possible, as they greatly simplify the bleeding operation, and reduce the risk of expelled air and fluid being drawn back into the system. If such a kit is not available, the basic (two-man) method must be used, which is described in detail below.

9 If a kit is to be used, prepare the vehicle as described previously, and follow the kit manufacturer's instructions, as the procedure may vary slightly according to the type being used; generally, they are as outlined below in the relevant sub-section.

Bleeding - basic (two-man) method

10 Collect a clean glass jar, a suitable length of plastic or rubber tubing which is a tight fit over the bleed screw, and a ring spanner to fit the screw. The help of an assistant will also be required.

11 Remove the dust cap from the bleed screw. Fit the spanner and tube to the screw, place the other end of the tube in the jar, and pour in sufficient fluid to cover the end of the tube.

12 Ensure that the fluid level is maintained at least above the lower level line in the reservoir throughout the procedure.

13 Have the assistant fully depress the clutch pedal several times to build up pressure, then maintain it on the final downstroke.

14 While pedal pressure is maintained, unscrew the bleed screw (approximately one turn) and allow the compressed fluid and air to flow into the jar. The assistant should maintain pedal pressure and should not release it until instructed to do so. When the flow stops, tighten the bleed screw again, have the assistant release the pedal slowly, and recheck the reservoir fluid level.

15 Repeat the steps given in paragraphs 13 and 14 until the fluid emerging from the bleed screw is free from air bubbles. If the master cylinder has been drained and refilled allow approximately five seconds between cycles for the master cylinder passages to refill.

16 When no more air bubbles appear, tighten the bleed screw securely, remove the tube and spanner, and refit the dust cap. Do not overtighten the bleed screw.

Bleeding - using a one-way valve kit

17 As their name implies, these kits consist of a length of tubing with a one-way valve fitted, to prevent expelled air and fluid being drawn back into the system; some kits include a translucent container, which can be positioned so that the air bubbles can be more easily seen flowing from the end of the tube.

18 The kit is connected to the bleed screw, which is then opened. The user returns to the driver's seat, depresses the clutch pedal with a smooth, steady stroke, and slowly releases it; this is repeated until the expelled fluid is clear of air bubbles.

19 Note that these kits simplify work so much that it is easy to forget the clutch fluid reservoir level; ensure that this is maintained at least above the lower level line at all times.

Bleeding - using a pressure-bleeding kit

20 These kits are usually operated by the reservoir of pressurised air contained in the spare tyre. However, note that it will probably be necessary to reduce the pressure to a lower level than normal; refer to the instructions supplied with the kit.

21 By connecting a pressurised, fluid-filled container to the clutch fluid reservoir, bleeding can be carried out simply by opening the bleed screw and allowing the fluid to flow out until no more air bubbles can be seen in the expelled fluid.

22 This method has the advantage that the large reservoir of fluid provides an additional safeguard against air being drawn into the system during bleeding.

All methods

23 When bleeding is complete, and correct pedal feel is restored, tighten the bleed screw securely and wash off any spilt fluid. Refit the dust cap to the bleed screw.

24 Check the hydraulic fluid level in the master cylinder reservoir, and top-up if necessary (see *"Weekly Checks"*).

25 Discard any hydraulic fluid that has been bled from the system; it will not be fit for re-use.

26 Check the operation of the clutch pedal. If the clutch is still not operating correctly, air must still be present in the system, and further bleeding is required. Failure to bleed satisfactorily after a reasonable repetition of the bleeding procedure may be due to worn master cylinder/release cylinder seals.

3 Master cylinder - removal and refitting

Note: *A new hydraulic pipe union sealing ring will be required on refitting.*

Removal

Right-hand drive models

1 To gain access to the master cylinder, remove the braking system vacuum servo unit as described in Chapter 9.

2 Remove all traces of dirt from the outside of the master cylinder and position some cloth beneath the cylinder to catch any spilt fluid.

3 Slide out the retaining clip and free the hydraulic pipe from the front of the master cylinder. Plug the pipe end and master cylinder port to minimise fluid loss and prevent the entry of dirt. Recover the sealing ring from the union and discard it; a new one must be used on refitting. Refit the retaining clip to the master cylinder groove, ensuring it is correctly located.

4 From inside the vehicle, remove the driver's side footwell trim below the facia (see Chapter 11), release the pedal return spring, slide off the retaining clip and remove the clevis pin securing the master cylinder pushrod to the pedal.

5 Return to the engine compartment then undo the retaining nuts and remove the master cylinder from the vehicle, along with its gasket. If the master cylinder is faulty it must be renewed; overhaul of the unit is not possible.

Left-hand drive models

6 To gain access to the master cylinder, unclip the relay box from the top of the ABS hydraulic modulator unit and position it clear. Access is still poor but can be further improved by removing the braking system vacuum servo unit (see Chapter 9).

7 Minimise fluid loss by first removing the master cylinder reservoir cap, and then tightening it down onto a piece of polythene, to obtain an airtight seal.

8 Wipe away all traces of dirt around the clutch master cylinder pipe union on the side of the fluid reservoir. Release the retaining clip then disconnect the pipe, catching any spilt fluid with a cloth. Plug or tape over the reservoir union and pipe end to prevent dirt entry and minimise fluid loss. Wipe off any spilt fluid immediately.

9 From inside the vehicle, unscrew the fasteners and remove the lower trim panel from underneath the driver's side of the facia to gain access to the clutch pedal.

10 Remove the master cylinder as described in paragraphs 2 to 5.

Refitting

Right-hand drive models

11 Ensure the cylinder and bulkhead mating surfaces are clean and dry and the gasket is in position.

12 Manoeuvre the master cylinder into position whilst ensuring that the pushrod clevis engages correctly with the pedal. Ensure the pushrod is correctly engaged then tighten the master cylinder retaining nuts to the specified torque.

13 Apply a smear of multi-purpose grease to the clevis pin then align the clevis and pedal and insert the pin. Secure the clevis pin in position with the retaining clip, making sure it is correctly located in the pin groove.

14 Fit a new sealing ring to the hydraulic pipe union and ensure the retaining clip is correctly located in the master cylinder groove. Ease the pipe union into position until the retaining clip is heard to 'click' then check that the pipe is securely retained.

15 Refit the braking system servo unit and master cylinder and bleed the hydraulic braking system as described in Chapter 9.

16 Once the braking system has been correctly bled, bleed the clutch hydraulic system as described in Section 2.

Left-hand drive models

17 Carry out the operations described in paragraphs 11 to 14.

18 Refit the lower trim panel to the driver's side of the facia.

19 Reconnect the master cylinder hose to the fluid reservoir and secure it in position with the retaining clip.

20 Bleed the hydraulic system as described in Section 2 then refit the relay box to the top of the modulator unit.

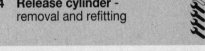

4 Release cylinder - removal and refitting

Note: *Refer to the warning concerning the dangers of asbestos dust at the beginning of Section 6.*

Removal

1 Unless the complete engine/transmission unit is to be removed from the car and separated for major overhaul (see Chapter 2), the clutch release cylinder can be reached by removing the transmission only, as described in Chapter 7.

2 Wipe clean the outside of the release cylinder then slacken the union nut and disconnect the hydraulic pipe **(see illustration)**. Wipe up any spilt fluid with a clean cloth.

3 Unscrew the three retaining bolts and slide the release cylinder off from the transmission input shaft. Remove the sealing ring which is fitted between the cylinder and transmission housing and discard it; a new one must be used on refitting. Whilst the cylinder is removed, take care not to allow any debris to enter the transmission unit.

4 The release cylinder is a sealed unit and cannot be overhauled. If the cylinder seals have gone or the release bearing is noisy or rough in operation, then the complete unit must be renewed.

Refitting

5 Ensure the release cylinder and trans-

mission mating surfaces are clean and dry and fit the new sealing ring to the transmission recess.

6 Lubricate the release cylinder seal with a smear of transmission oil then carefully ease the cylinder along the input shaft and into position. Ensure the sealing ring is still correctly seated in its groove then refit the release cylinder retaining bolts and tighten them to the specified torque.

7 Reconnect the hydraulic pipe to the release cylinder, tightening its union nut to the specified torque.

8 Refit the transmission unit as described in Chapter 7.

5 Clutch pedal - removal and refitting

Note: *The clutch pedal support and clutch pedal are one assembly and must be renewed as a complete unit. In the event of a frontal collision, the clutch pedal is released from its bearing in the support bracket to prevent injury to the driver's feet and legs (this also applies to the brake pedal). If an airbag has been deployed, inspect the clutch pedal assembly and if necessary renew the complete unit.*

Removal

1 Remove the braking system vacuum servo unit as described in Chapter 9. Ensure the clutch master cylinder fluid supply hose is securely clamped or plugged to prevent fluid loss and dirt entry.

2 Slide off the retaining clip and remove the clevis pin securing the master cylinder pushrod to the clutch pedal.

3 Carefully unhook the return spring from behind the pedal to release all tension in the spring.

4 On models with cruise control, disconnect the wiring connector from the clutch switch then remove the switch from the pedal bracket.

5 Slacken and remove the nuts securing the top of the pedal mounting bracket to the facia frame.

6 Return to the engine compartment then slacken and remove the clutch master cylinder retaining nuts. Leave the master cylinder in position; there is no need to remove or disconnect it.

7 Slacken and remove the remaining nuts securing the pedal mounting bracket to the bulkhead. Return to the inside of the vehicle and manoeuvre the pedal and mounting bracket assembly out of position.

8 Check the pedal mounting brackets for signs of damage or deformation (the brackets are designed to bend easily as a safety feature in the event of a collision) and check the pedal mounting bushes for signs of wear. If any components is worn or damage it

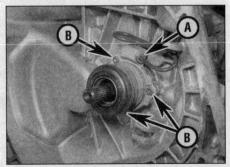

4.2 Clutch release cylinder hydraulic pipe union nut (A) and retaining bolts (B)

6

6.3 Slacken and remove the retaining bolts . . .

6.4 . . . and remove the clutch pressure plate and friction plate from the flywheel

should be renewed; the pedal and brackets can be separated once the bracket bolts have been unscrewed.

Refitting

9 If the pedal and bracket assembly has been dismantled, apply a smear of multi-purpose grease to the pedal pivot shaft and bushes prior to reassembly. Reassemble all components, making sure the pedal return spring is correctly engaged with the bracket, then securely tighten the bracket bolts. Check that the pedal pivots smoothly before refitting the assembly to the vehicle.

10 Manoeuvre the pedal and bracket assembly into position, engaging the pedal with the master cylinder pushrod, then loosely refit the nuts securing it to the facia frame.

11 Working in the engine compartment, refit the nuts securing the pedal mounting bracket and master cylinder to the bulkhead and tighten them to the specified torque setting.

12 From inside the vehicle, apply a smear of multi-purpose grease to the clevis pin then align the pushrod with the clutch pedal hole and insert the pin. Secure the pin in position with the retaining clip, making sure it is correctly located in the groove.

13 Tighten the nuts securing the pedal bracket to the facia to the specified torque setting.

14 Hook the return spring into position behind the clutch pedal.

15 Refit the braking system servo unit and master cylinder then bleed the hydraulic system as described in Chapter 9.

16 On models with cruise control, ensure the switch plunger is fully depressed then refit the switch to the bracket and connect the wiring connector. Fully depress the clutch pedal and extend the switch plunger then release the pedal to set the switch adjustment.

17 Refit the lower cover to the facia and check the operation of the clutch before using the vehicle on the road.

6 Clutch assembly - removal, inspection and refitting

Warning: Dust created by clutch wear and deposited on the clutch components may contain asbestos, which is a health hazard. DO NOT blow it out with compressed air, or inhale any of it. DO NOT use petrol or petroleum-based solvents to clean off the dust. Brake system cleaner or methylated spirit should be used to flush the dust into a suitable receptacle. After the clutch components are wiped clean with rags, dispose of the contaminated rags and cleaner in a sealed, marked container.
Note: *Although some friction materials may no longer contain asbestos, it is safest to assume that they do, and to take precautions accordingly.*

Removal

1 Unless the complete engine/transmission unit is to be removed from the car and separated for major overhaul (see Chapter 2), the clutch can be reached by removing the transmission as described in Chapter 7.

2 Before disturbing the clutch, use chalk or a marker pen to mark the relationship of the pressure plate assembly to the flywheel.

3 Working in a diagonal sequence, slacken the pressure plate bolts by half a turn at a time, until spring pressure is released and the bolts can be unscrewed by hand **(see illustration)**.

4 Remove the pressure plate assembly and collect the friction plate, noting which way round the friction plate is fitted **(see illustration)**.

Inspection

Note: *Due to the amount of work necessary to remove and refit clutch components, it is usually considered good practice to renew the clutch friction plate, pressure plate assembly*

and release bearing as a matched set, even if only one of these is actually worn enough to require renewal. It is also worth considering the renewal of the clutch components on a preventative basis if the engine and/or transmission have been removed for some other reason.

5 Remove the clutch assembly.

6 When cleaning clutch components, read first the warning at the beginning of this Section; remove dust using a clean, dry cloth, and working in a well-ventilated atmosphere.

7 Check the friction plate facings for signs of wear, damage or oil contamination. If the friction material is cracked, burnt, scored or damaged, or if it is contaminated with oil or grease (shown by shiny black patches), the friction plate must be renewed.

8 If the friction material is still serviceable, check that the centre boss splines are unworn, that the torsion springs are in good condition and securely fastened, and that all the rivets are tight. If any wear or damage is found, the friction plate must be renewed.

9 If the friction material is fouled with oil, this must be due to an oil leak from the crankshaft oil seal, from the sump-to-cylinder block joint, or from the release cylinder assembly (either the main seal or the sealing ring). Renew the crankshaft oil seal or repair the sump joint as described in Chapter 2, before installing the new friction plate. The clutch release cylinder is covered in Section 4.

10 Check the pressure plate assembly for obvious signs of wear or damage; shake it to check for loose rivets, or worn or damaged fulcrum rings, and check that the drive straps securing the pressure plate to the cover do not show signs of overheating (such as a deep yellow or blue discoloration). If the diaphragm spring is worn or damaged, or if its pressure is in any way suspect, the pressure plate assembly should be renewed.

11 Examine the machined bearing surfaces of the pressure plate and of the flywheel; they should be clean, completely flat, and free from

scratches or scoring. If either is discoloured from excessive heat, or shows signs of cracks, it should be renewed - although minor damage of this nature can sometimes be polished away using emery paper.

12 Check that the release cylinder bearing rotates smoothly and easily, with no sign of noise or roughness. Also check that the surface itself is smooth and unworn, with no signs of cracks, pitting or scoring. If there is any doubt about its condition, the clutch release cylinder should be renewed (it is not possible to renew the bearing separately).

Refitting

13 On reassembly, ensure that the bearing surfaces of the flywheel and pressure plate are completely clean, smooth, and free from oil or grease. Use solvent to remove any protective grease from new components.

14 Fit the friction plate so that its spring hub assembly faces away from the flywheel; there may also be a marking showing which way round the plate is to be refitted.

15 Refit the pressure plate assembly, aligning the marks made on dismantling (if the original pressure plate is re-used). Fit the pressure plate bolts, but tighten them only finger-tight so that the friction plate can still be moved.

16 The friction plate must now be centralised so that, when the transmission is refitted, its input shaft will pass through the splines at the centre of the friction plate.

17 Centralisation can be achieved by passing a screwdriver or other long bar through the friction plate and into the hole in the crankshaft; the friction plate can then be moved around until it is centred on the crankshaft hole. Alternatively, a clutch-aligning tool can be used to eliminate the guesswork; these can be obtained from most accessory shops. A home-made aligning tool can be fabricated from a length of metal rod or wooden dowel which fits closely inside the crankshaft hole, and has insulating tape wound around it to match the diameter of the friction plate splined hole.

18 When the friction plate is centralised, tighten the pressure plate bolts evenly and in a diagonal sequence to the specified torque setting.

19 Refit the transmission as described in Chapter 7.

Notes

Chapter 7 Part A:
Manual transmission

Contents

Degrees of difficulty

Easy, suitable for novice with little experience	Fairly easy, suitable for beginner with some experience	Fairly difficult, suitable for competent DIY mechanic	Difficult, suitable for experienced DIY mechanic	Very difficult, suitable for expert DIY or professional

Specifications

General

Type .... Manual, five forward speeds and reverse.
Synchromesh on all forward speeds

Identification code*:
  Petrol models:
    X16SZR F13
    X16XEL:
      Early models F15
      Later models F17
    X18XE1 .... F17
    X18XE and X20XEV F18
  Diesel models F18

*The transmission identification code is cast onto the top of the transmission housing, next to the selector mechanism cover

Lubrication

Oil type .... See "Weekly checks"
Oil capacity .... See Chapter 1A or 1B

Torque wrench settings

	Nm	lbf ft
Differential lower cover plate bolts:		
F18 transmission unit	40	30
All other transmission units:		
Models with an alloy cover plate	18	12
Models with a steel cover plate	30	22
Engine-to-transmission unit bolts:		
M8 bolts	20	15
M10 bolts	40	30
M12 bolts	60	44
Engine/transmission left-hand mounting bolts	60	44
Flywheel cover plate	8	6
Gearchange mechanism:		
Selector rod clamp bolt:		
Stage 1	12	9
Stage 2	Angle-tighten a further 180°	
Lever mounting bolts	6	4
Level plug	See Chapter 1A or 1B	
Reversing light switch	20	15
Roadwheel bolts	See Chapter 1A or 1B	

2.8a Unscrew the breather valve from the top of the transmission housing . . .

2.8b . . . and refill the transmission with the specified type and amount of oil

1 General information

1 The transmission is contained in a cast-aluminium alloy casing bolted to the engine's left-hand end, and consists of the gearbox and final drive differential - often called a transaxle.

2 Drive is transmitted from the crankshaft via the clutch to the input shaft, which has a splined extension to accept the clutch friction plate, and rotates in sealed ball-bearings. From the input shaft, drive is transmitted to the output shaft, which rotates in a roller bearing at its right-hand end, and a sealed ball-bearing at its left-hand end. From the output shaft, the drive is transmitted to the differential crownwheel, which rotates with the differential case and planetary gears, thus driving the sun gears and driveshafts. The rotation of the planetary gears on their shaft allows the inner roadwheel to rotate at a slower speed than the outer roadwheel when the car is cornering.

3 The input and output shafts are arranged side by side, parallel to the crankshaft and driveshafts, so that their gear pinion teeth are in constant mesh. In the neutral position, the output shaft gear pinions rotate freely, so that drive cannot be transmitted to the crownwheel.

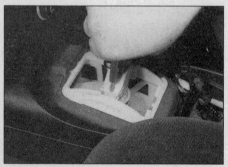

3.4 Lock the gearchange lever in position by inserting a punch through the clamp and locating it in the hole on the left-hand side of the lever

4 Gear selection is via a floor-mounted lever and selector linkage mechanism. The selector linkage cause the appropriate selector fork to move its respective synchro-sleeve along the shaft, to lock the gear pinion to the synchro-hub. Since the synchro-hubs are splined to the output shaft, this locks the pinion to the shaft, so that drive can be transmitted. To ensure that gear-changing can be made quickly and quietly, a synchro-mesh system is fitted to all forward gears, consisting of baulk rings and spring-loaded fingers, as well as the gear pinions and synchro-hubs. The synchro-mesh cones are formed on the mating faces of the baulk rings and gear pinions.

2 Transmission oil - draining and refilling

Note: *A new differential lower cover plate gasket will be required for this operation.*

1 Since the transmission oil is not renewed as part of the manufacturer's maintenance schedule, no drain plug is fitted to the transmission. If for any reason the transmission needs to be drained, the only way of doing so is to remove the differential lower cover plate.

2 This operation is much more efficient if the car is first taken on a journey of sufficient length to warm the engine/transmission up to normal operating temperature.

Caution: If the procedure is to be carried out on a hot transmission unit, take care not to burn yourself on the hot exhaust or the transmission/engine unit.

3 Park the car on level ground, switch off the ignition and apply the handbrake firmly. Jack up the front of the car and support it securely on axle stands. Where necessary, undo the retaining bolts and remove the undercover from beneath the engine/transmission unit.

4 Wipe clean the area around the differential cover plate and position a suitable container underneath the cover.

5 Evenly and progressively slacken and remove the retaining bolts then withdraw the cover plate and allow the transmission oil to drain in to the container. Remove the gasket and discard it; a new one should be used on refitting.

6 Allow the oil to drain completely into the container. If the oil is hot, take precautions against scalding. Remove all traces of dirt and oil from the cover and transmission mating surfaces and wipe clean the inside of the cover plate.

7 Once the oil has finished draining, ensure the mating surfaces are clean and dry then refit the cover plate to the transmission unit, complete with a new gasket. Refit the retaining bolts and evenly and progressively tighten them to the specified torque setting. Lower the vehicle to the ground.

8 The transmission is refilled via the breather aperture on the selector unit cover, on the top of the transmission. Wipe clean the area around the breather valve then unscrew the valve from the transmission unit. Refill the transmission with the specified type and amount of oil given in the Specifications, then refit the breather valve and tighten securely **(see illustrations)**.

9 Take the vehicle on a short journey so that the new oil is distributed fully around the transmission components.

10 On your return, park the vehicle on level ground and check the transmission oil level as described in Chapter 1.

3 Gearchange mechanism - adjustment

Note: *A 5 mm drill or punch will be required to carry out this procedure.*

1 Adjustment of the gearchange mechanism is not a routine operation and should only be needed if the mechanism has been removed. If the gearchange action is stiff or imprecise, check that it is correctly adjusted as follows.

2 The mechanism is adjusted via the clamp bolt which secures the selector rod to the transmission linkage (see Section 4). The bolt is located at the rear of the engine/transmission unit, just in front of the engine compartment bulkhead and, on most models, access to the bolt can be gained from above. If the bolt can not be reached from above, firmly apply the handbrake then jack up the front of the vehicle and support it securely on axle stands. Limited access can then be gained from underneath the vehicle.

3 Slacken the gearchange selector rod clamp bolt which is situated at the front of the rod. Do not remove the bolt completely.

4 From inside the vehicle, unclip the gearchange lever gaiter from the console and fold it back. Lock the gearchange lever in position by inserting a 5 mm drill or punch through the clamp on the left-hand side of the lever base and into its locating hole **(see illustration)**.

5 Lock the transmission selector mechanism in position by pressing in the spring-loaded locking pin on the selector mechanism cover, which is located on the top of the transmission unit **(see illustration)**.

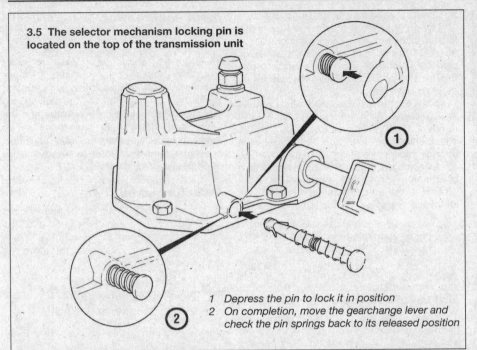

3.5 The selector mechanism locking pin is located on the top of the transmission unit

1 *Depress the pin to lock it in position*
2 *On completion, move the gearchange lever and check the pin springs back to its released position*

3 Using paint or a suitable marker pen, make alignment marks between the selector rod and the clamp on the front end of the rod. Loosen the clamp bolt by a couple of turns but do not remove it completely **(see illustration)**. Move the gearchange lever into the 4th gear position then free the selector rod from the clamp and slide off the rubber gaiter.
4 Remove the centre console as described in Chapter 11.
5 Undo the retaining screws and remove the switch panel from around the gearchange lever, disconnecting the wiring connectors as they become accessible (see Chapter 12).
6 Slacken and remove the four bolts securing the gearchange lever to the floor then manoeuvre the lever and selector rod assembly out of position.
7 To dismantle the lever and rod assembly, carefully release the retaining clip from the base of the lever then separate the rod and lever and remove them from the housing. Examine all components for signs of wear or damage, paying particular attention to the selector rod and lever locating pivot bushes, and renew as necessary.

Transmission linkage assembly

Note: *A new linkage to transmission lever pivot pin should be used on refitting.*

8 Separate the selector rod from its clamp as described in paragraph 3. The bolt is located at the rear of the engine/transmission unit, just in front of the engine compartment bulkhead and on most models access to the bolt can be gained from above. If the bolt can not be reached from above, firmly apply the handbrake then jack up the front of the vehicle and support it securely on axle stands. Limited access can then be gained from underneath the vehicle.
9 Depress the detent mechanism and remove the pivot pin connecting the linkage to the selector lever on the top of the transmission unit **(see illustrations)**. Discard the pivot pin, a new one should be used on refitting.
10 Slide off the retaining clips securing the linkage bracket to its mountings then manoeuvre the assembly upwards and out of position **(see illustration)**. If necessary, the mounting brackets can then be unbolted and removed.

6 With both the lever and transmission locked in position, tighten the selector rod clamp bolt to the specified torque stage 1 setting then tighten it through the specified stage 2 angle.
7 Remove the locking rod from the gearchange lever and check the operation of the gearchange mechanism; the transmission locking pin will automatically release when the lever is moved into the reverse position.
8 Ensure the transmission locking pin has released then (where necessary) lower the vehicle to the ground.

---

4 Gearchange mechanism - removal and refitting

Removal

1 The gearchange mechanism consists of the gearchange lever, the selector rod and the linkage assembly on the transmission. The lever and selector rod and the linkage assembly can be removed separately.

Gearchange lever and selector rod

2 Firmly apply the handbrake then jack up the front of the vehicle and support it on axle stands. Where necessary, undo the retaining bolts and remove the undercover from beneath the engine/transmission unit.

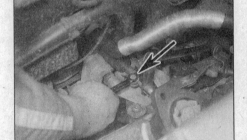

4.3 Slacken the clamp bolt (arrowed) securing the transmission linkage to the selector rod

4.9a Withdraw the pin connecting the linkage to the transmission unit selector lever . . .

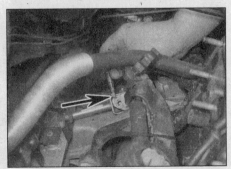

4.9b . . . noting that it is necessary to depress the detent mechanism (arrowed) in order to release the pin

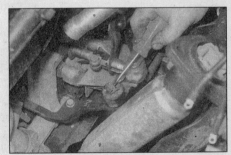

4.10 Carefully slide off the retaining clips securing the linkage bracket to its mountings and remove the assembly from the engine compartment

7A

4.11 Examine the linkage assembly for signs of wear and renew worn components as necessary

11 Examine the linkage assembly closely for signs of wear or damage, renewing worn components as necessary **(see illustration)**.

Refitting

Gearchange lever and selector rod

12 If necessary, reassemble the lever and rod, making sure the lever base is correctly located in the housing pivot, and secure them in position with the retaining clip.
13 Lubricate all pivot points and bearing surfaces with silicone grease then manoeuvre the assembly into position. Refit the housing retaining bolts and tighten them to the specified torque setting.
14 Refit the switch panel, making sure its wiring is correctly routed, then refit the centre console as described in Chapter 11.
15 From underneath the vehicle, slide the rubber gaiter onto the end of the selector rod and locate it securely in the bulkhead.
16 Engage the selector rod end with its linkage clamp. Align the marks made prior to removal and tighten the clamp bolt to the specified stage 1 torque then tighten it through the specified stage 2 angle.
17 Check the gearchange mechanism operation before lowering the vehicle to the ground. If the mechanism seems notchy or imprecise, adjust it as described in Section 3.

Transmission linkage assembly

18 Prior to refitting, lubricate the balljoints and pivot points with silicone grease.
19 Manoeuvre the assembly into position and locate the linkage bracket on its mountings.

Secure the assembly in position with the retaining clips, ensuring they are correctly located in the mounting bracket pin grooves.
20 Align the linkage with the transmission selector lever and insert the new pivot pin. Ensure the pin is securely retained by its detent mechanism.
21 Engage the selector rod end with its linkage clamp. Align the marks made prior to removal and tighten the clamp bolt to the specified stage 1 torque then tighten it through the specified stage 2 angle.
22 Check the gearchange mechanism operation before lowering the vehicle to the ground. If the mechanism seems notchy or imprecise, adjust it as described in Section 3.

5 Oil seals - renewal

Driveshaft oil seals

1 Chock the rear wheels, apply the handbrake, then jack up the front of the car and support it on axle stands. Remove the appropriate front roadwheel.
2 Drain the transmission oil as described in Section 2 or be prepared for oil loss as the seal is changed.
3 Remove the driveshaft as described in Chapter 8.
4 Note the correct fitted depth of the seal in its housing then carefully prise it out of position using a large flat-bladed screwdriver **(see illustration)**.
5 Remove all traces of dirt from the area around the oil seal aperture, then apply a smear of grease to the outer lip of the new oil seal. Ensure the seal is correctly positioned, with its sealing lip facing inwards, and tap it squarely into position, using a suitable tubular drift (such as a socket) which bears only on the hard outer edge of the seal **(see illustration)**. Ensure the seal is fitted at the same depth in its housing that the original was.
6 Refit the driveshaft as described in Chapter 8.
7 If the transmission was drained, refill the transmission with the specified type and amount of oil, as described in Section 2. If the oil was not drained top-up the transmission oil level and check as described in Chapter 1.

Input shaft oil seal

8 The input shaft oil seal is an integral part of the clutch release cylinder; if the seal is leaking the complete release cylinder assembly must be renewed. Before condemning the release cylinder, check that the leak is not coming from the sealing ring which is fitted between the cylinder and the transmission housing; the sealing ring can be renewed once the release cylinder assembly has been removed. Refer to Chapter 6 for removal and refitting details.

Selector rod oil seal

9 Renewal of the selector rod oil seal requires the selector mechanism cover to be unbolted from the transmission and dismantled. This is a difficult task and should therefore be entrusted to a Vauxhall dealer.

6 Reversing light switch - testing, removal and refitting

Testing

1 The reversing light circuit is controlled by a plunger-type switch that is screwed into the top of the transmission, towards the front of the housing. If a fault develops in the circuit, ensure that the fuse (No. 29) has not blown.
2 To test the switch, disconnect the wiring connector. Use a multimeter (set to the resistance function) or a battery-and-bulb test circuit to check that there is continuity between the switch terminals only when reverse gear is selected. If this is not the case, and there are no obvious breaks or other damage to the wires, the switch is faulty, and must be renewed.

Removal

3 To improve access to the switch, remove the battery and mounting plate (see Chapter 5).
4 Disconnect the wiring connector, then unscrew the switch and remove it from the transmission casing along with its sealing washer **(see illustration)**.

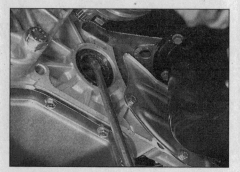

5.4 Prising out a driveshaft oil seal

5.5 Fitting a new driveshaft oil seal using a socket as a tubular drift

6.4 The reversing light switch is screwed into the top of the transmission (shown with battery and mounting plate removed)

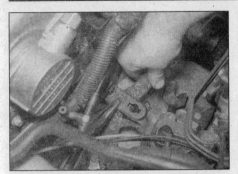

7.4 Disconnect the reversing light switch wiring connector and free the wiring from its retaining clips

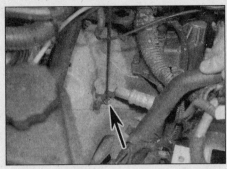

7.5a Carefully prise out the retaining clip (arrowed) . . .

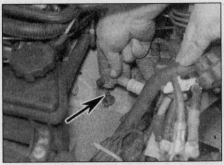

7.5b . . . then free the clutch pipe/hose end fitting from the transmission, noting the sealing ring (arrowed)

Refitting

5 Fit a new sealing washer to the switch, then screw it back into position in the top of the transmission housing and tighten it to the specified torque. Reconnect the wiring connector, then refit the battery (where removed) and test the operation of the circuit.

---

7 Transmission - removal and refitting

Removal

1 Chock the rear wheels, then firmly apply the handbrake. Jack up the front of the vehicle, and securely support it on axle stands. Remove both front roadwheels then, where necessary, undo the retaining bolts and remove the undercover from beneath the engine/transmission unit.

2 Drain the transmission oil as described in Section 2 or be prepared for oil loss as the transmission is removed.

3 Remove the battery and mounting plate and the starter motor (see Chapter 5).

4 Disconnect the wiring connector from the reversing light switch and free the wiring from the transmission unit and mounting brackets **(see illustration)**.

5 Minimise clutch fluid loss by clamping the master cylinder supply hose, which is connected to the side of the brake/clutch fluid reservoir. Prise out the retaining clip securing the clutch hydraulic pipe/hose end fitting to the top of the transmission bellhousing and detach the end fitting from the transmission. Clip the retaining clip back into position in the end fitting and discard the sealing ring from the pipe end; a new sealing ring must be used on refitting **(see illustrations)**. Plug/cover both the union and pipe ends to minimise fluid loss and prevent the entry of dirt into the hydraulic system. **Note:** *Whilst the hose/pipe is disconnected, do not depress the clutch pedal.*

6 Remove the gearchange mechanism linkage assembly from the top of the transmission unit as described in Section 4.

7 Remove the front suspension subframe assembly as described in Chapter 10, ensuring that the engine unit is securely supported **(see illustration)**.

8 Referring to Chapter 8, free the driveshaft inner constant velocity joints from the transmission unit and position them clear. Note that it is not necessary to remove the driveshafts, then can be left attached to the hub assemblies. **Note:** *Do not allow the shafts to hang down under their own weight as this could damage the constant velocity*

joints/gaiters. If the transmission has not been drained be prepared for fluid loss.

9 Undo the retaining bolts and remove the front, left-hand engine/transmission mounting assembly from the front of the transmission housing **(see illustration)**.

10 On models where a pressed steel sump is fitted to the engine, unbolt the flywheel cover plate and remove it from the base of the transmission unit.

11 On all models, place a jack with a block of wood beneath the transmission, and raise the jack to take the weight of the transmission.

12 Slacken and remove the upper and lower bolts securing the transmission housing to the engine. Note the correct fitted positions of each bolt, and the necessary brackets, as they are removed, to use as a reference on refitting. Make a final check that all components have been disconnected, and are positioned clear of the transmission so that they will not hinder the removal procedure.

13 With the bolts removed, move the trolley jack and transmission to the right, to free it from its locating dowels. Once the transmission is free, lower the jack and manoeuvre the unit out from under the car **(see illustration)**. Remove the locating dowels from the transmission or engine if they are loose, and keep them in a safe place.

7.7 Ensure that the engine unit is securely supported before removing the front suspension subframe

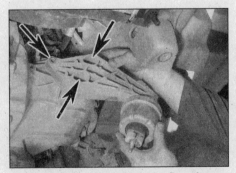

7.9 Undo the retaining bolts (locations arrowed) and remove the left-hand mounting assembly from the front of the transmission housing

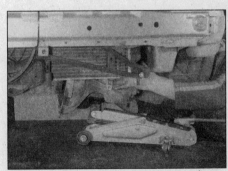

7.13 Free the transmission unit from the engine then lower it out of position and remove it from underneath the vehicle

7A

Refitting

14 The transmission is refitted by a reversal of the removal procedure, bearing in mind the following points.

a) *Ensure the locating dowels are correctly positioned prior to installation.*

b) *Tighten all nuts and bolts to the specified torque (where given).*

c) *Renew the driveshaft oil seals (see Section 5) before refitting the driveshafts.*

d) *Refit the front suspension subframe assembly as described in Chapter 10.*

e) *Fit a new sealing ring to the transmission clutch hydraulic pipe before clipping the hose/pipe end fitting into position. Ensure the end fitting is securely retained by its clip then bleed the hydraulic system as described in Chapter 6.*

f) *If the transmission was drained, refill the transmission with the specified type and amount of oil, as described in Section 2. If the oil was not drained, top-up the transmission oil and check the level as described in Chapter 1.*

g) *On completion, adjust the gearchange mechanism as described in Section 3.*

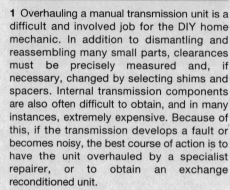

8 Transmission overhaul - general information

1 Overhauling a manual transmission unit is a difficult and involved job for the DIY home mechanic. In addition to dismantling and reassembling many small parts, clearances must be precisely measured and, if necessary, changed by selecting shims and spacers. Internal transmission components are also often difficult to obtain, and in many instances, extremely expensive. Because of this, if the transmission develops a fault or becomes noisy, the best course of action is to have the unit overhauled by a specialist repairer, or to obtain an exchange reconditioned unit.

2 Nevertheless, it is not impossible for the more experienced mechanic to overhaul the transmission, provided the special tools are available, and the job is done in a deliberate step-by-step manner, so that nothing is overlooked.

3 The tools necessary for an overhaul include internal and external circlip pliers, bearing pullers, a slide hammer, a set of pin punches, a dial test indicator, and possibly a hydraulic press. In addition, a large, sturdy workbench and a vice will be required.

4 During dismantling of the transmission, make careful notes of how each component is fitted, to make reassembly easier and more accurate.

5 Before dismantling the transmission, it will help if you have some idea what area is malfunctioning. Certain problems can be closely related to specific areas in the transmission, which can make component examination and replacement easier. Refer to the Fault diagnosis Section of this manual for more information.

Chapter 7 Part B:
Automatic transmission

Contents

Degrees of difficulty

Easy, suitable for novice with little experience	**Fairly easy,** suitable for beginner with some experience	**Fairly difficult,** suitable for competent DIY mechanic	**Difficult,** suitable for experienced DIY mechanic	**Very difficult,** suitable for expert DIY or professional

Specifications

General

Type . . . . Four-speed electronically-controlled automatic with three (normal, sport and winter) driving modes

Identification code*:
    1.6 litre (X16XEL and X16SZR) models AF13
    1.8 litre (X18XE1) models AF17
    1.8 and 2.0 litre (X18XE and X20XEV) models AF20
*The identification code is marked on the identification plate which is attached to the top of the transmission unit

Lubrication

Fluid type . . . . See "Weekly checks"
Fluid capacity . . . . See Chapter 1A

Torque wrench settings	Nm	lbf ft
Drain plug	35	26
Engine-to-transmission unit bolts:		
M8 bolts	20	15
M10 bolts	40	30
M12 bolts:		
1.6 litre models	60	44
1.8 and 2.0 litre models	75	55
Engine/transmission left-hand mounting bolts	60	44
Fluid filler tube to selector lever position switch (AF20)	20	15
Fluid filler tube to transmission (AF13/17)	75	55
Fluid lines to transmission or fluid cooler	22	16
Fluid pump to transmission	25	18
Fluid temperature sensor	25	18
Input shaft speed sensor bolt	6	4
Output shaft speed sensor bolt	6	4
Selector lever:		
Pivot crank nut	28	23
Lever-to-vehicle body bolts	10	7
Torque converter-to-driveplate bolts	55	41
Transmission selector shaft nuts:		
Main (starter/reversing light switch) nut	8	6
Selector lever nut	16	12
Starter inhibitor/reversing light switch bolt	25	18

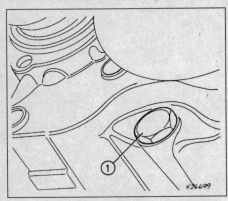

2.3 Automatic transmission fluid drain plug (1)

1 General information

1 Most models covered in this manual were offered with the option of a four-speed, electronically-controlled automatic transmission, consisting of a torque converter, an epicyclic geartrain, and hydraulically-operated clutches and brakes. The unit is controlled by the electronic control unit (ECU) via four electrically-operated solenoid valves. The transmission unit has three driving modes; normal (economy), sport and winter modes.

2 The normal (economy) mode is the standard mode for driving in which the transmission shifts up at relatively low engine speeds to combine reasonable performance with economy. If the transmission unit is switched into sport mode, using the button on the selector lever, the transmission shifts up only at high engine speeds, giving improved acceleration and overtaking performance. When the transmission is in sport mode, the indicator light in the instrument panel is illuminated. If the transmission is switched into winter mode, using the button on the selector lever indicator panel, the

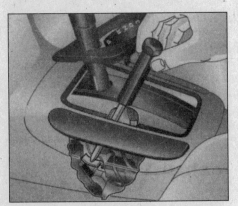

3.0 If it is necessary to move the selector lever from the 'P' position with the battery disconnected, manually release the detent lever as shown

transmission will select third gear as the vehicle pulls away from a standing start; this helps to maintain traction on very slippery surfaces.

3 The torque converter provides a fluid coupling between engine and transmission, which acts as an automatic clutch, and also provides a degree of torque multiplication when accelerating.

4 The epicyclic geartrain provides either of the four forward or one reverse gear ratios, according to which of its component parts are held stationary or allowed to turn. The components of the geartrain are held or released by brakes and clutches which are activated by the control unit. A fluid pump within the transmission provides the necessary hydraulic pressure to operate the brakes and clutches.

5 Driver control of the transmission is by a seven-position selector lever. The 'drive' D position, allows automatic changing throughout the range of all four gear ratios. An automatic kickdown facility shifts the transmission down a gear if the accelerator pedal is fully depressed. The transmission also has three 'hold' positions, 1 means only the first gear ratio can be selected, 2 allows both the first and second gear ratios position to be automatically selected and 3 allows automatic changing between the first three gear ratios. These 'hold' positions are useful for providing engine braking when travelling down steep gradients. Note, however, that the transmission should *never* be shifted down a position at high engine speeds.

6 Due to the complexity of the automatic transmission, any repair or overhaul work must be left to a Vauxhall dealer with the necessary special equipment for fault diagnosis and repair. The contents of the following Sections are therefore confined to supplying general information, and any service information and instructions that can be used by the owner.

2 Transmission fluid - draining and refilling

Draining

1 This operation is much quicker and more efficient if the vehicle is first taken on a journey of sufficient length to warm the engine/transmission up to normal operating temperature.

2 Park the vehicle on level ground, switch off the ignition, and apply the handbrake firmly. For improved access, jack up the front of the car and support it securely on axle stands.

3 Withdraw the dipstick, then position a container under the drain plug at the rear right-hand side of the transmission, below the driveshaft. Unscrew the plug and remove it along with its sealing washer **(see illustration)**.

4 Allow the fluid to drain completely into the container. If the fluid is hot, take precautions against scalding.

5 When the fluid has finished draining, clean the drain plug threads and those of the transmission casing, fit a new sealing washer and refit the drain plug, tightening it to the specified torque wrench setting. Where applicable, lower the vehicle to the ground.

Refilling

6 Refilling the transmission is an awkward operation, adding the specified type and amount of fluid to the transmission a little at a time via the dipstick tube. Use a funnel with a fine mesh gauze, to avoid spillage, and to ensure that no foreign matter enters the transmission. Allow plenty of time for the fluid level to settle properly.

7 Start the engine, and allow it to idle for a few minutes whilst moving the selector lever through its various positions. Switch off the engine and add sufficient fluid to bring the level up to the lower mark on the dipstick. Take the car on a short run to fully distribute the new fluid around the transmission, then recheck the fluid level as described in Chapter 1 with the transmission at normal operating temperature.

3 Selector cable - adjustment

Note: *If the battery is disconnected with the selector lever in the 'P' position, the lever will be locked in position. To manually release the lever, carefully prise out the selector lever surround from the top of the centre console then, using a flat-bladed screwdriver, depress the detent lever on the left-hand side of the selector lever* **(see illustration)**.

1 Operate the selector lever throughout its entire range and check that the transmission engages the correct gear indicated on the selector lever position indicator. If adjustment is necessary, continue as follows.

2 Position the selector lever in the 'P' (park) position.

3 Working in the engine compartment, to gain access to the transmission end of the selector cable, remove the battery and mounting plate (see Chapter 5).

4 Locate the selector cable mounting bracket on the top of the transmission unit and release the inner cable by carefully lifting the locking clip in the cable end fitting **(see illustration)**.

5 Ensure that the selector lever is locked in the 'P' position and move the lever on the transmission selector mechanism fully forwards so that the transmission is also positioned in the park position **(see illustration)**. With both the selector lever and transmission correctly positioned, lock the cable adjuster in position by pushing the locking clip firmly down until it clicks in position.

6 Refit the battery then check the operation of the selector lever and, if necessary, repeat the adjustment procedure.

4 Selector cable - removal and refitting

Removal

1 Remove the centre console as described in Chapter 11 then position the selector lever in the 'P' (park) position.

2 Using a flat-bladed screwdriver, carefully lever the selector cable end fitting off from the balljoint from the base of the lever. Slide out the retaining clip and release the cable from the front of the lever mounting plate **(see illustration)**.

3 Working in the engine compartment, to gain access to the transmission end of the selector cable, remove the battery and mounting plate (see Chapter 5).

4 Slide off the retaining clip (where fitted) then carefully unclip the selector cable end fitting from the transmission lever. Unclip the outer cable from its mounting bracket.

5 Work back along the cable, noting its correct routing, and free it from all the relevant retaining clips. Free the cable grommet from the bulkhead and remove it from the vehicle.

6 Examine the cable, looking for worn end fittings or a damaged outer casing, and for signs of fraying of the inner cable. Check the cable's operation; the inner cable should move smoothly and easily through the outer casing. Remember that a cable that appears serviceable when tested off the car may well be much heavier in operation when curved into its working position. Renew the cable if it shows any signs of excessive wear or any damage.

Refitting

7 Manoeuvre the cable into position, ensuring it is correctly routed and pass it through the bulkhead. Ensure the cable passes through the selector lever mounting plate then locate the grommet securely in the bulkhead.

8 Pass the transmission end of the cable through its mounting bracket and clip the outer cable securely in position. Align the inner cable end fitting with the transmission lever then clip it on the lever and (where necessary) secure it in position with the retaining clip.

9 From inside the vehicle, secure the outer cable in position with the retaining clip, and clip the inner cable end fitting securely onto the selector lever balljoint.

10 Adjust the selector cable as described in Section 3

11 Refit the centre console, as described in Chapter 11, and refit all components removed to gain access to the transmission end of the cable.

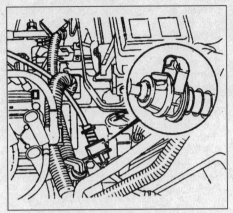

3.4 Release the selector cable inner cable by lifting the locking clip (inset)

5 Selector lever assembly - removal and refitting

Note: *Renewal of the sport and winter mode switches is covered in Section 8*

Removal

1 Remove the centre console, as described in Chapter 11, then position the selector lever in the 'P' (park) position.

2 Disconnect the wiring connectors from the selector lever mode switches and free the bulbholder from the indicator panel.

3 Using a flat-bladed screwdriver, carefully lever the selector cable end fitting off from the balljoint from the base of the lever. Slide out the retaining clip and release the cable from the front of the lever mounting plate.

4 Slacken and remove the mounting bolts then manoeuvre the lever assembly out of position.

5 Inspect the selector lever mechanism for signs of wear or damage. To dismantle, slacken and remove the nut and washer then withdraw the pivot crank assembly. Unclip the indicator panel then separate the lever

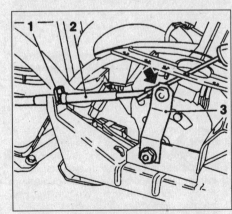

4.2 Remove the retaining clip (1) then lever the selector cable (2) off from the selector lever balljoint (3)

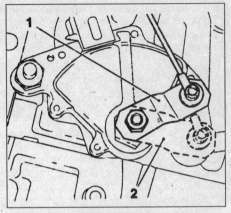

3.5 Move the transmission selector lever (1) fully forwards so that it is in the 'P' position (2)

assembly and mounting plate. No further dismantling is possible.

Refitting

6 Where necessary, reassemble the lever and mounting plate and insert the pivot crank. Ensure the crank is correctly engaged with the selector lever then refit the washer and tighten its retaining nut to the specified torque. Clip the indicator panel onto the mounting plate then check the operation of the lever before refitting it to the car.

7 Manoeuvre the lever assembly into position, engage it with the selector cable. Refit the retaining bolts and tighten them to the specified torque setting.

8 Secure the outer cable in position with the retaining clip and securely clip the cable end fitting onto the selector lever crank balljoint.

9 Ensuring the wiring is correctly routed, refit the bulbholder to the indicator panel and reconnect the switch wiring connectors.

10 Adjust the selector cable, as described in Section 3, then refit the centre console as described in Chapter 11.

6 Oil seals - renewal

Driveshaft oil seals

1 Refer to Chapter 7A.

Torque converter oil seal

2 Remove the transmission as described in Section 9.

3 Carefully slide the torque converter off of the transmission shaft whilst being prepared for fluid spillage.

4 Note the correct fitted position of the seal in the oil pump housing then carefully lever the seal out of position taking care not to mark the housing or input shaft.

5 Remove all traces of dirt from the area around the oil seal aperture then press the new seal into position, ensuring its sealing lip is facing inwards.

7B

6 Lubricate the seal with clean transmission fluid then carefully ease the torque converter into position.

7 Refit the transmission (see Section 9).

7 Fluid cooler - general information

1 The transmission fluid cooler is an integral part of the radiator assembly. Refer to Chapter 3 for removal and refitting details, if the cooler is damaged the complete radiator assembly must be renewed.

8 Transmission control system electrical components - removal and refitting

Starter inhibitor/ reversing light switch

1 The switch is a dual-function switch, performing the reversing light and starter inhibitor switch functions. The switch operates the reversing lights when reverse gear is selected and prevents the engine being started when the transmission is in gear. If at any time the reversing light operation becomes faulty, or it is noted that the engine can be started with the selector lever in any position other than 'P' (park) or 'N' (neutral), then it is likely that the switch is faulty. If adjustment fails to correct the fault then the complete switch must be renewed as a unit.

Removal

2 Position the selector lever in the 'N' (neutral) position.

3 To gain access to the switch, remove the battery and mounting plate as described in Chapter 5.

4 Slide off the retaining clip (where fitted) then carefully unclip the selector cable end fitting from the transmission lever. Unscrew the retaining nut and remove the lever from the transmission selector shaft.

5 Trace the wiring back from the switch and disconnect it at the wiring connector.

6 On AF20 transmissions, withdraw the fluid dipstick then undo the retaining nut and ease the dipstick out from the transmission. Remove the dipstick seal and discard it; a new one should be used on refitting.

7 Bend back the lockwasher (where fitted) then slacken and remove the main nut and washer(s) from the transmission selector shaft.

8 Slacken and remove the switch and wiring retaining plate bolts, and manoeuvre the switch assembly upwards and away from the transmission unit.

Refitting

9 Prior to refitting, first make sure that the transmission selector shaft is still in the 'N' (neutral) position. If there is any doubt, engage the selector lever with the transmission shaft and move the lever fully forwards (to the 'P' position) then move it two notches backwards.

10 Locate the switch on the transmission shaft then refit the wiring retaining plate. Refit the retaining bolts, tightening them by hand only at this stage.

11 Refit the washer(s) and main nut to the selector shaft. Tighten the nut to the specified torque setting and secure it in position by bending up the locking washer against one of its flats.

12 Adjust the switch as described in paragraph 18.

13 Once the switch is correctly adjusted, reconnect the wiring connector, ensuring that the wiring is correctly routed.

14 On AF20 transmission, fit a new seal to the transmission aperture then ease the dipstick tube into position. Securely tighten the dipstick retaining nut then refit the dipstick.

15 Refit the selector lever to the shaft and tighten its retaining nut to the specified torque. Clip the selector cable end fitting securely onto the lever balljoint.

16 Refit the battery and check the operation of the switch. If necessary, adjust the selector cable as described in Section 3.

Adjustment

Note: *Before adjusting the switch first ensure the selector cable is correctly adjusted (see Section 3).*

17 Carry out the operations described in paragraphs 2 to 4.

18 With the transmission in neutral, the flats on the selector shaft should be parallel to the marking on the switch assembly **(see illustration)**. If adjustment is necessary, slacken the switch retaining bolts and rotate the switch assembly as necessary before retightening the bolts to the specified torque setting.

19 Refit the selector lever to the shaft and tighten its retaining nut to the specified torque. Refit the selector cable end fitting securely onto the lever and (where necessary) secure it in position with the retaining clip.

20 Refit the battery and check the operation of the switch. If adjustment of the switch has not been successful, then the switch must be faulty and should be renewed.

Sport mode switch

Note: *A soldering iron and solder will be required to renew the switch.*

Removal

21 Remove the selector lever assembly as described in Section 5.

22 Push the switch out of the top of the selector lever by inserting a length of welding rod up through the selector lever bore **(see illustration)**.

23 Make identification marks between the switch and wires then carefully unsolder the wires from the switch terminals and remove the switch. The wiring can then be withdrawn from the base of the lever.

Refitting

24 Feed the wiring up through the selector lever bore until it appears at the top. Solder the wires to the terminals of the switch, using the marks made prior to removal to ensure they are correctly connected.

25 Push the switch securely into position then refit the selector lever as described in Section 5.

Winter mode switch

Removal

26 Unclip the storage compartment from the centre console to gain access to the selector lever trim cover screws. Slacken and remove the two screws from the rear of the cover and lift the cover off of the lever.

27 Release the retaining clips and free the selector lever position indicator panel from the lever mounting plate.

28 Trace the wiring back from the switch and disconnect it at the wiring connector. Unclip the switch from the indicator panel and remove it from the vehicle.

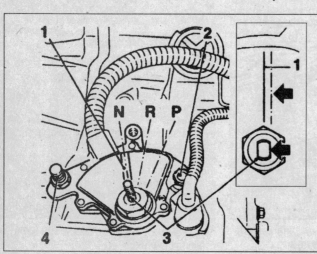

8.18 Starter inhibitor/ reversing light switch adjustment details

1 *Switch assembly marking*
2 *Retaining bolt*
3 *Selector shaft*
4 *Retaining bolt*

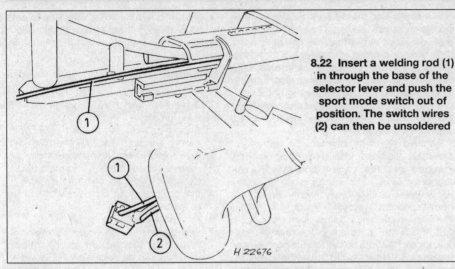

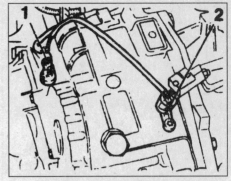

8.22 Insert a welding rod (1) in through the base of the selector lever and push the sport mode switch out of position. The switch wires (2) can then be unsoldered

8.35 Transmission input shaft speed sensor (1) and output shaft speed sensor (2) locations

Refitting

29 Refitting is the reverse of removal, ensuring the wiring is correctly routed.

Kickdown switch

30 The kickdown switch is an integral part of the accelerator cable and cannot be renewed separately. Refer to Chapter 4 for details of accelerator cable removal and refitting.

Electronic control unit (ECU)

Removal

31 The ECU is located in the front passenger footwell. Prior to removal, disconnect the battery negative terminal.

32 Prise out the retaining clips and remove the undercover from the passenger side of the facia. Remove the glovebox from the facia (see Chapter 11) to gain access to the ECU.

33 Release the retaining clip and disconnect the wiring connector from the ECU. Release the mounting bracket from the body and remove the ECU from the vehicle.

Refitting

34 Refitting is the reverse of removal, ensuring that the wiring is securely reconnected.

Transmission input and output shaft speed sensors

Removal

35 The speed sensors are fitted to the top of the transmission unit. The input shaft speed sensor is the front of the two sensors and is nearest to the left-hand end of the transmission. The output shaft sensor is the rear of the two (see illustration).

36 To gain access to the sensors, remove the battery and mounting plate as described in Chapter 5. Access can be further improved by unclipping the coolant expansion tank from its mountings and positioning it clear.

37 Disconnect the wiring connector and wipe clean the area around the relevant sensor.

38 Undo the retaining bolt and remove the sensor from the transmission. Remove the

sealing ring from the sensor and discard it, a new one should be used on refitting.

Refitting

39 Fit the new sealing ring to the sensor groove and lubricate it with a smear of transmission fluid.

40 Ease the sensor into position then refit the retaining bolt and tighten it to the specified torque setting. Reconnect the wiring connector.

41 Refit the battery and clip the expansion tank (where necessary) back into position.

Transmission fluid temperature sensor

Removal

42 The fluid temperature sensor is screwed into the base of the transmission unit, at the front. Before removing the sensor, disconnect the battery negative terminal.

43 Firmly apply the handbrake then jack up the front of the vehicle and support it on axle stands.

44 Trace the wiring back from the sensor, noting its correct routing. Disconnect the wiring connector and free the wiring from its retaining clips.

45 Undo the retaining bolts and remove the cover plate from the sensor (see illustration).

46 Wipe clean the area around the sensor and have a suitable plug ready to minimise fluid loss as the sensor is removed (see illustration).

47 Unscrew the sensor and remove it from the transmission unit along with its sealing washer. Quickly plug the transmission aperture and wipe up any spilt fluid.

Refitting

48 Fit a new sealing washer to the sensor then remove the plug and quickly screw the sensor into the transmission unit. Tighten the sensor to the specified torque and wipe up any spilt fluid. Refit the cover plate and securely tighten its retaining bolts.

49 Ensure the wiring is correctly routed and retained by all the necessary clips then securely reconnect the wiring connector.

50 Lower the vehicle to the floor and reconnect the battery. Check the transmission fluid level as described in Chapter 1.

9 Automatic transmission - removal and refitting

Note: New torque converter-to-driveplate bolts and fluid cooler union sealing rings will be required on refitting.

Removal

1 Chock the rear wheels, apply the handbrake, and place the selector lever in the 'N' (neutral) position. Jack up the front of the vehicle, and securely support it on axle stands. Remove both front roadwheels then remove the retaining screws and fasteners

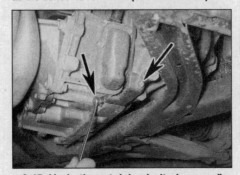

8.45 Undo the retaining bolts (arrowed) and remove the cover plate . . .

8.46 . . . to gain access to the fluid temperature sensor (arrowed)

7B

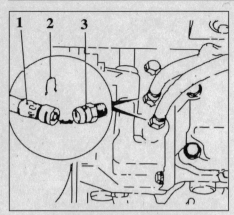

9.8a Transmission fluid cooler hose connections - 1.6 litre models

1 Hose end fitting
2 Retaining clip
3 Transmission union

and (where necessary) remove the undercover from beneath the engine/transmission unit.

2 Drain the transmission fluid as described in Section 2, then refit the drain plug and tighten it to the specified torque.

3 Remove the battery and mounting plate, and the starter motor as described in Chapter 5. To further improve access, unclip the coolant expansion tank from its mountings.

4 On 1.6 litre models, remove the DIS ignition module as described in Chapter 5.

5 Slide off the retaining clip (where fitted) then carefully unclip the selector cable end fitting from the transmission lever. Unclip the outer cable from its mounting bracket and position the cable clear of the transmission unit.

6 Trace the wiring back from the transmission switches and sensors and disconnect the various connectors by lifting their retaining clips. Release the main wiring harness from any clips or ties securing it to the transmission unit.

7 Disconnect the breather hose (where fitted) from the top of the transmission unit.

8 Make identification marks between the oil

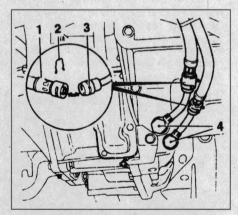

9.8b Transmission fluid cooler hose connections - 1.8 and 2.0 litre models

1 Hose end fitting
2 Retaining clip
3 Pipe end fitting
4 Transmission unions

cooler hoses and their unions on the front of the transmission housing. Using a flat-bladed screwdriver, prise out the retaining clips from each hose end fitting and detach both hoses from the transmission **(see illustrations)**. Clip the retaining clips back into position in the end fittings and discard the sealing rings; new sealing rings must be used on refitting. Plug/cover both the union and hose ends to prevent the entry of dirt.

9 Remove the front suspension subframe assembly as described in Chapter 10, ensuring that the engine unit is securely supported.

10 Referring to Chapter 8, free the driveshaft inner constant velocity joints from the transmission unit and position them clear. Note that it is not necessary to remove the driveshafts, then can be left attached to the hub assemblies. **Note:** *Do not allow the shafts to hang down under their own weight as this could damage the constant velocity joints/gaiters.*

11 Undo the retaining bolts and remove the left-hand engine/transmission mounting assembly from the front of the transmission housing.

12 Remove the rubber cover(s) from the cylinder block/sump flange to gain access to the torque converter retaining bolts. Slacken and remove the visible bolt(s) then, using a socket and extension bar to rotate the crankshaft pulley, undo the remaining bolts securing the torque converter to the driveplate as they become accessible. On 1.6 litre models there are three bolts in total and on 1.8 and 2.0 litre models there are six. Discard the bolts, new ones must be used on refitting.

13 To ensure that the torque converter does not fall out as the transmission is removed, slide the converter along the shaft and fully into the transmission housing.

14 Place a jack with a block of wood beneath the transmission, and raise the jack to take the weight of the transmission.

15 With the jack positioned beneath the transmission taking the weight, slacken and remove the upper and lower bolts securing the transmission housing to the engine. Note the correct fitted positions of each bolt, and the necessary brackets, as they are removed, to use as a reference on refitting. Make a final check that all components have been disconnected, and are positioned clear of the transmission so that they will not hinder the removal procedure.

16 With all the bolts removed, move the trolley jack and transmission to the right, to free it from its locating dowels. Once the transmission is free, lower the jack and manoeuvre the unit out from under the car, taking care to ensure that the torque

converter does not fall off. Remove the locating dowels from the transmission or engine if they are loose, and keep them in a safe place.

Refitting

17 The transmission is refitted by a reversal of the removal procedure, bearing in mind the following points.

a) *Prior to refitting, remove all traces of old locking compound from the torque converter threads by running a tap of the correct thread diameter and pitch down the holes. In the absence of a suitable tap, use one of the old bolts with slots cut in its threads.*

b) *Prior to refitting, ensure the engine/transmission locating dowels are correctly positioned and apply a smear of molybdenum disulphide grease to the torque converter locating pin and its centring bush in the crankshaft end.*

c) *Once the transmission and engine are correctly joined, refit the securing bolts, tightening them to the specified torque setting.*

d) *Fit the new torque converter to driveplate bolts and tighten them lightly only to start then go around and tighten them to the specified torque setting in a diagonal sequence.*

e) *Tighten all nuts and bolts to the specified torque (where given).*

f) *Renew the driveshaft oil seals (see Chapter 7A) and refit the driveshafts to the transmission as described in Chapter 8.*

g) *Fit new sealing rings to the fluid cooler hose unions and ensure both unions are securely retained by their clips.*

h) *On completion, refill the transmission with the specified type and quantity of fluid as described in Section 2 and adjust the selector cable as described in Section 3.*

10 Automatic transmission overhaul - general information

1 In the event of a fault occurring with the transmission, it is first necessary to determine whether it is of a mechanical or hydraulic nature, and to do this, special test equipment is required. It is therefore essential to have the work carried out by a Vauxhall dealer if a transmission fault is suspected.

2 Do not remove the transmission from the car for possible repair before professional fault diagnosis has been carried out, since most tests require the transmission to be in the vehicle.

Chapter 8
Driveshafts

Contents

Degrees of difficulty

Easy, suitable for novice with little experience		**Fairly easy,** suitable for beginner with some experience		**Fairly difficult,** suitable for competent DIY mechanic		**Difficult,** suitable for experienced DIY mechanic		**Very difficult,** suitable for expert DIY or professional	

Specifications

General

Driveshaft type . . . . Solid steel shafts with inner and outer constant velocity (CV) joints. Right-hand driveshaft is fitted with a vibration damper (except 1.6 litre models).

Lubricant:

  Type/specification . . . . Special grease (Vauxhall part number 19 41 521 (90 094 176) supplied in sachets with gaiter kits - joints are otherwise pre-packed with grease and sealed

  Quantity (per joint) . . . . 90 g

Torque wrench settings

	Nm	lbf ft
Front driveshaft retaining nut:		
Stage 1	130	96
Stage 2	Loosen completely	
Stage 3	20	15
Stage 4	Angle-tighten a further 90°	
Stage 5	If necessary loosen by approx. 9° to insert split pin	
Front suspension lower arm balljoint to hub carrier	See Chapter 10	
Steering track rod end to steering arm on hub carrier	See Chapter 10	

8

2.2 Use a cold chisel to tap off the driveshaft nut cap

2.3 Removing the split pin from the castellated driveshaft nut

1 General information

Drive is transmitted from the differential to the front wheels by means of two, unequal-length driveshafts.

Each driveshaft is fitted with an inner and outer constant velocity (CV) joint. Each outer joint is splined to engage with the wheel hub, and is retained by a large nut. The inner joint is also splined to engage with the differential sunwheel and is held in place by an internal circlip.

Except on 1.6 litre models, a vibration damper is bolted to the right-hand driveshaft.

Note: *On V6 engine models (not covered by this manual) the right-hand driveshaft incorporates an intermediate shaft which is supported by a bearing in a bracket bolted to the rear of the cylinder block.*

2 Driveshaft – removal and refitting

Removal

Note: *A new front driveshaft nut and inner joint circlip will be required on refitting. The driveshaft outer joint splines may be a tight fit in the hub and it is possible that a puller/extractor will be required to draw the hub assembly off the driveshaft during removal.*

1 Apply the handbrake, then jack up the front of the vehicle and support it on axle stands (see "Jacking and Vehicle Support"). Remove the roadwheel. It is an advantage to only jack up one side of the vehicle as this will prevent loss of oil from the transmission when the driveshaft is withdrawn.

2 Using a cold chisel or screwdriver, tap off the driveshaft nut cap **(see illustration)**.

3 Extract the split pin from the castellated driveshaft nut on the end of the driveshaft **(see illustration)**.

4 The driveshaft nut must now be loosened. The nut is extremely tight, and an extension bar will be required to loosen it. To prevent the driveshaft from turning, insert two roadwheel bolts, and insert a metal bar between them to counterhold the hub. Remove the nut and washer from the driveshaft **(see illustrations)**.

5 Unscrew the nut securing the track rod end to the steering arm on the hub carrier, then use a balljoint separator tool to remove the track rod end.

6 Unscrew and remove the clamp bolt securing the front lower suspension arm to the hub carrier. Note that the bolt head faces the rear of the vehicle **(see illustration)**.

7 Using a chisel or screwdriver as a wedge, expand the balljoint clamp at the bottom of the hub carrier **(see illustration)**.

8 Using a lever, push down on the suspension lower arm to free the balljoint from the hub carrier, then move the hub carrier to one side and release the arm taking care not to damage the balljoint rubber boot.

9 The hub must now be freed from the end of the driveshaft. It should be possible to pull the hub off the driveshaft, but if the end of the driveshaft is tight in the hub, temporarily refit the driveshaft nut to protect the driveshaft threads, then tap the end of the driveshaft with a soft-faced hammer while pulling outwards on the hub carrier **(see illustration)**. Alternatively, use a suitable puller to press the driveshaft through the hub.

10 With the driveshaft detached from the hub carrier, tie the suspension strut to one side and support the driveshaft on an axle stand.

11 A lever will now be required to release the inner end of the driveshaft from the differential. Lever between the driveshaft and differential housing to release the driveshaft snap-ring **(see illustration)**.

2.4a Removing the driveshaft nut . . .

2.4b . . . and washer

2.6 Unscrewing the clamp bolt securing the front lower suspension arm to the hub carrier

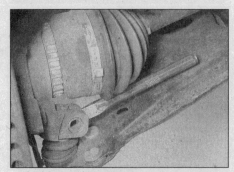

2.7 Using a cold chisel to expand the balljoint clamp at the bottom of the hub carrier

2.9 Use a soft-faced hammer to drive the driveshaft from the hub splines

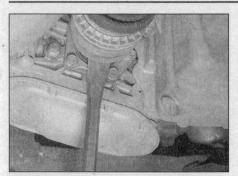

2.11 Carefully lever between the driveshaft and differential housing to release the driveshaft

2.13 Vibration damper fitted to the right-hand driveshaft on non-1.6 litre models

2.24a Insert the new split pin . . .

2.24b . . . and bend the legs to secure

12 Withdraw the driveshaft from the transmission, ensuring that the constant velocity joints are not placed under excessive strain, and remove the driveshaft from beneath the vehicle. Whilst the driveshaft is removed, plug or tape over the differential aperture to prevent dirt entry.

Caution: Do not allow the vehicle to rest on its wheels with one or both driveshafts removed, as damage to the wheel bearings(s) may result. If the vehicle must be moved on its wheels, clamp the wheel bearings using spacers and a long threaded rod to take the place of the driveshaft.

13 All models except 1.6 litre models have a vibration damper fitted to the right-hand driveshaft. If the damper is transferred to a new driveshaft, measure its fitted position before removing and locate it in the same position on the new driveshaft **(see illustration)**.

Refitting

14 Before refitting the driveshaft, examine the oil seal in the transmission housing and renew it if necessary as described in Chapter 7A or 7B.

15 Remove the circlip from the end of the driveshaft inner joint splines and discard it. Fit a new circlip, making sure it is correctly located in the groove.

16 Thoroughly clean the driveshaft splines, and the apertures in the transmission and hub assembly. Apply a thin film of grease to the oil seal lips, and to the driveshaft splines and shoulders. Check that all gaiter clips are securely fastened.

17 Offer up the driveshaft, and engage the inner joint splines with those of the differential sun gear, taking care not to damage the oil seal. Push the joint fully into position, then check that the circlip is correctly located and securely holds the joint in position. If necessary, use a soft-faced mallet or drift to drive the driveshaft inner joint fully into position.

18 Align the outer constant velocity joint splines with those of the hub, and slide the joint back into position in the hub.

19 Using the lever push down on the lower suspension arm, then re-locate the balljoint

and release the arm. Make sure that the balljoint stub is fully entered in the hub carrier.

20 Insert the clamp bolt with its head facing the rear of the vehicle, and tighten it to the specified torque.

21 Refit the track rod end to the steering arm on the hub carrier and tighten the nut to the specified torque.

22 Refit the washer to the end of the driveshaft, then screw on a new nut and tighten moderately at this stage.

23 Refit the roadwheel and lower the vehicle to the ground.

24 Tighten the driveshaft nut in the stages given in the Specifications, and fit a new split pin. Bend the outer leg of the split pin over the end of the driveshaft, then cut the inner leg as necessary and bend it inwards **(see illustrations)**.

25 Tap the driveshaft nut cap into position then refit the wheel trim.

26 Check and if necessary top-up the oil level in the transmission as described in Chapter 1.

3 Driveshaft joint – checking and renewal

Checking

1 Road test the vehicle, and listen for a metallic clicking noise from the front as the vehicle is driven slowly in a circle on full-lock. If evident, this indicates wear in the outer

constant velocity joint which must be renewed.

2 To check for wear on the inner joint, apply the handbrake then jack up the front of the vehicle and support it on axle stands (see *"Jacking and Vehicle Support"*). Attempt to move the inner end of the driveshaft up and down, then hold the joint with one hand and attempt to rotate the driveshaft with the other. If excessive wear is evident, the joint must be renewed.

Renewal

3 With the driveshaft removed, as described in Section 2, release the metal securing bands and slide back the rubber gaiter from the worn joint. Where necessary, cut the bands free taking care not to damage the gaiter seating **(see illustration)**.

4 Using a screwdriver or circlip pliers, expand the circlip that secures the joint to the driveshaft **(see illustration)**.

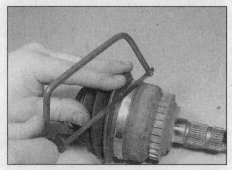

3.3 Cut free the gaiter securing bands with a small hacksaw

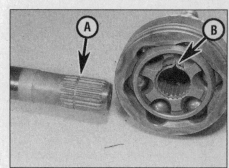

3.4 Driveshaft joint retaining circlip (B) and circlip groove (A)

8

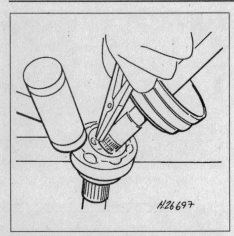

3.5 Tapping the joint from the driveshaft

5 Using a soft-faced mallet, tap the joint from the driveshaft **(see illustration)**.

6 Ensure that a new circlip is fitted to the new joint, then tap the new joint onto the driveshaft until the circlip engages in its groove.

7 Pack the joint with the specified type of grease.

8 Refit the rubber gaiter to the new joint, referring to Section 4, if necessary.

9 Refit the driveshaft to the vehicle, as described in Section 2.

4 Driveshaft joint gaiters – renewal

Renewal

1 With the driveshaft removed as described in Section 2, remove the relevant joint as described in Section 3. Note that if both gaiters on a driveshaft are to be renewed it is only necessary to remove one joint, however on the right-hand driveshaft it will also be necessary to remove the vibration damper after noting its location (except on 1.6 litre models).

2 Release the remaining securing band and slide the gaiter from the driveshaft. If the original Vauxhall band is fitted, use pincers to cut it free.

3 Clean the old grease from the joint, then re-pack the joint with the specified type of fresh grease. If excessively worn or damaged, the driveshaft joint should be renewed as described in Section 3.

4 Slide the new gaiter and new inner securing band onto the driveshaft so that the smaller diameter opening is located in the groove in the driveshaft **(see illustrations)**. **Note:** *Depending on model, there may be one or two grooves in the driveshaft; make sure that the gaiter is correctly located. On models with one groove, the inner end of the inner gaiter must be 135 mm from the end of the driveshaft. On models with two grooves, the inner end of the inner gaiter must be 123 mm from the end of the driveshaft.*

5 Pack the joint with the specified type of grease **(see illustration)**.

6 Refit the joint, using a new inner securing circlip **(see illustration)**. Tap the joint onto the driveshaft until the circlip engages in its groove.

7 Slide the gaiter over the joint, then release any excess air by carefully lifting the gaiter from the joint with a screwdriver.

8 Secure the gaiter using new securing bands. To fit a loop-type band, locate it over the gaiter then squeeze the raised loop using pincers - note that Vauxhall technicians use a special tool to do this, however careful use of pincers or a similar tool will be sufficient **(see illustrations)**. To fit a lug-and-slot type band, wrap it around the gaiter and while pulling on the band as tight as possible, engage the lug on the end of the band with one of the slots. Use a screwdriver if necessary to push the band as tight as possible before engaging the lug and slot. Finally tighten the band by compressing the raised square portion of the band with pliers, taking care not to cut the gaiter.

9 Refit the driveshaft to the vehicle, as described in Section 2.

4.4a Locate the new inner securing band on the driveshaft . . .

4.4b . . . followed by the new gaiter

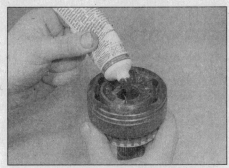

4.5 Pack the joint with the specified type of grease

4.6 Fitting the joint to the splines on the driveshaft

4.8a Fit the outer securing band . . .

4.8b . . . and tighten using a pair of pincers

Chapter 9
Braking system

Contents

Degrees of difficulty

Easy, suitable for novice with little experience		Fairly easy, suitable for beginner with some experience		Fairly difficult, suitable for competent DIY mechanic		Difficult, suitable for experienced DIY mechanic		Very difficult, suitable for expert DIY or professional

Specifications

System type

All models .... Front discs and rear drums (1.6 litre SOHC engine model) or rear discs (except 1.6 litre SOHC engine model) with vacuum servo assistance, 4-channel ABS (standard), operated via hydraulic modulator, dual hydraulic circuit split diagonally. Cable-operated handbrake on rear wheels

Front discs

Type .... Ventilated
Diameter:
  All models except 2.0 litre (X20XEV engine) .... 256 mm
  2.0 litre (X20XEV engine) .... 288 mm
Maximum disc run-out .... 0.1 mm
Minimum pad friction material thickness (including backing plate) .... 7.5 mm
Minimum disc thickness after machining: *
  All models except 2.0 litre (X20XEV engine) .... 22 mm
  2.0 litre (X20XEV engine) .... 23 mm

When this dimension is reached, only one further new set of brake pads is permissible, then renew the discs

Rear discs

Type	Solid
Diameter:	
All models except 2.0 litre (X20XEV engine)	270 mm
2.0 litre (X20XEV engine)	286 mm
Maximum disc run-out	0.1 mm
Minimum pad friction material thickness (including backing plate)	7.0 mm
Minimum disc thickness after machining *	9.0 mm
Minimum handbrake shoe friction material thickness (lining only)	1.0 mm

* When this dimension is reached, only one further new set of disc pads is permissible, then renew the discs

Rear drums

Internal diameter	230 mm
Maximum internal diameter	231 mm
Minimum shoe friction material thickness	0.5 mm above rivet heads

ABS system type

All models except 2.0 litre (X20XEV engine)	ABS 415 single-diaphragm servo
2.0 litre (X20XEV engine) model (with traction control)	ABS 5/TC tandem-diaphragm servo

Brake fluid type/specification

All models	Hydraulic fluid to DOT3 or DOT 4, or SAE J1703

Torque wrench settings

	Nm	lbf ft
ABS control unit to hydraulic modulator body:		
Stage 1	6	4
Stage 2	7	5
Brake disc securing screw	4	3
Brake fluid line unions	16	12
Caliper bleed screw	9	7
Caliper hose banjo bolt	40	30
Front caliper guide bolts	30	22
Front caliper mounting bracket to hub carrier	95	70
Handbrake lever mounting	10	7
Handbrake lever warning switch	2.5	1.8
Hydraulic modulator (ABS)	8	6
Master cylinder to servo	22	16
Pedal support	20	15
Rear brake drum securing screw	4	3
Rear caliper mounting	80	59
Rear wheel cylinder	9	7
Roadwheel bolts	110	81
Wheel speed sensor	8	6
Vacuum hose to inlet manifold	18	13
Vacuum hose to vacuum pump (diesel engine models)	18	13
Vacuum servo mounting nuts/bolts	20	15
Vacuum servo pushrod locknut	18	13

1 General information

The braking system is of servo-assisted, dual-circuit hydraulic type split diagonally. The arrangement of the hydraulic system is such that each circuit operates one front and one rear brake from a tandem master cylinder. Under normal circumstances, both circuits operate in unison. However, in the event of hydraulic failure in one circuit, full braking force will still be available at two wheels.

All models are fitted with front disc brakes, with rear drum brakes on the 1.6 litre SOHC engine model and rear disc brakes on all other models. The front disc brakes are actuated by single-piston sliding type calipers, which ensure that equal pressure is applied to each disc pad, whilst the rear calipers use twin-piston fixed calipers. The rear drum brakes (1.6 litre SOHC engine model) incorporate leading and trailing shoes, which are actuated by twin-piston wheel cylinders. A self-adjust mechanism is incorporated, to automatically compensate for brake shoe wear. As the brake shoe linings wear, the footbrake operation automatically operates the adjuster mechanism, which effectively lengthens the shoe strut and repositions the brake shoes, to reduce the lining-to-drum clearance.

All models are fitted with a 4-channel ABS (Anti-lock Braking System) incorporating a wheel speed sensor at each wheel. When the ignition is switched on, an 'ABS' symbol illuminates in the instrument panel for a short time while the system performs a self-test. The system comprises an electronic control unit, roadwheel sensors, hydraulic modulator, and the necessary valves and relays. The purpose of the system is to stop wheel(s) locking during heavy brake applications. This is achieved by automatic release of the brake on the locked wheel, followed by re-application of the brake. This procedure is carried out several times a second by the hydraulic modulator. The modulator is controlled by the electronic control unit, which itself receives signals from the wheel sensors, which monitor the locked or unlocked state of the wheels. The ABS unit is fitted between the brake master cylinder and the brakes. The master cylinder fitted to models with traction control (X20XEV engine models) is different to that fitted to models without traction control.

If the 'ABS' symbol, in the instrument panel stays lit, or if it comes on whilst driving, there is a fault in the system and the vehicle must be taken to a Vauxhall dealer for assessment using specialist diagnostic equipment.

The handbrake is cable-operated on the rear brakes by a lever mounted between the front seats.

On diesel engine models, since there is no throttling of the inlet manifold, the manifold is not a suitable source of vacuum to operate the vacuum servo unit. The servo unit is therefore connected to a separate vacuum pump - on 1.7 litre diesel engines the pump is attached to the alternator and driven by a central spline, however on 2.0 litre diesel engines the pump is bolted to the left-hand end of the cylinder head and driven by the camshaft.

 Warning: When servicing any part of the system, work carefully and methodically; also observe scrupulous cleanliness when overhauling any part of the hydraulic system. Always renew components (in axle sets, where applicable) if in doubt about their condition, and use only genuine Vauxhall replacement parts, or at least those of known good quality. Note the warnings given in "Safety first" and at relevant points in this Chapter concerning the dangers of asbestos dust and hydraulic fluid.

2 Hydraulic system - bleeding

 Warning: Hydraulic fluid is poisonous; wash off immediately and thoroughly in the case of skin contact, and seek immediate medical advice if any fluid is swallowed or gets into the eyes. Certain types of hydraulic fluid are inflammable, and may ignite when allowed into contact with hot components; when servicing any hydraulic system, it is safest to assume that the fluid is inflammable, and to take precautions against the risk of fire as though it is petrol that is being handled. Hydraulic fluid is also an effective paint stripper, and will attack plastics; if any is spilt, it should be washed off immediately, using copious quantities of fresh water. Finally, it is hygroscopic (it absorbs moisture from the air) - old fluid may be contaminated and unfit for further use. When topping-up or renewing the fluid, always use the recommended type, and ensure that it comes from a freshly-opened sealed container.

General

1 The correct operation of any hydraulic system is only possible after removing all air from the components and circuit; this is achieved by bleeding the system.

2 During the bleeding procedure, add only clean, unused hydraulic fluid of the recommended type; never re-use fluid that has already been bled from the system.

Ensure that sufficient fluid is available before starting work.

3 If there is any possibility of incorrect fluid being already in the system, the brake components and circuit must be flushed completely with uncontaminated, correct fluid, and new seals should be fitted to the various components.

4 If hydraulic fluid has been lost from the system, or air has entered because of a leak, ensure that the fault is cured before proceeding further.

5 Park the vehicle over an inspection pit or on car ramps. Alternatively, apply the handbrake then jack up the front and rear of the vehicle and support it on axle stands (see "*Jacking and Vehicle Support*"). For improved access with the vehicle jacked up, remove the roadwheels.

6 Check that all pipes and hoses are secure, unions tight and bleed screws closed. Clean any dirt from around the bleed screws.

7 Unscrew the master cylinder reservoir cap, and top the master cylinder reservoir up to the "MAX" level line; refit the cap loosely, and remember to maintain the fluid level at least above the "MIN" level line throughout the procedure, otherwise there is a risk of further air entering the system.

8 There are a number of one-man, do-it-yourself brake bleeding kits currently available from motor accessory shops. It is recommended that one of these kits is used whenever possible, as they greatly simplify the bleeding operation, and also reduce the risk of expelled air and fluid being drawn back into the system. If such a kit is not available, the basic (two-man) method must be used, which is described in detail below.

9 If a kit is to be used, prepare the vehicle as described previously, and follow the kit manufacturer's instructions, as the procedure may vary slightly according to the type being used; generally, they are as outlined below in the relevant sub-section.

10 Whichever method is used, the same sequence must be followed (paragraphs 11 and 12) to ensure the removal of all air from the system.

Bleeding sequence

11 If the system has been only partially disconnected, and suitable precautions were taken to minimise fluid loss, it should be necessary only to bleed that part of the system (ie the primary or secondary circuit).

12 If the complete system is to be bled, then it should be done working in the following sequence:

   a) *Left-hand rear brake.*
   b) *Right-hand front brake.*
   c) *Right-hand rear brake.*
   d) *Left-hand front brake.*

Bleeding - basic (two-man) method

13 Collect together a clean glass jar, a suitable length of plastic or rubber tubing

2.14 Dust cap on a bleed screw (arrowed)

which is a tight fit over the bleed screw, and a ring spanner to fit the screw. The help of an assistant will also be required.

14 Remove the dust cap from the first bleed screw in the sequence **(see illustration)**. Fit the spanner and tube to the screw, place the other end of the tube in the jar, and pour in sufficient fluid to cover the end of the tube.

15 Ensure that the master cylinder reservoir fluid level is maintained at least above the "MIN" level line throughout the procedure.

16 Have the assistant fully depress the brake pedal several times to build up pressure, then maintain it on the final downstroke.

17 While pedal pressure is maintained, unscrew the bleed screw (approximately one turn) and allow the compressed fluid and air to flow into the jar. The assistant should maintain pedal pressure, following it down to the floor if necessary, and should not release it until instructed to do so. When the flow stops, tighten the bleed screw again, have the assistant release the pedal slowly, and recheck the reservoir fluid level.

18 Repeat the steps given in paragraphs 16 and 17 until the fluid emerging from the bleed screw is free from air bubbles. If the master cylinder has been drained and refilled, and air is being bled from the first screw in the sequence, allow approximately five seconds between cycles for the master cylinder passages to refill.

19 When no more air bubbles appear, securely tighten the bleed screw, remove the tube and spanner, and refit the dust cap. Do not overtighten the bleed screw.

20 Repeat the procedure on the remaining screws in the sequence, until all air is removed from the system and the brake pedal feels firm again.

Bleeding - using a one-way valve kit

21 As the name implies, these kits consist of a length of tubing with a one-way valve fitted, to prevent expelled air and fluid being drawn back into the system; some kits include a translucent container, which can be positioned so that the air bubbles can be more easily seen flowing from the end of the tube.

9

22 The kit is connected to the bleed screw, which is then opened **(see illustration)**. The user returns to the driver's seat, depresses the brake pedal with a smooth, steady stroke, and slowly releases it; this is repeated until the expelled fluid is clear of air bubbles.

23 Note that these kits simplify work so much that it is easy to forget the master cylinder reservoir fluid level; ensure that this is maintained at least above the "MIN" level line at all times.

Bleeding - using a pressure-bleeding kit

24 These kits are usually operated by a reservoir of pressurised air contained in the spare tyre. However, note that it will probably be necessary to reduce the pressure to a lower level than normal; refer to the instructions supplied with the kit.

25 By connecting a pressurised, fluid-filled container to the master cylinder reservoir, bleeding can be carried out simply by opening each screw in turn (in the specified sequence), and allowing the fluid to flow out until no more air bubbles can be seen in the expelled fluid.

26 This method has the advantage that the large reservoir of fluid provides an additional safeguard against air being drawn into the system during bleeding.

27 Pressure-bleeding is particularly effective when bleeding "difficult" systems, or when bleeding the complete system at the time of routine fluid renewal.

All methods

28 When bleeding is complete, and firm pedal feel is restored, wash off any spilt fluid, securely tighten the bleed screws, and refit the dust caps.

29 Check the hydraulic fluid level in the master cylinder reservoir, and top-up if necessary (see "Weekly checks").

30 Discard any hydraulic fluid that has been bled from the system; it will not be fit for re-use.

31 Check the feel of the brake pedal. If it feels at all spongy, air must still be present in the system, and further bleeding is required. Failure to bleed satisfactorily after a reasonable repetition of the bleeding procedure may be due to worn master cylinder seals.

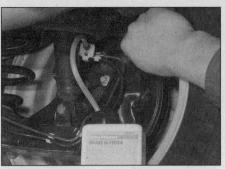

2.22 Using a one-way valve kit to bleed the rear brake

3 Hydraulic pipes and hoses - renewal

Note: *Before starting work, refer to the note at the beginning of Section 2 concerning the dangers of hydraulic fluid.*

1 If any pipe or hose is to be renewed, minimise fluid loss by first removing the master cylinder reservoir cap, then tightening it down onto a piece of polythene to obtain an airtight seal. Alternatively, hose clamps can be fitted to flexible hoses to isolate sections of the circuit; metal brake pipe unions can be plugged (if care is taken not to allow dirt into the system) or capped immediately they are disconnected. Place a wad of rag under any union that is to be disconnected, to catch any spilt fluid.

2 If a flexible hose is to be disconnected, unscrew the brake pipe union nut before removing the spring clip which secures the hose to its mounting bracket. Where applicable, unscrew the banjo union bolt securing the hose to the caliper and recover the copper washers. When removing the front flexible hose, pull out the spring clip and disconnect it from the strut **(see illustrations)**.

3 To unscrew union nuts, it is preferable to obtain a brake pipe spanner of the correct size; these are available from most motor accessory shops. Failing this, a close-fitting open-ended spanner will be required, though if the nuts are tight or corroded, their flats may be rounded-off if the spanner slips. In such a case, a self-

locking wrench is often the only way to unscrew a stubborn union, but it follows that the pipe and the damaged nuts must be renewed on reassembly. Always clean a union and surrounding area before disconnecting it. If disconnecting a component with more than one union, make a careful note of the connections before disturbing any of them.

4 If a brake pipe is to be renewed, it can be obtained, cut to length and with the union nuts and end flares in place, from Vauxhall dealers. All that is then necessary is to bend it to shape, following the line of the original, before fitting it to the car. Alternatively, most motor accessory shops can make up brake pipes from kits, but this requires very careful measurement of the original, to ensure that the replacement is of the correct length. The safest answer is usually to take the original to the shop as a pattern.

5 On refitting, do not overtighten the union nuts.

6 When refitting hoses to the calipers, always use new copper washers and tighten the banjo union bolts to the specified torque. Make sure that the hoses are positioned so that they will not touch surrounding bodywork or the roadwheels.

7 Ensure that the pipes and hoses are correctly routed, with no kinks, and that they are secured in the clips or brackets provided. After fitting, remove the polythene from the reservoir, and bleed the hydraulic system as described in Section 2. Wash off any spilt fluid, and check carefully for fluid leaks.

4 Front brake pads - renewal

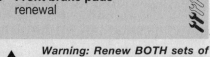

Warning: Renew BOTH sets of front brake pads at the same time - NEVER renew the pads on only one wheel, as uneven braking may result. Note that the dust created by wear of the pads may contain asbestos, which is a health hazard. Never blow it out with compressed air, and do not inhale any of it. An approved filtering mask should be worn when working on the brakes. DO NOT use petroleum-based

3.2a Pull out the spring clip . . .

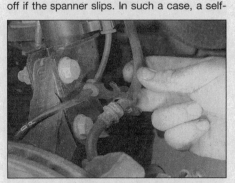

3.2b . . . and disconnect the flexible hose from the front suspension strut

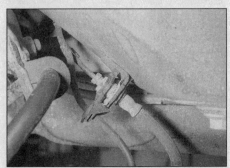

3.2c The rear flexible hose is connected to the rigid hydraulic line beneath the rear wheel arch

solvents to clean brake parts - use brake cleaner or methylated spirit only.

1 Apply the handbrake, then jack up the front of the vehicle and support it on axle stands (see *"Jacking and Vehicle Support"*). Remove the front roadwheels.

2 Using a screwdriver lever out the brake pad warning sensor and unclip it from the retainer.

3 Prise the retaining spring from the outer edge of the caliper, noting its correct fitted position **(see illustration)**.

4 Remove the dust caps from the inner ends of the guide bolts **(see illustration)**.

5 Unscrew the guide bolts from the caliper, and lift the caliper and inner pad away from the mounting bracket. Tie the caliper to the suspension strut using a suitable piece of wire **(see illustrations)**. Do not allow the caliper to hang unsupported on the flexible brake hose.

6 Remove the inner pad from the caliper piston, noting that it is retained by a spring clip attached to the pad backing plate, and recover the outer pad from the mounting bracket **(see illustration)**.

7 Brush the dirt and dust from the caliper, but take care not to inhale it. Carefully remove any rust from the edge of the brake disc.

8 Measure the thickness of each brake pad (friction material and backing plate) **(see illustration)**. If either pad is worn at any point to the specified minimum thickness or less, all four pads must be renewed. The pads should also be renewed if any are fouled with oil or grease; there is no satisfactory way of degreasing friction material, once contaminated. If any of the brake pads are

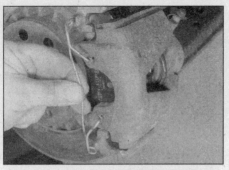

4.3 Removing the retaining spring from the front caliper

worn unevenly, or fouled with oil or grease, trace and rectify the cause before reassembly.

9 If the brake pads are still serviceable, carefully clean them using a clean, fine wire brush or similar, paying particular attention to the sides and back of the metal backing. Clean out the grooves in the friction material, and pick out any large embedded particles of dirt or debris. Carefully clean the pad locations in the caliper body/mounting bracket.

10 Prior to fitting the pads, check that the guide bolts are a snug fit in the caliper bushes. Brush the dust and dirt from the caliper and piston. Apply a little high-melting-point copper brake grease to the areas on the pad backing plates which contact the caliper and piston. Inspect the dust seal around the piston for damage, and the piston for evidence of fluid leaks, corrosion or damage. If attention to any of these components is necessary, refer to Section 10.

4.4 Remove the dust caps . . .

11 If new brake pads are to be fitted, the caliper piston must be pushed back into the cylinder to make room for them. We recommend that the caliper bleed screw is loosened and the excess fluid drained into a container, rather than forcing the fluid through the circuit into the reservoir. This method will prevent any sediment being forced back into the master cylinder. Either use a G-clamp or similar tool, or use suitable pieces of wood as levers to move the piston fully into the caliper bore. Tighten the bleed screw.

 Warning: Do not syphon the fluid by mouth, as it is poisonous; use a syringe or an old poultry baster.

12 Check that the cutaway recesses on the caliper piston are positioned as shown **(see illustration)**. If necessary, carefully turn the piston to its correct position.

4.5a . . . then unscrew the guide bolts . . .

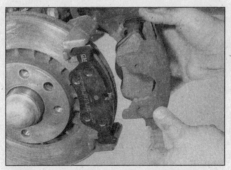

4.5b . . . and lift the caliper and inner pad away from the mounting bracket

4.5c Tie the caliper to the suspension strut, to avoid placing any strain on the hydraulic brake hose

4.6 Removing the outer pad from the mounting bracket

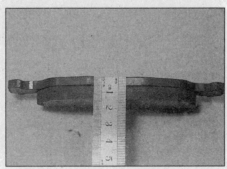

4.8 Measuring the brake pad thickness

4.12 Front brake caliper cutaway recess (arrowed) correctly positioned

9

4.13 Locate the clip in the front caliper piston when refitting the inner pad

4.16 Tightening the caliper guide bolts with a torque wrench

4.18 Make sure the retaining spring ends are correctly located in the caliper holes

13 Fit the inner pad to the caliper, ensuring that its clip is correctly located in the caliper piston **(see illustration)**.

14 Fit the outer pad to the caliper mounting bracket, ensuring that its friction material is facing the brake disc.

15 Slide the caliper and inner pad into position over the outer pad, and locate it in the mounting bracket.

16 Insert the caliper guide bolts, and tighten them to the specified torque setting **(see illustration)**.

17 Refit the guide bolt dust caps.

18 Refit the retaining spring to the caliper, ensuring that its ends are correctly located in the caliper holes **(see illustration)**.

19 Refit the brake pad warning sensor.

20 Depress the brake pedal repeatedly, until normal pedal pressure is restored.

21 Repeat the above procedure on the remaining front brake caliper.

5.2 Driving out the pad retaining pins from the rear brake caliper

22 Refit the roadwheels, then lower the vehicle to the ground and tighten the roadwheel bolts to the specified torque setting.

23 Check the hydraulic fluid level as described in *"Weekly checks"*.

5 Rear brake pads - renewal

> **Warning: Renew BOTH sets of rear brake pads at the same time - NEVER renew the pads on only one wheel, as uneven braking may result. Note that the dust created by wear of the pads may contain asbestos, which is a health hazard. Never blow it out with compressed air, and do not inhale any of it. An approved filtering mask should be worn when working on the brakes. DO NOT use petroleum-based solvents to clean brake parts - use brake cleaner or methylated spirit only.**

1 Chock the front wheels, then jack up the rear of the vehicle and support it on axle stands (see *"Jacking and Vehicle Support"*). Remove the rear roadwheels.

2 Note how the anti-rattle spring is located, then drive out the upper and lower pad retaining pins from the outside of the caliper using a punch **(see illustration)**.

3 Remove the anti-rattle spring **(see illustration)**.

4 Push the pads away from the disc slightly, then using a pair of pliers or removal tool,

withdraw the outboard pad from the caliper **(see illustration)**.

5 Withdraw the inboard pad from the caliper **(see illustration)**.

6 Brush the dirt and dust from the caliper, but take care not to inhale it. Carefully remove any rust from the edge of the brake disc.

7 Measure the thickness of each brake pad (friction material and backing plate). If either pad is worn at any point to the specified minimum thickness or less, all four pads must be renewed. The pads should also be renewed if any are fouled with oil or grease; there is no satisfactory way of degreasing friction material, once contaminated. If any of the brake pads are worn unevenly, or fouled with oil or grease, trace and rectify the cause before reassembly.

8 If the brake pads are still serviceable, clean them using a clean, fine wire brush or similar, paying particular attention to the sides and back of the metal backing. Carefully clean the pad locations in the caliper body/mounting bracket.

9 Prior to fitting the pads, clean and check the pad retaining pins. Brush the dust and dirt from the caliper and piston (see Warning at the beginning of this Section). Apply a little high-melting-point copper brake grease to the areas on the pad backing plates which contact the caliper and piston. Inspect the dust seal around the piston for damage, and the piston for evidence of fluid leaks, corrosion or damage. If attention to any of these components is necessary, refer to Section 11.

5.3 Removing a rear disc pad anti-rattle spring

5.4 Using a special removal tool to remove the rear brake disc pads

5.5 Using pliers to remove the inboard disc pad from the rear brake caliper

5.11 Checking a rear caliper piston cut-away recess angle with a card template

10 If new brake pads are to be fitted, the caliper piston must be pushed back into the cylinder to make room for them. We recommend that the caliper bleed screw is loosened and the excess fluid drained into a container, rather than forcing the fluid through the circuit into the reservoir. This method will prevent any sediment being forced back into the master cylinder. Either use a G-clamp or similar tool, or use suitable pieces of wood as levers to move the piston fully into the caliper bore. Tighten the bleed screw.

 Warning: Do not syphon the fluid by mouth, as it is poisonous; use a syringe or an old poultry baster.

11 Check that the cutaway recesses in the pistons are positioned at approximately 23° to the horizontal. A template made of card may be used to check the setting **(see illustration)**. If necessary, carefully turn the pistons to their correct positions.
12 Locate the new pads and the anti-squeal shims in the caliper. Ensure that the friction material faces the disc, and check that the pads are free to move slightly.
13 Locate the anti-rattle spring on the pads, then insert the pad retaining pins from the inside edge of the caliper, while depressing the spring. Tap the pins firmly into the caliper.
14 Depress the brake pedal repeatedly until normal pedal pressure is restored.

6.3 Checking the wear of the rear brake shoe friction material

15 Repeat the above procedure on the remaining rear brake caliper.
16 Refit the roadwheels, then lower the vehicle to the ground and tighten the roadwheel bolts to the specified torque setting.
17 Check the hydraulic fluid level as described in *"Weekly checks"*.

6 Rear brake shoes - renewal

 Warning: Brake shoes must be renewed on both rear wheels at the same time - never renew the shoes on only one wheel, as uneven braking may result. Also, the dust created by wear of the shoes may contain asbestos, which is a health hazard. Never blow it out with compressed air, and do not inhale any of it. An approved filtering mask should be worn when working on the brakes. DO NOT use petrol or petroleum-based solvents to clean brake parts; use brake cleaner or methylated spirit only.

1 Remove the rear brake drum as described in Section 9.
2 Taking precautions to avoid inhalation of dust, remove all traces of brake dust from the brake drum, shoes and backplate.
3 Measure the thickness of the friction material

6.5 Prior to disturbing the shoes, note the correct fitted locations of all components, paying particular attention to the adjuster strut components

of each brake shoe at several points; if either shoe is worn at any point to the specified minimum thickness or less, **all four** shoes must be renewed as a set **(see illustration)**. The shoes should also be renewed if any are fouled with oil or grease; there is no satisfactory way of degreasing friction material, once contaminated.
4 If any of the brake shoes are worn unevenly, or fouled with oil or grease, trace and rectify the cause before reassembly. If the shoes are to be renewed proceed as described below. If all is well refit the drums as described in Section 9.
5 Note the location and orientation of all components before dismantling, as an aid to reassembly **(see illustration)**.
6 Using a pair of pliers, carefully unhook the upper shoe return spring, and remove it from the brake shoes **(see illustration)**.
7 Prise the adjusting lever retaining spring out of the front shoe, and remove the retaining spring, lever and return spring from the brake shoe, noting each component's correct fitted position **(see illustration)**.
8 Prise the upper ends of the brake shoes apart, and withdraw the adjuster strut from between the shoes.
9 Using a pair of pliers, remove the front shoe retainer spring cup by depressing and turning it through 90°. With the cup removed, lift off the spring and withdraw the retainer pin.

6.6 Unhook the upper return spring, and remove it from the brake shoes

6.7 Remove the retaining spring, followed by the lever and return spring (arrowed)

6.11a Using pliers, remove the spring cup . . .

6.11b . . . then lift off the spring and retainer pin

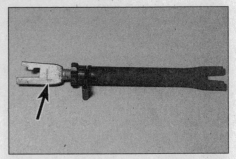

6.13 The left-hand adjuster strut assembly is marked "L" (arrow)

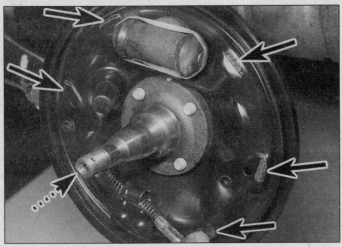

6.18 Apply a smear of anti-seize compound to the contact surfaces of the backplate (arrowed). Note the elastic band wrapped around the wheel cylinder

6.16 It may be necessary to transfer the adjusting lever pivot pin and clip (arrowed) from the original shoes to the new ones

10 Detach the front shoe from the lower return spring, and remove both the shoe and return spring.

11 Remove the rear shoe retainer spring cup, spring and retainer pin as described in paragraph 9, then remove the shoe, detaching it from the handbrake cable (see illustrations).

12 Do not depress the brake pedal with the shoes removed. As a precaution, wrap a strong elastic band around the wheel cylinder pistons to retain them.

13 If both brake assemblies are dismantled at the same time, take care not to mix them up. Note that the left-hand and right-hand adjuster components are marked as such; the threaded rod is marked "L" or "R", and the other "handed" components are colour-coded black for the left-hand side, and silver for the right-hand side (see illustration).

14 Dismantle and clean the adjuster strut. Apply a smear of silicone-based grease to the adjuster threads.

15 Examine the return springs. If they are distorted, or if they have seen extensive service, renewal is advisable. Weak springs may cause the brakes to bind.

16 If a new handbrake operating lever was not supplied with the new shoes (where applicable), transfer the lever from the old shoes. The lever may be secured with a pin and circlip, or by a rivet, which will have to be drilled out. It may also be necessary to transfer the adjusting lever pivot pin and clip from the original front shoe to the new shoe (see illustration).

17 Peel back the rubber protective caps, and check the wheel cylinder for fluid leaks or other damage. Ensure that both cylinder pistons are free to move easily. Refer to Section 12, if necessary, for information on wheel cylinder overhaul.

18 Prior to installation, clean the backplate thoroughly. Apply a thin smear of high-temperature copper-based brake grease or anti-seize compound to the shoe contact surfaces on the backplate and wheel cylinder pistons (see illustration). Do not allow the grease to foul the friction lining material.

19 Ensure that the handbrake cable is correctly retained by the clip on the lower brake shoe pivot point, then engage the rear shoe with the cable. Locate the shoe on the backplate (see illustration).

20 Install the rear shoe retainer pin and spring, and secure it in position with the spring cup.

21 Hook the lower return spring onto the rear shoe, then engage the front shoe with the return spring. Locate the front shoe on the backplate, and secure it in position with its retainer pin, spring and spring cup (see illustrations).

6.19 Engage the rear brake shoe with the handbrake cable, and locate the shoe on the backplate

6.21a Install the front shoe and lower return spring . . .

6.21b . . . and secure it in position with the retainer pin, spring and spring cup

6.23 Refit the adjuster strut, noting that the longer, straight part of the fork (arrowed) must be behind the shoe

6.24 Refit the adjusting lever and spring, making sure that the spring is correctly engaged in the front brake shoe hole (arrowed)

6.25 Make sure that both shoes are correctly aligned with the wheel cylinder, then install the upper return spring

22 Screw the adjuster strut wheel fully onto the forked end of the adjuster, so that the adjuster strut is set to its shortest possible length. Back the wheel off a half a turn, and check that it is free to rotate easily.

23 Manoeuvre the adjuster strut assembly into position between the brake shoes. Make sure that both ends of the strut are correctly engaged with the shoes, noting that the forked end of the strut must be positioned so that its longer, straight fork is to the rear of the shoe **(see illustration)**.

24 Engage the adjusting lever return spring with the front shoe and adjusting lever, and locate the lever on its pivot pin **(see illustration)**. Check that the lever and spring are correctly located, and secure the lever in position with the retaining spring, making sure the spring ends are securely located in the retaining pin and shoe.

25 Remove the rubber band from the wheel cylinder. Make sure that both shoes are correctly positioned on the wheel cylinder pistons, then fit the upper return spring **(see illustration)**.

26 Ensure that the handbrake operating lever stop peg is correctly positioned against the edge of the shoe web, then refit the brake drum as described in Section 9.

27 Repeat the operation on the remaining brake.

28 Once both sets of rear shoes have been renewed, with the handbrake fully released, adjust the lining-to-drum clearance by repeatedly depressing the brake pedal at least 20 to 25 times. Whilst depressing the pedal, have an assistant listen to the rear drums, to

check that the adjuster strut is functioning correctly; if so, a clicking sound will be emitted by the strut as the pedal is depressed.

29 Check and, if necessary, adjust the handbrake as described in Section 17.

30 On completion, check the hydraulic fluid level as described in *"Weekly checks"*.

Caution: New shoes will not give full braking efficiency until they have bedded-in. Be prepared for this, and avoid hard braking as far as possible for the first hundred miles or so after shoe renewal.

7 Handbrake shoes (rear disc brakes) - inspection, removal and refitting

⚠ *Warning: Brake shoes must be renewed on both rear wheels at the same time to ensure correct operation of the handbrake. Also, the dust created by wear of the shoes may contain asbestos, which is a health hazard. Never blow it out with compressed air, and do not inhale any of it. An approved filtering mask should be worn when working on the brakes. DO NOT use petrol or petroleum-based solvents to clean brake parts; use brake cleaner or methylated spirit only.*

Inspection

1 On models fitted with rear disc brakes, the handbrake operates independently of the footbrake, using brake shoes on the inside of the disc in a similar way to rear drum brake models.

2 Remove the brake disc (Section 8).

3 With the disc removed, check that the friction material has not worn down to less than the specified minimum.

4 If any one of the shoes has worn below the specified limit, all four handbrake shoes must be renewed as a set, as follows.

Removal

5 Clean the dust and dirt from the brake shoes and backplate (see Warning at the beginning of this Section).

6 Remove the shoe hold-down pins, springs and cups by depressing the cups and turning them through 90° using a pair of pliers **(see illustrations)**. This is a difficult task due to the strong spring tension and limited access, and an alternative method is to use a small socket through the holes in the hub flange to depress

7.6a Handbrake shoe hold-down spring and cup (arrowed)

7.6b Using a pair of pliers . . .

7.6c . . . to remove the handbrake shoe hold-down springs

9

7.7 Removing the adjuster from the top of the handbrake shoes

7.8 Unhook the upper return spring from the shoes with long nose pliers

7.9a Unhook the lower return spring and remove the leading . . .

the springs. **Note:** *The front hold-down pin can be removed through the rear of the brake backplate, however the rear pin can only be removed after removing the rear hub and bracket (see Chapter 10).*

7 Note the fitted position of all components then remove the adjuster from between the upper ends of the shoes **(see illustration)**.
8 Using a pair of pliers unhook the upper return spring from the shoes **(see illustration)**.

9 Unhook the lower return spring and remove the leading and trailing shoes **(see illustrations)**.
10 Disconnect the handbrake cable at the special clip using a small screwdriver then unhook the return spring from the backplate

7.9b . . . and trailing shoes from the backplate

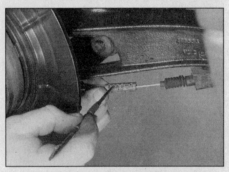

7.10a Using a small screwdriver to prise the rear cable from the special clip

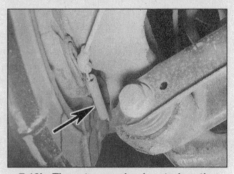

7.10b The return spring located on the rear of the backplate (arrowed)

7.13 With the rear hub removed, temporarily hold the backplate in position using two bolts

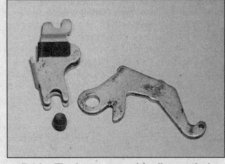

7.14a The lever assembly dismantled

7.14b The lever assembled

7.14c Refitting the lever assembly to the backplate

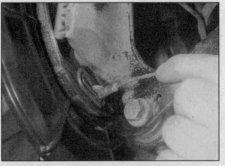

7.15a Hooking the rear cable onto the lever . . .

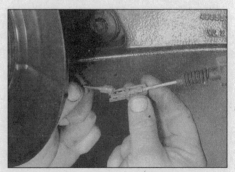

7.15b . . . and connector . . .

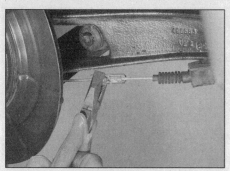

7.15c . . . and squeezing the connector with a pair of pliers

7.15d Refitting the return spring

7.16 Apply copper-based grease to the contact surfaces on the backplate

and remove the lever assembly **(see illustrations)**.

11 If both handbrake assemblies are dismantled at the same time, take care not to mix them up.

7.17a Locate the front (trailing) shoe on the backplate . . .

12 Dismantle and clean all components. Examine the return springs. Renew worn or damaged components.

Refitting

13 Prior to installation, clean the backplate thoroughly. The handbrake shoes can be reassembled using a reversal of the dismantling procedure, however improved access is possible by removing the rear hub assembly as described in Chapter 10 and temporarily holding the backplate in position on the trailing arm using two bolts **(see illustration)**. After reassembly the rear hub can then be refitted.

14 Reassemble the lever assembly and apply a little copper grease to the contact surfaces, then refit to the backplate and insert through the rubber grommet **(see illustrations)**.

15 Refit the cable to the lever and connector and use a pair of pliers to squeeze the clip together, then refit the return spring **(see illustrations)**.

16 Apply a thin smear of high-temperature copper-based brake grease or anti-seize compound to the shoe contact surfaces on the backplate **(see illustration)**.

17 With the pins already fitted to the backplate, refit the front (trailing) shoe and secure with the hold-down spring and cup **(see illustration)**.

18 Locate the rear (leading) shoe on the lever assembly and refit the lower return spring **(see illustrations)**.

19 Refit the hold-down spring and cup to secure the leading shoe to the backplate **(see illustration)**.

20 Refit the adjuster between the upper ends of the shoes **(see illustration)**.

7.17b . . . then refit the spring and cup . . .

7.17c . . . and use a pair of pliers to depress and turn the cup

7.18a Refit the rear (leading) shoe and the lower return spring

7.18b Engage the bottom of the shoe on the lever . . .

7.19 . . . then refit the hold-down spring and cup

7.20 Refit the adjuster between the upper ends of the shoes

9

7.21 Hook the upper return spring on the shoes

7.22 The handbrake shoes assembled ready for refitting of the rear hub

7.23 Using a screwdriver through the hole in the drive flange to turn the serrated nut on the adjuster

21 Hook the upper return spring on the shoes **(see illustration)**.

22 Where removed the rear hub can now be refitted **(see illustration)**.

23 Temporarily refit the disc over the shoes to determine the adjustment, then if necessary use a screwdriver to turn the serrated adjuster nut until it is just possible to refit the disc over the shoes without them binding **(see illustration)**.

24 Refit the brake disc with reference to Section 8.

25 Adjust the handbrake as described in Section 17.

26 Refit the roadwheels and lower the vehicle to the ground.

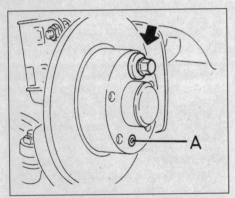

8.2 Refit a wheel bolt and spacer (arrowed) opposite the disc securing screw (A) before checking the brake disc run-out

8 Front/rear brake disc - inspection, removal and refitting

Note: *Before starting work, refer to the warning at the beginning of Section 4 or 5 concerning the dangers of asbestos dust. If either disc requires renewal, both should be renewed at the same time together with new pads, to ensure even and consistent braking.*

Inspection

1 Remove the wheel trim, then loosen the roadwheel bolts. If checking a front disc, apply the handbrake, and if checking a rear disc, chock the front wheels, then jack up the relevant end of the vehicle and support on axle stands (see *"Jacking and Vehicle Support"*). Remove the roadwheel.

2 Check that the brake disc securing screw is tight, then fit a spacer approximately 10.0 mm thick to one of the roadwheel bolts, and refit and tighten the bolt in the hole opposite the disc securing screw **(see illustration)**.

3 Rotate the brake disc, and examine it for deep scoring or grooving. Light scoring is normal, but if excessive, the disc should be removed and either renewed or machined (within the specified limits) by an engineering works. The minimum thickness is stamped on the outer face of the rear disc **(see illustration)**.

4 Using a dial gauge, or a flat metal block and feeler blades, check that the disc run-out

does not exceed the figure given in the Specifications. Measure the run-out 10.0 mm (0.4 in) in from the outer edge of the disc.

5 If the rear disc run-out is excessive, check the rear wheel bearing adjustment, as described in Chapter 10.

6 If the front disc run-out is excessive, remove the disc as described later, and check that the disc-to-hub surfaces are perfectly clean. Refit the disc and check the run-out again.

7 If the run-out is still excessive, the disc should be renewed.

8 To remove a disc, proceed as follows.

Front disc

Removal

9 Remove the roadwheel bolt and spacer used when checking the disc.

10 Unbolt and remove the front brake caliper complete with disc pads and tie it to one side. Also remove the front brake caliper mounting bracket with reference to Section 10 **(see illustration)**.

11 Remove the securing screw and withdraw the disc from the hub **(see illustrations)**.

Refitting

12 Refitting is a reversal of removal, but make sure that the mating faces of the disc and hub are perfectly clean, and apply a little locking fluid to the threads of the securing screw.

13 Refit the disc pads, as described in Section 4.

8.3 The minimum thickness is stamped on the outer face of the rear disc

8.10 Tie the front brake caliper to one side when removing the disc

8.11a Using an impact driver to unscrew the front disc securing screw

8.11b Removing a front brake disc

8.17a Unscrew the securing screw . . .

8.17b . . . and remove the rear disc from the hub drive flange

Rear disc

Removal

14 Where applicable, remove the roadwheel bolt and spacer used when checking the disc.
15 Remove the rear brake pads, as described in Section 5.
16 Remove the rear brake caliper with reference to Section 11, but leave the hydraulic fluid pipe connected. Move the caliper to one side, and suspend it using wire or string to avoid straining the pipe.
17 Remove the securing screw and withdraw the disc from the hub **(see illustrations)**. If the disc is tight, back off the handbrake shoes by inserting a screwdriver through the adjuster hole in the disc and turning the adjuster wheel located at the top of the backplate.

Refitting

18 Refitting is a reversal of removal, but make sure that the mating faces of the disc and hub are perfectly clean, and apply a little locking fluid to the threads of the securing screw. Refit the disc pads, as described in Section 5.

| 9 | **Rear brake drum -** removal, inspection and refitting |

Note: *Before starting work, refer to the warning at the beginning of Section 6 concerning the dangers of asbestos dust.*

Removal

1 Remove the relevant wheel trim, then loosen the rear roadwheel bolts and chock the front wheels. Jack up the rear of the vehicle, and support on axle stands (see *"Jacking and Vehicle Support"*) positioned under the body side members. Remove the roadwheel.
2 Fully release the handbrake.
3 Extract the drum securing screw and remove the drum. If the drum is tight, remove the plug from the inspection hole in the brake backplate, and push the handbrake operating lever away from the brake shoe to allow the shoes to move away from the drums. If necessary, slacken the handbrake cable adjuster on the lever inside the vehicle.

Inspection

4 Brush the dirt and dust from the drum, taking care not to inhale it.
5 Examine the internal friction surface of the drum. If deeply scored, or so worn that the drum has become ridged to the width of the shoes, then both drums must be renewed.
6 Regrinding of the friction surface may be possible provided the maximum diameter given in the Specifications is not exceeded.

Refitting

7 Before refitting the drum, make sure that the handbrake operating lever is returned to its normal.
8 Refit the brake drum and tighten the securing screw. If necessary, back off the adjuster wheel on the strut until the drum will pass over the shoes.
9 Adjust the brakes by operating the footbrake a number of times. A clicking noise will be heard at the drum as the automatic adjuster operates. When the clicking stops, adjustment is complete.
10 Refit the roadwheel and lower the vehicle to the ground.

| 10 | **Front brake caliper -** removal, overhaul and refitting |

Note: *New brake hose copper washers will be required when refitting. Before starting work, refer to the note at the beginning of Section 2 concerning the dangers of hydraulic fluid, and*

10.5a Unscrew the bolts . . .

to the warning at the beginning of Section 4 concerning the dangers of asbestos dust.

Removal

1 Apply the handbrake, then jack up the front of the vehicle and support it on axle stands (see *"Jacking and Vehicle Support"*). Remove the roadwheel.
2 Minimise fluid loss by first removing the master cylinder reservoir cap, then tightening it down onto a piece of polythene to obtain an airtight seal. Alternatively, use a brake hose clamp, a G-clamp or a similar tool to clamp the flexible hose leading to the brake caliper.
3 Clean the area around the caliper brake hose union. Unscrew and remove the union bolt, and recover the sealing washer from each side of the hose union. Discard the washers; new ones must be used on refitting. Plug the hose end and caliper hole, to minimise fluid loss and prevent the ingress of dirt into the hydraulic system.
4 Remove the brake pads as described in Section 4, then remove the caliper from the vehicle.
5 If necessary, unbolt the caliper mounting bracket from the hub carrier **(see illustrations)**.

Overhaul

6 With the caliper on the bench, wipe it clean with a cloth rag.
7 Withdraw the partially-ejected piston from the caliper body, and remove the dust seal. The piston can be withdrawn by hand, or if necessary pushed out by applying compressed air to the brake hose union hole.

10.5b . . . and remove the front brake caliper mounting bracket

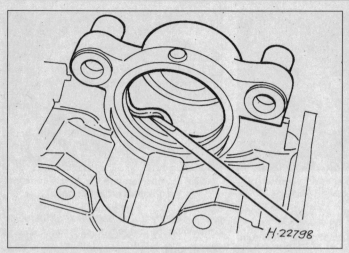

10.8 Removing the piston seal from the caliper body

10.16 The raised sectors (arrowed) must be positioned vertical when refitting the front brake caliper

Only low pressure should be required, such as is generated by a foot pump.

8 Using a small screwdriver, carefully remove the piston seal from the caliper, taking care not to mark the bore **(see illustration)**.

9 Carefully press the guide bushes out of the caliper body.

10 Thoroughly clean all components, using only methylated spirit or clean hydraulic fluid. Never use mineral-based solvents such as petrol or paraffin, which will attack the rubber components of the hydraulic system. Dry the components using compressed air or a clean, lint-free cloth. If available, use compressed air to blow clear the fluid passages.

 Warning: Wear eye protection when using compressed air!

11 Check all components, and renew any that are worn or damaged. If the piston and/or cylinder bore are scratched excessively, renew the complete caliper body. Similarly check the condition of the guide bushes and bolts; both bushes and bolts should be undamaged and (when cleaned) a reasonably tight sliding fit. If there is any doubt about the condition of any component, renew it.

12 If the caliper is fit for further use, obtain the necessary components from your Vauxhall/Opel dealer. Renew the caliper seals

and dust covers as a matter of course; these should never be re-used.

13 On reassembly, ensure that all components are absolutely clean and dry.

14 Dip the piston and the new piston seal in clean hydraulic fluid, and smear clean fluid on the cylinder bore surface.

15 Locate the new seal in the cylinder bore groove, using only the fingers to manipulate it into position.

16 Fit the new dust seal to the piston, then insert the piston into the cylinder bore using a twisting motion to ensure it enters the seal correctly. Make sure the piston enters squarely into the bore with the raised sectors positioned vertically as shown **(see illustration)**. Locate the dust seal in the body groove, and push the piston fully into the caliper bore.

17 Insert the guide bushes into position in the caliper body.

Refitting

18 Locate the caliper mounting bracket on the hub carrier, then insert and tighten the bolts (with locking fluid applied to their threads) to the specified torque **(see illustration)**.

19 Refit the brake pads as described in Section 4, together with the caliper which at this stage will not have the hose attached.

20 Position a new copper sealing washer on each side of the hose union, and connect the brake hose to the caliper. Ensure that the hose is correctly positioned against the caliper body lug, then install the union bolt and tighten it to the specified torque setting.

21 Remove the brake hose clamp or the polythene, where fitted, and bleed the hydraulic system as described in Section 2. Note that, providing the precautions described were taken to minimise brake fluid loss, it should only be necessary to bleed the relevant front brake.

22 Refit the roadwheel, then lower the vehicle to the ground and tighten the roadwheel bolts to the specified torque.

11 Rear brake caliper - removal, overhaul and refitting

Note: *Before starting work, refer to the note at the beginning of Section 2 concerning the dangers of hydraulic fluid, and to the warning at the beginning of Section 4 concerning the dangers of asbestos dust.*

Removal

1 Chock the front wheels, then jack up the rear of the vehicle and support on axle stands (see *"Jacking and Vehicle Support"*). Remove the roadwheel.

2 Minimise fluid loss by first removing the master cylinder reservoir cap, then tightening it down onto a piece of polythene to obtain an airtight seal.

3 Clean the area around the hydraulic line union nut, then loosen the nut **(see illustration)**. Do not fully unscrew the nut at this stage.

4 Remove the brake pads as described in Section 5.

5 Unscrew and remove the mounting bolts securing the caliper to the trailing arm **(see illustration)**.

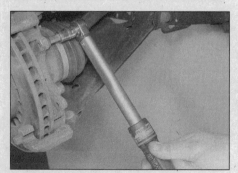

10.18 Tightening the front brake caliper mounting bracket bolts

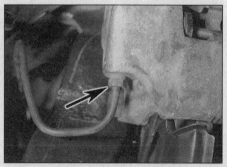

11.3 Hydraulic brake line union nut on the rear brake caliper

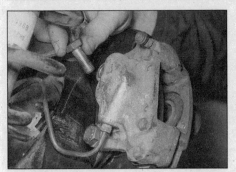

11.5 Unscrewing the bolts securing the rear brake caliper to the trailing arm

11.6 Removing the rear brake caliper from the trailing arm and disc

6 Fully unscrew the union nut and disconnect the hydraulic line from the caliper, then withdraw the caliper from the disc **(see illustration)**. Tape over or plug the hydraulic line to prevent entry of dust and dirt.

Overhaul

7 With the caliper on the bench, wipe it clean with a cloth rag.
8 Withdraw the partially-ejected pistons from the caliper body, and remove the dust seals. The pistons can be withdrawn by hand, or if necessary pushed out by applying compressed air to the brake line union hole. Only low pressure should be required, such as is generated by a foot pump.
9 Using a small screwdriver, carefully remove the piston seals from the caliper, taking care not mark the bore.
10 Thoroughly clean all components, using only methylated spirit or clean hydraulic fluid. Never use mineral-based solvents such as petrol or paraffin, which will attack the rubber components of the hydraulic system.
11 Dry the components using compressed air or a clean, lint-free cloth. If available, use compressed air to blow clear the fluid passages.

 Warning: Wear eye protection when using compressed air!

12 Check all components, and renew any that are worn or damaged. If the pistons and/or cylinder bores are scratched excessively, renew the complete caliper body.
13 If the caliper is fit for further use, obtain the necessary components from your Vauxhall/Opel dealer. Renew the caliper seals and dust covers as a matter of course; these should never be re-used.
14 On reassembly, ensure that all components are absolutely clean and dry.
15 Working on one piston at a time, dip the piston and the new piston seal in clean hydraulic fluid, and smear clean fluid on the cylinder bore surface.
16 Locate the new seal in the cylinder bore groove, using only the fingers to manipulate it into position.
17 Fit the new dust seal to the piston, then insert the piston into the cylinder bore using a twisting motion to ensure it enters the seal correctly. Make sure the piston enters squarely into the bore with the raised sectors positioned as described in Section 5 **(see illustration)**. Locate the dust seal in the body groove, and push the piston fully into the caliper bore.

Refitting

18 Locate the caliper over the disc, then insert the hydraulic line and screw in the union nut. Do not fully tighten the nut at this stage.
19 Apply a little locking fluid to the threads of the mounting bolts, then refit them and tighten to the specified torque.
20 Refit the brake pads (see Section 5).
21 Fully tighten the hydraulic union nut.
22 Remove the polythene, where fitted, and bleed the hydraulic system as described in Section 2. Note that, providing the precautions described were taken to minimise brake fluid loss, it should only be necessary to bleed the relevant rear brake.
23 Refit the roadwheel, then lower the vehicle to the ground and tighten the roadwheel bolts to the specified torque.

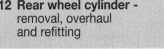

12 Rear wheel cylinder - removal, overhaul and refitting

Note: *Before starting work, refer to the note at the beginning of Section 2 concerning the dangers of hydraulic fluid, and to the warning at the beginning of Section 4 concerning the dangers of asbestos dust.*

11.17 Check that the piston (arrowed) is correctly positioned before refitting the rear brake caliper

Removal

1 Remove the brake drum (see Section 9).
2 Minimise fluid loss by first removing the master cylinder reservoir cap, and then tightening it down onto a piece of polythene, to obtain an airtight seal. Alternatively, use a brake hose clamp, a G-clamp or a similar tool to clamp the flexible hose at the nearest convenient point to the wheel cylinder.
3 Carefully unhook the brake shoe upper return spring, and remove it from both brake shoes. Pull the upper ends of the shoes away from the wheel cylinder to disengage them from the pistons.
4 Wipe away all traces of dirt around the brake pipe union nut at the rear of the wheel cylinder, and unscrew the nut. Carefully ease the pipe out of the wheel cylinder, and plug or tape over its end to prevent dirt entry. Wipe off any spilt fluid immediately.
5 Unscrew the retaining bolt from the rear of the backplate, and remove the wheel cylinder, taking great care not to allow surplus hydraulic fluid to contaminate the brake shoe linings.

Overhaul

6 Brush the dirt and dust from the wheel cylinder, but take care not to inhale it.
7 Pull the rubber dust seals from the ends of the cylinder body **(see illustration)**.
8 The pistons will normally be ejected by the pressure of the coil spring, but if they are not, tap the end of the cylinder body on a piece of wood, or apply low air pressure (eg, from a foot pump) to the hydraulic fluid union hole to eject the pistons from their bores.
9 Inspect the surfaces of the pistons and their bores in the cylinder body for scoring, or evidence of metal-to-metal contact. If evident, renew the complete wheel cylinder assembly.
10 If the pistons and bores are in good condition, discard the seals and obtain a repair kit, which will contain all the necessary renewable items.
11 Lubricate the piston seals with clean brake fluid, and insert them into the cylinder bores, with the spring between them, using finger pressure only.
12 Dip the pistons in clean brake fluid, and insert them into the cylinder bores.

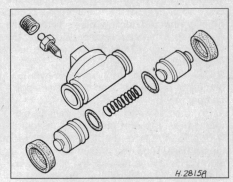

H.28158

12.7 Exploded view of the rear brake wheel cylinder

13 Fit the dust seals, and check that the pistons can move freely in their bores.

Refitting

14 Ensure that the backplate and wheel cylinder mating surfaces are clean, then spread the brake shoes and manoeuvre the wheel cylinder into position.

15 Insert the brake pipe, and screw in the union nut two or three turns to ensure that the thread has started.

16 Insert the wheel cylinder retaining bolt, and tighten to the specified torque setting. Now tighten the brake pipe union nut to the specified torque.

17 Remove the clamp from the flexible brake hose, or the polythene from the master cylinder reservoir (as applicable).

18 Ensure that the brake shoes are correctly located in the cylinder pistons, then carefully refit the brake shoe upper return spring.

19 Refit the brake drum as described in Section 9.

20 Bleed the brake hydraulic system as described in Section 2. Providing suitable precautions were taken to minimise loss of fluid, it should only be necessary to bleed the relevant rear brake.

---

13 Master cylinder -
removal, overhaul
and refitting

Note: *Before starting work, refer to the warning at the beginning of Section 2 concerning the dangers of hydraulic fluid.*

Removal

1 Exhaust the vacuum present in the brake servo unit by repeatedly depressing the brake pedal.

2 Remove the master cylinder reservoir cap and syphon the hydraulic fluid from the reservoir.

⚠ *Warning: Do not syphon the fluid by mouth, as it is poisonous; use a syringe or an old poultry baster.*

Alternatively, open any convenient bleed screw in the system, and gently pump the brake pedal to expel the fluid through a plastic tube connected to the bleed screw (see Section 2). Where applicable, disconnect the wiring connector from the brake fluid level sender unit.

3 Detach the relay box from the hydraulic modulator on the left-hand side of the engine compartment.

4 On models with manual transmission, release the clip and disconnect the clutch hydraulic pipe from the fluid reservoir **(see illustration)**. Tape over or plug the outlet.

5 Place cloth rags beneath the fluid reservoir then carefully prise it from the top of the master cylinder and withdraw from the engine compartment.

6 Identify the brake lines for position, then unscrew the union nuts and move the lines to one side. Tape over or plug the line outlets.

7 Unscrew the mounting nuts and withdraw the master cylinder from the front of the vacuum servo. Recover the seal. Take care not to spill fluid on the vehicle paintwork.

Overhaul

8 At the time of writing, master cylinder overhaul is not possible as no spares are available.

9 The only parts available individually are the fluid reservoir, its mounting seals, the filler cap and the master cylinder mounting seal.

10 If the master cylinder is worn excessively, it must be renewed.

Refitting

11 Ensure that the mating surfaces are clean and dry then fit the new seal to the rear of the master cylinder.

12 Fit the master cylinder to the servo unit, ensuring that the servo unit pushrod enters the master cylinder piston centrally. Fit the retaining nuts and tighten them to the specified torque setting.

13 Refit the brake lines and tighten the union nuts securely.

14 Smear a little brake fluid on the rubber seals in the top of the master cylinder, then press the fluid reservoir firmly into the seals.

15 On manual transmission models, reconnect the clutch hydraulic pipe and tighten the clip.

16 Refit the relay box to the hydraulic modulator.

17 Where applicable, reconnect the wiring connector to the brake fluid level sender unit.

18 Top-up the reservoir with fresh hydraulic fluid to the "MAX" mark (see *"Weekly checks"*).

19 Bleed the hydraulic system as described in Section 2 then refit the filler cap. Thoroughly check the operation of the braking system before using the vehicle on the road. **Note:** *The clutch hydraulic system uses the same reservoir as the brake system, bleed the clutch as described in Chapter 6, Section 2.*

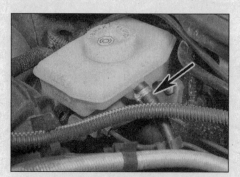

13.4 On manual transmission models, disconnect the clutch hydraulic pipe (arrowed) from the fluid reservoir

---

14 Brake pedal -
removal and refitting

Removal

1 Remove the vacuum servo unit as described in Section 15.

2 Unscrew the nuts securing the brake pedal assembly to the bulkhead.

3 Disconnect the wiring from the stop lamp switch on the pedal bracket.

4 Under the facia, unscrew the mounting bolts from the rear of the pedal bracket.

5 Withdraw the pedal assembly from inside the vehicle.

6 Note the location of the return spring and bearings, then unscrew the nuts from the ends of the pivot shaft, withdraw the shaft and remove the pedal components from the bracket.

7 Inspect the pedal for signs of wear or damage, paying particular attention to the pivot bearings, and renew worn components as necessary.

Refitting

8 Apply some multi-purpose grease to the bearing surfaces of the pedal, pivot shaft and bearings. Fit the pedal and components to the bracket then refit the nuts and tighten securely.

9 Locate the pedal assembly on the bulk-head. Fit the rear mounting bolts and tighten.

10 Reconnect the wiring to the stop lamp switch.

11 Refit the front mounting nuts and tighten to the specified torque.

12 Refit the vacuum servo unit as described in Section 15.

13 Check the operation of the brake pedal and stop lamp switch before using the vehicle on the road.

---

15 Vacuum servo unit -
testing, removal
and refitting

Testing

1 To test the operation of the servo unit, with the engine off, depress the footbrake several times to exhaust the vacuum. Now start the engine, keeping the pedal firmly depressed. As the engine starts, there should be a noticeable "give" in the brake pedal as the vacuum builds up. Allow the engine to run for at least two minutes, then switch it off. The brake pedal should now feel normal, but further applications should result in the pedal feeling firmer, the pedal stroke decreasing with each application.

2 If the servo does not operate as described, first inspect the servo unit check valve as described in Section 16.

3 If the servo unit still fails to operate

satisfactorily, the fault lies within the unit itself. Repairs to the unit are not possible; if faulty, the servo unit must be renewed.

Removal

Left-hand drive models

4 Remove the lower facia trim panel with reference to Chapter 11.

5 Working under the driver's side of the facia, prise out the locking plate then remove the pivot pin and disconnect the brake pedal from the servo piston rod.

6 Remove the rubber gaiter from the bulkhead.

7 Remove the brake master cylinder as described in Section 13.

8 Remove the wiring harness conduit from above the servo unit in the engine compartment.

9 Remove the ABS hydraulic modulator and control unit as described in Section 23. Unbolt the modulator mounting bracket. On some models it may be necessary to disconnect the hydraulic lines from the modulator.

10 Carefully prise the non-return valve or adapter from the rubber grommet in the servo unit.

11 Unscrew the mounting nuts from the bracket and recover the washers, then withdraw the unit forwards and upwards from the engine compartment.

Right-hand drive models

12 Remove the lower facia trim panel with reference to Chapter 11.

13 Working under the driver's side of the facia, prise out the clip and disconnect the pedal pushrod from the vacuum servo piston.

14 Remove the bonnet as described in Chapter 11, and the windscreen front deflector as described in Chapter 12, Section 16, when removing the wiper motor linkage.

15 Remove the air cleaner and duct assembly as described in Chapter 4.

16 As applicable, unbolt the engine torque support brackets from the right-hand side of the engine.

17 Remove the brake master cylinder as described in Section 13.

18 Prise the vacuum non-return valve or adapter and elbow from the rubber grommet in the vacuum servo **(see illustration)**.

19 Remove the wiper motor as described in Chapter 12.

20 Unscrew the mounting nuts and bolt located on the right-hand side of the bulkhead and beneath the servo.

21 Release the hydraulic brake lines from the clips on the bulkhead, then withdraw the vacuum servo unit from the engine compartment.

Refitting

22 Before refitting the servo, check that the pushrod setting dimension is correct, as follows.

23 Measure the distance from the end face of the servo casing to the end of the pushrod with reference to the illustration **(see illustrations)**. This distance should be 149.5 mm on left-hand drive models and 152.4 mm on right-hand drive models.

24 If adjustment is necessary, slacken the locknut, and turn the pushrod to give the specified dimension. Hold the pushrod and tighten the locknut to the specified torque.

25 Inspect the servo unit check valve sealing grommet for signs of damage or deterioration, and renew if necessary as described in Section 16.

Left-hand drive models

26 Ensure that the servo mounting faces are clean and dry.

27 Locate the servo on the bulkhead and align with the pedal pushrod, then refit the mounting nuts and tighten to the specified torque.

28 Refit the non-return valve or adapter in the rubber grommet.

29 Refit the ABS hydraulic modulator and control unit together with the mounting bracket with reference to Section 23.

15.18 Vacuum hose adapter location (arrowed) in the vacuum servo unit

Reconnect the hydraulic lines where necessary.

30 Refit the wiring harness conduit.

31 Refit the brake master cylinder with reference to Section 13.

32 Refit the rubber gaiter to the bulkhead.

33 Reconnect the brake pedal to the servo piston rod and refit the locking plate.

34 Refit the lower facia trim panel with reference to Chapter 11.

35 Bleed the brake hydraulic system as described in Section 2.

36 On completion, start the engine and check for air leaks at the vacuum hose-to-servo unit connection. Check the operation of the braking system.

Right-hand drive models

37 Ensure that the servo mounting faces are clean and dry.

38 Locate the servo unit on the bulkhead then refit the mounting nuts and bolt and tighten to the specified torque.

39 Refit the wiper motor (Chapter 12).

40 Refit the non-return valve or adapter and elbow to the rubber grommet in the vacuum servo.

41 Refit the brake master cylinder with reference to Section 13.

42 Refit the hydraulic brake lines in the clips on the bulkhead.

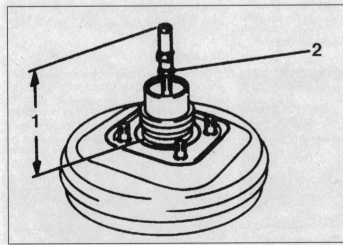

15.23a Pushrod setting dimension (1) and locknut (2) on LHD models

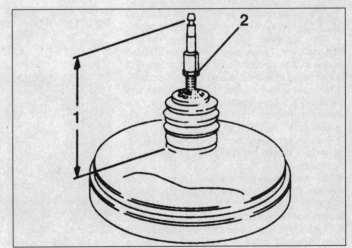

15.23b Pushrod setting dimension (1) and locknut (2) on RHD models

9

43 Refit the engine torque support brackets and tighten the mounting bolts to the specified torque.

44 Refit the air cleaner and duct assembly with reference to Chapter 4.

45 Refit the windscreen front deflector as described in Chapter 12, Section 16, and the bonnet as described in Chapter 11.

46 Refit the clip securing the pedal pushrod to the vacuum servo piston.

47 Refit the lower facia trim panel with reference to Chapter 11.

48 Bleed the brake hydraulic system as described in Section 2.

49 On completion, start the engine and check for air leaks at the vacuum hose-to-servo unit connection. Check the operation of the braking system.

16 Vacuum servo unit check valve and hose - removal, testing and refitting

Removal

1 Carefully ease the non-return valve or adapter from its rubber grommet on the front of the servo unit.

2 Disconnect the hose from the non-return valve/adapters as necessary and unscrew the union nut from the inlet manifold (petrol engines) or vacuum pump (diesel engines). If the hose is tight it may be necessary to cut it free.

Testing

3 Examine the check valve and hose(s) for signs of damage, and renew if necessary. The valve(s) may be tested by blowing through them in both directions. Air should flow through the valve in one direction only - when blown through from the servo unit end. Renew the valves and hoses as necessary.

4 Examine the servo unit rubber sealing grommet for signs of damage or deterioration, and renew as necessary.

Refitting

5 Refitting is a reversal of removal but make sure that the arrows on the non-return valve points towards the inlet manifold (petrol engines) or vacuum pump (diesel engines). Tighten the union nut on the inlet manifold or vacuum pump to the specified torque.

6 On completion, start the engine and check that there are no air leaks.

17 Handbrake - adjustment

1 It is only necessary to adjust the handbrake after renewing or dismantling the rear brake shoes, or renewing the drum/disc.

Rear drum brake models

2 Chock the front wheels, then jack up the rear of the vehicle and support on axle stands (see "Jacking and Vehicle Support").

3 Fully release the handbrake lever, then apply the footbrake firmly several times to ensure that the self-adjust mechanism is fully adjusted. Apply the handbrake lever to the 7th notch, and check that both rear wheels are locked firmly by attempting to rotate them by hand.

4 If adjustment is necessary, release the gaiter from the centre console and withdraw it over the handbrake lever for access to the adjustment nut.

5 Set the handbrake to the 4th notch, then tighten the adjustment nut on the handbrake lever (on the front of the primary cable) until the rear wheels can just be turned by hand.

6 Apply the handbrake lever to the 7th notch and check that both rear wheels are locked firmly. If necessary, repeat the adjustment procedure.

7 Refit the gaiter and lower the vehicle to the ground.

Rear disc brake models

8 Chock the front wheels, then jack up the rear of the vehicle and support on axle stands (see "Jacking and Vehicle Support").

9 Fully release the handbrake lever, then apply it to the 7th notch. Check that both rear wheels are locked firmly by attempting to rotate them.

10 If adjustment is necessary, first fully release the handbrake then release the gaiter from the centre console and withdraw it over the handbrake lever for access to the adjustment nut. Back off the nut to the end of the primary cable.

11 Remove both rear wheels.

12 Working on one side at a time, position the hole in the disc over the serrated adjustment nut on the adjuster at the top of the backplate. Using a screwdriver inserted through the hole, turn the nut to lock the disc then back it off until the disc just moves freely **(see illustration)**. Repeat the adjustment on the remaining rear brake.

13 Inside the vehicle, screw on the adjustment nut on the handbrake lever several turns then apply the lever to the 7th notch **(see illustration)**. Check that both rear wheels are firmly locked. If adjustment is necessary, release the handbrake and turn the adjustment nut as required, then recheck the adjustment.

14 After fitting new handbrake shoes, the shoes should be bedded-in by driving a short distance (approximately 300 meters) at low speed with the handbrake lever lightly applied. Check and if necessary adjust the handbrake again after completing the bedding-in.

15 Refit the rear wheels, refit the gaiter to the handbrake lever, and lower the vehicle to the ground.

17.12 Adjusting the handbrake shoes using a screwdriver through the hole in the disc/flange

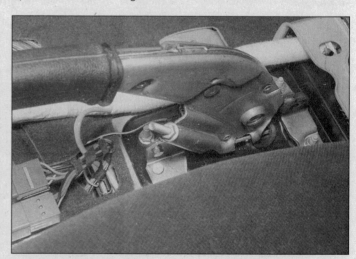

17.13 Adjustment nut on the handbrake lever

18 Handbrake lever - removal and refitting

Removal

1 Jack up the vehicle and support on axle stands (see "*Jacking and Vehicle Support*").
2 Remove the exhaust system as described in Chapter 4.
3 Unbolt and remove the heatshield for access to the handbrake lever compensator. With the handbrake lever fully released, push the compensator forwards and unhook the primary cable from it.
4 Inside the vehicle, remove the centre console and handbrake lever gaiter as described in Chapter 11.
5 Unscrew the adjustment nut from the front end of the primary cable and withdraw the cable from the handbrake lever.
6 Unscrew and remove the lever mounting nuts, then disconnect the wiring from the warning light switch and withdraw the lever from inside the vehicle **(see illustration)**.
7 The handbrake "on" warning lamp switch can be removed from the lever assembly after unscrewing the securing bolt.

Refitting

8 Refitting is a reversal of removal, but adjust the handbrake as described in Section 17.

19 Handbrake cables - removal and refitting

Removal

1 The handbrake cable consists of three main sections, a short front (primary) section which connects the lever to the equalizer plate and the left- and right-hand rear (secondary) sections which link the equalizer plate to the rear brakes. Short cables connect the rear of the secondary cables to the levers on the rear brake shoes with a special spring clip. Each section can be removed individually as follows.

Primary (front) cable

2 Firmly chock the front wheels, then jack up the rear of the vehicle and support it on axle stands (see "*Jacking and Vehicle Support*").
3 Inside the vehicle, release the gaiter from the centre console and withdraw it over the handbrake lever.
4 With the handbrake lever fully released, unscrew the adjustment nut from the front end of the primary cable.
5 Working beneath the vehicle, remove the rear exhaust system from the catalytic converter as described in Chapter 4.
6 Unbolt and remove the heatshield from the underbody for access to the handbrake compensator plate.

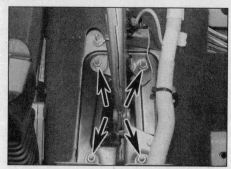

18.6 Handbrake lever mounting nuts (arrowed)

7 Turn the end stop of the primary cable through 90° and disconnect it from the compensator plate.
8 Disconnect the rubber boot from the underbody, and withdraw the primary cable. Remove the boot from the cable.

Secondary (rear) cable

Note: *The secondary cables are supplied as one part together with the compensator plate.*
9 Firmly chock the front wheels, then jack up the rear of the vehicle and support it on axle stands (see "*Jacking and Vehicle Support*"). Fully release the handbrake lever.
10 Working beneath the vehicle, remove the rear exhaust system from the catalytic converter as described in Chapter 4.
11 Unbolt and remove the heatshield from the underbody for access to the handbrake compensator plate.
12 Push the compensator plate forwards, then turn the end stop of the primary cable through 90° and disconnect it from the compensator plate.
13 Disconnect the rear of each secondary cable from the rear cables at the connectors using a small screwdriver to prise them out. Examine the connectors and if necessary renew them.
14 Bend up the retaining clips and release the cable assembly from the guides on the underbody.
15 Withdraw the assembly from under the vehicle.

Rear cable

16 Firmly chock the front wheels, then jack up the rear of the vehicle and support it on axle stands (see "*Jacking and Vehicle Support*"). Fully release the handbrake lever.
17 Disconnect the rear cable from the connector using a small screwdriver to prise out the end fitting. Examine the connector and if necessary renew it.
18 Unhook the cable from the rear brake shoe lever.
19 If necessary, remove the rubber boot from the lever.

Refitting

20 Refitting is a reversal of the removal procedure, but adjust the handbrake as described in Section 17.

20 Stop-light switch - removal, refitting and adjustment

Removal

1 The stop-light switch is located on the pedal bracket in the driver's footwell.
2 To remove the switch, first remove the lower facia trim panel (see Chapter 11), then disconnect the heating duct for access to the switch.
3 Disconnect the wiring plug from the top of the switch, then twist the switch and remove it from the pedal bracket.

Refitting and adjustment

4 Before refitting the switch, push the actuation pin fully in.
5 Screw the switch into the pedal bracket and tighten moderately.
6 Depress the brake pedal then pull the actuation pin fully out of the switch so that it contacts the pedal. Now release the pedal to set the pin.
7 Refit the heating duct and the lower facia trim panel. Check the operation of the stop-light.

21 Handbrake "on" warning light switch - removal and refitting

Removal

1 Unclip the handbrake lever gaiter from the centre console and withdraw it over the handbrake lever.
2 Disconnect the wiring then unscrew the mounting bolt and remove the switch from the handbrake lever bracket **(see illustration)**.

Refitting

3 Refitting is a reversal of removal.

21.2 Disconnect the wiring (arrowed) from the handbrake "on" warning light switch

22 Anti-lock Braking and Traction Control systems - general information

ABS is fitted as standard to all models. Traction control is fitted as standard to 2.0 litre petrol engine models.

The ABS system comprises a hydraulic modulator and electronic control unit together with four roadwheel sensors. The hydraulic modulator contains the electronic control unit (ECU), the hydraulic solenoid valves (one set for each brake) and the electrically-driven pump. The purpose of the system is to prevent the wheel(s) locking during heavy braking. This is achieved by automatic release of the brake on the relevant wheel, followed by re-application of the brake.

The solenoid valves are controlled by the ECU, which itself receives signals from the four wheel sensors which monitor the speed of rotation of each wheel. By comparing these signals, the ECU can determine the speed at which the vehicle is travelling. It can then use this speed to determine when a wheel is decelerating at an abnormal rate, compared to the speed of the vehicle, and therefore predicts when a wheel is about to lock. During normal operation, the system functions in the same way as a non-ABS braking system.

If the ECU senses that a wheel is about to lock, it operates the relevant solenoid valve(s) in the hydraulic unit, which then isolates from the master cylinder the relevant brake(s) on the wheel(s) which is/are about to lock, effectively sealing-in the hydraulic pressure.

If the speed of rotation of the wheel continues to decrease at an abnormal rate, the ECU operates the electrically-driven pump which pumps the hydraulic fluid back into the master cylinder, releasing the brake. Once the speed of rotation of the wheel returns to an acceptable rate, the pump stops, and the solenoid valves switch again, allowing the hydraulic master cylinder pressure to return to the caliper/wheel cylinder (as applicable), which then re-applies the brake. This cycle can be carried out many times-a-second.

The action of the solenoid valves and return pump creates pulses in the hydraulic circuit. When the ABS system is functioning, these pulses can be felt through the brake pedal.

On 2.0 litre petrol models equipped with ABS, the hydraulic unit incorporates an additional set of solenoid valves which operate the traction control system. The system operates at speeds up to approximately 30 mph (60 km/h) using the signals supplied by the wheel sensors. If the ECU senses that a driving wheel is about to lose traction, it prevents this by momentarily applying the relevant front brake.

The operation of the ABS and the traction control system is entirely dependent on electrical signals. To prevent the system responding to any inaccurate signals, a built-in safety circuit monitors all signals received by the ECU. If an inaccurate signal or low battery voltage is detected, the system is automatically shut down, and the warning light on the instrument panel is illuminated, to inform the driver that the system is not operational. Normal braking is still available, however.

If a fault develops in the ABS/traction control system, the vehicle must be taken to a Vauxhall/Opel dealer for fault diagnosis and repair.

23 Anti-lock Braking and Traction Control system components - removal and refitting

Hydraulic modulator and electronic control unit (models without traction control)

Removal

1 Remove the battery as described in Chapter 5A.
2 Remove the relay box and bracket from the hydraulic modulator.
3 Unscrew and remove the filler cap from the brake fluid reservoir, then draw out all of the hydraulic fluid using a poultry baster or old battery hydrometer.
4 Disconnect the special multiplug from the top of the hydraulic modulator by lifting the clip and unhooking the multiplug.
5 Unscrew the union nuts securing the hydraulic lines to the master cylinder and withdraw the lines a little way. Ideally, a special split ring spanner should be used to unscrew the nuts as they may be tight. Be prepared for some loss of fluid by placing cloth rags beneath the lines.
6 Unscrew and remove the three mounting bolts, then withdraw the modulator and control unit upwards from the engine compartment. Take care not to spill any hydraulic fluid on the vehicle's paintwork.

Refitting

7 Refitting is a reversal of removal, but finally bleed the hydraulic system as described in Section 2. **Note:** *The clutch hydraulic system uses the same reservoir as the brake system, bleed the clutch as described in Chapter 6, Section 2.*

Hydraulic modulator and electronic control unit (models with traction control)

Removal

8 Disconnect the battery negative (earth) lead (see Chapter 5A).
9 Disconnect the vacuum hose from the brake vacuum servo unit.
10 Remove the relay together with its base.
11 Remove the relay box from the hydraulic modulator.
12 Remove the brake master cylinder as described in Section 13.
13 Unscrew the upper brake line union nuts and release the lines a little way from the modulator. Ideally, a special split ring spanner should be used to unscrew the nuts as they may be tight. Loosen only the lower brake line union nuts.
14 Disconnect the earth cable from the modulator.
15 Disconnect the special wiring multiplug from the control unit by lifting the clip and unhooking the multiplug.
16 Loosen the clip and disconnect the small hose from the coolant expansion tank. Plug the hose to prevent loss of coolant. Remove the clip then position the expansion tank to one side.
17 Unscrew the mounting nut, then carefully move the brake lines to one side as necessary and lift the modulator and control unit upwards from the engine compartment.

Refitting

18 Refitting is a reversal of removal, but finally bleed the hydraulic system as described in Section 2. **Note:** *The clutch hydraulic system uses the same reservoir as the brake system, bleed the clutch as described in Chapter 6, Section 2. If necessary, top-up the cooling system (see "Weekly checks").*

Wheel sensor

Removal

19 To remove the rear wheel sensor, remove the wheel hub as described in Chapter 10.
20 To remove the front wheel sensor, first apply the handbrake, then jack up the front of the vehicle and support it on axle stands (see "Jacking and Vehicle Support"). Remove the relevant roadwheel.

23.22a Unscrew the bolt using a Torx key . . .

23.22b . . . and remove the wheel sensor

24.1 The vacuum pump is on the left-hand end of the cylinder head (2.0 litre diesel engine)

24.3 Unscrew the union nut (arrowed) and disconnect the pipe from the vacuum pump (2.0 litre diesel engine)

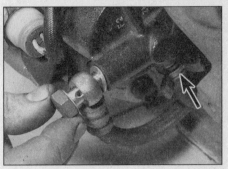

24.4 Disconnecting the oil feed line from the vacuum pump. Return line arrowed (1.7 litre diesel engine)

21 Disconnect the sensor wiring and release it from the clips on the front suspension strut and wheel arch.
22 Unscrew the mounting bolt using a Torx key and remove the sensor from the mounting bracket **(see illustrations)**.

Refitting

23 Refitting is a reversal of removal, but tighten the mounting bolt to the specified torque.

Traction Control switch

Removal

24 Carefully prise the switch from the facia panel, using a small screwdriver. Use card or cloth to prevent damage to the facia.

Refitting

25 Refitting is a reversal of removal.

ABS Control Unit

Removal

26 Remove the hydraulic modulator and electronic control unit as previously described in this Section.
27 Disconnect the wiring then unscrew the mounting bolts and carefully remove the ABS control unit from the hydraulic body taking care not to damage the coil carrier.
28 Recover the seal from between the coil carrier and control unit.

Refitting

29 Insert the new seal, then carefully position the ABS control unit on the body and tighten

the bolts to the specified torque in the stages given. **Note:** *Do not tilt the control unit when positioning it on the body.*
30 The remaining procedure is a reversal of the removal procedure.

24 Vacuum pump (diesel engine models) - removal and refitting

Removal

1 On the 1.7 litre diesel engine the vacuum pump is attached to the rear of the alternator, however on the 2.0 litre diesel engine it is bolted directly to the cylinder head **(see illustration)**. Access to the pump on the 1.7 litre engine can be improved by removal of the exhaust pipe heatshield adjacent to it, or alternatively, the alternator may be removed as described in Chapter 5A.
2 On the 1.7 litre engine, apply the handbrake then jack up the front of the vehicle and support it on axle stands (see *"Jacking and Vehicle Support"*).
3 Disconnect the servo vacuum pipe from the pump by counterholding the large union nut and unscrewing the small one **(see illustration)**.
4 On the 1.7 litre engine, unscrew the union nut and disconnect the oil feed line from the pump **(see illustration)**.
5 Release the clip and disconnect the oil return line. Allow any oil to drain into a suitable container and plug or cap all lines.

6 Unscrew the mounting bolts, taking note of any cable clips/supports fitted beneath them, and withdraw the pump from the alternator drive spline (1.7 litre engine) or cylinder head (2.0 litre engine) **(see illustrations)**.
7 Remove the O-ring from the alternator (1.7 litre engine) or groove in the pump (2.0 litre engine) **(see illustration)**. Discard the O-ring and obtain a new one.

Refitting

8 Refitting is a reversal of removal, noting the following points.
a) *On the 1.7 litre engine, before fitting the pump pour approximately 5 cc of clean engine oil into the oil feed aperture.*
b) *Clean the mating faces of the pump and alternator or cylinder head (as applicable) and fit a new O-ring.*
c) *On the 1.7 litre engine, with the pump fitted to the alternator ensure that the alternator pulley can be turned easily by hand.*

25 Vacuum pump (diesel engine models) - testing and overhaul

Note: *A vacuum gauge will be required for this check.*
1 The operation of the braking system vacuum pump can be checked using a vacuum gauge.

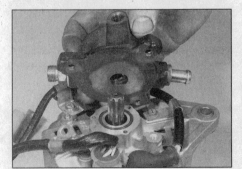

24.6a Removing the vacuum pump from the alternator (1.7 litre diesel engine)

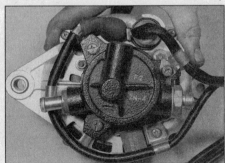

24.6b Ensure that the electrical cables are correctly routed around the vacuum pump (1.7 litre diesel engine)

24.7 Renew the O-ring (arrowed) in the alternator casing (1.7 litre diesel engine)

9

2 Disconnect the vacuum pipe from the pump, and connect the gauge to the pump union using a suitable length of hose.

3 Start the engine and allow it to idle, then measure the vacuum created by the pump. As a guide, after one minute, a minimum of approximately 500 mm Hg should be recorded. If the vacuum registered is significantly less than this, it is likely that the pump is faulty. However, seek the advice of a Vauxhall/Opel dealer before condemning the pump.

4 Overhaul of the vacuum pump is not possible, since no components are available separately for it. If faulty, the complete pump assembly must be renewed.

Chapter 10
Suspension and steering

Contents

Degrees of difficulty

| Easy, suitable for novice with little experience | | Fairly easy, suitable for beginner with some experience | | Fairly difficult, suitable for competent DIY mechanic | | Difficult, suitable for experienced DIY mechanic | | Very difficult, suitable for expert DIY or professional | |

Specifications

General

Front suspension type . . . . Independent, with MacPherson struts, gas-filled shock absorbers and anti-roll bar

Rear suspension type . . . . Independent, with trailing arms, coil springs, gas-filled shock absorbers, upper and lower transverse arms and anti-roll bar

Steering type . . . . Rack and pinion. Power steering standard on all models.

Rear wheel bearings

Bearing play (maximum) . . . . 0.3 mm
Bearing lateral run-out . . . . 0.05 mm
Bearing radial run-out . . . . 0.05 mm

Front wheel alignment

Camber . . . . -1°05' ± 45'
  Max. difference between sides . . . . 1°
Castor (non-adjustable):
  Saloon . . . . +3°50' ± 1°
  Estate . . . . +3°30' ± 1°
  Max. difference between sides . . . . 1°
Toe in . . . . +0°10' ± 10'
Toe-in on turns (inner wheel turned in 20°) . . . . 1°10' ± 45'

10

Rear wheel alignment

Camber (non-adjustable):
Up to 1997 models .... -1°20' ± 35'
From 1997 models:
    Saloon .... -1°27' ± 35'
    Estate .... -1°19' ± 35'
Max. difference between sides .... 35'
Toe in:
Up to 01/96 .... +0°16' ± 10'
01/96 to 1997 models .... +0°25' ± 10'
From 1997 models:
    Saloon .... +0°27' ± 10'
    Estate .... +0°26' ± 10'
Max. difference between sides .... 15'

Steering

Ratio .... 16.5 : 1
Power steering drivebelt tension (measured with Vauxhall special gauge):
New belt .... 250 to 300 N
Used belt .... 450 N

Wheels and tyres

Wheel size .... 5½J x 14 or 6J x 15
Tyre size:
5½J x 14 wheels .... 175/70 R14-84T, 185/70 R14-88 H, 185/70 R14-88 T
6J x 15 wheels .... 195/65 R15-91 H, 195/65 R15-91 T, 195/65 R15-91 V, 205/60 R15-91 V

Torque wrench settings

	Nm	lbf ft
Front suspension		
Brake splash guard	4	3
Front anti-roll bar link:		
To strut	65	48
To anti-roll bar	65	48
Front anti-roll bar to subframe	20	15
Front subframe:		
Bolts 1,3, 4, 5 (ie all except engine mounting nuts): *		
Stage 1	100	74
Stage 2	Angle-tighten 45°	
Stage 3	Angle-tighten 15°	
Bolts 2 (ie engine mounting nuts)	45	33
Front suspension lower arm to subframe: *		
Stage 1	90	66
Stage 2	Angle-tighten 75°	
Stage 3	Angle-tighten 15°	
Front suspension lower balljoint to hub carrier	100	74
Front suspension lower balljoint to lower arm	35	26
Front suspension strut upper mounting	55	41
Hydraulic line to steering gear	28	21
Strut to hub carrier: *		
Stage 1	50	37
Stage 2	90	66
Stage 3	Angle-tighten 45°	
Stage 4	Angle-tighten 15°	
Support bearing to shock absorber piston rod	70	52
Rear suspension		
Anti-roll bar	55	41
Rear suspension strut to trailing arm: *		
Stage 1	150	111
Stage 2	Angle-tighten 30°	
Stage 3	Angle-tighten 15°	
Rear suspension strut upper mounting bracket to body	55	41
Rear shock absorber upper retaining nut	20	15
Trailing arm front mounting bracket to underbody: *		
Stage 1	90	66
Stage 2	Angle-tighten 30°	
Stage 3	Angle-tighten 15°	
Trailing arm to front mounting bracket: *		
Stage 1	90	66
Stage 2	Angle-tighten 60°	
Stage 3	Angle-tighten 15°	

Torque wrench settings (continued)

Rear suspension (continued)

	Nm	lbf ft
Rear suspension upper arm to trailing arm and subframe: *		
Stage 1	90	66
Stage 2	Angle-tighten 60°	
Stage 3	Angle-tighten 15°	
Rear suspension lower arm to trailing arm and subframe: *		
Stage 1	90	66
Stage 2	Angle-tighten 60°	
Stage 3	Angle-tighten 15°	
Rear suspension subframe to underbody: *		
Stage 1	90	66
Stage 2	Angle-tighten 60°	
Stage 3	Angle-tighten 15°	
Rear hub bracket to trailing arm: *		
Stage 1	50	37
Stage 2	Angle-tighten 30°	
Stage 3	Angle-tighten 15°	
Steering		
Hydraulic pressure line to power steering pump:		
Petrol engines	37.5	28
1.7 diesel engine	28	21
2.0 diesel engine	35	26
Rear engine mounting bracket to subframe	20	15
Steering gear to subframe	45	33
Steering wheel	25	19
Airbag unit to steering wheel	8	6
Steering column to crossmember	22	16
Steering column brace upper nut	22	16
Steering column intermediate shaft clamp bolt	22	16
Power steering pump to bracket:		
1.6 litre petrol engine models	20	15
1.8 and 2.0 litre petrol engine models	25	19
Diesel engine models	25	19
Power steering pump pulley: *		
Stage 1	20	15
Stage 2	Angle-tighten 30°	
Stage 3	Angle-tighten 45°	
Power steering pump tensioner	40	30
Track rod to steering gear rack:		
Saginaw	100	74
Servotronic	80 ± 8	60 ± 6
Track rod end to track rod	85	63
Track rod end locknut	60	44
Track rod end to hub carrier steering arm	60	44
Wheels		
All models	110	81

* Note: *The manufacturer states that all fasteners secured by the angle-tightening method must be renewed as a matter of course.*

1 General information and precautions

General information

The front suspension is of independent type, with a subframe, MacPherson struts, lower arms, and an anti-roll bar. The struts, which incorporate coil springs and integral gas-filled shock absorbers, are attached at their upper ends to the reinforced strut mountings on the body shell. The lower end of each strut is bolted to the top of a cast hub carrier, which carries the hub, and the brake disc and caliper. The hubs run within non-adjustable bearings in the hub carriers. The lower end of each hub carrier is attached, via a balljoint, to a pressed-steel lower arm assembly. The balljoints are bolted to the lower arms and attached to the hub carriers by a clamp bolt. Each lower arm is attached at its inboard end to the subframe with flexible rubber bushes, and controls both lateral and fore and aft movement of the front wheels. An anti-roll bar is fitted to all models. The anti-roll bar is mounted on the subframe, and is connected to the suspension struts by vertical drop links.

The rear suspension is of fully independent type, with a central crossmember, gas-filled shock absorbers incorporating coil springs, trailing arms, upper and lower transverse arms, and an anti-roll bar. The shock absorbers are attached at their upper ends to tower units located in the wheel arches; this design reduces the transfer of noise to the rear interior of the vehicle. The rear hub/stub axles are bolted to the trailing arms. The trailing arms and upper and lower transverse arms are located with flexible rubber bushes. A rear anti-roll bar is fitted to all models. The anti-roll bar is mounted on the central subframe and is connected to the trailing arms by drop links.

10

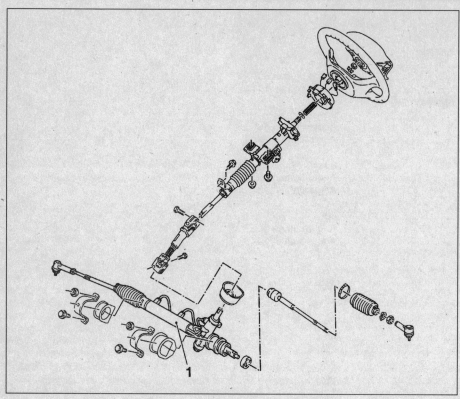

1.3 Steering gear and column components

The steering is of conventional rack-and-pinion type, incorporating a collapsible safety column (see illustration). The column is joined to the steering gear by an intermediate shaft incorporating two universal joints. The upper section of the column includes an outer slip coupling into which the steering lock engages. With the steering lock engaged, the coupling allows the column to turn at torques above 200 Nm only, so making it impossible to break the steering lock shear pin. However, at this torque it is not possible to control the vehicle. The steering gear is mounted on the front suspension subframe. The steering gear track-rods are attached to the steering arms on the hub carriers by track rod ends.

All models are fitted with power assisted steering. The power steering pump is belt-driven from the crankshaft pulley. The hydraulic fluid reservoir is either incorporated in the pump or located remotely according to model.

Precautions

An airbag is fitted to the steering wheel. To ensure it operates correctly should it ever be needed, and to avoid the risk of personal injury from it being accidentally triggered, the following precautions must be observed. Also refer to Chapter 12 for more information:

a) *Before carrying out any operations on the airbag system, disconnect the battery negative terminal, and wait at least 1 minute to ensure that the system capacitor has been discharged.*

b) *Note that the airbag must not be subjected to temperatures in excess of 90°C (194°F). When the airbag is removed, ensure that it is stored with the pad facing upwards.*

c) *Do not allow any solvents or cleaning agents to contact the airbag assembly. The unit must be cleaned using only a damp cloth.*

d) *The airbag and control unit are both sensitive to impact. If either is dropped from a height of more than 50 cm (20 in), they must be renewed.*

e) *Disconnect the airbag control unit wiring plug prior to using arc-welding equipment on the vehicle.*

f) *On vehicles fitted with a passenger side airbag, **do not** fit accessories in the airbag*

2.5 Tie the brake caliper to the coil spring while removing the front hub carrier

zone. Items like telephones, cassette storage boxes, additional mirrors, etc., can be ripped off and cause serious injury, if the airbag inflates.

2 Front hub carrier - removal and refitting

Note: *It is recommended that all mounting nuts and bolts are renewed. A balljoint separator tool will be required for this operation.*
Caution: The front wheel camber setting is controlled by the bolts securing the hub carrier to the front suspension strut. Before removing the bolts, mark the hub carrier in relation to the strut accurately. On completion, the camber setting must be checked and adjusted by a suitably equipped garage.

Removal

1 Apply the handbrake, then jack up the front of the vehicle and support it on axle stands (see *"Jacking and Vehicle Support"*). Remove the relevant front wheel.

2 Unscrew the nut securing the track rod end to the steering arm on the hub carrier. Using a balljoint separator, separate the track rod end from the steering arm.

3 Unscrew and remove the clamp bolt securing the front suspension lower arm balljoint in the hub carrier, noting which way round it is fitted.

4 Using a suitable lever, push down the lower arm and separate it from the hub carrier. When releasing the lower arm, take care not to damage the balljoint rubber boot on the bottom of the hub carrier; if necessary protect it with a piece of card or plastic. **Note:** *If the balljoint stub is tight in the hub carrier, use a screwdriver or cold chisel as a wedge to force the clamp apart.*

5 Remove the brake caliper with reference to Chapter 9, however, do not disconnect the hydraulic line from it. Tie the caliper to the coil on the front suspension strut using a length of wire or string (see illustration).

6 Unscrew the mounting bolt and remove the wheel speed sensor from the top of the hub carrier. Tie it to one side.

7 Carefully tap the protective cap from the centre of the hub, then extract the split pin and unscrew the driveshaft retaining nut while holding the hub stationary with a bar positioned between two wheel bolts temporarily refitted to the hub. **Note:** *The nut is tightened to a high torque.* Remove the nut and spacer.

8 Pull the hub carrier out while pressing the driveshaft through the hub. If it is tight use a suitable puller.

9 Mark the position of the strut on the hub carrier. This is important to maintain the camber setting.

2.10a Removing the bolts securing the hub carrier to the strut

2.10b Withdrawing the hub from the driveshaft

2.12 Front splash guard retaining screws

10 Unscrew and remove the two bolts securing the hub carrier to the strut noting which way round they are fitted. Now lift the hub carrier from under the front wing while withdrawing the hub from the driveshaft **(see illustrations)**. If necessary, use a soft faced mallet to drive the driveshaft through the hub.
11 Undo the screw and remove the front brake disc from the hub drive flange.
12 Undo the screws and remove the splash guard from the hub carrier **(see illustration)**.

Refitting

13 Refit the splash guard to the hub carrier and tighten the screws.
14 Refit the front brake disc to the hub drive flange and tighten the screw.
15 Ensure that the driveshaft outer constant velocity joint and hub splines are clean, then apply a little grease to the splines.
16 Lift the hub carrier into position and locate the hub on the splines on the end of the driveshaft. Locate the top of the hub carrier on the strut and insert the bolts making sure that the bolt heads are facing the front of the vehicle. With the hub carrier positioned as noted previously, tighten the bolts to the specified torque. If new components are being fitted, loosely tighten the bolts at this stage, and adjust the camber before using the vehicle on the road.
17 Refit the driveshaft retaining nut and spacer and hand-tighten the nut at this stage.
18 Refit the brake caliper with reference to Chapter 9.
19 Using a lever, push down the lower suspension arm then locate the balljoint in the bottom of the hub carrier and push the balljoint fully upwards. Insert the clamp bolt with its head facing to the rear and tighten to the specified torque.
20 Refit the track rod end to the steering arm and tighten the nut to the specified torque.
21 Refit the front wheel and lower the vehicle to the ground.
22 Fully tighten the driveshaft retaining nut to the specified torque in the stages given in the Specifications (see Chapter 8). Check that the castellated nut is aligned with the hole in the driveshaft - if necessary, loosen the nut slightly to the next castellation. Fit a new split pin and bend over its ends to secure.

23 Tap the protective cap on the centre of the hub.
24 Check and if necessary adjust the camber angle setting at the earliest opportunity.

3 Front wheel bearings - checking and renewal

Note: *A press, a suitable puller, or similar improvised tools will be required for this operation. Obtain a bearing overhaul kit before proceeding. A new bearing retaining circlip should be used on refitting.*

Checking

1 To check the front wheel bearings for wear, apply the handbrake then jack up the front of the vehicle and support it on axle stands (see *"Jacking and Vehicle Support"*). Spin the wheel by hand and check for a noisy or rough bearing. Grip the wheel and rock it to check for excessive play in the bearing, however be careful not to confuse wear in the suspension or steering joints with wear in the bearing.

Renewal

2 With the hub carrier removed as described in Section 2, proceed as follows.
3 The hub must now be removed from the bearing/hub carrier assembly. It is preferable to use a press to do this, but it is possible to drive out the hub using a metal tube of suitable diameter. Alternatively a suitable puller can be used.
4 Securely support the hub carrier, with the inner face uppermost then, using a metal bar or tube of suitable diameter, press or drive the hub from the hub bearing. Alternatively, use the puller to separate the hub from the bearing. Note that the part of the bearing inner race will remain on the hub.
5 Using a suitable puller, pull the half inner bearing race from the hub. Alternatively, support the bearing race on suitably thin metal bars, and press or drive the hub from the bearing race.
6 Remove the bearing retaining circlip from the inner face of the hub carrier - discard the circlip, a new one must be used on refitting.
7 Temporarily refit the half inner bearing race

to the bearing, making sure that the bearing cage and the seal are in position then, using a puller, pull the bearing from the hub carrier, applying pressure to the inner race. Alternatively, support the hub carrier, and press or drive out the bearing.
8 Before fitting the new bearing, thoroughly clean the bearing location in the hub carrier.
9 Using a press or a suitable puller, fit the new bearing to the hub carrier. The outer face of the bearing should contact the shoulder in the hub carrier. It may be possible to improvise a suitable puller using a socket, nut, washers, and length of threaded bar.
10 Fit a new bearing retaining clip to the inner face of the hub carrier.
11 Press or draw the hub into the bearing. The bearing inner track must be supported during this operation. This can be achieved using a socket, nut washers, and a length of threaded bar.
12 Refit the hub carrier as described in Section 2.

4 Front subframe - removal and refitting

Note: *Vauxhall/Opel technicians use special jigs to ensure that the engine/transmission is correctly aligned. Without the use of these tools it is important to note the position of the engine/transmission accurately before removal.*

Removal

1 Turn the steering to the straight-ahead position, then remove the ignition key and allow the steering lock to engage.
2 In the driver's footwell, unscrew the bolt securing the bottom of the steering column intermediate shaft to the steering gear pinion. Pull the shaft from the pinion and position to one side.
3 Syphon all the hydraulic fluid from the power steering fluid reservoir.
4 On manual transmission models, disconnect the gearchange rod from the transmission with reference to Chapter 7A. If preferred, the linkage can be disconnected at the bracket on the steering rack.

4.20 Front subframe side mounting bolt

5.4 Unclipping the brake pad wiring harness from the strut

5 On petrol models, disconnect the oxygen sensor wiring and position to one side.

6 Connect a hoist to the engine/transmission assembly and support its weight. If available, the type of support bar which locates in the engine compartment side channels is to be preferred, as this will ensure correct repositioning during refitting.

7 Remove the radiator grille (Chapter 11) then use cable-ties to tie the radiator to the air deflector panel/crossmember on the front of the engine compartment.

8 Remove the front bumper as described in Chapter 11.

9 Apply the handbrake, then jack up the front of the vehicle and support it on axle stands (see *"Jacking and Vehicle Support"*). Remove both front wheels.

10 Unscrew the nuts and disconnect the anti-roll bar links from the struts on both sides. Use a further spanner to hold the studs while the nuts are being loosened.

11 Disconnect the steering track rod ends from the hub carriers by unscrewing the nuts and using a balljoint separator tool.

12 Unscrew and remove the clamp bolts securing the front suspension lower arm balljoints in the hub carriers, noting which way round they are fitted.

13 Using a suitable lever, push down the lower arms and separate them from the hub carriers. When releasing the lower arms, take care not to damage the balljoint rubber boots on the bottom of the hub carriers; if necessary

protect them with a piece of card or plastic. **Note:** *If the balljoint stub is tight in the hub carrier, use a screwdriver or cold chisel as a wedge to force the clamp apart.*

14 Remove the front exhaust downpipe as described in Chapter 4.

15 Unscrew the three bolts securing the rear engine mounting bracket to the transmission. If preferred, the bracket can be unbolted from the subframe.

16 On models with air conditioning, disconnect the coolant lines from the subframe.

17 Release the clips and disconnect the power steering hydraulic lines from the right-hand side of the subframe.

18 Ideally, support the engine/transmission with a cradle on a trolley jack. Alternatively, two trolley jacks and the help of two assistants will be required.

19 Unscrew the bolts securing the transmission front mounting to the subframe. On petrol engine models, also unscrew the bolt securing the right-hand front mounting to the subframe.

20 Unscrew the subframe mounting bolts - note that the rear mounting brackets must be unbolted from the underbody **(see illustration)**. Slightly lower the subframe until the power steering gear hydraulic lines can be unscrewed and detached from the steering gear. Place a suitable container beneath the steering gear to catch the fluid. Tape over or plug the lines to prevent entry of dust and dirt then tie them to one side.

21 Lower the subframe to the ground. Remove the lower suspension arms with reference to Section 7, the anti-roll bar with reference to Section 6, the rear engine mounting with reference to Chapter 2, and the steering gear with reference to Section 21.

Refitting

22 Refitting is a reversal of removal, but tighten all nuts and bolts to the specified torque where necessary in the stages given. Make sure that the alignment holes in the subframe and underbody are correctly aligned before fully tightening the mounting bolts.

5 Front suspension strut - removal, overhaul and refitting

Note: *A balljoint separator tool will be required for this operation. Ideally, both front suspension struts should be renewed at the same time in order to maintain good steering and suspension characteristics. It is recommended that all mounting nuts and bolts are renewed.*

Removal

1 Apply the handbrake, then jack up the front of the vehicle and support it on axle stands (see *"Jacking and Vehicle Support"*). Remove the front wheel.

2 Unscrew the nut and disconnect the anti-roll bar link from the strut. Use a spanner on the special flats to hold the link while the nut is being loosened.

3 Pull out the clip and disconnect the brake hose from the bracket on the strut.

4 Unclip the brake pad wiring harness from the strut **(see illustration)**.

5 Mark the position of the strut on the hub carrier. This is important to maintain the camber setting.

6 Unscrew and remove the two bolts securing the hub carrier to the strut noting which way round they are fitted. With the two bolts removed, pull the hub carrier away from the strut and support on an axle stand **(see illustrations)**.

5.6a Counterhold the hub carrier-to-strut bolts when loosening the nut . . .

5.6b . . . then remove the bolt

5.6c Pull the hub carrier away from the strut

5.7a Remove the cap . . .

5.7b . . . then unscrew the upper mounting nut while counterholding the piston rod with a further spanner . . .

5.7c . . . and remove the nut . . .

5.7d . . . followed by the upper mounting

5.8 Withdrawing the front suspension strut from under the front wing

Overhaul

Note: *A spring compressor tool will be required for this operation.*

9 With the suspension strut resting on a bench, or clamped in a vice, fit a spring compressor tool, and compress the coil spring to relieve the pressure on the spring seats. Ensure that the compressor tool is securely located on the spring, in accordance with the tool manufacturer's instructions **(see illustrations)**.

10 Counterhold the strut piston rod with a spanner, and unscrew the piston rod nut **(see illustration)**.

11 Remove the upper damping ring with support bearing, upper spring seat, and buffer **(see illustrations)**.

12 Remove the spring from the strut **(see illustration)**.

7 Support the strut beneath the front wing. In the engine compartment remove the cap then unscrew the strut upper mounting nut while counterholding the piston rod with a further spanner. Recover the upper mounting from the suspension tower **(see illustrations)**.

8 Lower the strut and withdraw from under the front wing **(see illustration)**.

5.9a The front suspension strut removed from the vehicle

5.9b Make sure the spring compressor tool is safely fitted to the front coil spring

5.10 Remove the piston rod nut . . .

5.11a . . . upper damping ring and support bearing . . .

5.11b . . . upper spring seat . . .

5.11c . . . and buffer

10

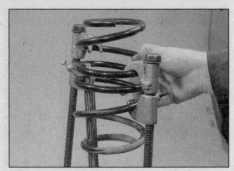

5.12 Removing the coil spring from the strut

5.17 Raised coil spring stop on the front suspension strut

5.21 Tightening the front suspension strut upper mounting nut with a torque wrench

13 With the strut assembly now completely dismantled, examine all the components for wear, damage or deformation, and check the support bearing for smoothness of operation. Renew any of the components as necessary.

14 Examine the strut for signs of fluid leakage. Check the strut piston for signs of pitting along its entire length, and check the strut body for signs of damage. While holding it in an upright position, test the operation of the strut by moving the piston through a full stroke, and then through short strokes of 50 to 100 mm. In both cases, the resistance felt should be smooth and continuous. If the resistance is jerky or uneven or if there is any visible sign of wear or damage to the strut, renewal is necessary.

15 If any doubt exists as to the condition of the coil spring, carefully remove the spring compressors and check the spring for distortion and signs of cracking. Renew the spring if it is damaged or distorted, or if there is any doubt as to its condition.

16 Inspect all other components for damage or deterioration, and renew any that are suspect.

17 With the spring compressed with the compressor tool, locate the spring on the strut making sure that it is correctly seated with its lower end on the raised stop **(see illustration)**.

18 Refit the buffer, upper spring seat, support bearing and upper damping ring.

19 Refit the piston rod nut and tighten it to the specified torque while counterholding the piston rod with a spanner.

20 Slowly slacken the spring compressor tool to relieve the tension in the spring. Check that the ends of the spring locate correctly against the stops on the spring seats. If necessary, turn the spring and the upper seat so that the components locate correctly before the compressor tool is removed. Remove the compressor tool when the spring is fully seated.

Refitting

21 Refitting is a reversal of removal, bearing in mind the following points.

a) Renew the two bolts securing the hub carrier to the strut, also the piston rod upper nuts. Note that the strut-to-hub carrier bolts must be fitted from front to rear.

b) Tighten all nuts and bolts to the specified torque **(see illustration)**.

c) On completion have the camber setting checked and adjusted by a suitably equipped garage.

6 Front suspension anti-roll bar and links - removal and refitting

Note: *It is recommended that all mounting nuts and bolts are renewed.*

Removal

1 Remove the front subframe as described in Section 4.

2 Identify the links side for side to ensure correct refitting, then unscrew the nuts and

remove the links from the anti-roll bar. Use a spanner on the special flats to hold the links while the nuts are being loosened **(see illustrations)**.

3 Unbolt the clamps securing the anti-roll bar to the subframe. **Note:** *If the bolts are rusted in position, they can be cut off and drilled out and new inserts fitted. Consult a Vauxhall/Opel dealer for more information.*

4 Lift the anti-roll bar from the subframe.

5 Note the position of the rubber bushes, then prise them from the anti-roll bar.

6 Examine the anti-roll bar, links, and rubber bushes for wear and damage and renew them if necessary.

Refitting

7 Refitting is a reversal of removal, but note the following points.

a) The slits of the rubber bushes must face forwards when fitted to the anti-roll bar.

b) Tighten all nuts and bolts to the specified torque.

c) Refit the front subframe with reference to Section 4.

7 Front suspension lower arm - removal, overhaul and refitting

Note: *The lower arm inner pivot bolts must be renewed when refitting.*

Removal

1 Apply the handbrake, then jack up the front of the vehicle and support it on axle stands (see *"Jacking and Vehicle Support"*). Remove the front wheel.

2 Unscrew and remove the clamp bolt securing the front suspension lower arm balljoint to the bottom of the hub carrier, noting which way round it is fitted.

3 Using a suitable lever, push down the lower arm and separate it from the hub carrier. When releasing the lower arm, take care not to damage the balljoint rubber boot on the bottom of the hub carrier; if necessary protect it with a piece of card or plastic. **Note:** *If the balljoint stub is tight in the hub carrier, use a screwdriver or cold chisel as a wedge to force the clamp apart.*

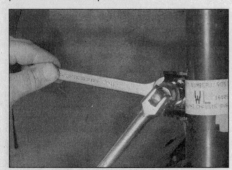

6.2a Use a spanner to counterhold the anti-roll bar link stub while loosening the nut

6.2b Disconnecting the anti-roll bar link from the front suspension strut

4 Note that the lower arm inner retaining bolt heads are facing the front of the vehicle. Unscrew and remove the bolts and withdraw the lower arm from the subframe **(see illustrations)**. It will be necessary to slightly press the arms to release the rubber mountings.

Overhaul

5 The lower balljoint may be renewed as described in Section 8. The rubber bushes are a tight fit in the arm and must be pressed out. If a press is not available, the bushes can be drawn out using a long bolt, nut, washers and a socket or length of metal tubing.

6 Prior to fitting the new bushes, coat them with silicone grease or soapy water. Press both bushes fully into the lower arm.

Refitting

7 Locate the lower arm on the subframe and fit the retaining bolts from the front of the vehicle. Hand tighten the bolts at this stage.

8 Locate the lower balljoint stub fully in the bottom of the hub carrier, then insert the clamp bolt from the rear and tighten its nut to the specified torque setting.

9 Refit the front wheel and lower the vehicle to the ground.

10 With the weight of the vehicle on the suspension, tighten the lower arm inner pivot bolts to the specified torque and in the stages given.

8 Front suspension lower balljoint - renewal

Note: *The original balljoint is riveted to the lower arm, however service replacements are bolted in position.*

1 Remove the front suspension lower arm as described in Section 7. **Note:** *If the fitted balljoint is a service replacement, it is not necessary to completely remove the arm but only to disconnect the balljoint from the bottom of the hub carrier then unbolt the old balljoint.*

2 Mount the lower arm in a vice, then drill the heads from the three rivets that secure the balljoint to the lower arm, using a 12.0 mm diameter drill **(see illustration)**.

3 If necessary, tap the rivets from the lower arm, then remove the balljoint.

4 Clean any rust from the rivet holes, and apply rust inhibitor.

5 The new balljoint must be fitted using three special bolts, spring washers and nuts, available from a Vauxhall/Opel parts centre.

6 Ensure that the balljoint is fitted the correct way up, noting that the securing nuts are positioned on the underside of the lower arm. Tighten the nuts to the specified torque.

7 Refit the front suspension lower arm as described in Section 7.

7.4a Front suspension lower arm front inner mounting bolt . . .

9 Rear hub and bracket - removal and refitting

Note: *New nuts will be required when refitting the rear hub bracket to the trailing arm.*

Removal

1 Remove the rear brake drum or disc as applicable as described in Chapter 9.

2 On the inside of the rear trailing arm, disconnect the wiring for the wheel speed sensor.

3 Support the rear brake backplate and shoes on an axle stand, then support the rear hub and unscrew the mounting nuts on the inside of the trailing arm **(see illustration)**. Withdraw the hub bracket from the rear trailing arm. Note that the locating studs are spaced so that the hub bracket will only fit in one position. If required, the backplate and handbrake shoes may be removed with reference to Chapter 9.

Refitting

4 Where removed, refit the backplate with reference to Chapter 9, then locate the hub bracket in the trailing arm and fit new nuts to secure. Tighten the nuts to the specified torque and angles in the stages given.

5 Reconnect the wiring for the wheel speed sensor.

8.2 The original lower balljoint is riveted to the lower arm, but service replacements are bolted to the arm

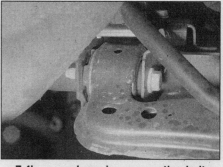

7.4b . . . and rear inner mounting bolt

6 Refit the rear brake drum or disc as applicable as described in Chapter 9. Where necessary, adjust the handbrake as described in Chapter 9.

10 Rear wheel bearings - checking and renewal

1 Chock the front wheels, then jack up the rear of the vehicle and support on axle stands (see *"Jacking and Vehicle Support"*). Remove the rear wheels.

2 On models with rear brake drums, remove the drums as described in Chapter 9.

3 A dial test indicator (DTI) or datum bar and feeler blades will be required to measure the amount of play in the bearing. On disc brake models zero the DTI on the brake disc, and on brake drum models zero it on the hub flange. Alternatively, position the datum bar against the surface and use a feeler blade to measure the clearance.

4 Lever the hub in and out and measure the amount of play in the bearing.

5 Now measure the run-out of the bearing by turning the disc or drum flange.

6 The lateral run-out is measured by locating the probe on the outer diameter of the hub centre aperture.

7 If the play or run-out exceeds the specified amounts, renew the hub bearing and bracket as described in Section 9.

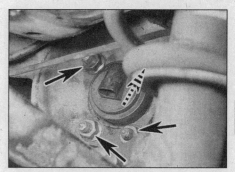

9.3 Rear hub bracket mounting nuts on the trailing arm

10

11.3 Unscrewing the rear suspension strut lower mounting bolt

11.4a Removing the rear suspension strut lower rear mounting bolt and bracket . . .

11.4b . . . and lower front mounting bolt

11 Rear suspension strut -
removal, overhaul and refitting

Note: *A spring compressor tool will be required for this operation. Ideally both rear suspension struts should be renewed at the same time in order to maintain good suspension characteristics. It is recommended that all mounting nuts and bolts are renewed.*

Removal

1 Chock the front wheels, then jack up the rear of the vehicle and support on axle stands (see *"Jacking and Vehicle Support"*). Remove the rear roadwheel and support the trailing arm on an axle stand.

2 Remove the liner from under the rear wheel arch.
3 Unscrew and remove the strut lower mounting bolt and disconnect the strut from the trailing arm. Recover the washer from the inner side of the strut **(see illustration)**.
4 Support the strut, then loosen only the two upper mounting bolts and remove the lower mounting bolts securing the strut upper carrier bracket to the inner body panel. Note the location of the bracket on the lower rear bolt **(see illustrations)**.
5 Lift the strut from under the rear wheel arch **(see illustration)**.

Overhaul

6 With the suspension strut resting on a bench, or clamped in a vice, fit a spring compressor tool, and compress the coil

spring to relieve the pressure on the spring seats. Ensure that the compressor tool is securely located on the spring, in accordance with the tool manufacturer's instructions **(see illustration)**.
7 Hold the piston rod stationary with a spanner on the hexagon, then unscrew and remove the nut from the top of the rod **(see illustrations)**.
8 Remove the shock absorber upper cup and bearing followed by the top carrier, lower bearing and sleeve, and lower cup **(see illustrations)**.
9 Remove the buffer from the piston rod then remove the coil spring from the lower seat on the shock absorber **(see illustration)**.
10 Remove the coil spring seat from the top carrier **(see illustration)**.

11.5 Lower the rear suspension strut from the loosened upper mounting bolts

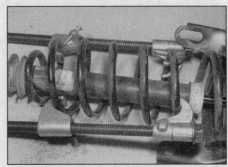

11.6 Compressor tool fitted to the rear suspension coil spring

11.7a Counterhold the piston rod while loosening the nut . . .

11.7b . . . then remove the nut from the top of the piston rod

11.8a Remove the upper cup . . .

11.8b . . . bearing . . .

11.8c . . . then lift off the top carrier . . .

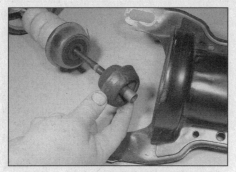

11.8d . . . and remove the lower bearing and sleeve . . .

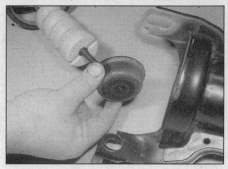

11.8e . . . lower cup . . .

11 On models fitted with an automatic self-levelling device, also remove the guard tube and damper ring from the shock absorber.

12 Note that the coil spring lower seat cannot be removed from the shock absorber.

13 With the strut assembly now completely dismantled, examine all the components for wear, damage or deformation. Renew the components as necessary.

14 Examine the strut for signs of fluid leakage. Check the strut piston for signs of pitting along its entire length, and check the strut body and carrier for signs of damage. While holding it in an upright position, test the operation of the strut by moving the piston through a full stroke, and then through short strokes of 50 to 100 mm. In both cases, the resistance felt should be smooth and continuous. If the resistance is jerky or uneven or if there is any visible sign of wear or damage to the strut, renewal is necessary.

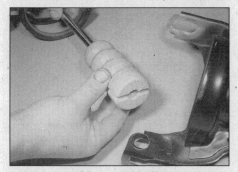

11.9 . . . and buffer

15 If any doubt exists as to the condition of the coil spring, carefully remove the spring compressors and check the spring for distortion and signs of damage. Renew the spring if necessary.

16 Inspect all other components for damage or deterioration, and renew as necessary.

17 If the spring compressor tool has been removed from the spring, refit it and compress the spring sufficiently to enable it to be refitted to the strut.

18 On models fitted with an automatic self-levelling device, refit the guard tube and damper ring to the shock absorber.

19 Locate the coil spring seat in the top carrier.

20 Locate the spring onto the shock absorber and position the lower end of the spring in the lower seat indentation.

21 Fit the buffer onto the piston rod.

22 To the shock absorber piston rod, fit the lower cup followed by the lower bearing and sleeve.

23 Locate the top carrier over the piston rod and onto the coil spring making sure that the end of the coil spring is located in the seat indentation **(see illustration)**.

24 Fit the shock absorber upper bearing and cup.

25 Fit the nut to the top of the piston rod and tighten to the specified torque while holding the rod with a spanner on the hexagon.

26 Slowly slacken the spring compressor tool to relieve the tension in the spring. Check that the ends of the spring locate correctly

against the indentations in the spring seats. Remove the compressor tool when the spring is fully seated.

Refitting

27 Refitting is a reversal of removal, but renew the strut-to-trailing arm lower mounting bolt. Hand-tighten the lower mounting bolt initially and tighten it to the specified torque with the weight of the vehicle on the suspension. The carrier mounting bolts can be fully tightened before lowering the vehicle to the ground but first lift the strut to the ends of the elongated slots in the carrier. Note also the location stud near the rear lower mounting bolt **(see illustration)**.

12 Rear suspension anti-roll bar and links - removal and refitting

Note: *It is recommended that all mounting nuts and bolts are renewed.*

Removal

1 Chock the front wheels, then jack up the rear of the vehicle and support on axle stands (see *"Jacking and Vehicle Support"*). Remove the rear wheels.

2 Note the fitted positions of the links, then unscrew and remove the bolts securing the links to the tops of the trailing arms **(see illustration)**.

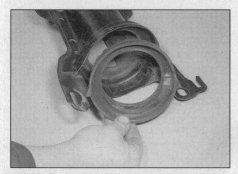

11.10 Removing the coil spring seat from the top carrier

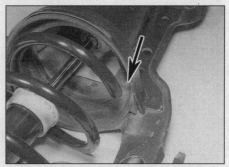

11.23 Make sure the end of the coil spring is located in the seat indentation

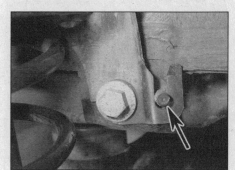

11.27 Location stud for the rear suspension strut top carrier

10

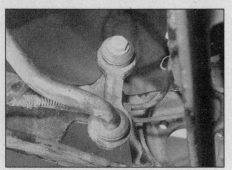

12.2 Rear anti-roll bar link and bolt securing the link to the trailing arm

3 Unscrew the nuts securing the anti-roll bar support clamps to the crossmember, then tilt the anti-roll bar and withdraw it from under the vehicle **(see illustration)**.
4 Unhook and remove the clamps.
5 Unbolt the links from the anti-roll bar. To ensure correct reassembly, mark the links for position.
6 Remove the rubber mountings from the anti-roll bar.
7 Examine the anti-roll bar, links, and rubber bushes for wear and damage and renew them if necessary.

Refitting

8 Refitting is a reversal of removal, but tighten all nuts and bolts to the specified torque with the weight of the vehicle on the suspension.

13.2 Rear suspension upper arm outer mounting bolt

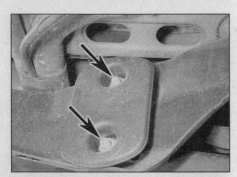

13.3 Mounting bolts in the crossmember for the rear suspension upper and lower arms

12.3 Rear anti-roll bar mounting bolt on the crossmember

13 Rear suspension upper arm - removal, overhaul and refitting

Note: *It is recommended that all mounting nuts and bolts are renewed.*

Removal

1 Chock the front wheels, then jack up the rear of the vehicle and support on axle stands (see *"Jacking and Vehicle Support"*). Remove the rear wheel on the relevant side of the vehicle.
2 Release the locking plate, then unscrew the outer bolt securing the upper arm to the trailing arm **(see illustration)**.
3 Unscrew the inner bolt and withdraw the upper arm from the crossmember and trailing arm **(see illustration)**.

Overhaul

4 To renew the inner rubber bush, grip the arm in a vice then use a long threaded bar, nuts and metal tubing to press the rubber bush from the arm. Alternatively, use a press to remove the bush. Insert a spacer in the arm to prevent it from being crushed while removing the bush.
5 Press the new bush into the arm using the tool used for removal.
6 The outer rubber bush may be removed from the trailing arm with reference to Section 15.

Overhaul

14.2 Rear suspension lower arm outer mounting bolt

Refitting

7 Refitting is a reversal of removal, but renew the locking plate and do not fully tighten the mounting bolts until the weight of the vehicle is on the suspension. Have the rear wheel toe-in setting checked and if necessary adjusted at the earliest opportunity.

14 Rear suspension lower arm - removal, overhaul and refitting

Note: *It is recommended that all mounting nuts and bolts are renewed.*

Removal

1 Chock the front wheels, then jack up the rear of the vehicle and support on axle stands (see *"Jacking and Vehicle Support"*). Remove the rear wheel on the relevant side of the vehicle.
2 Release the locking plate, then unscrew the outer bolt securing the lower arm to the trailing arm **(see illustration)**.
3 Unscrew the inner bolt and withdraw the lower arm from the crossmember and trailing arm.

Overhaul

4 To renew the inner rubber bush, grip the arm in a vice then use a long threaded bar, nuts and metal tubing to press the rubber bush from the arm. Alternatively, use a press to remove the bush. Insert a spacer in the arm to prevent it from being crushed while removing the bush.
5 Press the new bush into the arm using the tool used for removal.
6 The outer rubber bush may be removed from the trailing arm with reference to Section 15.

Refitting

7 Refitting is a reversal of removal, but renew the locking plate and do not fully tighten the mounting bolts until the weight of the vehicle is on the suspension. Have the rear wheel toe-in setting checked and if necessary adjusted at the earliest opportunity.

15 Rear suspension trailing arm - removal, overhaul and refitting

Note: *It is recommended that all mounting nuts and bolts are renewed.*

Removal

1 Chock the front wheels, then jack up the rear of the vehicle and support on axle stands (see *"Jacking and Vehicle Support"*). Remove the wheel on the relevant side of the vehicle.
2 With the handbrake released, disconnect the rear cable from the secondary cable by prising the fitting from the special clip.

3 Remove the secondary handbrake cable from the support on the trailing arm.

4 Remove the rear hub and bracket together with the brake backplate as described in Section 9.

5 Unbolt the brake hydraulic line support from the top of the trailing arm.

6 Release the ABS wheel speed sensor wiring from the trailing arm.

7 Unscrew the bolt securing the anti-roll bar link to the trailing arm.

8 Release the locking plates then unscrew the bolts securing the upper and lower arms to the trailing arm. Prise the arms free.

9 Unscrew the bolt securing the bottom of the strut to the trailing arm.

10 Accurately mark the position of the trailing arm front mounting plate on the underbody. This is important since the position of the plate determines the toe-in setting of the rear wheel.

11 Unscrew the front mounting bolts and withdraw the trailing arm from the underbody.

Overhaul

12 If it is required to remove the front mounting bracket from the trailing arm, first determine the rest position of the bracket in relation to the arm by measuring the distance from the rear of the bracket to the arm. Vauxhall/Opel technicians use a special tool to set the bracket position, however if the position of the bracket is noted before removal, the new bracket can be set to the same position.

13 Unscrew the bolt, noting which way round it is fitted, and separate the bracket from the arm.

14 To renew the rubber bushes, grip the arm in a vice then use a long threaded bar, nuts and metal tubing to press out the rubber bushes. Alternatively, use a press to remove the bushes.

15 Press in the new bushes using the tool used for removal.

16 Locate the bracket on the front of the trailing arm, and position it as noted during removal. Tighten the bolt to the specified torque and angle.

Refitting

17 Locate the trailing arm and front bracket on the underbody, and insert the bolts. Position the bracket as noted on removal, then tighten the bolts to the specified torque and angles.

18 Insert the bolt securing the bottom of the strut to the trailing arm and tighten to the specified torque and angles.

19 Locate the upper and lower arms on the trailing arm and insert the retaining bolts loosely at this stage.

20 Refit the anti-roll bar link and tighten the mounting bolt to the specified torque.

21 Attach the ABS wheel speed sensor wiring to the trailing arm.

22 Refit the brake hydraulic line support to the top of the trailing arm and tighten the bolt.

23 Refit the rear hub and bracket together with the brake backplate as described in Section 9.

24 Insert the handbrake secondary cable in the support, then connect the inner cable to the rear cable by pressing the end fitting into the special clip.

25 Refit the wheel then lower the vehicle to the ground. Apply the handbrake.

26 With the weight of the vehicle on the suspension, fully tighten the upper and lower arm outer retaining bolts.

27 Have the rear wheel toe-in setting checked and if necessary adjusted at the earliest opportunity.

16 Rear suspension crossmember - removal and refitting

Note: *It is recommended that all mounting nuts and bolts are renewed.*

Removal

1 Chock the front wheels, then jack up the rear of the vehicle and support on axle stands (see *"Jacking and Vehicle Support"*). Remove both rear wheels.

2 Remove the rear exhaust system as described in Chapter 4.

3 Clamp the brake rear hydraulic hoses using hose clamps, or alternatively remove the brake fluid reservoir cap and tighten it down onto a piece of polythene. This will prevent the loss of fluid while the brake lines are disconnected.

4 Unscrew the union nuts attaching the rigid brake lines to the flexible hoses on the trailing arms, then pull out the retaining spring clips and detach the hoses from the supports. Plug the hoses and lines to prevent entry of dust and dirt. Be prepared for some loss of fluid by placing cloth rags or a container beneath the hoses.

5 Disconnect the handbrake secondary cables from the rear cables by prising the cable fittings from the special clip.

6 Disconnect the wiring from the ABS wheel speed sensors on both sides of the vehicle.

7 Accurately mark the positions of the trailing arm front mounting plates on the underbody. This is important since the position of the plates determines the toe-in setting of the rear wheels. Working on each trailing arm in turn, unscrew and remove the bolts securing the arm front brackets to the underbody. Support the arms on axle stands.

8 Using a trolley jack, support the weight of the crossmember. If necessary, use a length of wood positioned beneath the crossmember.

9 Unscrew the bolts securing the bottom of the struts to the trailing arms on each side.

10 With the help of an assistant, unscrew the four mounting bolts and carefully lower the crossmember to the floor **(see illustration)**.

11 Remove the upper and lower arms from the crossmember together with the trailing arms and rear hubs, with reference to Sections 13 and 14.

12 Remove the anti-roll bar from the crossmember with reference to Section 12.

Refitting

13 Refitting is a reversal of removal, but note the following points.

a) Before lifting the crossmember into position, check the condition of the captive mounting nuts in the underbody and renew them if necessary.

b) Delay fully tightening the upper and lower arm inner bolts until the weight of the vehicle is on the suspension.

c) Bleed the brake hydraulic system as described in Chapter 9.

d) Have the rear wheel toe-in setting checked and if necessary adjusted at the earliest opportunity.

17 Steering wheel - removal and refitting

Note: *A puller will be required to draw the steering wheel off the column splines. A new retaining nut lockwasher will be required when refitting.*

Models without an airbag

Removal

1 Disconnect the battery negative (earth) lead (see Chapter 5A).

2 Set the front wheels in the straight-ahead position, and release the steering lock by inserting the ignition key.

3 Carefully ease the horn button out from the steering wheel, and disconnect its wiring.

4 Using a screwdriver, prise back the tabs on the retaining nut lockwasher.

5 Unscrew the retaining nut, and lift off the lockwasher. Discard the lockwasher; a new one should be used on refitting.

6 Make alignment marks between the steering wheel and steering column shaft.

7 A two-legged puller will now be required to free the steering wheel from its splines.

16.10 Rear suspension crossmember mounting

10

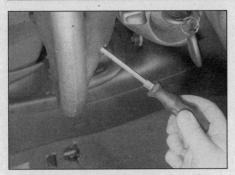

17.16a Remove the screws from the steering wheel . . .

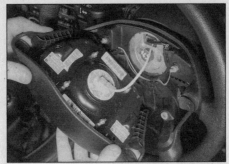

17.16b . . . then remove the airbag/horn-push . . .

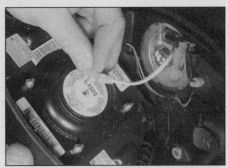

17.16c . . . and disconnect the wiring

Locate the legs of the puller in the holes in the centre of the wheel, and draw the steering wheel off the column splines. Lift off the steering wheel, and remove the spring from the column shaft.

Refitting

8 Check that the indicator cancelling lug/horn button contact pad fitted to the rear of steering wheel is in good condition, and if necessary renew it. To release the pad, depress the two clips located inside the steering wheel. Apply a little copper grease to the contact pad before refitting it.

9 Ensure that the indicator switch stalk is in its central (OFF) position. Failure to do this could lead to the steering wheel lug breaking the switch tab as the steering wheel is refitted.

10 Fit the spring to the column, then locate the wheel on the column splines, aligning the marks made on removal.

11 Fit the new lockwasher, and screw on the retaining nut. Tighten the retaining nut to the specified torque, and secure it in position with the lockwasher tabs.

12 Reconnect the wiring connectors to the horn button, and refit the button in the centre of the steering wheel.

13 Reconnect the battery, and check the operation of the horn.

Models with an airbag

 Warning: Before removing the steering wheel, observe the safety precautions given in Chapter 12 and in Section 1 of this Chapter.

Removal

14 Disconnect the battery negative (earth) lead (see Chapter 5A).
Caution: Wait at least one minute before

proceeding. This is necessary to allow the airbag condenser to fully discharge.

15 Set the front wheels in the straight-ahead position, then lock the column in position after removing the ignition key.

16 Unscrew and remove the two screws from the rear of the steering wheel and carefully lift the airbag/horn-push from the steering wheel. Disconnect the wiring from the airbag **(see illustrations)**. Position the airbag in a safe place where it cannot be tampered with, making sure that the padded side is facing upwards.

17 Where fitted, disconnect the wiring from the radio control switches **(see illustration)**.

18 Using a screwdriver, prise back the tabs on the retaining nut lockwasher **(see illustration)**.

19 Unscrew the retaining nut, and lift off the lockwasher **(see illustrations)**. Discard the lockwasher; a new one should be used on refitting.

20 Make alignment marks between the steering wheel and steering column shaft.

21 A two-legged puller will now be required to free the steering wheel from its splines. Locate the legs of the puller in the holes in the centre of the wheel, and draw the steering wheel off the column splines. Lift off the steering wheel, and remove the spring from the column shaft. As the steering wheel is removed, guide the wiring for the contact unit (and radio control if fitted) through the hole **(see illustrations)**.

22 With the steering wheel removed, do not disturb the contact unit. If necessary hold it in its central position with tape.

17.17 Disconnect the wiring from the radio control switches

17.18 Prise back the tabs on the retaining nut lockwasher . . .

17.19a . . . then loosen the steering wheel mounting nut . . .

17.19b . . . and remove it . . .

17.19c . . . together with the lockwasher

17.21a Using a two-legged puller to remove the steering wheel from the column

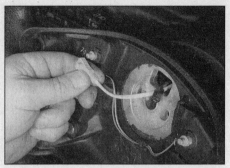

17.21b As the steering wheel is removed, feed the airbag wiring through the hole

Refitting

23 Check that the contact unit is positioned with the arrows aligned with each other. If it has been disturbed, return it to its central position by depressing the detent on top of the unit and carefully turning the centre part of the unit anti-clockwise until resistance is felt. Now turn it 2.5 turns clockwise and align the arrows on the centre part and outer edge.

24 Offer the steering wheel onto the column splines and guide the wiring for the contact unit (and radio control if fitted) through the hole.

25 Ensure that the indicator switch stalk is in its central (OFF) position, then refit the steering wheel to the column, aligning the marks made prior to removal. When locating the steering wheel on the splines, make sure that the contact unit is correctly engaged with both the steering column and indicator switch.

26 Fit the new lockwasher, and screw on the retaining nut. Tighten the retaining nut to the specified torque, and secure it in position with the lockwasher tabs.

27 Reconnect the wiring for the radio control switches where fitted.

28 Refit the airbag/horn-push and reconnect the wiring. Insert the two screws and tighten to the specified torque.

29 Release the steering lock, then reconnect the battery negative lead.

Removal

Note: *A new shear bolt must be used on refitting.*

1 Remove the steering wheel as described in Section 17. Alternatively, the steering wheel may remain in position, but it will have to turned for access to the end face screws.

2 Remove the steering column shrouds by unscrewing the tilt steering lever, then removing the two screws from the end face and three screws from the bottom shroud. Recover the ignition key position indicator from the ignition switch **(see illustrations)**.

3 On models with an airbag, remove the contact unit as follows. Using a small screwdriver lift off the locking plate, then disconnect the wiring plug. Release the four rear clips and pull the contact unit from the top of the column. **Note:** *Make sure that the contact unit halves remain in their central position with the arrows aligned at the bottom. If necessary, apply tape to the halves to hold them.*

4 Unclip and remove the turn signal switch and wiper switch (refer to Chapter 12 if necessary).

18.2a Removing the tilt steering lever

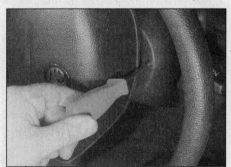

18.2b With the steering wheel turned 90° from the straight-ahead position, undo the end face screws from the shrouds

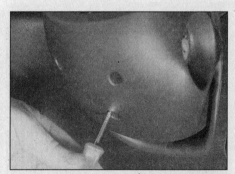

18.2c Undo the three screws from the bottom of the shrouds

18.2d Removing the upper shroud . . .

18.2e . . . and lower shroud

18.2f Removing the ignition key position indicator

10

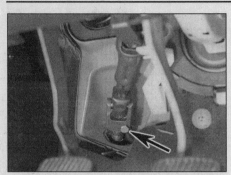

18.8 Clamp bolt securing the intermediate shaft to the bottom of the upper column

5 Remove the ignition switch and lock cylinder as described in Chapter 12.
6 Remove the trim panel from under the driver's side of the facia, then pull out the air distribution duct leading to the heater unit.
7 Remove the screws and withdraw the driver's footwell inner trim panel for access to the steering column support brace. Unscrew the lower bolt and the upper nuts and remove the brace.
8 Mark the intermediate shaft in relation to the upper column. Unscrew and remove the clamp bolt and disconnect the column intermediate shaft from the splines on the bottom of the upper column **(see illustration)**.
9 The upper column mounting is secured with a shear bolt or a standard bolt. Either drill out the shear bolt or loosen it using a small cold chisel. **Note:** *A new shear bolt must be used on refitting.*
10 Unscrew the remaining mounting bolts and withdraw the steering column from the bulkhead. Remove the column from inside the vehicle.

Refitting

11 Commence refitting by locating the steering column on the bulkhead and inserting the mounting bolts loosely. Screw in the new shear bolt finger-tight.
12 Check that the column is correctly located then tighten the standard bolts to the specified torque. Tighten the shear bolt until its head breaks off.
13 Slide the intermediate shaft onto the splines on the bottom of the upper column. Clean the threads of the clamp bolt then apply

20.2 Steering gear rubber gaiter outer securing clip

a little locking fluid to them. Position the intermediate shaft then insert the clamp bolt and tighten to the specified torque.
14 Refit the steering column support brace and screw on the nuts loosely. Apply a little locking fluid to the threads of the bolt then insert it and tighten to the specified torque. Tighten the nuts to the specified torque.
15 Refit the air distribution duct and the trim panel to the driver's footwell.
16 Refit the ignition switch and lock cylinder as described in Chapter 12.
17 Refit the turn signal switch and wiper switch as described in Chapter 12.
18 On models with an airbag refit the contact unit to the top of the column (if necessary refer to Chapter 12). Make sure that the alignment arrows are positioned correctly and that the contact unit is not tilted but retained by the clips correctly.
19 Refit the steering column shrouds and tighten the retaining screws.
20 Refit the steering wheel (Section 17).

19 Steering column intermediate shaft - removal and refitting

Removal

1 Set the front wheels in the straight-ahead position. Remove the ignition key and allow the steering lock to engage.
2 Remove the trim panel from under the driver's side of the facia, then pull out the air distribution duct leading to the heater unit.
3 Using paint or a suitable marker pen, make alignment marks between the intermediate shaft joints and the steering column and steering gear pinion.
4 Unscrew and remove the upper and lower clamp bolts.
5 Disengage the shaft universal joint from the steering column, then slide the shaft from the steering gear pinion and remove it from the vehicle.

Inspection

6 Inspect the intermediate shaft universal joints for excessive wear or damage. If either joint is worn or damaged, the complete shaft assembly must be renewed.

Refitting

7 Check that the front wheels are still in the straight-ahead position, and that the steering wheel is correctly positioned.
8 Aligning the marks made on removal, engage the shaft universal joints with the steering gear pinion and column. Insert the clamp bolts and tighten them to the specified torque.
9 Refit the air distribution duct and trim panel.
10 Make sure that the front wheels are pointing straight-ahead with the steering wheel in the straight-ahead position. If not, reposition the steering wheel with reference to Section 17.

20 Steering gear rubber gaiters - renewal

1 Remove the relevant track-rod end as described in Section 24.
2 Remove the inner and outer securing clips, then slide the gaiter off the end of the track-rod **(see illustration)**.
3 Thoroughly clean the track-rod, then slide the new gaiter into position. Note that a groove is provided in the track rod for the outer end of the gaiter to locate in.
4 Fit the gaiter securing clips, using new clips if necessary, making sure that the gaiter is not twisted.
5 Refit the track-rod end (Section 24).
6 Have the front wheel toe-in and camber setting checked and adjusted at the earliest opportunity.

21 Steering gear - removal and refitting

Removal

1 Set the front wheels in the straight-ahead position. Remove the ignition key and allow the steering lock to engage.
2 Remove the front subframe as described in Section 4.
3 Unbolt the rear engine mounting bracket from the subframe.
4 Mark the steering gear mounting clamps for position to ensure correct refitting, then unscrew the mounting bolts and remove the clamps **(see illustration)**.
5 Lift the steering gear from the subframe.
6 Prise the rubber mountings from the steering gear, noting their fitted positions.
7 Examine the mountings for wear and damage and renew them if necessary.

Refitting

8 Locate the rubber mountings on the steering gear in the positions noted on removal.
9 Fit the clamps over the mountings, then insert the bolts and tighten to the specified torque.

21.4 Steering gear mounting clamp

10 Refit the rear engine mounting bracket and tighten the bolts to the specified torque.

11 Refit the front subframe as described in Section 4.

12 Have the front wheel toe-in and camber setting checked and adjusted at the earliest opportunity.

22 Power steering pump - removal and refitting

1.6, 1.8 and 2.0 litre petrol engine models

Removal

1 Remove the air cleaner assembly as described in Chapter 4.

2 Unscrew the cap from the power steering hydraulic fluid reservoir, then syphon the fluid into a container. An old poultry baster or hydrometer can be used to draw out the fluid.

3 Remove the auxiliary drivebelt as described in Chapter 1. Mark the drivebelt with the direction of travel to ensure correct refitting.

4 Position a container beneath the power steering pump to catch spilled fluid, then unscrew the union bolt and disconnect the pressure line from the pump. Release the pressure line from the support bracket.

5 Release the clip and disconnect the return line from the bottom of the reservoir. Plug the fluid lines and openings to prevent entry of dust and dirt.

6 Unscrew the four mounting bolts and withdraw the power steering pump together with the hydraulic fluid reservoir from the engine. Wrap the pump in cloth rags to prevent fluid being spilt on the vehicle paintwork.

Refitting

7 Locate the power steering pump on the mounting brackets, then insert the bolts and tighten to the specified torque.

8 Reconnect the return line to the bottom of the reservoir and fit the clip.

9 Reconnect the pressure line and refit the union bolt. Tighten the union bolt to the specified torque, and locate the line in the support bracket.

10 Refit and tension the auxiliary drivebelt as described in Chapter 1.

11 Refit the air cleaner assembly as described in Chapter 4.

12 Fill the hydraulic fluid reservoir with fresh fluid and bleed the system as described in Section 23.

1.7 litre diesel engine models

Removal

13 Remove the air cleaner assembly as described in Chapter 4.

14 On models with air conditioning, remove the compressor as described in Chapter 3.

15 Using hose clamps, clamp both the supply and return hoses near the reservoir.

Alternatively, unscrew the cap from the power steering hydraulic fluid reservoir, then syphon the fluid into a container. An old poultry baster or hydrometer can be used to draw out the fluid.

16 Remove the auxiliary drivebelt as described in Chapter 1 and remove the tensioning screw. Mark the drivebelt with the direction of travel to ensure correct refitting.

17 Position a container beneath the power steering pump to catch spilled fluid, then unscrew the union bolt and disconnect the pressure line from the pump.

18 Release the clip and disconnect the return line from the pump. Plug the fluid lines and openings to prevent entry of dust and dirt.

19 Unscrew the mounting bolt and withdraw the power steering pump together with the retaining tie from the bracket on the engine. Wrap the pump in cloth rags to prevent fluid being spilt on the vehicle paintwork.

Refitting

20 Locate the power steering pump and retaining tie on the bracket, then insert the bolt and tighten to the specified torque.

21 Reconnect the return line and secure with the clip.

22 Reconnect the pressure line and refit the union bolt. Tighten the union bolt to the specified torque. Remove any hose clamps fitted.

23 Refit the tensioning screw then refit and tension the auxiliary drivebelt as described in Chapter 1.

24 On models with air conditioning, refit the compressor as described in Chapter 3.

25 Refit the air cleaner as described in Chapter 4.

26 Fill the hydraulic fluid reservoir with fresh fluid and bleed the system as described in Section 23.

2.0 litre diesel engine models

Removal

Note: *Do not detach the power steering pump from its support bracket. New pumps are supplied together with the support bracket.*

27 Using hose clamps, clamp both the supply and return hoses near the reservoir **(see illustration)**. Alternatively, unscrew the cap from the power steering hydraulic fluid reservoir, then syphon the fluid into a container. An old poultry baster or hydrometer can be used to draw out the fluid.

28 Remove the auxiliary drivebelt and the tensioner as described in Chapter 1. Mark the drivebelt with the direction of travel to ensure correct refitting.

29 Remove the air conditioning compressor as described in Chapter 3.

30 Position a container beneath the power steering pump to catch spilled fluid, then unscrew the union bolt and disconnect the pressure line from the pump.

31 Release the clip and disconnect the return line from the pump. Plug the fluid lines and

openings to prevent entry of dust and dirt.

32 Unscrew the bolt securing the engine oil level dipstick tube to the pump, then pull the tube from the cylinder block.

33 Unscrew the bracket-to-engine mounting bolts and withdraw the power steering pump and bracket downwards from the engine. Wrap the pump in cloth rags to prevent fluid being spilt.

34 If a new pump is being fitted, unbolt the pulley for transfer to the new pump.

Refitting

35 Locate the pulley on the new pump, insert the bolts, and tighten to the specified torque while holding the pulley stationary with an oil filter strap.

36 Locate the pump and bracket on the engine and insert the mounting bolts. Tighten the bolts to the specified torque.

37 Check the condition of the oil seals on the dipstick tube and renew them if necessary. Refit the tube to the cylinder block and secure it to the pump with the bolt.

38 Reconnect the return line to the pump and refit the clip.

39 Reconnect the pressure line, insert the union bolt and tighten to the specified torque.

40 Refit the air conditioning compressor as described in Chapter 3.

41 Refit and tension the auxiliary drivebelt as described in Chapter 1.

42 Remove the hose clamps, then fill the hydraulic fluid reservoir with fresh fluid and bleed the system as described in Section 23.

23 Power steering hydraulic system - bleeding

1 Check and top-up the power steering fluid level to the 'MAX' mark as described in *"Weekly checks"*.

2 Turn the steering wheel quickly from lock-to-lock several times, then re-check the fluid level and top-up if necessary.

3 Start the engine and allow it to idle, then *slowly* turn the steering wheel from lock-to-lock several times - do not hold the steering wheel on full lock for more than 15 seconds at a time. Check for air bubbles in the fluid

22.27 The power steering hydraulic fluid reservoir is mounted on the top of the radiator on 2.0 litre diesel models

10

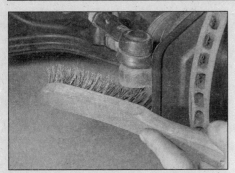

24.2 Remove rust from the track-rod end mounting nut with a wire brush

reservoir - if air bubbles are visible, the system requires further bleeding.

4 Stop the engine, then re-check the fluid level.

5 If air bubbles appear in the reservoir when the system is operated, or if the pump is noisy in operation (not to be confused with a slipping drivebelt), repeat the bleeding procedure.

24 Track-rod end - removal and refitting

Note: *A balljoint separator tool will be required for this operation.*

Removal

1 Remove the relevant front wheel trim or the wheel centre plate (alloy wheels), then slacken the wheel bolts. Apply the handbrake, then jack up the front of the vehicle, and support securely on axle stands (see *"Jacking and Vehicle Support"*). Remove the roadwheel.

2 Loosen the track-rod end securing locknut on the track rod a quarter turn. If necessary, use a wire brush to remove rust from the nut and threads and lubricate the threads with penetrating oil before unscrewing the nut **(see illustration)**.

3 Slacken the track-rod end balljoint nut, but leave the nut in place at the end of the thread to protect it from the risk of damage from the balljoint separator tool.

24.4 Using a balljoint separator tool to release the track-rod end from the steering arm

4 Disconnect the track-rod end balljoint from the steering arm on the hub carrier using a balljoint separator tool, taking care not to damage the balljoint boot. Once the balljoint has been released, remove the balljoint nut and remove the balljoint from the steering arm **(see illustration)**.

5 Unscrew the track-rod end from the track-rod, counting the number of turns necessary to remove it and taking care not to disturb the locknut. **Note:** *The track rod ends are handed side for side. The right-hand track-rod end is marked with an 'R' and has a right-hand thread, whereas the left-hand one is marked with an 'L' and has a left-hand thread.*

Refitting

6 Screw the track-rod end onto the track-rod the number of turns noted during removal.

7 Insert the track-rod end balljoint in the steering arm on the hub carrier, then fit the nut and tighten to the specified torque. If the balljoint stud turns as the nut is being tightened, press down on the track rod end to force the stud into the arm.

8 Tighten the track-rod end securing locknut on the track rod to the specified torque.

9 Refit the roadwheel, then lower the vehicle to the ground, and tighten the wheel nuts.

10 Have the front wheel alignment checked and adjusted at the earliest opportunity.

25 Track-rod - removal and refitting

Removal

1 Remove the steering gear as described in Section 21.

2 Remove the relevant track-rod end with reference to Section 24.

3 Measure the distance from the track-rod end locknut to the end of the track rod, then unscrew and remove the locknut.

4 Release the clips and remove the rubber bellows from the steering gear and track rod.

5 Unscrew the inner balljoint from the rack and remove the track rod.

Refitting

6 Apply locking fluid to the threads, then screw the track rod inner balljoint on the rack and tighten to the specified torque.

7 Refit the bellows making sure that the inner end is pushed fully onto the steering gear and the outer end is seated in the groove on the track rod.

8 Screw on the locknut to the position noted on removal.

9 Refit the track-rod end with reference to Section 24.

10 Refit the steering gear as described in Section 21.

11 Have the front wheel alignment checked and adjusted at the earliest opportunity.

26 Wheel alignment and steering angles - general information

Front wheel alignment

1 Accurate front wheel alignment is essential to good steering and for even tyre wear. Before considering the steering angles, check that the tyres are correctly inflated, that the front wheels are not buckled, the hub bearings are not worn and that the steering linkage is in good order without slackness or wear at the joints. The fuel tank must be half full and each front seat must be loaded with 70 kg.

2 Wheel alignment consists of four factors **(see illustration)**:

Camber, is the angle at which the roadwheels are set from the vertical when viewed from the front or rear of the vehicle. Positive camber is the angle (in degrees) that the wheels are tilted outwards at the top from the vertical. Negative camber is the angle that the wheels are tilted inwards at the top from the vertical. The camber angle is adjusted by loosening the two bolts securing the bottom of the front suspension struts to the hub carriers, then lowering the weight of the vehicle onto the front wheels until the correct camber angle is achieved. The bolt holes are not slotted and only minimal adjustment is possible (±1°).

Castor, is the angle between the steering axis and a vertical line when viewed from each side of the vehicle. Positive castor is indicated when the steering axis is inclined towards the rear of the vehicle at its upper end. This angle is not adjustable.

Steering axis inclination (kingpin inclination), is the angle, when viewed from the front or rear of the vehicle, between the vertical and an imaginary line drawn between the upper and lower front suspension strut mountings. This angle is not adjustable.

Toe, is the amount by which the distance between the front inside edges of the roadwheel rim differs from that between the rear inside edges. If the distance between the front edges is less than that at the rear, the wheels are said to toe-in. If the distance between the front inside edges is greater than that at the rear, the wheels toe-out.

3 Owing to the need for precision gauges to measure the small angles of the steering and suspension settings, it is preferable that checking of camber and castor is left to a service station having the necessary equipment. Castor is set during production of the vehicle, and any deviation from the specified angle will be due to accident damage or gross wear in the suspension mountings.

4 To check the front wheel alignment, first make sure that the lengths of both track-rods are equal when the steering is in the straight-ahead position. The track-rod lengths can be

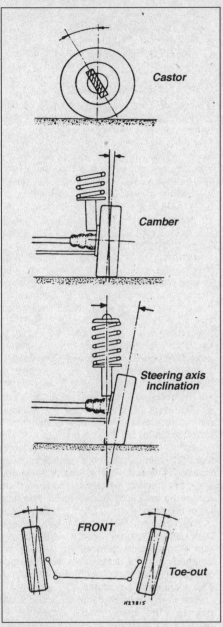

26.2 Wheel alignment and steering angles

adjusted if necessary by releasing the locknuts from the track-rod ends and rotating the track-rods. If necessary, self-locking grips can be used to rotate the track-rods.

5 Obtain a tracking gauge. These are available in various forms from accessory stores, or one can be fabricated from a length of steel tubing suitably cranked to clear the sump and transmission, and having a setscrew and locknut at one end.

6 With the gauge, measure the distances between the two wheel inner rims (at hub height) at the rear of the wheel. Push the vehicle forward to rotate the wheel through 180° (half a turn) and measure the distance between the wheel inner rims, again at hub height, at the front of the wheel. This last measurement should differ from the first by the appropriate toe-in which is given in the Specifications. The vehicle must be on level ground.

7 If the toe-in is found to be incorrect, release the track-rod end locknuts and turn both track-rods equally. Only turn them a quarter-of-a-turn at a time before re-checking the alignment. If necessary use self-locking grips to turn the track-rods - **do not** grip the threaded part of the track-rod during adjustment. It is important not to allow the track-rods to become unequal in length during adjustment, otherwise the alignment of the steering wheel will become incorrect and tyre scrubbing will occur on turns.

8 On completion tighten the locknuts without disturbing the setting. Check that the balljoints are at the centre of their arcs of travel.

Rear wheel alignment

9 The rear wheel camber setting is given for reference only since no adjustment is possible.

10 Rear wheel toe setting is possible by repositioning the rear trailing arm front mounting brackets on the underbody. Vauxhall/Opel technicians use a special tool in one of the bolt holes (one bolt temporarily removed) to move the brackets.

10

Chapter 11
Bodywork and fittings

Contents

Degrees of difficulty

Easy, suitable for novice with little experience	**Fairly easy,** suitable for beginner with some experience	**Fairly difficult,** suitable for competent DIY mechanic	**Difficult,** suitable for experienced DIY mechanic	**Very difficult,** suitable for expert DIY or professional

Specifications

Torque wrench settings	Nm	lbf ft
Bonnet striker locknut:		
Black coating	22	16
Galvanized coating	40	30
Front seat belt to seat	20	15
Front seat belt-to-B-pillar upper mounting bolt	35	26
Front seat belt reel	35	26
Front seat belt tensioner	35	26
Front seat mounting screws	20	15
Rear seat belt mountings to floor	35	26
Rear seat belt reel	35	26
Rear seat belt height adjuster to C pillar	20	15
Sunroof glass side mounting screws	5	4

1 General information

The bodyshell is of four-door Notchback Saloon, five-door Hatchback Saloon or Estate configuration, and is made of high-strength low alloy sheet metal sections. The sections are alloy-galvanized on one or both sides, depending on their position on the vehicle. Most components are welded together, but some use is made of structural adhesives. The front wings are bolted on.

The bonnet, doors and some other vulnerable panels are made of zinc-coated metal, and are further protected by being coated with an anti-chip primer prior to being sprayed. The front and rear doors incorporate safety bars as protection in the event of a side impact.

Except on Envoy models, electrically operated front windows are fitted, however electrically operated rear windows are only fitted to CDX models. The electric windows can be operated from the outside of the vehicle using the infrared remote control or alternatively the door lock key may be held in the locking position for longer than 1 second. The electric window mechanism incorporates a safety feature which stops the window if it meets an obstruction.

Extensive use is made of plastic materials, mainly in the interior, but also in exterior components. The front and rear bumpers and the front grille are injection-moulded from a synthetic material which is very strong, and yet light. Plastic components such as wheel arch liners are fitted to the underside of the vehicle, to improve the body's resistance to corrosion.

2 Maintenance - bodywork and underframe

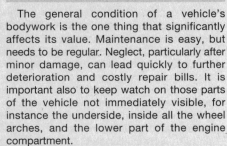

The general condition of a vehicle's bodywork is the one thing that significantly affects its value. Maintenance is easy, but needs to be regular. Neglect, particularly after minor damage, can lead quickly to further deterioration and costly repair bills. It is important also to keep watch on those parts of the vehicle not immediately visible, for instance the underside, inside all the wheel arches, and the lower part of the engine compartment.

The basic maintenance routine for the bodywork is washing - preferably with a lot of water, from a hose. This will remove all the loose solids which may have stuck to the vehicle. It is important to flush these off in such a way as to prevent grit from scratching the finish. The wheel arches and underframe need washing in the same way, to remove any accumulated mud which will retain moisture and tend to encourage rust. Paradoxically

enough, the best time to clean the underframe and wheel arches is in wet weather, when the mud is thoroughly wet and soft. In very wet weather, the underframe is usually cleaned of large accumulations automatically, and this is a good time for inspection.

Periodically, except on vehicles with a wax-based underbody protective coating, it is a good idea to have the whole of the underframe of the vehicle steam-cleaned, engine compartment included, so that a thorough inspection can be carried out to see what minor repairs and renovations are necessary. Steam-cleaning is available at many garages, and is necessary for the removal of the accumulation of oily grime, which sometimes is allowed to become thick in certain areas. If steam-cleaning facilities are not available, there are one or two excellent grease solvents available, which can be brush-applied; the dirt can then be simply hosed off. Note that these methods should not be used on vehicles with wax-based underbody protective coating, or the coating will be removed. Such vehicles should be inspected annually, preferably just prior to Winter, when the underbody should be washed down, and any damage to the wax coating repaired. Ideally, a completely fresh coat should be applied. It would also be worth considering the use of such wax-based protection for injection into door panels, sills, box sections, etc, as an additional safeguard against rust damage, where such protection is not provided by the vehicle manufacturer.

After washing paintwork, wipe off with a chamois leather to give an unspotted clear finish. A coat of clear protective wax polish will give added protection against chemical pollutants in the air. If the paintwork sheen has dulled or oxidised, use a cleaner/polisher combination to restore the brilliance of the shine. This requires a little effort, but such dulling is usually caused because regular washing has been neglected. Care needs to be taken with metallic paintwork, as special non-abrasive cleaner/polisher is required to avoid damage to the finish. Always check that the door and ventilator opening drain holes and pipes are completely clear, so that water can be drained out. Brightwork should be treated in the same way as paintwork. Windscreens and windows can be kept clear of the smeary film which often appears, by the use of proprietary glass cleaner. Never use any form of wax or other body or chromium polish on glass.

3 Maintenance - upholstery and carpets

Mats and carpets should be brushed or vacuum-cleaned regularly, to keep them free of grit. If they are badly stained, remove them from the vehicle for scrubbing or sponging, and make quite sure they are dry before

refitting. Seats and interior trim panels can be kept clean by wiping with a damp cloth. If they do become stained (which can be more apparent on light-coloured upholstery), use a little liquid detergent and a soft nail brush to scour the grime out of the grain of the material. Do not forget to keep the headlining clean in the same way as the upholstery. When using liquid cleaners inside the vehicle, do not over-wet the surfaces being cleaned. Excessive damp could get into the seams and padded interior, causing stains, offensive odours or even rot. If the inside of the vehicle gets wet accidentally, it is worthwhile taking some trouble to dry it out properly, particularly where carpets are involved. *Do not leave oil or electric heaters inside the vehicle for this purpose.*

4 Minor body damage - repair

Note: *For more detailed information about bodywork repair, Haynes Publishing produce a book titled "The Car Bodywork Repair Manual" (Book No 9864). This incorporates information on such aspects as rust treatment, painting and glass-fibre repairs, as well as details on more ambitious repairs involving welding and panel beating.*

Repairs of minor scratches in bodywork

If the scratch is very superficial, and does not penetrate to the metal of the bodywork, repair is very simple. Lightly rub the area of the scratch with a paintwork renovator, or a very fine cutting paste, to remove loose paint from the scratch, and to clear the surrounding bodywork of wax polish. Rinse the area with clean water.

Apply touch-up paint to the scratch using a fine paint brush; continue to apply fine layers of paint until the surface of the paint in the scratch is level with the surrounding paintwork. Allow the new paint at least two weeks to harden, then blend it into the surrounding paintwork by rubbing the scratch area with a paintwork renovator or a very fine cutting paste. Finally, apply wax polish.

Where the scratch has penetrated right through to the metal of the bodywork, causing the metal to rust, a different repair technique is required. Remove any loose rust from the bottom of the scratch with a penknife, then apply rust-inhibiting paint, to prevent the formation of rust in the future. Using a rubber or nylon applicator, fill the scratch with bodystopper paste. If required, this paste can be mixed with cellulose thinners, to provide a very thin paste which is ideal for filling narrow scratches. Before the stopper-paste in the scratch hardens, wrap a piece of smooth cotton rag around the top of a finger. Dip the finger in cellulose thinners, and quickly sweep it across the surface of the stopper-paste in the scratch; this will ensure that the surface of the stopper-paste is slightly hollowed. The scratch can now be painted over as described earlier in this Section.

Repairs of dents in bodywork

When deep denting of the vehicle's bodywork has taken place, the first task is to pull the dent out, until the affected bodywork almost attains its original shape. There is little point in trying to restore the original shape completely, as the metal in the damaged area will have stretched on impact, and cannot be reshaped fully to its original contour. It is better to bring the level of the dent up to a point which is about 3 mm below the level of the surrounding bodywork. In cases where the dent is very shallow anyway, it is not worth trying to pull it out at all. If the underside of the dent is accessible, it can be hammered out gently from behind, using a mallet with a wooden or plastic head. Whilst doing this, hold a suitable block of wood firmly against the outside of the panel, to absorb the impact from the hammer blows and thus prevent a large area of the bodywork from being "belled-out".

Should the dent be in a section of the bodywork which has a double skin, or some other factor making it inaccessible from behind, a different technique is called for. Drill several small holes through the metal inside the area - particularly in the deeper section. Then screw long self-tapping screws into the holes, just sufficiently for them to gain a good purchase in the metal. Now the dent can be pulled out by pulling on the protruding heads of the screws with a pair of pliers.

The next stage of the repair is the removal of the paint from the damaged area, and from an inch or so of the surrounding "sound" bodywork. This is accomplished most easily by using a wire brush or abrasive pad on a power drill, although it can be done just as effectively by hand, using sheets of abrasive paper. To complete the preparation for filling, score the surface of the bare metal with a screwdriver or the tang of a file, or alternatively, drill small holes in the affected area. This will provide a really good "key" for the filler paste.

To complete the repair, see the Section on filling and respraying.

Repairs of rust holes or gashes in bodywork

Remove all paint from the affected area, and from an inch or so of the surrounding "sound" bodywork, using an abrasive pad or a wire brush on a power drill. If these are not available, a few sheets of abrasive paper will do the job most effectively. With the paint removed, you will be able to judge the severity of the corrosion, and therefore decide whether to renew the whole panel (if this is possible) or to repair the affected area. New body panels are not as expensive as most people think, and it is often quicker and more

satisfactory to fit a new panel than to attempt to repair large areas of corrosion.

Remove all fittings from the affected area, except those which will act as a guide to the original shape of the damaged bodywork (eg headlamp shells etc). Then, using tin snips or a hacksaw blade, remove all loose metal and any other metal badly affected by corrosion. Hammer the edges of the hole inwards, in order to create a slight depression for the filler paste.

Wire-brush the affected area to remove the powdery rust from the surface of the remaining metal. Paint the affected area with rust-inhibiting paint; if the back of the rusted area is accessible, treat this also.

Before filling can take place, it will be necessary to block the hole in some way. This can be achieved by the use of aluminium or plastic mesh, or aluminium tape.

Aluminium or plastic mesh, or glass-fibre matting is probably the best material to use for a large hole. Cut a piece to the approximate size and shape of the hole to be filled, then position it in the hole so that its edges are below the level of the surrounding bodywork. It can be retained in position by several blobs of filler paste around its periphery.

Aluminium tape should be used for small or very narrow holes. Pull a piece off the roll, trim it to the approximate size and shape required, then pull off the backing paper (if used) and stick the tape over the hole; it can be overlapped if the thickness of one piece is insufficient. Burnish down the edges of the tape with the handle of a screwdriver or similar, to ensure that the tape is securely attached to the metal underneath.

Bodywork repairs - filling and respraying

Before using this Section, see the Sections on dent, deep scratch, rust holes and gash repairs.

Many types of bodyfiller are available, but generally speaking, those proprietary kits which contain a tin of filler paste and a tube of resin hardener are best for this type of repair. A wide, flexible plastic or nylon applicator will be found invaluable for imparting a smooth and well-contoured finish to the surface of the filler.

Mix up a little filler on a clean piece of card or board - measure the hardener carefully (follow the maker's instructions on the pack), otherwise the filler will set too rapidly or too slowly. Using the applicator, apply the filler paste to the prepared area; draw the applicator across the surface of the filler to achieve the correct contour and to level the surface. As soon as a contour that approximates to the correct one is achieved, stop working the paste - if you carry on too long, the paste will become sticky and begin to "pick-up" on the applicator. Continue to add thin layers of filler paste at 20-minute

intervals, until the level of the filler is just proud of the surrounding bodywork.

Once the filler has hardened, the excess can be removed using a metal plane or file. From then on, progressively-finer grades of abrasive paper should be used, starting with a 40-grade production paper, and finishing with a 400-grade wet-and-dry paper. Always wrap the abrasive paper around a flat rubber, cork, or wooden block - otherwise the surface of the filler will not be completely flat. During the smoothing of the filler surface, the wet-and-dry paper should be periodically rinsed in water. This will ensure that a very smooth finish is imparted to the filler at the final stage.

At this stage, the "dent" should be surrounded by a ring of bare metal, which in turn should be encircled by the finely "feathered" edge of the good paintwork. Rinse the repair area with clean water, until all of the dust produced by the rubbing-down operation has gone.

Spray the whole area with a light coat of - this will show up any imperfections in the surface of the filler. Repair these imperfections with fresh filler paste or bodystopper, and once more smooth the surface with abrasive paper. If bodystopper is used, it can be mixed with cellulose thinners, to form a really thin paste which is ideal for filling small holes. Repeat this spray-and-repair procedure until you are satisfied that the surface of the filler, and the feathered edge of the paintwork, are perfect. Clean the repair area with clean water, and allow to dry fully.

The repair area is now ready for final spraying. Paint spraying must be carried out in a warm, dry, windless and dust-free atmosphere. This condition can be created artificially if you have access to a large indoor working area, but if you are forced to work in the open, you will have to pick your day very carefully. If you are working indoors, dousing the floor in the work area with water will help to settle the dust which would otherwise be in the atmosphere. If the repair area is confined to one body panel, mask off the surrounding panels; this will help to minimise the effects of a slight mis-match in paint colours. Bodywork fittings (eg chrome strips, door handles etc) will also need to be masked off. Use genuine masking tape, and several thicknesses of newspaper, for the masking operations.

Before commencing to spray, agitate the aerosol can thoroughly, then spray a test area (an old tin, or similar) until the technique is mastered. Cover the repair area with a thick coat of primer; the thickness should be built up using several thin layers of paint, rather than one thick one. Using 400 grade wet-and-dry paper, rub down the surface of the primer until it is really smooth. While doing this, the work area should be thoroughly doused with water, and the wet-and-dry paper periodically rinsed in water. Allow to dry before spraying on more paint.

11

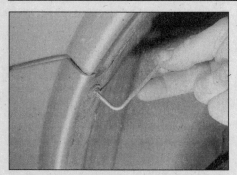

6.2a Remove the side Torx screws and pull back the wheel arch liners

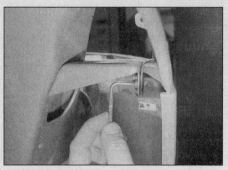

6.2b Unscrewing the Torx side mounting screws on the front bumper

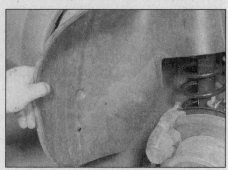

6.2c Removing the complete wheel arch liner

Spray on the top coat, again building up the thickness by using several thin layers of paint. Start spraying in the centre of the repair area, and then, using a circular motion, work outwards until the whole repair area and about 2 inches of the surrounding original paintwork is covered. Remove all masking material 10 to 15 minutes after spraying on the final coat of paint.

Allow the new paint at least two weeks to harden, then, using a paintwork renovator or a very fine cutting paste, blend the edges of the paint into the existing paintwork. Finally, apply wax polish.

Plastic components

With the use of more and more plastic body components by the vehicle manufacturers (eg bumpers. spoilers, and in some cases major body panels), rectification of more serious damage to such items has become a matter of either entrusting repair work to a specialist in this field, or renewing complete components. Repair of such damage by the DIY owner is not really feasible, owing to the cost of the equipment and materials required for effecting such repairs. The basic technique involves making a groove along the line of the crack in the plastic, using a rotary burr in a power drill. The damaged part is then welded back together, using a hot air gun to heat up and fuse a plastic filler rod into the groove. Any excess plastic is then removed, and the area rubbed down to a smooth finish. It is important that a filler rod of the correct plastic is used, as body components can be made of

a variety of different types (eg polycarbonate, ABS, polypropylene).

Damage of a less serious nature (abrasions, minor cracks etc) can be repaired by the DIY owner using a two-part epoxy filler repair. Once mixed in equal, this is used in similar fashion to the bodywork filler used on metal panels. The filler is usually cured in twenty to thirty minutes, ready for sanding and painting.

If the owner is renewing a complete component himself, or if he has repaired it with epoxy filler, he will be left with the problem of finding a suitable paint for finishing which is compatible with the type of plastic used. At one time, the use of a universal paint was not possible, owing to the complex range of plastics encountered in body component applications. Standard paints, generally speaking, will not bond to plastic or rubber satisfactorily, but suitable paints to match any plastic or rubber finish, can be obtained from dealers. However, it is now possible to obtain a plastic body parts finishing kit which consists of a pre-primer treatment, a primer and coloured top coat. Full instructions are normally supplied with a kit, but basically, the method of use is to first apply the pre-primer to the component concerned, and allow it to dry for up to 30 minutes. Then the primer is applied, and left to dry for about an hour before finally applying the special-coloured top coat. The result is a correctly-coloured component, where the paint will flex with the plastic or rubber, a property that standard paint does not normally possess.

5 Major body damage - repair

Where serious damage has occurred, or large areas need renewal due to neglect, it means that complete new panels will need welding-in, and this is best left to professionals. If the damage is due to impact, it will also be necessary to check completely the alignment of the bodyshell, and this can only be carried out accurately by a Vauxhall/Opel dealer using special jigs. If the body is left misaligned, it is primarily dangerous, as the car will not handle properly, and secondly, uneven stresses will be imposed on the steering, suspension and possibly transmission, causing abnormal wear, or complete failure, particularly to such items as the tyres.

6 Bumpers - removal and refitting

Front bumper

Removal

1 Remove the radiator grille as described in Section 7.
2 Working beneath the front wheel arches, using a Torx key remove the screws, then pull back the liners for access to the front bumper side mounting screws. If preferred, the liners can be completely removed by releasing the plastic retainers (press the centre pins through the clips) **(see illustrations)**. Unscrew and remove the side mounting screws.
3 Remove the plastic clips securing the bottom of the front bumper to the front valance. To do this, pull out the centre pins using a pair of pliers **(see illustrations)**.
4 Unscrew and remove the upper mounting bolts, then carefully withdraw the front bumper from the front of the vehicle.
5 Where a spoiler is fitted, prise off the special clips then compress the lugs and separate the spoiler from the front bumper.
Note: *New front bumpers are supplied in base colour and require painting in the correct colour before fitting.*

6.3a Use a pair of pliers to pull out the centre pins . . .

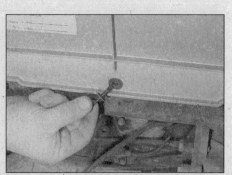

6.3b . . . then pull the plastic clips from the bottom of the front bumper

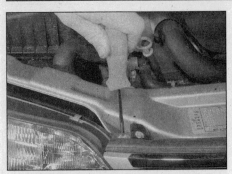

7.1 Unscrew the upper mounting screws . . .

7.2 . . . then lift the radiator grille and release the clips from the front bumper

Refitting

6 Refitting is a reversal of removal but tighten the screws securely.

Rear bumper

Removal

7 Open the bootlid or tailgate as applicable.
8 Pull up the weatherstrip to provide access to the rear bumper upper mounting screws.
9 Using a Torx key, unscrew the screws securing the front of the rear bumper to the rear wheel arch on both sides. On Estate models also remove the screws from the lower corners.
10 Using the key, unscrew the screws securing the bottom of the rear bumper to the rear valance.
11 Unscrew the upper mounting screws then carefully withdraw the rear bumper from the

rear of the vehicle. **Note:** *New rear bumpers are supplied in base colour and require painting in the correct colour before fitting.*

Refitting

12 Refitting is a reversal of removal but tighten the screws securely.

7 Radiator grille - removal and refitting

Removal

1 Open the bonnet, then use a Torx screwdriver to unscrew the radiator grille upper mounting screws **(see illustration)**.
2 Lift the radiator grille and release the clips from the front bumper **(see illustration)**.

Refitting

3 Refitting is a reversal of removal but tighten the screws securely.

8 Bonnet and support struts - removal, refitting and adjustment

Bonnet

Removal

1 Open the bonnet, and have an assistant support it.

2 Using a marker pen or paint, mark around the hinge positions on the bonnet.
3 Disconnect the windscreen washer fluid hose at the connector and support **(see illustration)**.
4 With the aid of the assistant, unscrew the bolts securing the bonnet to the hinges on both sides **(see illustration)**.
5 Lift off the bonnet taking care not to damage the vehicle paintwork.

Refitting

6 With the aid of the assistant, align the marks made on the bonnet before removal with the hinges, then refit and tighten the bonnet securing bolts.
7 Reconnect the windscreen washer fluid hose.
8 Check the bonnet adjustment as follows.

Adjustment

9 Close the bonnet, and check that there is an equal gap at each side, between the bonnet and the wing panels. Check also that the bonnet sits flush in relation to the surrounding body panels.
10 The bonnet should close smoothly and positively without excessive pressure. If this is not the case, adjustment will be required.
11 To adjust the bonnet alignment, loosen the bonnet mounting bolts, and move the bonnet on the bolts as required (the bolt holes in the hinges are enlarged). To adjust the bonnet front height in relation to the front wings, adjustable rubber bump stops are fitted to the front corners of the bonnet. These may be screwed in or out as necessary. After making an adjustment, the bonnet striker must be adjusted so that the lock spring holds the bonnet firmly against the rubber bump stops. Loosen the locknut and screw the striker in or out as necessary **(see illustrations)**.

Support struts

Removal

12 Open the bonnet, and have an assistant support it.

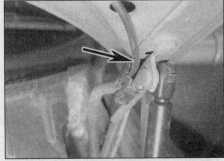

8.3 Windscreen washer fluid hose and clip on the bonnet

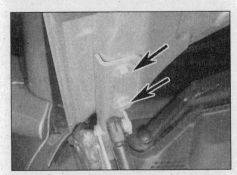

8.4 Bolts securing the bonnet to the hinges

8.11a The bonnet rubber bump stops are located at the front corners

8.11b Bonnet striker and safety catch

11

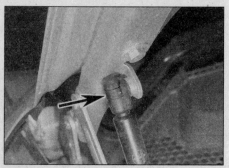

8.13 Prise the spring clip from the bonnet support strut to disconnect it from the ball

13 Using a screwdriver prise out the retaining spring clips and disconnect the strut from the bonnet and body. Note which way round the strut is fitted **(see illustration)**.

Refitting

14 Refitting is a reversal of removal.

9 Bonnet release cable - removal and refitting

Removal

1 Remove the lower trim panel from under the driver's side of the facia.
2 Remove the radiator grille as described in Section 7.
3 Disconnect the front end of the release cable from the bonnet lock spring.
4 Disconnect the rear end of the release cable from the release lever in the driver's footwell. Access is very limited and the use of a mirror will help.
5 Release the cable from the support clips in the engine compartment, then withdraw the cable through the rubber grommet and withdraw into the engine compartment. As an aid to refitting, tie a length of string to the cable before removing it and leave the string in position ready for refitting.

Refitting

6 Refitting is a reversal of removal, but tie the string to the release lever end of the cable, and use the string to pull the cable into position. Ensure that the cable is routed as noted before removal, and make sure that the grommet is correctly seated.

10 Bonnet lock spring - removal and refitting

Removal

1 The bonnet is held in its locked position with a strong spring which engages with the striker on the front edge of the bonnet. The release cable is connected to the end of the spring.
2 The striker may be removed from the bonnet by unscrewing the locknut, however measure its fitted length first as a guide to refitting it.
3 To remove the lock spring, first remove the radiator grille (see Section 7) then disconnect the cable and unhook the spring from the front crossmember.

Refitting

4 Refitting is a reversal of removal.

11 Door - removal and refitting

Removal

1 The door hinges are welded onto the door frame and the body pillar. Where necessary, adjustment is carried out using special tools to bend the hinges.
2 Open the door to gain access to the wiring connector which is fitted to the front edge of the door. Disconnect the wiring connector from the front edge of the door. To do this, unscrew the connector locking ring, then pull the connector away from the door **(see illustration)**.
3 Unscrew and remove the bolt securing the door check link to the vehicle body **(see illustration)**.
4 Remove the plastic covers from the door hinge pins. Have an assistant support the door, then drive both hinge pins out of

position using a hammer and suitable punch.
Note: *Vauxhall/Opel technicians use a special hinge pin removal tool which acts like a slide hammer.* Remove the door from the vehicle.
5 Inspect the hinge pins for signs of wear or damage, and renew if necessary.

Refitting

6 Refitting is a reversal of removal, but check that when shut the door is positioned centrally within the body aperture. If the hinge pins have been renewed and adjustment is still required, the hinges will have to be re-aligned using special tools. This work must be carried out by a Vauxhall/Opel dealer, however minor adjustment may be possible by physically lifting the door on its hinges. After adjustment, make sure that the door lock engages correctly with the striker on the body pillar. If necessary loosen the striker retaining screws using a Torx key, then reposition the striker and tighten the screws **(see illustration)**.

12 Door inner trim panel - removal and refitting

Front door

Removal

1 Disconnect the battery negative (earth) lead (see Chapter 5A).
2 With the front door open carefully pull off the exterior mirror adjustment handle, then prise off the triangular plastic cover taking care not to damage the retaining clips. Remove the foam padding **(see illustrations)**.
3 Prise the plastic cover from the inside of the interior door handle grip. Also prise out the small plastic cover or electric mirror switch (as applicable) from the outside of the grip - disconnect the wiring where necessary **(see illustrations)**.
4 Prise off the small loudspeaker grille **(see illustration)**.
5 Undo the retaining screws and remove the door handle surround/grip. Disconnect the wiring from the loudspeaker **(see illustrations)**.

11.2 Wiring connector on the front door

11.3 Front door check link

11.6 Rear door striker

12.2a Pull off the exterior mirror adjustment handle . . .

12.2b . . . then prise off the triangular plastic cover . . .

12.2c . . . and remove the foam padding

6 On base models, remove the window regulator handle by first closing the window and noting the fitted angle of the handle. Using a piece of cloth rag inserted behind the handle, release the clip then withdraw the

handle from the splined shaft.

7 Unscrew and remove the screws from the bottom edge of the trim panel, then use a wide-bladed screwdriver or removal tool to carefully prise the panel clips from the door.

Unhook the top of the panel and remove it from the door **(see illustrations)**.

8 If necessary, carefully peel the protective plastic membrane from the door **(see illustration)**.

12.3a Prise off the plastic cover from the inside of the interior front door handle grip . . .

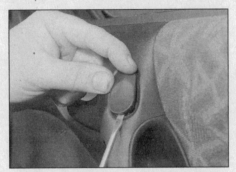

12.3b . . . then prise out the upper plastic cover from the outside of the grip

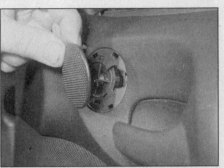

12.4 Prise off the small loudspeaker grille from the front door

12.5a Undo the retaining screws . . .

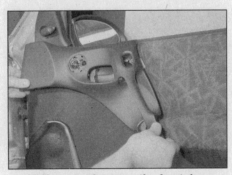

12.5b . . . and remove the front door handle surround/grip . . .

12.5c . . . then disconnect the wiring from the loudspeaker

12.7a Undo the screws from the bottom edge of the front door trim panel . . .

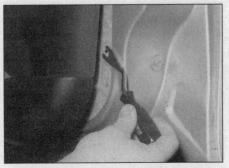

12.7b . . . then prise out the panel clips and remove the trim panel from the door

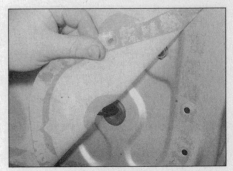

12.8 Peel the protective plastic membrane from the front door

11

12.11 Prise off the small loudspeaker grille from the rear door

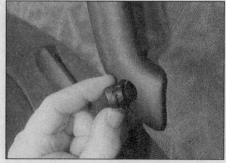

12.12a Prise out the lower plastic plug . . .

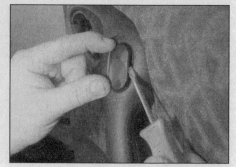

12.12b . . . the upper plastic plug from the rear door inner trim panel

Refitting

9 Refitting is a reversal of removal.

Rear door

Removal

10 Disconnect the battery negative (earth) lead (see Chapter 5A).

11 With the rear door open use a small screwdriver to carefully prise off the small loudspeaker grille **(see illustration)**.

12 Prise out the lower plastic plug and upper plug or electric window switch (as applicable) from the interior handle surround - disconnect the wiring where necessary **(see illustrations)**.

13 Unscrew and remove the three retaining screws and remove the door handle surround/ grip **(see illustrations)**.

14 Where a manual window regulator is

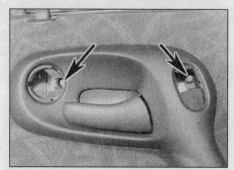

12.13a Undo the retaining screws (upper two screws arrowed) . . .

fitted, fully close the window and note the position of the regulator handle. The handle must now be removed from the splined shaft. To do this, locate a cloth rag between the handle and the trim panel and pull it to one

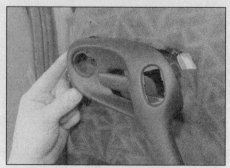

12.13b . . . and remove the rear door handle surround/grip

side to release the spring clip. The handle can now be removed from the splined shaft and the escutcheon removed **(see illustrations)**.

15 Prise the triangular plastic cover from the upper rear of the trim panel **(see illustration)**.

12.14a Locate a cloth rag between the handle and the trim panel . . .

12.14b . . . then pull it to one side to release the spring clip, and remove the handle from the splined shaft . . .

12.14c . . . and remove the escutcheon

12.15 Prise off the triangular plastic cover from the upper rear of the rear door

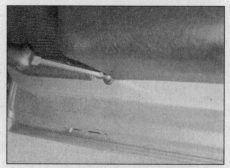

12.16a Remove the screws from the bottom edge of the rear door . . .

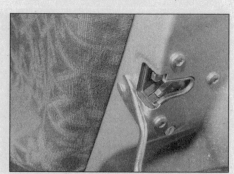

12.16b . . . then carefully prise away the inner trim panel . . .

12.16c . . . and unhook it from the locking knob

16 Unscrew and remove the screws from the bottom edge of the trim panel, then use a wide-bladed screwdriver or removal tool to carefully prise the inner trim panel clips from the inside of the rear door. Unhook the top of

13.3 Unhook the interior handle from the linkage

12.17 Peel the protective plastic membrane from the door

the panel from the locking knob and remove it from the door **(see illustrations)**.
17 If necessary, carefully peel the protective plastic membrane from the door **(see illustration)**.

Refitting

18 Refitting is a reversal of removal.

---

13 Door handles and lock components -
removal and refitting

Door interior handle

Removal

1 Remove the door inner trim panel, and peel back the protective plastic sheeting as described in Section 12.

2 Press the interior handle forwards to release it from the elongated slots in the door panel.
3 Unhook the handle from the linkage **(see illustration)**.

Refitting

4 Refitting is a reversal of removal.

Front door exterior handle

Removal

5 Remove the door inner trim panel, and peel back the protective plastic sheeting as described in Section 12.
6 With the window closed, pull out the guide rubber then unscrew the retaining screws and lower the rear window guide from the window. Withdraw the guide from the aperture in the door **(see illustrations)**.
7 Unscrew the nuts from the rear of the exterior handle using a socket inserted through the aperture provided for access to the rear nut **(see illustration)**.
8 Carefully withdraw the exterior handle from the door taking care not to damage the paintwork **(see illustration)**.
9 Unhook the linkage from the inner cover/ lock cylinder housing and withdraw through the aperture in the door **(see illustrations)**.

Refitting

10 Refitting is a reversal of removal, but before refitting the inner trim panel, screw down the knurled nut on the handle linkage until it is free of play.

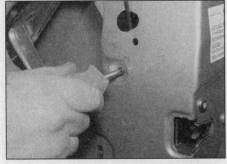

13.6a Undo the upper mounting screw . . .

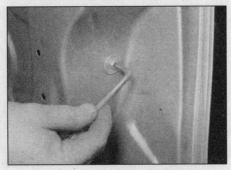

13.6b . . . and lower rear mounting screw . . .

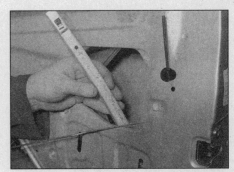

13.6c . . . then withdraw the guide from the aperture in the door

13.7 Unscrew the nuts using a socket through the hole in the door . . .

13.8 . . . then withdraw the front door exterior handle from the outside of the door . . .

13.9a . . . and unhook the linkage . . .

11

13.9b . . . and withdraw the handle through the aperture in the door

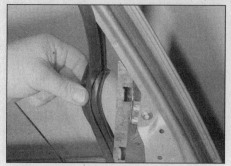

13.12 Pull the weatherstrip from the guide . . .

13.13 . . . then unscrew the retaining screws and withdraw the guide

Rear door exterior handle

Removal

11 Remove the door inner trim panel, and peel back the protective plastic sheeting as described in Section 12.

12 Lower the rear window. Pull the window weatherstrip from the rear of the window aperture and pull it upwards from the window guide **(see illustration)**.

13 Unscrew the retaining screws and withdraw the window guide from the top of the door. Note the lower retaining screw is accessed through the special hole in the door **(see illustration)**.

14 Unscrew the nuts from the rear of the exterior handle using a socket inserted through the aperture provided for access to the rear nut. Withdraw the inner cover/security plate through the aperture in the door **(see illustrations)**.

15 Disconnect the linkage arms from the door lock by prising up the plastic clips.

16 Withdraw the handle from the door taking care not to damage the paintwork **(see illustration)**.

Refitting

17 Refitting is a reversal of removal, but before refitting the inner trim panel, screw down the knurled nut on the handle linkage until it is free of play.

Front door lock cylinder

Removal

18 Remove the exterior handle as described previously in this Section.

19 Insert the key in the lock cylinder, then prise off the circlip and remove the arm from the rear of the cylinder.

20 Pull the lock cylinder from the inner cover/security plate.

Refitting

21 Refitting is a reversal of removal.

Front door lock

Removal

22 Remove the door inner trim panel, and peel back the protective plastic sheeting as described in Section 12.

23 With the window closed, unscrew the retaining screws and lower the rear window guide from the window. Withdraw the guide from the aperture in the door.

24 Where fitted, disconnect the central locking wiring from the lock by levering up the plastic retainer and separating the connector **(see illustration)**.

25 Undo the three retaining screws then disconnect the linkage arms for the outer door handle and lock cylinder from the lock.

26 Withdraw the lock from inside the door

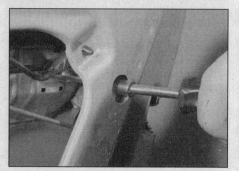

13.14a Unscrew the nuts . . .

13.14b . . . and withdraw the inner cover/security plate from the door

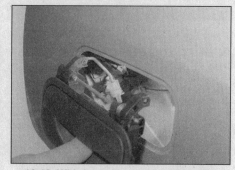

13.16 Withdraw the rear door exterior handle from the outside of the door

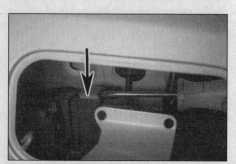

13.24 Use a screwdriver to lever up the plastic retainer in order to separate the central locking wiring from the lock

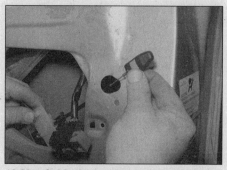

13.26a Guide the locking knob through the hole . . .

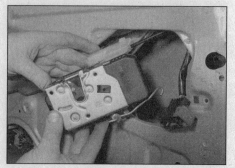

13.26b . . . while withdrawing the lock from the front door

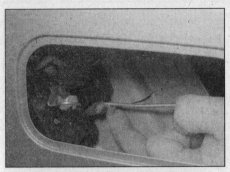

13.31 Release the plastic clip and disconnect the locking knob extension from the rear door lock

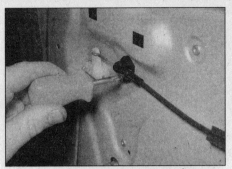

13.32a Undo the screw and disconnect the front end of the locking knob cable from the intermediate lever . . .

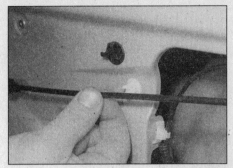

13.32b . . . then release the cable from the support

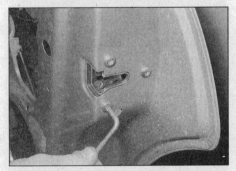

13.33a Unscrew the mounting screws . . .

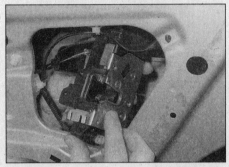

13.33b . . . and withdraw the lock through the rear door inner aperture

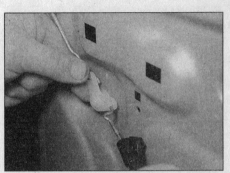

13.35 Removing the rear door locking knob intermediate lever

while guiding the locking knob through the hole provided (see illustrations).
27 Disconnect the inner door handle cable.

Refitting

28 Refitting is a reversal of removal.

Rear door lock

Removal

29 Remove the door inner trim panel, and peel back the protective plastic sheeting as described in Section 12.
30 Remove the rear door exterior handle as described previously in this Section.
31 Disconnect the locking knob extension linkage from the lock by releasing the plastic clip (see illustration).
32 Undo the screw and disconnect the front end of the locking knob cable from the intermediate lever. Release the cable from the support (see illustrations).

33 Unscrew the lock mounting screws and withdraw the lock through the door inner aperture (see illustrations).
34 Disconnect the central locking wiring by levering up the plastic retainer and separating the connector.
35 If necessary, remove the locking knob intermediate lever (see illustration).

Refitting

36 Refitting is a reversal of removal.

14 Door window regulator and glass - removal and refitting

Window regulator

Note: New rivets will be required to secure the regulator mechanism to the door on refitting.

Removal

1 Remove the door inner trim panel, and peel back the protective plastic sheeting as described in Section 12.
2 When removing the front regulator on models fitted with side airbags, remove the side airbag sensor bracket with reference to Chapter 12.
3 Using strong adhesive tape, secure the window fully closed (see illustration).
4 On models with electric window regulators, disconnect the wiring connector by squeezing the retaining tags (see illustration).
5 Mark the position of the regulator guide rail in the elongated slot, then unscrew and remove the adjustment screw (see illustration).
6 Drill out the rivets then slide the arm extensions from the channel at the bottom of the glass (see illustrations).

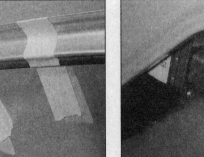

14.3 Secure the window glass fully closed using strong adhesive tape

14.4 Disconnecting the wiring from the electric window regulator

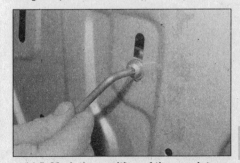

14.5 Mark the position of the regulator guide rail in the elongated slot before unscrewing it

11

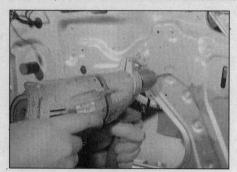

14.6a Drill out the rivets . . .

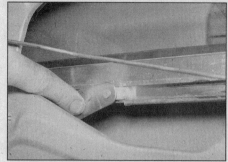

14.6b . . . then slide the arm extensions from the channel at the bottom of the glass

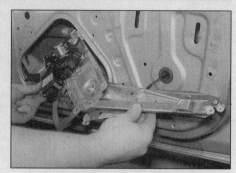

14.7a Removing a front door window regulator mechanism . . .

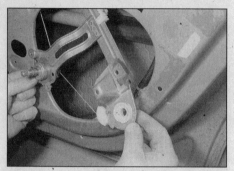

14.7b . . . and rear door window regulator mechanism

7 Manoeuvre the regulator mechanism out from the aperture in the door inner panel **(see illustrations)**.

Refitting

8 Refitting is a reversal of removal but use a pop riveter to secure the regulator with new pop rivets **(see illustrations)**. Before refitting the inner trim panel and protective plastic sheeting, adjust the position of the regulator by inserting the adjustment screw hand-tight then raising and lowering the window fully. Tighten the adjustment screw and check that the window opens and closes correctly. Finally refit the inner trim panel and plastic sheeting.

9 On models with electric window regulators the winder must be reprogrammed as follows. Fully close the window then hold the switch down for a further 5 seconds.

Window glass

Removal

10 Remove the regulator as previously described in this Section.

11 Remove the window seal on the outer edge of the door, then tilt the window glass down at the front and carefully lift it upwards from the door **(see illustration)**.

Refitting

12 Refitting is a reversal of removal.

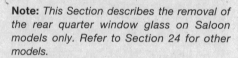

15 Rear quarter window glass - removal and refitting

Note: *This Section describes the removal of the rear quarter window glass on Saloon models only. Refer to Section 24 for other models.*

Removal

1 Remove the inner trim panel for access to the rear quarter window glass with reference to Section 29.

2 Unscrew the nuts and remove the window glass from the body. On Notchback models there are 4 nuts; on Hatchback models there are 7 nuts.

Refitting

3 Refitting is a reversal of removal.

16 Fuel filler flap lock and release cable - removal and refitting

Removal

1 Open the fuel flap and remove the filler cap.

2 Undo the two screws and withdraw the fuel filler flap.

3 Release the rubber boot from the body and withdraw it over the filler neck.

4 The catch can be removed after unscrewing the two screws.

Refitting

5 Refitting is a reversal of removal but use suitable adhesive to stick the rubber boot to the body. Clean away all old adhesive first. Note that a new flap must be painted with the body colour before fitting.

17 Bootlid - removal, refitting and adjustment

Removal

1 Open the bootlid, then disconnect the wiring at the connector.

2 Using a pencil or marker pen, mark around the hinges on the bootlid as a guide for refitting.

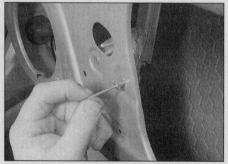

14.8a Fit new pop rivets . . .

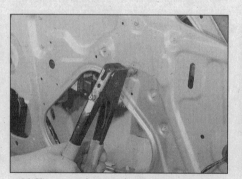

14.8b . . . and secure with a pop riveter

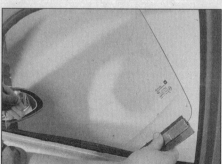

14.11 Removing a front door window glass

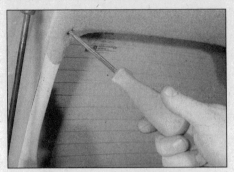

19.8a Undo the upper screws . . .

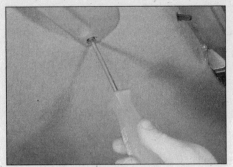

19.8b . . . and lower screws . . .

19.8c . . . then prise the trim panel from the inside of the tailgate (Estate models)

3 With the aid of an assistant, unscrew the mounting bolts then lift the bootlid from the hinges.

4 The hinges can be removed if required by unhooking the return springs and unbolting the hinges from the body.

Refitting and adjustment

5 Refitting is a reversal of removal, but make sure that the hinges are positioned as noted on removal and tighten the mounting bolts securely. With the bootlid closed, check that it is positioned centrally within the body aperture. If adjustment is necessary, loosen the mounting bolts and reposition the bootlid, then retighten the bolts. Check that the striker enters the lock centrally, and if necessary adjust the striker position by loosening the mounting bolt. Tighten the bolt on completion.

---

18 Bootlid lock components - removal and refitting

Lock

Removal

1 Open the bootlid then undo the screws and remove the trim panel by prising carefully using a wide-bladed screwdriver.

2 Disconnect the private lock linkage rod by prising up the plastic retainer.

3 Using a Torx key unscrew the mounting bolts, then withdraw the lock from inside the bootlid.

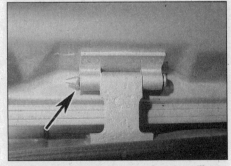

19.15 Location of clip securing the tailgate hinge pin (Estate models)

Refitting

4 Refitting is a reversal of removal. Check that when closed the bootlid lock engages the lock striker centrally. If necessary loosen the bolt and adjust the position of the striker, then tighten the bolt.

Lock cylinder

Removal

5 Open the bootlid and remove the trim panel as previously described.

6 Disconnect the central locking linkage rod by prising up the plastic retainer.

7 Unscrew the hexagon headed mounting bolts, then unhook the lock cylinder from the lock linkage rod and remove from the bootlid.

Refitting

8 Refitting is a reversal of removal.

---

19 Tailgate and support struts - removal, refitting and adjustment

Tailgate (Hatchback models)

Removal

1 Disconnect the battery negative (earth) lead (see Chapter 5A).

2 Open the tailgate and disconnect the wiring harness at the connectors.

3 Disconnect the tailgate washer hose.

4 Have an assistant support the tailgate, then disconnect the tops of the support struts by prising out the spring clips with a small screwdriver. Lower the struts to the body.

5 Extract the clips from the hinge pivot pins, then drive out the pins with a suitable drift while the assistant supports the tailgate. Withdraw the tailgate from the body.

Refitting

6 Refitting is a reversal of removal, but check that when closed the tailgate is positioned centrally within the body aperture and flush with the surrounding bodywork. If necessary, remove the trim from the rear of the roof headlining and loosen the hinge mounting bolts. Reposition the tailgate then tighten the bolts and refit the trim. If necessary, adjust the

---

position of the rubber supports so that the tailgate is flush with the surrounding bodywork. After making adjustments, check that the striker enters the lock centrally and if necessary loosen the striker bolts to reposition it. Tighten the bolts on completion.

Tailgate (Estate models)

Removal

7 Disconnect the battery negative (earth) lead (see Chapter 5A).

8 Open the tailgate then remove the trim panel by removing the screws and carefully prising the panel free from the clips **(see illustrations)**.

9 Disconnect the wiring at the connector just below the tailgate glass.

10 Release the cable ties and unbolt the earth cable.

11 Disconnect the wiring from the heated rear screen, interior light switch, number plate lamp, wiper motor, central door locking drive and anti-theft warning system switch.

12 Attach a piece of string to the end of the wiring harness, then withdraw it from the top of the tailgate. Untie the string and leave it in position inside the tailgate to aid refitting.

13 Disconnect the tailgate washer hose.

14 Have an assistant support the tailgate, then disconnect the tops of the support struts by prising out the spring clips with a small screwdriver. Lower the struts to the body.

15 Extract the clips from the hinge pivot pins, then drive out the pins with a suitable drift while the assistant supports the tailgate. Withdraw the tailgate from the body **(see illustration)**.

Refitting

16 Refitting is a reversal of removal, but check that when closed the tailgate is positioned centrally within the body aperture and flush with the surrounding bodywork. If necessary, remove the trim from the rear of the roof headlining and loosen the hinge mounting bolts. Reposition the tailgate then tighten the bolts and refit the trim. If necessary, adjust the position of the rubber supports so that the tailgate is flush with the surrounding bodywork. After making adjustments, check that the striker enters the lock centrally and if necessary loosen the striker bolts to reposition

11

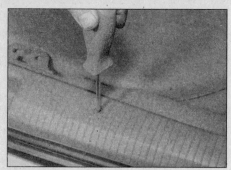

19.16a Undo the screws and remove the rear trim panel . . .

19.16b . . . for access to the tailgate lock striker

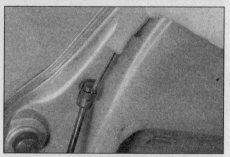

19.18 Use a screwdriver to prise out the spring clip from the top of the tailgate support strut

it. Remove the rear trim panel where necessary. Tighten the bolts and refit the trim on completion **(see illustrations)**.

Support struts

Removal

17 Open the tailgate and note which way round the struts are fitted. Have an assistant support the tailgate in its open position.
18 Using a small screwdriver, prise the spring clip from the top of the strut and disconnect it from the ball on the tailgate **(see illustration)**.
19 Similarly prise the spring clip from the bottom of the strut and disconnect it from the ball on the body. Withdraw the strut.

Refitting

20 Refitting is a reversal of removal but make sure that the exposed rod is at the top of the strut.

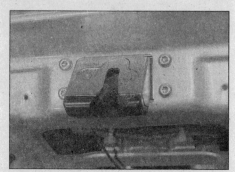

20.3 Tailgate lock and mounting bolts

20 Tailgate lock components - removal and refitting

Lock

Removal

1 Open the tailgate and remove the trim panel.
2 Disconnect the linkage by prising up the plastic retainer.
3 Using a Torx key unscrew the mounting bolts then withdraw the lock from the tailgate **(see illustration)**.

Refitting

4 Refitting is a reversal of removal.

Lock cylinder assembly

Removal

5 Open the tailgate and remove the trim panel.
6 Disconnect the central locking linkage by prising up the plastic retainer **(see illustration)**.
7 Unscrew the hexagon headed mounting nuts, then unhook the lock cylinder assembly from the lock linkage rod and remove from the tailgate **(see illustrations)**.

Refitting

8 Refitting is a reversal of removal.

21 Central locking system components - removal and refitting

Door servo motor

Removal and refitting

1 The servo motors are integral with the door locks. Refer to Section 13 for removal and refitting information.

Control unit

Note: *The central locking control unit is combined with the anti-theft warning system.*

Removal

2 Remove the trim panel from the right-hand front footwell.
3 Release the catch and disconnect the wiring from the bottom of the control unit **(see illustration)**.
4 Unscrew the mounting nuts and remove the control unit from inside the vehicle.

Refitting

5 Refitting is a reversal of removal, but tighten the mounting nuts securely.

Bootlid servo motor

Removal

6 Open the bootlid, then disconnect the central locking linkage from the servo motor by prising up the plastic retainer.
7 Disconnect the wiring connector(s) from the motor.

20.6 Disconnecting the central locking linkage rod from the lock cylinder assembly

20.7a Unscrew the nuts . . .

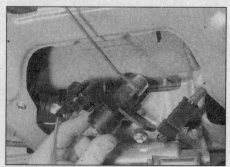

20.7b . . . and withdraw the lock cylinder assembly from the tailgate

21.3 Central locking/anti-theft alarm systems control unit

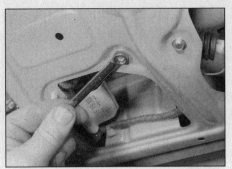

21.12 Unscrew the mounting bolts . . .

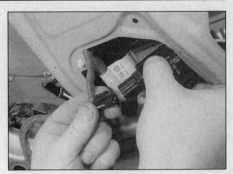

21.13 . . . and remove the servo motor from the tailgate

8 Unscrew the mounting bolts and remove the servo motor from the bootlid.

Refitting

9 Refitting is a reversal of removal, but tighten the mounting bolts securely.

Tailgate servo motor

Removal

10 Open the tailgate and remove the trim panel.
11 Disconnect the servo motor linkage from the lock cylinder by prising up the plastic retainer.
12 Unscrew the mounting bolts **(see illustration)**.
13 Disconnect the wiring connector from the motor and remove the servo motor from the tailgate **(see illustration)**.

Refitting

14 Refitting is a reversal of removal, but tighten the mounting bolts securely.

Fuel filler flap servo motor (Hatchback and Estate models)

Removal

15 Open the right-hand side luggage compartment side trim lid, then disconnect the wiring plug from the servo motor **(see illustration)**.
16 Unscrew the two mounting bolts and remove the servo motor from the rear quarter panel. Withdraw from inside the vehicle.

21.15 Fuel filler flap servo motor located behind the right-hand side luggage compartment side trim lid (Hatchback and Estate models)

Refitting

17 Refitting is a reversal of removal, but tighten the mounting bolts securely.

Fuel filler flap servo motor (Notchback models)

Removal

18 Open the right-hand side luggage compartment side trim lid, then remove the jack.
19 Detach the interior trim panel then disconnect the wiring plug from the servo motor.
20 Unbolt the retainer and the servo motor and withdraw from inside the vehicle.

Refitting

21 Refitting is a reversal of removal, but tighten the mounting bolts securely.

22 Electric window components - removal and refitting

Note: *After reconnecting the battery, renewing fuses or reconnecting the window winder wiring plugs, each window winder motor must be reprogrammed.*

Centre console control switch

Removal

1 Carefully prise the storage compartment panel from under the handbrake lever on the centre console.
2 Disconnect the relevant wiring plug, then carefully lever out the control switch and remove it together with the wiring from the centre console.

Refitting

3 Refitting is a reversal of removal.

Rear door control switch

Removal

4 Using two small screwdrivers, carefully lever the rear door control switch from the plastic door grip. Also prise out the speaker grille and the lower plastic plug.
5 Unscrew the bolts and remove the door grip while feeding the switch wiring through.

6 Disconnect the wiring and remove the switch.

Refitting

7 Refitting is a reversal of removal.

Window winder motor

Removal

8 Remove the window regulator as described in Section 14.
9 Unbolt the motor from the regulator.

Refitting

10 Refitting is a reversal of removal.

Programming

11 After refitting a window winder motor or reconnecting the battery, each motor must be programmed with its fully closed position.
12 With the ignition switched on, close all doors.
13 Working on each window in turn, completely close the window by pressing and holding down the rocker switch, then hold the switch down for at least a further 2 seconds.

23 Exterior mirrors and associated components - removal and refitting

Exterior mirror

Removal

1 On models with electrically-controlled and heated exterior mirrors, remove the door inner trim panel and protective sheeting as described in Section 12 then disconnect the wiring for the mirror.
2 On models with non-electric exterior mirrors, carefully pull off the control knob then prise off the triangular trim from the inside of the exterior mirror and remove the padding.
3 Support the mirror then unscrew the three mounting bolts and lift the mirror from the door. Note that the front bolt is located on the edge of the door **(see illustrations)**.

Refitting

4 Refitting is a reversal of removal.

11

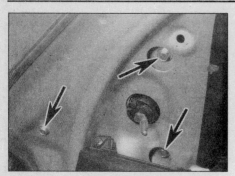

23.3a Unscrew the mounting bolts (arrowed) . . .

23.3b . . . and lift the exterior mirror from the front door

23.5 Disconnecting the exterior mirror glass from the centre retainer and control cable ends

Mirror glass

Removal

5 Using a wad of cloth, press the upper inner corner of the glass inwards so that the glass is forced out from the centre retainer and control cable ends **(see illustration)**.
6 Disconnect the mirror heating wiring and withdraw the mirror from the housing.

Refitting

7 Refitting is a reversal of removal. Carefully press the mirror into the housing until the centre retainer and control cable ends are engaged **(see illustration)**.

Servo motor

Removal

8 Remove the mirror as described earlier in this Section.
9 Remove the mirror glass as described earlier in this Section.
10 Remove the front cover by prising out the upper and lower corners until the lug is released, then pulling the rear out of the eccentric. Lever out the wiring plug then undo the three screws and withdraw the servo motor.

Refitting

11 Refitting is a reversal of removal.

Mirror actuation switch (where fitted to driver's door)

Removal

12 Prise the plastic cover from the inside of the interior door handle grip. Also prise out the switch from the outside of the grip - disconnect the wiring where necessary.
13 Prise off the small loudspeaker grille.
14 Unscrew and remove the retaining screws and remove the door handle surround/grip while feeding the switch wiring through the hole. Disconnect the wiring from the loudspeaker.
15 Disconnect the wiring and remove the switch.

Refitting

16 Refitting is a reversal of removal.

Mirror adjusting cable

Removal

17 Remove the mirror glass as described earlier.
18 Detach the covers from the housing.
19 Note the position of the guide grooves, then push the control cable guides apart and remove from the rear of the mirror housing. Note that the upper cable fitting is coloured white and the lower one is coloured black.

Refitting

20 Refitting is a reversal of removal, but note that the cable guides must be located in the second groove on the driver's side and in the first groove on the passenger's side.

24 Windscreen and fixed window glass - general information

The windscreen, rear/tailgate screen and rear quarter window glass (Estate models) are cemented in position with a special adhesive and require the use of specialist equipment for their removal and refitting. Renewal of such fixed glass is considered beyond the scope of the home mechanic. Owners are strongly advised to have the work carried out by one of the many specialist windscreen fitting specialists.

On Estate models the rear quarter window

23.7 When fitting a new glass, press it firmly into the housing until the centre retainer and control cable ends are engaged

glass incorporates a breakage sensor which is linked to the anti-theft security system, and the rear screen incorporates an aerial for the radio.

25 Sunroof components - removal and refitting

1 Either a manually-operated or electrically-operated sunroof may be fitted.

Sunroof glass

Removal

2 Slide back the sun screen and half open the sunroof.
3 Undo the screws from the front edge of the sunroof and remove the trim.
4 Close the sunroof then unclip the side trim using a screwdriver.
5 Mark the position of the side screws then unscrew them and withdraw the glass.

Refitting

6 Refitting is a reversal of removal but adjust the height of the glass as follows. With the side screws loose, position the glass so that the front edge is flush with the front of the roof or a maximum of 1.0 mm below the roof and the rear edge is flush with the rear of the roof or a maximum of 1.0 mm above the roof. Tighten the screws to the specified torque with the glass in this position.

Sunroof screen

Removal

7 Remove the sunroof glass as described earlier.
8 Remove the water deflector panel.
9 Remove the front sliders, then pull the screen forwards and remove the rear sliders.
10 Withdraw the screen from the roof.

Refitting

11 Refitting is a reversal of removal.

Wind deflector

Removal

12 Half open the glass then use pliers to release the lugs at the front of the opening.

13 Lever off the retaining ring and extract the pin, then remove the deflector.

Refitting

14 Refitting is a reversal of removal.

Sunroof crank drive

Removal

15 Remove the interior lamp as described in Chapter 12.
16 Undo the centre screw and remove the crank handle from the splined shaft.
17 Undo the screws and remove the control unit cover.
18 Undo the screws and remove the crank drive.

Refitting

19 Refitting is a reversal of removal, however first adjust the drive by temporarily locating the crank handle on the splines and turning the drive clockwise as far as possible. Now turn the handle back three full turns to the catch position. **Note:** *On manual versions, the crank handle stops after 8 turns clockwise after which the button must be depressed and the handle turned a further 2 turns for the glass to reach its end position.*

Sunroof electric drive unit

Removal

20 Remove the control unit panel then disconnect the wiring harness plug from the drive unit.
21 Unbolt and remove the electric drive unit.

Refitting

22 Refitting is a reversal of removal. It is recommended that new bolts are used to secure the drive unit.

Sunroof assembly and control cables

Removal and refitting

23 Removal and refitting of the complete sunroof assembly and control cables is considered beyond the scope of the average home mechanic as it involves the removal of the headlining. This work should be carried out by a Vauxhall/Opel dealer.

26 Body exterior fittings - removal and refitting

Scuttle cover panel

Removal

1 Open the bonnet then remove the windscreen wiper arms as described in Chapter 12.
2 Pull the rubber weatherstrip from the front of the scuttle.
3 Release the side clips and withdraw the scuttle cover panel.

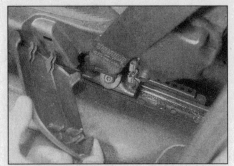

27.1 Prise off the cover for access to the seat belt mounting on the front seat

Refitting

4 Refitting is a reversal of removal.

Wheel arch liners

Removal and refitting

5 The wheel arch liners are secured by a combination of self-tapping screws, push-fit clips and nuts. Removal is self-evident after supporting the vehicle on axle stands and removing the roadwheel (see *"Jacking and Vehicle Support"*). The clips are removed by pushing the centre pins through, and are secured by inserting the pins and pushing them in flush.

Body trim strips and badges

Removal and refitting

6 The various body trim strips and badges are held in position with a special adhesive. Removal requires the trim/badge to be heated, to soften the adhesive, and then cut away from the surface. Due to the high risk of damage to the vehicle paintwork during this operation, it is recommended that this task should be entrusted to a Vauxhall/Opel dealer.

27 Seats - removal and refitting

Front seat

⚠️ **Warning: The front seats are fitted with seat belt tensioners which are triggered by the airbag control system. Before removing the front seats, disconnect the battery and wait at least 1 minute to allow the system capacitors to discharge.**

Removal

1 Carefully prise the cover from the outer side of the front seat **(see illustration)**.
2 Using a Torx key unscrew the mounting bolt and disconnect the belt from the front seat. Recover the special washer.
3 Adjust the seat fully forwards, then use the Torx key to unscrew the rear mounting screws **(see illustration)**.
4 Tilt the seat forward and release it from the front mountings.

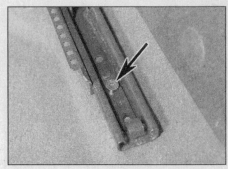

27.3 The front seats are secured to the floor with Torx screws

5 Disconnect the wiring and remove the front seat from inside the vehicle.

Refitting

6 Refitting is a reversal of removal but tighten the mounting screws to the specified torque.

Rear seat cushion

Removal

7 Fold the rear seat cushion forwards to expose the front hinge pins **(see illustration)**.
8 Extract the circlips then drive out the hinge pins using a suitable drift.
9 Withdraw the rear seat from inside the vehicle.

Refitting

10 Refitting is a reversal of removal.

Rear seat backrest

Removal

11 Fold the rear seat cushion forwards and detach the seat belt buckles from the backrest.
12 Where necessary detach the rubber cable.
13 Fold the backrest forwards then prise out the clips and pull back the carpet from the rear outer corners **(see illustrations)**.
14 Using a Torx key undo the screws and detach the side hinges.
15 Undo the screws and detach the centre hinges **(see illustration)**.
16 Withdraw the rear seat backrest from inside the vehicle.

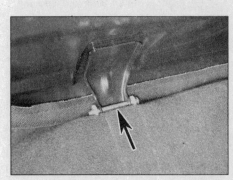

27.7 Rear seat cushion front hinge pins

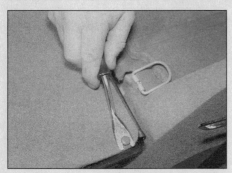

27.13a Use a screwdriver or removal tool . . .

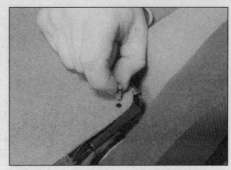

27.13b . . . to remove the plastic clips . . .

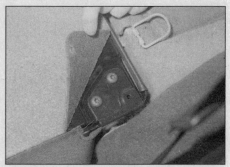

27.13c . . . then pull back the carpet to expose the rear seat backrest side hinges

Refitting

17 Refitting is a reversal of removal.

28 Seat belt components - removal and refitting

Front seat belt and reel

Removal

1 Carefully prise the cover from the outer side of the front seat.
2 Using a Torx key unscrew the mounting bolt and disconnect the belt from the front seat. Recover the special washer.
3 Remove the upper trim panel from the B-pillar.
4 Unhook the seat belt from the shackle, then unscrew the upper mounting bolt and detach the seat belt - recover the special washer.

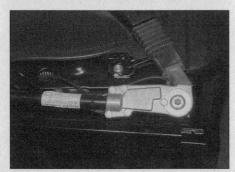

28.10 Front seat belt stalk and tensioner

5 Remove the lower trim panel from the B-pillar.
6 Prise the cover from the lower outside of the B-pillar for access to the front seat belt reel mounting nut. Using a deep socket, unscrew the nut taking care not to drop it inside the B-pillar. Note that an extension pin is provided to enable the nut to be removed safely.
7 With the nut removed, remove the reel from the inside of the pillar. As it is being removed, feed the belt through the hole in the trim panel.

Refitting

8 Refitting is a reversal of removal, but tighten the mounting bolts to the specified torque.

Front seat belt stalk and tensioner

Removal

9 Remove the front seat as described in Section 27.
10 Disconnect the wiring plug and release the cable tie, then unbolt and remove the tensioner (see illustration).

Refitting

11 Refitting is a reversal of removal but tighten the mounting bolt to the specified torque.

Rear seat belt and reel

Removal

12 Open the rear door and pull the weatherstrip from the door aperture in the area of the wheel arch (see illustration).

27.15 Rear seat backrest centre hinge mounting screws

13 On Estate and 5-door models, remove the retaining clamp for the rear seat backrest, and remove the load compartment cover.
14 On Estate models remove the rear quarter inner panel.
15 Remove the cover from the seat belt reel then unbolt and remove the reel from behind the backrest (see illustration). On Notchback models thread the seat belt through the inner panel.
16 Remove the sill inner trim panel, then unscrew the bolt securing the outer belt to the floor (see illustration).
17 Remove the cover, then unscrew the bolt securing the seat belt to the height adjuster, noting the location of the spacers (see illustration).
18 Fold the rear seat cushion forwards, then unbolt the centre seat belt stalks from the floor (see illustration).

28.12 Pull the weatherstrip from the door aperture and remove the trim . . .

28.15 . . . for access to the rear seat belt reel mounting

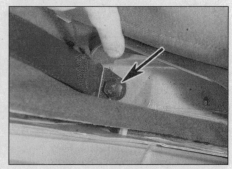

28.16 Rear seat belt outer mounting on the floor

28.17 Removing the cover from the rear seat belt height adjuster

Refitting

19 Refitting is a reversal of removal, but tighten the mounting bolts to the specified torque.

29 Interior trim - removal and refitting

1 The interior trim panels are secured by a combination of clips and screws. Removal and refitting is generally self-explanatory, noting that it may be necessary to remove or loosen surrounding panels to allow a particular panel to be removed. The following paragraphs describe the removal and refitting of the major panels in more detail.

Front footwell side trim panel

Removal

2 Open the front door and pull the weatherstrip away from the side trim panel.
3 Undo the crosshead screw and press the centre pin through the clip, then remove the side trim panel.

Refitting

4 Refitting is a reversal of removal.

B-pillar trim panel

Removal

5 Where fitted, carefully lever off the movement sensor and disconnect the wiring.
6 Unbolt the front seat belt from the height adjuster with reference to Section 28.
7 Pull the door weatherstrip away from the trim.
8 Prise the upper trim panel from the B-pillar and feed the seat belt through.
9 Remove the trim panel from the sill, then prise away the B-pillar trim.

Refitting

10 Refitting is a reversal of removal.

Rear quarter glass trim panel

Removal

11 On Estate and Hatchback models remove the rear luggage compartment cover.
12 Pull the weatherstrip from the front of the trim panel.

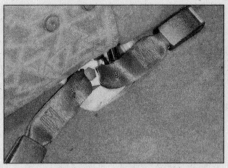

28.18 Rear seat belt centre stalks

13 Remove the rear seat belt from the C-pillar with reference to Section 28.
14 Carefully prise away the rear quarter glass trim panel. On Notchback models, feed the seat belt through the panel.

Refitting

15 Refitting is a reversal of removal.

Sill inner trim panel

Removal

16 Remove the relevant front seat as described in Section 27.
17 Pull away the door weatherstrip from the top of the trim panel.
18 The trim panel is secured with 7 clips. Carefully prise away the panel using a screwdriver to release the clips.

Refitting

19 Refitting is a reversal of removal.

Luggage compartment side trim panel (Hatchback models)

Removal

20 Remove the rear luggage compartment cover.
21 Fold the rear seat backrest forwards.
22 Undo the retaining screws, then prise out the trim panel using a screwdriver to release the retaining clips.
23 Disconnect the wiring for the interior lamp, and withdraw the trim panel.

Refitting

24 Refitting is a reversal of removal.

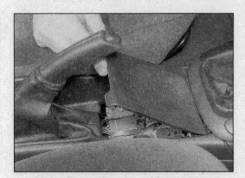

30.2a Removing the oddments tray

Luggage compartment side trim panel (Estate models)

Removal

25 Remove the rear luggage compartment cover.
26 Undo the screws then prise out the side trim panel using a screwdriver to release the retaining clips.

Refitting

27 Refitting is a reversal of removal.

Luggage compartment side trim panel (Notchback models)

Removal

28 Open the bootlid and remove the vehicle tools.
29 Remove the rear seat backrest release bracket, the rubber buffer and the hinge pin.
30 Remove the luggage compartment carpet.
31 The side trim panels are secured with clips and nuts. After removing them prise the panels away from the body.

Refitting

32 Refitting is a reversal of removal.

Carpets

Removal

33 The front and rear carpets can be removed after removing the front seats, centre console and rear footwell air distribution ducts together with side trim panels and remaining brackets.
34 On Estate models the rear luggage compartment carpet can be removed by releasing the clips located on the backrest and rear valance then removing the tools and spare wheel cover.

Refitting

35 Refitting is a reversal of removal.

Headlining

36 The headlining is secured to the roof with clips and screws, and can be withdrawn once all fittings such as the grab handles, sun visors, sunroof, front, centre and rear pillar trim panels, and associated components have been removed. The door and tailgate aperture weatherseals will also have to be prised clear.
37 Note that headlining removal requires considerable skill and experience if it is to be carried out without damage, and is therefore best entrusted to an expert.

30 Centre console - removal and refitting

Removal

1 Disconnect the battery negative (earth) lead (see Chapter 5A).
2 Carefully prise out the oddments tray from under the handbrake lever then unclip the gaiter and surround and remove from the top of the handbrake lever (see illustrations).

11

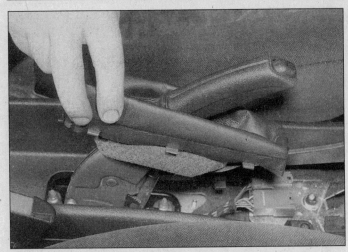

30.2b Removing the gaiter and surround from the handbrake lever

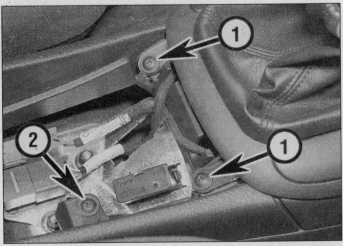

30.3 Gear lever/selector lever surround panel securing screws (1) and centre console middle mounting screw (2)

3 Undo the screws and remove the gear lever/selector lever surround panel. Where necessary also disconnect the wiring from the electric window switches **(see illustration)**.

4 Using a small screwdriver carefully prise out the covers from the centre console side retaining screws then undo the screws. Two are located on each side of the front of the console and a further two are located at the rear of the console. Also unscrew the middle mounting screw **(see illustrations)**.

5 Withdraw the console slightly from the facia, then carefully prise off the covers at each side of the ashtray.

6 Prise out the ashtray and can holder insert retaining clamp.

7 Disconnect the wiring for the ashtray illumination and cigar lighter.

8 Fully apply the handbrake lever, then withdraw the centre console upwards and remove from inside the vehicle **(see illustration)**.

Refitting

9 Refitting is a reversal of removal.

31 Glovebox - removal and refitting

Removal

1 Open the glovebox lid and undo the two upper mounting screws securing the top of the glovebox to the facia panel.

2 Undo the two lower screws and withdraw the glovebox from the facia panel sufficient to disconnect the wiring from the illumination lamp.

3 Where fitted, disconnect the wiring from the CD changer. On models fitted with air conditioning detach the hose from the cooling slider.

4 Withdraw the glovebox from inside the vehicle.

Refitting

5 Refitting is a reversal of removal.

32 Facia assembly - removal and refitting

Removal

1 Disconnect the battery negative (earth) lead (see Chapter 5A).

 Warning: Wait for at least 1 minute after disconnecting the battery to allow the airbag control system capacitors to discharge.

2 Remove the steering wheel as described in Chapter 10.

3 Remove the airbag contact unit as described in Chapter 12.

4 Remove the wiper and indicator switches from the steering column as described in Chapter 12. Also remove the switch mounting bracket.

5 Remove the ignition switch as described in Chapter 12.

6 Remove the anti-theft immobiliser transceiver unit as described in Chapter 12, Section 4.

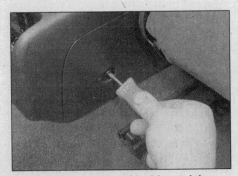

30.4a Unscrewing the side retaining screws . . .

30.4b . . . and middle retaining screw

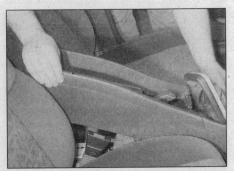

30.8 Removing the centre console

32.7a Remove the clips . . .

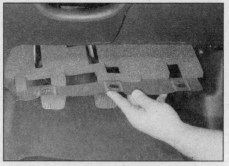

32.7b . . . and remove the lower trim panel from under the facia on the driver's side

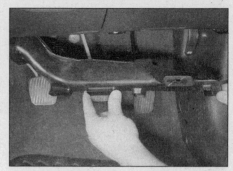

32.7c Prise out the air distribution duct

7 On the driver's side remove the lower trim panel from under the facia then prise out the air distribution duct **(see illustrations)**.
8 Remove the radio as described in Chapter 12.
9 Remove the heating controls as described in Chapter 3.
10 Remove the centre air vents as described in Chapter 3 and the instrument panel as described in Chapter 12.
11 Remove the glovebox as described in Section 31.
12 Remove the centre console with reference to Section 30.
13 Where fitted, remove the passenger side airbag as described in Chapter 12.
14 Remove the inner panels from the A-pillars with reference to Section 29.

15 Remove the coolant line cover from under the facia.
16 Carefully prise the windscreen airflow cover from the front of the facia.
17 Remove the trim panels from the outer sides of each front footwell.
18 Remove the heating air ducts from the left- and right-hand sides.
19 Unclip the wiring loom and support then unbolt the support brace from below the centre of the facia assembly **(see illustrations)**.
20 Disconnect the wiring harness plug located in the right-hand side of the engine compartment.
21 Unscrew the bolt and disconnect the earth cable from the bottom of the A-pillar. Also detach the earth cable from the steering column bracket.

22 Where necessary, remove the brake ABS hydraulic modulator with reference to Chapter 9, then disconnect the wiring harness plug and withdraw the wiring into the passenger compartment.
23 Remove the fusebox cover and unbolt the fusebox.
24 Unscrew the bolts securing the facia to the bulkhead and body, and withdraw it together with the wiring **(see illustration)**. Remove from inside the vehicle.

Refitting

25 Refitting is a reversal of removal, referring to the relevant Chapters where necessary. If a new facia assembly is fitted, make sure that the airbag warning stickers are transferred from the old facia

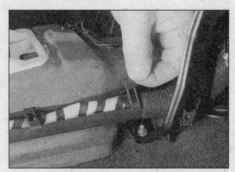

32.19a Release the clips . . .

32.19b . . . and remove the wiring support . . .

32.19c . . . then unscrew the support brace lower mounting nuts . . .

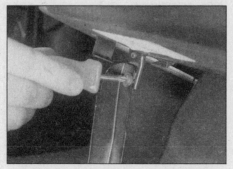

32.19d . . . and upper mounting screws

32.24 Facia panel lower mounting bolt

11

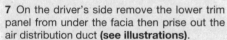

Notes

Chapter 12
Body electrical system

Contents

Degrees of difficulty

| **Easy,** suitable for novice with little experience | | **Fairly easy,** suitable for beginner with some experience | | **Fairly difficult,** suitable for competent DIY mechanic | | **Difficult,** suitable for experienced DIY mechanic | | **Very difficult,** suitable for expert DIY or professional |

Specifications

System type . . . . 12-volt negative earth

Wiper blades

Type (windscreen and tailgate) . . . . 19 in (Champion X-48)

Fuses

Fuse	Rating (colour)	Circuits protected
1	-	-
2	30 A (Green)	Air conditioning system, cooling fan
3	40 A (Orange)	Heated rear window
4	-	-
5	-	-
6	10 A (Red)	Dipped beam (right), headlamp range adjustment
7	10 A (Red)	Parking and tail lamps, right
8	10 A (Red)	Main beam, right
9	30 A (Green)	Headlamp wash system *
10	20 A (Yellow)	Horn
11	30 A (Green)	Central locking system *
12	20 A (Yellow)	Fog lamps *
13	-	-
14	30 A (Green)	Windscreen wipers
15	-	-
16	10 A (Red)	Fog tail lamp *
17	30 A (Green)	Electrically operated windows *
18	10 A (Red)	Number plate lamp
19	20 A (Yellow)	Fuel pump
20	30 A (Green)	Electrically operated windows *
21	-	-
22	20 A (Yellow)	Hazard warning flashers, information display, trip computer *, courtesy lamp, cooling fan, radio *, control indicators
23	-	-
24	10 A (Red)	Dipped beam (left), headlamp range adjustment
25	10 A (Red)	Parking and tail lamps, left
26	10 A (Red)	Main beam, left
27	-	-
28	-	-
29	10 A (Red)	Hazard warning flashers, reversing lamps, electrically adjustable exterior mirrors *, electrically operated windows, sun roof *, cruise control *, courtesy lamp
30	30 A (Green)	Sun roof *
31	-	-
32	10 A (Red)	Daylight running lamps (Scandinavia) *
33	20 A (Yellow)	Terminal 30; constant current for caravan/trailer
34	20 A (Yellow)	CD changer *
35	10 A (Red)	ABS *, TC *, automatic transmission *
36	20 A (Yellow)	Cigarette lighter and heated front seats*
37	-	-
38	10 A (Red)	Brake lamps, automatic transmission *, information display *, cruise control *
39	10 A (Red)	Automatic transmission *
40	10 A (Red)	Cooling fan, heated rear window
41	10 A (Red)	Heated exterior mirrors

* *Not all items fitted to all models*

Torque wrench settings

	Nm	lbf ft
Tailgate wiper motor retaining nut	10	7
Airbag to steering wheel	8	6
Passenger side airbag	5	4
Side airbag	5	4
Airbag control unit	10	7

1 General information and precautions

Warning: Before carrying out any work on the electrical system, read through the precautions given in Safety first! at the beginning of this manual, and in Chapter 5.

1 The electrical system is of 12-volt negative earth type. Power for the lights and all electrical accessories is supplied by a lead acid type battery, which is charged by the alternator.

2 This Chapter covers repair and service procedures for the various electrical components not associated with the engine. Information on the battery, alternator and starter motor can be found in Chapter 5.

3 It should be noted that, before working on any component in the electrical system, the battery negative terminal should first be disconnected, to prevent the possibility of electrical short-circuits and/or fires.

4 At regular intervals, carefully check the routing of the wiring harness, ensuring that it is correctly secured by the clips or ties provided so that it cannot chafe against other components. If evidence is found of the harness having chafed against other components, repair the damage and ensure that the harness is secured or protected so that the problem cannot occur again.

Caution: If the radio/cassette player fitted to the vehicle is one with an anti-theft security code, refer to Radio/cassette player anti-theft system - a precaution in the Reference Section of this manual before disconnecting the battery.

2 Electrical fault-finding - general information

Note: *Refer to the precautions given in Safety first! (at the beginning of this manual) and to Section 1 of this Chapter before starting work. The following tests relate to testing of the main electrical circuits, and should not be used to test delicate electronic circuits (such as anti-lock braking systems), particularly where an electronic control module is used.*

General

1 A typical electrical circuit consists of an electrical component, any switches, relays, motors, fuses, fusible links or circuit breakers related to that component, and the wiring and connectors that link the component to both the battery and the chassis. To help to pinpoint a problem in an electrical circuit, wiring diagrams are included at the end of this chapter.

2 Before attempting to diagnose an electrical fault, first study the appropriate wiring diagram to obtain a complete understanding of the components included in the particular circuit concerned. The possible sources of a fault can be narrowed down by noting whether other components related to the circuit are operating properly. If several components or circuits fail at one time, the problem is likely to be related to a shared fuse or earth connection.

3 Electrical problems usually stem from simple causes, such as loose or corroded connections, a faulty earth connection, a blown fuse, a melted fusible link, or a faulty relay (refer to Section 3 for details of testing relays). Visually inspect the condition of all fuses, wires and connections in a problem circuit before testing the components. Use the wiring diagrams to determine which terminal connections will need to be checked, to pinpoint the trouble-spot.

4 The basic tools required for electrical fault-finding include the following:

a) *a circuit tester or voltmeter (a 12-volt bulb with a set of test leads can also be used for certain tests).*

b) *a self-powered test light (sometimes known as a continuity tester).*

c) *an ohmmeter (to measure resistance).*

d) *a battery.*

e) *a set of test leads.*

f) *a jumper wire, preferably with a circuit breaker or fuse incorporated, which can be used to bypass suspect wires or electrical components.*

Before attempting to locate a problem with test instruments, use the wiring diagram to determine where to make the connections.

5 To find the source of an intermittent wiring fault (usually due to a poor or dirty connection, or damaged wiring insulation), a 'wiggle' test can be performed on the wiring. This involves wiggling the wiring by hand, to see if the fault occurs as the wiring is moved.

It should be possible to narrow down the source of the fault to a particular section of wiring. This method of testing can be used in conjunction with any of the tests described in the following sub-Sections.

6 Apart from problems due to poor connections, two basic types of fault can occur in an electrical circuit - open-circuit and short-circuit.

7 Open-circuit faults are caused by a break somewhere in the circuit, which prevents current from flowing. An open-circuit fault will prevent a component from working, but will not cause the relevant circuit fuse to blow.

8 Short-circuit faults are caused by a 'short' somewhere in the circuit, which allows the current flowing in the circuit to 'escape' along an alternative route, usually to earth. Short-circuit faults are normally caused by a breakdown in wiring insulation, which allows a feed wire to touch either another wire, or an earthed component such as the bodyshell. A short-circuit fault will normally cause the relevant circuit fuse to blow.

Finding an open-circuit

9 To check for an open-circuit, connect one lead of a circuit tester or voltmeter to either the negative battery terminal or a known good earth.

10 Connect the other lead to a connector in the circuit being tested, preferably nearest to the battery or fuse.

11 Switch on the circuit, remembering that some circuits are live only when the ignition switch is moved to a particular position.

12 If voltage is present (indicated either by the tester bulb lighting or a voltmeter reading, as applicable), this means that the section of the circuit between the relevant connector and the battery is problem-free.

13 Continue to check the remainder of the circuit in the same fashion.

14 When a point is reached at which no voltage is present, the problem must lie between that point and the previous test point with voltage. Most problems can be traced to a broken, corroded or loose connection.

Finding a short-circuit

15 To check for a short-circuit, first disconnect the load(s) from the circuit (loads are the components that draw current from a circuit, such as bulbs, motors, heating elements, etc.).

16 Remove the relevant fuse from the circuit, and connect a circuit tester or voltmeter to the fuse connections.

17 Switch on the circuit, remembering that some circuits are live only when the ignition switch is moved to a particular position.

18 If voltage is present (indicated either by the tester bulb lighting or a voltmeter reading, as applicable), this means that there is a short-circuit.

19 If no voltage is present, but the fuse still blows with the load(s) connected, this indicates an internal fault in the load(s).

Finding an earth fault

20 The battery negative terminal is connected to 'earth' (the metal of the engine/transmission and the car body), and most systems are wired so that they only receive a positive feed. The current returning through the metal of the car body. This means that the component mounting and the body form part of that circuit. Loose or corroded mountings can therefore cause a range of electrical faults, ranging from total failure of a circuit, to a puzzling partial fault. In particular, lights may shine dimly (especially when another circuit sharing the same earth point is in operation). Motors (eg wiper motors or the radiator cooling fan motor) may run slowly, and the operation of one circuit may have an affect on another. Note that on many vehicles, earth straps are used between certain components, such as the engine/transmission and the body, usually where there is no metal-to-metal contact between components, due to flexible rubber mountings, etc.

21 To check whether a component is properly earthed, disconnect the battery, and connect one lead of an ohmmeter to a known good earth point. Connect the other lead to the wire or earth connection being tested. The resistance reading should be zero; if not, check the connection as follows.

22 If an earth connection is thought to be faulty, dismantle the connection, and clean back to bare metal both the bodyshell and the wire terminal or the component earth connection mating surface. Be careful to remove all traces of dirt and corrosion, then use a knife to trim away any paint, so that a clean metal-to-metal joint is made. On reassembly, tighten the joint fasteners securely; if a wire terminal is being refitted, use serrated washers between the terminal and the bodyshell, to ensure a clean and secure connection. When the connection is remade, prevent the onset of corrosion in the future by applying a coat of petroleum jelly or silicone-based grease.

3 Fuses and relays - general information

General

Fuses

1 Fuses are designed to break a circuit when a predetermined current is reached, to protect the components and wiring which could be damaged by excessive current flow. Any excessive current flow will be due to a fault in the circuit, usually a short-circuit (see Section 2).

2 The main fuses and relays are located in a panel beneath a cover at the driver's end of the facia **(see illustration)**. Various fuses (usually the higher-rated ones protecting the engine circuits) are located in the engine compartment relay boxes.

3 The circuits protected by the various fuses and relays are marked on the inside of the panel cover.

12

3.2 The main fuses are located on the driver's side of the facia panel

3.5 Using the special tweezers to remove a fuse

3.10 The engine related relays are located in front of the battery on diesel models

3.12 Removing a relay from the main fusebox

4 A blown fuse can be recognised from its melted or broken wire.

5 To remove a fuse, first ensure that the relevant circuit is switched off. Then open the cover and pull the relevant fuse from the panel using the tweezers supplied **(see illustration)**. If desired, the lower end of the panel can be tilted forwards, after releasing the retaining clip, to improve access.

6 Before renewing a blown fuse, trace and rectify the cause, and always use a fuse of the correct rating. Never substitute a fuse of a higher rating, or make temporary repairs using wire or metal foil, as more serious damage or even fire could result.

7 Spare fuses are generally provided in the blank terminal positions in the fusebox.

8 Note that the fuses are colour-coded, see Specifications. Refer to the wiring diagrams for details of the fuse ratings and the circuits protected.

Relays

9 A relay is an electrically-operated switch, which is used for the following reasons:

 a) *A relay can switch a heavy current remotely from the circuit in which the control current is flowing, allowing the use of lighter-gauge wiring and control switch contacts.*

 b) *A relay can receive more than one control input, unlike a mechanical switch.*

 c) *A relay can have a timer function.*

10 The main relays are located on the main fusebox, although some engine-related relays are located in the engine compartment. The relay boxes are located in front of or to one side of the battery, and above the ABS control unit **(see illustration)**.

11 If a circuit or system controlled by a relay develops a fault, and the relay is suspect, operate the system. If the relay is functioning, it should be possible to hear it 'click' as it is energised. If this is the case, the fault lies with the components or wiring of the system. If the relay is not being energised, then either the relay is not receiving a main supply or a switching voltage, or the relay itself is faulty. Testing is by the substitution of a known good unit, but be careful - while some relays are identical in appearance and in operation, others look similar but perform different functions.

12 To remove a relay, first ensure that the relevant circuit is switched off. The relay can then simply be pulled out from the socket, and pushed back into position **(see illustration)**.

13 Incorporated in the fusebox is a multi-timer which combines the components and relays that were previously separate units. The timer slides into the side of the fusebox as a separate module. It controls the direction indicators (flasher relay) and hazard warning flashers, interior lighting delay, acoustic warning system, windscreen wiper delay, the heated rear window and the rear fog lamps. Where appropriate, it also controls the front fog lamps, the rear screen wiper delay and the exterior mirror heater circuits.

4 Switches - removal and refitting

Ignition switch/ steering column lock cylinder

Steering column lock cylinder

1 Remove the steering wheel. Alternatively, the steering wheel may remain in position, but it will have to turned for access to the end face screws of the shrouds.

2 Remove the steering column shrouds by unscrewing the tilt steering lever, then removing the two screws from the end face and three screws from the bottom shroud **(see illustrations)**. Recover the ignition key position indicator from the ignition switch.

3 Withdraw the anti-theft immobiliser transceiver unit from the lock and disconnect the wiring **(see illustration)**.

4 Insert the ignition key and turn it to position 'I'.

5 Using a small screwdriver or pin punch, depress the locking pin through the hole in the top of the column, then withdraw the lock cylinder using the key **(see illustrations)**.

4.2a Undo the retaining screws (also on lower shroud) . . .

4.2b . . . and remove the steering column shrouds

4.3 Disconnecting the wiring from the anti-theft immobiliser transceiver

4.5a Depress the locking pin . . .

4.5b . . . and withdraw the lock cylinder using the key

4.6 Pressing the steering lock pin down with a screwdriver before inserting the lock cylinder

6 To refit the lock cylinder, push the assembly into the lock housing, until the locking pin engages, then turn the ignition key to position '0' and withdraw the key. If the steering lock pin engages with the steering column as the cylinder is removed, it will not be possible to insert the cylinder so that the locking pin engages. In this case, use a screwdriver in the housing to press the steering lock pin down before inserting the lock cylinder **(see illustration)**.

Ignition switch

7 To remove the ignition switch, disconnect the battery negative (earth) lead (see Chapter 5A) then remove the lock cylinder as previously described.

8 Undo the small grub screw and remove the switch from the steering column.

9 Disconnect the wiring from the switch, using a screwdriver to lever it out if necessary **(see illustration)**.

10 Refitting is a reversal of removal.

Turn signal/ wiper switch assembly

11 The turn signal and wiper switch assemblies are removed identically.

12 Remove the steering wheel. Alternatively, the steering wheel may remain in position, but it will have to be turned for access to the end face screws of the shrouds.

13 Remove the steering column shrouds by unscrewing the tilt steering lever, then removing the two screws from the end face and three screws from the bottom shroud. Recover the ignition key position indicator from the ignition switch.

14 Carefully slide the switch from the top of the housing, then disconnect the wiring and remove it from the vehicle **(see illustrations)**. On models with cruise control, disconnect the additional plugs.

15 Refitting is a reversal of removal.

Facia-mounted pushbutton switches (except hazard warning)

16 A small, hooked instrument or length of welding rod is required to pull the switch from the facia.

17 Carefully insert the hooked instrument between the switch and surround, then pull out the switch **(see illustration)**.

18 Disconnect the wiring from the switch.

19 Refitting is a reversal of removal.

Lighting and fog lamp switch

20 Using a small screwdriver, carefully prise the lighting switch from the facia **(see illustrations)**. Take care not to damage the facia by placing a wad of cloth beneath the screwdriver. If the switch is tight, use a screwdriver inserted on each side of the switch. Note that the terminals on the rear of the switch locate directly in the sockets in the housing. To remove the fog lamp switch, release the tab.

4.9 Disconnecting the wiring from the ignition switch

4.14a Slide the turn signal/wiper switch from the top of the housing . . .

4.14b . . . and disconnect the wiring

4.17 Removing a facia-mounted pushbutton switch

4.20a Use a screwdriver and wad of cloth . . .

4.20b . . . to prise out the lighting switch

12

4.21 Removing the vent/switch rear housing from the facia

4.24 Use a hooked instrument to prise out the hazard switch

4.29a Undo the screw and remove the courtesy light switch . . .

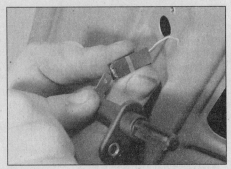

4.29b . . . then disconnect the wiring

4.36 Press the window switch from the surround

21 If necessary, the housing can be removed by removing the air vent, then undoing the screw and withdrawing the housing **(see illustration)**. Disconnect the wiring.

22 Refitting is a reversal of removal.

Hazard warning switch

23 It is easier to remove the hazard warning switch when in the ON position.

24 Insert screwdrivers into the channel on either side of the switch and carefully prise it from the facia, or use a small, hooked instrument or length of welding rod to remove the switch **(see illustration)**.

25 On some models the switch cover will separate from the switch, but removal is otherwise the same.

26 Refitting is a reversal of removal.

Heater blower motor switch

27 Refer to Chapter 3.

Stop light switch and handbrake 'on' warning light switch

28 Refer to Chapter 9.

Courtesy light switch and rear luggage compartment switch

29 Undo the retaining screw and withdraw the switch **(see illustrations)**.

30 Disconnect the wiring and tape it to the panel to prevent it dropping out of reach.

31 Make sure that the retaining screw makes good contact with the body and switch. If necessary clean the contact points.

32 Refitting is a reversal of removal.

Electrically-operated window switch

33 Prise the small storage compartment from beneath the handbrake lever on the centre console.

34 Disconnect the relevant wiring plug.

35 Undo the two screws and lift out the gear knob surround.

36 Press the switch from the surround **(see illustration)**.

37 Refitting is a reversal of removal.

5 Bulbs (exterior lights) - renewal

1 Whenever a bulb is renewed, note the following points.
 a) *Remember that, if the light has just been in use, the bulb may be extremely hot.*
 b) *Do not touch the bulb glass with the fingers, as this can result in early failure or a dull reflector.*
 c) *Always check the bulb contacts and holder, ensuring that there is clean metal-to-metal contact between the bulb and its live(s) and earth. Clean off any corrosion or dirt before fitting a new bulb.*
 d) *Ensure that the new bulb is of the correct rating.*

Headlight

2 With the bonnet open, remove the cover from the rear of the relevant headlight **(see illustration)**. Note that the outer headlight is for dipped beam and the inner headlight is for the main beam. If working on the left-hand front headlight, it is necessary to temporarily remove the relay box from the front of the battery.

3 Disconnect the wiring plug from the bulb **(see illustrations)**.

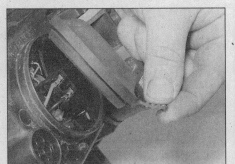

5.2 Removing the cover from the rear of the headlight

5.3a Disconnecting the wiring from the dipped beam headlight . . .

5.3b . . . and main beam headlight

5.4a Unhook the clip . . .

5.4b . . . and withdraw the main beam bulb from the headlight

5.4c Unhook the clip . . .

5.4d . . . and withdraw the dipped beam bulb from the headlight

5.8 Removing the sidelight bulbholder from the rear of the headlight

5.13 Remove the front direction indicator light bulbholder . . .

4 Depress and unhook the retaining clip, then withdraw the bulb from the headlight **(see illustrations)**.

5 When handling the new bulb, use a tissue or clean cloth, to avoid touching the glass with the fingers; moisture and grease from the skin can cause blackening and rapid failure of this type of bulb. If the glass is accidentally touched, wipe it clean using methylated spirit.

6 Fit the new bulb using a reversal of the removal procedure, but make sure that the bulb is seated correctly in the cut-outs in the headlight.

Front sidelight

7 The front sidelight bulb is located on the outer main beam headlight. First remove the cover the rear of the headlight.

8 Withdraw the sidelight bulbholder from the

rear of the headlight **(see illustration)**.

9 Remove the bulb from the holder.

10 Fit the new bulb using a reversal of the removal procedure.

Front direction indicator light

11 With the bonnet open, use a screwdriver to release the upper retaining clip from the outer side of the headlight.

12 Carefully slide the front direction indicator light forwards from the location slots in the headlight.

13 Twist the bulbholder to remove it from the light unit **(see illustration)**.

14 Depress and twist the bulb and remove it from the bulbholder **(see illustration)**.

15 Fit the new bulb using a reversal of the removal procedure.

Front foglight

16 Remove the cover from the rear of the foglight located in the front bumper.

17 Disconnect the wiring, then release the spring clip and remove the bulb from the foglight.

18 Fit the new bulb using a reversal of the removal procedure.

Front direction indicator side repeater light

19 Using a small screwdriver, carefully lever the side repeater light from the front wing moulding **(see illustration)**.

20 Hold the bulbholder, then twist the lens to remove it **(see illustration)**.

21 Pull the wedge-type bulb from the bulbholder **(see illustration)**.

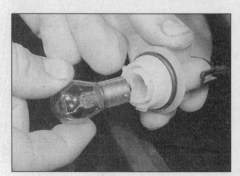

5.14 . . . then remove the bulb

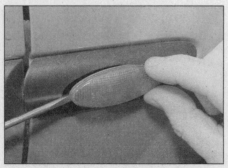

5.19 Prise the side repeater light from the front wing moulding . . .

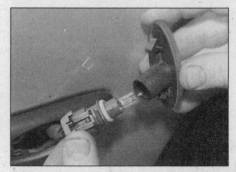

5.20 . . . then twist the lens to remove it . . .

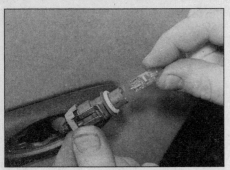

5.21 . . . and pull out the wedge-type bulb

5.24 Depress the retaining lug to release the rear light cluster bulbholder

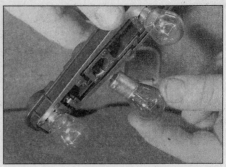

5.25 Removing the bulb from the rear light cluster bulbholder

22 Fit the new bulb using a reversal of the removal procedure.

Rear light cluster

23 In the luggage compartment, remove the side trim cover. If working on the right-hand side, remove the first aid kit and warning triangle. On Estate models, the left-hand cover is removed by twisting the fastener.
24 Depress the retaining lug in the middle of the rear light cluster, and withdraw the bulbholder from the rear light **(see illustration)**.
25 Depress and twist the relevant bulb to remove it **(see illustration)**.
26 Fit the new bulb using a reversal of the removal procedure.

Rear number plate light - Saloon and Hatchback models

27 Open the bootlid or tailgate, then insert a screwdriver vertically between the right-hand edge of the light and the rear bumper. Exert slight outwards pressure on the screwdriver to release the retaining clip, then withdraw the light upwards from the bumper.
28 Depress the clip and remove the lens from the light unit.
29 Depress and twist the bulb to remove it.
30 Fit the new bulb using a reversal of the removal procedure.

Rear number plate light - Estate models

31 Open the tailgate halfway, then undo the

screws from the relevant light and withdraw the light unit from under the handle moulding.
32 Release the festoon type bulb from the spring contacts.
33 Fit the new bulb using a reversal of the removal procedure. Make sure that the bulb is held firmly between the spring contacts, and if necessary pretension the contacts before fitting the bulb.

High level stop light - Saloon and Hatchback models

34 Unclip the cover from the high level stop light. On Saloon models, first pull down the rear centre head restraint.
35 Unclip the bulbholder bracket from the housing then remove the bulbholder.
36 Remove the bulb(s) as necessary.
37 Fit the new bulb using a reversal of the removal procedure.

High level stop light - Estate models

38 With the tailgate open, remove the inner trim panelling with reference to Chapter 11.
39 Prise out the screw covers then undo the screws and remove the edging panel together with the high level stop light **(see illustrations)**.
40 Unclip the stop light from the panel **(see illustration)**.
41 Release the cover from the bulbholder then use a screwdriver to release the tabs and withdraw the bulb strip from the holder **(see illustrations)**.

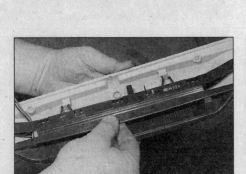

5.39a Remove the screw covers . . .

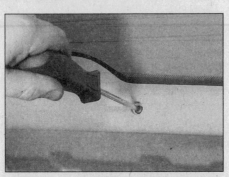

5.39b . . . and undo the screws from the edging panel

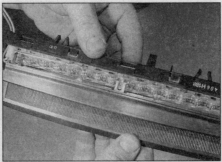

5.40 Unclip the stop light

5.41a Release the cover . . .

5.41b . . . then prise open the tabs with a screwdriver . . .

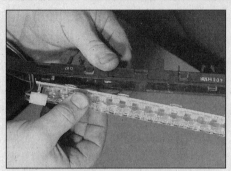

5.41c . . . and withdraw the bulb strip

42 Disconnect the wiring and remove the bulb strip **(see illustration)**.
43 Fit the new bulb using a reversal of the removal procedure.

6 Bulbs (interior lights) - renewal

1 Whenever a bulb is renewed, note the following points.

a) *Remember that, if the light has just been in use, the bulb may be extremely hot.*
b) *Do not touch the bulb glass with the fingers, as this can result in early failure or a dull reflector.*
c) *Always check the bulb contacts and holder, ensuring that there is clean metal-to-metal contact between the bulb and its live(s) and earth. Clean off any corrosion*

5.42 Disconnecting the wiring from the bulb strip

or dirt before fitting a new bulb.
d) *Ensure that the new bulb is of the correct rating.*

Front interior light

2 Carefully prise the interior light from the headlining using a screwdriver **(see illustrations)**.
3 Remove the festoon type bulb from the spring contacts **(see illustration)**.
4 Fit the new bulb using a reversal of the removal procedure. Make sure that the bulb is held firmly between the spring contacts. If necessary, pretension the contacts before fitting the bulb.

Rear interior light

5 Carefully prise the interior light from the surround in the headlining.
6 Remove the festoon type bulb from the spring contacts **(see illustration)**.

7 Fit the new bulb using a reversal of the removal procedure. Make sure that the bulb is held firmly between the spring contacts. If necessary, pretension the contacts before fitting the bulb.

Luggage compartment interior light

8 Carefully prise the light from the side trim **(see illustration)**.
9 Remove the festoon type bulb from the spring contacts **(see illustration)**.
10 Fit the new bulb using a reversal of the removal procedure. Make sure that the bulb is held firmly between the spring contacts. If necessary, pretension the contacts before fitting the bulb.

Glovebox light

11 With the glovebox open, carefully prise out the light unit.
12 Remove the festoon type bulb from the spring contacts.
13 Fit the new bulb using a reversal of the removal procedure. Make sure that the bulb is held firmly between the spring contacts. If necessary, pretension the contacts before fitting the bulb.

Rear reading light (where fitted)

14 Undo the screws and remove the grip from the headlining.
15 Disconnect the wiring or remove the heat shield, then remove the bulb.
16 Fit the new bulb using a reversal of the removal procedure.

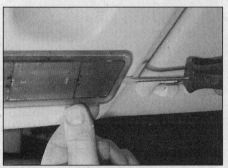

6.2a Use a screwdriver to prise out the front interior light . . .

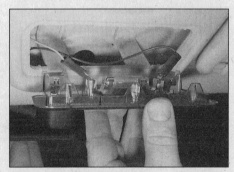

6.2b . . . and remove it from the headlining

6.3 Removing the festoon type bulb from the front interior light

6.6 Rear interior light and festoon type bulb

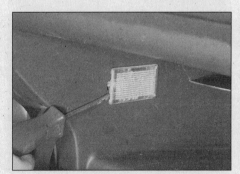

6.8 Prising the luggage compartment interior light from the side trim

6.9 Removing the festoon type bulb from the luggage compartment interior light

12

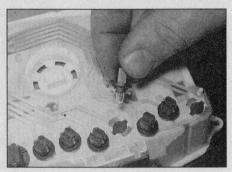

6.26a Removing a small warning bulbholder . . .

6.26b . . . and large warning bulbholder from the instrument panel

6.26c The large bulbs can be removed from their bulbholders

Door mounted interior light

17 Carefully lever the light from the door trim panel.

18 Disconnect the wiring or remove the heat shield, then remove the festoon type bulb from the spring contacts.

19 Fit the new bulb using a reversal of the removal procedure. Make sure that the bulb is held firmly between the spring contacts. If necessary, pretension the contacts before fitting the bulb.

Cigarette lighter bulb

20 Remove the centre console as described in Chapter 11.

21 Undo the screws and remove the storage compartment together with the ashtray.

22 Disconnect the upper wiring from the rear of the lighter, remove the bulbholder and remove the bulb.

6.29 Removing the illumination bulb from the rear of the lighting switch

23 Fit the new bulb using a reversal of the removal procedure.

Instrument panel illumination and warning light bulbs

24 Remove the instrument panel as described in Section 9.

25 The central (white) bulbholders are for the instrument illumination and the lower (black) bulbholders on the circuit board are the warning lights. The centre lower (black) bulbholder is for the odometer display illumination and LCD illumination (according to model).

26 To remove the bulbs twist and turn the bulbholder and remove from the instrument panel, then where possible remove the bulb from the bulbholder. Note that some bulbs cannot be removed from their bulbholders (see illustrations).

27 Fit the new bulb using a reversal of the removal procedure.

Light switch illumination

28 Remove the light switch as described in Section 4.

29 Using a screwdriver, twist the bulbholder from the rear of the switch (see illustration).

30 Fit the new bulb using a reversal of the removal procedure.

Clock/multi-function display unit illumination

31 Remove the instrument panel as described in Section 9. The clock/multi-function display unit is located on the rear of the instrument panel.

32 Using a pair of pliers twist the relevant bulbholder from the rear of the display unit (see illustrations).

33 Fit the new bulb using a reversal of the removal procedure.

Heater control illumination

34 Remove the heater control assembly as described in Chapter 3.

35 Pull out the relevant wedge-type bulb from the assembly (see illustration).

36 Fit the new bulb using a reversal of the removal procedure.

---

7 Exterior light units -
  removal and refitting

Headlight

Removal

1 Remove the front direction indicator light as described later in this Section.

2 Remove the radiator grille as described in Chapter 11.

3 Disconnect the wiring plugs from the rear of the headlight (see illustrations). If working on the left-hand headlight, remove the relay box from the front of the battery first.

4 Unscrew the headlight mounting bolts located on each side of the unit, and withdraw the headlight from the front of the vehicle (see illustrations).

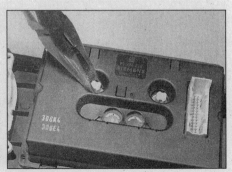

6.32a Use a pair of pliers . . .

6.32b . . . to remove the bulbholder from the clock/multi-function display unit

6.35 Removing a wedge-type bulb from the heater control assembly

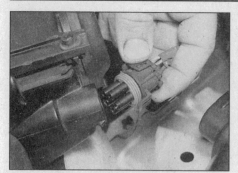

7.3a Disconnecting the bulb wiring . . .

7.3b . . . and servo motor wiring from the rear of the headlight

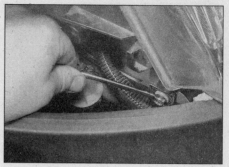

7.4a Unscrew the outer mounting bolt . . .

5 If necessary, the headlight range control servo may be removed by twisting it anti-clockwise **(see illustration)**.

Refitting

6 Refitting is a reversal of removal, but make sure that the locating lug on the headlight engages with the corresponding hole in the front valance and, on completion, have the headlight beam alignment checked at the earliest opportunity **(see illustration)**.

Front direction indicator light

Removal

7 Using a screwdriver inserted between the top of the direction indicator light and headlight, release the retaining clip then withdraw the light by sliding it forward from the location holes in the headlight **(see illustration)**.

8 Disconnect the wiring and remove the light unit.

Refitting

9 Refitting is a reversal of removal. Push the light unit into the location holes until the upper retaining clip engages.

Front foglight

Removal

10 Remove the front bumper as described in Chapter 11.

11 Unscrew the three mounting bolts and remove the foglight from the bumper, then disconnect the wiring.

Refitting

12 Refitting is a reversal of removal.

Front direction indicator side repeater light

13 The procedure is described in Section 5.

Rear light cluster

Removal

14 In the luggage compartment, remove the side trim cover. If working on the right-hand side, remove the first aid kit and warning triangle. On Estate models, the left-hand cover is removed by twisting the fastener.

15 Depress the retaining lug in the middle of the rear light cluster, and withdraw the bulbholder from the rear light.

16 Unscrew the mounting nuts and withdraw the light cluster from the rear of the vehicle **(see illustrations)**. Take care not to damage the vehicle paintwork.

7.4b . . . and the inner mounting bolt . . .

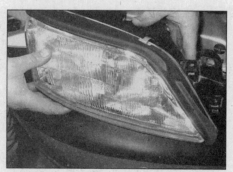

7.4c . . . and withdraw the headlight from the front of the vehicle

7.5 Removing the headlight range control servo from the headlight

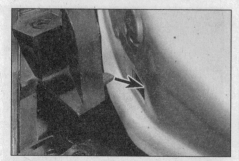

7.6 Make sure that the locating lug on the headlight engages with the corresponding hole in the front valance

7.7 Slide the front direction indicator light from the location holes in the headlight

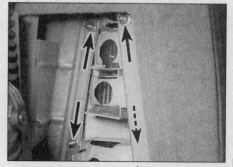

7.16a Mounting nuts for the rear light cluster

12

7.16b Removing the rear light cluster

Refitting

17 Refitting is a reversal of removal.

Rear number plate light

18 The procedure is described in Section 5.

High level stop light

19 The procedure is described in Section 5.

8 Headlight beam alignment - general information

1 Accurate adjustment of the headlight beam is only possible using optical beam-setting equipment, and this work should therefore be carried out by a Vauxhall/Opel dealer or suitably-equipped workshop.
2 For reference, the headlights can be adjusted using the adjuster assemblies fitted

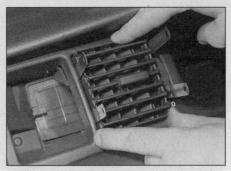

9.2 Using feeler blades to remove the centre air vents

to the front upper outer mounting and to the rear inner mounting. The inner screw is for horizontal adjustment and the outer one for vertical adjustment.
3 All models have an electrically-operated headlight beam adjustment range system, controlled via a switch in the facia. The recommended settings are as follows.

  0 Front seat(s) occupied
  1 All seats occupied
  2 All seats occupied, and load in luggage compartment
  3 Driver's seat occupied and load in the luggage compartment

Note: *When adjusting the headlight aim, ensure that the switch is set to position 0.*
4 On Estate models with automatic self-levelling control, the headlight range adjustment should be reduced by one setting after completing approximately 3 km (1.8 miles).

9 Instrument panel - removal and refitting

Removal

1 Remove the steering column shrouds. To do this, first remove the steering wheel. Alternatively, the steering wheel may remain in position, but it will have to turned for access to the end face screws of the shrouds. Unscrew the tilt steering lever, then removing the two screws from the end face and three screws from the bottom shroud. Remove the shrouds and recover the ignition key position indicator from the ignition switch.
2 Carefully prise the centre and driver's side air vents from the facia, using a small screwdriver or alternatively feeler blades to depress the side clips **(see illustration)**. Where applicable, place a wad of cloth beneath the screwdriver to prevent damage.
3 Remove the light switch as described in Section 4.
4 Undo the mounting screws and remove the centre surround and side surround/light switch housing from the facia. Disconnect the wiring **(see illustrations)**.
5 Undo the two mounting screws and withdraw the instrument panel from the facia **(see illustrations)**.
6 Disconnect the wiring from the rear of the instrument panel and withdraw the unit **(see illustration)**.

9.4a Undo the inner screws . . .

9.4b . . . and the outer screws . . .

9.4c . . . then remove the surround

9.4d The side surround/light switch housing screws

9.5a Undo the mounting screws . . .

9.5b . . . and withdraw the instrument panel from the facia

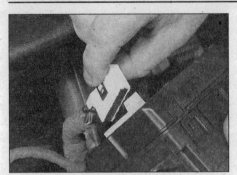

9.6 Disconnecting the wiring from the instrument panel

Refitting

7 Refitting is a reversal of removal, but check the operation of all the warning and illumination bulbs on completion.

10 Instrument panel components - removal and refitting

Note: *The speedometer fitted to all Vectra models is electrically-actuated using the signals from the ABS wheel sensors. Therefore, no speedometer cable or mechanical drive is fitted.*

Removal

1 With the instrument panel removed as described in Section 9, remove the warning and illumination bulbs as described in Section 6.
2 Remove the multi-function display unit as described in Section 11.
3 Carefully release the clips using a screwdriver, then release the front frame from the main housing.
4 Further dismantling of the instrument panel is not recommended.

Refitting

5 Refitting is a reversal of removal.

11 Clock/multi-function display components - removal and refitting

Note: *If fitting a new display unit, the vehicle will have to be taken to a dealer for it to be programmed via the diagnostic socket.*

Removal

1 To remove the display unit, first remove the instrument panel as described in Section 9. Undo the screws and remove the multi-info display unit, the triple-info display unit, or the digital clock as required from the rear of the instrument panel.
2 To remove the ambient temperature sensor, remove the radiator grille as described in Chapter 11. Unclip the sensor from the retainer then disconnect the wiring.
3 To remove the bulb check sensor, first remove the glovebox as described in Chapter 11. Remove the sensor from the retainer on the bulkhead and disconnect the wiring.

The trailer bulb control sensor is located above the bulb check sensor and may be pulled from its base if required.
4 The brake fluid level and coolant level sensors are part of the multi-function display. To remove the brake fluid level sensor, unscrew the filler cap from the brake hydraulic fluid reservoir and disconnect the wiring. To remove the coolant level sensor, unscrew and remove the filler cap from the expansion tank (note the precautions given in Chapter 3), and draw off the coolant until the level is just below the sensor. Remove the sensor from the tank. Refitting of the sensors is a reversal of the removal procedure.

Refitting

5 Refitting is a reversal of removal.

12 Cigarette lighter - removal and refitting

Removal

1 Remove the centre console as described in Chapter 11.
2 Undo the screws and remove the storage compartment together with the ashtray, then pull out the cigarette lighter element and disconnect the wiring from the rear of the lighter.
3 Using a small screwdriver, release the retainer and ring then remove the cigarette lighter.

Refitting

4 Refitting is a reversal of removal.

13 Acoustic warning system - general

1 The acoustic warning system has three functions as described in the following paragraphs. The multi-timer described in Section 3 operates the system.
2 If the parking or low beam lights are on and the front door is opened, a warning buzzer is sounded to prompt the driver to switch off the lights.
3 With the parking lights on (using the indicator switch), a warning buzzer is sounded for 2 seconds when the door is opened. This reminds

14.1 The horn is located behind the front bumper on the right-hand side on RHD models

the driver that the parking lights are on.
4 With the ignition key inserted in the steering lock, a warning buzzer is sounded when the door is opened to remind the driver that the ignition key is still inserted.

14 Horn(s) - removal and refitting

Removal

1 The horn is located behind the front bumper on the right-hand side on RHD models or on the left-hand side on LHD models **(see illustration)**. One or two horns are fitted according to model. First apply the handbrake, then jack up the front of the vehicle and support it on axle stands (see *"Jacking and Vehicle Support"*).
2 Disconnect the wiring from the horn.
3 Unscrew the mounting nut securing the horn to the bracket and remove the horn.

Refitting

4 Refitting is a reversal of removal.

15 Wiper arm - removal and refitting

Windscreen wiper arm

Removal

1 Operate the wiper motor, then switch it off so that the wiper arm returns to the at-rest position.

> **HAYNES HINT** *Stick a piece of masking tape on the windscreen, along the edge of the wiper blade, to use as an alignment aid on refitting.*

2 Using a screwdriver prise the cover from the spindle end of the wiper arm **(see illustrations)**.
3 Unscrew the spindle nut and recover the small washer **(see illustrations)**.

15.2a Use a screwdriver . . .

15.2b ... to prise off the cover ...

15.3a ... then remove the nut ...

15.3b ... and small washer ...

15.4 ... and remove the wiper arm from the spindle

15.10 Unscrew the retaining nut ...

15.11 ... and pull the tailgate wiper arm from the spindle splines

4 Lift the blade off the glass, and pull the wiper arm off its spindle **(see illustration)**. Note that the wiper arms may be very tight on the spindle splines - if necessary, lever the arm off the spindle, using a flat-bladed screwdriver (take care not to damage the scuttle cover panel).

5 If necessary, remove the blade from the arm with reference to Chapter 1.

Refitting

6 If removed, refit the wiper blade to the arm at this stage. This will prevent any damage to the windscreen from the upper end of the arm.

7 Ensure that the wiper arm and spindle splines are clean and dry, then refit the arm to the spindle and align the blade with the previously noted rest position.

8 Refit the washer and spindle nut, and tighten it securely. Refit the cover.

Tailgate wiper arm

Removal

9 Operate the wiper motor, then switch it off so that the wiper arm returns to the at-rest position.

> **HAYNES HINT** *Stick a piece of masking tape on the window, along the edge of the wiper blade, to use as an alignment aid on refitting.*

10 Lift the cover from the base of the wiper arm and unscrew the retaining nut **(see illustration)**.

11 Lift the blade off the glass, and pull the wiper arm off its spindle **(see illustration)**.

12 If necessary, remove the blade from the arm with reference to Chapter 1.

Refitting

13 If removed, refit the wiper blade to the arm at this stage. This will prevent any damage to the rear window from the upper end of the arm.

14 Ensure that the wiper arm and spindle splines are clean and dry, then refit the arm to the spindle and align the blade with the previously noted rest position.

15 Refit the spindle nut, and tighten it securely. Close the cover on the base of the arm.

16 Windscreen wiper motor and linkage - removal and refitting

Removal

1 Remove the wiper arms as described in Section 15.

2 Pull the rubber weatherstrip from the rear of the engine compartment, then unscrew the nuts securing the scuttle cover panel to the wiper spindle housings. Unclip and remove the panel **(see illustrations)**.

3 Disconnect the wiring at the wiper motor **(see illustration)**.

4 Unscrew the bolts securing the wiper motor assembly to the scuttle, and withdraw the assembly **(see illustrations)**.

5 The motor can be removed from the linkage assembly by prising free the rod from the crank and unbolting the motor. The remaining

16.2a Unscrew and remove the spindle housing nuts ...

16.2b ... then remove the scuttle cover panel

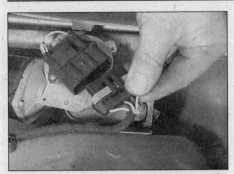

16.3 Disconnecting the wiring from the wiper motor

16.4a Unscrew the central mounting bolt . . .

16.4b . . . and outer linkage mounting bolt . . .

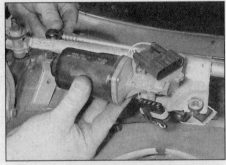

16.4c . . . and withdraw the windscreen wiper motor and linkage from the scuttle

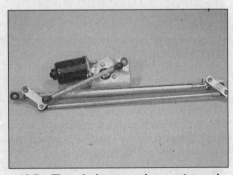

16.5a The windscreen wiper motor and linkage removed from the vehicle

16.5b Windscreen wiper motor and linkage mounting bolts/nut

linkage rods can also be dismantled if necessary **(see illustrations)**.

6 Clean the assembly and examine the spindles and joints for wear and damage. Renew the components as required.

Refitting

7 Refitting is a reversal of removal, but lubricate the joints with a little grease before assembling them. Refit the wiper arms with reference to Section 15.

17 Tailgate wiper motor - removal and refitting

Removal

1 Remove the wiper arm from the tailgate as described in Section 15.
2 Remove the trim panelling from the inside of the tailgate with reference to Chapter 11.
3 Remove the rubber cap from the wiper spindle **(see illustration)**.
4 Unscrew the nut securing the spindle housing to the tailgate, and remove the washer and cover **(see illustrations)**.
5 Disconnect the wiring at the plug **(see illustration)**.
6 Unscrew the mounting bolts and withdraw the wiper motor while sliding the spindle housing through the rubber grommet **(see illustrations)**.

17.3 Remove the rubber cap . . .

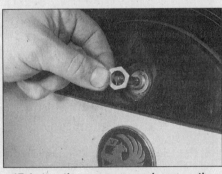

17.4a . . . then unscrew and remove the nut . . .

17.4b . . . remove the washer . . .

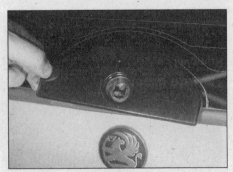

17.4c . . . and withdraw the cover

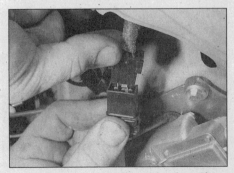

17.5 Disconnecting the wiring from the tailgate wiper motor

17.6a Unscrew the mounting bolts . . .

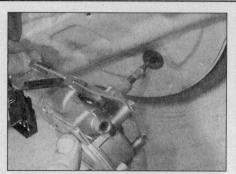

17.6b . . . and withdraw the wiper motor from the tailgate

17.7 Check the rubber grommet in the tailgate before refitting the motor

7 If necessary remove the rubber grommet from the tailgate. Examine the grommet for wear and damage and renew it if necessary **(see illustration)**.

Refitting

8 Refitting is a reversal of removal; tighten the mounting nut to the specified torque. Refit the wiper arm with reference to Section 15.

18 Windscreen/tailgate/headlight washer system components - removal and refitting

Washer fluid reservoir

Removal

1 Remove the front bumper as described in Chapter 11.
2 Remove the left-hand front wheel arch liner as described in Chapter 11.
3 Position a container beneath the washer fluid pump and reservoir to collect the fluid.
4 Disconnect the wiring from the top of the pump and position to one side **(see illustration)**.
5 Disconnect the hose from the pump and allow the fluid to drain into the container.
6 On models with a multi-function display unit, disconnect the wiring from the level sensor on the fluid reservoir.
7 On models with a headlight washer system, disconnect the wiring and hose from the additional pump on the reservoir.

8 Disconnect the filler neck(s) from the reservoir.
9 Release the wiring from the clips on top of the reservoir **(see illustration)**.
10 Unscrew the mounting bolts and withdraw the reservoir from the front valance **(see illustration)**.

Refitting

11 Refitting is a reversal of removal. Fill the reservoir with washer fluid with reference to "Weekly checks".

Washer fluid pump

Removal

12 Remove the front bumper as described in Chapter 11.
13 Remove the left-hand front wheel arch liner as described in Chapter 11.
14 Position a suitable container beneath the washer fluid pump and reservoir to collect the fluid.
15 Disconnect the wiring from the top of the pump and position to one side.
16 Disconnect the hose from the pump and allow the fluid to drain into the container.
17 Pull the pump to the side and extract it from the reservoir.
18 If necessary, remove the grommet from the reservoir.

Refitting

19 Refitting is a reversal of removal. Fill the reservoir with washer fluid with reference to "Weekly checks".

Windscreen washer nozzle

Removal

20 With the bonnet open, disconnect the wiring and supply hose from the bottom of the nozzle.
21 Release the nozzle from the bonnet and remove it upwards.

Refitting

22 Refitting is a reversal of removal.

Tailgate washer nozzle

Removal

23 On Hatchback models, carefully lever the nozzle out of the aerial base with a small screwdriver, then disconnect the nozzle from the hose.
24 On Estate models, carefully insert a small screwdriver between the nozzle and the rubber seal. Depress the lugs and remove the nozzle from the tailgate.
25 Disconnect the nozzle from the hose.

Refitting

26 Refitting is a reversal of removal.

Headlight washer nozzle

Removal

27 Remove the headlight as described in Section 7.
28 Release the supply hose from the support and remove it from the nozzle.
29 Pull out the clip and remove the nozzle from the front bumper.

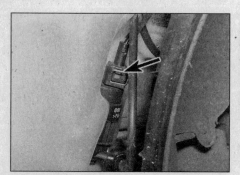

18.4 The washer fluid reservoir and pump is located behind the front bumper

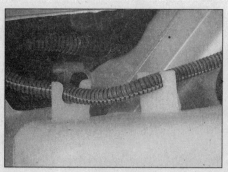

18.9 Release the wiring from the top of the reservoir

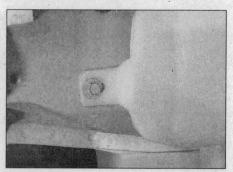

18.10 Washer fluid reservoir mounting bolt

Refitting

30 Refitting is a reversal of removal.

19 Radio/cassette/CD player - removal and refitting

Note: *On models with a security-coded radio/cassette player, once the battery has been disconnected, the unit cannot be re-activated until the appropriate security code has been entered. Do not remove the unit unless the appropriate code is known. The following information applies to radio/cassette players having standard DIN fixings. Two DIN removal tools will be required for this operation.*

Radio/cassette player

Removal

1 Using an Allen key, undo the grub screws from the four holes in each corner of the radio front face **(see illustration)**.
2 Insert the two DIN removal tools into the holes on each side of the radio until they are felt to engage with the retaining strips **(see illustration)**.
3 Carefully withdraw the radio/cassette player from the facia.
4 Disconnect the wiring and aerial from the rear of the radio.
5 Remove the removal tools and refit the grub screws.

19.1 Removing the grub screws before fitting the DIN removal tools

Refitting

6 Reconnect the wiring plugs and the aerial lead, then push the unit into its housing until the securing clips engage.
7 On completion, enter the security code.

CD player

Removal

8 Remove the glovebox as described in Chapter 11.
9 Disconnect the wiring plug.
10 Unscrew the mounting bolts and withdraw the CD player from behind the facia.

Refitting

11 Refitting is a reversal of removal.

20 Loudspeakers - removal and refitting

Front door-mounted low frequency loudspeakers

Removal

1 Remove the front door inner trim panel, as described in Chapter 11.
2 Undo the mounting screws and withdraw the loudspeaker from the door inner panel **(see illustration)**.
3 Disconnect the wiring from the loudspeaker **(see illustration)**.

Refitting

4 Refitting is a reversal of removal.

19.2 Using the DIN removal tools to remove the radio/cassette player

Front door-mounted high-frequency ('tweeter') loudspeakers

Removal

5 Remove the front door inner handle grip with reference to Chapter 11.
6 Disconnect the wiring, then release the loudspeaker from the grip.

Refitting

7 Refitting is a reversal of removal.

Rear door loudspeaker

Removal

8 Remove the rear door inner trim panel, as described in Chapter 11.
9 Undo the mounting screws and withdraw the loudspeaker from the door inner panel **(see illustration)**.
10 Disconnect the wiring from the loudspeaker **(see illustration)**.

Refitting

11 Refitting is a reversal of removal.

21 Radio aerial - removal and refitting

Removal

1 Remove the headlining moulding from the rear of the luggage compartment.
2 Disconnect the lead from the aerial.

20.2 Undo the mounting screws . . .

20.3 . . . then disconnect the wiring from the rear of the loudspeaker

20.9 Removing a rear door loudspeaker

20.10 Disconnecting the wiring from the rear door loudspeaker

3 Remove the hose for the rear screen wash/wipe, then unscrew the nut and remove the aerial from the roof.

Refitting

4 Refitting is a reversal of removal.

22 Anti-theft alarm system and engine immobiliser - general information

1 All models have an engine immobiliser which effectively prevents the engine from being started when the ignition key is in the OFF position or removed from the steering lock. The system is activated by the ignition key and an electronic sensor mounted on the steering lock. The driver's door lock barrel is freewheeling - if an attempt is made to forcefully turn the lock without the correct key, it will just turn within its housing.
2 The anti-theft alarm system monitors the doors, bootlid or tailgate, bonnet, radio, ignition, and on some models the passenger compartment. The control unit for the system is shared with the central locking system - see Section 21 of Chapter 11. On higher specification models an ultrasonic sensor is located at the top of each B-pillar. The anti-theft alarm system horn is located on the bulkhead in the engine compartment and the power sounder is located beneath the left-hand front wing. On Estate models, a glass breakage detector is fitted to the luggage compartment rear side windows.
3 To remove the ultrasonic sensor, carefully lever it out of its housing using a screwdriver then disconnect the wiring.
4 To remove the warning horn, disconnect the wiring and unscrew the mounting nut.
5 To remove the bonnet contact, disconnect the wiring then detach the contact from the bulkhead.
6 To remove the power sounder, disconnect the battery negative lead, as described in Chapter 5A, within 15 seconds of switching off the ignition. Remove the wheel arch liner from under the left-hand front wing, then disconnect the wiring and unbolt the bracket and power sounder.
7 Refitting of the components is a reversal of the removal procedure.

24.5 Disconnecting the wiring from the airbag

8 Any faults with the system should be referred to a Vauxhall/Opel dealer.

23 Airbag system - general information, precautions and system de-activation

General information

A driver's side airbag is fitted as standard equipment on all models. The airbag is fitted to the steering wheel centre pad. Similarly, a passenger's side airbag is also fitted as standard equipment, or as an option, depending on model. On certain later models, side airbags are fitted.

The system is armed only when the ignition is switched on, however, a reserve power source maintains a power supply to the system in the event of a break in the main electrical supply. The system is activated by a 'g' sensor (deceleration sensor), incorporated in the electronic control unit. Note that the electronic control unit also controls the front seat belt tensioners.

The airbags are inflated by gas generators, which force the bags out from their locations in the steering wheel, and the passenger's side facia, where applicable.

In the event of a fault occurring in the airbag system (warning light illuminated on the instrument panel), seek the advice of a Vauxhall/Opel dealer.

Precautions

 Warning: The following precautions must be observed when working on vehicles equipped with an airbag system, to prevent the possibility of personal injury.

General precautions

The following precautions **must** be observed when carrying out work on a vehicle equipped with an airbag.

a) *Do not disconnect the battery with the engine running.*
b) *Before carrying out any work in the vicinity of the airbag, removal of any of the airbag components, or any welding work on the vehicle, de-activate the system as described in the following sub-Section.*
c) *Do not attempt to test any of the airbag system circuits using test meters or any other test equipment.*
d) *If the airbag warning light comes on, or any fault in the system is suspected, consult a Vauxhall/Opel dealer without delay. Do not attempt to carry out fault diagnosis, or any dismantling of the components.*

Precautions to be taken when handling an airbag

a) *Transport the airbag by itself, bag upward.*
b) *Do not put your arms around the airbag.*

c) *Carry the airbag close to the body, bag outward.*
d) *Do not drop the airbag or expose it to impacts.*
e) *Do not attempt to dismantle the airbag unit.*
f) *Do not connect any form of electrical equipment to any part of the airbag circuit.*
g) *Do not allow any solvents or cleaning agents to contact the airbag assembly. The unit must be cleaned using only a damp cloth.*

Precautions to be taken when storing an airbag unit

a) *Store the unit in a cupboard with the airbag upward.*
b) *Do not expose the airbag to temperatures above 90°C.*
c) *Do not expose the airbag to flames.*
d) *Do not attempt to dispose of the airbag - consult a Vauxhall/Opel dealer.*
e) *Never refit an airbag which is known to be faulty or damaged.*

De-activation of airbag system

The system must be de-activated as follows, before carrying out any work on the airbag components or surrounding area.
a) *Switch off the ignition.*
b) *Remove the ignition key.*
c) *Switch off all electrical equipment.*
d) *Disconnect the battery negative lead (see Chapter 5A).*
e) *Insulate the battery negative terminal and the end of the battery negative lead to prevent any possibility of contact.*
f) *Wait for at least one minute before carrying out any further work. This will allow the system capacitor to discharge.*

24 Airbag system components - removal and refitting

Driver's side airbag unit

 Warning: Refer to the precautions given in Section 23 before attempting to carry out work on the airbag components.

Removal

1 The airbag unit is an integral part of the steering wheel centre pad.
2 De-activate the airbag system as described in Section 23.
3 Set the front wheels in the straight-ahead position, then lock the column in position after removing the ignition key.
4 Unscrew and remove the two screws from the rear of the steering wheel and carefully lift the airbag/horn-push from the steering wheel.
5 Disconnect the wiring from the airbag **(see illustration)**. Position the airbag in a safe place where it cannot be tampered with, making sure that the padded side is facing upwards.

Refitting

6 Refitting is a reversal of removal, but make sure that the wiring connector is securely reconnected and tighten the retaining screws to the specified torque.

Passenger's side airbag unit

 Warning: Refer to the precautions given in Section 23 before attempting to carry out work on the airbag components.

Removal

7 De-activate the airbag system as described in Section 23.
8 Remove the glovebox and passenger side air distribution duct from under the facia with reference to Chapter 11.
9 Unscrew the lower mounting screws and remove the airbag cover in an outwards direction.
10 Disconnect the wiring from the airbag.
11 Undo the three lower screws and lift the airbag from the facia.

Refitting

12 Refitting is a reversal of removal, but make sure that the wiring connector is securely reconnected and tighten the retaining screws to the specified torque.

Side airbag unit

 Warning: Refer to the precautions given in Section 23 before attempting to carry out work on the airbag components.

Removal

13 The side airbag is located in the front seat backrest. To remove it first de-activate the airbag system as described in Section 23.
14 Carefully pull back the upholstery to expose the side airbag unit.
15 Disconnect the wiring from the airbag.
16 Unscrew the three securing nuts and remove the airbag from the seat backrest.

24.22 Use a screwdriver to release the four rear clips . . .

Refitting

17 Refitting is a reversal of removal, but make sure that the wiring connector is securely reconnected and tighten the retaining nuts to the specified torque.

Airbag contact unit (on steering column)

Removal

18 Remove the driver's airbag unit as described earlier in this Section.
19 Remove the steering wheel as described in Chapter 10.
20 Remove the steering column shrouds by unscrewing the tilt steering lever, then removing the two screws from the end face and three screws from the bottom shroud. Recover the ignition key position indicator from the ignition switch.
21 Using a small screwdriver lift off the locking plate, then disconnect the wiring plug.
22 Release the four rear clips and remove the contact unit from the top of the column (see illustrations). Note: *Make sure that the contact unit halves remain in their central position with the arrows aligned at the bottom. If necessary, apply tape to the halves to hold them.*

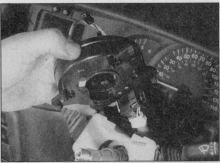

24.22b . . . then remove the airbag contact unit from the top of the column

Refitting

23 Before refitting the contact unit, if the centre position has been lost or if a new unit is being fitted, determine the centre position as follows. Depress the detent on top of the unit and carefully turn the centre part of the unit anti-clockwise until resistance is felt. Now turn it 2.5 turns clockwise and align the arrows on the centre part and outer edge (see illustration).
24 If a new unit is fitted, first remove the transport clip.
25 Locate the contact unit on the top of the steering column making sure that the guide pins locate in the holes provided. Press the unit in until the clips engage (see illustration). Note: *The clips must not be damaged in any way. If they are, the unit must be renewed.*
26 Reconnect the wiring while depressing the slider.
27 Refit the ignition key position indicator, then refit the steering column shrouds and tighten the securing screws. Refit and tighten the tilt steering lever.
28 Refit the steering wheel as described in Chapter 10.
29 Refit the driver's airbag unit as described earlier.

24.23 Centre position arrows on the airbag contact unit

24.25 Contact unit located on the top of the steering column

24.32 Airbag electronic control unit

Electronic control unit

Removal

30 De-activate the airbag system as described in Section 23.
31 Remove the centre console as described in Chapter 11.
32 Disconnect the wiring from the control unit, then unscrew the mounting nuts and remove the unit from inside the vehicle (see illustration).

Refitting

33 Refitting is a reversal of removal but tighten the mounting nuts to the specified torque.

Side airbag sensor

Removal

34 De-activate the airbag system as described in Section 23.
35 Remove the front door inner trim panel as described in Chapter 11.
36 Pull back the water membrane for access to the sensor.
37 Disconnect the wiring, then unscrew the mounting bolts and remove the sensor.

Refitting

38 Refitting is a reversal of removal.

Wiring diagrams

Explanation of abbreviations used

Note: Not all items apply

AB	Airbag	HB	Hatchback	PBSL	Parking/brake lockout
ABS	Anti-lock braking system	HRL	Luggage compartment lamp	P/N	Park/Neutral (starter inhibitor - automatic transmission)
AC	Air conditioning	HS	Heated rear window		
ASP	Outside mirror	HSF	Glovebox	POT	Potentiometer
AT	Automatic transmission	HW	Rear screen wiper	RC	Ride control
ATC	Automatic temperature control	HZG	Heating	RFS	Reversing lights
AZV	Trailer hitch	ID	Info-Display	RHD	Right-hand drive
BR	On-board computer	IMO	Immobiliser	S	Sweden
CC	Check control	INS	Instrument	SA	Saudi Arabia
CD	CD changer	IRL	Interior light	SD	Sliding sunroof
CRC	Cruise control	J	Japan	SH	Seat heating
D	Diesel	KAT	Catalytic converter	SLP	Secondary air pump
DID	Dual information display	KBS	Wiring harness	SM	Engine control unit
DIM	Dimmer display	KV	Contact, distributor	SRA	Headlight washer
DIS	Direct ignition system	KW	Estate	TANK	Fuel gauge
DS	Theft protection	L3.1	Fuel injection (Bosch L3.1-Jetronic)	TC	Traction Control
DWA	Anti-theft warning system	LED	Light-emitting diode	TD	Turbodiesel
DZM	Tachometer	LCD	LCD instrument	TEL	Telephone
E	Release	LHD	Left-hand drive	TEMP	Temperature gauge
ECC	Electronic Climate Control	LWR	Headlamp range control	TID	Triple Info Display
EFC	Electric folding roof (Convertible)	M1.5	Fuel injection (Bosch Motronic M1.5)	TFL	Day running lights
EKP	Fuel pump	M2.5	Fuel injection (Bosch Motronic M2.5)	TKS	Door courtesy light switch
EKS	Pinch guard (electric windows)	MID	Multi-information display	TSZI	High-energy ignition (HEI)
EMP	Radio/cassette	MOT	Motronic system (general)	V	Lock
ETC	Electronic traction control	MT	Manual transmission	VGS	Carburettor
EUR	Euronorm engine	MUL	Fuel injection (Multec)	WEG	Mileometer frequency sensor
EZ +	El Plus with self-diagnosis	MUT	Multitimer	WHR	Vehicle level control
EZV	Ecotronic	N	Norway	WS	Warning buzzer
FH	Electric windows	NB	Notchback	ZIG	Cigarette lighter
FI	Petrol	NSL	Rear foglight	ZV	Central locking
FT	Driver's door	NSW	Front foglight	ZYL	Cylinder
FV	Pre-fuse	OEL	Oil pressure switch	4WD	Four-wheel-drive
GB	Great Britain	OPT	Optional equipment		

Wiring identification

Example: GE WS 1.5
GE - Basic colour

WS - Identification colour
1.5 - Wire cross-section (mm²)

Colour code

BL	Blue	GR	Grey	SW	Black
BR	Brown	HBL	Light blue	VI	Violet
GE	Yellow	LI	Lilac	WS	White
GN	Green	RT	Red		

Circuit interconnections

A framed number - eg 180 - refers to a grid reference (track) at which the circuit is continued

Key to wiring diagrams

Not all items fitted to all models

No	Description	Track	No	Description	Track
E1	Sidelight, left	338	F39	Fuse, automatic transmission	155
E2	Tail light, left	341	F40	Fuse, terminal 15A	115
E3	Number plate light	347 to 350	F41	Fuse, mirror	157
E4	Sidelight, right	352	F50	Fuse, radiator fan	1562, 1596, 1622, 1660, 1691
E5	Tail light, right	355	F52	Fuse, radiator fan	1505, 1516, 1544, 1578, 1605, 1641, 1672
E7	Headlight main beam, left	301	F56	Fuse, filter heating	194
E8	Headlight main beam, right	304	F59	Fuse, engine control unit	196
E9	Headlight dipped beam, left	307	FV1	Pre-fuse, terminal 30	103
E10	Headlight dipped beam, right	310	FV2	Pre-fuse, terminal 30	136
E11	Instrument lighting	714 to 716	FV3	Pre-fuse, terminal 30	125
E12	Automatic transmission selector illumination	644, 645	FV4	Fuse, ABS/TC	103
E13	Luggage compartment light	1328	FV5	Fuse, secondary air induction	103
E15	Glovebox light	1350	FV6	Fuse, engine control	103
E16	Cigarette lighter illumination	1356	G1	Battery	101
E17	Reversing light, left	1344	G2	Alternator	112 to 114
E18	Reversing light, right	1345	H1	Radio	1701 to 1731, 1742 to 1759
E19	Heated rear window	803, 1723	H3	Direction indicator warning light	721
E20	Foglight, front left	650, 871	H4	Oil pressure warning light	736
E21	Foglight, front right	651, 873	H5	Brake fluid warning light	731
E24	Foglight, rear left	645, 877	H7	Alternator/no-charge warning light	734
E25	Seat heating, left	1886	H8	Headlight main beam warning light	725
E27	Rear reading light, left	1331, 1332	H9	Stop-light, left	1253, 1285
E28	Rear reading light, right	1334, 1335	H10	Stop-light, right	1256, 1288
E30	Seat heating, right	1893	H11	Direction indicator light, front left	379
E37	Sun visor lamp, left	1338	H12	Direction indicator light, rear left	380
E39	Foglight, rear right	879	H13	Direction indicator light, front right	386
E40	Sun visor lamp, right	1340	H14	Direction indicator light, rear right	387
E41	Passenger compartment light delay	1322 to 1325	H15	Low fuel/fuel reserve warning light	714
E42	Coolant heating	1472 to 1489	H16	Glow plug warning light	740
E42.1	Add-on heater control unit	1472 to 1489	H17	Trailer direction indicator warning light	719
E42.2	Fan motor	1478	H18	Horn (twin-tone)	1067, 1069
E42.3	Glow plug	1480	H22	Rear foglamp warning light	727
E42.4	Coolant sensor flame sensor	1482	H23	Airbag warning light	746
E42.5	Coolant sensor	1484	H24	Anti-theft warning siren	961 to 963
E42.6	Overheat sensor	1486	H26	ABS warning light	738
E50	Door light, driver's	1306	H27	Safety check buzzer	1878 to 1880
E51	Door light, passenger's	1309	H28	Seatbelt warning light	748
E52	Door light, rear left	1313	H30	Engine warning light	729
E53	Door light, rear right	1317	H33	Direction indicator side repeater light left	381
F2	Fuse, fan motor	122	H34	Direction indicator side repeater light right	388
F3	Fuse, heated rear window	137	H36	Stop-light, centre	1249, 1281
F6	Fuse, low beam, right	310	H37	Loudspeaker, front left	1703 to 1705
F7	Fuse, parking light, right	352	H38	Loudspeaker, front right	1707 to 1709
F8	Fuse, high beam, right	304	H39	Loudspeaker, rear left	1711 to 1713
F9	Fuse, headlamp washer pump	126	H40	Loudspeaker, rear right	1715 to 1717
F10	Fuse, horn	139	H42	Automatic transmission warning light	744
F11	Fuse, central locking	141	H46	Catalytic converter temperature warning light	719
F12	Fuse, foglamps	128	H47	Anti-theft alarm horn	952
F14	Fuse, wiper	175	H51	Electronic traction control (ETC) warning light	742
F16	Fuse, rear foglamps	130	H52	Tweeter, front left	1703 to 1705
F17	Fuse, electric window	143	H53	Tweeter, front right	1707 to 1709
F18	Fuse, number plate lamp	348	H57	Tweeter, rear left	1711 to 1713
F20	Fuse, electric window	145	H58	Tweeter, rear right	1715 to 1717
F21	Fuse, terminal W	104	H65	Foglamp warning light	723
F22	Fuse, terminal 30	132	H66	Middle tone speaker, front left	1703, 1705
F24	Fuse, low beam left	307	H67	Middle tone speaker, front right	1707, 1709
F25	Fuse, parking light, left	338	K1	Heated rear window relay	381, 382, 803
F26	Fuse, high beam, left	301	K5	Front foglight relay	385, 386, 871
F28	Fuse, coolant heating	147	K6	Air conditioning relay	1146 to 1148, 1815 to 1817, 1851 to 1853
F29	Fuse, terminal 15	160	K7	Fan relay	1819, 1820, 1855, 1856
F30	Fuse, sunroof	149	K12	Secondary air induction relay	255 to 257
F32	Fuse, daytime running lights	323	K14	Cruise control unit	1052 to 1058
F33	Fuse, trailer terminal 30	151	K28	Radiator fan relay	1614 to 1616
F34	Fuse, CD changer	153	K31	Airbag control unit	1080 to 1098
F35	Fuse, ABS/TC	164	K34	Radiator fan time delay relay	1542 to 1544, 1576 to 1578
F36	Fuse, terminal 15	167	K37	Central door locking control unit	901 to 954
F37	Fuse, cigarette lighter	169	K43	Injection valves relay	243, 244, 293, 294, 440, 441
F38	Fuse, terminal 15	171			

12

No	Description	Track
K44	Fuel pump relay	247, 248, 298, 299, 444, 445
K50	ABS control unit	1001 to 1030
K51	Radiator fan relay	1561 to 1562, 1595, 1596, 1622, 1623, 1660, 1661, 1691, 1392
K52	Radiator fan relay	1557 to 1559, 1591 to 1593, 1618 to 1620, 1656 to 1658, 1687 to 1689
K53	Radiator fan relay	1547 to 1549, 1581 to 1583, 1609 to 1611, 1644 to 1646, 1675 to 1677
K57	Multec single-point control unit	471 to 498, 503 to 544, 576 to 596
K58	Fuel pump relay (Multec single-point)	475, 476, 507, 508, 579, 580
K59	Day running light relay	323 to 328
K60	Air conditioning compressor relay	1153 to 1155, 1810 to 1812, 1846 to 1848
K61	Motronic control unit	202 to 247, 268 to 297
K63	Twin-tone horn relay	1069, 1070
K64	Air conditioning fan relay	1824, 1825, 1860, 1861
K67	Radiator fan relay	1520, 1521, 1625, 1626
K69	Simtec control unit	402 to 445, 402 to 445
K70	Diesel control unit	1404 to 1459
K73	High beam relay	315, 316
K74	Radiator fan relay	1649, 1650, 1680, 1681
K76	Glow time control unit	1415 to 1419
K80	Fuel filter heating relay (diesel)	1461, 1462
K85	Automatic transmission control unit	613 to 641
K87	Radiator fan relay	1515, 1516, 1604, 1605, 1640, 1641, 1671, 1672
K88	Catalytic converter temperature control unit	651 to 653
K89	Rear foglight relay	387, 388, 877
K94	Anti-theft alarm control unit	901 to 954
K95	ABS & TC system control unit	1001 to 1030
K96	Radiator fan relay	1552 to 1554, 1586 to 1588, 1652 to 1654, 1683 to 1685
K97	Headlight washer delay relay	1219 to 1221
K101	Mirror parking position mirror	856 to 859
K114	Engine main relay	1465, 1466
K117	Immobiliser control unit	1038 to 1043
K120	Rear wiper relay	377, 378, 1226
K121	Heated mirror relay	382, 384, 831, 854
K122	Left indicator relay	381 to 383
K123	Right indicator relay	388 to 390
K124	Windscreen wiper relay	379, 380, 1204, 1205
K128	Injection pump control unit	1442 to 1445
L1	Ignition coil	572, 573
L2	Ignition coil (DIS)	201 to 204, 267 to 269, 401 to 403, 469 to 472, 501 to 504
M1	Starter motor	105, 106
M2	Windscreen wiper motor	1202 to 1205
M3	Heater fan motor	1778 to 1781
M4	Radiator cooling fan motor	1519, 1520, 1559, 1560, 1593, 1594, 1620, 1621, 1658, 1659, 1689, 1690
M8	Tailgate wiper motor	1224 to 1226
M10	Air conditioning fan motor	1134 to 1139, 1820 to 1823, 1856 to 1859
M11	Radiator cooling fan motor	1582 to 1584, 1645 to 1647, 1676 to 1678
M12	Radiator fan motor	1548 to 1550, 1610 to 1612
M13	Sunroof motor	1182 to 1188
M18	Central locking motor, driver's door	901 to 910
M19	Central locking motor, left rear door	918 to 920
M20	Central locking motor, right rear door	922 to 924
M21	Fuel pump	261
M24	Headlight washer pump	1221
M27	Secondary air induction pump	256
M30	Electric mirror (driver's side)	822 to 825, 842 to 848
M30.1	Electric mirror motor	822 to 824, 842 to 844
M30.2	Mirror heater	825, 845
M30.3	Mirror motor, parking position	847, 848
M31	Electric mirror (passenger side)	828 to 830, 851 to 857
M31.1	Electric mirror motor	828 to 831, 851 to 853
M31.2	Mirror heater	831, 854
M31.3	Mirror motor, parking position	856, 858
M32	Central locking motor, front passenger door	913 to 915
M33	Idle speed actuator/power unit	283, 284, 423, 424, 445 to 488, 527 to 530, 583 to 586
M35	Radiator cooling fan motor	1505
M39	Headlight levelling motor, left	312 to 314
M40	Headlight levelling motor, right	317 to 319
M41	Central locking motor, fuel filler flap	918
M47	Electric window motor, driver's door	967 to 970
M48	Electric window motor, passenger's door	985 to 988
M49	Electric window motor, rear left	973 to 976
M50	Electric window motor, rear right	991 to 995
M54	Coolant pump timing control	1638
M55	Windscreen/tailgate washer pump	1213
M57	Coolant pump	250
M69	Fuel pump metering	1489
M74	Actuator, defrost	1104 to 1107
M74	Actuator, leg room	1109 to 1112
M74	Actuator, ventilator	1114 to 1117
M74	Actuator, mixed air flap	1119 to 1122
P1	Fuel gauge	702
P2	Coolant temperature gauge	704
P4	Fuel level sensor	702
P5	Coolant temperature sensor	704
P7	Tachometer	707
P13	Ambient air temperature sensor	771
P17	Wheel sensor, front left	1001
P18	Wheel sensor, front right	1004
P19	Wheel sensor, rear left	1007
P20	Wheel sensor, rear right	1010
P23	MAP sensor	484 to 486, 520 to 522, 590 to 592
P24	Engine oil temperature sensor	1438
P25	Bulb test sensor	308, 309, 342 to 357, 1253 to 1256, 1285 to 1288
P27	Brake pad wear sensor, front left	793
P28	Brake pad wear sensor, front right	793
P29	Inlet manifold temperature sensor	218, 291, 421, 525
P30	Coolant temperature sensor	219, 292, 423, 474, 507, 588, 1436
P32	Exhaust gas oxygen sensor (heated)	241, 242, 436 to 429
P33	Exhaust gas oxygen sensor	497, 539
P34	Throttle valve potentiometer	221, 222, 294, 295, 414 to 416, 481, 482, 517, 518, 593 to 595
P35	Crankshaft impulse sensor	232 to 234, 273 to 275, 425 to 428, 490 to 492, 535 to 537, 579 to 581, 1409 to 1411
P36	Exhaust gas oxygen sensor (heated)	244, 245
P38	Automatic transmission fluid temperature sensor	632
P39	Bulb test sensor, trailer	1260 to 1262, 1292 to 1294
P41	Outlet temperature sensor	1128
P43	Speedometer	710
P44	Air mass meter	247, 248, 297, 298, 443 to 446, 1403 to 1407
P45	Automatic transmission engine speed sensor	623, 624
P46	Knock sensor	213, 214, 287, 288, 410, 411, 488, 489, 527, 528
P47	Hall sensor (cylinder identification)	235 to 237, 431 to 433, 530 to 532
P48	Automatic transmission distance sensor	621, 622
P50	Catalytic converter temperature sensor	652, 653
P51	Sun sensor	1125
P53	Anti-theft sensor, driver's side	942 to 945
P53	Anti-theft sensor, passenger's side	949 to 952
P56	Knock sensor	215, 216
P57	Aerial	1752
P58	Anti-theft alarm glass breakage sensor, rear left	954
P59	Anti-theft alarm glass breakage sensor, rear right	954
P65	Load pressure sensor	1452, 1453
P67	Pedal position sensor	1415 to 1423
P69	Power steering pressure sensor	224, 225
P71	Airbag sensor, driver's side	1093 to 1095
P72	Airbag sensor, passenger's side	1096 to 1098
R3	Cigarette lighter	1355

No	Description	Track
R5	Glow plugs	1416 to 1419
R19	Pre-resistor, radiator cooling fan motor	1649, 1680
S1	Ignition/starter switch	103 to 109
S2	Light switch assembly	349 to 365
S3	Heater fan switch	1778 to 1784
S4	Rear window & mirror switch	811 to 813
S5	Direction indicator switch assembly	
S5.2	Headlight dipped beam switch	316, 317
S5.3	Direction indicator switch	392, 393
S5.4	Sidelight switch	337 to 339
S7	Reversing light switch	1344
S8	Stop-light switch	1241, 1273
S9	Wiper switch assembly	
S9.1	Wiper switch (windscreen)	1202 to 1205
S9.5	Tailgate wash/wipe switch	1214 to 1216
S10	Automatic transmission selector switch	602 to 611
S11	Brake fluid level switch	732
S13	Handbrake 'on' switch	731
S14	Oil pressure sender/switch	736
S15	Luggage compartment light switch	1328
S16	Courtesy light switch, driver's door	1303, 1304
S17	Courtesy light switch, passenger's door	1308, 1309
S20	Pressure switch	1161 to 1163, 1808, 1830, 1866
S20.1	Compressor low pressure switch	1163, 1830, 1866
S20.2	Compressor high pressure switch	1163, 1830, 1866
S20.3	Compressor high pressure fan switch	1161, 1808
S24	Air conditioning fan switch	1820 to 1827, 1856 to 1863
S29	Coolant temperature switch	1505, 1543
S30	Seat heating switch, front left	1886 to 1888
S31	Courtesy light switch, left rear door	1312, 1313
S32	Courtesy light switch, right rear door	1316, 1317
S33	ETC system switch	1029, 1030
S37	Electric window switch assembly (in driver's door)	968 to 994
S37.1	Electric window switch, driver's window	968 to 970
S37.2	Electric window switch, passenger window	986 to 988
S37.3	Electric window switch, rear left	974 to 976
S37.4	Electric window switch, rear right	992 to 994
S37.5	Electric window safety switch	972, 973
S37.7	Electric window automatic control	978 to 982
S41	Anti-theft locking switch, driver's door	907, 908
S43	Cruise control switch	1055 to 1058, 1446 to 1449
S45	Cruise control clutch switch	1052, 1452
S52	Hazard warning light (hazard flashers) switch	395 to 397
S55	Seat heating switch, front right	1893 to 1895
S57	Sunroof switch	1180 to 1183
S59	Trailer socket, fog lamps	884 to 886
S63	Info display switch	796, 797
S63.1	Switch reset	796
S63.2	Function select switch	797
S64	Horn switch	1072
S65	Coolant pressure switch	1613 to 1617, 1648 to 1652, 1679 to 1683
S66	Coolant temperature switch	1674 to 1676
S67	Radio remote control switch	1060 to 1066
S68	Electric mirror switch assembly	820 to 825, 840 to 847
S68.1	Electric mirror adjustment switch	821 to 825, 841 to 845
S68.2	Electric mirror left/right switch	821 to 825, 841 to 845
S68.4	Electric mirror parking position switch	846
S69	Inlet air heating switch	1476
S70	Air recirculation limit switch	1784
S78	Electric window switch, rear left	977 to 979
S79	Electric window switch, rear right	995 to 997
S82	Washer fluid level switch	791
S84	Selector lever switch	648
S85	Ignition key switch	646
S86	Anti-theft switch, passenger compartment	935 to 937
S88	Coolant temperature switch	1515, 1516, 1547, 1548, 1608, 1609, 1643, 1644
S89	Seat belt switch	1884, 1891
S92	Boot lock switch	931 to 933
S93	Coolant level switch	789
S95	Engine oil level switch	787
S101	Air conditioning compressor switch	1124 to 1126, 1829, 1830, 1865, 1866
S102	Air recirculation switch	1132 to 1134, 1788 to 1790, 1834 to 1836, 1870 to 1872
S104	Automatic transmission kickdown switch	636
S105	Automatic transmission Winter switch	640 to 642
S106	Automatic transmission Economy/Sport switch	638
S116	Stop-light switch	1244, 1245, 1276, 1277
S120	Anti-theft alarm bonnet switch	939
S121	Temperature lever limit switch	1824, 1860
S128	Coolant temperature switch	1603, 1604, 1636, 1637
S131	Defroster lever limit switch	1827, 1863
U12	Heated fuel filter assembly	1462
U13	Automatic transmission solenoid valve block	626 to 631
U13.1	2/3 shift solenoid valve	627
U13.2	1/2, 3/4 shift solenoid valve	628
U13.3	Converter clutch solenoid valve	629
U13.4	Hydraulic pressure control solenoid valve	630
U13.5	Neutral control solenoid valve	626
U15	Clock/radio display unit	770 to 797
U16	Clock/radio/computer display unit	515 to 533
U17	Aerial amplifier	1728, 1729
U18	Aerial amplifier, rear window	1726 to 1725
U20	Airbag contact	1073 to 1082
U21	Airbag, driver's side	1080 to 1082
U21.1	Airbag, driver's side squib	1080 to 1082
U22	Airbag, passenger's side	1084 to 1086
U22.1	Airbag, passenger's side squib	1084 to 1086
U24	CD changer	1740 to 1749
U25	Multi-timer	370 to 397
U26	Seatbelt pretensioner, driver's side	1095, 1096
U26.1	Seatbelt pretensioner, driver's side squib	1095, 1096
U27	Seatbelt pretensioner, passenger's side	1098, 1099
U27.1	Seatbelt pretensioner, passenger's side squib	1098, 1099
U28	Electronic climate control adjustment unit	1103 to 1140
U28.1	Compartment temperature sensor	1129
U29	Transmitter	1753 to 1757
U30	Side airbag, driver's side	1087 to 1089
U30.1	Side airbag, driver's side squib	1087 to 1089
U31	Side airbag, passenger's side	1090 to 1092
U31.1	Side airbag, passenger's side squib	1090 to 1092
V8	Compressor diode	1152, 1806, 1842
V21	Anti-theft warning diode	1071
X1 to X99	Wiring connectors	Various
Y1	Air conditioning compressor clutch	1154, 1809, 1844
Y7	Fuel injectors	222 to 233, 283 to 290, 426 to 433, 517 to 524
Y14	Coolant solenoid valve	1137, 1824, 1860
Y18	EGR solenoid valve	227 to 230, 419, 420, 476 to 479, 511 to 514, 1427
Y19	Inlet manifold solenoid valve	238, 417, 418
Y21	Stroke magnet - unlock ignition key	140 to 144, 201 to 208
Y23	Distributor (HEI system)	140 to 144, 201 to 208
Y28	Spin level regulation solenoid valve	1425
Y29	Boost pressure regulation solenoid valve	1423
Y32	Single-point fuel injector	473, 577
Y33	Distributor (MHDI system)	570 to 572
Y34	Fuel tank ventilation valve	236, 292, 421, 422, 479, 511
Y35	Air recirculation solenoid valve	1788, 1789, 1834, 1835, 1870, 1871
Y46	Inlet manifold solenoid valve	240
Y47	Selector lever lifting magnet	648

12

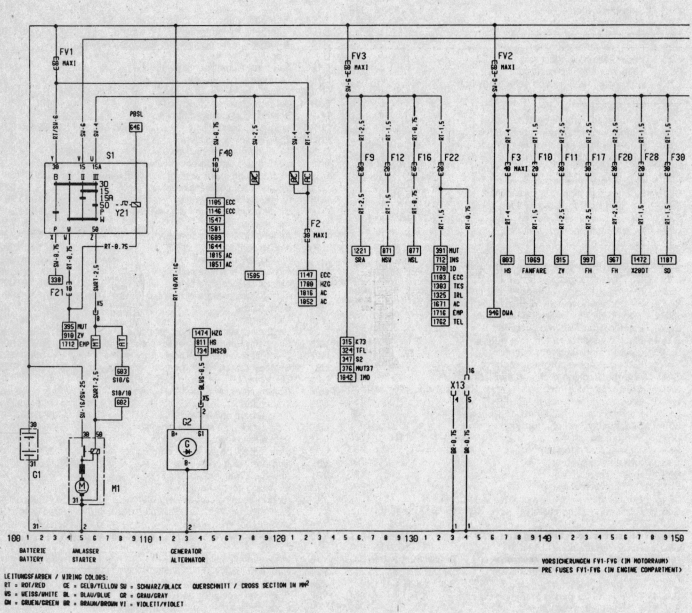

Typical wiring diagram - Current track 0100 - 0150

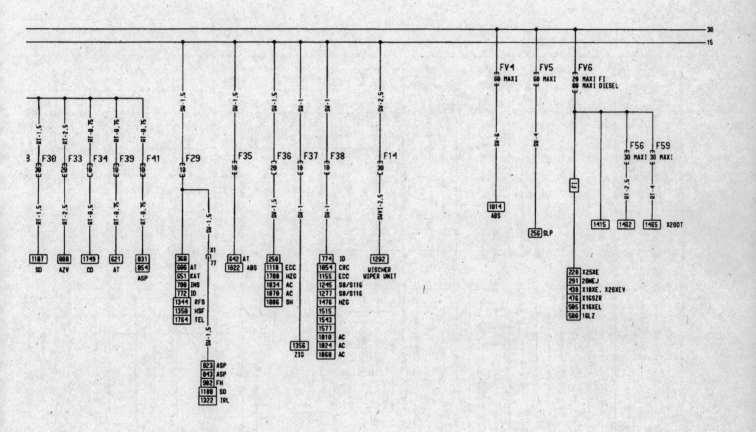

Typical wiring diagram - Current track 0150 - 0199

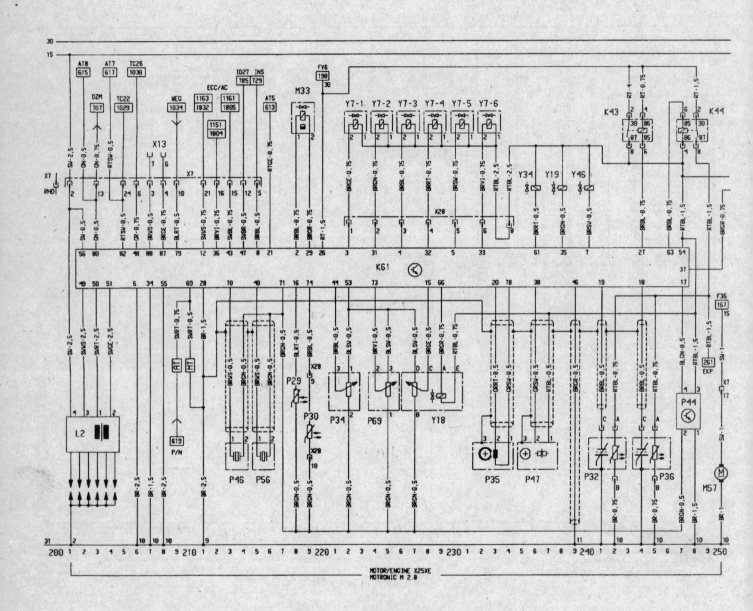

Typical wiring diagram - Current track 0200 - 0250

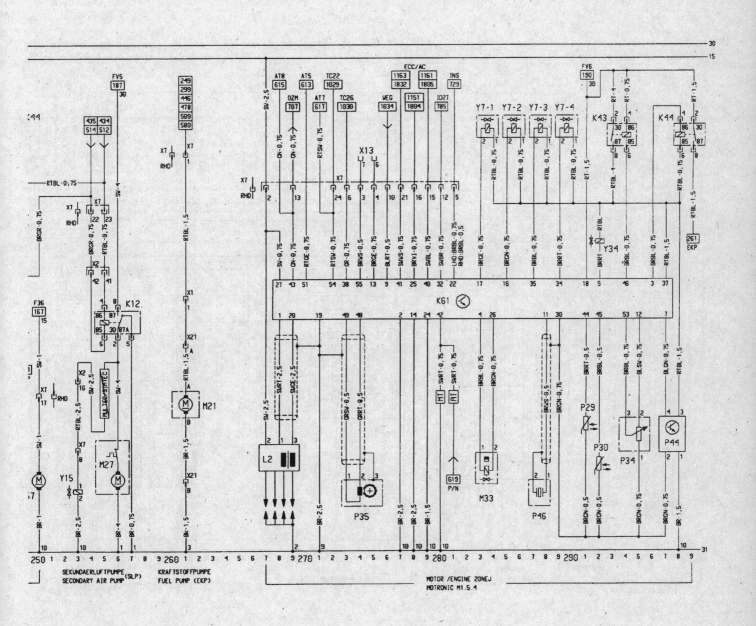

Typical wiring diagram - Current track 0250 - 0299

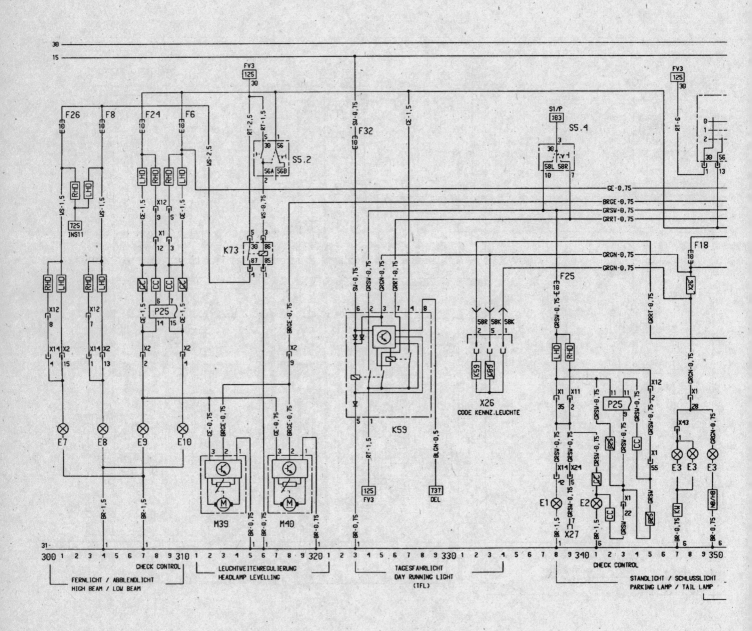

Typical wiring diagram - Current track 0300 - 0350

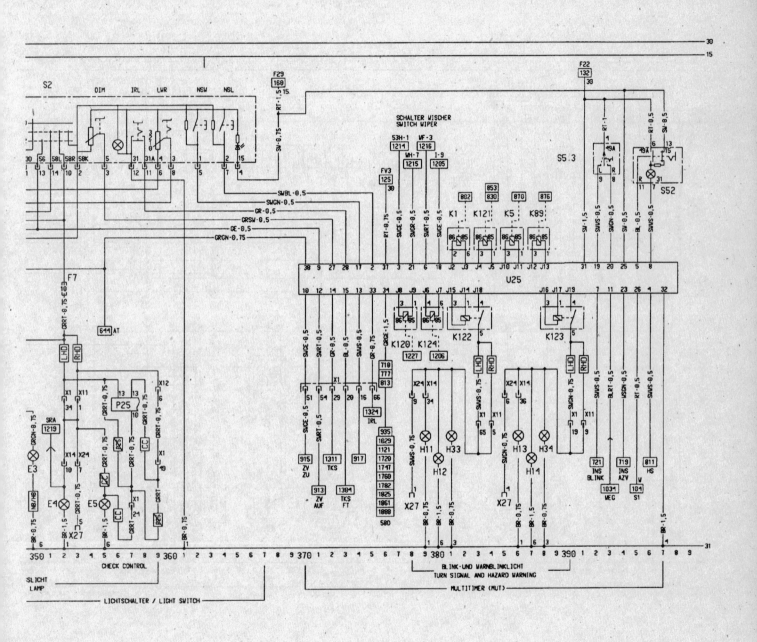

Typical wiring diagram - Current track 0350 - 0399

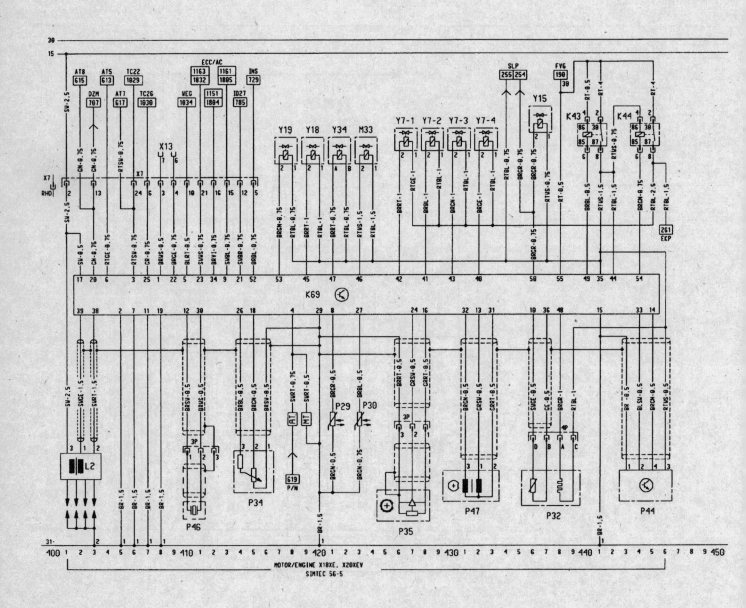

Typical wiring diagram - Current track 0400 - 0450

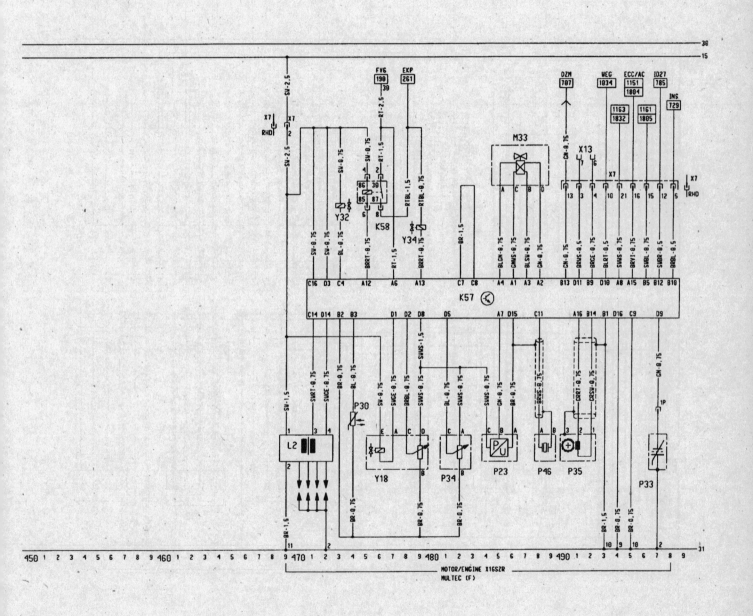

Typical wiring diagram - Current track 0450 - 0499

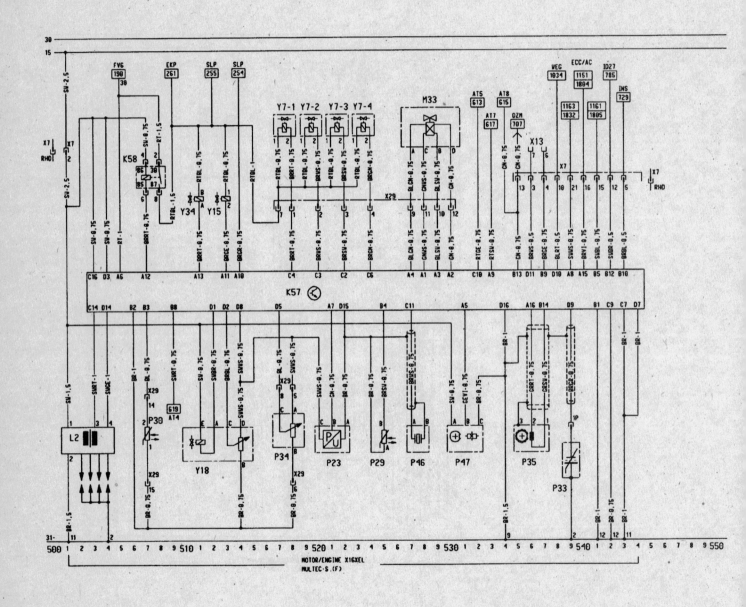

Typical wiring diagram - Current track 0500 - 0550

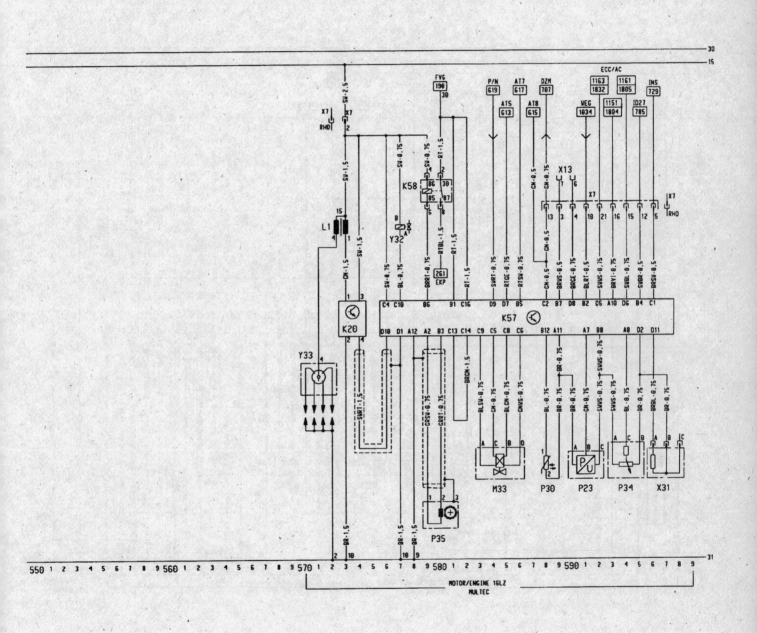

Typical wiring diagram - Current track 0550 - 0599

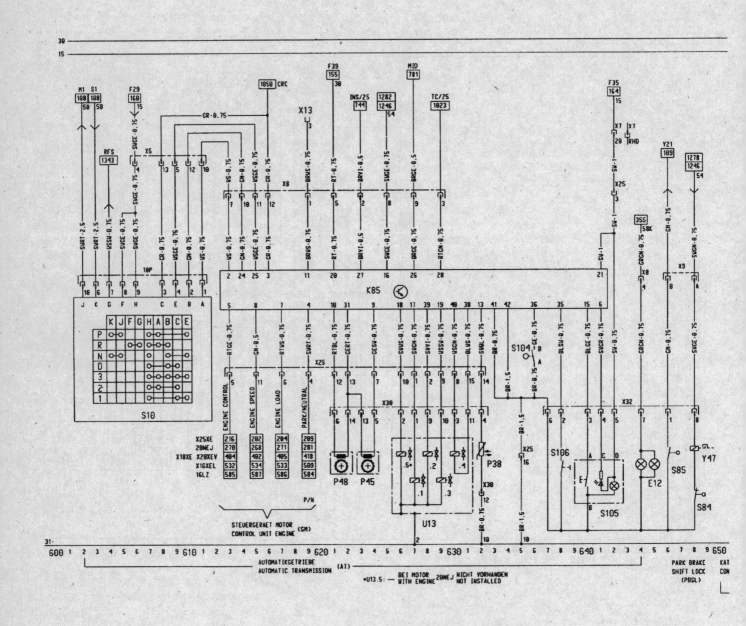

Typical wiring diagram - Current track 0600 - 0650

Typical wiring diagram - Current track 0650 - 0699

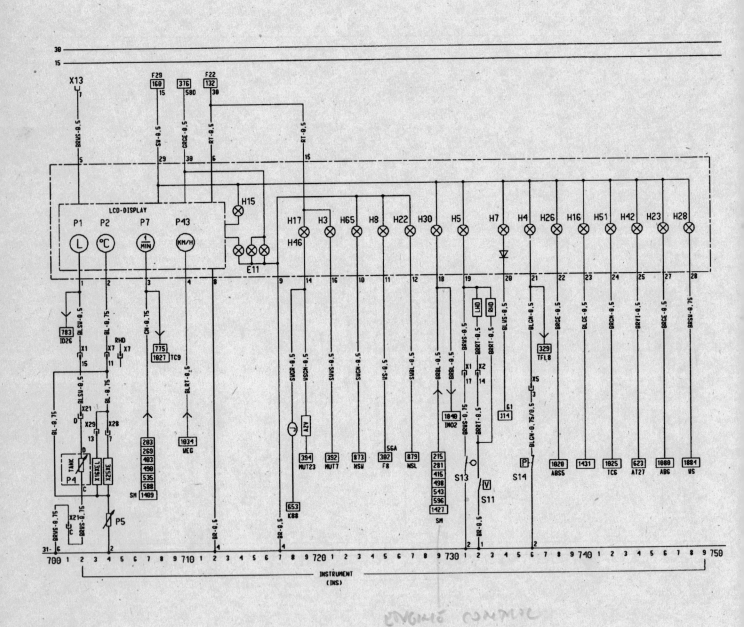

Typical wiring diagram - Current track 0700 - 0750

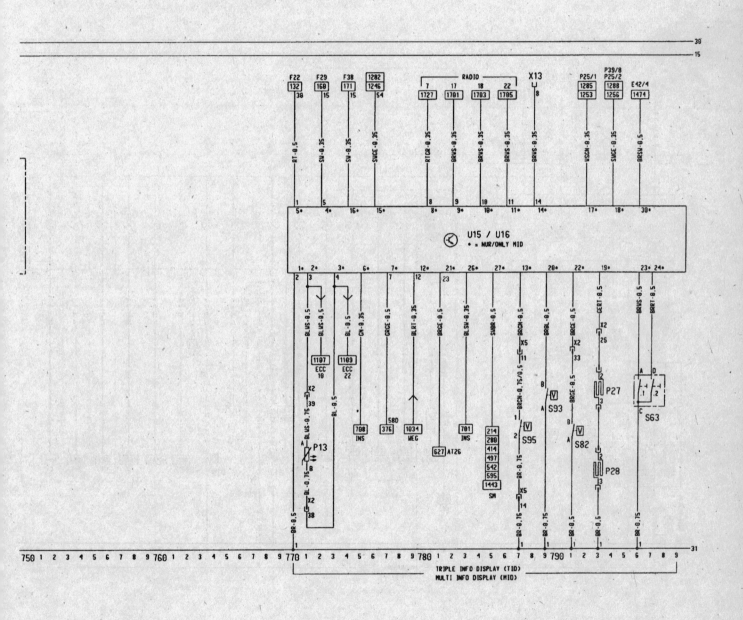

Typical wiring diagram - Current track 0750 - 0799

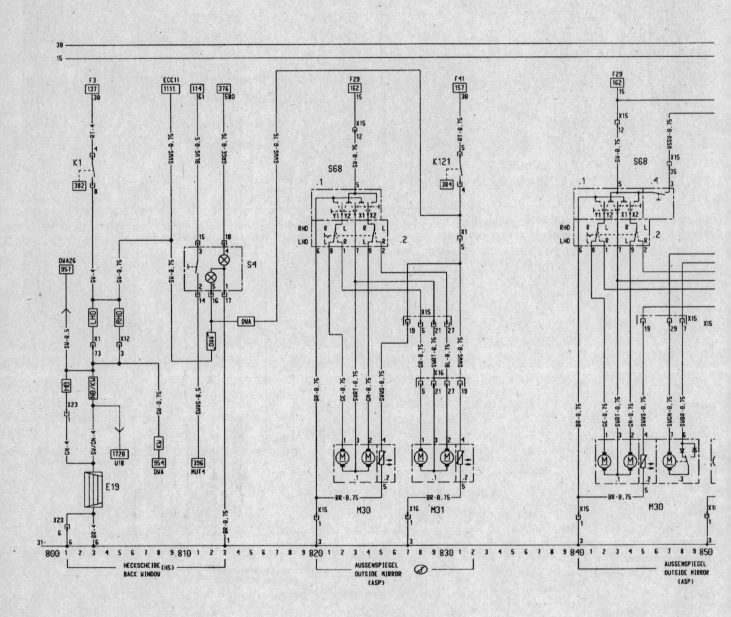

Typical wiring diagram - Current track 0800 - 0850

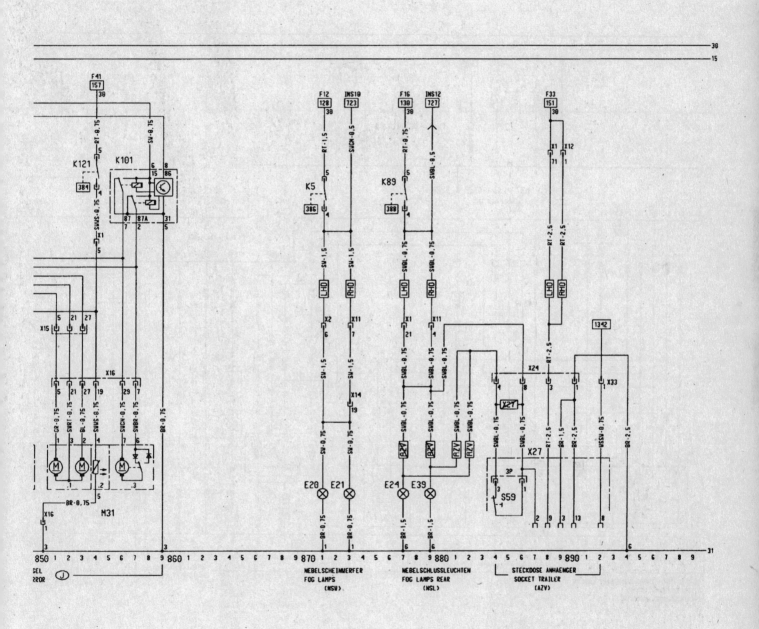

Typical wiring diagram - Current track 0850 - 0899

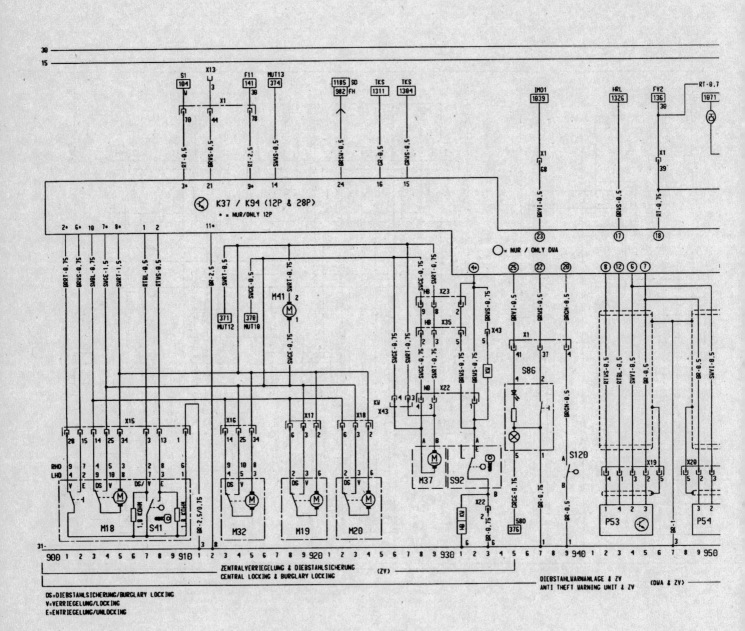

Typical wiring diagram - Current track 0900 - 0950

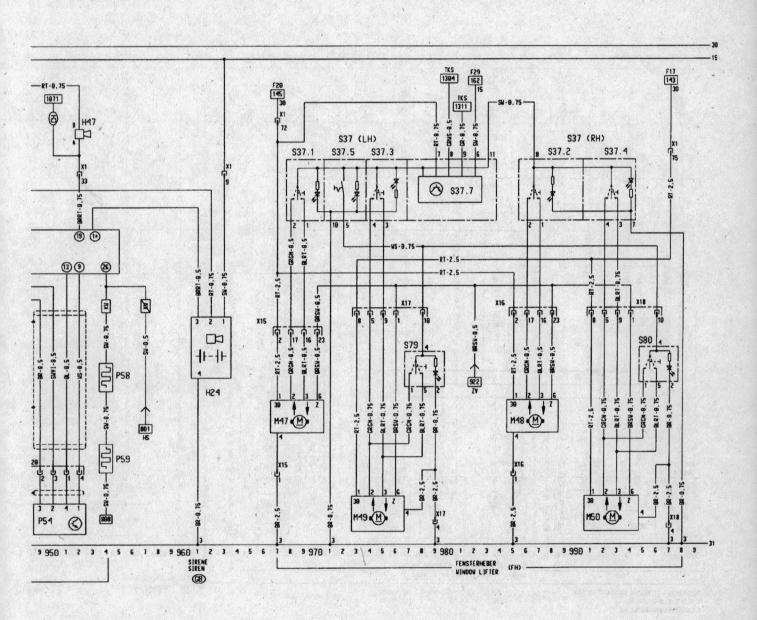

Typical wiring diagram - Current track 0950 - 0999

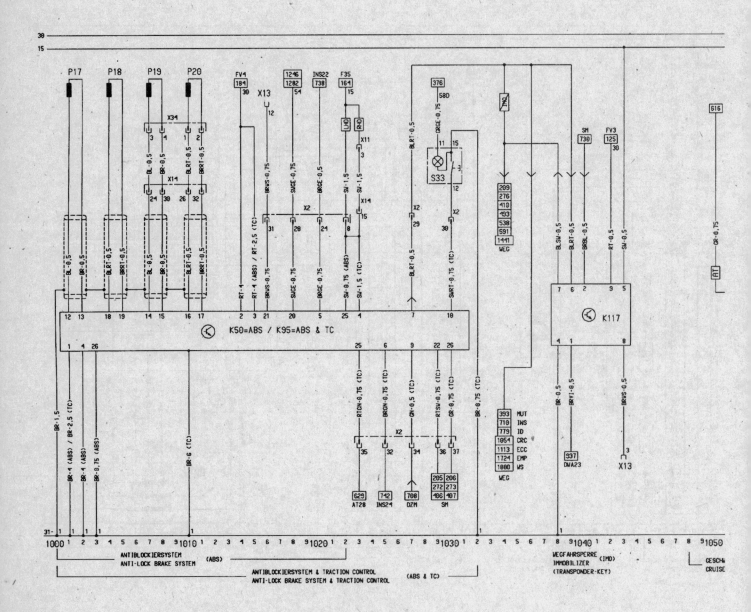

Typical wiring diagram - Current track 1000 - 1050

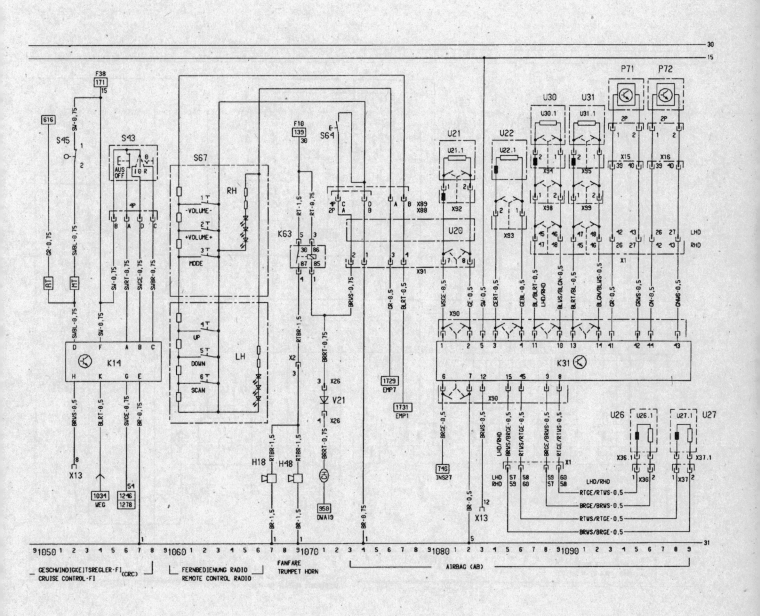

Typical wiring diagram - Current track 1050 - 1099

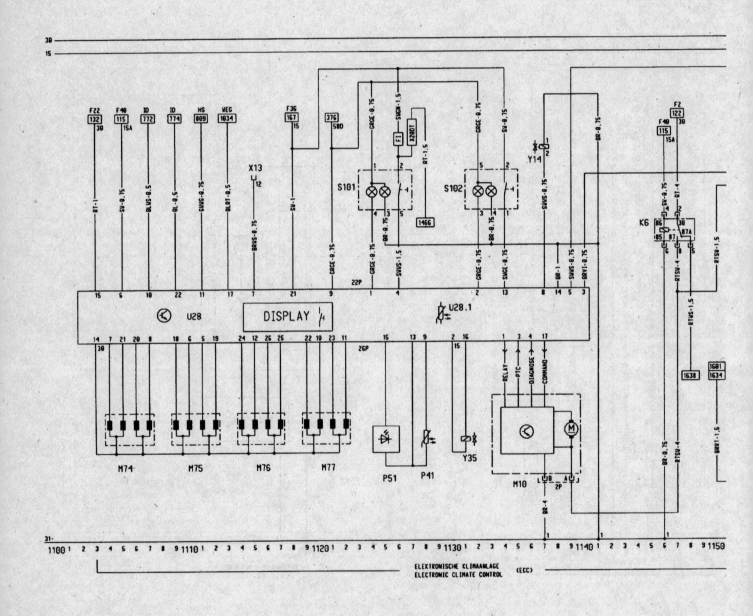

Typical wiring diagram - Current track 1100 - 1150

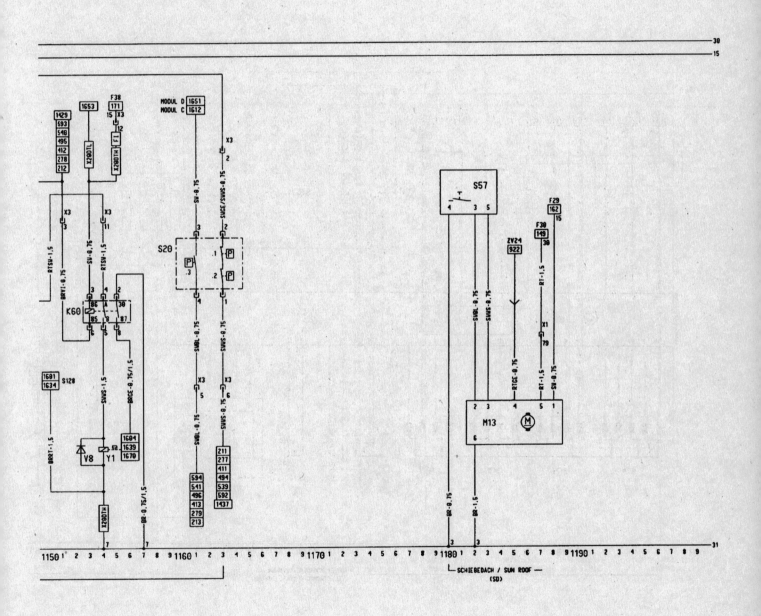

Typical wiring diagram - Current track 1150 - 1199

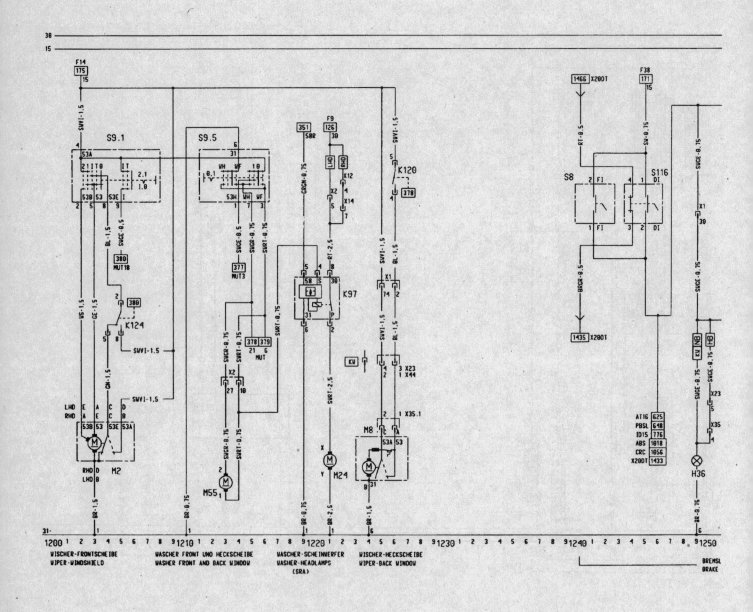

Typical wiring diagram - Current track 1200 - 1250

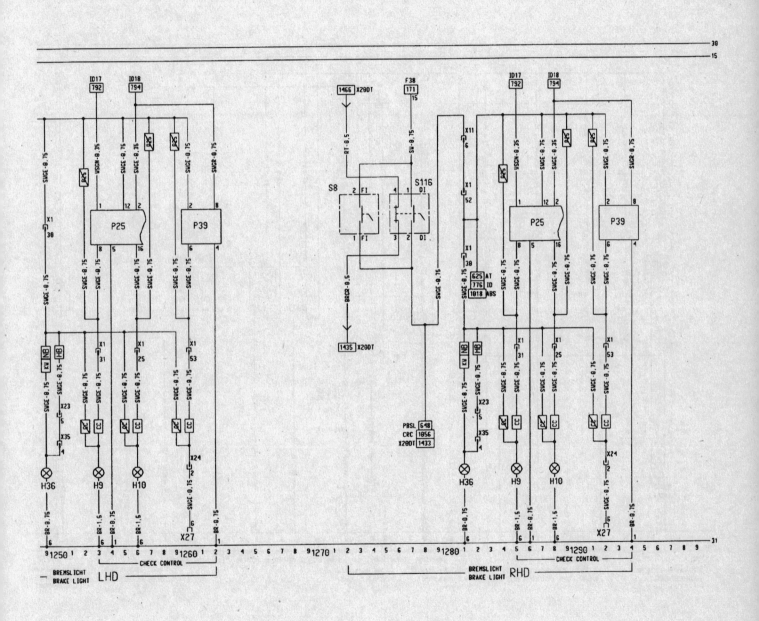

Typical wiring diagram - Current track 1250 - 1299

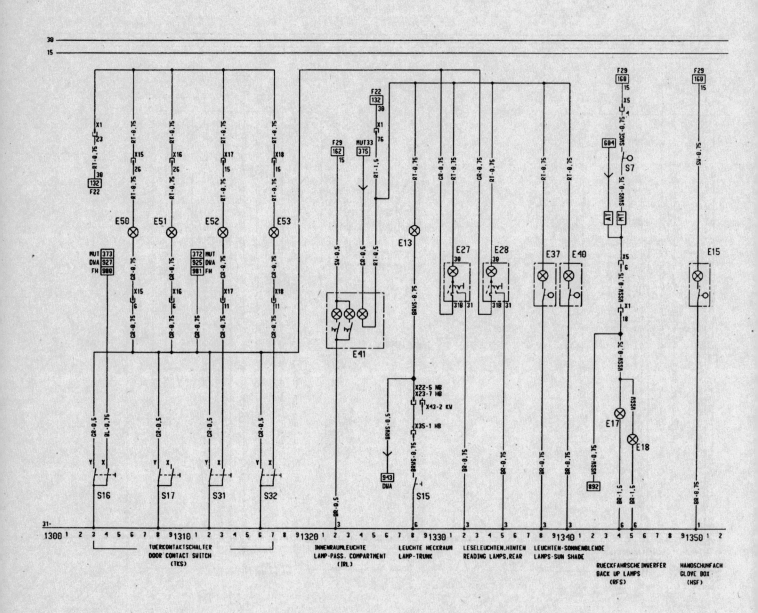

Typical wiring diagram - Current track 1300 - 1350

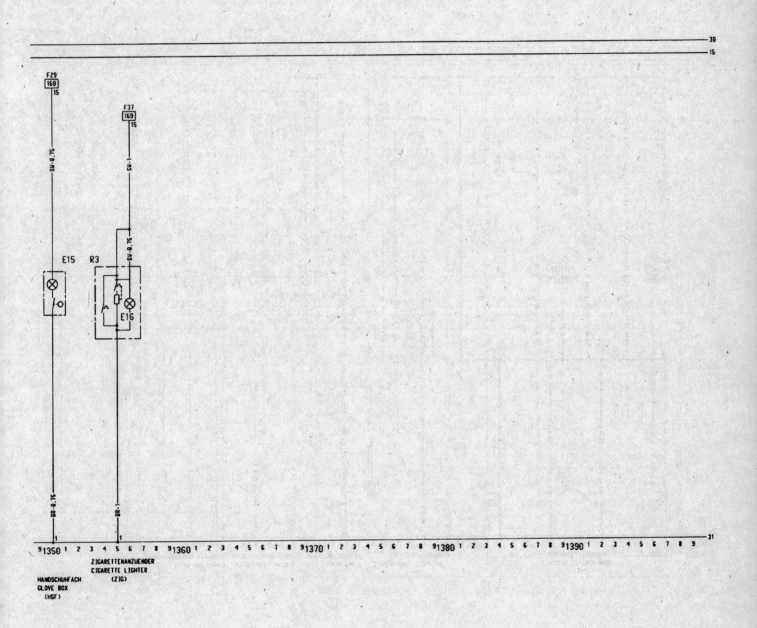

Typical wiring diagram - Current track 1350 - 1399

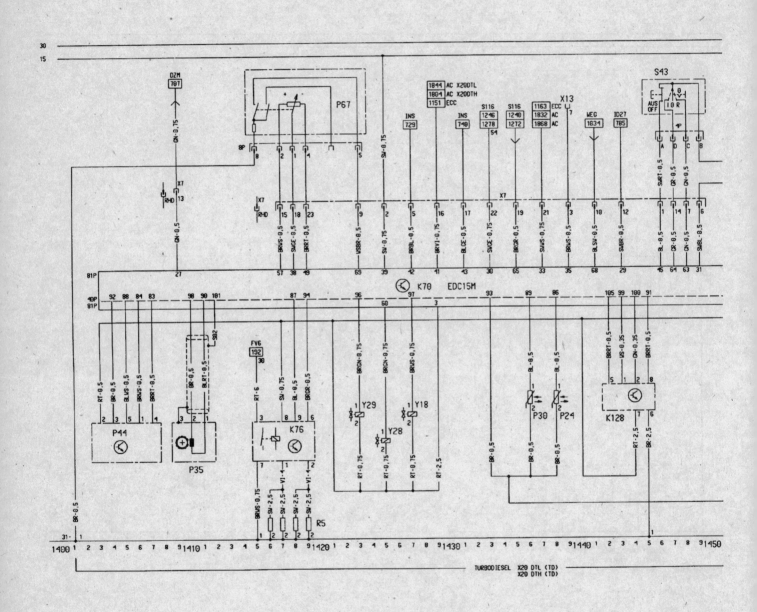

Typical wiring diagram - Current track 1400 - 1450

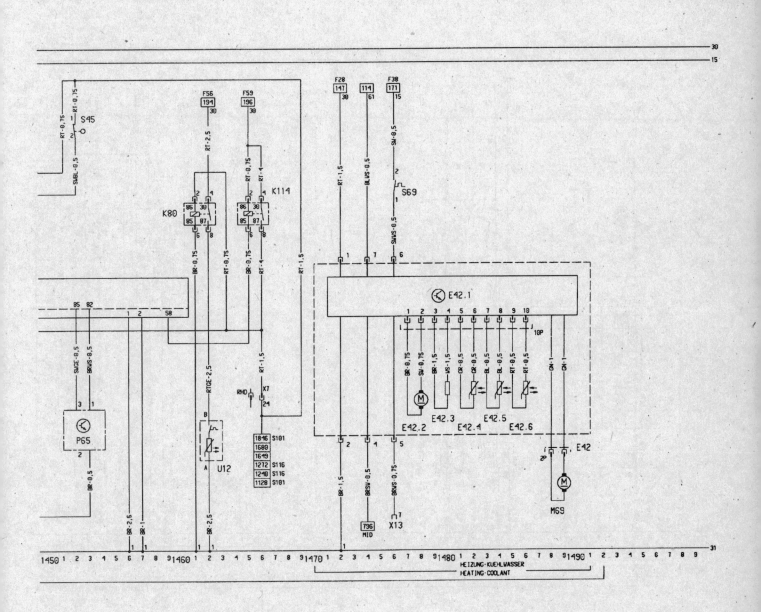

Typical wiring diagram - Current track 1450 - 1499

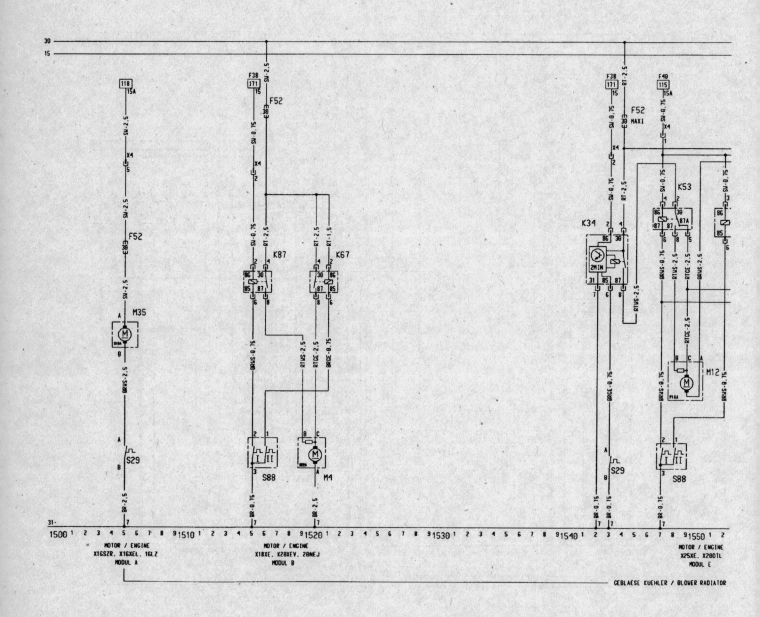

Typical wiring diagram - Current track 1500 - 1550

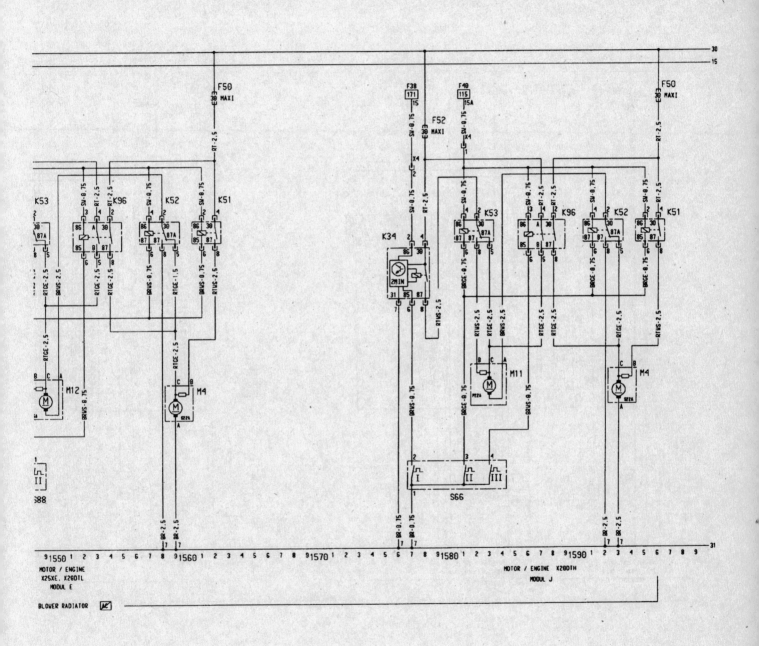

Typical wiring diagram - Current track 1550 - 1599

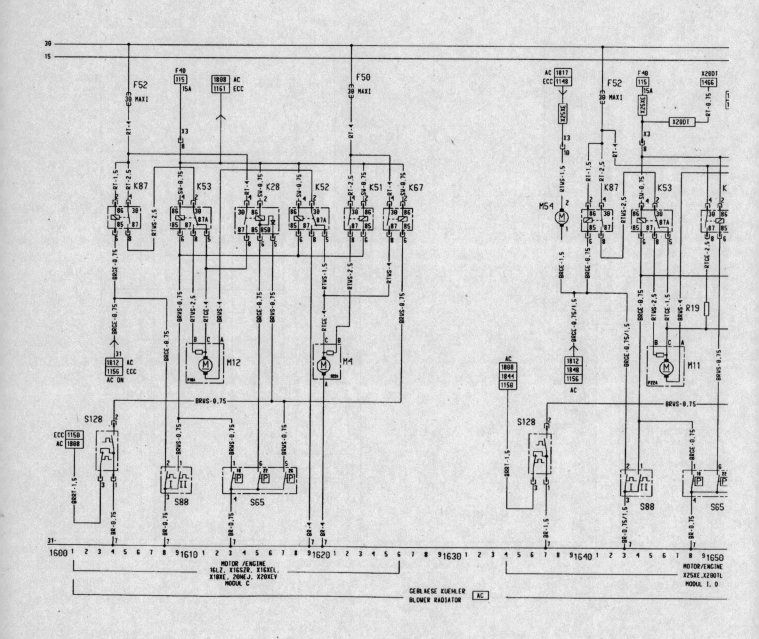

Typical wiring diagram - Current track 1600 - 1650

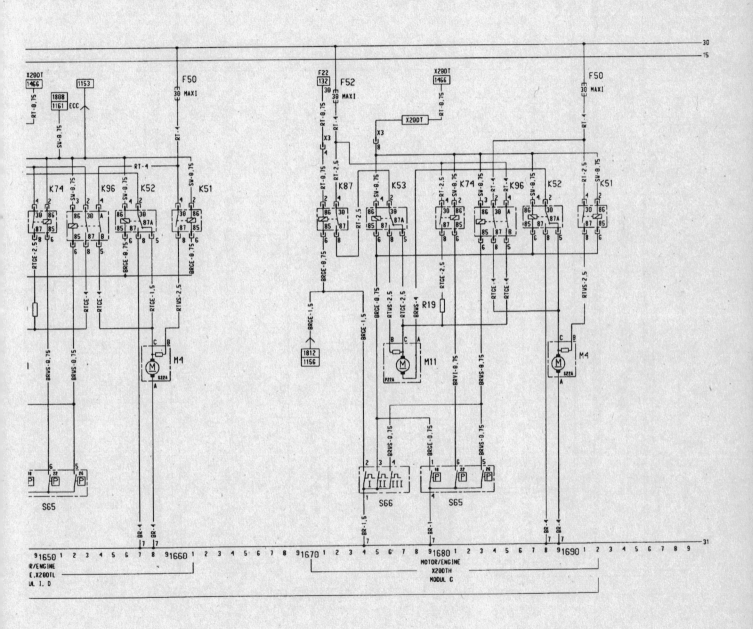

Typical wiring diagram - Current track 1650 - 1699

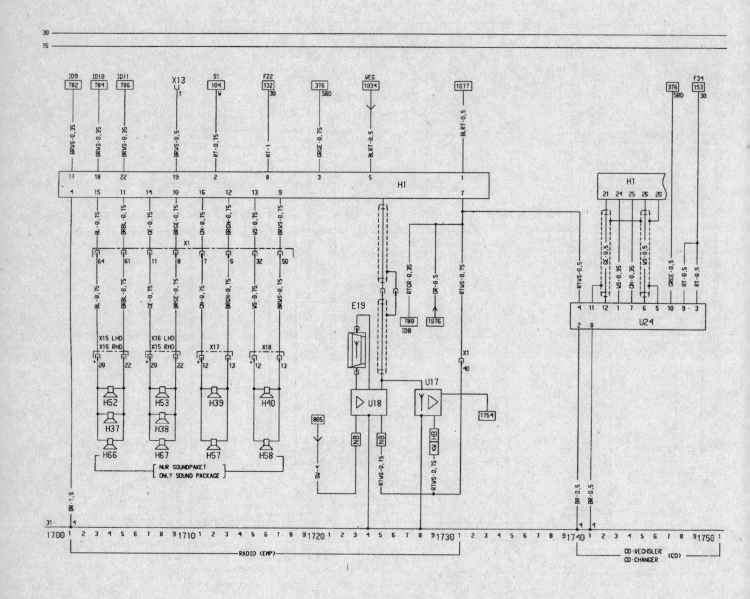

Typical wiring diagram - Current track 1700 - 1750

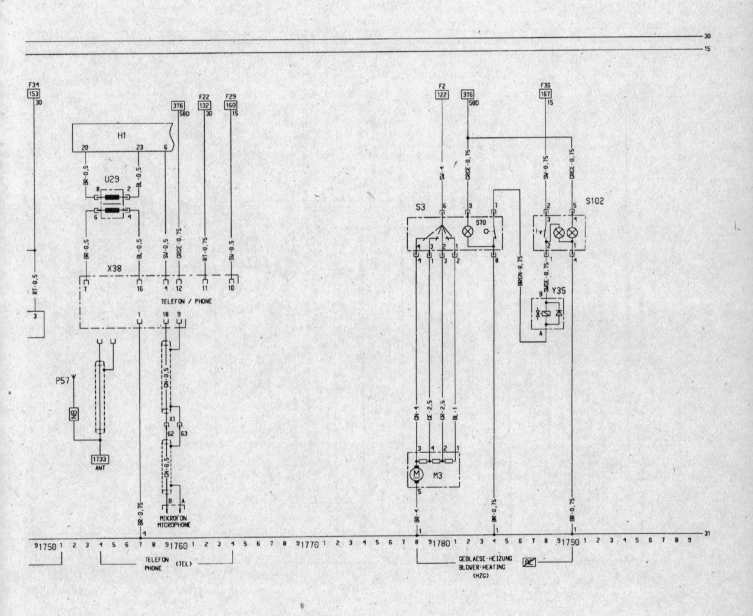

Typical wiring diagram - Current track 1750 - 1799

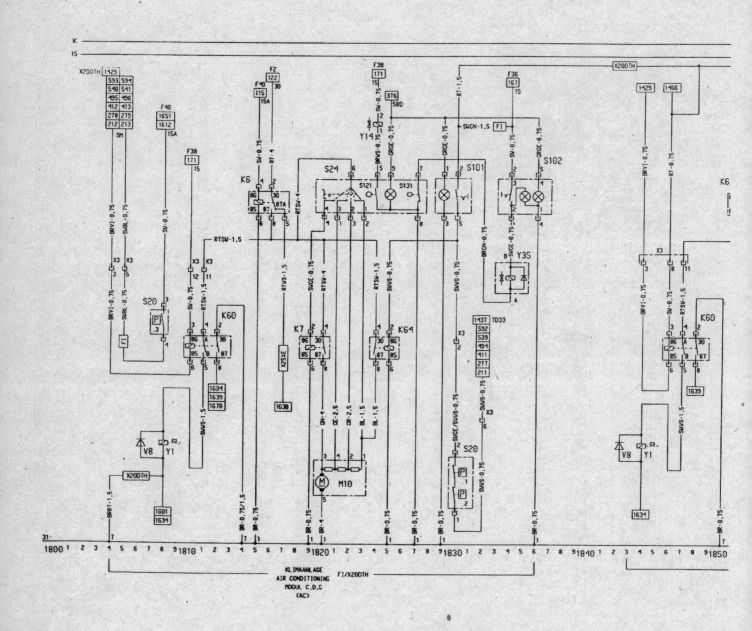

Typical wiring diagram - Current track 1800 - 1850

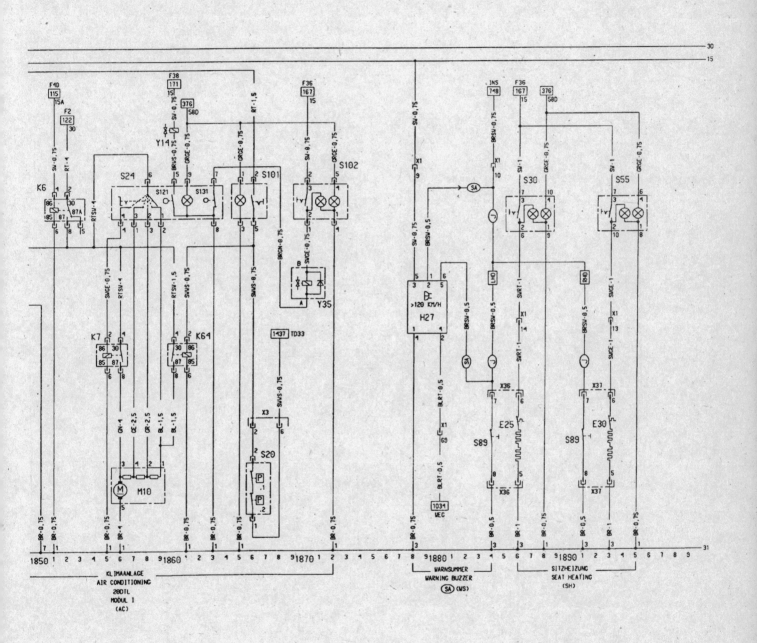

Typical wiring diagram - Current track 1850 - 1899

Dimensions and weights

Note: *All figures are approximate, and vary according to model. Refer to manufacturer's data for exact figures.*

Dimensions

Overall length:	
Saloon	4477 mm
Estate	4490 mm
Overall width (excluding wing mirrors)	1841 mm
Overall height (unladen):	
Saloon	1425 mm
Estate	1490 mm
Wheelbase	2637 mm
Track width:	
Front	1463 mm
Rear	1450 mm

Weights

Kerb weight:	
1.6 litre SOHC petrol engine models:	
Saloon	1245 kg
Hatchback	1260 kg
Estate	1280 kg
1.6 litre DOHC petrol engine models:	
Saloon	1280 kg
Hatchback	1295 kg
Estate	1320 to 1350 kg
1.8 litre petrol engine models:	
Saloon	1320 kg
Hatchback	1335 kg
Estate	1360 kg
2.0 litre petrol engine models:	
Saloon	1360 kg
Hatchback	1375 kg
Estate	1395 kg
1.7 litre diesel engine models:	
Saloon	1350 kg
Hatchback	1365 kg
2.0 litre diesel engine models:	
Saloon	1395 kg
Hatchback	1410 kg
Estate	1435 kg
Maximum towing weight:	
Unbraked trailer	620 kg (Envoy) to 700 kg (CDX)
Braked trailer	1000 kg (Envoy) to 1500 kg (CDX)
Maximum roof rack load	100 kg

Conversion factors

Length (distance)

Inches (in)	x 25.4	= Millimetres (mm)	x 0.0394	=	Inches (in)
Feet (ft)	x 0.305	= Metres (m)	x 3.281	=	Feet (ft)
Miles	x 1.609	= Kilometres (km)	x 0.621	=	Miles

Volume (capacity)

Cubic inches (cu in; in³)	x 16.387	= Cubic centimetres (cc; cm³)	x 0.061	=	Cubic inches (cu in; in³)
Imperial pints (Imp pt)	x 0.568	= Litres (l)	x 1.76	=	Imperial pints (Imp pt)
Imperial quarts (Imp qt)	x 1.137	= Litres (l)	x 0.88	=	Imperial quarts (Imp qt)
Imperial quarts (Imp qt)	x 1.201	= US quarts (US qt)	x 0.833	=	Imperial quarts (Imp qt)
US quarts (US qt)	x 0.946	= Litres (l)	x 1.057	=	US quarts (US qt)
Imperial gallons (Imp gal)	x 4.546	= Litres (l)	x 0.22	=	Imperial gallons (Imp gal)
Imperial gallons (Imp gal)	x 1.201	= US gallons (US gal)	x 0.833	=	Imperial gallons (Imp gal)
US gallons (US gal)	x 3.785	= Litres (l)	x 0.264	=	US gallons (US gal)

Mass (weight)

Ounces (oz)	x 28.35	= Grams (g)	x 0.035	=	Ounces (oz)
Pounds (lb)	x 0.454	= Kilograms (kg)	x 2.205	=	Pounds (lb)

Force

Ounces-force (ozf; oz)	x 0.278	= Newtons (N)	x 3.6	=	Ounces-force (ozf; oz)
Pounds-force (lbf; lb)	x 4.448	= Newtons (N)	x 0.225	=	Pounds-force (lbf; lb)
Newtons (N)	x 0.1	= Kilograms-force (kgf; kg)	x 9.81	=	Newtons (N)

Pressure

Pounds-force per square inch (psi; lbf/in²; lb/in²)	x 0.070	= Kilograms-force per square centimetre (kgf/cm²; kg/cm²)	x 14.223	=	Pounds-force per square inch (psi; lbf/in²; lb/in²)
Pounds-force per square inch (psi; lbf/in²; lb/in²)	x 0.068	= Atmospheres (atm)	x 14.696	=	Pounds-force per square inch (psi; lbf/in²; lb/in²)
Pounds-force per square inch (psi; lbf/in²; lb/in²)	x 0.069	= Bars	x 14.5	=	Pounds-force per square inch (psi; lbf/in²; lb/in²)
Pounds-force per square inch (psi; lbf/in²; lb/in²)	x 6.895	= Kilopascals (kPa)	x 0.145	=	Pounds-force per square inch (psi; lbf/in²; lb/in²)
Kilopascals (kPa)	x 0.01	= Kilograms-force per square centimetre (kgf/cm²; kg/cm²)	x 98.1	=	Kilopascals (kPa)
Millibar (mbar)	x 100	= Pascals (Pa)	x 0.01	=	Millibar (mbar)
Millibar (mbar)	x 0.0145	= Pounds-force per square inch (psi; lbf/in²; lb/in²)	x 68.947	=	Millibar (mbar)
Millibar (mbar)	x 0.75	= Millimetres of mercury (mmHg)	x 1.333	=	Millibar (mbar)
Millibar (mbar)	x 0.401	= Inches of water (inH₂O)	x 2.491	=	Millibar (mbar)
Millimetres of mercury (mmHg)	x 0.535	= Inches of water (inH₂O)	x 1.868	=	Millimetres of mercury (mmHg)
Inches of water (inH₂O)	x 0.036	= Pounds-force per square inch (psi; lbf/in²; lb/in²)	x 27.68	=	Inches of water (inH₂O)

Torque (moment of force)

Pounds-force inches (lbf in; lb in)	x 1.152	= Kilograms-force centimetre (kgf cm; kg cm)	x 0.868	=	Pounds-force inches (lbf in; lb in)
Pounds-force inches (lbf in; lb in)	x 0.113	= Newton metres (Nm)	x 8.85	=	Pounds-force inches (lbf in; lb in)
Pounds-force inches (lbf in; lb in)	x 0.083	= Pounds-force feet (lbf ft; lb ft)	x 12	=	Pounds-force inches (lbf in; lb in)
Pounds-force feet (lbf ft; lb ft)	x 0.138	= Kilograms-force metres (kgf m; kg m)	x 7.233	=	Pounds-force feet (lbf ft; lb ft)
Pounds-force feet (lbf ft; lb ft)	x 1.356	= Newton metres (Nm)	x 0.738	=	Pounds-force feet (lbf ft; lb ft)
Newton metres (Nm)	x 0.102	= Kilograms-force metres (kgf m; kg m)	x 9.804	=	Newton metres (Nm)

Power

Horsepower (hp)	x 745.7	= Watts (W)	x 0.0013	=	Horsepower (hp)

Velocity (speed)

Miles per hour (miles/hr; mph)	x 1.609	= Kilometres per hour (km/hr; kph)	x 0.621	=	Miles per hour (miles/hr; mph)

Fuel consumption*

Miles per gallon (mpg)	x 0.354	= Kilometres per litre (km/l)	x 2.825	=	Miles per gallon (mpg)

Temperature

Degrees Fahrenheit = (°C x 1.8) + 32   Degrees Celsius (Degrees Centigrade; °C) = (°F - 32) x 0.56

It is common practice to convert from miles per gallon (mpg) to litres/100 kilometres (l/100km), where mpg x l/100 km = 282

Spare parts are available from many sources, including maker's appointed garages, accessory shops, and motor factors. To be sure of obtaining the correct parts, it will sometimes be necessary to quote the vehicle identification number. If possible, it can also be useful to take the old parts along for positive identification. Items such as starter motors and alternators may be available under a service exchange scheme - any parts returned should be clean.

Our advice regarding spare parts is as follows.

Officially appointed garages

This is the best source of parts which are peculiar to your car, and which are not otherwise generally available (eg, badges, interior trim, certain body panels, etc). It is also the only place at which you should buy parts if the vehicle is still under warranty.

Accessory shops

These are very good places to buy materials and components needed for the maintenance of your car (oil, air and fuel filters, light bulbs, drivebelts, greases, brake pads, tough-up paint, etc). Components of this nature sold by a reputable shop are of the same standard as those used by the car manufacturer.

Besides components, these shops also sell tools and general accessories, usually have convenient opening hours, charge lower prices, and can often be found close to home. Some accessory shops have parts counters where components needed for almost any repair job can be purchased or ordered.

Motor factors

Good factors will stock all the more important components which wear out comparatively quickly, and can sometimes supply individual components needed for the overhaul of a larger assembly (eg, brake seals and hydraulic parts, bearing shells, pistons, valves). They may also handle work such as cylinder block reboring, crankshaft regrinding, etc.

Tyre and exhaust specialists

These outlets may be independent, or members of a local or national chain. They frequently offer competitive prices when compared with a main dealer or local garage, but it will pay to obtain several quotes before making a decision. When researching prices, also ask what 'extras' may be added - for instance fitting a new valve and balancing the wheel are both commonly charged on top of the price of a new tyre.

Other sources

Beware of parts or materials obtained from market stalls, car boot sales or similar outlets. Such items are not invariably sub-standard, but there is little chance of compensation if they do prove unsatisfactory. In the case of safety-critical components such as brake pads, there is the risk not only of financial loss, but also of an accident causing injury or death.

Second-hand components or assemblies obtained from a car breaker can be a good buy in some circumstances, but his sort of purchase is best made by the experienced DIY mechanic.

Vehicle identification

Modifications are a continuing and unpublicised process in vehicle manufacture, quite apart from major model changes. Spare parts manuals and lists are compiled upon a numerical basis, the individual vehicle identification numbers being essential to correct identification of the component concerned.

When ordering spare parts, always give as much information as possible. Quote the car model, year of manufacture, body and engine numbers as appropriate.

The *Vehicle Identification Number (VIN)* is stamped on a plate riveted to the engine compartment front crossmember, behind the radiator. It is also stamped into the body floor panel between the driver's seat and the door sill panel; lift the flap in the carpet to see it. On some non-UK models the plate may be attached to the front door frame **(see illustrations)**.

The *Engine number* is stamped on the front left-hand side of the cylinder block on petrol engines, and on the front right-hand side of the cylinder block beneath the injection pump on diesel engines.
Note: *When new, the car is provided with a Car Pass (similar to a credit card) having all the vehicle's data recorded on a magnetic strip.*

The *Vehicle Identification Number (VIN)* is stamped on a plate riveted to the engine compartment front crossmember

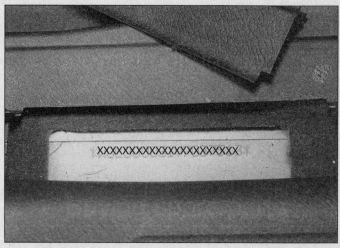

The *VIN* is also stamped into the body floor panel next to the driver's seat

Whenever servicing, repair or overhaul work is carried out on the car or its components, observe the following procedures and instructions. This will assist in carrying out the operation efficiently and to a professional standard of workmanship.

Joint mating faces and gaskets

When separating components at their mating faces, never insert screwdrivers or similar implements into the joint between the faces in order to prise them apart. This can cause severe damage which results in oil leaks, coolant leaks, etc upon reassembly. Separation is usually achieved by tapping along the joint with a soft-faced hammer in order to break the seal. However, note that this method may not be suitable where dowels are used for component location.

Where a gasket is used between the mating faces of two components, a new one must be fitted on reassembly; fit it dry unless otherwise stated in the repair procedure. Make sure that the mating faces are clean and dry, with all traces of old gasket removed. When cleaning a joint face, use a tool which is unlikely to score or damage the face, and remove any burrs or nicks with an oilstone or fine file.

Make sure that tapped holes are cleaned with a pipe cleaner, and keep them free of jointing compound, if this is being used, unless specifically instructed otherwise.

Ensure that all orifices, channels or pipes are clear, and blow through them, preferably using compressed air.

Oil seals

Oil seals can be removed by levering them out with a wide flat-bladed screwdriver or similar implement. Alternatively, a number of self-tapping screws may be screwed into the seal, and these used as a purchase for pliers or some similar device in order to pull the seal free.

Whenever an oil seal is removed from its working location, either individually or as part of an assembly, it should be renewed.

The very fine sealing lip of the seal is easily damaged, and will not seal if the surface it contacts is not completely clean and free from scratches, nicks or grooves. If the original sealing surface of the component cannot be restored, and the manufacturer has not made provision for slight relocation of the seal relative to the sealing surface, the component should be renewed.

Protect the lips of the seal from any surface which may damage them in the course of fitting. Use tape or a conical sleeve where possible. Lubricate the seal lips with oil before fitting and, on dual-lipped seals, fill the space between the lips with grease.

Unless otherwise stated, oil seals must be fitted with their sealing lips toward the lubricant to be sealed.

Use a tubular drift or block of wood of the appropriate size to install the seal and, if the seal housing is shouldered, drive the seal down to the shoulder. If the seal housing is unshouldered, the seal should be fitted with its face flush with the housing top face (unless otherwise instructed).

Screw threads and fastenings

Seized nuts, bolts and screws are quite a common occurrence where corrosion has set in, and the use of penetrating oil or releasing fluid will often overcome this problem if the offending item is soaked for a while before attempting to release it. The use of an impact driver may also provide a means of releasing such stubborn fastening devices, when used in conjunction with the appropriate screwdriver bit or socket. If none of these methods works, it may be necessary to resort to the careful application of heat, or the use of a hacksaw or nut splitter device.

Studs are usually removed by locking two nuts together on the threaded part, and then using a spanner on the lower nut to unscrew the stud. Studs or bolts which have broken off below the surface of the component in which they are mounted can sometimes be removed using a stud extractor. Always ensure that a blind tapped hole is completely free from oil, grease, water or other fluid before installing the bolt or stud. Failure to do this could cause the housing to crack due to the hydraulic action of the bolt or stud as it is screwed in.

When tightening a castellated nut to accept a split pin, tighten the nut to the specified torque, where applicable, and then tighten further to the next split pin hole. Never slacken the nut to align the split pin hole, unless stated in the repair procedure.

When checking or retightening a nut or bolt to a specified torque setting, slacken the nut or bolt by a quarter of a turn, and then retighten to the specified setting. However, this should not be attempted where angular tightening has been used.

For some screw fastenings, notably cylinder head bolts or nuts, torque wrench settings are no longer specified for the latter stages of tightening, "angle-tightening" being called up instead. Typically, a fairly low torque wrench setting will be applied to the bolts/nuts in the correct sequence, followed by one or more stages of tightening through specified angles.

Locknuts, locktabs and washers

Any fastening which will rotate against a component or housing during tightening should always have a washer between it and the relevant component or housing.

Spring or split washers should always be renewed when they are used to lock a critical component such as a big-end bearing retaining bolt or nut. Locktabs which are folded over to retain a nut or bolt should always be renewed.

Self-locking nuts can be re-used in non-critical areas, providing resistance can be felt when the locking portion passes over the bolt or stud thread. However, it should be noted that self-locking stiffnuts tend to lose their effectiveness after long periods of use, and should then be renewed as a matter of course.

Split pins must always be replaced with new ones of the correct size for the hole.

When thread-locking compound is found on the threads of a fastener which is to be re-used, it should be cleaned off with a wire brush and solvent, and fresh compound applied on reassembly.

Special tools

Some repair procedures in this manual entail the use of special tools such as a press, two or three-legged pullers, spring compressors, etc. Wherever possible, suitable readily-available alternatives to the manufacturer's special tools are described, and are shown in use. In some instances, where no alternative is possible, it has been necessary to resort to the use of a manufacturer's tool, and this has been done for reasons of safety as well as the efficient completion of the repair operation. Unless you are highly-skilled and have a thorough understanding of the procedures described, never attempt to bypass the use of any special tool when the procedure described specifies its use. Not only is there a very great risk of personal injury, but expensive damage could be caused to the components involved.

Environmental considerations

When disposing of used engine oil, brake fluid, antifreeze, etc, give due consideration to any detrimental environmental effects. Do not, for instance, pour any of the above liquids down drains into the general sewage system, or onto the ground to soak away. Many local council refuse tips provide a facility for waste oil disposal, as do some garages. If none of these facilities are available, consult your local Environmental Health Department, or the National Rivers Authority, for further advice.

With the universal tightening-up of legislation regarding the emission of environmentally-harmful substances from motor vehicles, most vehicles have tamperproof devices fitted to the main adjustment points of the fuel system. These devices are primarily designed to prevent unqualified persons from adjusting the fuel/air mixture, with the chance of a consequent increase in toxic emissions. If such devices are found during servicing or overhaul, they should, wherever possible, be renewed or refitted in accordance with the manufacturer's requirements or current legislation.

OIL CARE
FOLLOW THE CODE

OIL BANK LINE
0800 66 33 66
www.oilbankline.org.uk

Note: It is antisocial and illegal to dump oil down the drain. To find the location of your local oil recycling bank, call this number free.

The jack supplied with the vehicle tool kit should only be used for changing the roadwheels - see *"Wheel changing"* at the front of this manual. When carrying out any other kind of work, raise the vehicle using a hydraulic trolley jack, and always supplement the jack with axle stands positioned under the vehicle jacking points.

When using a trolley jack or axle stands, always position the jack head or axle stand head under, or adjacent to one of the relevant wheel changing jacking points under the sills. Use a block of wood between the jack or axle stand and the sill - the block of wood should have a groove cut into it, in which the welded flange of the sill will locate **(see illustrations)**.

Do not attempt to jack the vehicle under the front crossmember, the sump, or any of the suspension components.

The jack supplied with the vehicle locates in the jacking points on the underside of the sills - see *"Wheel changing"* at the front of this manual. Ensure that the jack head is correctly engaged before attempting to raise the vehicle.

Never work under, around, or near a raised vehicle, unless it is adequately supported in at least two places.

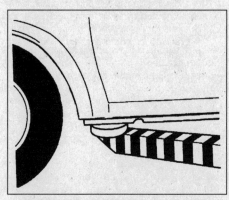

Front jacking point for hydraulic jack or axle stands

Rear jacking point for hydraulic jack or axle stands

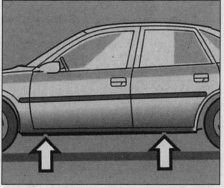

Wheel changing jacking points (arrowed)

Radio/cassette unit anti-theft system - precautions

The radio/cassette unit fitted may be equipped with a built-in security code, to deter thieves. If the power source to the unit is cut, the anti-theft system will activate. Even if the power source is immediately reconnected, the radio/cassette unit will not function until the correct security code has been entered. Therefore if you do not know the correct security code for the unit, **do not** disconnect the battery negative lead, or remove the radio/cassette unit from the vehicle.

If the security code is lost or forgotten, seek the advice of your Vauxhall dealer. On presentation of proof of ownership, a Vauxhall dealer will be able to provide you with a new security code.

Introduction

A selection of good tools is a fundamental requirement for anyone contemplating the maintenance and repair of a motor vehicle. For the owner who does not possess any, their purchase will prove a considerable expense, offsetting some of the savings made by doing-it-yourself. However, provided that the tools purchased meet the relevant national safety standards and are of good quality, they will last for many years and prove an extremely worthwhile investment.

To help the average owner to decide which tools are needed to carry out the various tasks detailed in this manual, we have compiled three lists of tools under the following headings: *Maintenance and minor repair*, *Repair and overhaul*, and *Special*. Newcomers to practical mechanics should start off with the *Maintenance and minor repair* tool kit, and confine themselves to the simpler jobs around the vehicle. Then, as confidence and experience grow, more difficult tasks can be undertaken, with extra tools being purchased as, and when, they are needed. In this way, a *Maintenance and minor repair* tool kit can be built up into a *Repair and overhaul* tool kit over a considerable period of time, without any major cash outlays. The experienced do-it-yourselfer will have a tool kit good enough for most repair and overhaul procedures, and will add tools from the *Special* category when it is felt that the expense is justified by the amount of use to which these tools will be put.

Maintenance and minor repair tool kit

The tools given in this list should be considered as a minimum requirement if routine maintenance, servicing and minor repair operations are to be undertaken. We recommend the purchase of combination spanners (ring one end, open-ended the other); although more expensive than open-ended ones, they do give the advantages of both types of spanner.

- [ ] *Combination spanners:*
  Metric - 8 to 19 mm inclusive
- [ ] *Adjustable spanner - 35 mm jaw (approx.)*
- [ ] *Spark plug spanner (with rubber insert) - petrol models*
- [ ] *Spark plug gap adjustment tool - petrol models*
- [ ] *Set of feeler gauges*
- [ ] *Brake bleed nipple spanner*
- [ ] *Screwdrivers:*
  Flat blade - 100 mm long x 6 mm dia
  Cross blade - 100 mm long x 6 mm dia
  Torx - various sizes (not all vehicles)
- [ ] *Combination pliers*
- [ ] *Hacksaw (junior)*
- [ ] *Tyre pump*
- [ ] *Tyre pressure gauge*
- [ ] *Oil can*
- [ ] *Oil filter removal tool*
- [ ] *Fine emery cloth*
- [ ] *Wire brush (small)*
- [ ] *Funnel (medium size)*
- [ ] *Sump drain plug key (not all vehicles)*

Repair and overhaul tool kit

These tools are virtually essential for anyone undertaking any major repairs to a motor vehicle, and are additional to those given in the *Maintenance and minor repair* list. Included in this list is a comprehensive set of sockets. Although these are expensive, they will be found invaluable as they are so versatile - particularly if various drives are included in the set. We recommend the half-inch square-drive type, as this can be used with most proprietary torque wrenches.

The tools in this list will sometimes need to be supplemented by tools from the *Special* list:

- [ ] *Sockets (or box spanners) to cover range in previous list (including Torx sockets)*
- [ ] *Reversible ratchet drive (for use with sockets)*
- [ ] *Extension piece, 250 mm (for use with sockets)*
- [ ] *Universal joint (for use with sockets)*
- [ ] *Flexible handle or sliding T "breaker bar" (for use with sockets)*
- [ ] *Torque wrench (for use with sockets)*
- [ ] *Self-locking grips*
- [ ] *Ball pein hammer*
- [ ] *Soft-faced mallet (plastic or rubber)*
- [ ] *Screwdrivers:*
  Flat blade - long & sturdy, short (chubby), and narrow (electrician's) types
  Cross blade - long & sturdy, and short (chubby) types
- [ ] *Pliers:*
  Long-nosed
  Side cutters (electrician's)
  Circlip (internal and external)
- [ ] *Cold chisel - 25 mm*
- [ ] *Scriber*
- [ ] *Scraper*
- [ ] *Centre-punch*
- [ ] *Pin punch*
- [ ] *Hacksaw*
- [ ] *Brake hose clamp*
- [ ] *Brake/clutch bleeding kit*
- [ ] *Selection of twist drills*
- [ ] *Steel rule/straight-edge*
- [ ] *Allen keys (inc. splined/Torx type)*
- [ ] *Selection of files*
- [ ] *Wire brush*
- [ ] *Axle stands*
- [ ] *Jack (strong trolley or hydraulic type)*
- [ ] *Light with extension lead*
- [ ] *Universal electrical multi-meter*

Sockets and reversible ratchet drive

Brake bleeding kit

Torx key, socket and bit

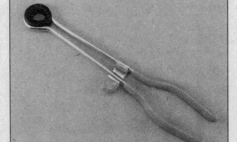

Hose clamp

Angular-tightening gauge

Special tools

The tools in this list are those which are not used regularly, are expensive to buy, or which need to be used in accordance with their manufacturers' instructions. Unless relatively difficult mechanical jobs are undertaken frequently, it will not be economic to buy many of these tools. Where this is the case, you could consider clubbing together with friends (or joining a motorists' club) to make a joint purchase, or borrowing the tools against a deposit from a local garage or tool hire specialist. It is worth noting that many of the larger DIY superstores now carry a large range of special tools for hire at modest rates.

The following list contains only those tools and instruments freely available to the public, and not those special tools produced by the vehicle manufacturer specifically for its dealer network. You will find occasional references to these manufacturers' special tools in the text of this manual. Generally, an alternative method of doing the job without the vehicle manufacturers' special tool is given. However, sometimes there is no alternative to using them. Where this is the case and the relevant tool cannot be bought or borrowed, you will have to entrust the work to a dealer.

- ☐ Angular-tightening gauge
- ☐ Valve spring compressor
- ☐ Valve grinding tool
- ☐ Piston ring compressor
- ☐ Piston ring removal/installation tool
- ☐ Cylinder bore hone
- ☐ Balljoint separator
- ☐ Coil spring compressors (where applicable)
- ☐ Two/three-legged hub and bearing puller
- ☐ Impact screwdriver
- ☐ Micrometer and/or vernier calipers
- ☐ Dial gauge
- ☐ Stroboscopic timing light
- ☐ Dwell angle meter/tachometer
- ☐ Fault code reader
- ☐ Cylinder compression gauge
- ☐ Hand-operated vacuum pump and gauge
- ☐ Clutch plate alignment set
- ☐ Brake shoe steady spring cup removal tool
- ☐ Bush and bearing removal/installation set
- ☐ Stud extractors
- ☐ Tap and die set
- ☐ Lifting tackle
- ☐ Trolley jack

Buying tools

Reputable motor accessory shops and superstores often offer excellent quality tools at discount prices, so it pays to shop around.

Remember, you don't have to buy the most expensive items on the shelf, but it is always advisable to steer clear of the very cheap tools. Beware of 'bargains' offered on market stalls or at car boot sales. There are plenty of good tools around at reasonable prices, but always aim to purchase items which meet the relevant national safety standards. If in doubt, ask the proprietor or manager of the shop for advice before making a purchase.

Care and maintenance of tools

Having purchased a reasonable tool kit, it is necessary to keep the tools in a clean and serviceable condition. After use, always wipe off any dirt, grease and metal particles using a clean, dry cloth, before putting the tools away. Never leave them lying around after they have been used. A simple tool rack on the garage or workshop wall for items such as screwdrivers and pliers is a good idea. Store all normal spanners and sockets in a metal box. Any measuring instruments, gauges, meters, etc, must be carefully stored where they cannot be damaged or become rusty.

Take a little care when tools are used. Hammer heads inevitably become marked, and screwdrivers lose the keen edge on their blades from time to time. A little timely attention with emery cloth or a file will soon restore items like this to a good finish.

Working facilities

Not to be forgotten when discussing tools is the workshop itself. If anything more than routine maintenance is to be carried out, a suitable working area becomes essential.

It is appreciated that many an owner-mechanic is forced by circumstances to remove an engine or similar item without the benefit of a garage or workshop. Having done this, any repairs should always be done under the cover of a roof.

Wherever possible, any dismantling should be done on a clean, flat workbench or table at a suitable working height.

Any workbench needs a vice; one with a jaw opening of 100 mm is suitable for most jobs. As mentioned previously, some clean dry storage space is also required for tools, as well as for any lubricants, cleaning fluids, touch-up paints etc, which become necessary.

Another item which may be required, and which has a much more general usage, is an electric drill with a chuck capacity of at least 8 mm. This, together with a good range of twist drills, is virtually essential for fitting accessories.

Last, but not least, always keep a supply of old newspapers and clean, lint-free rags available, and try to keep any working area as clean as possible.

Micrometers

Dial test indicator ("dial gauge")

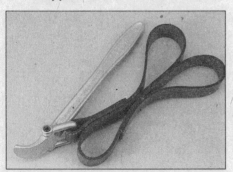
Strap wrench

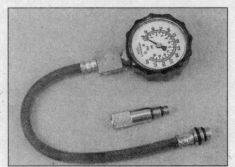
Compression tester

Fault code reader

MOT test checks

This is a guide to getting your vehicle through the MOT test. Obviously it will not be possible to examine the vehicle to the same standard as the professional MOT tester. However, working through the following checks will enable you to identify any problem areas before submitting the vehicle for the test.

Where a testable component is in borderline condition, the tester has discretion in deciding whether to pass or fail it. The basis of such discretion is whether the tester would be happy for a close relative or friend to use the vehicle with the component in that condition. If the vehicle presented is clean and evidently well cared for, the tester may be more inclined to pass a borderline component than if the vehicle is scruffy and apparently neglected.

It has only been possible to summarise the test requirements here, based on the regulations in force at the time of printing. Test standards are becoming increasingly stringent, although there are some exemptions for older vehicles.

An assistant will be needed to help carry out some of these checks.

The checks have been sub-divided into four categories, as follows:

1 Checks carried out **FROM THE DRIVER'S SEAT**

2 Checks carried out **WITH THE VEHICLE ON THE GROUND**

3 Checks carried out **WITH THE VEHICLE RAISED AND THE WHEELS FREE TO TURN**

4 Checks carried out on **YOUR VEHICLE'S EXHAUST EMISSION SYSTEM**

---

1 Checks carried out **FROM THE DRIVER'S SEAT**

Handbrake

□ Test the operation of the handbrake. Excessive travel (too many clicks) indicates incorrect brake or cable adjustment.

□ Check that the handbrake cannot be released by tapping the lever sideways. Check the security of the lever mountings.

Footbrake

□ Depress the brake pedal and check that it does not creep down to the floor, indicating a master cylinder fault. Release the pedal, wait a few seconds, then depress it again. If the pedal travels nearly to the floor before firm resistance is felt, brake adjustment or repair is necessary. If the pedal feels spongy, there is air in the hydraulic system which must be removed by bleeding.

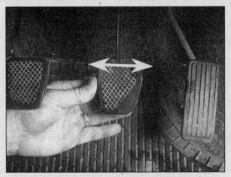

□ Check that the brake pedal is secure and in good condition. Check also for signs of fluid leaks on the pedal, floor or carpets, which would indicate failed seals in the brake master cylinder.

□ Check the servo unit (when applicable) by operating the brake pedal several times, then keeping the pedal depressed and starting the engine. As the engine starts, the pedal will move down slightly. If not, the vacuum hose or the servo itself may be faulty.

Steering wheel and column

□ Examine the steering wheel for fractures or looseness of the hub, spokes or rim.

□ Move the steering wheel from side to side and then up and down. Check that the steering wheel is not loose on the column, indicating wear or a loose retaining nut. Continue moving the steering wheel as before, but also turn it slightly from left to right.

□ Check that the steering wheel is not loose on the column, and that there is no abnormal

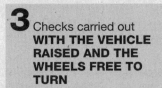

movement of the steering wheel, indicating wear in the column support bearings or couplings.

Windscreen, mirrors and sunvisor

□ The windscreen must be free of cracks or other significant damage within the driver's field of view. (Small stone chips are acceptable.) Rear view mirrors must be secure, intact, and capable of being adjusted.

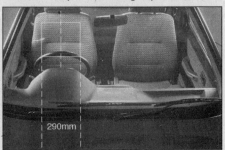

□ The driver's sunvisor must be capable of being stored in the "up" position.

Seat belts and seats

Note: *The following checks are applicable to all seat belts, front and rear.*

☐ Examine the webbing of all the belts (including rear belts if fitted) for cuts, serious fraying or deterioration. Fasten and unfasten each belt to check the buckles. If applicable, check the retracting mechanism. Check the security of all seat belt mountings accessible from inside the vehicle.

☐ Seat belts with pre-tensioners, once activated, have a "flag" or similar showing on the seat belt stalk. This, in itself, is not a reason for test failure.

☐ The front seats themselves must be securely attached and the backrests must lock in the upright position.

Doors

☐ Both front doors must be able to be opened and closed from outside and inside, and must latch securely when closed.

2 Checks carried out WITH THE VEHICLE ON THE GROUND

Vehicle identification

☐ Number plates must be in good condition, secure and legible, with letters and numbers correctly spaced – spacing at (A) should be at least twice that at (B).

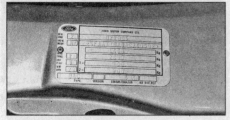

☐ The VIN plate and/or homologation plate must be legible.

Electrical equipment

☐ Switch on the ignition and check the operation of the horn.

☐ Check the windscreen washers and wipers, examining the wiper blades; renew damaged or perished blades. Also check the operation of the stop-lights.

☐ Check the operation of the sidelights and number plate lights. The lenses and reflectors must be secure, clean and undamaged.

☐ Check the operation and alignment of the headlights. The headlight reflectors must not be tarnished and the lenses must be undamaged.

☐ Switch on the ignition and check the operation of the direction indicators (including the instrument panel tell-tale) and the hazard warning lights. Operation of the sidelights and stop-lights must not affect the indicators - if it does, the cause is usually a bad earth at the rear light cluster.

☐ Check the operation of the rear foglight(s), including the warning light on the instrument panel or in the switch.

☐ The ABS warning light must illuminate in accordance with the manufacturers' design. For most vehicles, the ABS warning light should illuminate when the ignition is switched on, and (if the system is operating properly) extinguish after a few seconds. Refer to the owner's handbook.

Footbrake

☐ Examine the master cylinder, brake pipes and servo unit for leaks, loose mountings, corrosion or other damage.

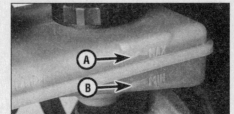

☐ The fluid reservoir must be secure and the fluid level must be between the upper (**A**) and lower (**B**) markings.

☐ Inspect both front brake flexible hoses for cracks or deterioration of the rubber. Turn the steering from lock to lock, and ensure that the hoses do not contact the wheel, tyre, or any part of the steering or suspension mechanism. With the brake pedal firmly depressed, check the hoses for bulges or leaks under pressure.

Steering and suspension

☐ Have your assistant turn the steering wheel from side to side slightly, up to the point where the steering gear just begins to transmit this movement to the roadwheels. Check for excessive free play between the steering wheel and the steering gear, indicating wear or insecurity of the steering column joints, the column-to-steering gear coupling, or the steering gear itself.

☐ Have your assistant turn the steering wheel more vigorously in each direction, so that the roadwheels just begin to turn. As this is done, examine all the steering joints, linkages, fittings and attachments. Renew any component that shows signs of wear or damage. On vehicles with power steering, check the security and condition of the steering pump, drivebelt and hoses.

☐ Check that the vehicle is standing level, and at approximately the correct ride height.

Shock absorbers

☐ Depress each corner of the vehicle in turn, then release it. The vehicle should rise and then settle in its normal position. If the vehicle continues to rise and fall, the shock absorber is defective. A shock absorber which has seized will also cause the vehicle to fail.

Exhaust system

☐ Start the engine. With your assistant holding a rag over the tailpipe, check the entire system for leaks. Repair or renew leaking sections.

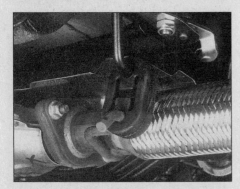

3 Checks carried out **WITH THE VEHICLE RAISED AND THE WHEELS FREE TO TURN**

Jack up the front and rear of the vehicle, and securely support it on axle stands. Position the stands clear of the suspension assemblies. Ensure that the wheels are clear of the ground and that the steering can be turned from lock to lock.

Steering mechanism

☐ Have your assistant turn the steering from lock to lock. Check that the steering turns smoothly, and that no part of the steering mechanism, including a wheel or tyre, fouls any brake hose or pipe or any part of the body structure.
☐ Examine the steering rack rubber gaiters for damage or insecurity of the retaining clips. If power steering is fitted, check for signs of damage or leakage of the fluid hoses, pipes or connections. Also check for excessive stiffness or binding of the steering, a missing split pin or locking device, or severe corrosion of the body structure within 30 cm of any steering component attachment point.

Front and rear suspension and wheel bearings

☐ Starting at the front right-hand side, grasp the roadwheel at the 3 o'clock and 9 o'clock positions and rock gently but firmly. Check for free play or insecurity at the wheel bearings, suspension balljoints, or suspension mountings, pivots and attachments.
☐ Now grasp the wheel at the 12 o'clock and 6 o'clock positions and repeat the previous inspection. Spin the wheel, and check for roughness or tightness of the front wheel bearing.

☐ If excess free play is suspected at a component pivot point, this can be confirmed by using a large screwdriver or similar tool and levering between the mounting and the component attachment. This will confirm whether the wear is in the pivot bush, its retaining bolt, or in the mounting itself (the bolt holes can often become elongated).

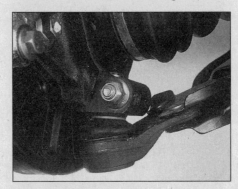

☐ Carry out all the above checks at the other front wheel, and then at both rear wheels.

Springs and shock absorbers

☐ Examine the suspension struts (when applicable) for serious fluid leakage, corrosion, or damage to the casing. Also check the security of the mounting points.
☐ If coil springs are fitted, check that the spring ends locate in their seats, and that the spring is not corroded, cracked or broken.
☐ If leaf springs are fitted, check that all leaves are intact, that the axle is securely attached to each spring, and that there is no deterioration of the spring eye mountings, bushes, and shackles.

☐ The same general checks apply to vehicles fitted with other suspension types, such as torsion bars, hydraulic displacer units, etc. Ensure that all mountings and attachments are secure, that there are no signs of excessive wear, corrosion or damage, and (on hydraulic types) that there are no fluid leaks or damaged pipes.
☐ Inspect the shock absorbers for signs of serious fluid leakage. Check for wear of the mounting bushes or attachments, or damage to the body of the unit.

Driveshafts (fwd vehicles only)

☐ Rotate each front wheel in turn and inspect the constant velocity joint gaiters for splits or damage. Also check that each driveshaft is straight and undamaged.

Braking system

☐ If possible without dismantling, check brake pad wear and disc condition. Ensure that the friction lining material has not worn excessively, (A) and that the discs are not fractured, pitted, scored or badly worn (B).

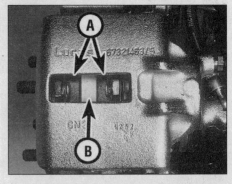

☐ Examine all the rigid brake pipes underneath the vehicle, and the flexible hose(s) at the rear. Look for corrosion, chafing or insecurity of the pipes, and for signs of bulging under pressure, chafing, splits or deterioration of the flexible hoses.
☐ Look for signs of fluid leaks at the brake calipers or on the brake backplates. Repair or renew leaking components.
☐ Slowly spin each wheel, while your assistant depresses and releases the footbrake. Ensure that each brake is operating and does not bind when the pedal is released.

☐ Examine the handbrake mechanism, checking for frayed or broken cables, excessive corrosion, or wear or insecurity of the linkage. Check that the mechanism works on each relevant wheel, and releases fully, without binding.

☐ It is not possible to test brake efficiency without special equipment, but a road test can be carried out later to check that the vehicle pulls up in a straight line.

Fuel and exhaust systems

☐ Inspect the fuel tank (including the filler cap), fuel pipes, hoses and unions. All components must be secure and free from leaks.

☐ Examine the exhaust system over its entire length, checking for any damaged, broken or missing mountings, security of the retaining clamps and rust or corrosion.

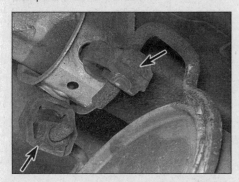

Wheels and tyres

☐ Examine the sidewalls and tread area of each tyre in turn. Check for cuts, tears, lumps, bulges, separation of the tread, and exposure of the ply or cord due to wear or damage. Check that the tyre bead is correctly seated on the wheel rim, that the valve is sound and properly seated, and that the wheel is not distorted or damaged.

☐ Check that the tyres are of the correct size for the vehicle, that they are of the same size and type on each axle, and that the pressures are correct.

☐ Check the tyre tread depth. The legal minimum at the time of writing is 1.6 mm over at least three-quarters of the tread width. Abnormal tread wear may indicate incorrect front wheel alignment.

Body corrosion

☐ Check the condition of the entire vehicle structure for signs of corrosion in load-bearing areas. (These include chassis box sections, side sills, cross-members, pillars, and all suspension, steering, braking system and seat belt mountings and anchorages.) Any corrosion which has seriously reduced the thickness of a load-bearing area is likely to cause the vehicle to fail. In this case professional repairs are likely to be needed.

☐ Damage or corrosion which causes sharp or otherwise dangerous edges to be exposed will also cause the vehicle to fail.

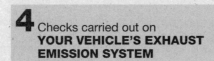

4 Checks carried out on **YOUR VEHICLE'S EXHAUST EMISSION SYSTEM**

Petrol models

☐ Have the engine at normal operating temperature, and make sure that it is in good tune (ignition system in good order, air filter element clean, etc).

☐ Before any measurements are carried out, raise the engine speed to around 2500 rpm, and hold it at this speed for 20 seconds. Allow the engine speed to return to idle, and watch for smoke emissions from the exhaust tailpipe. If the idle speed is obviously much too high, or if dense blue or clearly-visible black smoke comes from the tailpipe for more than 5 seconds, the vehicle will fail. As a rule of thumb, blue smoke signifies oil being burnt (engine wear) while black smoke signifies unburnt fuel (dirty air cleaner element, or other carburettor or fuel system fault).

☐ An exhaust gas analyser capable of measuring carbon monoxide (CO) and hydrocarbons (HC) is now needed. If such an instrument cannot be hired or borrowed, a local garage may agree to perform the check for a small fee.

CO emissions (mixture)

☐ At the time of writing, for vehicles first used between 1st August 1975 and 31st July 1986 (P to C registration), the CO level must not exceed 4.5% by volume. For vehicles first used between 1st August 1986 and 31st July 1992 (D to J registration), the CO level must not exceed 3.5% by volume. Vehicles first

used after 1st August 1992 (K registration) must conform to the manufacturer's specification. The MOT tester has access to a DOT database or emissions handbook, which lists the CO and HC limits for each make and model of vehicle. The CO level is measured with the engine at idle speed, and at "fast idle". The following limits are given as a general guide:

> *At idle speed -*
>> CO level no more than 0.5%
> *At "fast idle" (2500 to 3000 rpm) -*
>> CO level no more than 0.3%
>> (Minimum oil temperature 60ºC)

☐ If the CO level cannot be reduced far enough to pass the test (and the fuel and ignition systems are otherwise in good condition) then the carburettor is badly worn, or there is some problem in the fuel injection system or catalytic converter (as applicable).

HC emissions

☐ With the CO within limits, HC emissions for vehicles first used between 1st August 1975 and 31st July 1992 (P to J registration) must not exceed 1200 ppm. Vehicles first used after 1st August 1992 (K registration) must conform to the manufacturer's specification. The MOT tester has access to a DOT database or emissions handbook, which lists the CO and HC limits for each make and model of vehicle. The HC level is measured with the engine at "fast idle". The following is given as a general guide:

> *At "fast idle" (2500 to 3000 rpm) -*
>> HC level no more than 200 ppm
>> (Minimum oil temperature 60ºC)

☐ Excessive HC emissions are caused by incomplete combustion, the causes of which can include oil being burnt, mechanical wear and ignition/fuel system malfunction.

Diesel models

☐ The only emission test applicable to Diesel engines is the measuring of exhaust smoke density. The test involves accelerating the engine several times to its maximum unloaded speed.

Note: *It is of the utmost importance that the engine timing belt is in good condition before the test is carried out.*

☐ The limits for Diesel engine exhaust smoke, introduced in September 1995 are:
Vehicles first used before 1st August 1979:
> Exempt from metered smoke testing, but must not emit "dense blue or clearly visible black smoke for a period of more than 5 seconds at idle" or "dense blue or clearly visible black smoke during acceleration which would obscure the view of other road users".
Non-turbocharged vehicles first used after
> *1st August 1979:* 2.5m^{-1}
Turbocharged vehicles first used after
> *1st August 1979:* 3.0m^{-1}

☐ Excessive smoke can be caused by a dirty air cleaner element. Otherwise, professional advice may be needed to find the cause.

Engine

- ☐ Engine fails to rotate when attempting to start
- ☐ Engine rotates, but will not start
- ☐ Engine difficult to start when cold
- ☐ Engine difficult to start when hot
- ☐ Starter motor noisy or excessively-rough in engagement
- ☐ Engine starts, but stops immediately
- ☐ Engine idles erratically
- ☐ Engine misfires at idle speed
- ☐ Engine misfires throughout the driving speed range
- ☐ Engine hesitates on acceleration
- ☐ Engine stalls
- ☐ Engine lacks power
- ☐ Engine backfires
- ☐ Oil pressure warning light illuminated with engine running
- ☐ Engine runs-on after switching off
- ☐ Engine noises

Cooling system

- ☐ Overheating
- ☐ Overcooling
- ☐ External coolant leakage
- ☐ Internal coolant leakage
- ☐ Corrosion

Fuel and exhaust systems

- ☐ Excessive fuel consumption
- ☐ Fuel leakage and/or fuel odour
- ☐ Excessive noise or fumes from the exhaust system

Clutch

- ☐ Pedal travels to floor - no pressure or very little resistance
- ☐ Clutch fails to disengage (unable to select gears)
- ☐ Clutch slips (engine speed increases, with no increase in vehicle speed)
- ☐ Judder as clutch is engaged
- ☐ Noise when depressing or releasing clutch pedal

Manual transmission

- ☐ Noisy in neutral with engine running
- ☐ Noisy in one particular gear
- ☐ Difficulty engaging gears
- ☐ Jumps out of gear
- ☐ Vibration
- ☐ Lubricant leaks

Automatic transmission

- ☐ Fluid leakage
- ☐ Transmission fluid brown, or has burned smell
- ☐ Engine will not start in any gear, or starts in gears other than Park or Neutral
- ☐ General gear selection problems
- ☐ Transmission will not downshift (kickdown) with accelerator pedal fully depressed
- ☐ Transmission slips, shifts roughly, is noisy, or has no drive in forward or reverse gears

Driveshafts

- ☐ Vibration when accelerating or decelerating
- ☐ Clicking or knocking noise on turns (at slow speed on full-lock)

Braking system

- ☐ Vehicle pulls to one side under braking
- ☐ Noise (grinding or high-pitched squeal) when brakes applied
- ☐ Excessive brake pedal travel
- ☐ Brake pedal feels spongy when depressed
- ☐ Excessive brake pedal effort required to stop vehicle
- ☐ Judder felt through brake pedal or steering wheel when braking
- ☐ Pedal pulsates when braking hard
- ☐ Brakes binding
- ☐ Rear wheels locking under normal braking

Steering and suspension

- ☐ Vehicle pulls to one side
- ☐ Wheel wobble and vibration
- ☐ Excessive pitching and/or rolling around corners, or during braking
- ☐ Wandering or general instability
- ☐ Excessively-stiff steering
- ☐ Excessive play in steering
- ☐ Lack of power assistance
- ☐ Tyre wear excessive

Electrical system

- ☐ Battery will not hold a charge for more than a few days
- ☐ Ignition/no-charge warning light remains illuminated with engine running
- ☐ Ignition/no-charge warning light fails to come on
- ☐ Lights inoperative
- ☐ Instrument readings inaccurate or erratic
- ☐ Horn inoperative, or unsatisfactory in operation
- ☐ Windscreen/tailgate wipers inoperative, or unsatisfactory in operation
- ☐ Windscreen/tailgate washers inoperative, or unsatisfactory in operation
- ☐ Electric windows inoperative, or unsatisfactory in operation
- ☐ Central locking system inoperative, or unsatisfactory in operation

Introduction

The vehicle owner who does his or her own maintenance according to the recommended service schedules should not have to use this section of the manual very often. Modern component reliability is such that, provided those items subject to wear or deterioration are inspected or renewed at the specified intervals, sudden failure is comparatively rare. Faults do not usually just happen as a result of sudden failure, but develop over a period of time. Major mechanical failures in particular are usually preceded by characteristic symptoms over hundreds or even thousands of miles. Those components which do occasionally fail without warning are often small and easily carried in the vehicle.

With any fault-finding, the first step is to decide where to begin investigations. Sometimes this is obvious, but on other occasions, a little detective work will be necessary. The owner who makes half a dozen haphazard adjustments or replacements may be successful in curing a fault (or its symptoms), but will be none the wiser if the fault recurs, and ultimately may have spent more time and money than was necessary. A calm and logical approach will be found to be more satisfactory in the long run. Always take into account any warning signs or abnormalities that may have been noticed in the period preceding the fault - power loss, high or low gauge readings, unusual smells, etc - and remember that failure of components such as fuses or spark plugs may only be pointers to some underlying fault.

The pages which follow provide an easy-reference guide to the more common problems which may occur during the operation of the vehicle. These problems and their possible causes are grouped under headings denoting various components or systems, such as Engine, Cooling system, etc. The Chapter and/or Section which deals with the problem is also shown in brackets. Whatever the fault, certain basic principles apply. These are as follows:

Verify the fault. This is simply a matter of being sure that you know what the symptoms are before starting work. This is particularly important if you are investigating a fault for someone else, who may not have described it very accurately.

Don't overlook the obvious. For example, if the vehicle won't start, is there fuel in the tank? (Don't take anyone else's word on this particular point, and don't trust the fuel gauge either!) If an electrical fault is indicated, look for loose or broken wires before digging out the test gear.

Cure the disease, not the symptom. Substituting a flat battery with a fully-charged one will get you off the hard shoulder, but if the underlying cause is not attended to, the new battery will go the same way. Similarly, changing oil-fouled spark plugs for a new set will get you moving again, but remember that the reason for the fouling (if it wasn't simply an incorrect grade of plug) will have to be established and corrected.

Don't take anything for granted. Particularly, don't forget that a 'new' component may itself be defective (especially if it's been rattling around in the boot for months), and don't leave components out of a fault diagnosis sequence just because they are new or recently-fitted. When you do finally diagnose a difficult fault, you'll probably realise that all the evidence was there from the start.

Engine

Engine fails to rotate when attempting to start

☐ Battery terminal connections loose or corroded (see *"Weekly checks"*).
☐ Battery discharged or faulty (Chapter 5A).
☐ Broken, loose or disconnected wiring in the starting circuit (Chapter 5A).
☐ Defective starter solenoid or switch (Chapter 5A).
☐ Defective starter motor (Chapter 5A).
☐ Starter pinion or flywheel ring gear teeth loose or broken (Chapters 2 and 5A).
☐ Engine earth strap broken or disconnected (Chapter 5A).

Engine rotates, but will not start

☐ Fuel tank empty.
☐ Battery discharged (engine rotates slowly) (Chapter 5A).
☐ Battery terminal connections loose or corroded (see *"Weekly checks"*).
☐ Ignition components damp or damaged - petrol models (Chapters 1A and 5B).
☐ Broken, loose or disconnected wiring in the ignition circuit - petrol models (Chapters 1A and 5B).
☐ Worn, faulty or incorrectly-gapped spark plugs - petrol models (Chapter 1A).
☐ Preheating system faulty - diesel models (Chapter 5C).
☐ Fuel injection system faulty - petrol models (Chapter 4A).
☐ Stop solenoid faulty - diesel models (Chapter 4B).
☐ Air in fuel system - diesel models (Chapter 4B).
☐ Major mechanical failure (eg camshaft drive) (Chapter 2).

Engine difficult to start when cold

☐ Battery discharged (Chapter 5A).
☐ Battery terminal connections loose or corroded (see *"Weekly checks"*).
☐ Worn, faulty or incorrectly-gapped spark plugs - petrol models (Chapter 1A).
☐ Preheating system faulty - diesel models (Chapter 5C).
☐ Fuel injection system faulty - petrol models (Chapter 4A).
☐ Other ignition system fault - petrol models (Chapters 1A and 5B).
☐ Low cylinder compressions (Chapter 2).

Engine difficult to start when hot

☐ Air filter element dirty or clogged (Chapter 1).
☐ Fuel injection system faulty - petrol models (Chapter 4A).
☐ Low cylinder compressions (Chapter 2).

Starter motor noisy or excessively-rough in engagement

☐ Starter pinion or flywheel ring gear teeth loose or broken (Chapters 2 and 5A).
☐ Starter motor mounting bolts loose or missing (Chapter 5A).
☐ Starter motor internal components worn or damaged (Chapter 5A).

Engine starts, but stops immediately

☐ Loose or faulty electrical connections in the ignition circuit - petrol models (Chapters 1A and 5B).
☐ Vacuum leak at the throttle body or inlet manifold - petrol models (Chapter 4A).
☐ Blocked injector/fuel injection system fault - petrol models (Chapter 4A).

Engine idles erratically

☐ Air filter element clogged (Chapter 1).
☐ Vacuum leak at the throttle body, inlet manifold or associated hoses - petrol models (Chapter 4A).
☐ Worn, faulty or incorrectly-gapped spark plugs - petrol models (Chapter 1A).
☐ Uneven or low cylinder compressions (Chapter 2).
☐ Camshaft lobes worn (Chapter 2).
☐ Timing belt/chain incorrectly fitted (Chapter 2).
☐ Blocked injector/fuel injection system fault - petrol models (Chapter 4A).
☐ Faulty injector(s) - diesel models (Chapter 4B).

Engine misfires at idle speed

☐ Worn, faulty or incorrectly-gapped spark plugs - petrol models (Chapter 1A).
☐ Faulty spark plug HT leads - petrol models (Chapter 1A).
☐ Vacuum leak at the throttle body, inlet manifold or associated hoses - petrol models (Chapter 4A).
☐ Blocked injector/fuel injection system fault - petrol models (Chapter 4A).
☐ Faulty injector(s) - diesel models (Chapter 4B).
☐ Uneven or low cylinder compressions (Chapter 2).
☐ Disconnected, leaking, or perished crankcase ventilation hoses (Chapter 4C).

Engine (continued)

Engine misfires throughout the driving speed range
- ☐ Fuel filter choked (Chapter 1).
- ☐ Fuel pump faulty, or delivery pressure low - petrol models (Chapter 4A).
- ☐ Fuel tank vent blocked, or fuel pipes restricted (Chapter 4).
- ☐ Vacuum leak at the throttle body, inlet manifold or associated hoses - petrol models (Chapter 4A).
- ☐ Worn, faulty or incorrectly-gapped spark plugs - petrol models (Chapter 1A).
- ☐ Faulty spark plug HT leads - petrol models (Chapter 1A).
- ☐ Faulty injector(s) - diesel models (Chapter 4B).
- ☐ Faulty ignition coil - petrol models (Chapter 5B).
- ☐ Uneven or low cylinder compressions (Chapter 2).
- ☐ Blocked injector/fuel injection system fault - petrol models (Chapter 4A).

Engine hesitates on acceleration
- ☐ Worn, faulty or incorrectly-gapped spark plugs - petrol models (Chapter 1A).
- ☐ Vacuum leak at the throttle body, inlet manifold or associated hoses - petrol models (Chapter 4A).
- ☐ Blocked injector/fuel injection system fault - petrol models (Chapter 4A).
- ☐ Faulty injector(s) - diesel models (Chapter 4B).

Engine stalls
- ☐ Vacuum leak at the throttle body, inlet manifold or associated hoses - petrol models (Chapter 4A).
- ☐ Fuel filter choked (Chapter 1).
- ☐ Fuel pump faulty, or delivery pressure low - petrol models (Chapter 4A).
- ☐ Fuel tank vent blocked, or fuel pipes restricted (Chapter 4).
- ☐ Blocked injector/fuel injection system fault - petrol models (Chapter 4A).
- ☐ Faulty injector(s) - diesel models (Chapter 4B).

Engine lacks power
- ☐ Timing belt/chain incorrectly fitted or tensioned (Chapter 2).
- ☐ Fuel filter choked (Chapter 1).
- ☐ Fuel pump faulty, or delivery pressure low - petrol models (Chapter 4A).
- ☐ Uneven or low cylinder compressions (Chapter 2).
- ☐ Worn, faulty or incorrectly-gapped spark plugs - petrol models (Chapter 1A).
- ☐ Vacuum leak at the throttle body, inlet manifold or associated hoses - petrol models (Chapter 4A).
- ☐ Blocked injector/fuel injection system fault - petrol models (Chapter 4A).
- ☐ Faulty injector(s) - diesel models (Chapter 4B).
- ☐ Injection pump timing incorrect - diesel models (Chapter 4B).
- ☐ Brakes binding (Chapters 1 and 9).
- ☐ Clutch slipping (Chapter 6).

Engine backfires
- ☐ Timing belt/chain incorrectly fitted or tensioned (Chapter 2).
- ☐ Vacuum leak at the throttle body, inlet manifold or associated hoses - petrol models (Chapter 4A).
- ☐ Blocked injector/fuel injection system fault - petrol models (Chapter 4A).

Oil pressure warning light illuminated with engine running
- ☐ Low oil level, or incorrect oil grade ("Weekly checks").
- ☐ Faulty oil pressure sensor (Chapter 5A).
- ☐ Worn engine bearings and/or oil pump (Chapter 2).
- ☐ High engine operating temperature (Chapter 3).
- ☐ Oil pressure relief valve defective (Chapter 2).
- ☐ Oil pick-up strainer clogged (Chapter 2).

Engine runs-on after switching off
- ☐ Excessive carbon build-up in engine (Chapter 2).
- ☐ High engine operating temperature (Chapter 3).
- ☐ Fuel injection system faulty - petrol models (Chapter 4A).
- ☐ Faulty stop solenoid - diesel models (Chapter 4B).

Engine noises

Pre-ignition (pinking) or knocking during acceleration or under load
- ☐ Ignition timing incorrect/ignition system fault - petrol models (Chapters 1A and 5B).
- ☐ Incorrect grade of spark plug - petrol models (Chapter 1A).
- ☐ Incorrect grade of fuel (Chapter 4).
- ☐ Vacuum leak at the throttle body, inlet manifold or associated hoses - petrol models (Chapter 4A).
- ☐ Excessive carbon build-up in engine (Chapter 2).
- ☐ Blocked injector/fuel injection system fault - petrol models (Chapter 4A).

Whistling or wheezing noises
- ☐ Leaking inlet manifold or throttle body gasket - petrol models (Chapter 4A).
- ☐ Leaking exhaust manifold gasket or pipe-to-manifold joint (Chapter 4).
- ☐ Leaking vacuum hose (Chapters 4, 5 and 9).
- ☐ Blowing cylinder head gasket (Chapter 2).

Tapping or rattling noises
- ☐ Worn valve gear or camshaft (Chapter 2).
- ☐ Ancillary component fault (coolant pump, alternator, etc) (Chapters 3, 5, etc).

Knocking or thumping noises
- ☐ Worn big-end bearings (regular heavy knocking, perhaps less under load) (Chapter 2).
- ☐ Worn main bearings (rumbling and knocking, perhaps worsening under load) (Chapter 2).
- ☐ Piston slap (most noticeable when cold) (Chapter 2).
- ☐ Ancillary component fault (coolant pump, alternator, etc) (Chapters 3, 5, etc).

Cooling system

Overheating

- [ ] Insufficient coolant in system (*"Weekly Checks"*).
- [ ] Thermostat faulty (Chapter 3).
- [ ] Radiator core blocked, or grille restricted (Chapter 3).
- [ ] Electric cooling fan or thermostatic switch faulty (Chapter 3).
- [ ] Inaccurate temperature gauge sender unit (Chapter 3).
- [ ] Airlock in cooling system (Chapter 3).
- [ ] Expansion tank pressure cap faulty (Chapter 3).

Overcooling

- [ ] Thermostat faulty (Chapter 3).
- [ ] Inaccurate temperature gauge sender unit (Chapter 3).

External coolant leakage

- [ ] Deteriorated or damaged hoses or hose clips (Chapter 1).
- [ ] Radiator core or heater matrix leaking (Chapter 3).
- [ ] Pressure cap faulty (Chapter 3).
- [ ] Coolant pump internal seal leaking (Chapter 3).
- [ ] Coolant pump-to-block seal leaking (Chapter 3).
- [ ] Boiling due to overheating (Chapter 3).
- [ ] Core plug leaking (Chapter 2).

Internal coolant leakage

- [ ] Leaking cylinder head gasket (Chapter 2).
- [ ] Cracked cylinder head or cylinder block (Chapter 2).

Corrosion

- [ ] Infrequent draining and flushing (Chapter 1).
- [ ] Incorrect coolant mixture or inappropriate coolant type (see *"Weekly checks"*).

Fuel and exhaust systems

Excessive fuel consumption

- [ ] Air filter element dirty or clogged (Chapter 1).
- [ ] Fuel injection system faulty - petrol models (Chapter 4A).
- [ ] Faulty injector(s) - diesel models (Chapter 4B).
- [ ] Ignition timing incorrect/ignition system faulty - petrol models (Chapters 1A and 5B).
- [ ] Tyres under-inflated (see *"Weekly checks"*).

Fuel leakage and/or fuel odour

- [ ] Damaged or corroded fuel tank, pipes or connections (Chapter 4).

Excessive noise or fumes from the exhaust system

- [ ] Leaking exhaust system or manifold joints (Chapters 1 and 4).
- [ ] Leaking, corroded or damaged silencers or pipe (Chapters 1 and 4).
- [ ] Broken mountings causing body or suspension contact (Chapter 1).

Clutch

Pedal travels to floor - no pressure or very little resistance

☐ Air in hydraulic system/faulty master or slave cylinder (Chapter 6).
☐ Faulty hydraulic release system (Chapter 6).
☐ Broken clutch release bearing or arm (Chapter 6).
☐ Broken diaphragm spring in clutch pressure plate (Chapter 6).

Clutch fails to disengage (unable to select gears)

☐ Air in hydraulic system/faulty master or slave cylinder (Chapter 6).
☐ Faulty hydraulic release system (Chapter 6).
☐ Clutch disc sticking on gearbox input shaft splines (Chapter 6).
☐ Clutch disc sticking to flywheel or pressure plate (Chapter 6).
☐ Faulty pressure plate assembly (Chapter 6).
☐ Clutch release mechanism worn or incorrectly assembled (Chapter 6).

Clutch slips (engine speed increases, with no increase in vehicle speed)

☐ Faulty hydraulic release system (Chapter 6).
☐ Clutch disc linings excessively worn (Chapter 6).
☐ Clutch disc linings contaminated with oil or grease (Chapter 6).
☐ Faulty pressure plate or weak diaphragm spring (Chapter 6).

Judder as clutch is engaged

☐ Clutch disc linings contaminated with oil or grease (Chapter 6).
☐ Clutch disc linings excessively worn (Chapter 6).
☐ Faulty or distorted pressure plate or diaphragm spring (Chapter 6).
☐ Worn or loose engine or gearbox mountings (Chapter 2).
☐ Clutch disc hub or gearbox input shaft splines worn (Chapter 6).

Noise when depressing or releasing clutch pedal

☐ Worn clutch release bearing (Chapter 6).
☐ Worn or dry clutch pedal pivot (Chapter 6).
☐ Faulty pressure plate assembly (Chapter 6).
☐ Pressure plate diaphragm spring broken (Chapter 6).
☐ Broken clutch friction plate cushioning springs (Chapter 6).

Manual transmission

Noisy in neutral with engine running

☐ Input shaft bearings worn (noise apparent with clutch pedal released, but not when depressed) (Chapter 7A).*
☐ Clutch release bearing worn (noise apparent with clutch pedal depressed, possibly less when released) (Chapter 6).

Noisy in one particular gear

☐ Worn, damaged or chipped gear teeth (Chapter 7A).*

Difficulty engaging gears

☐ Clutch faulty (Chapter 6).
☐ Worn or damaged gear linkage (Chapter 7A).
☐ Worn synchroniser units (Chapter 7A).*

Jumps out of gear

☐ Worn or damaged gear linkage (Chapter 7A).
☐ Worn synchroniser units (Chapter 7A).*
☐ Worn selector forks (Chapter 7A).*

Vibration

☐ Lack of oil (Chapter 1).
☐ Worn bearings (Chapter 7A).*

Lubricant leaks

☐ Leaking oil seal (Chapter 7A).
☐ Leaking housing joint (Chapter 7A).*
☐ Leaking input shaft oil seal (Chapter 7A).*

Although the corrective action necessary to remedy the symptoms described is beyond the scope of the home mechanic, the above information should be helpful in isolating the cause of the condition, so that the owner can communicate clearly with a professional mechanic.

Automatic transmission

Note: *Due to the complexity of the automatic transmission, it is difficult for the home mechanic to properly diagnose and service this unit. For problems other than the following, the vehicle should be taken to a dealer service department or automatic transmission specialist. Do not be too hasty in removing the transmission if a fault is suspected, as most of the testing is carried out with the unit still fitted.*

Fluid leakage

☐ Automatic transmission fluid is usually dark in colour. Fluid leaks should not be confused with engine oil, which can easily be blown onto the transmission by airflow.

☐ To determine the source of a leak, first remove all built-up dirt and grime from the transmission housing and surrounding areas using a degreasing agent, or by steam-cleaning. Drive the vehicle at low speed, so airflow will not blow the leak far from its source. Raise and support the vehicle, and determine where the leak is coming from. The following are common areas of leakage:
 a) *Oil pan (Chapter 1A and 7B).*
 b) *Dipstick tube (Chapter 1A and 7B).*
 c) *Transmission-to-fluid cooler pipes/unions (Chapter 7B).*

Transmission fluid brown, or has burned smell

☐ Transmission fluid level low, or fluid in need of renewal (Chapter 1A and 7B).

Engine will not start in any gear, or starts in gears other than Park or Neutral

☐ Incorrect starter/inhibitor switch adjustment (Chapter 7B).
☐ Incorrect selector cable adjustment (Chapter 7B).

General gear selection problems

☐ Chapter 7B deals with checking and adjusting the selector cable on automatic transmissions. The following are common problems which may be caused by a poorly-adjusted cable:
 a) *Engine starting in gears other than Park or Neutral.*
 b) *Indicator panel indicating a gear other than the one actually being used.*
 c) *Vehicle moves when in Park or Neutral.*
 d) *Poor gear shift quality or erratic gear changes.*
☐ Refer to Chapter 7B for the selector cable adjustment procedure.

Transmission will not downshift (kickdown) with accelerator pedal fully depressed

☐ Low transmission fluid level (Chapter 1A).
☐ Incorrect selector cable adjustment (Chapter 7B).

Transmission slips, shifts roughly, is noisy, or has no drive in forward or reverse gears

☐ There are many probable causes for the above problems, but the home mechanic should be concerned with only one possibility - fluid level. Before taking the vehicle to a dealer or transmission specialist, check the fluid level and condition of the fluid as described in Chapter 1A, or 7B, as applicable. Correct the fluid level as necessary, or change the fluid and filter if needed. If the problem persists, professional help will be necessary.

Driveshafts

Vibration when accelerating or decelerating

☐ Worn inner constant velocity joint (Chapter 8).
☐ Bent or distorted driveshaft (Chapter 8).
☐ Worn intermediate bearing - where applicable (Chapter 8).

Clicking or knocking noise on turns (at slow speed on full-lock)

☐ Worn outer constant velocity joint (Chapter 8).
☐ Lack of constant velocity joint lubricant, possibly due to damaged gaiter (Chapter 8).

Braking system

Note: *Before assuming that a brake problem exists, make sure that the tyres are in good condition and correctly inflated, that the front wheel alignment is correct, and that the vehicle is not loaded with weight in an unequal manner. Apart from checking the condition of all pipe and hose connections, any faults occurring on the anti-lock braking system should be referred to a dealer for diagnosis.*

Vehicle pulls to one side under braking

- ☐ Worn, defective, damaged or contaminated front or rear brake pads/shoes on one side (Chapters 1 and 9).
- ☐ Seized or partially-seized front or rear brake caliper/wheel cylinder piston (Chapter 9).
- ☐ A mixture of brake pad/shoe lining materials fitted between sides (Chapter 9).
- ☐ Brake caliper or rear brake backplate mounting bolts loose (Chapter 9).
- ☐ Worn or damaged steering or suspension components (Chapters 1 and 10).

Noise (grinding or high-pitched squeal) when brakes applied

- ☐ Brake pad/shoe friction lining material worn down to metal backing (Chapters 1 and 9).
- ☐ Excessive corrosion of brake disc or drum - may be apparent after the vehicle has been standing for some time (Chapters 1 and 9).
- ☐ Foreign object (stone chipping, etc) trapped between brake disc and shield (Chapters 1 and 9).

Excessive brake pedal travel

- ☐ Faulty rear drum brake self-adjust mechanism (Chapter 9).
- ☐ Faulty master cylinder (Chapter 9).
- ☐ Air in hydraulic system (Chapter 9).
- ☐ Faulty vacuum servo unit (Chapter 9).
- ☐ Faulty vacuum pump - diesel models (Chapter 9).

Brake pedal feels spongy when depressed

- ☐ Air in hydraulic system (Chapter 9).
- ☐ Deteriorated flexible rubber brake hoses (Chapters 1 and 9).
- ☐ Master cylinder mountings loose (Chapter 9).
- ☐ Faulty master cylinder (Chapter 9).

Excessive brake pedal effort required to stop vehicle

- ☐ Faulty vacuum servo unit (Chapter 9).
- ☐ Disconnected, damaged or insecure brake servo vacuum hose (Chapters 1 and 9).
- ☐ Faulty vacuum pump - diesel models (Chapter 9).
- ☐ Primary or secondary hydraulic circuit failure (Chapter 9).
- ☐ Seized brake caliper or wheel cylinder piston(s) (Chapter 9).
- ☐ Brake pads/shoes incorrectly fitted (Chapter 9).
- ☐ Incorrect grade of brake pads/shoes fitted (Chapter 9).
- ☐ Brake pads/shoe linings contaminated (Chapter 9).

Judder felt through brake pedal or steering wheel when braking

- ☐ Excessive run-out or distortion of brake disc(s) or drum(s) (Chapter 9).
- ☐ Brake pad/shoe linings worn (Chapters 1 and 9).
- ☐ Brake caliper or rear brake backplate mounting bolts loose (Chapter 9).
- ☐ Wear in suspension or steering components or mountings (Chapters 1 and 10).

Pedal pulsates when braking hard

- ☐ Normal feature of ABS - no fault

Brakes binding

- ☐ Seized brake caliper/wheel cylinder piston(s) (Chapter 9).
- ☐ Incorrectly-adjusted handbrake mechanism (Chapter 9).
- ☐ Faulty master cylinder (Chapter 9).

Rear wheels locking under normal braking

- ☐ Rear brake pad/shoe linings contaminated (Chapters 1 and 9).
- ☐ Rear brake discs/drums warped (Chapters 1 and 9).

Steering and suspension

Note: *Before diagnosing suspension or steering faults, be sure that the trouble is not due to incorrect tyre pressures, mixtures of tyre types, or binding brakes.*

Vehicle pulls to one side

- ☐ Defective tyre (see *"Weekly checks"*).
- ☐ Excessive wear in suspension or steering components (Chapters 1 and 10).
- ☐ Incorrect front wheel alignment (Chapter 10).
- ☐ Accident damage to steering or suspension components (Chapters 1 and 10).

Wheel wobble and vibration

- ☐ Front roadwheels out of balance (vibration felt mainly through the steering wheel) (Chapter 10).
- ☐ Rear roadwheels out of balance (vibration felt throughout the vehicle) (Chapter 10).
- ☐ Roadwheels damaged or distorted (Chapter 10).
- ☐ Faulty or damaged tyre (*"Weekly Checks"*).
- ☐ Worn steering or suspension joints, bushes or components (Chapters 1 and 10).
- ☐ Wheel bolts loose (Chapter 1 and 10).

Excessive pitching and/or rolling around corners, or during braking

- ☐ Defective shock absorbers (Chapters 1 and 10).
- ☐ Broken or weak coil spring and/or suspension component (Chapters 1 and 10).
- ☐ Worn or damaged anti-roll bar or mountings (Chapter 10).

Wandering or general instability

- ☐ Incorrect front wheel alignment (Chapter 10).
- ☐ Worn steering or suspension joints, bushes or components (Chapters 1 and 10).
- ☐ Roadwheels out of balance (Chapter 10).
- ☐ Faulty or damaged tyre (*"Weekly Checks"*).
- ☐ Wheel bolts loose (Chapter 10).
- ☐ Defective shock absorbers (Chapters 1 and 10).

Excessively-stiff steering

- ☐ Seized track rod end balljoint or suspension balljoint (Chapters 1 and 10).
- ☐ Broken or incorrectly adjusted auxiliary drivebelt (Chapter 1).
- ☐ Incorrect front wheel alignment (Chapter 10).
- ☐ Steering gear damaged (Chapter 10).

Excessive play in steering

- ☐ Worn steering column universal joint(s) (Chapter 10).
- ☐ Worn steering track rod end balljoints (Chapters 1 and 10).
- ☐ Worn steering gear (Chapter 10).
- ☐ Worn steering or suspension joints, bushes or components (Chapters 1 and 10).

Lack of power assistance

- ☐ Broken or incorrectly-adjusted auxiliary drivebelt (Chapter 1).
- ☐ Incorrect power steering fluid level (*"Weekly Checks"*).
- ☐ Restriction in power steering fluid hoses (Chapter 10).
- ☐ Faulty power steering pump (Chapter 10).
- ☐ Faulty steering gear (Chapter 10).

Tyre wear excessive

Tyres worn on inside or outside edges

- ☐ Tyres under-inflated (wear on both edges) (*"Weekly Checks"*).
- ☐ Incorrect camber or castor angles (wear on one edge only) (Chapter 10).
- ☐ Worn steering or suspension joints, bushes or components (Chapters 1 and 10).
- ☐ Excessively-hard cornering.
- ☐ Accident damage.

Tyre treads exhibit feathered edges

- ☐ Incorrect toe setting (Chapter 10).

Tyres worn in centre of tread

- ☐ Tyres over-inflated (*"Weekly Checks"*).

Tyres worn on inside and outside edges

- ☐ Tyres under-inflated (*"Weekly Checks"*).
- ☐ Worn shock absorbers (Chapter 10).

Tyres worn unevenly

- ☐ Tyres/wheels out of balance (*"Weekly Checks"*).
- ☐ Excessive wheel or tyre run-out (Chapter 10).
- ☐ Worn shock absorbers (Chapters 1 and 10).
- ☐ Faulty tyre (*"Weekly Checks"*).

Electrical system

Note: *For problems associated with the starting system, refer to the faults listed under "Engine" earlier in this Section.*

Battery will not hold a charge for more than a few days

- ☐ Battery defective internally (Chapter 5A).
- ☐ Battery electrolyte level low - where applicable ("*Weekly Checks*").
- ☐ Battery terminal connections loose or corroded ("*Weekly Checks*").
- ☐ Auxiliary drivebelt worn - or incorrectly adjusted, where applicable (Chapter 1).
- ☐ Alternator not charging at correct output (Chapter 5A).
- ☐ Alternator or voltage regulator faulty (Chapter 5A).
- ☐ Short-circuit causing continual battery drain (Chapters 5 and 12).

Ignition/no-charge warning light remains illuminated with engine running

- ☐ Auxiliary drivebelt broken, worn, or incorrectly adjusted (Chapter 1).
- ☐ Internal fault in alternator or voltage regulator (Chapter 5A).
- ☐ Broken, disconnected, or loose wiring in charging circuit (Chapter 5A).

Ignition/no-charge warning light fails to come on

- ☐ Warning light bulb blown (Chapter 12).
- ☐ Broken, disconnected, or loose wiring in warning light circuit (Chapter 12).
- ☐ Alternator faulty (Chapter 5A).

Lights inoperative

- ☐ Bulb blown (Chapter 12).
- ☐ Corrosion of bulb or bulbholder contacts (Chapter 12).
- ☐ Blown fuse (Chapter 12).
- ☐ Faulty relay (Chapter 12).
- ☐ Broken, loose, or disconnected wiring (Chapter 12).
- ☐ Faulty switch (Chapter 12).

Instrument readings inaccurate or erratic

Instrument readings increase with engine speed

- ☐ Faulty voltage regulator (Chapter 12).

Fuel or temperature gauges give no reading

- ☐ Faulty gauge sender unit (Chapters 3 and 4).
- ☐ Wiring open-circuit (Chapter 12).
- ☐ Faulty gauge (Chapter 12).

Fuel or temperature gauges give continuous maximum reading

- ☐ Faulty gauge sender unit (Chapters 3 and 4).
- ☐ Wiring short-circuit (Chapter 12).
- ☐ Faulty gauge (Chapter 12).

Horn inoperative, or unsatisfactory in operation

Horn operates all the time

- ☐ Horn contacts permanently bridged or horn push stuck down (Chapter 12).

Horn fails to operate

- ☐ Blown fuse (Chapter 12).
- ☐ Cable or cable connections loose, broken or disconnected (Chapter 12).
- ☐ Faulty horn (Chapter 12).

Horn emits intermittent or unsatisfactory sound

- ☐ Cable connections loose (Chapter 12).
- ☐ Horn mountings loose (Chapter 12).
- ☐ Faulty horn (Chapter 12).

Windscreen/tailgate wipers inoperative, or unsatisfactory in operation

Wipers fail to operate, or operate very slowly

- ☐ Wiper blades stuck to screen, or linkage seized or binding ("*Weekly Checks*" and Chapter 12).
- ☐ Blown fuse (Chapter 12).
- ☐ Cable or cable connections loose, broken or disconnected (Chapter 12).
- ☐ Faulty relay (Chapter 12).
- ☐ Faulty wiper motor (Chapter 12).

Electrical system (continued)

Wiper blades sweep over too large or too small an area of the glass

☐ Wiper arms incorrectly positioned on spindles (Chapter 12).
☐ Excessive wear of wiper linkage (Chapter 12).
☐ Wiper motor or linkage mountings loose or insecure (Chapter 12).

Wiper blades fail to clean the glass effectively

☐ Wiper blade rubbers worn or perished (*"Weekly Checks"*).
☐ Wiper arm tension springs broken, or arm pivots seized (Chapter 12).
☐ Insufficient windscreen washer additive to adequately remove road film (*"Weekly Checks"*).

Windscreen/tailgate washers inoperative, or unsatisfactory in operation

One or more washer jets inoperative

☐ Blocked washer jet (Chapter 12).
☐ Disconnected, kinked or restricted fluid hose (Chapter 12).
☐ Insufficient fluid in washer reservoir (*"Weekly Checks"*).

Washer pump fails to operate

☐ Broken or disconnected wiring or connections (Chapter 12).
☐ Blown fuse (Chapter 12).
☐ Faulty washer switch (Chapter 12).
☐ Faulty washer pump (Chapter 12).

Washer pump runs for some time before fluid is emitted from jets

☐ Faulty one-way valve in fluid supply hose (Chapter 12).

Electric windows inoperative, or unsatisfactory in operation

Window glass will only move in one direction

☐ Faulty switch (Chapter 12).

Window glass slow to move

☐ Regulator seized or damaged, or in need of lubrication (Chapter 11).
☐ Door internal components or trim fouling regulator (Chapter 11).
☐ Faulty motor (Chapter 11).

Window glass fails to move

☐ Blown fuse (Chapter 12).
☐ Faulty relay (Chapter 12).
☐ Broken or disconnected wiring or connections (Chapter 12).
☐ Faulty motor (Chapter 12).

Central locking system inoperative, or unsatisfactory in operation

Complete system failure

☐ Blown fuse (Chapter 12).
☐ Faulty relay (Chapter 12).
☐ Broken or disconnected wiring or connections (Chapter 12).
☐ Faulty motor (Chapter 11).

Latch locks but will not unlock, or unlocks but will not lock

☐ Faulty switch (Chapter 12).
☐ Broken or disconnected latch operating rods or levers (Chapter 11).
☐ Faulty relay (Chapter 12).
☐ Faulty motor (Chapter 11).

One solenoid/motor fails to operate

☐ Broken or disconnected wiring or connections (Chapter 12).
☐ Faulty motor (Chapter 11).
☐ Broken, binding or disconnected lock operating rods or levers (Chapter 11).
☐ Fault in door lock (Chapter 11).

A

ABS (Anti-lock brake system) A system, usually electronically controlled, that senses incipient wheel lockup during braking and relieves hydraulic pressure at wheels that are about to skid.

Air bag An inflatable bag hidden in the steering wheel (driver's side) or the dash or glovebox (passenger side). In a head-on collision, the bags inflate, preventing the driver and front passenger from being thrown forward into the steering wheel or windscreen.

Air cleaner A metal or plastic housing, containing a filter element, which removes dust and dirt from the air being drawn into the engine.

Air filter element The actual filter in an air cleaner system, usually manufactured from pleated paper and requiring renewal at regular intervals.

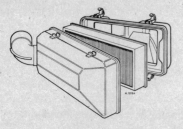

Air filter

Allen key A hexagonal wrench which fits into a recessed hexagonal hole.

Alligator clip A long-nosed spring-loaded metal clip with meshing teeth. Used to make temporary electrical connections.

Alternator A component in the electrical system which converts mechanical energy from a drivebelt into electrical energy to charge the battery and to operate the starting system, ignition system and electrical accessories.

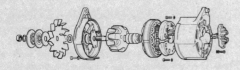

Alternator (exploded view)

Ampere (amp) A unit of measurement for the flow of electric current. One amp is the amount of current produced by one volt acting through a resistance of one ohm.

Anaerobic sealer A substance used to prevent bolts and screws from loosening. Anaerobic means that it does not require oxygen for activation. The Loctite brand is widely used.

Antifreeze A substance (usually ethylene glycol) mixed with water, and added to a vehicle's cooling system, to prevent freezing of the coolant in winter. Antifreeze also contains chemicals to inhibit corrosion and the formation of rust and other deposits that

would tend to clog the radiator and coolant passages and reduce cooling efficiency.

Anti-seize compound A coating that reduces the risk of seizing on fasteners that are subjected to high temperatures, such as exhaust manifold bolts and nuts.

Anti-seize compound

Asbestos A natural fibrous mineral with great heat resistance, commonly used in the composition of brake friction materials. Asbestos is a health hazard and the dust created by brake systems should never be inhaled or ingested.

Axle A shaft on which a wheel revolves, or which revolves with a wheel. Also, a solid beam that connects the two wheels at one end of the vehicle. An axle which also transmits power to the wheels is known as a live axle.

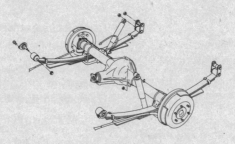

Axle assembly

Axleshaft A single rotating shaft, on either side of the differential, which delivers power from the final drive assembly to the drive wheels. Also called a driveshaft or a halfshaft.

B

Ball bearing An anti-friction bearing consisting of a hardened inner and outer race with hardened steel balls between two races.

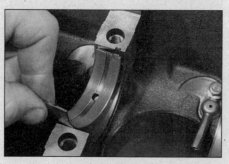

Bearing

Bearing The curved surface on a shaft or in a bore, or the part assembled into either, that permits relative motion between them with minimum wear and friction.

Big-end bearing The bearing in the end of the connecting rod that's attached to the crankshaft.

Bleed nipple A valve on a brake wheel cylinder, caliper or other hydraulic component that is opened to purge the hydraulic system of air. Also called a bleed screw.

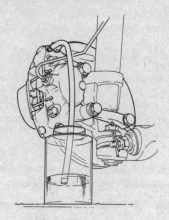

Brake bleeding

Brake bleeding Procedure for removing air from lines of a hydraulic brake system.

Brake disc The component of a disc brake that rotates with the wheels.

Brake drum The component of a drum brake that rotates with the wheels.

Brake linings The friction material which contacts the brake disc or drum to retard the vehicle's speed. The linings are bonded or riveted to the brake pads or shoes.

Brake pads The replaceable friction pads that pinch the brake disc when the brakes are applied. Brake pads consist of a friction material bonded or riveted to a rigid backing plate.

Brake shoe The crescent-shaped carrier to which the brake linings are mounted and which forces the lining against the rotating drum during braking.

Braking systems For more information on braking systems, consult the *Haynes Automotive Brake Manual*.

Breaker bar A long socket wrench handle providing greater leverage.

Bulkhead The insulated partition between the engine and the passenger compartment.

C

Caliper The non-rotating part of a disc-brake assembly that straddles the disc and carries the brake pads. The caliper also contains the hydraulic components that cause the pads to pinch the disc when the brakes are applied. A caliper is also a measuring tool that can be set to measure inside or outside dimensions of an object.

Camshaft A rotating shaft on which a series of cam lobes operate the valve mechanisms. The camshaft may be driven by gears, by sprockets and chain or by sprockets and a belt.

Canister A container in an evaporative emission control system; contains activated charcoal granules to trap vapours from the fuel system.

Canister

Carburettor A device which mixes fuel with air in the proper proportions to provide a desired power output from a spark ignition internal combustion engine.

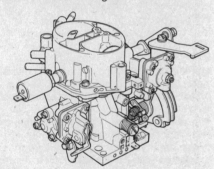

Carburettor

Castellated Resembling the parapets along the top of a castle wall. For example, a castellated balljoint stud nut.

Castellated nut

Castor In wheel alignment, the backward or forward tilt of the steering axis. Castor is positive when the steering axis is inclined rearward at the top.

Catalytic converter A silencer-like device in the exhaust system which converts certain pollutants in the exhaust gases into less harmful substances.

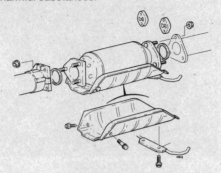

Catalytic converter

Circlip A ring-shaped clip used to prevent endwise movement of cylindrical parts and shafts. An internal circlip is installed in a groove in a housing; an external circlip fits into a groove on the outside of a cylindrical piece such as a shaft.

Clearance The amount of space between two parts. For example, between a piston and a cylinder, between a bearing and a journal, etc.

Coil spring A spiral of elastic steel found in various sizes throughout a vehicle, for example as a springing medium in the suspension and in the valve train.

Compression Reduction in volume, and increase in pressure and temperature, of a gas, caused by squeezing it into a smaller space.

Compression ratio The relationship between cylinder volume when the piston is at top dead centre and cylinder volume when the piston is at bottom dead centre.

Constant velocity (CV) joint A type of universal joint that cancels out vibrations caused by driving power being transmitted through an angle.

Core plug A disc or cup-shaped metal device inserted in a hole in a casting through which core was removed when the casting was formed. Also known as a freeze plug or expansion plug.

Crankcase The lower part of the engine block in which the crankshaft rotates.

Crankshaft The main rotating member, or shaft, running the length of the crankcase, with offset "throws" to which the connecting rods are attached.

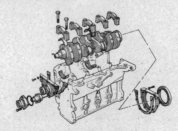

Crankshaft assembly

Crocodile clip See Alligator clip

D

Diagnostic code Code numbers obtained by accessing the diagnostic mode of an engine management computer. This code can be used to determine the area in the system where a malfunction may be located.

Disc brake A brake design incorporating a rotating disc onto which brake pads are squeezed. The resulting friction converts the energy of a moving vehicle into heat.

Double-overhead cam (DOHC) An engine that uses two overhead camshafts, usually one for the intake valves and one for the exhaust valves.

Drivebelt(s) The belt(s) used to drive accessories such as the alternator, water pump, power steering pump, air conditioning compressor, etc. off the crankshaft pulley.

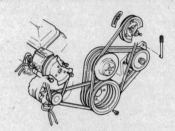

Accessory drivebelts

Driveshaft Any shaft used to transmit motion. Commonly used when referring to the axleshafts on a front wheel drive vehicle.

Driveshaft

Drum brake A type of brake using a drum-shaped metal cylinder attached to the inner surface of the wheel. When the brake pedal is pressed, curved brake shoes with friction linings press against the inside of the drum to slow or stop the vehicle.

Drum brake assembly

E

EGR valve A valve used to introduce exhaust gases into the intake air stream.

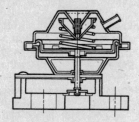
EGR valve

Electronic control unit (ECU) A computer which controls (for instance) ignition and fuel injection systems, or an anti-lock braking system. For more information refer to the *Haynes Automotive Electrical and Electronic Systems Manual*.

Electronic Fuel Injection (EFI) A computer controlled fuel system that distributes fuel through an injector located in each intake port of the engine.

Emergency brake A braking system, independent of the main hydraulic system, that can be used to slow or stop the vehicle if the primary brakes fail, or to hold the vehicle stationary even though the brake pedal isn't depressed. It usually consists of a hand lever that actuates either front or rear brakes mechanically through a series of cables and linkages. Also known as a handbrake or parking brake.

Endfloat The amount of lengthwise movement between two parts. As applied to a crankshaft, the distance that the crankshaft can move forward and back in the cylinder block.

Engine management system (EMS) A computer controlled system which manages the fuel injection and the ignition systems in an integrated fashion.

Exhaust manifold A part with several passages through which exhaust gases leave the engine combustion chambers and enter the exhaust pipe.

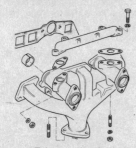
Exhaust manifold

F

Fan clutch A viscous (fluid) drive coupling device which permits variable engine fan speeds in relation to engine speeds.

Feeler blade A thin strip or blade of hardened steel, ground to an exact thickness, used to check or measure clearances between parts.

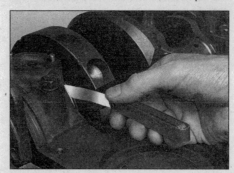
Feeler blade

Firing order The order in which the engine cylinders fire, or deliver their power strokes, beginning with the number one cylinder.

Flywheel A heavy spinning wheel in which energy is absorbed and stored by means of momentum. On cars, the flywheel is attached to the crankshaft to smooth out firing impulses.

Free play The amount of travel before any action takes place. The "looseness" in a linkage, or an assembly of parts, between the initial application of force and actual movement. For example, the distance the brake pedal moves before the pistons in the master cylinder are actuated.

Fuse An electrical device which protects a circuit against accidental overload. The typical fuse contains a soft piece of metal which is calibrated to melt at a predetermined current flow (expressed as amps) and break the circuit.

Fusible link A circuit protection device consisting of a conductor surrounded by heat-resistant insulation. The conductor is smaller than the wire it protects, so it acts as the weakest link in the circuit. Unlike a blown fuse, a failed fusible link must frequently be cut from the wire for replacement.

G

Gap The distance the spark must travel in jumping from the centre electrode to the side

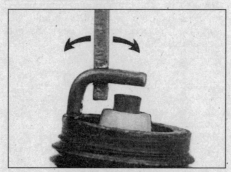
Adjusting spark plug gap

electrode in a spark plug. Also refers to the spacing between the points in a contact breaker assembly in a conventional points-type ignition, or to the distance between the reluctor or rotor and the pickup coil in an electronic ignition.

Gasket Any thin, soft material - usually cork, cardboard, asbestos or soft metal - installed between two metal surfaces to ensure a good seal. For instance, the cylinder head gasket seals the joint between the block and the cylinder head.

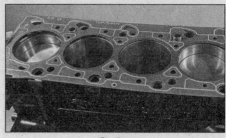
Gasket

Gauge An instrument panel display used to monitor engine conditions. A gauge with a movable pointer on a dial or a fixed scale is an analogue gauge. A gauge with a numerical readout is called a digital gauge.

H

Halfshaft A rotating shaft that transmits power from the final drive unit to a drive wheel, usually when referring to a live rear axle.

Harmonic balancer A device designed to reduce torsion or twisting vibration in the crankshaft. May be incorporated in the crankshaft pulley. Also known as a vibration damper.

Hone An abrasive tool for correcting small irregularities or differences in diameter in an engine cylinder, brake cylinder, etc.

Hydraulic tappet A tappet that utilises hydraulic pressure from the engine's lubrication system to maintain zero clearance (constant contact with both camshaft and valve stem). Automatically adjusts to variation in valve stem length. Hydraulic tappets also reduce valve noise.

I

Ignition timing The moment at which the spark plug fires, usually expressed in the number of crankshaft degrees before the piston reaches the top of its stroke.

Inlet manifold A tube or housing with passages through which flows the air-fuel mixture (carburettor vehicles and vehicles with throttle body injection) or air only (port fuel-injected vehicles) to the port openings in the cylinder head.

J

Jump start Starting the engine of a vehicle with a discharged or weak battery by attaching jump leads from the weak battery to a charged or helper battery.

L

Load Sensing Proportioning Valve (LSPV) A brake hydraulic system control valve that works like a proportioning valve, but also takes into consideration the amount of weight carried by the rear axle.

Locknut A nut used to lock an adjustment nut, or other threaded component, in place. For example, a locknut is employed to keep the adjusting nut on the rocker arm in position.

Lockwasher A form of washer designed to prevent an attaching nut from working loose.

M

MacPherson strut A type of front suspension system devised by Earle MacPherson at Ford of England. In its original form, a simple lateral link with the anti-roll bar creates the lower control arm. A long strut - an integral coil spring and shock absorber - is mounted between the body and the steering knuckle. Many modern so-called MacPherson strut systems use a conventional lower A-arm and don't rely on the anti-roll bar for location.

Multimeter An electrical test instrument with the capability to measure voltage, current and resistance.

N

NOx Oxides of Nitrogen. A common toxic pollutant emitted by petrol and diesel engines at higher temperatures.

O

Ohm The unit of electrical resistance. One volt applied to a resistance of one ohm will produce a current of one amp.

Ohmmeter An instrument for measuring electrical resistance.

O-ring A type of sealing ring made of a special rubber-like material; in use, the O-ring is compressed into a groove to provide the sealing action.

O-ring

Overhead cam (ohc) engine An engine with the camshaft(s) located on top of the cylinder head(s).

Overhead valve (ohv) engine An engine with the valves located in the cylinder head, but with the camshaft located in the engine block.

Oxygen sensor A device installed in the engine exhaust manifold, which senses the oxygen content in the exhaust and converts this information into an electric current. Also called a Lambda sensor.

P

Phillips screw A type of screw head having a cross instead of a slot for a corresponding type of screwdriver.

Plastigage A thin strip of plastic thread, available in different sizes, used for measuring clearances. For example, a strip of Plastigage is laid across a bearing journal. The parts are assembled and dismantled; the width of the crushed strip indicates the clearance between journal and bearing.

Plastigage

Propeller shaft The long hollow tube with universal joints at both ends that carries power from the transmission to the differential on front-engined rear wheel drive vehicles.

Proportioning valve A hydraulic control valve which limits the amount of pressure to the rear brakes during panic stops to prevent wheel lock-up.

R

Rack-and-pinion steering A steering system with a pinion gear on the end of the steering shaft that mates with a rack (think of a geared wheel opened up and laid flat). When the steering wheel is turned, the pinion turns, moving the rack to the left or right. This movement is transmitted through the track rods to the steering arms at the wheels.

Radiator A liquid-to-air heat transfer device designed to reduce the temperature of the coolant in an internal combustion engine cooling system.

Refrigerant Any substance used as a heat transfer agent in an air-conditioning system. R-12 has been the principle refrigerant for many years; recently, however, manufacturers have begun using R-134a, a non-CFC substance that is considered less harmful to the ozone in the upper atmosphere.

Rocker arm A lever arm that rocks on a shaft or pivots on a stud. In an overhead valve engine, the rocker arm converts the upward movement of the pushrod into a downward movement to open a valve.

Rotor In a distributor, the rotating device inside the cap that connects the centre electrode and the outer terminals as it turns, distributing the high voltage from the coil secondary winding to the proper spark plug. Also, that part of an alternator which rotates inside the stator. Also, the rotating assembly of a turbocharger, including the compressor wheel, shaft and turbine wheel.

Runout The amount of wobble (in-and-out movement) of a gear or wheel as it's rotated. The amount a shaft rotates "out-of-true." The out-of-round condition of a rotating part.

S

Sealant A liquid or paste used to prevent leakage at a joint. Sometimes used in conjunction with a gasket.

Sealed beam lamp An older headlight design which integrates the reflector, lens and filaments into a hermetically-sealed one-piece unit. When a filament burns out or the lens cracks, the entire unit is simply replaced.

Serpentine drivebelt A single, long, wide accessory drivebelt that's used on some newer vehicles to drive all the accessories, instead of a series of smaller, shorter belts. Serpentine drivebelts are usually tensioned by an automatic tensioner.

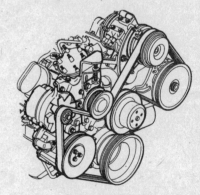
Serpentine drivebelt

Shim Thin spacer, commonly used to adjust the clearance or relative positions between two parts. For example, shims inserted into or under bucket tappets control valve clearances. Clearance is adjusted by changing the thickness of the shim.

Slide hammer A special puller that screws into or hooks onto a component such as a shaft or bearing; a heavy sliding handle on the shaft bottoms against the end of the shaft to knock the component free.

Sprocket A tooth or projection on the periphery of a wheel, shaped to engage with a chain or drivebelt. Commonly used to refer to the sprocket wheel itself.

Starter inhibitor switch On vehicles with an automatic transmission, a switch that prevents starting if the vehicle is not in Neutral or Park.

Strut See MacPherson strut.

T

Tappet A cylindrical component which transmits motion from the cam to the valve stem, either directly or via a pushrod and rocker arm. Also called a cam follower.

Thermostat A heat-controlled valve that regulates the flow of coolant between the cylinder block and the radiator, so maintaining optimum engine operating temperature. A thermostat is also used in some air cleaners in which the temperature is regulated.

Thrust bearing The bearing in the clutch assembly that is moved in to the release levers by clutch pedal action to disengage the clutch. Also referred to as a release bearing.

Timing belt A toothed belt which drives the camshaft. Serious engine damage may result if it breaks in service.

Timing chain A chain which drives the camshaft.

Toe-in The amount the front wheels are closer together at the front than at the rear. On rear wheel drive vehicles, a slight amount of toe-in is usually specified to keep the front wheels running parallel on the road by offsetting other forces that tend to spread the wheels apart.

Toe-out The amount the front wheels are closer together at the rear than at the front. On front wheel drive vehicles, a slight amount of toe-out is usually specified.

Tools For full information on choosing and using tools, refer to the *Haynes Automotive Tools Manual*.

Tracer A stripe of a second colour applied to a wire insulator to distinguish that wire from another one with the same colour insulator.

Tune-up A process of accurate and careful adjustments and parts replacement to obtain the best possible engine performance.

Turbocharger A centrifugal device, driven by exhaust gases, that pressurises the intake air. Normally used to increase the power output from a given engine displacement, but can also be used primarily to reduce exhaust emissions (as on VW's "Umwelt" Diesel engine).

U

Universal joint or U-joint A double-pivoted connection for transmitting power from a driving to a driven shaft through an angle. A U-joint consists of two Y-shaped yokes and a cross-shaped member called the spider.

V

Valve A device through which the flow of liquid, gas, vacuum, or loose material in bulk may be started, stopped, or regulated by a movable part that opens, shuts, or partially obstructs one or more ports or passageways. A valve is also the movable part of such a device.

Valve clearance The clearance between the valve tip (the end of the valve stem) and the rocker arm or tappet. The valve clearance is measured when the valve is closed.

Vernier caliper A precision measuring instrument that measures inside and outside dimensions. Not quite as accurate as a micrometer, but more convenient.

Viscosity The thickness of a liquid or its resistance to flow.

Volt A unit for expressing electrical "pressure" in a circuit. One volt that will produce a current of one ampere through a resistance of one ohm.

W

Welding Various processes used to join metal items by heating the areas to be joined to a molten state and fusing them together. For more information refer to the *Haynes Automotive Welding Manual*.

Wiring diagram A drawing portraying the components and wires in a vehicle's electrical system, using standardised symbols. For more information refer to the *Haynes Automotive Electrical and Electronic Systems Manual*.

Note: *References throughout this index are in the form - "Chapter number" • "Page number"*

Haynes Manuals – The Complete List

Title	Book No.
ALFA ROMEO	
Alfa Romeo Alfasud/Sprint (74 - 88) up to F	0292
Alfa Romeo Alfetta (73 - 87) up to E	0531
AUDI	
Audi 80, 90 (79 - Oct 86) up to D & Coupe (81 - Nov 88) up to F	0605
Audi 80, 90 (Oct 86 - 90) D to H & Coupe (Nov 88 - 90) F to H	1491
Audi 100 (Oct 82 - 90) up to H & 200 (Feb 84 - Oct 89) A to G	0907
Audi 100 & A6 Petrol & Diesel (May 91 - May 97) H to P	3504
Audi A4 (95 - Feb 00) M to V	3575
AUSTIN	
Austin A35 & A40 (56 - 67)*	0118
Austin Allegro 1100, 1300, 1.0, 1.1 & 1.3 (73 - 82)*	0164
Austin Healey 100/6 & 3000 (56 - 68)*	0049
Austin/MG/Rover Maestro 1.3 & 1.6 (83 - 95) up to M	0922
Austin/MG Metro (80 - May 90) up to G	0718
Austin/Rover Montego 1.3 & 1.6 (84 - 94) A to L	1066
Austin/MG/Rover Montego 2.0 (84 - 95) A to M	1067
Mini (59 - 69) up to H	0527
Mini (69 - 01) up to X-reg	0646
Austin/Rover 2.0 litre Diesel Engine (86 - 93) C to L	1857
BEDFORD	
Bedford CF (69 - 87) up to E	0163
Bedford/Vauxhall Rascal & Suzuki Supercarry (86 - Oct 94) C to M	3015
BMW	
BMW 1500, 1502, 1600, 1602, 2000 & 2002 (59 - 77)*	0240
BMW 316, 320 & 320i (4-cyl) (75 - Feb 83) up to Y	0276
BMW 320, 320i, 323i & 325i (6-cyl) (Oct 77 - Sept 87) up to E	0815
BMW 3-Series (Apr 91 - 96) H to N	3210
BMW 3- & 5-Series (sohc) (81 - 91) up to J	1948
BMW 520i & 525e (Oct 81 - June 88) up to E	1560
BMW 525, 528 & 528i (73 - Sept 81) up to X *	0632
CHRYSLER	
Chrysler PT Cruiser (00 - 03) W-reg onwards	4058
CITROËN	
Citroën 2CV, Ami & Dyane (67 - 90) up to H	0196
Citroën AX Petrol & Diesel (87 - 97) D to P	3014
Citroën BX (83 - 94) A to L	0908
Citroën C15 Van Petrol & Diesel (89 - Oct 98) F to S	3509
Citroën CX (75 - 88) up to F	0528
Citroën Saxo Petrol & Diesel (96 - 01) N to X	3506
Citroën Visa (79 - 88) up to F	0620
Citroën Xantia Petrol & Diesel (93 - 98) K to S	3082
Citroën XM Petrol & Diesel (89 - 00) G to X	3451
Citroën Xsara Petrol & Diesel (97 - Sept 00) R to W	3751
Citroën Xsara Picasso Petrol & Diesel (00 - 02) W-reg. onwards	3944
Citroën ZX Diesel (91 - 98) J to S	1922
Citroën ZX Petrol (91 - 98) H to S	1881
Citroën 1.7 & 1.9 litre Diesel Engine (84 - 96) A to N	1379
FIAT	
Fiat 126 (73 - 87)*	0305
Fiat 500 (57 - 73) up to M	0090
Fiat Bravo & Brava (95 - 00) N to W	3572
Fiat Cinquecento (93 - 98) K to R	3501
Fiat Panda (81 - 95) up to M	0793
Fiat Punto Petrol & Diesel (94 - Oct 99) L to V	3251
Fiat Regata (84 - 88) A to F	1167
Fiat Tipo (88 - 91) E to J	1625
Fiat Uno (83 - 95) up to M	0923
Fiat X1/9 (74 - 89) up to G	0273

Title	Book No.
FORD	
Ford Anglia (59 - 68)*	0001
Ford Capri II (& III) 1.6 & 2.0 (74 - 87) up to E	0283
Ford Capri II (& III) 2.8 & 3.0 (74 - 87) up to E	1309
Ford Cortina Mk III 1300 & 1600 (70 - 76)*	0070
Ford Cortina Mk IV (& V) 1.6 & 2.0 (76 - 83)*	0343
Ford Cortina Mk IV (& V) 2.3 V6 (77 - 83)*	0426
Ford Escort Mk I 1100 & 1300 (68 - 74)*	0171
Ford Escort Mk I Mexico, RS 1600 & RS 2000 (70 - 74)*	0139
Ford Escort Mk II Mexico, RS 1800 & RS 2000 (75 - 80)*	0735
Ford Escort (75 - Aug 80)*	0280
Ford Escort (Sept 80 - Sept 90) up to H	0686
Ford Escort & Orion (Sept 90 - 00) H to X	1737
Ford Fiesta (76 - Aug 83) up to Y	0334
Ford Fiesta (Aug 83 - Feb 89) A to F	1030
Ford Fiesta (Feb 89 - Oct 95) F to N	1595
Ford Fiesta (Oct 95 - 01) N-reg. onwards	3397
Ford Focus (98 - 01) S to Y	3759
Ford Galaxy Petrol & Diesel (95 - Aug 00) M to W	3984
Ford Granada (Sept 77 - Feb 85) up to B	0481
Ford Granada & Scorpio (Mar 85 - 94) B to M	1245
Ford Ka (96 - 02) P-reg. onwards	3570
Ford Mondeo Petrol (93 - 99) K to T	1923
Ford Mondeo (Oct 00 - 03) X-reg. onwards	3990
Ford Mondeo Diesel (93 - 96) L to N	3465
Ford Orion (83 - Sept 90) up to H	1009
Ford Sierra 4 cyl. (82 - 93) up to K	0903
Ford Sierra V6 (82 - 91) up to J	0904
Ford Transit Petrol (Mk 2) (78 - Jan 86) up to C	0719
Ford Transit Petrol (Mk 3) (Feb 86 - 89) C to G	1468
Ford Transit Diesel (Feb 86 - 99) C to T	3019
Ford 1.6 & 1.8 litre Diesel Engine (84 - 96) A to N	1172
Ford 2.1, 2.3 & 2.5 litre Diesel Engine (77 - 90) up to H	1606
FREIGHT ROVER	
Freight Rover Sherpa (74 - 87) up to E	0463
HILLMAN	
Hillman Avenger (70 - 82) up to Y	0037
Hillman Imp (63 - 76) *	0022
HONDA	
Honda Accord (76 - Feb 84) up to A	0351
Honda Civic (Feb 84 - Oct 87) A to E	1226
Honda Civic (Nov 91 - 96) J to N	3199
Honda Civic (Mar 95 - 01) M to X	4050
HYUNDAI	
Hyundai Pony (85 - 94) C to M	3398
JAGUAR	
Jaguar E Type (61 - 72) up to L	0140
Jaguar MkI & II, 240 & 340 (55 - 69)*	0098
Jaguar XJ6, XJ & Sovereign; Daimler Sovereign (68 - Oct 86) up to D	0242
Jaguar XJ6 & Sovereign (Oct 86 - Sept 94) D to M	3261
Jaguar XJ12, XJS & Sovereign; Daimler Double Six (72 - 88) up to F	0478
JEEP	
Jeep Cherokee Petrol (93 - 96) K to N	1943
LADA	
Lada 1200, 1300, 1500 & 1600 (74 - 91) up to J	0413
Lada Samara (87 - 91) D to J	1610
LAND ROVER	
Land Rover 90, 110 & Defender Diesel (83 - 95) up to N	3017
Land Rover Discovery Petrol & Diesel (89 - 98) G to S	3016
Land Rover Freelander (97 - 02) R-reg. onwards	3929
Land Rover Series IIA & III Diesel (58 - 85) up to C	0529
Land Rover Series II, IIA & III Petrol (58 - 85) up to C	0314
MAZDA	
Mazda 323 (Mar 81 - Oct 89) up to G	1608

Title	Book No.
Mazda 323 (Oct 89 - 98) G to R	3455
Mazda 626 (May 83 - Sept 87) up to E	0929
Mazda B-1600, B-1800 & B-2000 Pick-up (72 - 88) up to F	0267
Mazda RX-7 (79 - 85)*	0460
MERCEDES-BENZ	
Mercedes-Benz 190, 190E & 190D Petrol & Diesel (83 - 93) A to L	3450
Mercedes-Benz 200, 240, 300 Diesel (Oct 76 - 85) up to C	1114
Mercedes-Benz 250 & 280 (68 - 72) up to L	0346
Mercedes-Benz 250 & 280 (123 Series) (Oct 76 - 84) up to B	0677
Mercedes-Benz 124 Series (85 - Aug 93) C to K	3253
Mercedes-Benz C-Class Petrol & Diesel (93 - Aug 00) L to W	3511
MG	
MGA (55 - 62)*	0475
MGB (62 - 80) up to W	0111
MG Midget & AH Sprite (58 - 80) up to W	0265
MITSUBISHI	
Mitsubishi Shogun & L200 Pick-Ups (83 - 94) up to M	1944
MORRIS	
Morris Ital 1.3 (80 - 84) up to B	0705
Morris Minor 1000 (56 - 71) up to K	0024
NISSAN	
Nissan Almera (Oct 95 - Feb 00) N - V reg	4053
Nissan Bluebird (May 84 - Mar 86) A to C	1223
Nissan Bluebird (Mar 86 - 90) C to H	1473
Nissan Cherry (Sept 82 - 86) up to D	1031
Nissan Micra (83 - Jan 93) up to K	0931
Nissan Micra (93 - 99) K to T	3254
Nissan Primera (90 - Aug 99) H to T	1851
Nissan Stanza (82 - 86) up to D	0824
Nissan Sunny (May 82 - Oct 86) up to D	0895
Nissan Sunny (Oct 86 - Mar 91) D to H	1378
Nissan Sunny (Apr 91 - 95) H to N	3219
OPEL	
Opel Ascona & Manta (B Series) (Sept 75 - 88) up to F	0316
Opel Ascona (81 - 88) (Not available in UK see Vauxhall Cavalier 0812)	3215
Opel Astra (Oct 91 - Feb 98) (Not available in UK see Vauxhall Astra 1832)	3156
Opel Astra & Zafira Diesel (Feb 98 - Sept 00) (See Astra & Zafira Diesel Book No. 3797)	
Opel Astra & Zafira Petrol (Feb 98 - Sept 00) (See Vauxhall/Opel Astra & Zafira Petrol Book No. 3758)	
Opel Calibra (90 - 98) (See Vauxhall/Opel Calibra Book No. 3502)	
Opel Corsa (83 - Mar 93) (Not available in UK see Vauxhall Nova 0909)	3160
Opel Corsa (Mar 93 - 97) (Not available in UK see Vauxhall Corsa 1985)	3159
Opel Frontera Petrol & Diesel (91 - 98) (See Vauxhall/Opel Frontera Book No. 3454)	
Opel Kadett (Nov 79 - Oct 84) up to B	0634
Opel Kadett (Oct 84 - Oct 91) (Not available in UK see Vauxhall Astra & Belmont 1136)	3196
Opel Omega & Senator (86 - 94) (Not available in UK see Vauxhall Carlton & Senator 1469)	3157
Opel Omega (94 - 99) (See Vauxhall/Opel Omega Book No. 3510)	
Opel Rekord (Feb 78 - Oct 86) up to D	0543
Opel Vectra (Oct 88 - Oct 95) (Not available in UK see Vauxhall Cavalier 1570)	3158
Opel Vectra Petrol & Diesel (95 - 98) (Not available in UK see Vauxhall Vectra 3396)	3523

* Classic reprint

Title	Book No.
PEUGEOT	
Peugeot 106 Petrol & Diesel (91 - 02) J-reg. onwards	1882
Peugeot 205 Petrol (83 - 97) A to P	0932
Peugeot 206 Petrol and Diesel (98 - 01) S to X	3757
Peugeot 305 (78 - 89) up to G*	0538
Peugeot 306 Petrol & Diesel (93 - 99) K to T	3073
Peugeot 309 (86 - 93) C to K	1266
Peugeot 405 Petrol (88 - 97) E to P	1559
Peugeot 405 Diesel (88 - 97) E to P	3198
Peugeot 406 Petrol & Diesel (96 - 97) N to R	3394
Peugeot 406 Petrol & Diesel (Mar 99 - 02) T-reg onwards	3982
Peugeot 505 (79 - 89) up to G	0762
Peugeot 1.7/1.8 & 1.9 litre Diesel Engine (82 - 96) up to N	0950
Peugeot 2.0, 2.1, 2.3 & 2.5 litre Diesel Engines (74 - 90) up to H	1607
PORSCHE	
Porsche 911 (65 - 85) up to C	0264
Porsche 924 & 924 Turbo (76 - 85) up to C	0397
PROTON	
Proton (89 - 97) F to P	3255
RANGE ROVER	
Range Rover V8 (70 - Oct 92) up to K	0606
RELIANT	
Reliant Robin & Kitten (73 - 83) up to A	0436
RENAULT	
Renault 4 (61 - 86)*	0072
Renault 5 (Feb 85 - 96) B to N	1219
Renault 9 & 11 (82 - 89) up to F	0822
Renault 18 (79 - 86) up to D	0598
Renault 19 Petrol (89 - 96) F to N	1646
Renault 19 Diesel (89 - 96) F to N	1946
Renault 21 (86 - 94) C to M	1397
Renault 25 (84 - 92) B to K	1228
Renault Clio Petrol (91 - May 98) H to R	1853
Renault Clio Diesel (91 - June 96) H to N	3031
Renault Clio Petrol & Diesel (May 98 - May 01) R to Y	3906
Renault Espace Petrol & Diesel (85 - 96) C to N	3197
Renault Fuego (80 - 86)*	0764
Renault Laguna Petrol & Diesel (94 - 00) L to W	3252
Renault Mégane & Scénic Petrol & Diesel (96 - 98) N to R	3395
Renault Mégane & Scénic Petrol & Diesel (Apr 99 - 02) T-reg onwards	3916
ROVER	
Rover 213 & 216 (84 - 89) A to G	1116
Rover 214 & 414 (89 - 96) G to N	1689
Rover 216 & 416 (89 - 96) G to N	1830
Rover 211, 214, 216, 218 & 220 Petrol & Diesel (Dec 95 - 98) N to R	3399
Rover 414, 416 & 420 Petrol & Diesel (May 95 - 98) M to R	3453
Rover 618, 620 & 623 (93 - 97) K to P	3257
Rover 820, 825 & 827 (86 - 95) D to N	1380
Rover 3500 (76 - 87) up to E	0365
Rover Metro, 111 & 114 (May 90 - 98) G to S	1711
SAAB	
Saab 90, 99 & 900 (79 - Oct 93) up to L	0765
Saab 95 & 96 (66 - 76)*	0198
Saab 99 (69 - 79)*	0247
Saab 900 (Oct 93 - 98) L to R	3512
Saab 9000 (4-cyl) (85 - 98) C to S	1686
SEAT	
Seat Ibiza & Cordoba Petrol & Diesel (Oct 93 - Oct 99) L to V	3571
Seat Ibiza & Malaga (85 - 92) B to K	1609

Title	Book No.
SKODA	
Skoda Estelle (77 - 89) up to G	0604
Skoda Favorit (89 - 96) F to N	1801
Skoda Felicia Petrol & Diesel (95 - 01) M to X	3505
SUBARU	
Subaru 1600 & 1800 (Nov 79 - 90) up to H	0995
SUNBEAM	
Sunbeam Alpine, Rapier & H120 (67 - 76)*	0051
SUZUKI	
Suzuki SJ Series, Samurai & Vitara (4-cyl) (82 - 97) up to P	1942
Suzuki Supercarry & Bedford/Vauxhall Rascal (86 - Oct 94) C to M	3015
TALBOT	
Talbot Alpine, Solara, Minx & Rapier (75 - 86) up to D	0337
Talbot Horizon (78 - 86) up to D	0473
Talbot Samba (82 - 86) up to D	0823
TOYOTA	
Toyota Carina E (May 92 - 97) J to P	3256
Toyota Corolla (Sept 83 - Sept 87) A to E	1024
Toyota Corolla (80 - 85) up to C	0683
Toyota Corolla (Sept 87 - Aug 92) E to K	1683
Toyota Corolla (Aug 92 - 97) K to P	3259
Toyota Hi-Ace & Hi-Lux (69 - Oct 83) up to A	0304
TRIUMPH	
Triumph Acclaim (81 - 84)*	0792
Triumph GT6 & Vitesse (62 - 74)*	0112
Triumph Herald (59 - 71)*	0010
Triumph Spitfire (62 - 81) up to X	0113
Triumph Stag (70 - 78) up to T	0441
Triumph TR2, TR3, TR3A, TR4 & TR4A (52 - 67)*	0028
Triumph TR5 & 6 (67 - 75)*	0031
Triumph TR7 (75 - 82)*	0322
VAUXHALL	
Vauxhall Astra (80 - Oct 84) up to B	0635
Vauxhall Astra & Belmont (Oct 84 - Oct 91) B to J	1136
Vauxhall Astra (Oct 91 - Feb 98) J to R	1832
Vauxhall/Opel Astra & Zafira Diesel (Feb 98 - Sept 00) R to W	3797
Vauxhall/Opel Astra & Zafira Petrol (Feb 98 - Sept 00) R to W	3758
Vauxhall/Opel Calibra (90 - 98) G to S	3502
Vauxhall Carlton (Oct 78 - Oct 86) up to D	0480
Vauxhall Carlton & Senator (Nov 86 - 94) D to L	1469
Vauxhall Cavalier 1300 (77 - July 81)*	0461
Vauxhall Cavalier 1600, 1900 & 2000 (75 - July 81) up to W	0315
Vauxhall Cavalier (81 - Oct 88) up to F	0812
Vauxhall Cavalier (Oct 88 - 95) F to N	1570
Vauxhall Chevette (75 - 84) up to B	0285
Vauxhall Corsa (Mar 93 - 97) K to R	1985
Vauxhall/Opel Corsa (Apr 97 - Oct 00) P to X	3921
Vauxhall/Opel Frontera Petrol & Diesel (91 - Sept 98) J to S	3454
Vauxhall Nova (83 - 93) up to K	0909
Vauxhall/Opel Omega (94 - 99) L to T	3510
Vauxhall/Opel Vectra Petrol & Diesel (95 - Feb 99) N to S	3396
Vauxhall/Opel Vectra (Mar 99 - May 02) T-reg. onwards	3930
Vauxhall/Opel 1.5, 1.6 & 1.7 litre Diesel Engine (82 - 96) up to N	1222
VOLKSWAGEN	
Volkswagen 411 & 412 (68 - 75)*	0091
Volkswagen Beetle 1200 (54 - 77) up to S	0036
Volkswagen Beetle 1300 & 1500 (65 - 75) up to P	0039

Title	Book No.
Volkswagen Beetle 1302 & 1302S (70 - 72) up to L	0110
Volkswagen Beetle 1303, 1303S & GT (72 - 75) up to P	0159
Volkswagen Beetle Petrol & Diesel (Apr 99 - 01) T-reg onwards	3798
Volkswagen Golf & Bora Petrol & Diesel (April 98 - 00) R to X	3727
Volkswagen Golf & Jetta Mk 1 1.1 & 1.3 (74 - 84) up to A	0716
Volkswagen Golf, Jetta & Scirocco Mk 1 1.5, 1.6 & 1.8 (74 - 84) up to A	0726
Volkswagen Golf & Jetta Mk 1 Diesel (78 - 84) up to A	0451
Volkswagen Golf & Jetta Mk 2 (Mar 84 - Feb 92) A to J	1081
Volkswagen Golf & Vento Petrol & Diesel (Feb 92 - Mar 98) J to R	3097
Volkswagen LT vans & light trucks (76 - 87) up to E	0637
Volkswagen Passat & Santana (Sept 81 - May 88) up to E	0814
Volkswagen Passat Petrol & Diesel (May 88 - 96) E to P	3498
Volkswagen Passat 4-cyl Petrol & Diesel (Dec 96 - Nov 00) P to X	3917
Volkswagen Polo & Derby (76 - Jan 82) up to X	0335
Volkswagen Polo (82 - Oct 90) up to H	0813
Volkswagen Polo (Nov 90 - Aug 94) H to L	3245
Volkswagen Polo Hatchback Petrol & Diesel (94 - 99) M to S	3500
Volkswagen Scirocco (82 - 90) up to H	1224
Volkswagen Transporter 1600 (68 - 79) up to V	0082
Volkswagen Transporter 1700, 1800 & 2000 (72 - 79) up to V	0226
Volkswagen Transporter (air-cooled) (79 - 82) up to Y	0638
Volkswagen Transporter (water-cooled) (82 - 90) up to H	3452
Volkswagen Type 3 (63 - 73)*	0084
VOLVO	
Volvo 120 & 130 Series (& P1800) (61 - 73)*	0203
Volvo 142, 144 & 145 (66 - 74) up to N	0129
Volvo 240 Series (74 - 93) up to K	0270
Volvo 262, 264 & 260/265 (75 - 85)*	0400
Volvo 340, 343, 345 & 360 (76 - 91) up to J	0715
Volvo 440, 460 & 480 (87 - 97) D to P	1691
Volvo 740 & 760 (82 - 91) up to J	1258
Volvo 850 (92 - 96) J to P	3260
Volvo 940 (90 - 96) H to N	3249
Volvo S40 & V40 (96 - 99) N to V	3569
Volvo S70, V70 & C70 (96 - 99) P to V	3573
AUTOMOTIVE TECHBOOKS	
Automotive Air Conditioning Systems	3740
Automotive Carburettor Manual	3288
Automotive Diagnostic Fault Codes Manual	3472
Automotive Diesel Engine Service Guide	3286
Automotive Electrical and Electronic Systems Manual	3049
Automotive Engine Management and Fuel Injection Systems Manual	3344
Automotive Gearbox Overhaul Manual	3473
Automotive Service Summaries Manual	3475
Automotive Timing Belts Manual – Austin/Rover	3549
Automotive Timing Belts Manual – Ford	3474
Automotive Timing Belts Manual – Peugeot/Citroën	3568
Automotive Timing Belts Manual – Vauxhall/Opel	3577
Automotive Welding Manual	3053
In-Car Entertainment Manual (3rd Edition)	3363

Classic reprint

Preserving Our Motoring Heritage

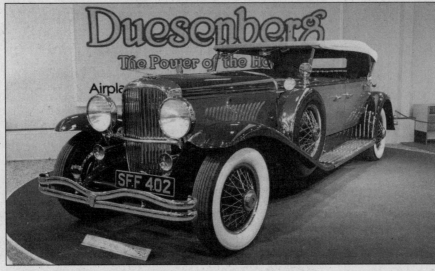

< The Model J Duesenberg
Derham Tourster.
Only eight of these
magnificent cars were
ever built – this is the
only example to be found
outside the United States
of America

Almost every car you've ever loved, loathed or desired is gathered under one roof at the Haynes Motor Museum. Over 300 immaculately presented cars and motorbikes represent every aspect of our motoring heritage, from elegant reminders of bygone days, such as the superb Model J Duesenberg to curiosities like the bug-eyed BMW Isetta. There are also many old friends and flames. Perhaps you remember the 1959 Ford Popular that you did your courting in? The magnificent 'Red Collection' is a spectacle of classic sports cars including AC, Alfa Romeo, Austin Healey, Ferrari, Lamborghini, Maserati, MG, Riley, Porsche and Triumph.

A Perfect Day Out

Each and every vehicle at the Haynes Motor Museum has played its part in the history and culture of Motoring. Today, they make a wonderful spectacle and a great day out for all the family. Bring the kids, bring Mum and Dad, but above all bring your camera to capture those golden memories for ever. You will also find an impressive array of motoring memorabilia, a comfortable 70 seat video cinema and one of the most extensive transport book shops in Britain. The Pit Stop Cafe serves everything from a cup of tea to wholesome, home-made meals or, if you prefer, you can enjoy the large picnic area nestled in the beautiful rural surroundings of Somerset.

John Haynes O.B.E.,
Founder and
Chairman of the
museum at the wheel
of a Haynes Light 12.

< Graham Hill's Lola
Cosworth Formula 1
car next to a 1934
Riley Sports.

The Museum is situated on the A359 Yeovil to Frome road at Sparkford, just off the A303 in Somerset. It is about 40 miles south of Bristol, and 25 minutes drive from the M5 intersection at Taunton.
Open 9.30am - 5.30pm (10.00am - 4.00pm Winter) 7 days a week, *except Christmas Day, Boxing Day and New Years Day*
Special rates available for schools, coach parties and outings Charitable Trust No. 292048